Transnational Management
Text and Cases in Cross-Border Management

Transnational Management provides an integrated conceptual framework to guide students and instructors through the challenges facing today's multinational enterprises. Through text narrative and cases, the authors skilfully examine the development of strategy, organizational capabilities, and management roles and responsibilities for operating in the global economy.

The key concepts are developed in eight chapters that are supplemented by carefully selected practical case studies from world-leading case writers. All chapters have been revised and updated for this eighth edition to reflect the latest thinking in transnational management while retaining the book's strong integrated conceptual framework. Ten new cases have been added, and four others updated. A full range of online support materials are available, including detailed case teaching notes, almost 200 PowerPoint slides, and a test bank.

Suitable for MBA, executive education, and senior undergraduate students studying international management, international business, or global strategy courses, *Transnational Management* offers a uniquely global perspective on the subject.

Christopher A. Bartlett is Professor Emeritus at Harvard Business School. His research and teaching have focused on strategic and organizational challenges confronting managers in multinational corporations. He is the author or co-author of nine books, including *Managing Across Borders: The Transnational Solution* (co-authored with Sumantra Ghoshal 2002), which was named by the *Financial Times* as one of the 50 most influential business books of the twentieth century. He has also researched and written over 100 case studies and teaching notes, and is Harvard's best-selling case author with over 6 million copies sold. In 2001, he received the Academy of Management's International Division's Distinguished Scholar Award. He is a Fellow of the Academy of Management, the Academy of International Business, the Strategic Management Society, and the World Economic Forum.

Paul W. Beamish is the Canada Research Chair in International Business at the Ivey Business School, University of Western Ontario. He has received best research awards from the Academy of Management and the Academy of International Business. He was previously Editor-in-Chief of the *Journal of International Business Studies*. His cases have been studied over 3 million times, with over 20 winning awards. In 2012, he was the recipient of the International Management Outstanding Educator Award and, in 2017, the recipient of the International Management Eminent Scholar Award, both from the Academy of Management. He is the editorial director of Ivey Publishing, and director of Ivey's International Business Institute. He is a Fellow of the Academy of International Business, Royal Society of Canada, and Asia Pacific Foundation of Canada.

Transnational Management

Text and Cases in Cross-Border Management

CHRISTOPHER A. BARTLETT
Harvard University, Massachusetts

PAUL W. BEAMISH
University of Western Ontario

CAMBRIDGE
UNIVERSITY PRESS

CAMBRIDGE
UNIVERSITY PRESS

University Printing House, Cambridge CB2 8BS, United Kingdom

One Liberty Plaza, 20th Floor, New York, NY 10006, USA

477 Williamstown Road, Port Melbourne, VIC 3207, Australia

314–321, 3rd Floor, Plot 3, Splendor Forum, Jasola District Centre, New Delhi – 110025, India

79 Anson Road, #06-04/06, Singapore 079906

Cambridge University Press is part of the University of Cambridge.

It furthers the University's mission by disseminating knowledge in the pursuit of education, learning, and research at the highest international levels of excellence.

www.cambridge.org
Information on this title: www.cambridge.org/9781108422437
DOI: 10.1017/9781108500067

This book was previously published by Harvard Business Review Press 1991, 1998
This book was previously published by McGraw-Hill Education 2000, 2003, 2007, 2010, 2013
Eighth edition first published by Cambridge University Press 2018

Printed in the United States of America by Sheridan Books, Inc.

A catalogue record for this publication is available from the British Library.

ISBN 978-1-108-42243-7 Hardback
ISBN 978-1-108-43669-4 Paperback

Additional resources for this publication at www.cambridge.org/bartlett&beamish.

CONTENTS

LIST OF FIGURES

LIST OF TABLES

PREFACE

This book grew out of the authors' strongly held belief that the best research in the academic fields of international business and cross-border management did more than capture the activities, challenges, and best practices from the field. It also translated those findings into practical and relevant lessons for managers and students of management. That philosophy and commitment has shaped the content of *Transnational Management* over the 25 years since it was first published, and remains at the core of this eighth edition.

Indeed, it was our commitment to deliver current, relevant, and practical research in an engaging format to the students who will be tomorrow's business leaders that led us to make an important change with this new edition. As we became increasingly concerned that many textbooks – including this one – were being priced beyond the means of many of those we were trying to reach, we decided to work with a publisher whose commitments more closely aligned with ours. So this eighth edition of *Transnational Management* begins our exciting new relationship with Cambridge University Press, a publisher that shares our values.

In the quarter-century since the first edition of *Transnational Management* was published, much has changed in the field of multinational enterprise management. In the rapidly evolving global environment, new external demands have required innovative new strategic responses, flexible new organizational capabilities, and adaptive new management capabilities. But many seasoned observers who have operated in the global business environment for decades will insist that despite these differences, the core agenda remains remarkably constant. They make a convincing case that beyond ongoing and inevitable adjustments and refinements, the tensions that characterize cross-border management remain much as they have always been: understanding the world's inexorable evolution toward an integrated strategic whole, yet being sensitive to the constantly evolving impediments and constraints to that ideal; recognizing global and regional opportunities while also being aware of cross-cultural differences and responsive to host country demands; developing the ability to be fast, flexible, and adaptive while also overcoming the barriers to such seamless implementation due to the reality of the distance, language, time, and culture that separate worldwide operations.

We are reminded of this debate with each revision of this volume, as faculty colleagues weigh in on both sides. They remind us that, in many ways, both views are correct. On the one hand, we receive passionate input from those anxious for brand new material that reflects the vibrancy of the field and keeps up with the latest developments. But we also hear from colleagues who recognize the importance of the ongoing cross-border management tensions, often best captured in classic cases that teach timeless international management issues.

Based on input that we constantly receive from the users of this text as well as from the valuable expert reviews to which each new edition is subjected, we have sought to maintain this balance. As you will see in the following pages, while we have maintained the intellectual integrity of the core concepts, we have also undertaken a major updating of each of the chapters to ensure they reflect the current global context. As a new feature, we have added an extended list of recommended practitioner-oriented readings at the end of each chapter. Where possible, we have used the authors' wording of their article abstracts. We have also provided expanded annotated footnotes of relevant theory. And we have retained our practice of changing about half the case material in this edition, aiming to capture the emerging issues to keep courses fresh, while retaining popular classic cases that have maintained their relevance and have a proven history of stimulating strong classroom engagement and learning.

We trust you will find that the new content, new format, and new publisher support we have assembled for the eighth edition offer a relevant, insightful, and stimulating framework through which to explore the rich territory of transnational management.

ACKNOWLEDGMENTS

Transnational Management has greatly benefited from comments, suggestions, and insights generously offered by colleagues at the hundreds of institutions around the world that have adopted this book. In particular, we would like to acknowledge the key role played by the Cambridge University Press panel of reviewers whose insights and suggestions for the chapter content of the eighth edition proved extremely helpful. They are listed on page xix as our Editorial Advisory Board.

We are also extraordinarily grateful to the colleagues who have contributed to this edition. Co-authors who have collaborated on our own case studies for this edition include faculty colleagues Professors Harold Crookell, Brian J. Hall, Isaiah A. Litvak, Aloysius Newenham-Kahindi, Albert Wöcke, and Michael Y. Yoshino, as well as Research Associates and doctoral students R. Azimah Ainuddin, Heather Beckham, Nicole Bennett, Carole Carlson, Nikhil Celly, Dwarka Chakravarty, Vincent Dessain, Charles Dhanaraj, Perry L. Fagan, Vanessa Hasse, Arar Han, Sarah McAra, Paul S. Myers, Michael Roberts, Anders Sjoman, Laura Winig, and Megan (Min) Zhang. We are also delighted to include additional new case studies authored by Luis Arciniega, Ivy Buche, Ramasastry Chandrasekhar, Meeta Dasgupta, Charles Dhanaraj, Tashmia Ismail, Srivardhini K. Jha, Rishikesha Krishnan, José Luis Rivas, Jean-Louis Schaan, and Margaret Sutherland.

Assembling a textbook always involves coordinating many components, but this is particularly true at a time of transition from one publisher to another. We could not have managed this without the great help provided by the skilled support staff who worked with us over many months to coordinate the flow of emails, phone calls, manuscripts, and other documents between the United States, Canada, and Australia. At Ivey, this includes PhD candidates Dwarka Chakravarty, Yamlaksira Getachew, Max Stallkamp, and Jenny Zhu. However, we would like to offer special thanks to Research Associate Mila Bojic for helping us through the long and arduous revision process.

This eighth edition also represents an important publishing landmark that merits recognition. As mentioned in the preface, we are delighted to be working with Cambridge University Press as our new publisher. To Valerie Appleby, our Commissioning Editor, and Caitlin Lisle, our Development Editor, we offer our grateful thanks not only for your helpful input and continual support, but also for your patience and tolerance through a long and challenging transition process. We look forward to continuing our productive working relationship for many years to come.

Finally, we would like to acknowledge the lasting contribution of our good friend and colleague, the late Sumantra Ghoshal, who passed away in 2004. Sumantra was a founding co-author of this book and left an enduring imprint on the field of international management and beyond. His wisdom and insights still glow brightly in this volume. But more than his sharp intelligence, we miss his warm, convivial, and energetic company.

Despite the best efforts of all the contributors, responsibility for any remaining shortcomings of the book rests with us. Our only hope is that they are outweighed by the value that you find in these pages and the exciting challenges that they represent in the constantly changing field of transnational management.

EDITORIAL ADVISORY BOARD

Introduction
So What Is Transnational Management?

Few managers operating in today's international business environment would dispute that this is an extremely exciting time to be engaged in almost any aspect of cross-border management. Fast-changing global developments have created big challenges that appear unusually complex, but at the same time they have opened up new opportunities that seem almost limitless.

Around the world, managers are asking questions like the following: How does the unraveling of the long anticipated Trans-Pacific Partnership (TPP) trade agreement affect our business? What can we do to manage the political disruption and economic dislocation following Brexit? How can we take advantage of the continued rise in Asian markets? How should we deal with the threat of new competitors emerging from developing countries? Can we exploit the impending boom in big data to track and exploit new global trends? How might we harness fast-growing social networks to leverage our cross-border management connections and organizational processes?

Before we launch into these and the other such rich and engaging discussions, perhaps we should step back for a moment to review the broad territory we will be exploring on our voyage of discovery. A good place to start might be with the title of this book. What exactly does *Transnational Management* mean?

Transnational: What Does That Imply?

The first word on the cover of this book may not be familiar to some. While the terms "multinational," "international," and "global" are in widespread general use, it may not be entirely clear to you why we chose to use the less familiar description "transnational" in the title of this book.

Good question. And we promise to respond to it by the end of Chapter 1. By the end of that opening chapter it should be clear to you that we use those four terms quite specifically. Furthermore, you will find that our distinction between "multinational," "international," "global," and "transnational" will become a strong theme that runs through this book in our discussion of strategy, organization, and management.

But more of that later. For the purpose of this introduction, let's just recognize that the "transnational" qualifier indicates that our focus will be on the management challenges that face companies whose operations extend across national boundaries. Indeed, the concepts we will be presenting in the text are grounded in extensive research published in a book titled *Managing Across Borders: The*

Transnational Solution. The challenging cross-border management issues identified in that five-year long, multicompany, worldwide research project supplemented with a large body of subsequent research frames our agenda.

So what is different about cross-border management? In what ways do the challenges facing a manager of a multinational enterprise (MNE) differ from those facing his or her counterpart in a purely domestic organization? There are many such differences, but let's begin by identifying half a dozen of the most important that will be reflected in the issues we explore throughout this book.

- The most obvious contrast derives from the fact that, by definition, MNEs have operations in multiple nation-states, a difference that has huge strategic, organizational, and management implications. Although domestic companies must take account of local and state governments, what distinguishes intercountry differences from the intracountry ones is the powerful force of national sovereignty. Unlike the local or regional bodies, the nation-state generally represents the ultimate rule-making authority against whom no appeal is feasible. Consequently, the MNE faces an additional and unique element of risk: the political risk of operating in countries with different legislative requirements, legal systems, and political philosophies regarding a host of issues including private property, free enterprise, human rights, and corporate responsibility – that a domestic company can simply take for granted.
- Cross-border management must also deal with a greater range of social and cultural differences. Again, domestic companies experience some regional cultural differences, but in cross-border operations the stakes are much higher. An MNE will quickly flounder unless management is not only embedded in the community and able to speak the local language, but also is both sensitive and responsive to local cultural norms, practices, preferences, and values.
- By having operations in foreign countries, an MNE is exposed to a wide range of economic systems and conditions that they must understand and to which they must adapt. The differences may be built into political systems ranging from unfettered free enterprise to highly regulated socialist economies; they may be reflected in various stages of economic development from advanced OECD countries to extremely poor less developed countries; and they may be facilitated or constrained by differences in national infrastructure ranging from subtle differences in technical standards to the quality of basic communications services. Each variation in the underlying standards or support systems demands significant modifications to an MNE's strategy and operations.
- Another major way in which cross-border management diverges from domestic management relates to differences in competitive strategy. The purely domestic company can respond to competitive challenges within the context of its single market; the MNE can, and often must, play a much more complex competitive game. Global-scale efficiencies or cross-border sourcing may be necessary to achieve a competitive position, implying the need for complex international logistical coordination. Furthermore, on the global chessboard, effective competitive strategy might require that a competitive challenge in one country might call

for a response in a different country – perhaps the competitor's home market. These are options and complexities a purely domestic company does not face.

- In terms of metrics, a purely domestic company can measure its performance in a single comparable unit – the local currency. But because currency values fluctuate against each other, the MNE is required to measure results with a flexible and sometimes distorted measuring stick. In addition, its results are exposed to the economic risks associated with shifts in both nominal and real exchange rates.
- Finally, the purely domestic company manages its activities through organizational structures and management systems that reflect its product and functional variety; the MNE organization is intrinsically more complex because it must provide for management control over its product, functional, and geographic diversity. And the resolution of this three-way tension must be accomplished in an organization whose managers are divided by barriers of distance and time, and impeded by differences in language and culture.

Management: Why This Focus?

The *Transnational* in the title is simply a qualifier for *Management* and, in the final analysis, that is what this book is really about. In many ways, it is a focus that distinguishes this volume from many others in the field. For that reason, let's take a moment to understand why.

The serious study of cross-border management is a relatively recent phenomenon. For many decades, international business research focused mainly on global environmental forces, international systems and structures, and powerful institutions like home- and host-country governments, all of which framed the context within which the MNE had to operate. In these studies, countries and industries rather than companies were the primary units of analysis, and most international policy attention (as well as academic research) focused on macro analysis of key indicators such as trade flows and foreign direct investment patterns.

During the 1960s and 1970s, this interest in global economic forces and international institutions began to be matched by an equal focus on the MNE as the primary driver of the rapidly expanding international economy. A decade later, as the task of running such companies became more complex, attention again expanded to encompass an understanding of the roles, responsibilities, and relationships of those running the MNEs.

And so there opened a field of management that had been largely neglected by both practitioners and researchers up to that point. Indeed, until the 1970s, many companies had staffed their international operations with aging or less competent managers, instructing them to simply take the most successful domestic products, strategies, and practices, and transfer them abroad. But in the closing decades of the twentieth century, as new offshore markets opened up, global competition intensified, and worldwide operations became more complex, it was clear that such an approach was doomed to failure. Only the most capable managers would be able to run the modern MNE.

This book builds on the lessons that came out of that burst of innovation in cross-border management that has continued into the first decades of the twenty-first century. So while we will reflect on the changes taking place in the macro global environment, and specifically on the way in which these forces affect MNEs, we will do so by adopting a management interpretation, viewing these fast-changing global forces through the eyes of the executives who operate in the thick of it.

It is this management perspective that has framed the design of this book and the pedagogy that supports it. But unlike many other courses in international management that have been constructed around the traditional functions of the company – R&D, manufacturing, marketing, etc. – we have rejected this conceptual approach. Our experience is that the most important issues facing today's business leaders rarely come packaged in such neatly defined and hermetically sealed bundles. Almost all real-world problems cut across functional boundaries and require executives to understand the issue in a broader and more systemic sense. Furthermore, they demand integrative solutions that bring together, rather than divide, the people working in their traditional functional silos. For that reason, our dominant perspective throughout this book will be that of a general manager – whether that is the CEO of the corporation, the global business vice-president, the national subsidiary manager, or the frontline country product manager.

By adopting the perspective of the transnational general manager, however, we do not ignore the important and legitimate perspectives, interests, and influences of other key actors both inside and outside the company. We view the effects of these other key players from the perspective of an MNE general manager, however, and focus on understanding how they shape or influence the strategic, organizational, and operational decisions that the general manager must take.

Text, Cases, and Readings: How Will We Learn?

If the title, *Transnational Management*, describes the field of study and the content of the book, the subtitle, *Text and Cases in Cross-Border Management*, provides clues to the teaching philosophy and materials that will be employed. Because this book may be different in structure and format from some others you have used, it's probably worth spending a little time describing the classroom materials you will find between these covers and the pedagogic philosophy we followed in assembling them.

As the previous paragraphs have suggested, taking on the responsibility of the general manager in a twenty-first century MNE may well represent the most complex task to which a manager could be assigned. So creating a course that prepares one for such a role requires some creativity. It's clear that the challenges cannot be reduced, for example, to a few global strategy recipes, a standardized international organization chart, or a simple check list of the six most important things a country manager must do to succeed.

But neither is it helpful to suggest that everything is too complex to reduce to specifics. In the chapters that follow, we will seek a middle way that presents some broad concepts, frameworks, and principles that allow some generalization and conceptualization of the issues. But we will also provide material that allows students to take these generalized models for a "test drive" to apply, adapt, enhance, and embed the ideas in a practice-based, decision-oriented approach that is both grounded and flexible.

The Structure

The book is structured into three parts, which are divided into eight integrated text chapters, each representing a topic that builds on the chapters that precede it. The basic outline is shown in Figure 1.

Part I of the book consists of three chapters that focus on the strategic imperatives facing the MNE.

- In Chapter 1, we will examine the internal strategic motivations that drive, attract, or compel MNEs to expand offshore.
- Chapter 2 helps us understand the complex and often conflicting external environmental forces that shape the strategy of the MNE as it expands abroad.

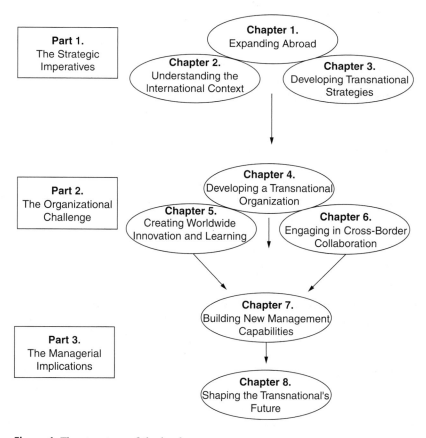

Figure 1 The structure of the book

- Chapter 3 explores how MNEs resolve the tension between their internal motivations and the external forces to develop a strategy based on building layers of competitive advantage.

Part II has three chapters that examine the organizational challenges flowing from the strategic imperatives.

- Chapter 4 examines the task of building an organization able to deliver the multilayered strategic capabilities required by a multidimensional transnational strategy.
- Chapter 5 focuses on the critical strategic task of developing the capability to advance and diffuse innovations on a worldwide platform.
- In Chapter 6, we explore the growing organizational challenge of managing collaborations across corporate boundaries.

Part III has two chapters focusing on the managerial implications of both the strategic imperatives and the organizational challenges we have identified.

- Chapter 7 allows us to explore the managerial roles and responsibilities required to build the capabilities MNEs need to successfully implement their strategies.
- Chapter 8 considers the evolving roles and responsibilities of transnational organizations that managers need to develop to negotiate the current and future global political economy.

The Learning Materials

To help us through this big agenda, the book is constructed around three major learning resources: the eight text chapters described above, 28 case studies relevant to the chapter topics, and a portfolio of recommended practitioner and academic supplemental readings. Let's briefly explain how each of these components contribute to the overall learning.

At the end of each chapter, there is a list of recommended readings drawn primarily from practitioner-oriented journals such as *Harvard Business Review* and the *McKinsey Quarterly*. These readings have been carefully selected to provide supplemental perspectives to those presented in the text chapters. Some are classic articles whose wisdom has endured over time, while others are contemporary and reflect the latest thinking on the topic being addressed. And for those interested in exploring the theoretical underpinnings of the arguments presented, the footnotes in each chapter provide a link to relevant academic articles. In all instances, the objective of these supplemental readings is to expand and enrich the mental maps being created as we progress on this voyage of discovery.

But, as we have emphasized, because the challenges facing the modern MNE represent perhaps the most complex environment in which a manager can operate, no amount of concepts, models, theories, or frameworks can capture the task. We believe that the most powerful way to allow students to enter this complexity is to employ real-life cases that require the complexity to be unraveled and decisions to be made. Most of those in this book provide the reader not only with data on the macro business and company context, but also with detailed information about the key actors and what they bring to the situation: their personal motivations, their strengths and weaknesses, their roles and responsibilities. In many instances, videos and follow-up cases lead to further insight.

Although a few of the cases have been disguised, all of them are real, and almost all have been prepared on the basis of detailed field research. While the vast majority of them document current best practice or illustrate managers facing contemporary challenges, we have also included a handful of classic cases, enduring favorites that have been shown to be effective in illustrating persistent issues in cross-border management.

For those who are less familiar with the use of cases in a classroom setting, it is worthwhile emphasizing that the purpose of this classroom material is to present you with the kinds of important challenges a manager might encounter only once a year, once in a decade, or even once in a career. They present you with an opportunity to go through the same process as the case protagonist – sorting through the information, analyzing the situation, evaluating the options, deciding on action, thinking through the implementation steps required to bring about the necessary change, and then convincing your colleagues of the wisdom of your approach. Repeating this process a couple of dozen times through the course can significantly increase one's ability to translate abstract concepts and general theories into real on-the-ground practice.

Getting Started

But enough overview, background, and analysis; it's time to launch headlong into this fascinating and exciting new world of transnational management. So let's begin our voyage to explore the challenges and opportunities of those who have the responsibility for the strategy and operations of organizations that stretch across the barriers of distance, language, and culture. It should be quite a trip.

Part I
The Strategic Imperatives

1 Expanding Abroad
Motivations, Means, and Mentalities

This chapter looks at a number of important questions that companies must resolve before taking the leap to operate outside their home environment. What market opportunities, sourcing advantages, or strategic imperatives provide the *motivation* for their international expansion? By what *means* will they expand their overseas presence – through modes such as exports, licensing, joint ventures, wholly owned subsidiaries, or some other means? And how will the management *mentalities* – their embedded attitudes, assumptions, and beliefs – that they bring to their international ventures affect their chances of success? Before exploring these important questions, however, we first need to develop a definition of this entity – the multinational enterprise (MNE) – that we plan to study and develop some sense of its size and importance in the global economy.

This book focuses on the management challenges associated with developing the strategies, building the organizations, and managing the operations of companies whose activities stretch across national boundaries. Clearly, operating in an international rather than a domestic arena presents managers with many new opportunities. Having worldwide operations not only gives a company access to new markets and low-cost resources, it also opens up new sources of information and knowledge, and broadens the options for strategic moves the company might make in competing with its domestic and international rivals. However, with all these new opportunities come the challenges of managing strategy, organization, and operations that are innately more complex, diverse, and uncertain.

Our starting point is to focus on the dominant vehicle of internationalization, the MNE, and briefly review its role and influence in the global economy.[1] Only after understanding the origins, interests, and objectives of this key actor will we be in a position to explore the strategies it pursues and the organization it develops to achieve them.

---

[1] Such entities are referred to variously – and often interchangeably – as *multinational, international,* and *global enterprises*. (Note that we use the term "enterprise" rather than "corporation" because some of the cross-border entities we will examine are non-profit organizations whose strategies and operations are every bit as complex as their corporate brethren's.) At the end of this chapter, we assign each of those terms – *multinational, international,* and *global* – specific meanings, but throughout the book, we adopt the widely used MNE abbreviation in a broader, more general, sense to refer to all enterprises whose operations extend across national borders.

In this chapter, we introduce the MNE by defining its key characteristics, discussing its origins, interests, and objectives, and reviewing its major role and influence in the global economy. We then describe the motivations that drive these companies abroad, the means they adopt to expand internationally, and the mentalities of management that shape the strategies MNEs pursue and the organizations they develop to achieve them.

The MNE: Definition, Scope, and Influence

An economic historian could trace the origins of international business back thousands of years to the sea-faring traders of Greece and Egypt,[2] through the merchant traders of medieval Venice, and the great British and Dutch trading companies of the seventeenth and eighteenth centuries. By the nineteenth century, the newly emerged capitalists in industrialized Europe began investing in the less developed areas of the world (including the United States) but particularly within the vast empires held by Britain, France, Holland, and Germany.

Definition

In terms of the working definition we use, few if any of these entities through history could be called true MNEs. Most early traders would be excluded by our first qualification, which requires that an MNE have *substantial direct investment* in foreign countries, not just the trading relationships of an import–export business. And even most of the companies that had established international operations in the nineteenth century would be excluded by our second criterion, which requires that they be engaged in the *active management* of these offshore assets rather than simply holding them in a passive investment portfolio.

Thus, though companies that source their raw materials offshore, license their technologies abroad, export their products into foreign markets, or even hold minor equity positions in overseas ventures without any management involvement may regard themselves as "international," by our definition they are not true MNEs unless they have substantial direct investment in foreign countries *and* actively manage and regard those operations as integral parts of the company, both strategically and organizationally.

Scope

According to our definition, the MNE is a very recent phenomenon, with the vast majority developing only in the post–World War II years. However, the motivations for international expansion and the nature of MNEs' offshore activities have evolved significantly over this relatively short period, and we will explore some of these changes later in this chapter.

[2] See Karl Moore and David Lewis, *The Origins of Globalization* (New York: Routledge, 2009).

It is interesting to observe how the United Nations (UN) has changed its definition of the MNE as these companies have grown in size and importance.[3] In 1973, it defined such an enterprise as one "which controls assets, factories, mines, sales offices, and the like in two or more countries." By 1984, it had changed the definition to an enterprise (a) comprising entities in two or more countries, regardless of the legal form and fields of activity of those entities; (b) which operates under a system of decision making permitting coherent policies and a common strategy through one or more decision-making centers; and (c) in which the entities are so linked, by ownership or otherwise, that one or more of them may be able to exercise a significant influence over the activities of the others, in particular to share knowledge, resources, and responsibilities.

In essence, the changing definition highlights the importance of both strategic and organizational integration, and thereby the *active, coordinated management* of operations located in different countries, as the key differentiating characteristic of an MNE. The resources committed to those units can take the form of skilled people or research equipment just as easily as plants and machinery or computer hardware. What really differentiates the MNE is that it creates an internal organization to carry out key cross-border tasks and transactions internally rather than depending on trade through the external markets, just as the companies in Table 1.1 do. This more recent UN definition also expands earlier assumptions of traditional ownership patterns to encompass a more varied set of financial, legal, and contractual relationships with different foreign affiliates. With this understanding, our definition of MNEs includes Apple, BP, and Honda Motors, but also Intercontinental Hotels, Deloitte Consulting, and McDonald's.

MNE Influence in the Global Economy

Most frequent international business travelers have had an experience like the following: She arrives on her Singapore Airlines flight, rents a Toyota at Hertz, and drives to the downtown Marriott Hotel. In her room, she flips on the LG television and absentmindedly gazes out at neon signs flashing "Pepsi," "Samsung," and "Lexus." The latest episode of *Modern Family* is flickering on the screen when room service delivers dinner along with the bottle of Perrier she ordered. All of a sudden, a feeling of disorientation engulfs her. Is she in Sydney, Shanghai, Sao Paulo, or San Francisco? Her surroundings and points of reference over the past few hours have provided few clues.

Such experiences, more than any data, provide the best indication of the enormous influence of MNEs in the global economy. As the cases in this book show, few sectors of the economy and few firms – not even those that are purely domestic in their operations – are free from this pervasive influence. Worldwide, there are over

---

[3] The generic term for companies operating across national borders in most UN studies is *transnational corporation* (TNC). Because we use that term very specifically, we continue to define the general form of organizations with international operations as MNEs.

Table 1.1 Selected indicators of FDI and international production, 2010–2015

Item	Value at current prices (billions of dollars)			Annual growth rate or change on return (%)		
	2010	2014	2015	2010	2014	2015
FDI inflows	1,244	1,277	1,762	4.9	−10.5	38.0
FDI outflows	1,323	1,318	1,474	13.1	0.6	11.8
FDI inward stock	19,141	25,113	24,983	6.6	2.4	−0.5
FDI outward stock	20,408	24,810	25,045	6.3	0.6	0.9
Income on inward FDI	1,137	1,595[a]	1,404[a]	20.3	4.5	−12.0
Rate of return on inward FDI[b]	7.3	6.7	6.0	0.3	0.2	−0.7
Income on outward FDI	1,251[b]	1,509[a]	1,351[a]	20.6	4.3	−10.5
Rate of return on outward FDI[b]	7.2	6.3	5.6	0.3	0.2	−0.7
Cross-border M&As	339	432	721	35.7	64.7	66.8
Sales of foreign affiliates	32,960[c]	34,149[d]	36,668[d]	9.1	7.2	7.4
Value-added (product) of foreign affiliates	6,636[c]	7,419[d]	7,903[d]	8.3	5.5	6.5
Total assets of foreign affiliates	56,998[c]	101,254[d]	105,778[d]	6.3	5.8	4.5
Exports of foreign affiliates	6,239[e]	7,688[e]	7,803[e]	18.6	2.9	1.5
Employment by foreign affiliates (thousands)	68,218[c]	76,821[d]	79,505[d]	2.3	6.3	3.5

Source: UNCTAD, *World Investment Report 2016*.

[a] Based on data from 174 countries for income on FDI and 143 countries for income on outward FDI in 2015, in both cases representing more than 90% of global inward and outward stocks.

[b] Calculated only for countries with both FDI income and stock data.

[c] Data for 2010 is estimated based on a fixed-effects panel regression of each variable against outward stock and a lagged dependent variable for the period 1980–2008.

[d] Data for 2014 and 2015 are estimated based on a fixed-effects panel regression of each variable against outward stock and a lagged dependent variable for the period 1980–2012.

[e] The share of exports of foreign affiliates in world exports in 1998 (33.3%) was applied to obtain values.

Note: Not included in this table is the value of worldwide sales by foreign affiliates associated with their parent firms through non-equity relationships and of the sales of the parent firms themselves. Worldwide sales, gross product, total assets, exports, and employment of foreign affiliates are sometimes estimated.

130 million firms.[4] While most of these are small, and focused on their home country, others are extremely large, with a global focus. In 2015, MNEs' foreign affiliates generated value-added of approximately $8 trillion, more than one-tenth of global GDP and 30% of world exports.

[4] The *World Investment Report 2016* published by the United Nations Conference on Trade and Development (UNCTAD) references the Bureau van Dijk's Orbis database. This database is the largest and most widely used database of its kind, covering 136 million active companies (at the time of extraction, in November 2015) across more than 200 countries and territories, and containing firm-level data sourced from national business registries, chambers of commerce, and various other official sources (UNCTAD, *World Investment Report 2016*, p. 145).

Table 1.2 Internationalization statistics of the 100 largest non-financial MNEs worldwide and from developing and transition economies
(Billions of dollars, thousands of employees, and percent)

	100 largest MNEs worldwide			100 largest MNEs from developing and transition economies	
	2013	2014	2015[a]	2013	2014
Assets					
Foreign	8,198	8,341	7,933	1,556	1,731
Total	13,382	13,231	12,854	5,540	5,948
Foreign as % of total	61	63	62	28	29
Sales					
Foreign	6,078	6,011	5,115	2,003	2,135
Total	9,292	9,042	7,863	4,170	4,295
Foreign as % of total	65	66	65	48	50
Employment					
Foreign	9,555	9,375	9,973	4,083	4,173
Total	16,461	15,816	17,304	11,447	11,534
Foreign as % of total	58	59	58	36	36

Source: UNCTAD, *World Investment Report 2016*.
Note: Data refer to fiscal year results reported between April 1 of the base year to March 31 of the following year. 2015 data are unavailable for the 100 largest MNEs from developing and transition economies due to lengthier reporting deadlines in these economies.
[a] Preliminary results.

Not all MNEs are large, but most large companies in the world are MNEs. Indeed, the largest 100 MNEs, excluding those in banking and finance, accounted for $12.9 trillion of total worldwide assets in 2015, of which $7.9 trillion was located outside their respective home countries.

Moreover, as Table 1.1 shows, international production is expanding, with sales, employment, and assets of foreign affiliates all increasing. The rate of return earned by MNEs on foreign direct investment (FDI) was 5.6% in 2015.

However, the importance of the developing and transition economies is rising. As Table 1.2 shows, while the total worldwide assets of the 100 largest MNEs (or TNCs as the UN refers to them) decreased by 1.1% to $13,231 billion between 2013 and 2014, in the same period, the total assets of the 100 largest TNCs from developing and transition economies increased by 7.4% to $5,948 billion. In addition, while the total employment of the 100 largest TNCs worldwide decreased by 3.9% to 15,816,000 between 2013 and 2014, in the same period, the total employment of the 100 largest TNCs from developing and transition economies increased by 0.8% to 11,534,000.

A different perspective on the size and potential impact of MNEs is provided in Table 1.3, which compares the overall revenues of several MNEs with the gross

Table 1.3 Comparison of top MNEs and selected countries: 2016

Company[a]	Revenues (millions USD)	Company rank	Country[b]	GDP (current millions USD)	Country GDP rank
Walmart	482,130	1	United States	18,036,648	1
State Grid[c]	329,601	2	China	11,007,721	2
China National Petroleum	299,271	3	Japan	4,123,258	3
Sinopec Group	294,344	4	Germany	3,363,447	4
Royal Dutch Shell	272,156	5	Nigeria	481,066	23
ExxonMobil	246,204	6	South Africa	314,572	31
Volkswagen	236,600	7	Denmark	295,091	35
Toyota Motor	236,592	8	Finland	231,950	42
Apple	233,715	9	Hungary	121,715	55
BP	225,982	10	Jamaica	14,262	112
Samsung Electronics	177,440	13	Moldova	6,568	142

Note: This table is illustrative of the economic importance of some of the world's largest MNEs. One has to be cautious when comparing the above company and country numbers. That is because country GDPs and company revenues are not perfectly comparable while country value-added and company value-added are. A country's GDP represents its value-added whereas a company's revenue is typically higher than its value-added. Thus from a comparison point of view, the above company numbers may be somewhat inflated relative to the country numbers.

[a] Data are from the Fortune Global 500 list of the world's largest corporation in 2016 by revenue http://beta.fortune.com/global500.

[b] Data are from World Development Indicators published by the World Bank http://data.worldbank.org/indicator/NY.GDP.MKTP.CD?year_high_desc=true.

[c] State Grid Corporation of China, established in 2002, is the world's largest utility company.

domestic products (GDPs) of selected countries. By comparing company revenues and country GDPs, it is clear that some of the world's largest MNEs are equivalent in their economic importance to medium-sized economies such as Nigeria, South Africa, and Denmark, and considerably more economically important than smaller or less developed economies such as Jamaica, Moldova, or Barbados. They have considerable influence on the global economy, employ a high percentage of business graduates, and pose the most complex strategic and organizational challenges for their managers. For the same reasons, they provide the focus for much of our attention in this book.

The Motivations: Pushes and Pulls to Internationalize

What motivates companies to expand their operations internationally?[5] Although occasionally the motives may be entirely idiosyncratic, such as the desire of the CEO

[5] In "Internalisation thinking: from multinational enterprise to the global factory," internalization thinking is traced from its inception, by Coase, through its application to multinational enterprises

to spend time in Mexico or link to old family ties in Europe, an extensive body of research suggests some more systematic patterns.

Traditional Motivations

Among the earliest motivations that drove companies to invest abroad was the need to *secure key supplies*. Aluminum producers needed to ensure their supply of bauxite, tire companies went abroad to develop rubber plantations, and oil companies wanted to open new fields in Canada, the Middle East, and Venezuela. By the early part of the nineteenth century, Standard Oil, Alcoa, Goodyear, Anaconda Copper, and International Nickel were among the largest of the emerging MNEs.

Another strong trigger for internationalization could be described as *market-seeking* behavior. This motivation was particularly strong for companies that had some intrinsic advantage, typically related to their technology or brand recognition, which gave them a competitive advantage in offshore markets. Their initial moves were often opportunistic, frequently originating with an unsolicited export order. However, many companies eventually realized that additional sales enabled them to exploit economies of scale and scope, thereby providing a source of competitive advantage over their domestic rivals. This market seeking was a particularly strong motive for some European multinationals whose small home markets were insufficient to support the volume-intensive manufacturing processes that were sweeping through industries from food and tobacco to chemicals and automobiles. Companies such as Philips, Volkswagen, and Unilever expanded internationally primarily in search of new markets.

Another traditional and important trigger of internationalization was the desire to *access low-cost factors* of production. Particularly as tariff barriers declined in the 1960s, the United States and many European countries, for which labor represented a major cost, found that their products were at a competitive disadvantage compared with imports. In response, a number of companies in clothing, electronics, household appliances, watch-making, and other such industries established offshore

and to the global factory. The general principles governing the internalization of markets are revisited and the focus on innovation, the dynamics of internalization, and its application to newer structures of firms such as the global factory are emphasized.

P. J. Buckley, "Internalisation thinking: from the multinational enterprise to the global factory," *International Business Review*, 18:3 (2009), 224–35.

"Uncertainty, imitation, and plant location: Japanese multinational corporations, 1990–1996," uses neoinstitutional theory and research on political institutions to explain organizational entry into new geographic markets. It extends neoinstitutional theory's proposition that prior decisions and actions by other organizations provide legitimization and information to a decision marked by uncertainty, showing that this effect holds when the uncertainty comes from a firm's lack of experience in a market but not when the uncertainty derives from the structure of a market's policymaking apparatus.

W. J. Henisz and A. Delios, "Uncertainty, imitation, and plant location: Japanese multinational corporations, 1990–1996," *Administrative Science Quarterly*, 46:3 (2001), 443–75.

sourcing locations to produce components or even complete product lines. For example, General Electric (GE) moved production from its lamp plant in Virginia to China and GE Healthcare, one of GE's most strategic businesses, invested in three world-class plants in India and more recently started manufacturing high-end computed tomography (CT) imaging systems there for India and the world.

Labor was not the only productive factor that could be sourced more economically overseas. For example, the availability of lower cost capital (often through a government investment subsidy) also became a strong force for internationalization. It was the provision of such government financial incentives that induced General Motors to expand its basic assembly operation in Brazil into a fully integrated operation that is now the company's fourth most important R&D facility worldwide.

These three motives were the main traditional driving force behind the overseas expansion of MNEs. The ways in which these motives interacted to push companies – particularly those from the United States – to become MNEs are captured in Vernon's well-known product cycle theory.[6]

This theory suggests that the starting point for an internationalization process is typically an innovation that a company creates in its home country. In the first phase of exploiting the development, the company – let's assume it is in the United States – builds production facilities in its home market not only because this is where its main customer base is located but also because of the need to maintain close linkages between research and production in this phase of its development cycle. In this early stage, some demand also may be created in other developed countries – in European countries, for example – where consumer needs and market developments are similar to those of the United States. These requirements normally would be met with home production, thereby generating exports for the United States.

During this pre-MNE stage, firms would typically establish an export unit within the home office, to oversee the growing export levels. Committing to this sort of organizational structure would in turn typically lead to stronger performance than would treating exports simply as a part of the domestic business.[7]

As the product matures and production processes become standardized, the company enters a new stage. By this time, demand in the European countries may have become quite sizable, and export sales, originally a marginal side benefit, have become an important part of the revenues from the new business. Furthermore, competitors probably begin to see the growing demand for the new product as a potential opportunity to establish themselves in the markets served by exports. To prevent or counteract such competition and to meet the foreign demand more effectively, the innovating company typically sets up production facilities in the importing countries, thereby making the transition from being an exporter to becoming a true MNE.

---

[6] Raymond Vernon, "International investment and international trade in the product cycle," *Quarterly Journal of Economics*, May (1966), 190–207.

[7] Paul W. Beamish, Lambros Karavis, Anthony Goerzen, and Christopher Lane, "The relationship between organizational structure and export performance," *Management International Review*, 39 (1999), 37–54.

Finally, in the third stage, the product becomes highly standardized, and many competitors enter the business. Competition focuses on price and, therefore, on cost. This trend activates the resource-seeking motive, and the company moves production to low-wage, developing countries to meet the demands of its customers in the developed markets at a lower cost. In this final phase, the developing countries may become net exporters of the product while the developed countries become net importers.

Although the product cycle theory provided a useful way to describe much of the internationalization of the postwar decades,[8] by the 1980s, its explanatory power was beginning to wane, as Vernon himself was quick to point out. As the international business environment became increasingly complex and sophisticated, companies developed a much richer rationale for their worldwide operations.

Emerging Motivations

Once MNEs had established international sales and production operations, their perceptions and strategic motivations gradually changed.[9] Initially, the typical attitude was that the foreign operations were mere strategic and organizational appendages to the domestic business and should be managed opportunistically. Gradually, however, managers began to think about their strategy in a more integrated, worldwide sense. In this process, the forces that originally triggered their expansion overseas often became secondary to a new set of motivations that underlay their emerging global strategies.

The first such set of forces was the increasing *scale economies, ballooning R&D investments,* and *shortening product life cycles* that transformed many industries into global rather than national structures and made a worldwide scope of activities not a matter of choice but an essential prerequisite for companies to survive in those businesses. These forces are described in detail in the next chapter.

A second factor that often became critical to a company's international strategy – though it was rarely the original motivating trigger – was its global *scanning and learning* capability.[10] A company drawn offshore to secure supplies of raw materials

---

[8] The record of international expansion of countries in the post-World War II era is quite consistent with the pattern suggested by the product cycle theory.

[9] "The governance of global value chains" article builds a theoretical framework to help explain governance patterns in global value chains. It draws on transaction costs economics, production networks, technological capability, and firm-level learning to identify three variables that play a large role in determining how global value chains are governed and change. These are: (1) the complexity of transactions, (2) the ability to codify transactions, and (3) the capabilities in the supply base. The theory generates five types of global value-chain governance – hierarchy, captive, relational, modular, and market – which range from high to low levels of explicit coordination and power asymmetry. The article highlights the dynamic and overlapping nature of global value-chain governance through four brief industry case studies: bicycles, apparel, horticulture, and electronics.
G. Gereffi, J. Humphrey, and T. Sturgeon, "The governance of global value chains," *Review of International Political Economy*, 12:1 (2005), 78–104.

[10] This motivation is highlighted by Raymond Vernon in "Gone are the cash cows of yesteryear," *Harvard Business Review*, November–December (1980), 150–5.

was more likely to become aware of alternative, low-cost production sources around the globe; a company tempted abroad by market opportunities was often exposed to new technologies or market needs that stimulated innovative product development. The very nature of an MNE's worldwide presence gave it a huge informational advantage that could result in it locating more efficient sources or more advanced product and process technologies. Thus a company whose international strategy was triggered by a technological or marketing advantage could enhance that advantage through the scanning and learning potential inherent in its worldwide network of operations. (This has become an increasingly important strategic advantage that we will explore in detail in Chapter 5.)

A third benefit that soon became evident was that being a multinational rather than a national company brought important advantages of *competitive positioning*. Certainly, the most controversial of the many global competitive strategic actions taken by MNEs in recent years have been those based on cross-subsidization of markets. For example, a Chinese energy company, such as China Petroleum and Chemical Group (Sinopec), could challenge a national company in the United States by subsidizing its US losses with funds from its profitable Middle East or South American operations.

If the US company did not have strong positions in the Chinese company's key Middle East and South American markets, its competitive response could only be to defend its home market positions – typically by seeking government intervention or matching or offsetting the Chinese challenger's competitive price reductions. Recognition of these competitive implications of multicountry operations led some companies to change the criteria for their international investment decisions to reflect not only market attractiveness or cost-efficiency choices but also the leverage such investments provided over competitors.[11]

Although for the purposes of analysis – and to reflect some sense of historical development – the motives behind the expansion of MNEs have been reduced to a few distinct categories, it should be clear that companies were rarely driven by a single motivating force. More adaptable companies soon learned how to capitalize on the potential advantages available from their international operations – ensuring critical supplies, entering new markets, tapping low-cost factors of production, leveraging their global information access, and capitalizing on the competitive advantage of their multiple market positions – and began to use these strengths to play a new strategic game that we will describe in later chapters as *global chess*.

The Means of Internationalization: Prerequisites and Processes

Having explored *why* an aspiring MNE wants to expand abroad (i.e., its motivation), we must now understand *how* it does so by exploring the means of

---

[11] These competitive aspects of global operations are discussed in detail in Chapter 3.

internationalization. Beyond the desire to expand offshore, a company must possess certain competencies – attributes that we describe as prerequisites – if it is to succeed in overseas markets. It must then be able to implement its desire to expand abroad through a series of decisions and commitments that define the internationalization process.

Prerequisites for Internationalization

In each national market, a foreign company suffers from some disadvantages in comparison with local competitors, at least initially. Because of their greater familiarity with the national culture, industry structure, government requirements, and other aspects of doing business in that country, domestic companies have a huge natural advantage. Their existing relationships with relevant customers, suppliers, regulators, and so on provide additional advantages that the foreign company must either match or counteract with some unique strategic capability. Most often, this countervailing strategic advantage comes from the MNE's superior knowledge or skills, which typically take the form of advanced technological expertise or specific marketing competencies. At other times, scale economies in R&D, production, or some other part of the value chain become the main source of the MNE's advantage over domestic firms. It is important to note, however, that the MNE cannot expect to succeed in the international environment unless it has some distinctive competency to overcome the liability of its foreignness.[12]

Such knowledge or scale-based strategic advantages are, by themselves, insufficient to justify the internationalization of operations. Often with much less effort, a company could sell or license its technology to foreign producers, franchise its brand name internationally, or sell its products abroad through general trading companies or local distributors, without having to set up its own offshore operations. This approach was explicitly adopted by Dunkin Donuts, which decided to proactively and aggressively franchise its brand domestically (in the United States) as well as internationally rather than solely set up its own domestic and international restaurants. Dunkin's founder, Bill Rosenberg, was so enamored by the franchising concept that he founded the International Franchise Association (IFA) in 1960. He believed that franchising is a wonderful way to expand further and faster. By 2016, Dunkin had more than 11,000 restaurants worldwide in 42 countries, around 8,000 of which were in the United States and 3,000 abroad. Approximately 99% of these restaurants were franchised operations. Dunkin claimed to serve more than 3 million customers a day! One may argue that Dunkin could not have grown domestically and internationally as fast were it not for the franchising strategy that it followed.

---

[12] The need for such strategic advantages for a company to become an MNE is highlighted by the *market imperfections theory of MNEs*. For a comprehensive review of this theory, see Richard E. Caves, *Multinational Enterprise and Economic Analysis*, 3rd edn (Cambridge: Cambridge University Press, 2007).

The other precondition for a company to become an MNE therefore is that it must have the organizational capability to leverage its strategic assets more effectively through its own subsidiaries than through contractual relations with outside parties. If superior knowledge is the main source of an MNE's competitive advantage, for example, it must have an organizational system that provides better returns from extending and exploiting its knowledge through direct foreign operations than the return it could get by selling or licensing that knowledge.[13]

To summarize, three conditions must be met for the existence of an MNE. First, some foreign countries must offer certain location-specific advantages to provide the requisite *motivation* for the company to invest there. Second, the company must have some *strategic competencies* or ownership-specific advantages to counteract the disadvantages of its relative unfamiliarity with foreign markets. Third, it must possess some *organizational capabilities* to achieve better returns from leveraging its strategic strengths internally rather than through external market mechanisms such as contracts or licenses.[14] Understanding these prerequisites is important not only because they explain why MNEs exist but also, as we show in Chapter 3, because they help define the strategic options for competing in worldwide businesses.

The Process of Internationalization

The process of developing these strategic and organizational attributes lies at the heart of the internationalization process through which a company builds its position in world markets.[15] This process is rarely well thought out in advance,

---

[13] The issue of organizational capability is the focus of what has come to be known as the *internalization theory of MNEs*. See Alan M. Rugman, "A new theory of the multinational enterprise: internationalization versus internalization," *Columbia Journal of World Business*, Spring (1982), 54–61. For a more detailed exposition, see Peter J. Buckley and Mark Casson, *The Future of the Multinational Enterprise* (London: MacMillan, 1976).

[14] These three conditions are highlighted in John Dunning's eclectic theory. See John H. Dunning and Sarianna M. Lundan, *Multinational Enterprises and the Global Economy*, 2nd edn (Cheltenham, UK: Edward Elgar, 2008).

[15] In "International expansion through flexible replication," Jonsson and Foss discuss how business organizations may expand internationally by replicating a part of their value chain, such as a sales and marketing format, in other countries. Based on a longitudinal in-depth study of Swedish home furnishing giant IKEA, they found that IKEA has developed organizational mechanisms that support an ongoing learning process aimed at frequent modification of the format for replication. They also observed that IKEA treats replication as hierarchical: lower level features (marketing efforts, pricing, etc.) are allowed to vary across IKEA stores in response to market-based learning, while higher level features (fundamental values, vision, etc.) are replicated in a uniform manner across stores, and change only very slowly (if at all) in response to learning ("flexible replication").

A. Jonsson and N. J. Foss, "International expansion through flexible replication: learning from the internationalization experience of IKEA," *Journal of International Business Studies*, 42:9 (2011), 1079–102.

In "International diversification and firm performance: the S-curve hypothesis," Lu and Beamish propose a theoretical framework for the study of multinationality and performance, which includes both benefits and costs of geographic expansion over different phases of internationalization. They find a consistent horizontal S-shaped relationship between multinationality and performance.

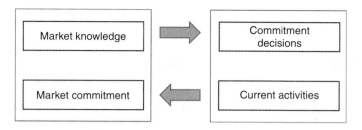

Figure 1.1 A learning model of internationalization
Source: Johanson and Vahlne, 1977.

and it typically builds on a combination of rational analysis, opportunism, and pure luck. Nonetheless, it is still possible to discern some general patterns of behavior that firms typically follow.

The most well-known model for internationalization was developed by two Swedish academics based in Uppsala, who described foreign market entry as a learning process.[16] The company makes an initial commitment of resources to the foreign market, and through this investment, it gains local market knowledge about customers, competitors, and regulatory conditions. On the basis of this market knowledge, the company is able to evaluate its current activities, the extent of its commitment to the market, and thus the opportunities for additional investment. It then makes a subsequent resource commitment, perhaps buying out its local distributor or investing in a local manufacturing plant, which allows it to develop additional market knowledge. Gradually, and through several cycles of investment, the company develops the necessary levels of local capability and market knowledge to become an effective competitor in the foreign country (see Figure 1.1).

Whereas many companies internationalize in the incremental approach depicted by the so-called Uppsala model, a great many do not.[17] Some companies invest in or acquire local partners to shortcut the process of building up local market knowledge. For example, Wal-Mart entered the UK by buying the supermarket chain ASDA rather than developing its own stores. Others speed up this process even more by starting up as "born globals" (see next page for a definition of a "born global" company). For example, Facebook, the social networking firm founded in

---

Further, firms investing more heavily in intangible assets, such as technology and advertising, achieved greater profitability gains from growth in FDI. Jane W. Lu and Paul W. Beamish, "International diversification and firm performance: the S-curve hypothesis," *Academy of Management Journal*, 47:4 (2004), 598–609.

[16] Jan Johanson and Jan-Erik Vahlne, "The internationalization process of the firm: a model of knowledge development and increasing foreign market commitments," *Journal of International Business Studies*, 88 (1977), 23–32. Jan Johanson and Jan-Erik Vahlne, "The Uppsala internationalization process model revisited: from liability of foreignness to liability of outsidership," *Journal of International Business Studies*, 40 (2009), 1411–31.

[17] Jonathan Calof and Paul W. Beamish, "Adapting to foreign markets: explaining internationalization," *International Business Review*, 4 (1995), 115–31.

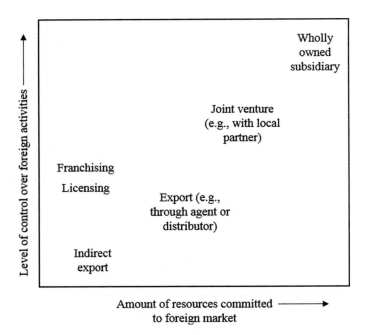

Figure 1.2 Approaches to foreign market entry
Derived from Johanson and Vahlne, 1977.

2004, became global at surprising speed because it was started as an internet company. By 2016, Facebook had around 1.79 billion monthly active users (MAUs) and around 1.18 billion daily active users (DAUs) and was available in more than 90 different languages. Its millions of users and thousands of advertisers and developers are managed from offices or data centers in over 30 countries. Cases such as these highlight the complexity of the decisions MNEs face in entering a foreign market.

One important set of factors is the assimilation of local market knowledge by the subsidiary unit, as suggested by the Uppsala model. But other, equally important factors to the MNE include its overall level of commitment to the foreign market in question, the required level of control of foreign operations, and the timing of its entry. To help make sense of these different factors, it is useful to think of the different modes of operating overseas in terms of two factors: the level of market commitment made and the level of control needed (see Figure 1.2).

Some companies internationalize by gradually moving up the scale, from exporting through joint venturing to direct foreign investment. Others, such as Wal-Mart, prefer to move straight to the high-commitment, high-control mode of operating, in part because they are entering mature markets in which it would be very difficult to build a business from nothing. Still others choose to adopt a low-commitment, low-control mode, such as some "born global" companies. "Born globals" establish significant international operations at or near their founding. Whether this is due to their internal orientation,[18] or the need to move quickly due to the nature of their product or services, such firms do not take such an incremental approach.

One of the most well-known "born globals" of our time is Google. Google was able to make this approach work because it started as an online search company whose users could access its web-based search engine from nearly any country in the world without Google's brick-and-mortar investment in that country. To be clear, none of these approaches is necessarily right or wrong, but they should be consistent with the overall strategic intentions and motivations of the MNE.

Similarly, not all MNEs are large firms. By definition, most large MNEs started out small. Yet many small- and medium-sized enterprises (SMEs) retain such a size, while still being MNEs in their own right. Other SMEs, observing a positive impact on performance as a consequence of their FDI activity, will grow.[19]

The Evolving Mentality: International to Transnational

Even from this brief description of the changing motivations for and means of internationalization, it should be clear that a gradual evolution has occurred in the strategic role that foreign operations play in emerging MNEs.[20] We can categorize this evolutionary pattern into four stages that reflect the way in which management thinking has developed over time as changes have occurred in both the international business environment and the MNE as a unique corporate form.

Although such a classification is necessarily generalized and somewhat arbitrary, it enables us to achieve two objectives. First, it highlights that, for most MNEs, the objectives that initially induced management to go overseas evolve into a very different set of motivations over time, thereby progressively changing management attitudes and actions. Second, such a classification provides a specific language

[18] Jane Lu and Paul W. Beamish, "Internationalization and performance of SMEs," *Strategic Management Journal*, 22 (2001), 565–86.

[19] In his *Ivey Business Journal* article entitled "Growing big by targeting small" Wunker (2012) argues that leaders of internationalizing firms are typically trained to focus on growing their companies in established, large, attractive markets. However, some of the greatest sources of firm growth arise from new markets that start out as small footholds. In support he shows that eight of the ten most valuable US companies started by serving very small new markets that they developed over time. And that following this strategy they grew with their markets to become giants.

[20] In "Home-region orientation in international expansion strategies," Banalieva and Dhanaraj draw on internalization theory to suggest that technological advantage and institutional diversity determine firms' home-region orientation (HRO), and posit a simultaneous relationship between HRO and performance. They apply insights from the firm heterogeneity literature of international trade to explain the influence of technology on HRO. They find a negative and non-linear impact of technological advantage on HRO driven by increasing returns logic, and a negative impact of institutional diversity on HRO driven by search and deliberation costs.

E. R. Banalieva and C. Dhanaraj, "Home-region orientation in international expansion strategies," *Journal of International Business Studies*, 44:2 (2013), 89–116.

system that we use throughout this book to describe the very different strategic approaches adopted by various MNEs.[21]

International Mentality

In the earliest stages of internationalization, many MNE managers tend to think of the company's overseas operations as distant outposts whose main role is to support the domestic parent company in different ways, such as contributing incremental sales to the domestic manufacturing operations. We label this approach the *international* strategic mentality.

The *international* terminology derives directly from the international product cycle theory, which reflects many of the assumptions implicit in this approach. Products are developed for the domestic market and only subsequently sold abroad; technology and other sources of knowledge are transferred from the parent company to the overseas operators; and offshore manufacturing represents a means to protect the company's home market. Companies with this mentality regard themselves fundamentally as domestic with some foreign appendages. Managers assigned to overseas operations may be selected because they happen to know a foreign language or have previously lived abroad. Decisions related to the foreign operations tend to be made in an opportunistic or ad hoc manner. Many firms at this stage will prefer to only enter countries where there is low "psychic distance" between it and the home market.

Multinational Mentality

The exposure of the organization to foreign environments and the growing importance of sales and profits from these sources gradually convince managers that international activities can provide opportunities of more than marginal significance. Increasingly, they also realize that to leverage those opportunities, they must do more than ship out old equipment, technology, or product lines that had been developed for the home market. The success of local competitors in the foreign markets and the demands of host governments often accelerate the learning of companies that would otherwise retain an unresponsive, international mentality for too long.

A *multinational* strategic mentality develops as managers begin to recognize and emphasize the differences among national markets and operating environments. Companies with this mentality adopt a more flexible approach to their international operations by modifying their products, strategies, and even management practices country by country. As they develop national companies that are increasingly sensitive and responsive to their local environments, these companies undertake a strategic approach that is literally multinational: their strategy is built on the foundation of the multiple, nationally responsive strategies of the company's worldwide subsidiaries.

---

[21] The terms *international, multinational, global,* and *transnational* have been used very differently – and sometimes interchangeably – by various writers. We want to give each term a specific and different meaning and ask that readers put aside their previous usage of the terms – at least for the duration of our exposition.

In companies operating with such a multinational mentality, managers of foreign operations tend to be highly independent entrepreneurs, often nationals of the host country. Using their local market knowledge and the parent company's willingness to invest in these growing opportunities, these entrepreneurial country managers often can build significant local growth and considerable independence from headquarters.

Global Mentality

Although the multinational mentality typically results in very responsive marketing approaches in the different national markets, it also gives rise to an inefficient manufacturing infrastructure within the company. Plants are built more to provide local marketing advantages or improve political relations than to maximize production efficiency. Similarly, the proliferation of products designed to meet local needs contributes to a general loss of efficiency in design, production, logistics, distribution, and other functional tasks.

In an operating environment of improving transportation and communication facilities and falling trade barriers, some companies adopt a very different strategic approach in their international operations. These companies think in terms of creating products for a world market and manufacturing them on a global scale in a few highly efficient plants, often at the corporate center.

We define this approach as a classic *global* strategy mentality, because it views the world, not individual national markets, as its basic unit of analysis. The underlying assumption is that national tastes and preferences are more similar than different or that they can be made similar by providing customers with standardized products at adequate cost and with quality advantages over those national varieties they know. Managers with this global strategic approach subscribe to Levitt's provocative argument in the mid-1980s that the future belongs to companies that make and sell "the same thing, the same way, everywhere."[22]

This strategic approach requires considerably more central coordination and control than the others and is typically associated with an organizational structure in which various product or business managers have worldwide responsibility. In such companies, research and development and manufacturing activities are typically managed from the headquarters, and most strategic decisions also take place at the center.

Transnational Mentality

In the closing decades of the twentieth century, many of these global companies seemed invincible, chalking up overwhelming victories over not only local companies but international and multinational competitors as well. Their success, however, created and strengthened a set of countervailing forces of localization.

To many host governments, for example, these global companies appeared to be a more powerful, and thus more threatening, version of earlier unresponsive companies with their unsophisticated international strategic mentality. Many host

[22] See Theodore Levitt, "The globalization of markets," *Harvard Business Review*, May–June (1983), 92–102.

governments increased both the restrictions and the demands they placed on global companies, requiring them to invest in, transfer technology to, and meet local content requirements of the host countries.

Customers also contributed to this strengthening of localizing forces by rejecting homogenized global products and reasserting their national preferences – albeit without relaxing their expectations of high quality levels and low costs that global products had offered. Finally, the increasing volatility in the international economic and political environments, especially rapid changes in currency exchange rates, undermined the efficiency of such a centralized global approach.

As a result of these developments, many worldwide companies recognized that demands to be responsive to local market and political needs *and* pressures to develop global-scale competitive efficiency were simultaneous, if sometimes conflicting, imperatives.

In these conditions, the either/or attitude reflected in both the multinational and the global strategic mentalities became increasingly inappropriate. The emerging requirement was for companies to become more responsive to local needs while capturing the benefits of global efficiency – an approach to worldwide management that we call the *transnational* strategic mentality.

In such companies, key activities and resources are neither centralized in the parent company nor so decentralized that each subsidiary can carry out its own tasks on a local-for-local basis. Instead, the resources and activities are dispersed but specialized, to achieve efficiency and flexibility at the same time. Furthermore, these dispersed resources are integrated into an interdependent network of world-wide operations.

In contrast to the global model, the transnational mentality recognizes the importance of flexible and responsive country-level operations – hence the return of national into the terminology. And compared with the multinational approach, it provides for means to link and coordinate those operations to retain competitive effectiveness and economic efficiency, as is indicated by the prefix *trans*. The resulting need for intensive, organization-wide coordination and shared decision making implies that this is a much more sophisticated and subtle approach to MNE management. In subsequent chapters, we will explore its strategic, organizational, and managerial implications.

It should be clear, however, that there is no inevitability in either the direction or the endpoint of this evolving strategic mentality in worldwide companies. Depending on the industry, the company's strategic position, the host countries' diverse needs, and a variety of other factors, a company might reasonably operate with any one of these strategic mentalities. More likely, bearing in mind that ours is an arbitrary classification, most companies probably exhibit some attributes of each of these different strategic approaches.[23]

---

[23] Professor Howard Perlmutter was perhaps the first to highlight the different strategic mentalities. See his article, "The tortuous evolution of the multinational corporation," *Columbia Journal of World Business*, January–February (1969), 9–18, referenced in the readings section of this chapter.

CONCLUDING COMMENTS

This chapter has provided the historical context of the nature of the MNE and has introduced a number of important concepts on which subsequent chapters will build. In particular, we have described the evolving set of *motivations* that led companies to expand abroad in the first place; the *means* of expansion, as shaped by the processes of internationalization they followed; and the typical *mentalities* that they developed. Collectively, these motivations, means, and mentalities are the prime drivers of what we call a company's *administrative heritage*, the unique and deeply embedded structural, process, and cultural biases that play an important part in shaping every company's strategic and organizational capabilities. We will explore this concept in more detail in later chapters.

☒ IVEY | Publishing

CASE 1.1 SHER-WOOD HOCKEY STICKS: GLOBAL SOURCING

Megan (Min) Zhang wrote this case under the supervision of Professor Paul W. Beamish solely to provide material for class discussion. The authors do not intend to illustrate either effective or ineffective handling of a managerial situation. The authors may have disguised certain names and other identifying information to protect confidentiality.

In early 2011, the senior executives of Sher-Wood Hockey (Sher-Wood), the venerable Canadian hockey stick manufacturer, were pondering whether to move the remaining high-end composite hockey and goalie stick production to its suppliers in China. Sher-Wood had been losing market share for its high-priced, high-end, one-piece composite sticks as retail prices continued to fall. Would outsourcing the production of the iconic Canadian-made hockey sticks to China help Sher-Wood to boost demand significantly? Was there any other choice?

The History of Ice Hockey[1]

From the time of early civilization in places as diverse as Rome, Scotland, Egypt and South America, the "ball and stick" game has been played. The game has had different names, but

---

[1] Summarized from Jacqueline L. Longe, *How Products Are Made*, Volume 4, Farmington Hills: Gale Research, 1998; www.historyhockey.net, accessed July 18, 2011; www.mcgilltribune.com, accessed July 18, 2011; and www.madehow.com, accessed July 18, 2011.

its basic idea has been the same; the Irish, for instance, used the word "hockie" to refer to the sport. Some reports trace the origins of the game to 4,000 years ago, but it has survived to the present.

The modern version of ice hockey emerged from the rules laid down by two Canadians, James Creighton and Henry Joseph, when they studied at McGill University in the late nineteenth century. Their rules were used in the first modern game, which was played in Montreal, Quebec in 1875. In 1892, Canada's governor general, Lord Stanley, introduced the game's first national title, the "Lord Stanley's Dominion Challenge Trophy," later simply referred to as the Stanley Cup. In 1917, the National Hockey League (NHL) was founded in Montreal.

Ice hockey found its way to the United States in 1893. By the early 1900s, it had also become prevalent in Europe. Ice hockey was played as a part of the Olympic Summer Games for the first time in April 1920 in Antwerp, Belgium.

By the late twentieth century, ice hockey represented an important source of national pride to Canadians, and it had become popular in other countries in the northern hemisphere, especially the United States, Czech Republic, Finland, Russia and Sweden.

Ice Hockey Stick[2]

In ice hockey, players use specialized equipment both to facilitate their participation in the game and for protection from injuries. The equipment can be classified into five categories: goalie, head/face (helmet, neck guard), protective (shoulder pads, shin pads, elbow pads, hockey pants and gloves), sticks and skates. "Head-to-toe equipment suppliers" typically offered all equipment except for goalie equipment. Among the five categories of equipment, sticks and skates drove the industry, accounting for almost two-thirds of global equipment sales.[3]

A hockey stick is a piece of equipment used to shoot, pass and carry the puck. It is composed of a long, slender shaft with a flat extension at one end called the blade. The goaltender (goalie) has a slightly modified shaft with a wider paddle. Hockey stick dimensions can vary to suit a player's comfort, size, usage and stickhandling skills.

Hockey sticks are manufactured either as one-piece sticks with the blade permanently fused to the shaft or as two-piece sticks, where the blade and shaft are made as separate pieces that are joined later in the manufacturing process. One-piece sticks emerged with the advent of new component materials.

The three qualities that players seek in a hockey stick are lightness, responsiveness and "the feel." There were three characteristics which professional players looked for: lie, flex and blade pattern. The lie of a stick refers to the angle between the shaft and the blade. Players usually seek a lie that will put the blade flat on the ice when they are in their skating stance. Hockey stick shafts are highly flexible, and this flexibility is a key component in their performance. Flex, bend, stiffness and whip are all terms used to describe the amount of force required to bend a given length of stick shaft.

Until the late 1950s, hockey stick blades were rarely curved. However, in the 1960s, players began asking their stick manufacturers to create sticks with pre-curved blades for better performance. Soon after, many NHL players became proponents of the "banana blade." In 2011, the legal limit for hockey blade curves in the NHL was 19 mm, or 3/4 of an inch. In addition, players generally expected a hockey stick to be light enough to use easily and flexibly.

To satisfy these qualities, the greatest change came in the materials used to make a hockey stick. One consequence of employing more advanced (composite) materials was that the manufacturing process became more complicated and required more innovations. Custom designs were prevalent among professional players who wanted their sticks to fit their own physical features (i.e., height and strength) and skills.

The three primary materials for manufacturing hockey sticks were wood, aluminum and

---

[2] Summarized from J.L. Longe, *How Products Are Made*, 1999, www.prohockeystuff.com, accessed July 18, 2011; and www.nhlhockeyice.com, accessed July 18, 2011.

[3] www.thehockeysource.tv, accessed July 18, 2011.

composite. The earliest hockey sticks were made with solid wood. These sticks were not very durable and were inconsistent in length and shape. In the 1940s, laminated sticks were created with layers of wood glued together to create a more flexible and durable design. In the 1960s, manufacturers began adding additional fibre-glass lamination or other synthetic coatings, which further enhanced the durability of the sticks.

In the early 1980s, Easton Hockey introduced single piece, all-aluminum sticks that were much lighter than wooden sticks. Because the stiff aluminum did not have the proper "feel" to players, manufacturers then developed a light aluminum shaft with a replaceable wooden blade. The design became popular in the late 1980s and early 1990s.

In the mid-1990s, advanced composite sticks were developed. Composites were comprised of reinforcing fibres, such as graphite (carbon) and Kevlar, and binders such as polyester, epoxy or other polymeric resins that held the fibres together. In the following decade, graphite had become by far the most popular material for sticks used in the NHL, and it was growing rapidly in popularity for amateur and recreational players. Although graphite sticks were originally sold as shafts alone while a separate blade was purchased by the hockey player, one-piece sticks that included both the shaft and the blade eventually predominated. Some manufacturers also used titanium to produce composite sticks. Moreover, Sher-Wood used foam materials, such as polyurethane, to fill blades and paddles of goalie sticks for shock absorption and stiffness.

New, lighter and more durable composites were always being developed. Ice hockey sticks, roller hockey sticks, lacrosse sticks, baseball bats, softball bats and hockey skates required similar technologies to manufacture because almost all of these athletic products incorporated composite materials. R&D, manufacturing and quality control processes continued to advance in the industry. Increasingly, precise technologies were employed throughout the production process.

For most composite and aluminum sticks, the stick's flex characteristic was expressed numerically. This number, which ranged from 50 through 120, was printed on the stick and corresponded to the amount of force (in pounds-force) that it took to deflect or bend the shaft one inch. By contrast, the flex characteristic of their wooden counterparts could not be derived precisely, because the sticks were produced using a high-volume production process that yielded sticks with variable flex properties.

Basics of Hockey Equipment Industry[4]

The global hockey equipment market was showing signs of maturity, growing at just 1 to 2 per cent per annum.[5] The global hockey equipment market in 2010 was $555 million, with skates and sticks accounting for an estimated 62 per cent of industry sales. Sales were driven primarily by global participation rates (registered and unregistered). There were about 600,000 hockey players in Canada in 2010. The number of registered hockey players in Canada between the ages of 5 and 25 was expected to shrink by 30,000 players, or 5 per cent, over the next five years. Nevertheless, some industry analysts believed that growth rates of casual and unregistered hockey participation, especially in the United States, as well as growth rates in Eastern Europe (particularly Russia) and women's hockey had exceeded that of the registered segment as a whole. Other drivers of equipment sales included demand creation efforts, the introduction of innovative products, a shorter product replacement cycle, general macroeconomic conditions and the level of consumer discretionary spending.

Relative to European football (soccer) or American baseball, all of the equipment required to participate in organized hockey was more

---

[4] Summarized from "Preliminary Prospectus of Bauer Performance Sports Ltd.," January 27, 2011, www.secure.globeadvisor.com/servlet/ArticleNews/story/gam/20110614/GIVOXBAUERMILSTEADATL, accessed July 18, 2011; www.sgma.com/press/93_Sanctioned-Team-Sports-Play-In-the-US-Remains-Strong,-But, accessed July 18, 2011; and www.ehow.com/way_5191903_ice-hockey-equipment-guide.html, accessed July 18, 2011.

[5] https://secure.globeadvisor.com/servlet/ArticleNews/story/gam/20110614/GIVOXBAUERMILSTEADATL, accessed July 18, 2011.

Exhibit 1
NHL Share of Hockey Stick Brands and their Manufacturing Sites

Company	NHL Share	Manufacturing Sites
Easton	45.1%	Tijuana, Mexico and China
Bauer	15.7%	Composite sticks made in China and Thailand
RBK/CCM	13.7%	Composites sticks in China, wooden sticks in Canada and Finland
Warrior	11.8%	Tijuana, Mexico (insourcing), China (outsourcing)
Sher-Wood	2.3%	Composite, high-end wood goalie sticks in Canada and China, most wood stick production in Eastern Europe
Louisville TPS, Mission, and others	11.4%	N/A

Source: www.usatoday.com/, January 2008, accessed May 29, 2011

expensive to purchase. Outfitting a teenager or an adult to play recreational hockey cost approximately $600. The equipment for younger players was less expensive. However, nearly 40 per cent of all ice hockey players lived in homes where the annual household income was more than $100,000 per year.

The hockey sticks endorsed by professional hockey players enjoyed a strong position in the hockey stick market. Children and amateur players liked to have sticks embossed with specific players' names. Hockey stick manufacturers typically paid NHL players to use their sticks and provided the players with custom designed sticks.

Competitor Brands and Strategies[6]

Before a Montreal company began manufacturing ice hockey sticks in the late 1880s, most players made their own. By the early twenty-first century, more than 20 brands of ice hockey sticks

[6] Summarized from "Preliminary Prospectus of Bauer Performance Sports Ltd.," www.fundinguniverse.com, accessed July 18, 2011; www.eastonbellsports.com, accessed July 18, 2011; www.bauer.com, accessed July 18, 2011; www.sher-wood.com, accessed July 18, 2011; www.adidas-group.corporate-publication.com, accessed July 18, 2011; www.warrior.com, accessed July 18, 2011; www.stickshack.com, accessed July 18, 2011; and www.hockeystickexpert.com, accessed July 18, 2011.

existed in North America and Europe, and many of the smaller equipment manufacturers had failed or been purchased by larger competitors. The main brands were Easton (Easton-Bell Sports), Bauer (Bauer Performance Sports), CCM (Reebok-CCM Hockey), Warrior (Warrior Sports), Sher-Wood (Sher-Wood Hockey), Mission ITECH (acquired by Bauer) and Louisville/TPS (acquired by Sher-Wood). Bauer, CCM and Sher-Wood originated in Canada, and Easton and Warrior originated in the United States.

Over 80 per cent of the ice hockey equipment market was shared by three major competitors: Bauer, Reebok (which owned both the Reebok and CCM brands) and Easton, each of which was a head-to-toe supplier offering players a full range of products (skates, sticks and full protective equipment). Moreover, Bauer and Reebok also provided goalie equipment. The balance of the equipment market was highly fragmented with many smaller equipment manufacturers, such as Warrior and Sher-Wood, offering specific products and catering to niche segments within the broader market. Exhibit 1 lists the proportion of NHL players using sticks made by the five major suppliers. Each of the five major companies sought new growth in diverse categories.

Easton-Bell Sports operated divisions dedicated to hockey, baseball, lacrosse and softball. Easton established itself as a worldwide leader in designing, developing and marketing performance sports equipment, as well as a broad spectrum of accessories for athletic and recreational activities. Easton Hockey's technical prowess made its stick the number one choice among NHL players and amateurs alike and kept its gloves, skates and helmets at the forefront of technological advance. For years, Easton Hockey had signed head-to-toe contract extensions with NHL players. Easton's innovation processes followed a unique routine – developing new technologies for composite ice hockey sticks first and then applying the advances in materials to skates, baseball bats and softball bats. In 2011, Easton-Bell offered 48 types of player and goalie sticks in its Synergy and Stealth lines. Net sales for 2006 were $639 million compared to $379.9 million in 2005, an increase of 68 per cent. Gross profit for 2006 was $212.9 million or 33.3 per cent of net sales, as compared to $134.9 million or 35.5 per cent of net sales for 2005.

Bauer Performance Sports manufactured ice hockey, roller hockey and lacrosse equipment as well as related apparel. Bauer was focused on building a leadership position and growing its market share in all ice hockey and roller hockey equipment products through continued innovation at all performance levels. It produced products at competitive prices using alternative materials, sourcing arrangements and supply-chain efficiencies. It also targeted emerging and underdeveloped consumer segments, including Russian players and female players. In 2008, Bauer Performance implemented several strategic acquisitions to enter new industries and to enhance its market leadership in its chosen categories. In 2011, Bauer offered 20 types of player and goalie sticks in its Supreme and Vapor lines. Bauer was the number one manufacturer of skates, helmets, protective gear and goalie equipment, and a close number two to Easton of sticks in 2010. It enjoyed a 45 per cent share of the global hockey equipment market. Bauer's profit margin as a percentage of net revenues was 37 per cent.

Reebok–CCM Hockey concentrated on providing hockey equipment and apparel. The company leveraged its multi-brand approach to target different consumer segments. In particular, it developed innovative technologies that appealed to image-conscious consumers. Its products were best suited to the physical side of the game and were frequently purchased by consumers seeking performance and quality. In 2011, they offered 32 types of player and goalie sticks. Reebok-CCM's net sales in 2010 were $280 million, and its key markets were Canada, the United States, Scandinavia and Russia.

Warrior Sports concentrated on providing lacrosse and ice hockey equipment, apparel and footwear. The company was dedicated to a core set of philosophies and strengths: technical superiority, grassroots marketing, original and creative youthful expression, and strong partnerships with retailers and suppliers. In 2011, Warrior offered 15 types of player and goalie sticks.

Generally, hockey companies provided one type of hockey stick at three different price points – junior, intermediate and senior. The reference retail prices of the five competitors' best senior composite sticks varied. The Bauer Supreme TotalOne Composite, Easton Stealth S19 Composite and Warrior Widow Composite Senior were all priced at $229.99. The CCM U+ Crazy Light Composite and Reebok 11K Sickkick III Composite came in at $209.99, while the Sher-Wood T90 Pro Composite was priced at $139.99.[7]

Global Sourcing in the Hockey Equipment Industry

Similar to other industries, the hockey industry eventually entered the global sourcing era. Global sourcing is the process by which the work is contracted or delegated to a company that may be situated anywhere in the world.[8] Sourcing activities can be categorized along both

---

[7] Source for all, www.amazon.com, accessed May 29, 2011.

[8] This paragraph is summarized from Ilan Oshri, Julia Kotlarsky, and Leslie P. Willcocks, *The Handbook of Global Outsourcing and Offshoring*, Hampshire, Macmillan, 2009; and Marc J. Schniederjans, Ashlyn M. Schniederjans, and Dara G. Schniederjans, *Outsourcing and Insourcing In An International Context*, New York, M.E. Sharpe, 2005.

Exhibit 2
Types of Global Sourcing

	Insourcing	Outsourcing
Offshoring	Keeping work in a wholly owned subsidiary in a distant country.	Contracting work with a service provider in a distant country.
Near-shoring	Keeping work in a wholly owned subsidiary in a neighbouring country.	Contracting work with a service provider in a neighbouring country
On-shoring	Keeping work in a wholly owned subsidiary in the home country.	Contracting work with a service provider in the home country.

Source: Derived from Oshri, Korlarksy, and Willcocks, *The Handbook of Global Outsourcing and Offshoring*, 2009; Macmillan Publishers.

Exhibit 3 Evaluation of Global Sourcing

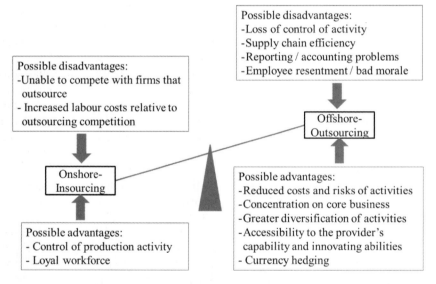

Possible disadvantages:
-Loss of control of activity
-Supply chain efficiency
-Reporting / accounting problems
-Employee resentment / bad morale

Possible disadvantages:
-Unable to compete with firms that outsource
- Increased labour costs relative to outsourcing competition

Offshore-Outsourcing

Onshore-Insourcing

Possible advantages:
- Control of production activity
- Loyal workforce

Possible advantages:
-Reduced costs and risks of activities
-Concentration on core business
-Greater diversification of activities
-Accessibility to the provider's capability and innovating abilities
- Currency hedging

Source: Adapted from Schniederjans, Schniederjans, and Schniederjans, *Outsourcing and Insourcing in an International Context*; 2005; M.E. Sharpe.

organizational and locational dimensions (Exhibit 2 lists several types of global sourcing). From an organizational perspective, the choice between insourcing and outsourcing involves deciding whether to keep the work within the firm or contract it out to an independent service provider. From a locational perspective, three choices are available – onshoring (within the nation), nearshoring (to a neighbouring country) and offshoring (to a geographically distant country). To optimize the overall benefits and hedge risks, companies often seek to balance their global outsourcing and insourcing activities. Exhibit 3 lists several of the factors typically considered by manufacturers faced with the decision of whether to onshore insource or offshore outsource.

As early as the 1980s, western sports equipment manufacturers, such as Nike and Reebok, started to outsource the manufacture of sporting goods, such as running shoes, to Asia. Nevertheless, before the year 2000, hockey companies preferred insourcing over outsourcing and executed this strategic focus through organic growth, strategic acquisitions and establishing company-owned factories in other countries; for example, Easton and Warrior had factories in Tijuana, Mexico. During the past decade, the hockey industry began to outsource. In 2004, Bauer Nike Hockey shut down or downsized three plants in Ontario and Quebec, eliminating 321 manufacturing jobs. The company outsourced about 90 per cent of its production to other makers in Canada and the rest to international suppliers. From 2002 to 2008, Reebok-CCM closed five plants in Ontario and Quebec and outsourced manufacturing to other countries, eliminating about 600 jobs. Easton and Warrior also outsourced part of their manufacturing to Asia but still kept their factories in Mexico. The capacity of Warrior's Mexican factory was estimated to be 4,000 composite sticks per week produced by 250 employees in 2008. (Exhibit 1 lists the manufacturing sites associated with several of the leading hockey stick brands.)

Global manufacturing outsourcing was characterized by some drawbacks. It separated manufacturing activities from R&D and marketing activities and challenged a company's ability to coordinate initiatives between these functions, such as product innovation, designing for manufacturability, supply chain efficiency and quality control. Especially in offshore outsourcing, cultural differences caused miscommunication, technology distance necessitated extra training, and geographic distance resulted in extra lead time or cycle time.[9] In March 2010,

Bauer Hockey recalled 13 models of junior hockey sticks, manufactured outside of Canada, due to excessive lead levels in the sticks' paint that was detected by public health officials in random testing.

Offshore outsourcing also threatened to negatively impact a company's public image if it reduced domestic employment. In November 2008, UNITE HERE[10] launched a national campaign to persuade Reebok to repatriate the production of its hockey equipment and jerseys.[11]

Additionally, global economic dynamics, such as changing labour costs, raw material costs and exchange rates, introduced new uncertainties into global sourcing. Exhibit 4 lists a sample of comparative labour rates prevailing in Canada, the United States, Mexico and China. In 2011, the Boston Consulting Group (BCG) concluded that with Chinese wages rising and the value of the Yuan continuing to increase, the gap between U.S. and Chinese wages was narrowing rapidly.

Industries other than sporting goods had already begun to practice repatriating manufacturing, also known as reshoring or backshoring. In fact, reshoring had been an alternative in global sourcing planning from the beginning. For German manufacturing companies in the period 1999 to 2006, every fourth to sixth offshoring activity was followed by a reshoring activity within the following four years, mainly due to lack of flexibility and quality problems at the foreign location. This served as a short-term correction of the prior location misjudgement rather than a long-term reaction to slowly emerging economic trends.[12]

---

[9] This paragraph is summarized from Masaaki Kotabe, *Global Sourcing Strategy: R&D, Manufacturing, and Marketing Interfaces*, New York, Quorum Books, 1992.

[10] UNITE HERE: a union representing 50,000 food service, apparel, textile, hotel and distribution workers across Canada.

[11] www.cbc.ca/news/story/2010/03/18/nike-hockeystick-recall.html, accessed July 18, 2011.

[12] S. Kinkel and S. Maloca. "Drivers and Antecedents of Manufacturing Offshoring and Backshoring: A German Perspective," *Journal of Purchasing and Supply Management* 15.3 (2009): 154–65.

Exhibit 4
Hourly Compensation Costs in Manufacturing (US$)

Year	China (Urban)	China[1]	Canada	USA	Mexico	Estonia	Finland
2002	0.95	0.41	18.05	27.36	5.59	3.11	22.62
2003	1.07	0.44	21.08	28.57	5.31	4.11	28.12
2004	1.19	0.45	23.67	29.31	5.26	4.86	32.47
2005	1.30	0.49	26.26	30.14	5.61	5.52	33.64
2006	1.47	0.53	28.58	30.48	5.88	6.58	35.23
2007	1.83	0.64	31.27	32.07	6.17	8.73	39.17
2008	2.38	0.82	32.06	32.78	6.47	10.56	43.85
2009	2.69	N/A	29.59	34.19	5.70	9.83	43.47
2010	3.16	N/A	34.60	34.81	6.14	9.42	41.10

[1] The data are for town or village
Source: www.bls.gov, accessed July 18, 2011

Sher-Wood Hockey: Company Timeline[13]

Sher-Wood Hockey Inc. manufactured and distributed hockey sticks and equipment in Canada. Based in Sherbrooke, Quebec, it was founded in 1949 and was formerly known as Sherwood-Drolet, Ltd. For more than 60 years, it had been one of Canada's best-known hockey equipment manufacturers. In 1976, Sherwood-Drolet introduced its flagship wooden stick, the PMP 5030, which was described as "the best stick in the world" by NHL legend Guy Lafleur. By 2007, the company had made more than 6 million PMP 5030s.

In 2006, Sherwood-Drolet sold about one million wooden and 350,000 composite sticks. The company anticipated that the composite stick business would continue to grow in terms of volume and profitability. Earlier, Sherwood-Drolet had started contracting out the production of its lower end wooden models to producers in the Ukraine. In 2007, it outsourced the production of PMP 5030 (mid to high end wooden) sticks to a local provider in Victoriaville, Quebec. Meanwhile, the company concentrated on making composite sticks fashioned from graphite, Kevlar and other synthetics. Notwithstanding the company's efforts to move its wooden stick production offshore, it claimed that it would continue to make custom wooden models for professional hockey players, such as Jason Spezza of the Ottawa Senators.

However, when Spezza learned that Sherwood-Drolet would no longer be manufacturing his favourite wooden sticks in Canada, he decided to move to another company. "They [local manufacturers] can get sticks to me in a week now. If it's over there [China], the process will probably be just too much," said Spezza.[14] Ultimately, Montreal-based Reebok designed and produced a stick for him that had a graphite shaft and wooden blade, but the look of a one-piece. In November 2008, Reebok issued a press release announcing that Spezza would start using their sticks, ". . .we are excited to work with Jason, not only on marketing initiatives, but also on the research, design and development of future Reebok Hockey equipment."[15]

[13] Summarized from www.sher-wood.com, accessed on July 18, 2011; http://hockeystickexpert.com, accessed July 18, 2011; www.canada.com/topics/sports/story.html?id=87c5d6b3-8872-496a-8d4f-01f5f4e36342, accessed July 18, 2011; and www.thestar.com/News/Canada/article/273561, accessed July 18, 2011.

[14] www.canada.com/topics/sports/story.html?id=87c5d6b3-8872-496a-8d4f-01f5f4e36342, accessed July 18, 2011.

[15] www.reebokhockey.com/labs/labs-blog/entries/2008/Nov/25/entry/jason-spezza-reebok-hockey-family/, accessed July 18, 2011.

By May 2008, Sherwood-Drolet had filed a proposal to its creditors under the Bankruptcy and Insolvency Act. CBC News reported, "It has been hurt in recent years by shift from wooden hockey sticks to composite sticks."[16] Richmond Hill, Ontario-based Carpe Diem Growth Capital bought the company and changed its name to Sher-Wood Hockey Inc.

In September 2008, Sher-Wood purchased the hockey novelty and licensed assets of Inglasco. In December that same year, it purchased TPS Sports Group, a leading manufacturer and distributor of hockey sticks and protective equipment. Sher-Wood transported TPS's assets from Wallaceburg and Strathroy, Ontario to Quebec, consolidated three companies and invested an additional $1.5 million to set up the new factory.

Production

As of March 2011,[17] Sher-Wood produced sticks (sticks, shafts, blades), protective equipment (gloves, pants, shoulder pads, elbow pads, shin pads), goalie gear (goalie pads, catcher, blocker, knee protector, arm and body protector, pants) and other accessories (pucks, bags, puck holders, mini sticks, bottles, carry cases) for ice hockey. The company also sold some equipment and accessories for street hockey (goalie kit, sticks, pucks, balls), as well as sports novelties for hockey fans.

The company introduced new sticks twice a year – in May/June and at the end of October. The life cycle of a product line in the market was about 18 to 24 months. By the end of 2010, Sher-Wood provided 27 types of player and goalie sticks. Thirteen of them were wooden.

Although Sher-Wood had targeted various NHL players in order to support the credibility of the brand, the company mostly targeted junior teams, AAA teams and a couple of senior leagues. Sher-Wood only conducted a low volume of

custom design for high-end players and mainly provided custom products from a cosmetic standpoint. For example, personalizing the graphic or colour of the sticks. Sher-Wood used to need two to three weeks to produce customized sticks for an NHL player.

In 2010, Sher-Wood sales volume for sticks produced in Sherbrooke dropped almost 50 per cent compared to 2009. Its Chinese partners manufactured most of their composite hockey sticks. Sher-Wood's plant manufactured the remaining high-end, one-piece composite sticks and goalie foam sticks, about 100,000 units annually, with 33 workers in the factory and seven staff in the office. The return on investment of the fixed cost in Canada was low.

Executives believed that they needed to provide a competitive retail price to boost the demand. To do so, they also needed to afford retailers a higher margin than their competitors did, so that retailers would help with product presentations in stores and marketing efforts. These approaches called for low cost production as well as decent quality. To reduce the cost and fully utilize the facilities, they could outsource the remaining production to the partner based in Victoriaville and move facilities there. However, according to regulations in Quebec, Sher-Wood did not have enough latitude to move or sell the equipment to their subcontractor in Quebec. They also considered backshoring the manufacturing out of China. They concluded that it would be more advantageous to stay in China from both cost reduction and R&D standpoints.

Chinese Partners' Condition and Collaboration

Sher-Wood's suppliers were located in Shanghai, Shenzhen and Zhongshan City near Hong Kong. They were producing tennis and badminton rackets, developing the expertise in composite technology and relevant sporting goods production. Sher-Wood began to cooperate with them about 10 years ago when it started selling composite sticks. For years, these suppliers manufactured one-piece and two-piece composite hockey

[16] www.cbc.ca/news/business/story/2008/05/05/sherwood-filing.html?ref=rss, accessed July 18, 2011.

[17] Summarized from www.sher-wood.com, accessed May 29, 2011.

sticks for hockey companies around the world. Gradually, they accumulated manufacturing capacity and R&D capability. Sher-Wood's main supplier in Zhongshan City operated two shifts for 10 hours a day, six days a week. Their annual capacity was more than 1 million units. Moreover, they possessed an R&D team with 10 to 15 engineers, which was able to produce a prototype within one day with full information. On the contrary, it would cost Sher-Wood four to five months with a team of two to three engineers to produce a similar prototype. More importantly, as a consequence of their long-term cooperation, the main supplier had developed a certain feeling about hockey so that language and cultural barriers were not problems any more. "They were becoming a partner rather than one section within the supply chain," said Eric Rodrigue, Sher-Wood's marketing vice president.

Sher-Wood and its Chinese supplier partner needed to collaborate closely. On one hand, Sher-Wood had to send their experts to China to coach the partner about how to produce sticks according to their specifications. On the other hand, although Sher-Wood and the partner had similar on-site labs to conduct product tests, Sher-Wood mainly focused on the feeling of the stick, that is, the reproduction of how the slap shot, passes, reception, etc., would feel when a player placed his or her hands a certain way on the stick. Sher-Wood also conducted tests on ice with professional players, something their supplier could not do.

Moreover, with young, passionate and knowledgeable new managers in management and marketing, company executives thought they were ready to meet the extra cost and effort in market collaboration between Sher-Wood, the partner in China and retailers.

Company executives were concerned with rising labour costs, material costs and the currency exchange rate in China. Nevertheless, the overall cost of manufacturing in China was still lower than the cost in Quebec. They estimated that cost reduction was 0 to 15 per cent per unit depending on the model, with good quality and fast turnaround time. Moreover, some industries such as textiles had started to relocate their manufacturing to new emerging countries, such as Vietnam and Cambodia, for low labour and equipment costs; however, there was no R&D advantage in composite materials in these alternative locales.

Executives were also concerned with other issues. First, although the main supplier was able to produce customized sticks for an NHL player within 24 hours, the shipping was quite expensive from China to Quebec. Second, the main supplier used to produce huge volumes fast but without product personalization. Third, the game of hockey was perceived as a Western cultural heritage sport, so anything relevant to hockey which was made in China had the potential to negatively influence the market perception. However, all their competitors had outsourced manufacturing to China for years.

The Challenge

In early 2011, the question for Sher-Wood senior executives was how to boost their hockey stick sales. They believed that they should cope with this challenge by providing sticks with better quality, better retail price and better margin for retailers. They wondered whether they should move the manufacturing of the remaining high-end composite sticks to their suppliers in China or whether there was any alternative.

If they decided to shift their remaining manufacturing outside of the company, they needed to deal with a variety of issues. To fully utilize the facilities in Sherbrooke, they needed to move equipment to China, which was difficult and time-consuming because of export regulations. To set up the manufacturing machines and guide the manufacturing team, they would need to send experts there. To complete the coming hockey season between September and April but still implement the decision, they needed to plan every phase precisely. They also needed to figure out what to say and do about the 40 affected employees. Many had worked for Sher-Wood for more than 30 years, and their average age was 56. How could this be communicated to the public? They needed to make a final decision soon.

⊗IVEY | Publishing
CASE 1.2 CAMERON AUTO PARTS: EARLY INTERNATIONALIZATION

Professor Paul Beamish revised this case (originally prepared by Professor Harold Crookell) solely to provide material for class discussion. The authors do not intend to illustrate either effective or ineffective handling of a managerial situation. The authors may have disguised certain names and other identifying information to protect confidentiality.

  Version: 2017–01–05

In the spring of 2013, Alex Cameron had just come back from a trip to Scotland with a signed contract for collaboration with one of his biggest European customers, McTaggart Supplies Ltd. As he pondered about the implications of this deal, he started reminiscing about the path that had brought him to this point.

Alex's first years in business were unusually harsh and turbulent. He graduated from a leading Michigan business school in 2010 when the American economy was just recovering from the Great Recession (2007–2009) caused by the subprime mortgage crisis and the collapse of the U.S. housing bubble. It was not that Alex had difficulty finding a job, however; it was that he took over the reins of the family business. His father timed his retirement to coincide with Alex's graduation and left him with the unenviable task of cutting back the workforce to match the severe sales declines the company was experiencing.

History

Cameron Auto Parts was founded in 1975 by Alex's father to seize opportunities created by the earlier signing of the Auto Pact between Canada and the United States. The Auto Pact permitted the Big Three automotive manufacturers to ship cars, trucks, and original equipment (OEM) parts between Canada and the United States tariff-free, as long as they maintained auto assembly facilities on both sides of the border. The Pact had been very successful with the result that a lot of auto parts firms sprang up in Canada to supply the Big Three. In 2001, the Auto Pact was abolished, superseded by the North American Free Trade Agreement, which continued to create favourable conditions for trade between the United States and Canada.

Cameron Auto Parts prospered in this environment until, by 2008, sales had reached $60 million[1] with profits of $1.75 million. The product focus was largely on small engine parts and auto accessories such as oil and air filters, fan belts and wiper blades, all sold as original equipment.

When Alex took over in 2010, the company's financial position was precarious. Sales in 2009 had dropped to $48 million and for the first six months of 2010 to $18 million. Not only were car sales declining in North America, but the Japanese were taking an increasing share of the market. As a result, the major North American auto producers were frantically trying to advance

---

[1] All currency in U.S. dollars unless specified otherwise.

their technology and to lower their prices at the same time. It was not a good year to be one of their suppliers. In 2009, Cameron Auto Parts lost $2.5 million, and had lost the same amount again in the first six months of 2010. Pressure for modernization and cost reduction had required close to $4 million in new investment in equipment and computer-assisted design and manufacturing systems. As a result, the company had taken up more than $10 million of its $12 million line of bank credit at an interest rate which stood at 3.25 per cent (U.S. prime rate charged by banks) in 2010.

Alex's first six months in the business were spent in what he later referred to as "operation survival." There was not much he could do about working capital management as both inventory and receivables were kept relatively low via contract arrangements with the Big Three. Marketing costs were negligible. Where costs had to be cut were in production and, specifically, in people, many of whom had been with the company for more than 15 years and were personal friends of Alex's father. Nevertheless, by the end of 2010, the workforce had been cut from 720 to 470, the losses had been stemmed, and the company had been saved from almost certain bankruptcy. Having to be the hatchet man, however, left an indelible impression on Alex. As things began to pick up during 2011 and 2012, he added as few permanent workers as possible, relying instead on overtime, part-timers, or subcontracting.

Recovery and Diversification

For Cameron Auto Parts, the year 2010 ended with sales of $38 million and losses of $3.5 million (see Exhibit 1). Sales began to pick up in 2011, reaching $45 million by year-end with a small profit. By mid-2012, it was clear that the recovery was well underway. Alex, however, while welcoming the turnaround, was suspicious of the basis for it. Cameron's own sales hit $27 million in the first six months of 2012 and company profits were over $2 million. Cameron was faced with increasingly aggressive competition from Canadian and offshore parts manufacturers. The short-term future for Cameron, however, seemed distinctly positive, but the popularity of Japanese cars left Alex feeling vulnerable to continued total dependence on the volatile automotive industry. Diversification was on his mind as early as 2010. He had an ambition to take the company public by 2016 and diversification was an important part of that ambition.

Unfortunately, working as an OEM parts supplier to the automotive industry did little to prepare Cameron to become more innovative. The auto industry tended to standardize its parts requirements to the point that Cameron's products were made to precise industry specifications and consequently, did not find a ready market outside the industry. Without a major product innovation, Cameron's dependence on the Big Three was likely to continue. Furthermore, the company had developed no "in-house" design and engineering strength from which to launch an attempt at new product development. Because product specifications had always come down in detail from the Big Three, Cameron had never needed to design and develop its own products and had never hired any design engineers.

In the midst of "operation survival" in 2010, Alex boldly decided to do something about diversification. He personally brought in a team of four design engineers and instructed them to concentrate on developing products related to the existing line but with a wider "non-automotive" market appeal. Their first year together showed little positive progress, and the question of whether to fund the team for another year (estimated budget $425,000) came to the management group:

Alex: Maybe we just expected too much in the first year. They did come up with the flexible coupling idea, but you didn't seem to encourage them, Andy (production manager).

Andy McIntyre: That's right! They had no idea at all how to produce such a thing in our facilities. Just a lot of ideas about how it could be used. When I told them a Canadian outfit

Exhibit 1
Income Statements
(for years ended December 31 ($000s))

	2010	2011	2012
Net Sales	$38,150	$45,200	$67,875
Cost of goods sold:			
Direct materials	6,750	8,050	12,400
Direct labour	12,900	10,550	12,875
Overheads (including depreciation)	16,450	19,650	27,600
Total	36,100	38,250	52,875
Gross Profit	2,050	6,950	15,000
Expenses:			
Selling and administration (includes design team)	3,150	3,800	6,200
Other (includes interest)	2,400	2,900	3,000
Total	5,500	6,700	9,200
Net Profit before Tax	(3,500)	250	5,800
Income Tax	(500)	-	200
Net Profit after Tax	$(3,000)	$ 250	$ 5,600

Note: Alex expected total sales to reach $85 million in 2013 with profits before tax of $10 million. Flexible couplings were expected to contribute sales of $30 million and profits of $5 million on assets of $12 million.
Source: Company files.

was already producing them, the team sort of lost interest.

John Ellis (Finance): We might as well face the fact that we made a mistake and cut it off before we sink any more money into it. This is hardly the time for unnecessary risks.

Alex: Why don't we shorten the whole process by getting a production license from the Canadian firm? We could start out that way and then build up our own technology over time.

Andy: The team looked into that, but it turned out the Canadians already have a subsidiary operating in United States – not too well from what I can gather – and they are not anxious to license anyone to compete with it.

Alex: Is the product patented?

Andy: Yes, but apparently it doesn't have long to run.

At this point a set of ideas began to form in Alex's mind, and in a matter of months he had lured away a key engineer from the Canadian firm with an $110,000 salary offer and put him in charge of the product development team. By mid-2012, the company had developed its own line of flexible couplings with an advanced design and an efficient production process using the latest in production equipment. Looking back, Alex commented: "We were very fortunate in the speed with which we got things done. Even then the project as a whole had cost us close to $1 million in salaries and related costs."

Marketing the New Product

Alex continued:

> We then faced a very difficult set of problems, because of uncertainties in the market place. We knew there was a good market for the flexible type of coupling because of its wide application across so many different industries. But, we didn't know how big the market was nor how much of it we could secure. This meant we weren't sure what volume to tool up for, what kind or size of equipment to purchase, or how to go about the marketing job. We were tempted to start small and grow as our share of market grew, but this could be costly too and could allow too much time for competitive response. Our Canadian engineer was very helpful here. He had a lot of confidence in our product and had seen it marketed in both Canada and the United States. At his suggestion we tooled up for a sales estimate of $30 million – which was pretty daring. In addition, we hired eight field sales representatives to back up the nation-wide distributor and soon afterwards hired several Canadian-based sales representatives to cover major markets. We found that our key Canadian competitor was pricing rather high and had not cultivated very friendly customer relations. We were surprised how quickly we were able to secure significant penetration into the Canadian market. It just wasn't being well-serviced.

During 2012, the company actually spent a total of $2.5 million on equipment for flexible coupling production. In addition, a fixed commitment of $1.5 million a year in marketing expenditures on flexible couplings arose from the hiring of sales representatives. A small amount of trade advertising was included in this sum. The total commitment represented a significant part of the company's resources and threatened serious damage to the company's financial position if the sales failed to materialize.

"It was quite a gamble at the time," Alex added. "By the end of 2012, it was clear that the gamble was going to pay off."

Sales by Market Sector ($ millions)

	OEM Parts Sales	Flexible Couplings Sales	Total Sales	After Tax Profits
2008	60	Nil	60	1.75
2009	48	Nil	48	(2.50)
2010	38	Nil	38	(3.50)
2011	45	Nil	45	0.25
2012	58	10 (six months)	68	5.80

Cameron's approach to competition in flexible couplings was to stress product quality, service, and speed of delivery, but not price. Certain sizes of couplings were priced slightly below the competition but others were not. In the words of one Cameron sales representative:

> Our job is really a technical function. Certainly, we help predispose the customer to buy and we'll even take orders, but we put them through our distributors. Flexible couplings can be used in almost all areas of secondary industry, by both large and small firms. This is why we need a large distributor with wide reach in the market. What we do is give our product the kind of emphasis a distributor can't give. We develop relationships with key buyers in most major industries, and we work with them to keep abreast of new potential uses for our product or of changes in size requirements or other performance characteristics. Then we feed this kind of information back to our design group. We meet with the design group quite often to find out what new types of couplings are being developed and what the intended uses are, etc. Sometimes they help us solve a customer's problem. Of course, these 'solutions' are usually built around the use of one of our products.

Financing Plant Capacity

When Alex first set his diversification plans in motion in 2010, the company's plant in suburban

Detroit was operating at 50 per cent capacity. However, by early 2013, sales of auto parts had recovered almost to pre-crisis levels (before 2007), and the flexible coupling line was squeezed for space. Andy McIntyre put the problem this way:

> I don't see how we can get sales of more than $85 million out of this plant without going to a permanent two-shift system, which Alex doesn't want to do. With two full shifts we could probably reach sales of $125 million. The problem is that both our product lines are growing very quickly. Auto parts could easily hit $80 million on their own this year, and flexible couplings! Well, who would have thought we'd sell $10 million in the first six months? Our salespeople are looking for $35 million to $40 million during 2013. It's wild! We just have to have more capacity.

There are two problems pressing us to consider putting flexible couplings under a different roof. The first is internal: we are making more and more types and sizes, and sales are growing to such a point that we may be able to produce more efficiently in a separate facility. The second is external: The Big Three like to tour our plant regularly and tell us how to make auto parts cheaper. Having these flexible couplings all over the place seems to upset them because they have trouble determining how much of our costs belong to Auto Parts. If it were left to me, I'd just let them be upset, but Alex feels differently. He's afraid of losing orders. Sometimes I wonder if he's right. Maybe we should lose a few orders to the Big Three and fill up the plant with our own product instead of expanding.

Flexible couplings were produced on a batch basis, and there were considerable savings involved as batches got larger. Thus as sales grew, and inventory requirements made large batches possible, unit production costs decreased, sometimes substantially. McIntyre estimated that unit production costs would decline by some 20 per cent as annual sales climbed from $20 million to $100 million and by a further 10 per cent at $250 million. Scale economies beyond sales of $250 million were not expected to be significant.

John Ellis, the company's financial manager, expressed his own reservations about new plant expansion from a cash flow perspective:

> We really don't have the balance sheet (see Exhibit 2) ready for major plant expansion yet. I think we should grow more slowly and safely for two more years and pay off our debts. If we could hold sales at $75 million for 2013 and $85 million for 2014, we would be able to put ourselves in a much stronger financial position. The problem is that people only look at the profits. They don't realize that every dollar of flexible coupling sales requires an investment in inventory and receivables of about 30 cents. It's not like selling to the Big Three. You have to manufacture to inventory and then wait for payment from a variety of sources.
>
> As it is, Alex wants to invest $10 million in a new plant and equipment right away to allow flexible coupling sales to grow as fast as the market will allow. We have the space on our existing site to add a separate plant for flexible couplings. It's the money I worry about.

Foreign Markets

As the company's market position in North America began to improve, Alex began to wonder about foreign markets. The company had always been a major exporter to Canada, but it had never had to market there. The Big Three placed their orders often a year or two in advance, and Cameron just supplied them. As Alex put it:

> It was different with the flexible coupling. We had to find our own way into the market. We did, however, start getting orders from Europe and South America, at first from the subsidiaries of our U.S. customers and then from a few other firms as word got around. We got $40,000 in orders during 2012 and the same amount during the first four months of 2013. This was a time when we were frantically busy and hopelessly understaffed in the management area, so all we did was fill the orders on a FOB (free-on-board), Detroit basis. The customers had to pay import duties of

Exhibit 2
Balance Sheets
(for years ended December 31 ($000s))

	2010	2011	2012
Assets			
Cash	$ 615	$ 430	$ 400
Accounts Receivable	5,850	6,850	10,400
Inventories	4,995	4,920	7,500
Total Current Assets	11,460	12,200	18,300
Property, Plant and Equipment (net)	10,790	11,800	13,000
Total Assets	22,250	24,000	31,300
Liabilities			
Accounts Payable	4,850	5,900	9,500
Bank Loan	11,500	12,000	10,000
Accrued Items (including taxes)	450	400	500
Total Current Liabilities	16,800	18,300	20,000
Common Stock (Held by Cameron family)	500	500	500
Retained Earnings	4,950	5,200	10,800
Total Equity	5,450	5,700	11,300
Total Liabilities	$22,250	$24,000	$31,300

Source: Company files.

approximately 3 per cent into most European countries and a value added tax (VAT) ranging between 15 per cent (Luxembourg) and 27 per cent (Hungary), with an average of about 21.5 per cent, on top of the freight and insurance, and still orders came in. The VAT for the United Kingdom was 20 per cent and France 19.6 per cent.

Seeing the growing potential in Europe, supported by clear signs of recovery from the financial crisis and the European debt crisis, Alex promptly took a European Patent from the European Patent Office in the United Kingdom. The cost of the whole process was under $10,000.

A Licensing Opportunity

In the spring of 2013, Alex made a vacation trip to Scotland and decided while he was there to drop in on one of the company's new foreign customers, McTaggart Supplies Ltd. Cameron Auto Parts had received unsolicited orders from overseas amounting to $40,000 in the first four months of 2013, and over 10 per cent of these had come from McTaggart. Alex was pleasantly surprised at the reception given to him by Sandy McTaggart, the 60-year-old head of the company.

Sandy: Come in! Talk of the devil. We were just saying what a shame it is you don't make those flexible couplings in this part of the world. There's a very good market for them. Why my men can even sell them to the English!

Alex: Well, we're delighted to supply your needs. I think we've always shipped your orders promptly, and I don't see why we can't continue . . .

Sandy: That's not the point! Those orders are already sold before we place them. The point

Exhibit 3
Data on McTaggart Supplies Ltd

2012 Sales	£35 million (down from £44 million in 2010).
Total Assets	£11 million: Equity £6.5 million
Net profit after tax	± £1.5 million
Control	McTaggart Family
Market coverage	15 sales representatives in United Kingdom, two in Europe, one in Australia, one in New Zealand, one in India.
Average factory wage rate	£9.00 per hour (which is below the United Kingdom mean of £12.92 due to the factory being located in a depressed area) (versus $19.54 in America).
Factory	Old and larger than necessary. Some very imaginative manufacturing know-how in evidence.
Reputation	Excellent credit record, business now 130 years old, good market contacts (high calibre sales force).
Other	Company sales took a beating during 2010–2011 as one of the company's staple products was badly hurt by a U.S. product of superior technology. Company filled out its line by distributing products obtained from other manufacturers. Currently about one-half of company sales are purchased from others. Company has capacity to increase production substantially.

Pricing	Index
Cameron's price to McTaggart	100
(same as net price to distributor in America)	
+ import duty	3
+ freight and insurance	10
import's cost	113
+ distributor's (McTaggart's) margin (30%)	34
+ VAT (20 % on cost plus margin)	29
= price charged by McTaggart	176
versus price charged by American distributor in the United States	120

Source: Company files.

is we can't really build the market here on the basis of shipments from America. There's a 3 per cent tariff coming in, freight and insurance cost us another 10 per cent on top of your price, then there's the matter of currency values. I get my orders in pounds (£)[2] but I have to pay you in dollars. And on top of

all that, I can never be sure how long exactly the goods will take to get here, especially with the ever-looming risk of strikes. I still remember the 2009 postal strikes. Listen, why don't you license us to produce flexible couplings here?

After a lengthy bargaining session, during which Alex secured the information (see Exhibit 3), he came round to the view that a license agreement with McTaggart might be a

---

[2] £1 was equivalent to US$ 1.54 in 2013 (average in the period between January 1, 2013 and April 30, 2013).

good way of achieving swift penetration of the U.K. market via McTaggart's sales force. McTaggart's production skills were not as up-to-date as Cameron's, but his plant showed evidence of a lot of original ideas to keep manufacturing costs down. Furthermore, the firm seemed committed enough to invest in some new equipment and to put a major effort into developing the U.K. market. At this point the two executives began to discuss specific terms of the license arrangements:

Alex: Let's talk about price. I think a figure around 3 per cent of your sales of flexible couplings would be about right.

Sandy: That's a bit high for an industrial license of this kind. I think one and a half per cent is more normal.

Alex: That may be, but we're going to be providing more than just blueprints. We'll have to help you choose equipment and train your operators as well.

Sandy: Aye, so you will. But we'll pay you for that separately. It's going to cost us £500,000 in special equipment as it is, plus, let's say, a $100,000 fee to you to help set things up. Now you have to give us a chance to price competitively in the market, or neither of us will benefit. With a royalty of one and a half per cent, I reckon we could reach sales of £500,000 in our first year and £1 million in our second.

Alex: The equipment will let you produce up to £4 million of annual output. Surely you can sell more than a million. We're getting unsolicited orders without even trying.

Sandy: With the right kind of incentive, we might do a lot better. Why don't we agree to a royalty of two and a half per cent on the first million in sales and one and a half per cent after that. Now mind you, we're to become exclusive agents for the U.K. market. We'll supply your present customers from our own plant.

Alex: But just in the United Kingdom! Now 2 per cent is as low as I'm prepared to go. You make those figures 3 per cent and 2 per cent and you have a deal. But it has to include a free technology flow-back clause in the event you make any improvements or adaptations to our manufacturing process.

Sandy: You drive a hard bargain! But it's your product, and we do want it. I'll have our lawyers draw up a contract accordingly. What do you say to a five-year deal, renewable for another five if we are both happy?

Alex: Sounds good. Let's do it.

Alex signed the contract the same week and then headed back to America to break the news. He travelled with mixed feelings, however. On the one hand, he felt he had got the better of Sandy McTaggart in the bargaining, while on the other, he felt he had no objective yardstick against which to evaluate the royalty rate he had agreed on. This was pretty much the way he presented the situation to his executive group when he got home.

Alex: ... so I think it's a good contract, and I have a cheque here for $100,000 to cover our costs in helping McTaggart get set up.

John: We can certainly use the cash right now. And there doesn't seem to be any risk (finance) involved. I like the idea, Alex.

Andy (production): Well, I don't. And Chuck (head of the Cameron design team) won't either when (production) he hears about it. I think you've sold out the whole U.K. market for a pittance. I thought you wanted to capture foreign markets directly.

Alex: But Andy, we just don't have the resources to capture foreign markets ourselves. We might as well get what we can through licensing, now that we've patented our process.

Andy: Well, maybe. But I don't like it. It's the thin edge of the wedge if you ask me. Our know-how on the production of this product is pretty special, and it's getting better all the time. I hate to hand it over to old McTaggart on a silver platter. I reckon we're going to sell over $20 million in flexible couplings in the United States alone during 2013.

As Alex walked back into his office after this conversation, he wondered whether signing the deal might have been premature.

IVEY | Publishing

CASE 1.3 MABE: LEARNING TO BE A MULTINATIONAL (A)

Jose Luis Rivas and Luis Arciniega wrote this case solely to provide material for class discussion. The authors do not intend to illustrate either effective or ineffective handling of a managerial situation. The authors may have disguised certain names and other identifying information to protect confidentiality.

Version: 2016–03–03

It was a sunny afternoon in March 2012, and Ramiro Perez, Mabe's international vice-president, was wondering what to do about Mabe's joint venture (JV) in Russia. It had been the firm's most difficult market entry in terms of return on time invested. The timing had certainly not helped, as the JV had occurred just before Lehman Brothers' fall in the summer of 2008. Mabe had chosen Russia based on the premise that it was the "last frontier," much like a Wild West gold-hunting opportunity in 19th century America. Backed by optimistic predictions of Russia's future, investment bankers and industry players contributed to fuelling this "wild frontier vision" of a vast territory boasting one of the world's largest populations, a highly educated workforce, an unlimited supply of energy and natural resources, and a political regime favourable to business. It had all seemed like a great idea – until the financial crises hit and the foundations of this last frontier started falling apart. Expanding Mabe to other Latin American countries and to Canada had been, to some extent, so natural and easy that Perez had a difficult time understanding how he could have done things differently when the company had entered Russia. Should Mabe have taken a more aggressive approach? Had Mabe become arrogant as a result of its past success?

History

Mabe was founded in 1946 by the Mabardi and Berrondo families. Although initially dedicated to building kitchen cabinets, in 1950, the company expanded to manufacture its first appliance, a stove. By 1968, the company had expanded its involvement in appliances and it began exporting fridges and stoves to Central America and the Caribbean. The first industrial plant for manufacturing refrigerators was built in Queretaro, Mexico, in 1976, the same year the company began exporting to the United States. By 1980, Mabe was the market leader of stoves and refrigerators in Mexico. General Electric (GE) acquired 48 per cent of Mabe in a JV in 1987. As part of the JV deal, Mabe retained full management responsibility and would build gas stoves for the U.S. market, in exchange for receiving U.S. technology and technical advice. By virtue of this deal, GE had become Mabe's main business partner and its largest customer.

In 1989, Mabe acquired Easy, one of the industry's key players, In 1990, Mabe opened a new stove plant spanning 1.5 million square feet in San Luis Potosi, Mexico. The production at this new plant would be mostly devoted to the U.S. market.

In 1994, the company decided to embark on an expansion to Latin America, and Mabe's mission was redefined to include the label "Leaders in Latin America" with a focus in the Andean Pact countries – Venezuela, Colombia, Peru and Ecuador. Mabe acquired appliances plants in Ecuador, Argentina and Colombia. In Venezuela, Mabe decided to compete using a GE plant and through a joint venture with Ceteco, a Dutch firm that already had a presence in the Latin American market. The purchased plant in Colombia was bought from Phillips. In Ecuador, Mabe established a JV with the Orrantia family through their Durex brand. In Peru, a representation office was opened to import appliances.

In 1998, Mabe acquired the Spanish manufacturer Fagor's operations in Argentina. In 1999–2000 the U.S. Energy Department issued a regulation requiring energy consumption to be decreased by 30 per cent. When GE considered the investment required to shift its U.S. production plant, it decided instead to source from a new plant to be built in Celaya, Mexico. Thus, in 2000, a high-end refrigerator plant began its operations there. The output from this plant would cover demand from both the domestic and international markets under the Mabe and GE brands. In 1994, a research and development (R&D) centre opened in the city of Queretaro, Mexico. The centre's main purpose was to decrease reliance on GE for R&D and to develop higher and more sophisticated technical skills to support GE's technology team in its R&D and product development efforts. Another goal was the development of proprietary technology. Also in 2000, the San Luis Potosi plant was enlarged to accommodate the production of electric stoves for GE's U.S. market.

In 2002, Mabe entered Latin America's main market through two acquisitions: Dako (GE's operation in Brazil) and CCE appliances.

By early 2003, more than a third of all gas and electric ranges and refrigerators sold in the United States had been manufactured in Mabe plants. Its side-by-side refrigerators could also be found in one of every four American homes.[1]

In 2005, Mabe's entered the only North American market where it did not yet have a presence. Camco Canada was acquired, and with this acquisition, Mabe started exporting dishwashing machines and clothes dryers to the U.S. market.

As part of Mabe's internationalization strategy, a brand portfolio was established with the GE brand in the upper segment, Mabe in the middle and some regional brands, such as Easy, Dako, Patrick and Durex, in the middle and lower segments.

In 2008, Mabe acquired ATLAS Costa Rica, a manufacturer of refrigerators and stoves. That same year, two representation offices were opened: one in Chile and one in Russia. The main purpose of a representation office was to import appliances from other producing countries. In the case of Russia, because of the market's importance and cultural distance, Mabe decided to open the representation office in a 50–50 deal with Spain's Fagor.

Due to the financial crisis, in 2008, GE considered selling its appliance business worldwide. Several bidders expressed interest, including Mabe. In the end, however, GE's board decided to keep the appliance business.

In 2009, Mabe became Brazil's second industry player by acquiring Bosch's Brazilian operations. With this acquisition, the Brazilian market also became Mabe's number-two worldwide market, after the United States. The Mexican market at that time was approximately $650 million,[2] while the Brazilian market was at almost $1 billion. Brazil had become Mabe's most complex experience, due to the following factors:

- GE's large operation with Brazilian-American executives

---

[1] J. David Hunger, "U.S. Major Home Appliance Industry in 2002: Competition Becomes Global," in T. Wheelen and J. Hunger (eds.), *Strategic Management and Business Policy*, Prentice Hall, Upper Saddle River, NJ, 2003.

[2] All currency amounts are expressed in U.S. dollars unless otherwise indicated.

Exhibit 1 Mabe's Company History, 1946 to 2009

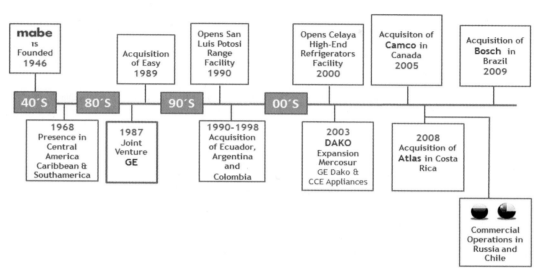

mabe   COMPANY HISTORY

Source: Company files.

- Mabe arrived with Mexican-Americans
- Bosch mostly had German-Brazilian executives

The challenge in Brazil was the result of different cultures having to come together. Thus, Mabe's chief executive officer (CEO) in Brazil was the former corporate head of human resources.

In 2012, Mabe was the largest appliance manufacturer in Latin America and held an important share of demand for the U.S. market. Mabe manufactured all the stoves that GE sold in the United States plus high-end side-by-side and bottom-freezer refrigerators and all of GE's clothes dryers. Mabe was also in charge of R&D for those products alongside GE's Canadian operations, where GE held 17 per cent of the market and was present in every Latin American country. Exhibits 1 and 2 contain a summary of Mabe's history and revenues.

One of the lessons Mabe learned through this expansion was that the best people to operate businesses are the locals who know the industry. Corporate managers needed to visit the foreign operations only to solve specific problems. Another lesson was the importance of instilling the firm's culture into the acquired firms. Perez was conscious of the value of cultural integration and knew it would be a complex issue to work through. A final lesson was that, in terms of culture, an internationalization process needed be taken very seriously, which meant a long-term commitment to the task and the involvement of the CEO, top managers and board members in all stages of the process.

The Alliance with GE

In 1987 GE acquired 48 per cent of Mabe. GE's main interest was to decrease its production costs.

Exhibit 2 Mabe's Historical Revenues, 1987 to 2010

US $ B

Joint Venture GE ('87)

Mexican Economic Crisis

Durex Ecuador

Commercial operations Peru

Fagor Argentina

Integration in LA

Opens Celaya Refrigerators Facility

Ceteco Venezuela

Subsidiaries in Brazil

Camco Canada

GE Chile

Atlas Costa Rica

Bosch Brazil

$0.1

$0.3

$0.6

$1.3

$1.9

$3.1

$3.9

$3.5

$3.6

'90   '92   '94   '96   '98   '00   '02   '04   '06   '08   '10

Source: Company files.

At the time, GE was using Electrolux as its main provider of stoves for the U.S. market. Mabe, on the other hand, wanted both to learn from a giant such as GE and to be able to penetrate new markets. One of the first decisions of the joint venture was to build a plant to manufacture stoves for the new markets. As it turned out, the new San Luis Potosi facility became the largest manufacturer of its kind in the world. Mabe and GE faced the challenge of training U.S. suppliers that were not accustomed to exporting components to a developing country such as Mexico.

As part of this joint venture, a new breed of executives joined Mabe, where graduate degrees were still rare. For many years, the norm had been for employees to work their way through the ranks. After the JV, all the new incoming cadre of hires were engineering graduates and, following the catchphrase "all students, all teachers," they were first assigned to teams headed by seasoned Mabe and GE executives, who were initially suspicious of the experiment. Five of these new executives were selected as the pilot group to receive training in Kentucky's GE facilities, while the rest of the group stayed in Mexico to continue working with their U.S. counterparts. Finally, as part of this process, Mabe would also manage GE's Canadian operations; the research and development activities of GE's stoves, refrigerators and dryers; and the global procurement of strategic components for both GE and Mabe. Exhibit 3 provides a breakdown of Mabe's regional sources of income.

At the beginning of the 1990s, Mabe convinced GE that Latin America was a natural market for expansion: the language, culture and the degree of economic development were similar

Exhibit 3 Mabe Income by Region, 1990 to 2011

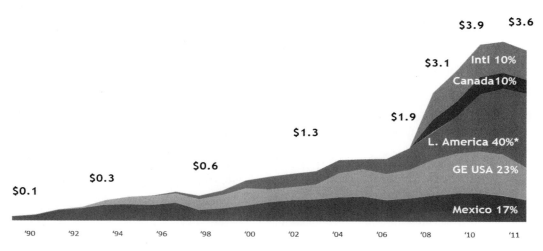

Source: Company files.

among the region's large economies. To rapidly consolidate the markets, Mabe used GE's methodology of "action learning," whereby multidisciplinary teams of executives collaborated to recommend ways to enter new markets. Each team travelled to the target market for a six- to eight–week stay. At the end of this time period, each team formulated its recommendations, and top management decided which markets to pursue. Since the late 1980s, GE had used this methodology at its Crotonville leadership centre to train and select executive talent.

Mabe and GE were to apply this methodology, using one team to recommend entry strategies to the board and top management team.

Throughout the expansion process in Latin America, Mabe and GE also worked closely on strategic programs for the North American markets, such as the new side-by-side bottom freezers, refrigerators, electric stoves and – with

the acquisition of Camco in Canada – the production and supply of clothes dryers. Exhibits 4 and 5 provide balance sheets and income statements for 2006 through 2008. Additionally, sales for global appliance players can be seen in Exhibit 6.

The BRIC Countries

Early in the 2000s, observers predicted that Brazil, Russia, India and China (i.e., the BRIC countries) would overtake the largest industrialized countries in size by 2050. Some predictions had subsequently shortened the timeline to 2018. In 2011, China surpassed Japan as the second world economy in terms of size. Exhibits 7 and 8 show the sizes and profitability of selected BRIC countries.

Russia had the largest land mass in the world and a gross domestic product (GDP) of almost $1.5 trillion in 2010, compared with India's $1.4

Exhibit 4
Mabe's Balance Sheet 2006–2008 (000s USD)

Balance Sheet

December 31st (USD)	2006	2007	2008
ASSETS			
Cash And Equivalents	149,100	211,055	204,883
Total Cash & ST Investments	**149,100**	**211,055**	**204,883**
Accounts Receivable	890,903	989,319	912,774
Other Receivables	-	-	22,789
Total Receivables	**890,903**	**989,319**	**935,562**
Inventory	412,894	492,095	539,670
Prepaid Exp.	12,764	14,931	7,189
Total Current Assets	**1,465,662**	**1,707,399**	**1,687,304**
Net Property, Plant & Equipment	**674,744**	**715,333**	**704,727**
Goodwill	197,382	208,398	163,547
Other Long-Term Assets	208,759	365,315	363,830
Total Assets	**2,546,547**	**2,996,445**	**2,919,408**
LIABILITIES			
Accounts Payable	904,777	1082,663	989,910
Accrued Exp.	4,625	3,939	3,235
Short-term Borrowings	54,294	186,322	637,870
Curr. Income Taxes Payable	34,130	49,649	49,028
Other Current Liabilities	12,487	14,473	13,587
Total Current Liabilities	**1,010,313**	**1,337,046**	**1,693,630**
Long-Term Debt	733,663	692,065	429,249
Pension & Other Post-Retire. Benefits	142,163	142,352	109,127
Def. Tax Liability, Non-Curr.	27,656	32,244	39,826
Other Non-Current Liabilities	78,990	128,703	95,684
Total Liabilities	**1,992,785**	**2,332,411**	**2,367,517**
Common Stock	553,762	616,950	534,782
Total Common Equity	**553,762**	**616,859**	**534,782**
Minority Interest	-	47,176	17,110
Total Equity	**553,762**	**664,035**	**551,891**
Total Liabilities And Equity	**2,546,547**	**2,996,445**	**2,919,408**

Note: Exp. = Expenses; Inc. = Income; EBT = Earnings before taxes; Excl. = Excluding; Incl. = Including; Cont. Ops. = Continuing operations
Source: www.capitaliq.com/home.aspx, accessed November 21, 2012.

trillion, Brazil's $2.2 trillion and China's $5.7 trillion. Russia's 2010 per capita income was slightly higher than Brazil's, double that of China and approximately nine times India's. Russia had the world's largest gas reserves and second largest oil reserves. Russia's discretionary income was 30 per cent higher than Brazil's, 10 times that of India and four times that of China.[3] Moscow and other major Russian cities were

[3] Sheila M. Puffer & Daniel McCarthy, "Two Decades of Russian Business and Management Research: An Institutional Theory Perspective," *Academy of Management Perspectives*, 2011, pp. 21–35.

Exhibit 5
Mabe's Income Statement 2006–2008 (000s USD)

Income Statement

December 31st (000s USD)	2006	2007	2008
Total Revenue	3,156,260	3788,084	3404,803
Cost Of Goods Sold	2,441,751	2,940,567	2,499,649
Gross Profit	714,517	847,517	905,153
Selling General & Admin Exp.	492,716	592,034	683,088
Other Operating Exp., Total	492,716	592,034	683,088
Operating Income	221,801	255,482	222,065
Interest Expense	-81,700	-88,800	-86,800
Interest and Invest. Income	12,394	13,649	11,646
Net Interest Exp.	-69,300	-75,100	-75,200
Currency Exchange Gains (Loss)	-5,500	9,344	-101,400
Other Non-Operating Inc. (Exp.)	-30,900	-16,900	-6,800
EBT Excl. Unusual Items	116,173	172,856	38,604
EBT Incl. Unusual Items	116,173	172,856	38,604
Income Tax Expense	34,685	46,168	27,174
Earnings from Cont. Ops.	81,487	126,688	11,430
Net Income to Company	81,487	126,688	11,430

Note: ST = Short-term; Exp. = expenses; Post-Retire. = Post-Retirement
Source: www.capitaliq.com/home.aspx, accessed Nov 21st, 2012

Exhibit 6
Global Appliance Players, 2011

Company	Headquarters	Sales
1. Whirlpool	United States	14,000,000
2. Electrolux	Sweden	11,000,000
3. BSHI	Germany	10,000,000
4. Samsung	South Korea	9,000,000
5. Midea	China	8,000,000
6. LG	South Korea	7,000,000
7. Haier	China	6,000,000
8. GE	US	4,000,000
9. Mabe	Mexico	4,000,000

Source: Annual reports and press releases.

experiencing a consumer boom, spurred on by rising incomes of the middle class.

The Russian government established in 2011 a $10 billion fund to be used to attract foreign investment. Russia's outward foreign direct investment was almost $50 billion between 2007 and 2009, and Russian multinational corporations (MNCs) owned $203 billion in assets outside of

Exhibit 7
Appliances Market Size in China, India, and Russia 2005 to 2010

Country	2005	2006	2007	2008	2009e	2010e
China	63,687,000	71,381,700	79,654,800	86,378,000	93,421,300	104,157,600
India	5,930,900	6,725,300	7,756,200	9,377,200	11,467,300	13,404,200
Russia	11,043,300	12,368,300	13,408,400	11,369,000	11,706,400	12,597,600

Source: Euromonitor International, *Major Appliances: Recovery and the Future for Core Categories*, April 2011.

Exhibit 8
Marginal Contribution Per Appliance in China, India, and Russia 2008 (per cent)

China	16–18
India	6–8
Russia	10–12

Source: Company files.

Russia, more than that of any other BRIC country. Additionally, Russia had recently introduced an innovation program that included a centre for innovation – Skolkovo – and several techno parks and economic zones throughout the country.

During the past two decades, Russia had faced struggles on two fronts: a decreasing population and the deterioration of human capital. According to Rosstat, the Russian agency of statistics, since 1992, Russia had 12.5 million more deaths than births, the equivalent of three funerals per each birth for the past 20 years. Worldwide, in the period after the Second World War, only one population decrease had been more alarming: in China, between 1959 and 1961, as a result of Mao Tse-Tung's "big jump-ahead program." Thus, between 1993 and 2010, Russia's population decreased from 148.6 million to 141.9 million.

Several industrialized countries were also experiencing population decreases: Germany, Italy and Japan were either bordering on population decreases or were beginning to show signs of a decrease. The difference between these countries and Russia was that the former countries faced this crisis at a time of unprecedented levels of public health, whereas Russia was experiencing an extraordinary crisis of mortality. According to the Human Mortality Database[4], life expectancy in Russia was lower in 2009 than in 1961. In 2009, the life expectancy in Russia at age 15 was lower than in Bangladesh or Madagascar. The main causes of Russian deaths were cardiovascular diseases, fatal injuries, accidents and suicides. Cardiovascular diseases in Russia were almost three times the levels in Western Europe, and deaths due to injuries and violence were similar to those experienced by some African societies, such as Liberia and Sierra Leone.

The second front of problems for Russia was its deterioration of human capital. Globally, higher levels of education typically correlate with increased levels of public health. Russia's adult

[4] www.mortality.org/cgi-bin/hmd/country.php?cntr= RUS&level=1, accessed April 3, 2013.

population was 30 percentage points above the OECD average but with a life expectancy similar to that in Senegal. Part of the problem might be the quality of Russian education; international standardized tests have revealed that Russian elementary and high-school education is below the levels in Turkey, which has among the lowest ratings for education among the OECD's list of countries. In 2008, Russian authors published fewer scientific articles than authors from Brazil, China or India. Indeed, Russia represented a new and curious reality in today's globalized world: a society characterized by high levels of education but low levels of health and knowledge. Beyond affecting individual levels of wellbeing, this triple problem could also have serious economic implications. Even despite Russia's vast natural resources, in today's globalized economy, a country's wealth is represented by its human capital. Natural resources can increase the level of wealth in an already rich human capital society, such as Norway or Canada; but, natural resources cannot on their own replace the value of human capital, nor is there a single example of a super world power that has developed solely on the basis of its natural resources. Each year, Russia earns less than Belgium for its exports. To complicate things further, in Russia, the state's share of the economy is 56 per cent, a high rate that is seen only in China, where state-owned companies also account for more than half of the total value of the stock market.[5]

Today, many multinationals consider an entry into Russia to be of strategic importance in their efforts to truly achieve global competitiveness. However, a survey of 158 corporate investors and non-investors in Russia indicated that respondents viewed doing business in Russia to be more risky and less profitable than doing business in China, India or South East Asia.[6] The respondents' main concerns were weak

legislative and enforcement regimes and the incidents of corruption and bribery at all levels of state bureaucracy. Indeed, Russia was ranked 147th out of 180 countries in Transparency International's 2008 Corruption Perception Index.[7] A 2009 survey by the Foreign Investment Advisory Council (FIAC) of 50 executives from large companies[8] reported concern about Russia's political interference in business, arbitrariness in the application of laws, complexity of the tax system and lack of skilled staff. Over the past decade, the Russian state had exerted a far stronger influence over business activity than the previous Yeltsin administration. The lack of clear direction and instability had created a volatile environment for managers, as had the corrupt law enforcement and judicial systems, weak capital market institutions and poor protection of private property rights.[9] Russia's flawed privatization process of the early 1990s was seen as having caused the problems that persisted in the country's business environment, including the low credibility of formal institutions.

An in-depth field study found that Russians' low trust of outsiders inhibited communication with the foreign managers of Western subsidiaries and undermined organizational initiatives.[10] As a consequence of the low levels of trust, outsiders needed to spend considerable time and effort building particularized trust.

Russians continued to be heavily influenced by their history and to manifest many cultural influences from their Soviet and Czarist past, including collectivism, paternalism, admiration of strong leaders, fear of responsibility, mistrust of outsiders and reliance on one's own networks. Indeed, compared with managers from the four

[5] Ruchir Sharma, *Breakout Nations: In Pursuit of the Next Economic Miracles*, WW Norton & Co. Ltd., New York, 2012.

[6] N. Buckley, "Huge gains but also a lot of pain," *Financial Times*, October 11, 2005.

[7] www.transparency.org/research/cpi/cpi_2009, accessed April 3, 2013.

[8] www.fiac.ru/surveys-2008.php, accessed April 3, 2013.

[9] Sheila M. Puffer and Daniel J. McCarthy, "Two Decades of Russian Business and Management Research: An Institutional Theory Perspective," *Academy of Management Perspectives*, May 2011, pp. 21–36.

[10] Angela Ayios, *Trust and Western-Russian Business Relationships*, Ashgate Publishing Ltd., Farnham, UK, 2004.

major developed economies, Russian managers have been found to be more oriented to the short term and to place little emphasis on competitive strategy, formal strategic planning or financial planning.[11]

A study that compared the informal institutions of Brazil, Russia, India and China[12] concluded that, of the four countries, Russia was in the worst position. Russian formal institutions and governance codes were, on paper, comparable with those in OECD countries; however, in practice, their informal institutions of networks (known as *blat*) between leading shareholders, the business groups and the state competed with the formal arrangements.

Russia had no middle ground. The proportion of small and medium-sized enterprises in relation to all enterprises was lower in Russia than in any other major emerging market. Compared with Europe, Russia had no truly modern banks. The country's financial system was dominated by one big bank, and very few Russians invested at home, so loans of any kind were difficult to acquire. The mortgage market was virtually nonexistent, representing only three per cent of GDP, the lowest of any emerging market. The financial market resembled that of frontier markets, such as Nigeria, rather than the financial market of a major developing country. Money flowed into Russia from 2004 to 2008, but then reversed in 2009, leading to a net foreign direct investment of *negative* $9.5 billion in 2010. Russia was probably the only emerging market that had suffered a large and accelerating outflow of private capital: based on Russian central bank estimates, the outflow hit $80 billion in 2011, up from $42 billion in 2006.

Vladimir Putin was probably the man in the best position to save Russia from chaos in 1999, when the economy was in crisis and the war with Chechnya was raging, but it was not clear whether he had the appropriate vision to take Russia to the next level of economic development. Putin had moved from the presidency to being the prime minister, and was again president. He could hold that office for two terms, until 2024, which would extend his reign to a quarter century. Putin's disapproval rating had doubled since 2008, to 40 per cent at the end of 2011. Of all the major emerging markets, Russia was the last to recoup the output lost during the recession of 2008, with the economy returning to its pre-crisis peak by the end of 2011.[13]

Mabe and Russia

Around 2004, Mabe started to explore new regions of the world for expansion. Economies of scale were a key success driver in the appliance industry and virtually all global players had a multiregional presence.

Mabe considered several possibilities. They already had a procurement office in China but Mabe's management thought the Chinese market was too big and complex to enter. India and Eastern Europe were strong candidates. While Mabe pursued market research in Eastern Europe, several industry players had referred to Russia as the "last frontier" market, which had caught the attention of Ramiro Perez, Mabe's international VP. To decrease the risk of foreignness and to leverage its competitor capabilities, Mabe invited Spain's Fagor to form a joint venture. Mabe would source stoves and fridges from Mexico and Brazil and microwave ovens from China. Fagor would contribute with its frontline washing machines that were made in its Polish plant. Initially, only a representative office would be established, and all appliances would be imported, which would provide the new joint venture with an opportunity to learn about the Russian market. One of the venture's first decisions was to have two expatriates, one Brazilian,

[11] Chris Carr, "Russian Strategic Investment Decision Practices Compared to Those of Great Britain, Germany, the United States and Japan," *International Studies of Management and Organization*, vol. 36, no. 4, pp. 82–110.

[12] Saul Estrin and Martha Prevezer, "The Role of Informal Institutions in Corporate Governance: Brazil, Russia, India and China Compared," *Asia Pacific Journal of Management*, vol. 28, pp. 41–67.

[13] Ruchir Sharma, *Breakout Nations: In Pursuit of the Next Economic Miracles*, WW Norton & Co. Ltd., New York, 2012.

the other Spanish, as the JV's CEO and chief financial officer (CFO), respectively. As was customary, Mabe introduced an "action learning" team to determine the type of products that the new JV would import to Russia. The team determined that a broad line of products strategy would serve the Russian market well.

One of the main challenges faced by global firms starting operations in Russia was understanding the vastness of the country. With a population of 142 million, the minorities were of "country size." For example, although Russia was usually considered to be predominantly Orthodox, it also had more than 20 million Muslims. This vast country had more than 20,000 linear kilometres of borders with 14 country neighbours, 83 regions and diverse religions. Russia shared borders with such diverse countries as China, Pakistan, Afghanistan and North Korea. Due to the misconception of the size and diversity of Russia, foreign companies tended to enter Moscow and Saint Petersburg first, the two most crowded markets in Russia. These two cities concentrated a large proportion of the population, whose consumption patterns and styles differed from those of the average Russian citizen, according to Nicolay Shkolyar[14], head of the Commercial Office of the Russian embassy in Mexico City. On another hand, the country was also one of the 20 least densely populated countries in the world and had only five cities with the critical mass of people and income necessary to draw in global brands.[15]

Russia could be a hostile environment for foreign investors. For example, to obtain a work visa, an AIDS test was required. Nonetheless, the appliance market was attractive due to its size (i.e., US$3 billion) and profitability (i.e., two times the average operating margin). The downside was that manufacturing locally was necessary to achieve cost advantages over the other industry players. The main local producers were Indesit (Italy), Bosch-Siemens (Germany) and LG (South Korea). Samsung (South Korea) and Mabe-Fagor both had a local office and imported appliances from several of their manufacturing facilities worldwide.

Business Culture

Until the early nineties, one of the rituals of trust among Russian executives was the sealing of deals by toasting with vodka in a *banya* (i.e., a sauna). The rationale was that if you were naked and drunk, you could not hide anything from your partners. A young Russian entrepreneur added:

> In Latin countries, people use charm to gain trust, but as a citizen of a country where most foreigners are considered suspicious, you don't really know what is behind an apparent friendly smile. Russians could be considered rude, cold and unfriendly, but one thing you can be sure is that what you see is what you get with them. Any foreigner coming to Russia for business needs to adapt to our cultural cues to be considered trustworthy.[16]

Russia's low unemployment rate acted to demotivate firm loyalty. The Communist culture continued to prevail among Russians for more than 40 years. As a result, a strong sense of distrust for private enterprises dominated the business environment and was more significant toward foreign firms.

Russians in their late twenties were a generation dissimilar to their predecessors. They tended to be money-oriented, with strong aspirations to accumulate wealth and to escape from the modest life that had characterized their socialist-style childhoods. Their top aspirations include escaping from their small apartments in huge blocks of grey, cold concrete and driving a German-made car. The second cluster of their lists included dining in fancy restaurants and vacationing in the Mediterranean, essentially behaving like other "European yuppies." One additional way of standing out among the crowd

[14] Nicolay Shkolyar, head of the commercial office, Russian embassy Mexico, June 2011.

[15] Ruchir Sharma, *Breakout Nations: In Pursuit of the Next Economic Miracles*, WW Norton & Co. Ltd., New York, 2012.

[16] Gleb Kouznetsov, Russian entrepreneur, Mexico, July 2011.

and showing their achievements was through the Russian version of the social-media site Facebook (www.odnoklassniki.ru). In their spirit of feeling European, many young Russians rotated jobs, selling themselves to the highest bidder. Contrary to their preceding generations, they openly criticized norms and avoided environments where discipline was heavily enforced.

Compensation did not mean everything in this high power distance country, remarked Glev Kuznetzov,

> I've heard from my elementary school classmates, talk about friends that moved to another company because of job titles. It was cooler to show a business card that said you are a VP, than a simple Manager, even when the latter was a position in a multinational and the former in a local small firm.

Young Russian professionals, with their high aspirations, acquired European style and anti-*status quo* spirit, collided against the more disciplined and submissive "older" Russians. In fact, Russians in their mid-thirties and forties tended to speak only Russian and had mostly been educated under a different mindset. Thus, when younger Russians led an organizational structure, they tended to be more selective when recruiting new talent. That is, they felt more comfortable working among Russians like themselves, not Russians like their parents.

In the process of recruiting and selection, these younger Russians paid more attention to candidates' family origins even when the candidates themselves were young and had a college degree. According to a common rule of thumb, if the potential hire came from a family of the intellectual elite – i.e., musicians, artists, scientists or academics – they would easily fit with the new generation, but if they came from a family of workers from the Soviet era, the potential of conflict still existed, notwithstanding the age or educational level of the candidate.

Global Trends in Major Appliances

Due to the contraction of GDP in major industrialized countries during 2008/09, emerging markets, led by China, Brazil and India, overtook the developed countries in terms of volume sales. This trend was expected to continue until 2015. Some emerging markets, such as Russia, experienced important volume declines in 2009. Even with a recovery after 2010, the ageing demographics would probably not allow Russia to recover from its pre-crisis levels until 2014.

Growth in the consumption of fresh food and ready-to-eat meals would likely lead to a decrease in freezer sales. Even with reduced disposable incomes, the market for ready-to-eat meals increased in Russia.

The emerging markets that offered the best growth potential were those with strong mid-term fundamentals, in terms of demographics, low percentages of appliance ownership and an ability to resist exogenous shocks. For example, Latin America, Turkey, Egypt, China and India were expected to grow 7 to 10 per cent between 2010 and 2015. Sales in many emerging markets would be influenced by the entrance of more affordable products that addressed market-specific needs. Government stimulus packages could also act as boosters in these markets.

Some of the key success factors for the future of the appliances sector were (a) energy and water efficiency and technological innovation and (b) location. For example, manufacturers such as Haier and Midea, which were based close to the Asia Pacific markets, would probably increase their market share. Another important change to consider was Samsung's push in Eastern Europe following the construction of its first non-Korean appliance factory.

Mabe and Russia in 2012

In 2012, the only foreign employee in Mabe's Russian JV was the CEO. After four years of working to understand the culture and nature of the Russian business people, a solid management team seemed to be in place. The product line offering was trimmed to only those products that truly offered a competitive advantage over other competitors' offers, and commercial best practices were implemented with key distributors. A lesson for Ramiro Perez was that when an

Exhibit 9 Mabe's Product Line in Russia

Source: Company files.

Exhibit 10 Main Appliance Players in Russia

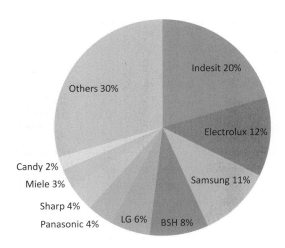

Indesit 20%
Others 30%
Electrolux 12%
Candy 2%
Miele 3%
Samsung 11%
Sharp 4%
Panasonic 4%
LG 6%
BSH 8%

Source: www.gfk.com/Industries/consumer-goods/home-appliances/Pages/default.aspx, accessed November 25, 2012.

Action Learning team analysed a new market, they should not do it with a "linear mindset," whereby they attempted to place a large set of the JV's offerings. In other words, the team needed to take an incremental approach, starting from scratch and delving deeper into what the market really needed. Thus, the JV started with a broad line of product offerings that needed to be trimmed down to products that truly offered the Mabe JV a competitive advantage. In Russia, being competitive in 2012 meant having access to local manufacturing. In 2011, the JV's sales in Russia were close to US$70 million and were expected to reach US$80 million in 2012. The products offered included stoves, which had a four per cent market share, and refrigerators and washing machines, which each had a market share of two per cent. Altogether, the JV's market share increased from 0.9 per cent in 2008 to 4.9 per cent at the end of 2012. A selection of images from the different offerings can be seen in Exhibit 9. Exhibit 10 shows the main appliance players in Russia during 2008.

A current advantage of the JV was its workforce. Mabe and Fagor had recognized early the potential problems in personnel recruitment and decided to have only two types of salespeople: a senior position requiring 8 to 10 years of experience and a junior position requiring one to three years of experience. For both positions, the average age was less than 42 years; candidates over that age were more likely to exhibit Soviet-era mentalities.

Because of the financial crisis of 2008, market demand in developed markets had decreased. In Western Europe, for example, demand had decreased 30 per cent in Spain and 18 per cent in Italy. This decrease had forced many of the industry's players to accelerate their international diversification to the most promising global markets: Malaysia, Philippines, Egypt, China, India, Russia, Brazil, Peru, Mexico and Argentina. As a consequence, the Russian market had expanded capacity, and the seemingly attractive profit margins of 2008 had dropped substantially.

Mabe's marketing strategy in Russia had been geared toward distributors and not toward the end consumers. In 2012, Mabe changed its strategy from using wholesalers to using regional distributors (while maintaining its presence in national and regional chains). Mabe's product offering catered to the high-end market segments in 2008 and gradually changed to the medium-end segments with such brands as De Dietrich and

Exhibit 11
Mabe's Entry Strategy and Positioning, 2008 and 2012

	2008	2012
PRODUCT	Cooking: Built-in; Wall Ovens, Cooktops, Ranges, Cooker Hoods & Dishwashers	Wall Ovens & Ranges
	Refrigerators: 2-Door, Top Mount	Refrigerators: 2-Door, Top Mount
	Laundry: Top-Load Washers & Washer/Dryers	Top-Load Washer
DISTRIBUTION CHANNEL	National & Regional Chains	National & Regional Chains
	Wholesalers	Regional Distributors
	Chef's Distribution Channel	
MARKET SHARE (at year's end)	0.90%	4.90%
PRICE POSITIONING	High	Medium
VALUE PROPOSITION	Products for market niches	Positioned with De Dietrich brand
	Complementary products from Mabe/Fagor lines	Post-sales service expertise
	Experience in international markets	Integration with external logistics operator
	De Dietrich and GE brands for luxury segments	Focused to medium market segments
	Access to low cost resources	Product quality
	Post-sales service expertise	
	Niche market (high-end, built-in, comfort products)	
	Excellent image of an European product (GE)	
	Integration with an external logistics operator	
	Distributor willingness to introduce new products and brands	
	Product quality	

Source: Company files.

Brandt that were part of Fagor's product portfolio. Mabe's entry and positioning strategy in 2008 and in 2012 are compared listed in Exhibit 11.

Vladimir Putin won the presidential election in 2012, and many foreign investors preferred to wait until the new government was in power before making any significant investment decisions. Mabe's JV was expected to finally turn in a small profit for 2012.

As Perez reclined his chair and glanced over Mabe's Mexico City skyline, sundown started. What should he do about this Russian JV? Was Fagor the right partner? Should the JV lower its prices to increase market share faster? Was it time to manufacture some products locally? What lessons had he learned for choosing future markets? Could another emerging market have been a better investment than Russia?

Chapter 1 Recommended Practitioner Readings

- Daniel J. Isenberg, "The global entrepreneur: a new breed of entrepreneur is thinking across borders – from day one," *Harvard Business Review*, 86:12 (2008), 107–11.

  In "The global entrepreneur," Isenberg describes the unconventional business thinking and behavior of the global entrepreneur; how they see the opportunity in the *distance* challenge; and the challenges faced and skills needed to succeed.

- Pankaj Ghemawat, "Distance still matters: the hard reality of global expansion," *Harvard Business Review*, 79:8 (2001), 137–47.

  In "Distance still matters," Ghemawat introduces the CAGE distance framework. The intent of this cultural, administrative, geographic, and economic distance framework is to help managers understand which attributes create distance, and the impact on various industries.

- Howard V. Perlmutter, "The tortuous evolution of the multinational corporation," *Columbia Journal of World Business*, 4 (1969), 9–18.

  In "The tortuous evolution of the multinational corporation," Perlmutter introduces the primary types of headquarters orientation toward subsidiaries: ethnocentric, polycentric, and geocentric, and the forces that move an organization toward – or away from – a geocentric mindset.

- Paul W. Beamish, *Note on International Licensing.* (Ivey Publishing, 2016).

  In *Note on International Licensing*, licensing is outlined as a strategy for technology transfer, and an approach to internationalization that requires less time or depth of involvement in foreign markets compared to exports, joint ventures, and foreign direct investment. This note examines when licensing is employed, risks associated with it, intellectual property rights, costs of licensing, unattractive markets for licensing, and the major elements of the license agreement.

- Paul W. Beamish, *Where Have You Been? An Exercise to Assess Your Exposure to the Rest of the World's Peoples* (Ivey Publishing, 2017).

  The *Where Have You Been?* exercise assesses one's exposure to the rest of the world's peoples. A series of worksheets require the respondents to check off the number and names of countries they have visited and the corresponding percentage of world population that each country represents. By summing a group's collective exposure to the world's peoples, the result will inevitably be the recognition that together they have seen much, even if individually some have seen little.

- Fons Trompenaars and Peter Woolliams, "Lost in translation," *Harvard Business Review*, April (2011).

  In "Lost in translation," Trompenaars and Woolliams describe how people vary enormously in how they perceive and respond to failure, and those perceptions and responses are shaped by the cultures in which they grew up or now work.

Any business with global aspirations must take seriously cultural differences in general and around failure in particular. The authors identify the dimensions along which people from various cultures differ regarding failure: (1) Do we view our environment as internally or externally controlled? (2) Which is more important – rules or relationships? (3) Are failures the responsibility of the individual or of the team? (4) How much do we identify with our failures? (5) Do we grant status according to performance or to position? Some forward-looking companies are managing to reconcile cultural differences to create a powerful platform for innovation.

All these readings are intended to underscore the motivations, means, and mentalities required to expand abroad.

2 Understanding the International Context
Responding to Conflicting Environmental Forces

This chapter shifts our focus from the internal forces that drive companies to expand to the larger, external, international environment in which they must operate. In particular, we consider three sets of macro forces that drive, constrain, and shape the industries in which entities compete globally. First, we examine the pressures – mostly economic – that drive companies in many industries to integrate and coordinate their activities across national boundaries to capture scale economies or other sources of competitive advantage. Second, we explore the forces – often social and political – that shape other industries and examine how they can drive MNEs to disaggregate their operations and activities to respond to national, regional, and local needs and demands. And third, we examine how, in an information-based, knowledge-intensive economy, players in a growing number of industries must adapt to opportunities or threats wherever they occur in the world by developing innovative responses and initiatives that they diffuse rapidly and globally to capture a knowledge-based competitive advantage.

Continual change in the international business environment has always character-ized the task facing MNE managers, and the situation at the end of the second decade of the twenty-first century is no different. Important shifts in political, social, economic, and technological forces have combined to create management challenges for today's MNEs that differ fundamentally from those facing companies just a couple of decades ago. Yet despite intense study by academics, consultants, and practicing managers, both the nature of the various external forces and their strategic and organizational implications are still widely disputed.

When Levitt's classic *Harvard Business Review* article, "The globalization of markets," was first published, his ideas provoked widespread debate. In Levitt's view, technological, social, and economic trends were combining to create a unified world marketplace that was driving companies to develop globally standardized products that would enable them to capture global economies. Critics, however, claimed that Levitt presented only one side of the story. They suggested that, like many managers, he had become so focused on the forces for globalization that he was blind to their limitations and equally powerful countervailing forces.

The ensuing debate helped better define the diverse, changeable, and often contradictory forces that reshaped so many industries. In this chapter, we summar-ize a few of the most powerful of these environmental forces, trace their historical evolution, and suggest how they have collectively led to a new and complex set of challenges that require managers of MNEs to respond to three simultaneous yet often conflicting sets of external demands: the need for cross-market integration, national responsiveness, and worldwide innovation and learning.

Forces for Global Integration and Coordination

The phenomenon of globalization in certain industries, as described by Levitt, was not a sudden or discontinuous development. It was simply the latest round of change brought about by economic, technological, and competitive factors that, 100 years earlier, had transformed the structures of many industries from regional to national in scope. Economies of scale, economies of scope, and differences in the availability and cost of productive resources were the three principal economic forces that drove this process of structural transformation of businesses. Globalization was simply the latest stage of this long transformation.[1] The impact of these forces on MNE strategy had been facilitated by the increasingly liberal trading environment of the 1980s, 1990s, and 2000s. We will now examine these forces of change in more detail.

Forces of Change: Scale, Scope, and Factor Costs

The Industrial Revolution created pressures for much larger plants that could capture the benefits of the *economies of scale* offered by the new technologies it spawned. Cheap and abundant energy combined with good transportation networks and new production technologies to restructure capital-intensive industries. For the first time, companies combined intermediate processes into single plants and developed large-batch or continuous-process technologies to achieve low-cost volume production.

As those pressures continued into the twentieth century, the level of scale intensity often increased further. In industries such as fine chemicals, automobiles, airframes, electronics, and oil refining, production at scale-economy volumes often exceeded the sales levels that individual companies could achieve in all but the largest nations, pushing them to seek markets abroad. Even in industries in which the leading companies could retain a large enough share of their domestic markets to achieve scale economies without exports, those on the next rung were forced to seek markets outside their home countries if they were to remain competitive.

In less capital-intensive industries, companies that were largely unaffected by scale economies were often transformed by the opportunities for *economies of scope* that were opened by more efficient, worldwide communication and transportation networks.

---

[1] For a more detailed analysis of these environmental forces, see Alfred D. Chandler Jr., "The evolution of the modern global corporation," in Michael Porter (ed.), *Competition in Global Industries* (Boston: Harvard Business School Press, 1986), pp. 405–48. For an even more detailed exposition, see Chandler's book, *Scale and Scope* (Cambridge, MA: Harvard University Press, 1990).

One classic example of how such economies could be exploited internationally was provided by trading companies that handled consumer goods. By exporting the products of many companies, they achieved a greater volume and lower per unit cost than any narrow-line manufacturer could in marketing and distributing its own products abroad.

In many industries, MNEs discovered that there were opportunities to exploit both scale and scope economies. For example, consumer electronics companies, such as Panasonic (at the time known as Matsushita), derived scale advantages from their highly specialized plants producing TVs, video recorders, and DVD players, and scope advantages through their marketing and sales networks that offered service, repair, and credit for a broad range of consumer electronics.

With changes in technology and markets came the requirement for access to new resources at the best possible prices, making differences in *factor costs* a powerful driver of globalization. Often no home-country key inputs were available to companies wishing to expand into new industry segments. European petroleum companies, for example, explored the Middle East because of Europe's limited domestic crude oil sources. Other companies went overseas in search of bauxite from which to produce aluminum, rubber to produce tires for a growing automobile industry, or tea to be consumed by an expanding middle class.

Labor-intensive industries such as textiles, apparel, and shoes turned to international markets as a source of cheap labor. The increased costs of transportation and logistics management were more than offset by much lower production costs. However, companies usually found that, once educated, the cheap labor rapidly became more expensive. Indeed no country remains a source of cheap labor indefinitely, as experience in China has demonstrated in recent decades. Therefore companies seeking the source of competitive advantage often chased cheap labor from Southern Europe to Central America to the Far East to Eastern Europe.

Forces of Change: Free Trade

In Ricardo's free trade theory of competitive advantage, if each country specializes in areas of advantage, and trades with other countries for the products/services in which they specialize, there is an *overall* gain for each country.

Whereas the economics of scale and scope and the differences in factor costs between countries provided the initial motivation for global coordination, the *liberalization of world trade* agreements became an equally powerful source of change. Beginning with the formation of the General Agreement on Tariffs and Trade (GATT) in 1945 and moving through various rounds of trade talks, the creation of regional free trade agreements such as the European Union (EU) and North American Free Trade Agreement (NAFTA), the formation of the World Trade Organization (WTO), and the signing in 2017 of CETA (Comprehensive Economic and Trade Agreement) between the EU and Canada, the dominant trend had been toward the reduction of barriers to international trade. While few new multicountry trading agreements have been reached during the 2000s, there has been a dramatic rise in the number of bilateral agreements involving the emerging markets in Asia and South America.

The result is that the international trading environment of the twenty-first century was less restricted than in recent decades, which enabled MNEs to realize most of the potential economic benefits that arise from global coordination.

In 2016, attitudes toward free trade in the United States and UK swung in the direction of greater protectionism. This shift was driven in part by a perception – some would say misperception – that job losses were primarily the result of globalization.

But what portion of domestic job loss has anything to do with foreign companies? What are the primary sources of job loss? Most objective analyses would suggest that there are a multitude of reasons for changes in the employment picture. Among the most commonly cited are:

- Automation – consider the increased use of self-services, whether it is ATMs in banking, rather than more tellers; self check-out at grocery stores, rather than cashiers; or retail shopping using the internet, rather than visiting a store; consider also the use of robotics in various sectors.
- Productivity and technology advances – consider the costs and features available on computers and smart phones, compared to a decade ago.
- Economic conditions – consider the recession of 2007 to 2009 resulting from the made-in-America subprime mortgage crisis, during which many jobs were lost.

None of these reasons can necessarily be attributed to globalization, particularly since the source of each is typically either the home country, or other developed economies.

The principal source of employment loss that most relates to globalization is the outsourcing of jobs to lower cost countries. When foreign labor is materially cheaper, and labor cost is a significant portion of total cost, outsourcing is often considered. Frequently the outsourced jobs are those held by less skilled, less educated workers. It is these workers who are the most vulnerable, with few available high-paying alternatives. Advocates of outsourcing will point to the overall benefits from reduced consumer prices, the fact that imports often include parts/inputs from their country, and the fact that more competitive pricing actually allows home-country jobs to be preserved. Such overall benefits are of no comfort, though, to those who have lost their jobs, and have no other job to go to. In some, but not all, countries this reality is addressed by greater emphasis on education, job training, and job retraining.

A protectionist stance of building walls, taxing exports, reducing the use of international supply chains and outsourcing, will result in a backlash with one's trading partners, and create a more expensive and less efficient domestic manufacturing base.

The opening of world markets has coincided with the growing opportunities presented by the high economic growth rates of emerging markets, which are attracting a new round of MNE investment. Once attracted to countries such as China and India as sources of low-cost labor, MNEs now recognize them as key sources of growth in coming decades. Today, the strategic role of developing countries has radically changed for many MNEs. Not only have they played a key role in the reconfiguration of their worldwide assets as companies continue to seek access to low-cost factors of production, they are now becoming important sources of revenue growth and drivers of global-scale efficiency.

Driving an Expanding Spiral of Globalization

During the 1970s and 1980s, these forces began to globalize the structure and competitive characteristics of a variety of industries. In some, the change was driven by a major technological innovation that forced a fundamental realignment of industry economics. For example, in the 1960s transistors and integrated circuits revolutionized the design and production of radios, televisions, and other consumer electronics and drove the minimum efficient scale of production beyond the demand of most single markets.

Later, advances in semiconductor technology led to the boom in the PC industry, and innovations in wireless technology resulted in the creation of the mobile phone industry. Advances in both of these latter technologies triggered by convergence of the telecommunications and consumer electronics industry resulted in the smart phone. Today, the growing dominance of digital media for music and books coupled with the rapid growth of social media are combining to transform the publishing and music industries, as well as creating an online retail distribution industry capable of low-cost, seamless global distribution.

In market terms also, the spread of global forces expanded from businesses in which the global standardization of products was relatively easy (e.g., watches, cameras) to others in which consumers' preferences and habits only slowly converged (e.g., automobiles, appliances). Again, major external discontinuities often facilitated the change process, as in the case of the 2005 global oil price increases, which triggered a worldwide demand for smaller, more fuel-efficient or alternative energy cars. An entirely different event initiated another major restructuring of the worldwide auto industry when the 2008 financial crisis saw the bankruptcy of General Motors (GM). Leaner and more efficient automakers, such as Hyundai Motors, took advantage of the ensuing industry shake-up to increase the US market share of its Hyundai and Kia product lines from 5.2% in 2008 to 9% in 2011.

Global Competitors as Change Agents

As the previous section highlighted, many industries were driven to become more globally integrated primarily through external forces of change. But other industries less affected by such external imperatives were transformed primarily through the internal restructuring efforts of competitors who recognized that by so doing they could gain significant competitive advantage. This led to a further wave of globalization as companies in industries as diverse as automobiles, office equipment, industrial bearings, construction equipment, and machine tools rolled out initiatives that involved rationalizing their product lines, standardizing parts design, and specializing in manufacturing operations. By capturing scale economies beyond national markets, these company-initiated actions led to the global transformation of their industries.

Competitors have even been successful in changing the structure of industries in which national tastes or behaviors traditionally varied widely around the world and were not susceptible to global convergence. Food tastes and eating habits were long thought to be the most culture bound of all consumer behaviors. Yet, as companies like McDonald's, Coca-Cola, and Starbucks have shown, in Eastern and Western countries alike, even these culturally linked preferences can be changed with the result that the restaurant industry around the world has been transformed.

Other companies in traditionally local businesses have also begun to exploit the opportunities for capturing economies beyond their national borders. Rather than responding to the enduring differences in consumer practices and market structures across European countries, many large branded packaged goods companies, such as Procter & Gamble (P&G) and Unilever, have recognized that there were potential economies that could transform traditionally national businesses like soap and detergent manufacturing. By standardizing product formulations, rationalizing package sizes, and printing multilingual labels, they have been able to restructure and specialize their nationally dominated plant configurations and achieve substantial scale economies giving them significant advantages over purely local competitors.

Even labor-intensive local industries, such as office cleaning and catering, are not immune to the forces of globalization. For example, the Danish cleaning services company ISS has built a successful international business by transferring practices and know-how across countries and thereby offering consistent, high-quality service to its international customers.

But beyond these initiatives to capture global-scale advantages there has been another competitor-driven force that has accelerated the global integration of many industries. In the closing decades of the twentieth century, there emerged a new competitive strategy that some called *global chess* and that could be played only by companies that implemented a coordinated global strategy by managing their worldwide operations as interdependent units. Unlike the traditional multinational strategic approach based on the assumption that each national market was unique and independent of the others, these global competitive games assumed that a company's competitive position in all markets was linked, and that funds generated in one market could be used to subsidize its position in another. While strategists called this approach "global chess" and economists referred to it as cross-subsidization of markets, politicians simply labeled it "dumping."

Whereas the classic exponents of this strategy were the Japanese companies that used the profit sanctuary of a protected home market to subsidize their loss-making expansions abroad in the 1980s, many others soon learned to play "global chess." For example, British Airways grew in part because its dominant position at Heathrow Airport enabled it to make large profits on its long-haul routes (particularly the trans-Atlantic route) and essentially subsidize its lower margin or loss-making UK and European business. For a time, it could fend off new entrants in Europe by pushing its prices down there while not putting its most profitable routes at risk. With deregulation and the rise of low-cost carriers, this changed dramatically. In early 2017, Europe's largest carrier (in terms of passengers carried) was Ryanair, a company only founded in 1985. Although few challenged the existence or growing influence of these diverse globalizing forces that were transforming the nature of competition worldwide, some questioned the unidimensionality of their influence and the universality of their strategic implications. They took issue, for example, with Levitt's suggestions that "the world's needs and desires have been irrevocably homogenized," that "no one is exempt and nothing can stop the process," and that "the commonality of preference leads inescapably to the standardization of products, manufacturing, and the institution of trade and commerce." Critics argued that, although these might indeed be long-term trends in many industries, there were important short- and medium-term impediments and countertrends that had to be taken into account if companies were to operate successfully in an international economy that jolts along – *perhaps* eventually toward Levitt's "global village," but perhaps not.

Forces for Local Differentiation and Responsiveness

There are many different stories of multinational companies making major blunders in transferring their successful products or ideas from their home countries to foreign markets. General Motors is reported to have faced difficulties in selling the popular Chevrolet Nova in Mexico, where the product name sounded like "no va," meaning "does not go" in Spanish.[2] Similarly, when managers began investigating why the advertising campaign built around the highly successful "come alive with Pepsi" theme was not having the expected impact in Thailand, they discovered that the Thai copy translation read more like "come out of the grave with Pepsi." Although these and other such cases have been widely cited, they represent extreme examples of an important strategic task facing managers of all MNEs: how to sense, respond to, and even exploit the differences in the environments of the many different countries in which their company operates.[3]

National environments differ on many dimensions. For example, there are clear differences in the per capita gross national product or the industry-specific technological capabilities of Japan, Australia, Brazil, and Poland. They also differ in terms of political systems, government regulations, social norms, and the cultural values of their people. It is these differences that require managers to be sensitive and responsive to national, social, economic, and political characteristics of the host countries in which they operate.

Far from being overshadowed by the pressures of globalization, the impact of these localizing forces have been felt with increasing intensity and urgency

---

[2] For this and many other such examples of international marketing problems, see David A. Ricks, *Blunders in International Business*, 4th edn. (Cornwall: Blackwell Publishing, 2006).

[3] In *Language in International Business*, Piekkari, Welch, and Welch present a case for recognizing and appreciating the importance of language, its multifaceted role, and the range of effects it may have on internationalizing firms.

    Rebecca Piekkari, Denice E. Welch, and Lawrence S. Welch, *Language in International Business: The Multilingual Reality of Global Business Expansion* (Northampton: Edward Elgar, 2014).

throughout recent decades. Even companies that had been most committed to global integration began to change. In the early 1990s, many Japanese companies that had so successfully ridden the wave of globalization began to feel the strong need to become much more sensitive to host-country economic and political forces. This shift led to a wave of investment abroad, as Japanese companies sought to become closer to their export markets and more responsive to host governments.

By the millennium, many North American and European companies also realized that they had pushed the logic of globalization too far and that a reconnection with the local environments in which they were doing business was necessary. For example, Coca-Cola's incoming CEO, Douglas Daft, explained his company's shift in policy in the *Financial Times*: "As the 1990s were drawing to a close, the world had changed course, and Coca-Cola had not. We were operating as a big, slow, insulated, sometimes even insensitive 'global' company; and we were doing it in an era when nimbleness, speed, transparency, and local sensitivity had become absolutely essential."

In an effort to catch up with Unilever's leading market share in developing countries, P&G has begun a major effort to emulate its old competitor's ability to adapt its products to local markets. For example, in India it has introduced Guard, a very inexpensive razor that comes with a small comb in front of the blade to make the local practice of weekly shaving more comfortable.

And Unilever CEO Paul Polman said in early 2017 that it was directing even more resources to local markets. He noted that Unilever "has seen the world become more 'multipolar' with local tastes and nationalism playing a bigger role in consumers' lives."[4]

Cultural Differences

A large body of academic research provides strong evidence that nationality plays an important and enduring role in shaping the assumptions, beliefs, and values of individuals. The most celebrated work describing and categorizing these differences in the orientations and values of people in different countries is Geert Hofstede's classic research. Hofstede originally described national cultural differences along four key dimensions: power distance, uncertainty avoidance, individualism, and "masculinity," later adding the fifth and sixth dimensions of long-term orientation and indulgence.[5] The study demonstrates how distinct cultural differences across

[4] Leonie Roderick, "Unilever responds to 'return of nationalism' with local products focus," *Marketing Week*, January 26, 2017. Accessed March 13, 2017, www.marketingweek.com/2017/01/26/unilever-responds-return-nationalism.

[5] For a more detailed exposition, see Hofstede's books *Culture's Consequences*, 2nd edn. (Beverly Hills, CA: Sage Publications, 2001) and *Cultures and Organizations: Software of the Mind*, 3rd edn. (McGraw Hill, 2010) or https://geert-hofstede.com/national-culture.html. For managerial implications of such differences in national culture, see also Nancy J. Adler and A. Gundersen, *International Dimensions of Organizational Behavior*, 5th edn. (Mason, OH: Thomson South-Western, 2008), and Fons Trompenaars and Charles Hampden-Turner, *Riding the Waves of Culture*, 3rd edn. (McGraw Hill, 2012).

countries result in wide variations in social norms and individual behavior (e.g., the Japanese respect for elders, the culturally embedded American response to time pressure) and is reflected in the effectiveness of different organizational forms (e.g., the widespread French difficulty with the dual-reporting relationships of a matrix organization) and management systems (e.g., the Swedes' egalitarian culture leading them to prefer flatter organizations and smaller wage differentials). More recently, the GLOBE Study[6] has refined Hofstede's landmark work and developed new measures of organizational culture and leadership, and the division of societies into cultural clusters.

However, cultural differences are also reflected in nationally differentiated consumption patterns, including the way people dress or the foods they prefer. Take the example of tea as a beverage consumed around the globe. The British drink their tea hot and diluted with milk, whereas Americans consume it primarily as a summer drink served over ice, and Saudi Arabians drink theirs as a thick, hot, heavily sweetened brew. To succeed in a world of such diversity, companies often must modify their quest for global efficiency through standardization and find ways to respond to the needs and opportunities created by cultural differences. So Unilever produces 20 separate brands of black tea, each blended to meet the specific tastes of local consumers around the world. It adapted its Lipton brand to offer a canned iced tea drink in the United States, and sells Lipton Cold Brew tea bags in markets around the world. Even more ambitious is the Starbucks strategy of serving green tea lattes in its Chinese outlets in a bid to eventually get that traditionally tea-drinking nation hooked on coffee.

Chinese giants such as Alibaba, Baidu, and WeChat understand the culture of their country and how to manage a business there. Alibaba, for example, held a 24-hour sales event on November 11, 2016, which recorded sales of US$17.73 billion. That is higher than the combined sales in the United States around the major Thanksgiving shopping days of Cyber Monday and Black Friday. Alibaba also has more active users than the combined populations of the United States and Canada.

Government Demands

Inasmuch as cultural differences among countries have been an important localizing force, the diverse demands and expectations of home and host governments have perhaps been the most severe constraint to the global strategies of many MNEs. Traditionally, the interactions between companies and host governments have had many attributes of classic love–hate relationships. See Table 2.1 for regulatory changes that have affected foreign investment around the world.

The "love" of the equation was built on the benefits each could bring to the other. To the host government, the MNE represented an important source of funds,

---

[6] R. J. House, P. W. Dorfman, M. Javidan, P. J. Hanges, and M. Sully de Luque (eds.), *Strategic Leadership Across Cultures: Globe Study of CEO Leadership Behaviour and Effectiveness in 24 Countries* (Thousand Oaks, CA: Sage, 2013).

Table 2.1 Changes in national investment policies, selected years 2003–2015

Item	2003	2006	2009	2012	2015
Number of countries that introduced changes	59	70	46	57	46
Number of regulatory changes	125	126	89	92	96
Liberalization/promotion	113	104	61	65	71
Restriction/regulation	12	22	24	21	13
Neutral/indeterminate[a]	–	–	4	6	12

Source: UNCTAD, *World Investment Report 2016*, Investment Policy Monitor database.
[a] In some cases, the expected impact of the policy measures on the investment is undetermined.

technology, and expertise that could help further national priorities, such as regional development, employment, import substitution, and export promotion. To the MNE, the host government represented the key to local market or resource access, which provided new opportunities for profit, growth, and improvement of its competitive position.

The "hate" side of the relationship – more often emerging as frustration rather than outright antagonism – arose from the differences in the motivations and objectives of the two partners. To be effective global competitors, MNEs sought three important operating objectives: unrestricted access to resources and markets throughout the world; the freedom to integrate manufacturing and other operations across national boundaries; and the unimpeded right to coordinate and control all aspects of the company on a worldwide basis. The host government, in contrast, sought to develop an economy that could survive and prosper in a competitive international environment. At times, this objective led to the designation of another company – perhaps a "national champion" – as its standard bearer in the specific industry, bringing it into direct conflict with the MNE.

This conflict is particularly visible in the international airline business, in which flag-carrying companies – from struggling developing country airlines such as Air Malawi or Pakistan International Airlines to Gulf State powerhouses such as Emirates, Etihad, Qatar or Gulf Air – compete only after receiving substantial government subsidies. But it also has been a thorny issue among their biggest suppliers, with Boeing complaining to the WTO that Airbus is violating free trade agreements through the support it receives from various European governments.

Even when the host government does not have such a national champion and is willing to permit and even support an MNE's operations within its boundaries, it usually does so only at a price. Although both parties might be partners in the search for global competitiveness, the MNE typically tried to achieve that objective within its global system, whereas the host government strove to capture it within its national boundaries, thereby leading to conflict and mutual resentment.

The potential for conflict between the host government and the MNE arose not only from economic but also from social, political, and cultural issues. MNE operations often cause social disruption in the host country through rural exodus, rising consumerism, rejection of indigenous values, or a breakdown of traditional community structures.

Similarly, even without the maliciousness of MNEs that, in previous decades, blatantly tried to manipulate host government structures or policies (e.g., ITT's attempt to overthrow the Allende government in Chile), MNEs can still represent a political threat because of their size, power, and influence – particularly in developing economies.

Because of these differences in objectives and motivations, MNE–host government relationships are often seen as a zero-sum game in which the outcome depends on the balance between the government's power (arising from its control over local market access and competition among different MNEs for that access) and the MNE's power (arising from its financial, technological, and managerial resources and the competition among national governments for those resources).

If, in the 1960s, the multinational companies had been able to hold "sovereignty at bay,"[7] by the 1980s, the balance had tipped in the other direction. In an effort to stem the flood of imports, many countries began bending or sidestepping trade agreements signed in previous years. By the early 1980s, even the US government, traditionally one of the strongest advocates of free trade, began to negotiate a series of orderly marketing agreements and voluntary restraints on Japanese exports, while threats of sanctions were debated with increasing emotion in legislative chambers around the globe. And countries became more sophisticated in the demands they placed on inward-investing MNEs. Rather than allowing superficial investment in so-called "screwdriver plants" that provided only limited, low-skill employment, governments began to specify the levels of local content, technology transfer, and a variety of other conditions, from re-export commitment to plant location requirements.

In the 1990s, however, the power of national governments was once again on the wane. The success of countries such as Ireland and Singapore in driving their economic development through foreign investment led many other countries – both developed and developing – to launch aggressive inward investment policies of their own.

This increased demand for investment allowed MNEs to play countries off one another and, in many cases, to extract a high price from the host country. For example, according to *The Economist,* the incentives paid by Alabama to Mercedes for its 1993 auto plant cost the state $167,000 per direct employee. This was not an isolated example. In 2015, Volvo announced a plant opening in South Carolina. The company would receive about $200 million in incentives.

In the first years of the new millennium, the once-troublesome issue of MNE–country bargaining power evolved into a relatively efficient market system for inward investment, at least in the developed world. However, the developing world was a rather different story, with MNEs continuing to be embroiled in political disputes. Global Witness, a UK watchdog, documented a total of 185 environmental

---

[7] Raymond Vernon, *Sovereignty at Bay* (New York: Basic Books, 1971).

activists killed across 16 countries (Brazil and the Philippines suffered the most) in 2015. The mining industry had the largest number of deaths with other industries including agribusiness, hydroelectric dams, and logging. Demand for minerals, timber, and palm oil is increasing around the world and governments, companies, and criminal gangs are able to seize land despite the fact that there are individuals living on it.[8]

In addition, MNEs have regularly attracted the brunt of criticism from so-called antiglobalization protestors during WTO meetings. The antiglobalization movement included a diverse mix of groups with different agendas but united in their belief that the increasing liberalization of trade through the WTO was being pursued for the benefit of MNEs and at the expense of people and companies in less developed parts of the world.

Although this movement did not have a coherent set of policy proposals of its own, it provided a salutary reminder to policymakers and the executives managing MNEs that the globalization of business remains a contentious issue. The rewards are not spread evenly, and for many people in many parts of the world, the process of globalization often makes things worse before it makes them better. This forced MNEs to rethink their more contentious policies and encouraged them to articulate the benefits they bring to less developed countries. By 2016, more than 9,000 companies from 160 countries had signed the UN Global Compact, committing themselves to aligning their operations and strategies with ten aspirational principles in the areas of human rights, labor, environment, and anti-corruption.[9]

A new trend is emerging that is set to alter the MNE–government relationship during the 2010s. Cash-rich governments and their nationally owned corporations in emerging markets, particularly China, are looking to invest in foreign resources, with such investments often packaged as part of a government-to-government diplomatic relationship. Not only are the government investors looking to earn returns on investments but, perhaps more importantly, they are securing the natural resources to ensure the future economic security of their own countries, and particularly the need to continue to grow and prosper. This policy-based partnership of governments and national corporations engaging in the global business arena via such mechanisms as Sovereign Wealth Funds is significantly different from the "national champion" strategy of an earlier era, and is certain to have important global competitive implications over the next decades.

Growing Pressures for Localization

Although there is no doubt that the increasing frequency of world travel and the ease with which communication linkages occur across the globe have done a great deal to reduce the effects of national consumer differences, it would be naïve to believe that worldwide tastes, habits, and preferences have become anywhere near

[8] Oliver Holmes, "Environmental activist murders set record as 2015 became deadliest year," *Guardian*, June 20, 2016.
[9] www.unglobalcompact.org

homogeneous. One need only look at the breakfast buffet items on display at any major hotel in Beijing. These hotels need to appeal to large groups of consumers from within China, from North America, from Europe, from Japan, and elsewhere. So separate breakfast stations will variously provide steamed breads and noodles, bacon and eggs, cold cuts and cheese, and miso soup.

Although many companies have succeeded in appealing to – and accelerating – convergence worldwide,[10] even the trend toward standardized products that are designed to appeal to a lowest common denominator of consumer demand has a flip side. In industry after industry, a large group of consumers has emerged to reject the homogenized product design and performance of standardized global products.

By reasserting traditional preferences for more differentiated products, they have created openings – often very profitable ones – for companies willing to respond to, and even expand, the need for products and services that are more responsive to those needs.

When the US-based office supply retail chain Office Depot issued a request of its vendors for refrigerators that could be locked for improved security in US offices and dormitories, it was Haier that was willing to create such a customized product.[11] The fact that such an innovation originated in a firm from China also underscores how localization solutions may appear from previously unlikely locales. Increasingly, it is MNEs from emerging markets that seem best equipped to compete in other emerging markets.

Other consumer and market trends are emerging to counterbalance the forces of global standardization of products. In an increasing number of markets, from telecommunications to office equipment to consumer electronics, consumers are not so much buying individual products as selecting systems. With advances in wireless, 4G, and other internet technologies, for example, the television is becoming part of a home entertainment and information network, connected through a home computer, smart phone, or gaming system, to an online databank of music, video, texts, and social media. This transformation is forcing companies to adapt their standard hardware-oriented products to more flexible and locally differentiated systems that consist of hardware plus software plus services. In such an environment, the competitive edge lies less with the company that has the most

---

[10] When going and operating abroad, firms face the challenge of finding the optimal balance between standardizing and adapting their marketing strategies across national borders in order to be successful. This paper introduces a theoretical framework combined with the concept of situation–strategy fit. The authors argue that a high degree of international product standardization is likely to enhance foreign product profit, as compared to all alternative strategies, if there is (1) a high cross-national homogeneity of demand, (2) a high potential for cross-national economies of scale, (3) a high cost of product modification, (4) a high foreign price elasticity of demand, (5) a small perceptual error of the managers, and (6) a high quality of strategy execution.

Stefan Schmid and Thomas Kotulla, "50 years of research on international standardization and adaptation – From a systematic literature analysis to a theoretical framework," *International Business Review*, 20:5 (2011), 491–507.

[11] For further detail, see Peter J. Williamson and Ming Zeng, *Dragons at Your Door: How Chinese Cost Innovation is Disrupting Global Competition* (Boston: Harvard Business School Press, 2007).

scale-efficient global production capability and more with the one that is sensitive and responsive to local requirements and able to develop the software and services. Unsurprisingly, it is also in the downstream parts of the value chain where most of the profit lies.

In addition to such barriers to global standardization, other important impediments exist. Although the benefits of scale economies obviously must outweigh the additional costs of supplying markets from a central point, companies often ignore that those costs consist of more than just freight charges. In particular, the administrative costs of coordination and scheduling worldwide demand through global-scale plants usually is quite significant and must be taken into account. For some products, lead times are so short or market service requirements so high that these scale economies may well be offset by other such costs.

More significantly, developments in computer-aided design and manufacturing, robotics, and other advanced production technologies have made the concept of flexible manufacturing a viable reality. Companies that previously had to produce tens or hundreds of thousands of standardized printed circuit boards (PCBs) in a central, global-scale plant now can achieve the minimum efficient scale in smaller, distributed, national plants closer to their customers. When linked to the consumer's growing disenchantment with homogenized global products, this technology appears to offer multinational companies an important tool that will enable them to respond to localized consumer preferences and national political constraints without compromising their economic efficiency.

The pressure for localization can extend down to the regional or city level in some countries. The growth opportunities in many national markets are not evenly distributed throughout each country. As a result, there is considerable intracountry variance in infrastructure development, industry structure, demographics, and consumer characteristics among cities or cluster of cities. For example, McKinsey segmented China into "22 city clusters, each homogeneous enough to be considered one market for strategic decision making. Prioritizing several clusters or sequencing the order in which they are targeted can help a company boost the effectiveness of its distribution networks, supply chains, sales forces, and media and marketing strategies."[12] Similarly, when Interbrew (now part of Anheuser-Busch InBev) was establishing Stella Artois as a global brand, their efforts were concentrated on 20 major cities around the world.

Forces for Worldwide Innovation and Learning

The trends we have described have created an extremely difficult competitive environment in many industries, and only those firms that have been able to adapt to the often conflicting forces for global coordination and national differentiation

---

[12] Yuval Atsmon, Ari Kertesz, and Ireena Vittal, "Is your emerging-market strategy local enough?" *McKinsey Quarterly*, 2 (2011), 50–61.

have been able to survive and prosper. But on top of these forces, another set of competitive demands has been growing rapidly around the need for fast, globally coordinated innovation. Indeed, in the emerging competitive game, and particularly in technology-intensive industries, victory most often goes to the company that can most effectively harness its access to information and expertise around the globe to develop and diffuse innovative products and processes on a worldwide basis.

This ability to develop worldwide innovation and learning is such a vital strategic capability for MNEs today that we will simply outline the issue here, and return to examine it in greater detail in Chapter 5.

The trends driving this shift in the competitive game in many ways derive from the globalizing and localizing forces we described previously. The increasing cost of R&D, coupled with shortening life cycles of new technologies and the products they spawn, have combined to reinforce the need for companies to seek global volume to amortize their heavy research investments as quickly as possible. At the same time, even the most advanced technology has often diffused rapidly around the globe, particularly during the past few decades. In part, this trend has been a response to the demands, pressures, and coaxing of host governments as they bargain for increasing levels of national production and high levels of local content in the leading-edge products being sold in their markets. But the high cost of product and process development has also encouraged companies to transfer new technologies voluntarily, with licensing becoming an important source of funding, cross-licensing a means to fill technology gaps, and joint development programs and strategic alliances a strategy for rapidly building global competitive advantage.

When coupled with converging consumer preferences worldwide, this diffusion of technology has had an important effect on both the pace and locus of innovation. No longer can US-based companies assume that their domestic environment provides them with the most sophisticated consumer needs and the most advanced technological capabilities, and thus the most innovative environment in the world. Today, the newest consumer trend or market need might emerge in Australia or Italy, and the latest technologies to respond to those needs may be located in South Korea or Sweden. Innovations are springing up worldwide, and companies are recognizing that they can gain competitive advantage by sensing needs in one country, responding with capabilities located in a second, and diffusing the resulting innovation to markets around the globe.

A related trend is the increasing importance of global standards in such industries as computer software, telecommunications, consumer electronics, and even consumer goods. The winners in the battle for a new standard – from software platforms to razor-blade cartridges – can build and defend dominant competitive positions that can endure worldwide for decades. First-mover advantages have increased substantially and provided strong incentives for companies to focus attention not only on the internal task of rapidly creating and diffusing innovations within their own worldwide operations but also on the external task of establishing the new product as an industry standard. As indicated previously, we will return to examine this vital strategic issue in greater detail in Chapter 5.

Responding to the Diverse Forces Simultaneously

Trying to distill key environmental demands in large and complex industries is a hazardous venture but, at the risk of oversimplification, we can make the case that until the late 1980s, most worldwide industries presented relatively unidimensional environmental requirements. This led to the development of industries with very different characteristics – those we distinguish as global, multinational, and international industries. More recently, however, this differentiation has been eroding with important consequences for companies' strategies.

Global, Multinational, and International Industries

In some businesses, the economic forces of globalization were historically strong enough to dominate other environmental demands. For example, in the consumer electronics industry, the invention of the transistor led to decades of inexorable expansion in the benefits of scale economics: successive rounds of technological change such as the introduction of integrated circuits and microprocessors led to a huge increase in the minimum efficient scale of operations for television sets. In an environment of falling transportation costs, low tariffs, and increasing homogenization of national market demand, these huge-scale economies dominated the strategic tasks for managers of consumer electronics companies in the closing decades of the twentieth century.

Such industries, in which the economic forces of globalization are dominant, we designate as *global industries*. In these businesses, success typically belongs to companies that adopt the classic *global strategies* of capitalizing on highly centralized, scale-intensive manufacturing and R&D operations and leveraging them through worldwide exports of standardized global products.

In other businesses, the localizing forces of national, cultural, social, and political differences dominate the development of industry characteristics. In laundry detergents, for example, R&D and manufacturing costs were relatively small parts of a company's total expenses, and all but the smallest markets could justify an investment in a detergent tower and benefit from its scale economies. At the same time, sharp differences in laundry practices, perfume preferences, phosphate legislation, distribution channels, labeling requirements, and other such attributes of different national markets led to significant benefits from differentiating products and strategies on a country-by-country basis.

This differentiation is typical of what we call *multinational industries* – worldwide businesses in which the dominance of national differences in cultural, social, and political environments allow multiple national industry structures to flourish. Success in such businesses typically belongs to companies that follow *multinational strategies* of building strong and resourceful national subsidiaries that are sensitive to local market needs and opportunities and allow them to manage their local businesses by developing or adapting products and strategies to respond to the powerful localizing forces.

Finally, in some other industries, technological forces are central, and the need for companies to develop and diffuse innovations is the dominant source of competitive advantage. For example, the most critical task for manufacturers of telecommunications switching equipment has been the ability to develop and harness new technologies and exploit them worldwide. In these *international industries,* it is the ability to innovate and appropriate the benefits of those innovations in multiple national markets that differentiates the winners from the losers.

In such industries, the key to success lies in a company's ability to exploit technological forces by creating new products and to leverage the international life cycles of the product by effectively transferring technologies to overseas units. We describe this as an *international strategy* – the ability to effectively manage the creation of new products and processes in one's home market and sequentially diffuse those innovations to foreign affiliates.

Transition to Transnationality

Our portrayal of the traditional demands in some major worldwide industries is clearly oversimplified. Different tasks in the value-added chains of different businesses are subject to different levels of economic, political, cultural, and technological forces. We have described what can be called the *center of gravity* of these activities – the environmental forces that have the most significant impact on industry's strategic task demands.

By the closing years of the twentieth century, however, these external demands were undergoing some important changes. In many industries, the earlier dominance of a single set of environmental forces was replaced by much more complex environmental demand, in which each of the different sets of forces was becoming strong simultaneously. For example, new economies of scale and scope, and intensifying competition among a few competitors were enhancing the economic forces toward increased global integration in many multinational and international industries. In the detergent business, product standardization has become more feasible because the growing penetration and standardization of washing machines has narrowed the differences in washing practices across countries. Particularly in regional markets such as Europe or South America, companies have leveraged this potential for product standardization by developing regional brands, uniform product formulation, multilingual packaging, and common advertising themes, all of which have led to additional economies.

Similarly, localizing forces are growing in strength in global industries such as consumer electronics. Although the strengths of the economic forces of scale and scope have continued to increase, host government pressures and renewed customer demand for differentiated products are forcing companies with global strategies to reverse their earlier strategies, which were based on exporting standard products. To protect their competitive positions, they have begun to emphasize the local design and production of differentiated product ranges in different countries and for different international segments. And the growing need to supplement standard hardware-oriented products with more locally differentiated systems, software, and services is increasing the need for more flexibility and responsiveness in local markets.

Finally, in the emerging competitive battle among a few large firms with comparable capabilities in global-scale efficiency and nationally responsive strategies, the ability to innovate and exploit the resulting developments globally is becoming more and more important for building durable comparative advantage, even in industries in which global economic forces or local political and cultural influences had previously been dominant. In the highly competitive mobile phone business, for example, all surviving major competitors must have captured the minimum scale efficiency to play on the global field, as well as the requisite government relationships and consumer understanding to respond to market differences. Today, competition in this industry consists primarily of a company's ability to develop innovative new products – perhaps in response to a consumer trend in Japan, a government requirement in Germany, or a technological development in the United States – and then diffuse it rapidly around the world.

In the emerging international environment therefore there are fewer and fewer examples of pure global, textbook multinational, or classic international industries. Instead, more and more businesses are driven to a greater or lesser extent by *simultaneous* demands for global efficiency, national responsiveness, and worldwide innovation. These are the characteristics of what we call a *transnational industry.* In such industries, companies find it increasingly difficult to defend a competitive position on the basis of only one dominant capability. They need to develop their ability to respond effectively to all forces at the same time to manage the often conflicting demands for efficiency, responsiveness, and innovation without trading-off any one for the other.

The emergence of the transnational industry has not only made the needs for efficiency, responsiveness, and innovation simultaneous, it has also made the tasks required to achieve each of these capabilities more demanding and complex. Rather than achieve world-scale economies through centralized and standardized production, companies must instead build global efficiency through a worldwide infrastructure of distributed but specialized assets and capabilities that exploit comparative advantages, scale economies, and scope economies simultaneously. (In Chapter 4, we will return to elaborate on this challenging organization requirement.)

Consequently, in most industries, a few global competitors now compete head to head in almost all major markets.

To succeed in such an environment, companies must develop new strategic capabilities, including a mastery of the logic of global chess: the ability to build and defend profit sanctuaries that are impenetrable to competitors; to leverage existing strengths in order to cross-subsidize weaker products and market positions; to make high-risk, preemptive investments that raise the stakes and force out rivals with weaker stomachs and purse strings; and to form alliances and coalitions to isolate and outflank competitors. These and other similar maneuvers must now be combined with world-scale economies to develop and maintain global competitive efficiency.

Similarly, responsiveness through differentiated and tailor-made local-for-local products and strategies in each host environment is rarely necessary or feasible anymore. National customers no longer demand differentiation; they demand sensitivity to their needs, along with the level of cost and quality standards for global products to which they have become accustomed. At the same time, host governments' desire to build their national competitiveness dominates economic policy in many countries, and MNEs are frequently viewed as key instruments in the implementation of national competitive strategies. Changes in regulations, tastes, exchange rates, and related factors have become less predictable and more frequent. In such an environment, simple market-by-market responsiveness is usually inadequate. The flexibility to change product designs, sourcing patterns, and pricing policies to remain responsive to continually changing national environments has become essential for survival.

And, finally, exploiting centrally developed products and technologies is no longer enough. MNEs must build the capability to learn from the many environments to which they are exposed and to appropriate the benefits of such learning throughout their global operations. Although some products and processes must still be developed centrally for worldwide use and others must be created locally in each environment to meet purely local demands, MNEs must increasingly use their access to multiple centers of technologies and familiarity with diverse customer preferences in different countries to create truly transnational innovations. Similarly, environmental and competitive information acquired in different parts of the world must be collated and interpreted to become a part of the company's shared knowledge base and provide input to future strategies. (In Chapter 3, we will develop this discussion of the required strategic capabilities and highlight the need for MNEs to build layers of competitive advantage.)

CONCLUDING COMMENTS

The increasing complexity of forces in the global environment and the need to respond simultaneously to their diverse and often conflicting demands have created some major challenges for many MNEs. The classic global companies, such as many highly successful Japanese and Korean companies whose competitive advantage was historically rooted in a highly efficient and centralized system, have been forced to respond more effectively to the demands for national responsiveness and world-wide innovation. The traditional multinational companies – many of them European – long had the advantage of being the masters of national responsiveness but today face the challenge of exploiting global-scale economic and technological forces more effectively. And US companies, with their more international approach to leveraging home-country innovations abroad, have had to struggle to build more understanding of the cultural and political forces and respond to national differences more effectively while simultaneously enhancing global-scale efficiency through improved scale economies.

For most MNEs, the challenge of the 2000s is both strategic and organizational. On the one hand, they are forced to develop a more complex array of strategic capabilities that enable them to capture the competitive advantages that accrue to efficiency, responsiveness, and learning. On the other hand, the traditional organizational approaches of these companies, developed to support their earlier global, multinational, or international approaches, have become inadequate for the more complex strategic tasks they now must accomplish. In Chapters 3 and 4, we will discuss some of the ways in which companies can respond to these new strategic and organizational challenges.

 HARVARD | BUSINESS | SCHOOL   REV: MARCH 6, 2017

Christopher A. Bartlett and Sarah McAra

CASE 2.1 GLOBAL WINE WAR 2015: NEW WORLD VERSUS OLD

Emeritus Professor Christopher A. Bartlett prepared the original version of this case, "Global Wine War 2009: New World versus Old," HBS No. 910-405. This version was prepared by Professor Bartlett and Associate Case Researcher Sarah McAra (Case Research & Writing Group). This case was developed from published sources. Funding for the development of this case was provided by Harvard Business School and not by the company. HBS cases are developed solely as the basis for class discussion. Cases are not intended to serve as endorsements, sources of primary data, or illustrations of effective or ineffective management.

The new [EU] rules will enable the sector to continue to grow at the same time as recognizing the need to protect wines with geographical indication.[1]
— Thierry Coste, Chairman, Copa-Cogeca Wine Working Party

Everything we do will be evidence-based, data-driven, consumer-engaged and market-focused.[2]
— Brian Walsh, Chair of Australian Grape and Wine Authority

[1] Thierry Coste in Copa-Cogeca press release, "Copa and Cogeca Welcome Main Thrust of New EU Authorization Scheme for Vine Plantings and Call for Support Measures to Continue beyond 2018 to Improve Competitivity," April 9, 2015, via http://www.copa-cogeca.be/Main.aspx?page=Archive, accessed February 2016.

[2] Brian Walsh, "Strategic Plan 2015–2020 at a Glance," Australian Grape and Wine Authority, p. 2, https://wineaustralia.com/en/About%20Us/~/media/0000Industry%20Site/Documents/About%20Us/AGWA%20Board%20Candidate%20Info%202015/AGWA%20Strategic%20Plan%20At%20a%20glance%202015-2020.ashx, accessed February 2016.

In 2015, these two views reflected the different sentiments unleashed by a fierce competitive battle raging between traditional winemakers and newer industry players as they fought for a share of the €250 billion ($280 billion) global wine market.[3] In recent decades, Old World wine producers—Italy, France, and Spain, for example—had found themselves inhibited by old winemaking traditions, restrictive industry regulations, and complex national and European Union (EU) legislation. This, plus a shift in consumer tastes and market structures, let New World companies—from Australia, Chile, and the United States, for instance—challenge Old World producers with innovations across the value chain. Now these competitors faced each other on a new front in this global wine war—a battle for China, the fastest-growing and potentially biggest export market of all time.

In the Beginning[4]

Grape growing and winemaking have been human occupations for centuries. Under the Roman Empire, viticulture spread across the Mediterranean region, making wine a peasant's drink with everyday meals. Soon, wine became part of liturgical services, and monasteries planted vines and built wineries. By the Middle Ages, vineyards became a mark of prestige among the nobility, and they began competing in the quality of wine they served—the first niche market for premium wine.

Wine Production

Historically, tending and harvesting grapes was labor intensive, and one worker could typically look after only 3 hectares (ha), approximately 7.5 acres. The introduction of vineyard horses in the early nineteenth century led to more efficient tending, with one person now able to work a 7 ha plot. Yet despite these efficiencies, vineyards became smaller, not larger. Over the centuries, agricultural holdings were continually fragmented as land was parceled out by kings, taken in wars, or broken up through inheritance. During the French Revolution, large estates were seized, divided, and sold off. And after 1815, the Napoleonic Code prescribed how land had to be passed on to all rightful heirs. By the mid-nineteenth century, the average holding in France was 5.5 ha and was still being subdivided. In Italy, similar events left the average vineyard at 0.8 ha.

While the largest estates made their own wine, most small farmers sold their grapes to the local winemaker or *vintner*. With payment based on weight, there was little incentive to pursue quality by reducing yield. Some small growers formed cooperatives, hoping to participate in wine making's downstream profit, but grape growing and wine making remained highly fragmented.

Distribution and Marketing

Traditionally, wine was sold in bulk to merchant traders—*négociants* in France—who often blended and bottled the product before distributing it. But poor roads and complex toll and tax systems made cross-border shipping very expensive. In the early nineteenth century, a shipment of wine from Strasbourg, France, to the Dutch border had to pass through 31 toll stations.[5] And since wine did not travel well, much of it spoiled on long journeys. As a result, only the most sophisticated *négociants* could handle exports, and only the rich could afford the imported luxury.

Innovations in the eighteenth and nineteenth centuries, such as mass production of glass bottles, the use of cork stoppers, and the development of pasteurization, revolutionized the industry. With greater wine longevity, distribution to distant markets and bottle aging of good vintages became the norm. Additional vine plantings and production followed, and a global market for wine was born.

---

[3] "Global Wine—Industry Profile," MarketLine, May 2015, via Thomson ONE, accessed May 2016.

[4] Historical discussions are indebted to Harry W. Paul, *Science, Vine and Wine in Modern France* (Cambridge: Cambridge University Press, 1996), pp. 2–15; Jancis Robinson, ed., *The Oxford Companion to Wine,* 2nd edn (Oxford: Oxford University Press, 1999); and James Wilson, *Terroir* (Berkeley: University of California Press, 1998), pp. 10–45.

[5] Robinson, *The Oxford Companion to Wine,* p. 308.

Regulation and Classification

By the mid-eighteenth century in France, grape growing supported 1.5 million families and an equal number in wine-related businesses. Wine became France's second-largest export, accounting for one-sixth of its trading revenue. The industry's growing cultural and economic importance soon attracted political attention, and with it, laws and regulations to control most aspects of winemaking. For example, France's wine classification system was formed by a Bordeaux committee for the 1855 Exposition in Paris. To help consumers identify their finest wines, they classified 500 vineyards into five levels of quality, from *premier cru* (first growth) to *cinquième cru* (fifth growth).

Because it helped consumers negotiate the complexity of a fragmented market, this marketing tool gained wide recognition, leading the government to codify and expand it in the *Appellation d'Origine Contrôlée* (AOC) laws of 1935. These laws, still in force today, also defined regional boundaries and set tight growing and winemaking standards.[6] Eventually, more than 300 AOC designations were defined, from the well-known (Saint-Émilion or Beaujolais) to the obscure (Fitou or Saint-Péray).

Italy introduced a similar classification scheme defining 213 *denominazione di origine controllata* (DOC) regions, with regulations prescribing area, allowed grape varieties, yields, required growing practices, acceptable alcohol content, label design, and more.[7] Germany's wine classification scheme, dating from 1644, prescribed 65 classes of quality, with rules for everything from ripeness required for harvesting to minimum sugar content. As late as 1971, a new German law was passed requiring a government panel to taste each vineyard's annual vintage and assign it a quality level.[8]

Rather than resisting such government controls, producers often supported them as a way of differentiating their products and raising entry

barriers. Eventually, other French wine regions were given official recognition. The classification of *vins délimités de qualité supérieure* (VDQS) was of lower rank than AOC, but above *vins de pays*—good yet inexpensive table wine. The categories were quite rigid, with almost no movement across them. This was due to a belief that quality was linked to *terroir*, the almost mystical blend of soil, aspect, microclimate, rainfall, and cultivation that the French passionately believed gave wine from each region—and indeed, each vineyard—its unique character.

But *terroir* could not guarantee consistent quality. As an agricultural product, wine was always subject to the vagaries of weather and disease. In the late nineteenth century, a deadly insect, phylloxera, devastated the French vine stock. From a production level of 500 million liters in 1876, output dropped to just 2 million liters in 1885. But a solution was found in an unexpected quarter: French vines were grafted onto phylloxera-resistant vine roots native to the U.S. and imported from the upstart Californian wine industry. It was the first time many in the Old World acknowledged the existence of a New World wine industry. It would not be the last.

Stirrings in the New World

Although insignificant in both size and reputation compared with traditional wine-producing countries, vineyards and winemakers in many New World countries dated back to the eighteenth century. In the U.S., Thomas Jefferson became a leading voice for establishing vineyards in Virginia, while in Australia, vines were brought over in the first fleet carrying convicts and settlers in 1788. Nascent wine industries were also developing at this time in Argentina, Chile, and South Africa, usually under the influence of immigrants from the Old World wine countries.

Opening New Markets

While climate and soil allowed grape growing to flourish in the New World, some cultures did not immediately embrace local wine. In Australia, the hot climate and a dominant British heritage made beer the alcoholic beverage of preference.

---

[6] Dewey Markham, *1855: A History of the Bordeaux Classification* (New York: Wiley, 1998), p. 177.
[7] Robinson, *The Oxford Companion to Wine*, p. 235.
[8] Robinson, *The Oxford Companion to Wine*, p. 312.

The U.S. market was more complex: one segment followed a tradition from the rum trade era and drank hard liquor, while another group reflected the Puritan heritage of temperance. As a result, in the pre-World War II era, wine was mostly made by and sold to European immigrant communities in both these countries. But in other New World wine-producing countries, the beverage became part of the national culture. For example, per capita annual consumption reached 80 liters in Argentina and 50 liters in Chile in the 1960s—well behind the 110 liters per capita in Italy and France, but comparable with Spain.

In the postwar era, however, demand for wine increased rapidly in most New World producer countries. In the U.S., consumption grew from a post-prohibition per capita level of 1 liter per annum to 9 liters by 2006, while in Australia, it grew from less than 2 liters in 1960 to 24 liters by 2006. Such growth led to a domestic boom that boosted the young New World wine industry.

Challenging Production Norms

Riding the postwar economic boom, New World producers created wine industries quite different from their European counterparts. With widely available inexpensive land, they developed more extensive vineyards that lowered labor costs by allowing the use of equipment, such as mechanical harvesters and pruners. In 2006, the average vineyard holding in the U.S. was 213 ha, and in Australia, 167 ha. This compared to an average size of 1.3 ha in Italy and 7.4 ha in France.[9]

Unconstrained by regulation or tradition, New World producers also experimented with grape-growing practices. Controlled drip irrigation—a practice strictly forbidden under AOC regulations—allowed Australian vineyards not only to expand into marginal land, but also to reduce vintage variability. Innovative trellis systems allowed New World producers to plant vines at twice the traditional density, while fertilizers and pruning methods increased yield and improved grape flavor. These innovations, coupled with typically sunny climates, freed New World farmers from many of the stresses of their counterparts in regions like Bordeaux, where the rainy maritime climate made late autumn harvests risky and held wine producers hostage to wide year-to-year vintage variations.

New World wine companies also broke many winemaking traditions. Most large estates had on-site labs whose analysis guided growing and harvest decisions. In the 1990s, some experimented with a reverse osmosis technology to concentrate the juice, ensuring a deeper-colored, richer-tasting wine. The technique had been developed in France, but was forbidden under AOC regulations. New World winemakers also developed processes allowing fermentation and aging in computer-controlled, stainless steel tanks rather than in traditional oak barrels. To provide the oak flavor that barrel aging offered, some added oak chips to these tanks, a practice strictly forbidden in Old World countries.

The economic impact of these and other innovations became clear in a cost comparison of popular priced wines from France's Languedoc region and Australia's Riverina district. The French grape cost of €238 per ton was 74% higher than the Australian cost of €137,[10] which translated to a juice cost of €0.32 versus €0.18 per bottle. Subsequent wholesale, retail, and tax markups amplified the impact of this difference on the final price. (See **Exhibits 1a** and **1b**.) Indeed, the industry's bottle-price multiplier rule of thumb predicted that the grape cost per ton was 100 times the average retail bottle price of entry-level and commercial premium wines.[11] Reflecting the cost discrepancies, in 2010 the price of Australian entry-level wine in Europe was around €2 a bottle, while the French *vins de pays* was above €3.

[10] Heijbrock, *Changing Competitiveness in the Wine Industry*, p. 16.

[11] Bruce Bordelon, "Economics of Midwestern Grape Production," Purdue University College of Agriculture, https://ag.purdue.edu/hla/fruitveg/Documents/GrapEcon.pdf, accessed May 2016.

[9] Arend Heijbrock, *Changing Competitiveness in the Wine Industry*, Rabobank Research Publication, 2007, p. 5.

Exhibit 1a
Retail Price Structure of a Typical EU Wine in Select Export Markets (€ per bottle), 2014

	China		United Kingdom		Germany	
	%	€/bottle	%	€/bottle	%	€/bottle
Grape, winemaking and bottling cost		2.00		2.00		2.00
Transportation cost		1.10		0.18		0.20
Landed cost (inc. insurance and freight)		3.10		2.18		2.20
Add Customs duties	14%	3.53	0%	2.18	0%	2.20
Add Excise duties	10%	3.89	€2.42[a]	4.60	0%	2.20
Add VAT	17%	4.55	20%	5.52	19%	2.57
Add Importer's margin	25%	5.69	10%	6.07	10%	3.22
Add Retailer's margin	50%	8.53	32%	8.01	32%	4.83

Source: Adapted from COGEA S.r.l., "Study on the Competitiveness of European Wines," European Commission, October 2014, p. 94, http://ec.europa.eu/agriculture/external-studies/2014/eu-wines/fulltext_en.pdf, accessed May 2016.
[a] UK excise duty was calculated on volume and alcohol content, not as a percentage.

Exhibit 1b
Bottle Wine Segments by Retail Price (European Commission's Categories), 2014

	Medium Range			
Entry Level	Commercial Premium	Super Premium	Ultra-Premium	Top Range
≤ 4.99 €/lt	5.00–9.99 €/lt	10.00–14.99 €/lt	15.00–49.99 €/lt	50.00 €/lt and more

Source: COGEA S.r.l., "Study on the Competitiveness of European Wines," European Commission, October 2014, p. 66, http://ec.europa.eu/agriculture/external-studies/2014/eu-wines/fulltext_en.pdf, accessed March 2016.

Reinventing the Marketing Model

New World producers also innovated in packaging and marketing. While the Europeans targeted the huge entry-level wine segment by selling liter bottles of table wine, in 1965 the Australians developed the innovative "wine-in-a-box" package. Employing a collapsible plastic bag in a compact cardboard box with a dispensing spigot, the box's shape and weight not only saved shipping costs, but also made storage in the consumer's refrigerator more convenient. Australian producers also began replacing corks with screw caps, even on premium wines. Providing more than cost savings, the screw caps greatly reduced spoilage due to deficient corks, particularly in delicate whites.

From their earliest experiences in the marketplace, New World producers learned the value of making wines that appealed to unsophisticated palates. While dismissed by connoisseurs, products like Ripple in the U.S. and Barossa Pearl in Australia were wildly successful. Just as important, they provided valuable lessons in branding and marketing—rare industry skills at the time. By showing wine's mass-appeal potential, they enticed Coca-Cola to acquire Taylor California Cellars in 1977, soon followed by other experienced consumer marketers such as Nestlé, Pillsbury, and Seagram. But the challenge of

Exhibit 2 Wine Industry Value Chain

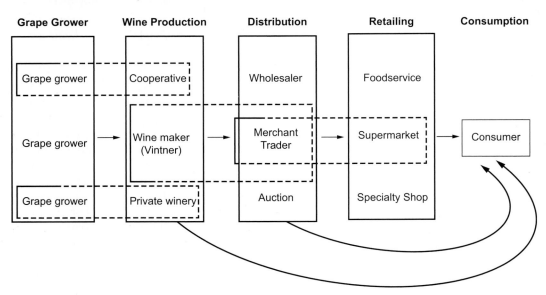

Source: Adapted from *The World Wine Business*, Rabobank Market Study, May 1999.

marketing the last largely unbranded major consumer product proved harder than expected. Within a decade the outsiders had sold out, but their influence endured in the consumer-focused attitudes and modern marketing skills they left behind.

The other big change driven by New World wine companies occurred in distribution. Historically, fragmented producers and tight government regulations had created a long, multilevel value chain, with service providers often lacking either the scale or expertise to operate efficiently. (See **Exhibit 2**.) In contrast, large New World wine companies typically controlled the full value chain, extracting margins at each stage and retaining bargaining power with the concentrated retailers. This also gave them an economic advantage by reducing handling stages and holding less inventory. Because their name was on the final product, they controlled quality at every step.

Traditionalists argued that the New World's drive for efficiency and desire to cater to simple palates had compromised the character of its wines. But they were shocked that these "engineered wines" were often sold under French

appellation names like Chablis, Burgundy, or Champagne. So when the EU took legal action, New World winemakers began identifying their wines by grape variety. Eventually, consumers learned to recognize varietal names and developed taste preferences defined by pinot noir versus merlot, or chardonnay versus sauvignon blanc. Indeed, many found this easier to understand than the complex regional designations that Old World winemakers used.

The Judgment of Paris

On May 24, 1976, a British wine merchant set up a blind-tasting panel to rate top wines from France and California. Despite the huge "home field advantage" of an event held in Paris with a judging panel of nine French wine critics, the American entries took top honors in both red and white competitions. When French producers complained that "The Judgment of Paris" was rigged, a new judging was held two years later. Again, Californian wines triumphed.[12]

---

[12] Gideon Rachman, "The Globe in a Glass," *The Economist*, December 18, 1999, p. 91.

The event was a watershed in the industry. To the great shock of those who dismissed the New World's innovative approaches, the event raised awareness that they produced quality wines. It was also a wake-up call to traditional producers who began taking these new challengers seriously. And finally, it gave confidence to New World producers that they could compete in global markets. In short, it was the bell for the opening round in a fight for export sales.

Maturing Markets, Changing Demand

"The Judgment of Paris" triggered a revolution in the wine industry that raged into the twenty-first century. In the decades that followed, traditional producers were shocked by alarming trends: a 14% drop in worldwide consumption from the 1980s to the 2010s,[13] radical changes in consumer tastes, consolidation in the distribution channels, and shifts in government support. But most New World producers saw the changes differently – as opportunities to disrupt the existing order.

Changing Global Demand Patterns

The most dramatic decline in demand occurred in the highest-consumption countries. Rates of per capita consumption in France and Italy in the 1970s more than halved by the end of the century.[14] (See Exhibit 3.) Causes included the different drinking preferences of a new generation, an older generation's concern about health issues, and stricter drunk-driving penalties. The downward trend continued into the twenty-first century. Between 2000 and 2012, consumption in France declined by 12%, by 27% in Italy, and by 34% in Spain. But in the same period, major importing countries were booming: UK demand was up by 29%, the U.S. by 37%, and China by an impressive 67%.[15] By 2014, China's consumption outpaced Spain's, Argentina's, and the UK's. (See Exhibit 4.) Its low per capita consumption clearly offered huge growth potential in a country of 1.3 billion people.

Rise of Fashion, Shift to Quality

As demand moved to new markets, consumption patterns shifted. A decline in working families' daily consumption of table wine was offset by upscale urban consumers' purchases, typically made on the basis of brand, grape variety, region–and, increasingly, fashion. The emphasis on lighter foods in the 1980s increased demand for white wines, which by the end of the decade represented over 75% of U.S. sales. But this changed dramatically following a 1991 *60 Minutes* TV report that identified red wine as part of the "French paradox"–low rates of heart disease in a country known for its rich food. Red wine's market share grew from 27% in 1991 to 43% in 1996. By 2010 white wine had lost its dominance, as red wine grapes reached 55% of global vineyard coverage.[16]

Demand for grape varieties also moved with fashion. During the white wine boom, chardonnay was the grape of choice, but by the late 1990s, sauvignon blanc emerged as a new trendy white varietal. In red wine, a love affair with cabernet sauvignon was followed by a mini-boom for merlot, which in turn was succeeded by a demand spike for pinot noir.

For Old World growers constrained by limited space and tight regulations, the inability to respond to these changes cost them dearly. Although vines had a productive life of 60 to 70 years, they could take 3 or 4 years to produce the first harvest, 5 to 7 years to reach full productive capacity, and 35 years to produce top-quality

13 "New Producers, New Consumers: The Revolution of the Global Wine Market," BNP Paribas press release, April 20, 2015, http://www.bnpparibas.com/en/news/press-release/new-producers-new-consumers-revolution-global-wine-market, accessed April 2016.

14 Barbara Insel, "The Evolving Global Wine Market," *Business Economics* 49, no. 1 (2014): 50, via Palgrave Macmillan, accessed January 2016.

15 Per Karlsson, "The World's Wine Consumption 2000–2012," *BKWine Magazine*, June 21, 2013, http://www.bkwine.com/features/more/global-wine-consumption-2000-2012/, accessed April 2016.

16 Mark Johanson, "What Are the Most Popular Wine Grapes in the World?," *International Business Times*, January 14, 2014, http://www.ibtimes.com/what-are-most-popular-wine-grapes-world-1540272, accessed February 2016.

Exhibit 3 Wine Consumption Per Capita, Selected Countries (1980–2014)

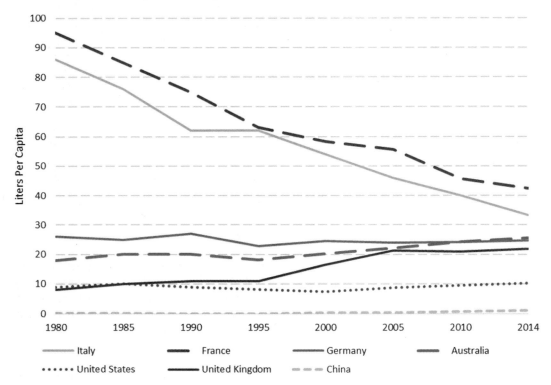

Source: Compiled by casewriter from *The World Wine Business*, Rabobank Market Study, May 1999; Wine Institute, "Statistics," http://www.wineinstitute.org/resources/statistics, accessed February 2016; and Kym Anderson and Signe Nelgen, *Global Wine Markets, 1961 to 2009: A Statistical Compendium* (Adelaide, Australia: University of Adelaide Press, 2011), https://www.adelaide.edu.au/wine-econ/databases/GWM/, accessed March 2016.

grapes. So, for example, a trend away from sweeter to drier white wines was disastrous for the German industry. With strict requirements on sugar content, German producers saw exports drop from over 3 million hectoliters in 1992 to under 2 million just five years later. In contrast, New World wine regions responded rapidly to demand shifts. For example, in the 1990s, California acreage planted with chardonnay increased 36%, and merlot plantings grew 31%.

Simultaneously, another market change emerged to challenge producers. Partially offsetting stalled volume growth, demand for higher-quality wines grew through the 2000s. (See **Exhibit 5.**) This was to some extent the result of the global financial crisis of 2008: while some consumers traded down to entry-level wines, others took the opportunity to try heavily discounted premium ones. Once the economy improved, many consumers opted to stay with the premium wines.[17]

Increasing Distribution Power

Because marketing was usually handled by *négociants*, Old World producers were often insulated from these trends. In contrast, most large New World wine companies controlled distribution

---

[17] Mike Veseth, "Trading Up? The New Conventional Wisdom about the U.S. Wine Market," *Wine Economist* blog, April 7, 2015, http://wineeconomist.com/?s=%22price+segment%22&submit=Search, accessed March 2016.

Exhibit 4
Wine Production and Consumption: Selected Old World and New World Countries, 2014

	Consumption		Production[b]	Exports		Imports	
	Liters per Capita	Total (khl[a])	Total (khl)	Volume (khl)	Value (€ millions)	Volume (khl)	Value (€ millions)
Argentina	23.5	9,900	15,197	2,626	631	-	-
Australia	24.5	5,400	12,000	7,301	1,262	840	443
China	1.2	15,800	11,178	-	-	4,578	1,145
France	42.5	27,900	46,698	14,387	2,468	6,453	620
Germany	24.8	20,200	9,334	3,863	968	15,171	2,505
Italy	33.3	20,400	44,739	20,540	5,078	2,440	310
Spain	21.3	10,000	41,620	22,560	2,468	470	153
UK	22	12,600	-	-	-	13,388	3,595
U.S.	10.3	30,700	22,300	4,045	1,103	10,739	4,032

Source: Compiled by casewriter from Wine Institute Statistics, 2015, http://www.wineinstitute.org/files/World_Per_Capita_Wine_Consumption_Revised_Nov_2015.pdf; "State of the Vitivinculture World Market," Organisation Internationale de la Vigne et du Vin, April 2015, http://www.oiv.int/public/medias/2935/oiv-noteconjmars2015-en.pdf; "EU-27 Wine Annual Report and Statistics 2015," Global Agricultural Information Network, February 24, 2015, http://gain.fas.usda.gov/Recent%20GAIN%20Publications/Wine%20Annual_Rome_EU-28_3-16-2015.pdf; and "Wine Industry Statistics," Winetitles Media, http://winetitles.com.au/statistics/default.asp, all accessed February 2016.
[a] kilo hectoliter (khl) was 1,000 hectoliters.
[b] In several European countries, production did not equal consumption (plus exports minus imports) due to excess production being subject to government purchase.

from vineyard to retailer. This allowed them to sense and respond to retailers' need for consistent supply, strong brands, good price/quality ratio, and strong promotion support.[18] Yet when fragmented French producers tried to respond, their lack of consumer knowledge and marketing skills was compounded by their limited bargaining power, often forcing them to compete on price.[19]

Even transport economics that once favored Old World suppliers' proximity to European markets changed. As trucking costs rose, container ship rates fell, making the cost of shipping wine from Australia to the UK similar to trucking it from southern France. Then Australia started shipping bulk wine in large plastic bags to be bottled at the destination, reducing shipping costs by up to €2.30 a case.[20] Bulk wine grew from one-third of New World exports in 2006 to nearly half in 2013.[21]

---

[18] Rachman, "The Globe in a Glass," p. 99.
[19] Annemiek Geene, Arend Heijbroek, Anne Lagerwerf, and Rafi Wazir, "The World Wine Business," Market Study, May 1999, available from Rabobank International.

[20] David Fickling, "Most Australian Wine Exports Ship in Giant Plastic Bladders," *Bloomberg Business*, February 7, 2013, http://www.bloomberg.com/bw/articles/2013-02-07/most-australian-wine-exports-ship-in-giant-plastic-bladders, accessed February 2016.
[21] Stephen Rannekleiv, Elena Saputo, and Marco Soccio, "Rabobank World Wine Map 2014," Rabobank, December 2014, p. 2, https://www.rabotransact.com/wps/portal/rtpubeu/!ut/p/a0/04_Sj9CPykssy0xPLMnMz0vMAfGjzOK9As09gt08TA39jcwNDDy9AlyDQoO9DA0CzfQLsh0VARhxnLM!/pw/Z7_JQ7HSFH51O2700IJPERUSJ1064/res/id=downloadWithToken/c=cacheLevelPage/=/?token=awCZimvzJjt22B0b8Pve&documentType=publication, accessed February 2016.

Exhibit 5 Global Wine Sales by Volume and Value (1999–2013)

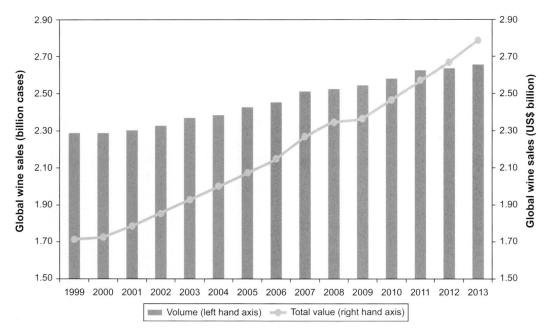

Source: Euromonitor International in Australian Grape and Wine Authority, "Strategic Plan 2015-2020," n.d., p. 33, https://www.wineaustralia.com/en/About%20Us/~/media/AGWA%20Strategic%20Plan%202015-2020.ashx, accessed January 2016.

Note: The average exchange rate over the period was $1 = €0.84. (In 1999, $1 = €0.93. In 2013, $1 = €0.75.)

Ascendancy of Brand Power

For years, the wine industry seemed ripe for branding. But extreme fragmentation in the European industry (Bordeaux alone had 20,000 producers) meant that few had the volume to support branding strategies. Historically, only the handful of Old World producers whose wines achieved icon status – Lafite, Veuve Cliquot, and Château d'Yquem, for example – were recognized brands based on image and quality. But these appealed to the elite, only a tiny fraction of the global market.

Government-supported classifications, such as France's AOC, had been partially successful in ensuring the quality and consistency that brands offered. But consumer confidence eroded over time as low-quality producers rode on the classification's prestige. For example, while most wine from Burgundy's most famous vineyard Chambertin was worthy of its *grand cru* status, wine

critic Robert Parker described some that sold at €140 a bottle under the Chambertin name as "thin, watery, and a complete rip-off."[22] In Italy, DOC regulations were so often violated that in 1980, the government had to introduce the DOCG classification where G stood for *garantita* (guaranteed). And in Germany, government standards were so diluted that, even in mediocre years, over 75% of wine was branded *Qualitätswein* (quality wine), while less than 5% was labeled the more modest *Tafelwein* (table wine).

Classification schemes were also impeded by their complexity – there were 327 designated AOC regions – requiring consumers to understand the intricacies of region, vintage, and vineyard reputation in order to choose a bottle. And even if they found a wine they liked, by their

[22] Robert M. Parker Jr., *Parker Wine Buyer's Guide*, 5th edn (New York: Fireside Press, 1999), p. 276.

Exhibit 6
Penfolds Red Wine U.S. Brand Structure, 2009

Label	Varietal Type	Years Before Release	Price Segment	Suggested U.S. Retail Price per Bottle ($US)
Rawson's Retreat	Varietal range[a]	1	Premium	$8.99
Koonunga Hill	Varietal range[a]	1-2	Premium	$10.99
Thomas Hyland	Varietal range[a]	1-2	Premium	$14.99
Bin 138	Shiraz Mourvedre Grenache	2	Super Premium	$19.00
Bin 128	Shiraz	3	Super Premium	$24.00
Bin 28	Shiraz	3	Super Premium	$24.00
Bin 389	Cabernet Shiraz	3	Super Premium	$26.00
Bin 407	Cabernet Sauvignon	3	Super Premium	$26.00
St. Henri	Shiraz	5	Ultra Premium	$39.00
Magill Estate	Shiraz	4	Ultra Premium	$50.00
RWT	Shiraz	4	Ultra Premium	$69.00
Bin 707	Cabernet Sauvignon	4	Ultra Premium	$80.00
Grange	Shiraz	6	Icon	$185.00

Source: Southcorp Wines, the Americas.

[a] Typical red varietal range of these brands included merlot, shiraz cabernet, and cabernet sauvignon. (These brands also offered a range of white wines.)

next purchase, it might not be in stock or a new vintage might be less appealing. Consumers were often faced with too many options and too little knowledge to make an informed choice.

Yet while global brands dominated soft drinks, beer, and liquor, no wine brand had ever captured even 5% of the global market. In the 1960s and 1970s, European producers had launched several mass-appeal brands such as Lancers, Blue Nun, and Mateus. But such initiatives had not endured. In contrast, New World producers had made branding a core marketing skill. For example, Australian winemaker Penfolds had built trust in its products by ensuring the vintage-to-vintage consistency that branding demanded. It then leveraged its trusted brand name by creating a hierarchy of wines, allowing consumers to move up each step from $9 to $185 (€6 to €130) wines as their tastes – and their budgets – developed. (See **Exhibit 6**.) Many other New World producers replicated this strategy.

By building marketing expertise in their home markets during the 1960s and 1970s, New World producers learned how to respond to consumer preferences for simpler, more fruit-driven wines that were easy to appreciate. They then took those wines and their marketing and branding skills into the export markets. For instance, in the 2000s, Yellow Tail, a full-bodied, fruit-driven wine with a trendy Australian label, came to dominate the low to middle segments of the U.S. market.

All these changes resulted in significant shifts in the world ranking of wine companies. Despite their newness and the comparative smallness of many of their home markets, the New World was home to 7 of the 10 top wine companies in the 2010s, a list previously dominated by the Old World. And by 2014, the world's top-10 wine brands all came from the New World. (See **Exhibits 7a and 7b**.)

Facing Challenges, Seeking Solutions

Of all these challenges, the biggest for traditional producers was that falling demand in their home markets and a loss of share in export markets had

Exhibit 7a
Top-10 Global Wine Companies by Volume, 2003 and 2014

	2003			2014	
Rank	Company	Country	Rank	Company	Country
1	Constellation Brands	U.S.	1	E&J Gallo Winery	U.S.
2	Bacardi & Co	Italy	2	Constellation Brands	U.S.
3	E & J Gallo Winery	U.S.	3	The Wine Group	U.S.
4	The Wine Group	U.S.	4	Treasury Wine Estates	Australia
5	Foster's Group	Australia	5	Accolade Wines	Australia
6	Les Grands Chais	France	6	Viña Concha y Toro	Chile
7	Pernod Ricard Groupe	France	7	Castel Groupe	France
8	Peñaflor	Argentina	8	Group Peñaflor	Argentina
9	Viña Concha y Toro	Argentina	9	Pernod Ricard Groupe	France
10	Castel Groupe	France	10	Cantine Riunite & CIV SC	Italy

Source: Compiled from Kym Anderson and Signe Nelgen, *Global Wine Markets, 1961 to 2009: A Statistical Compendium* (Adelaide, Australia: University of Adelaide Press, 2011), https://www.adelaide.edu.au/wine-econ/databases/GWM/; and Jeremy Cunnington, "Spirits and Wine: Corporate Overview," Euromonitor International, February 2016, p. 11, accessed February 2016.
Note: Treasury Wine Estates was formerly a part of Foster's Group.

Exhibit 7b
Top-10 Global Wine Brands, 2009 and 2014

	2009				2014		
	Brand	Brand Owner	Country		Brand	Brand Owner	Country
1	Gallo	E&J Gallo	U.S.	1	Barefoot	E&J Gallo	U.S.
2	Concha y Tora	Concha y Tora	Argentina	2	Gallo	E&J Gallo	U.S.
3	Moët et Chandon	LVMH	France	3	Concha y Toro	Concha y Toro	Chile
4	Veuve Cliquot	LVMH	France	4	Robert Mondavi	Constellation	U.S.
5	Robert Mondavi	Constellation	U.S.	5	Sutter Home	Trinchero Family Estates	U.S.
6	Yellowtail	Casella Wines	Australia	6	Yellow Tail	Casella Wines	Australia
7	Hardys	Constellation	Australia	7	Hardys	Accolade Wines	Australia
8	Beringer	Foster's Group	U.S.	8	Lindeman's	Treasury Wine Estates	Australia
9	Freixenet	Freixenet	Spain	9	Beringer	Treasury Wine Estates	Australia
10	Jacob's Creek	Pernot Ricard	Australia	10	Jacob's Creek	Pernod Ricard	Australia

Source: Compiled from Kym Anderson and Signe Nelgen, *Global Wine Markets, 1961 to 2009: A Statistical Compendium* (Adelaide: Australia: University of Adelaide Press, 2011), https://www.adelaide.edu.au/wine-econ/databases/GWM/; and Gabriel Stone, "Top 10 Wine Brands 2015," *The Drinks Business*, April 7, 2015, http://www.thedrinksbusiness.com/2015/04/top-10-wine-brands-2015/11/, accessed February 2016.

caused a structural wine surplus – dubbed the European wine lake. (For example, **Exhibit 4** shows that French wine production in 2014 was 46,698 kilo hectoliters (khl). Domestic consumption was 27,900 khl, including 6,453 khl of imports. Exports were 14,387 khl, leaving a surplus of 10,864 khl.) The EU's response was to pay farmers to uproot vineyards, with a parallel program to purchase excess for distillation into industrial alcohol. Yet after distilling 24.5 khl of wine from 2000 to 2008, the EU recognized that by guaranteeing a market for overproduction at attractive prices, the program exacerbated the problem.[23]

In 2008, the EU introduced policies to encourage commercially viable wines by phasing out crisis distillation, expanding uprooting efforts, and increasing its export promotion budget. The EU also created a new classification system, albeit one that could be superseded by a country's traditional system such as France's AOC. The top EU level of Protected Designation of Origin (PDO) required that all grapes be sourced from a defined region; next, the Protected Geographical Indication (PGI) level required that only 85% of grapes be from a protected region; and the third category, simply called "vin," had no geographic indication and could be identified by varietal. Yet one industry insider commented that "[t]he EU missed the chance to produce a new quality-based system . . . and has gone for the old terroir-based system, rehashed to frustrate New World producers."[24]

Meanwhile, New World producers were burdened by image problems born of their willingness to lower prices aggressively in an era of excess supply. Australia had enjoyed success from 1996 to 2006 – under the "Brand Australia" umbrella – as grape production more than doubled and exports grew 530% to 782 million liters, making it the world's number-four wine exporter. But growth eventually began to stagnate and average price eroded. Exports to the UK, its largest market, peaked at 807 million liters in 2007, then started to slide.[25] By 2009, Australia was producing 20 to 40 million cases more than it could sell.[26] Australian wine had become trapped by the "cheap and cheerful" image that brands like Yellow Tail had promoted so successfully.

Furthermore, increases in global energy prices and the cost of water in the midst of an ongoing drought boosted Australian production costs by $200 (€215) a ton. And appreciation of the Australian dollar from A$0.58 to €1 in 2001 to A$0.74 a decade later also increased export prices.[27] By 2010, Australian producers were forced to recognize that while they could land bulk table wine in the U.S. around $0.72 (€0.54) a liter, Chile's price was $0.58 (€0.44) a liter.[28] Australia's wine-governing bodies called for a restructuring of the industry with initiatives to manage supply and a commitment to undertake industrywide R&D, emphasizing research on the fast-growing market in China.

The Battle for the China Market

Squeezed by chronic oversupply and declining demand in mature markets, in the early twenty-first century, Old and New World producers were again locked in a competitive battle for export

---

[23] European Court of Auditors, "Special Report No 7/2012—The Reform of the Common Organization of the Market in Wine: Progress to Date," p. 19, http://www.eca.europa.eu/lists/ECADocuments/SR12_07/SR12_07_en.pdf, accessed January 2016.

[24] Bob Lindo, in Victoria Daskal, "EU Regulations," *Decanter*, August 21, 2009, http://www.decanter.com/features/eu-regulations-246636/, accessed January 2016.

[25] Australian Grape and Wine Authority, "Strategic Plan 2015–2020," p. 34, https://www.wineaustralia.com/en/About%20Us/~/media/AGWA%20Strategic%20Plan%202015-2020.ashx, accessed January 2016.

[26] Winemakers Federation of Australia, Wine Grape Growers Australia, Australian Wine and Brandy Corporation, and Grape and Wine Research and Development Corporation, "Wine Restructuring Action Agenda," November 10, 2009, http://www.wineaustralia.com/en/Winefacts%20Landing/Sector%20Overviews/Strategies%20and%20Plans/Wine%20Restructuring%20Action%20Agenda%20Statement.aspx, accessed February 2016.

[27] All exchange rates calculated from OANDA, https://www.oanda.com/currency/historical-rates/, accessed May 2016.

[28] "Italy Leads U.S. Wine Imports," Italian Wine & Food Institute press release, August 5, 2010, p. 3, http://www.winebusiness.com/content/file/PR%20-US%20Wine%20Imports.pdf, accessed March 2016.

Exhibit 8 Exports as % of Production Volume by Source: EU, New World, and Globally, 1961–2009

Source: Kym Anderson and Signe Nelgen, "Global Wine Markets at a Glance," Wine Economics Research Centre, University of Adelaide, 2011, p. 14, https://www.adelaide.edu.au/wine-econ/papers/GWM_SC_charts_043011.pdf, accessed May 2016.
Note: EU-15 included Austria, Belgium, Denmark, Finland, France, Germany, Greece, Ireland, Italy, Luxembourg, Netherlands, Portugal, Spain, Sweden, and the United Kingdom. NWE8 included Argentina, Australia, Canada, Chile, New Zealand, South Africa, United States, and Uruguay.

markets that accounted for 35% of global production.[29] But New World producers now exported 30% of their output, up from 3% in the 1980s.[30] (See Exhibit 8.) It was a situation that made China – called "the decade's most attractive wine market"[31]– a vital battleground in the global wine war.

Building on China's Wine Heritage

China's modern winemaking was born in 1892 when a wealthy Chinese businessman imported grapevines and winemakers from Europe to create Changyu Pioneer Wine (Changyu). Yet,

[29] BNP Paribas Wealth Management press release, "New Producers, New Consumers: The Revolution Of The Global Wine Market," April 20, 2015, http://www.bnpparibas.com/en/news/press-release/new-producers-new-consumers-revolution-global-wine-market, accessed February 2016.

[30] Tom Kierath and Crystal Wang, "The Global Wine Industry," Morgan Stanley, October 22, 2013, p. 3, http://blogs.reuters.com/counterparties/files/2013/10/Global-Wine-Shortage.pdf, accessed December 2015.

[31] Angelo A. Camillo, "A Strategic Investigation of the Determinants of Wine Consumption in China," *International Journal of Wine Business Research* 24, no. 1 (2012): 68–92.

for years, interest in wine was extremely limited, and the few who did drink it preferred either a fruity, syrup-like wine or wine made from grape juice concentrate and water. The wine industry resurfaced after the easing of Communist rule in 1978 as China opened up to the outside world. Economic reforms allowed the creation of new wine companies: in 1980, Dynasty Fine Wines Group (Dynasty) formed as a joint venture between state-owned Tianjin City Grape Garden and French producer Rémy Martin; and in 1983, state-owned China National Cereals Oils and Foodstuffs Corporation (COFCO) started the Great Wall Wine Company. Together, Changyu, Dynasty, and COFCO shaped the growing industry.

Wine consumption flourished in the 1990s as China chased aggressive gross domestic product (GDP) targets and household wealth increased. In 1996, Premier Li Peng toasted Congress with a glass of red wine and spoke of the health benefits of drinking wine over the harsh *baijiu*, a popular grain spirit. Some felt his motivation was also to protect China's grain supply, since it took two kilograms of staple crops like rice or barley to make one liter of *baijiu*. Grapes, in contrast, grew in soil unsuitable for other crops.[32] China's wine market took off and grew 20% a year from 2000 to 2009 – the fastest rate in the world.[33]

Establishing the Domestic Wine Industry

Most Chinese wine was priced to maximize volume and was below global standards, though some small wineries emerged with a focus on quality.[34] Part of the problem was sourcing: farmers, typically paid by weight, often produced grapes with sugar levels and acidity unsuitable for winemaking.[35] Since wines labeled "Product of China" required that only 10% of grapes be locally sourced, producers blended domestic wine with imported bulk wine, mostly from Australia and Chile. So while China's vineyard acreage doubled in the 2000s, wine production grew even faster.[36] In 2011, China's goal was to produce 2.2 billion liters annually by 2015, which some saw as a potential threat to the Old World.[37] At that time, France led global production at 5.2 billion liters.[38]

Investing heavily in marketing, the big domestic wine companies had broad brand recognition. Dynasty, for instance, typically committed 20% of its revenue to marketing, while COFCO leveraged its brand by becoming the exclusive wine supplier for the 2008 Beijing Olympics.[39,40] Local producers opened French-like châteaux in China and adopted labels that copied the French style.

Wine became a prestige product, commonly served at lavish banquets and given as high-status gifts among government officials. While this caused the top segment to grow, domestic entry-level wine dominated most other consumption. Red wine accounted for 90% of consumption, in part due to its ties with rich Western traditions, but also because it paired well with China's savory and spicy dishes.[41] Few drinkers understood varietal differences, but favored cabernet sauvignon and merlot.[42] China's brand-conscious consumers therefore made purchases based on image and price rather than taste, and it was common to mix wine with sweet sodas to make it palatable.

[32] Suzanne Mustacich, *Thirsty Dragon: China's Lust for Bordeaux and the Threat to the World's Best Wines* (New York: Henry Holt and Company, 2015), p. 14.

[33] Rabobank International, "Project Tannin–The Chinese Grape Wine Market," October 2010, http://research .wineaustralia.com/wp-content/uploads/2012/11/RI-0901.pdf, accessed January 2016.

[34] "Wine Production in China," May 2015, p. 13, via IBIS World, accessed December 2015.

[35] Mustacich, *Thirsty Dragon*, p. 76.

[36] Rudy Ruitenberg, "China's Vineyards Overtake France's as Europe Uproots Its Grapes," *Bloomberg Business*, April 28, 2015, http://www.bloomberg.com/news/ articles/2015-04-28/china-s-vineyards-overtake-france-s-as-europe-uproots-its-grapes, accessed December 2015.

[37] Mustacich, *Thirsty Dragon*, p. 208.

[38] Mustacich, *Thirsty Dragon*, p. 208.

[39] "Wine Production in China," May 2015, p. 21, via IBIS World, accessed December 2015.

[40] "Wine Production in China," May 2015, p. 27.

[41] "The Little Red Book–A Guide to How China Is Reshaping the Global Wine Industry," *Week in China*, Winter 2014, pp. 18–19, http://www.weekinchina.com/ wp-content/uploads/2014/10/China-Wine.pdf, accessed January 2016.

[42] Rabobank International, "Project Tannin," p. 17.

Navigating the Import Challenges

With domestic production lagging demand growth, a large import market opened up. But foreign producers had to navigate complex regulatory requirements: import laws varied by province and a bottle typically took four months to clear customs.[43] As a result, Hong Kong became a key entry point. After eliminating its 40% wine import tax in 2008, 40% of its imports were re-exported to China.[44]

Good local agents were vital. Large state-owned importers had experience clearing customs, but many lacked proper temperature-controlled transport equipment, sometimes leaving wine to spoil in the heat.[45] Importers often signed distribution agreements for foreign wines but did little to promote them, instead prioritizing a few that sold with little marketing – often their Bordeaux wines. So while imports were valued for their prestigious image, few achieved widespread brand recognition.[46]

Imports faced additional obstacles in the retail market. High markups were common: a €1 to €2 bottle in Europe could sell in China's stores for RMB 70 to RMB 100 (€9 to €12).[47] This was partly due to China's duty (up to 48%), but also reflected the uneducated consumer base.[48] At hotels, restaurants, and bars, imported wines were also subject to extra "introduction and promotion" fees. Foreign wine producers also faced another challenge: counterfeit wines. Local suppliers sold cheap local wine as premium imports under labels with fictitious French appellations or misspelt versions of prestigious brands. For example, a "Benfolds" brand mimicked the respected Australian Penfolds brand, and undiscerning consumers could not tell the difference.[49]

Local and foreign companies alike worked to develop a wine culture by educating consumers through classes and wine tastings. Wine drinkers gradually learned to appreciate and seek out better quality, and the volume of bottled wine imports finally surpassed bulk in 2009.[50] Although only 3% of the population drank wine,[51] China had become the world's fifth-largest wine market.

France: Capitalizing on a Premium Image

France stepped in to fill China's growing luxury segment, and its imports grew 15-fold from 2002 to 2008.[52] Chinese consumers admired France's prestigious wine reputation and relied on the AOC classification to determine quality, with ranking reflected in price. Bordeaux's Lafite led the surge; demand and prices soared with Chinese importers' huge orders. Lafite's prices peaked in 2010 at a Sotheby's auction in Hong Kong, where bottles worth a total of €1.8 million sold for €6.3 million.[53] Its 2008 vintage, labeled with the Chinese good luck number eight, sold for four times its value.[54]

As demand for Bordeaux spiked, the region's export promotional activities centered on the 200 most prominent châteaux, leaving its small and medium-sized wineries to promote on their own.[55] Already financially strained, and with some nearing bankruptcy, many offered their excess supply to *négociants,* who blended it into low-price wine sold in China with a Bordeaux label. This allowed France, with imports to China

43 Rabobank International, "Project Tannin." p. 111.
44 Rabobank International, "Project Tannin," p. 8.
45 Mustacich, *Thirsty Dragon*, p. 39.
46 "Wine Production in China," May 2015, p. 24.
47 Insel, "The Evolving Global Wine Market," p. 56.
48 Insel, "The Evolving Global Wine Market," p. 56.
49 Mark Hawthorne and Jared Lynch, "Fake Foods: Australian Producers Face Asian Retreat in Counterfeit Battle," *Sydney Morning Herald*, August 7, 2015, http://www.smh.com.au/business/the-economy/ australian-food-producers-face-asian-retreat-in-counterfeit-battle-20150806-gitb19.html, accessed February 2016.
50 Rabobank International, "Project Tannin," p. 26.
51 "Fine Wines Languish in China Warehouses as Consumers Cool: A Faltering Economy and the Crackdown on Graft Wilted Demand," *Business Times*, November 3, 2015, via ABI/ProQuest, accessed December 2015.
52 Andrew Peaple, "A Toast to China's Wine Industry," *Wall Street Journal*, December 26, 2009, p. B. 10, via ABI/ProQuest, accessed December 2015.
53 Mustacich, *Thirsty Dragon*, pp. 102, 108.
54 Mustacich, *Thirsty Dragon*, p. 106.
55 Mustacich, *Thirsty Dragon*, p. 82.

Exhibit 9a China Wine Sales Volume by Retail Sale Point and Country of Origin, 2009

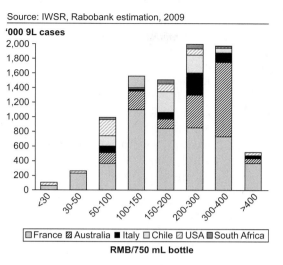

Source: Rabobank International, prepared for the Grape and Wine Research and Development Corporation, "Project Tannin—The Chinese Grape Wine Market," October 2010, p. 51, http://research.wineaustralia .com/wp-content/uploads/2012/11/RI-0901.pdf, accessed January 2016.

Exhibit 9b Bottle Wine Positioning in China by Price Segment and Area of Origin (%), 2014

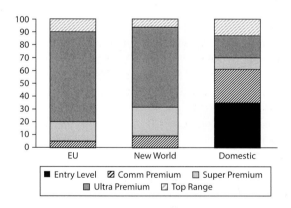

Source: Adapted by casewriter from COGEA S.r.l., "Study on the Competitiveness of European Wines," European Commission, October 2014, p. 68, http://ec.europa.eu/agriculture/external-studies/2014/eu-wines/fulltext_en.pdf, accessed May 2016.

totaling €135 million in 2009, to gain a position at both the high end (above RMB 400, or €40) and low end (under RMB 50, or €5) of the market.[56] (See **Exhibits 9a** and **9b.**) But wine was still a luxury product mainly purchased by China's urban upper-middle class, and some top French producers warned that the low-quality wine would dilute their image.[57]

[56] Rabobank International, "Project Tannin," p. 51.

[57] Mustacich, *Thirsty Dragon*, p. 82.

Other clouds were on the horizon. France's success in China resulted in its established customers being priced out of the market, with one American buyer saying that Bordeaux needed to reduce its prices "to fit the budgets of middle managers in Chicago rather than tycoons in Chengdu."[58] Then, some Chinese buyers started bypassing France's *négociant* system, with several châteaux offering buyers direct allocations. This raised fears that they would undermine France's strong worldwide distribution networks built over centuries.[59] Then, responding to buyer pressure, *négociants* sought Chinese joint-venture partners to protect profits. Meanwhile, Chinese investors were buying up Bordeaux châteaux, and from 2009 to 2014, 60 French châteaux came under Chinese control.[60]

Australia: Building a Value Image

During the 2000s, Australia also became a major exporter to China, largely by exporting surplus bulk wine, which accounted for 50% of its exports to China in 2009, up from 18% in 2008. This shift led to a drop in average price per liter from 3.75 Australian dollars (A$; €2.10) to A $1.40 (€0.80).[61] Much of the Australian bulk was blended to improve the quality of local Chinese wine, eliminating the Australian brand in the process.[62] Bulk wines the bottled under a Chinese label were slotted along with other New World offerings in the low-price segment, slightly above the domestic brands.[63]

At the same time, Australia looked to China as a potential market for its bottled wines. Because its wines did not yet command the same respect as France's, the Australian industry invested heavily in education through trade shows, social media campaigns, retail promotions, tasting roadshows, and classes.[64] These activities helped improve the image of Australian wine, and soon Chinese consumers started to recognize it as good value for the price.[65] China became a popular market for Australia's bottles over RMB 70 (€7), sales of which grew from A$4 million (€2.3 million) in 2005 to A$33 million (€18.7 million) in 2009 – a quarter of its Chinese export value that year.[66] By 2010, China was Australia's fastest-growing export market and its fourth largest by volume.

Austerity Restructures the Market

In 2012, as the Chinese economy began to slow, new austerity measures curtailed official banqueting and prohibited expensive gifts among government employees. Demand for fine wine plummeted and overall wine sales grew sluggish. Within a year, French imports fell by 18% in value[67] as Chinese buyers canceled orders worth millions of dollars.[68] As Chinese consumers started to look beyond Bordeaux, opportunities opened for less expensive yet still top-range imports, like France's Burgundy or Australia's Penfolds Grange.[69] So while Australia's exports to China slowed from 2012 to 2013, its average value per liter increased to A$6.76 (€4.90)—above France's €3.77.[70] Domestic producers also sought

[58] Mustacich, *Thirsty Dragon*, p. 181.

[59] Mustacich, *Thirsty Dragon*, p. 183.

[60] Alice Tidey, "In Search of Riches, France to Ply China with Wine," CNBC, March 25, 2014, http://www.cnbc.com/2014/03/25/in-search-of-riches-france-to-ply-china-with-wine.html, accessed February 2016.

[61] Rabobank International, "Project Tannin," p. 18.

[62] Global Agricultural Information Network, "Australia Wine Annual Report 2010," February 26, 2010, p. 3, http://gain.fas.usda.gov/Recent%20GAIN%20Publications/Wine%20Annual_Canberra_Australia_2-26-2010.pdf, accessed February 2016.

[63] Insel, "The Evolving Global Wine Market," p. 57.

[64] Winemakers Federation of Australia, Wine Grape Growers Australia, Australian Wine and Brandy Corporation, and Grape and Wine Research and Development Corporation, "Wine Restructuring Action Agenda," November 10, 2009.

[65] Rabobank International, "Project Tannin," p. 8.

[66] Rabobank International, "Project Tannin," p. 114.

[67] Jane Anson, "China Slowdown Knocks Bordeaux Wine Exports in 2013," *Decanter*, March 18, 2014, http://www.decanter.com/wine-news/china-slowdown-curbs-bordeaux-wine-exports-in-2013-29206/, accessed February 2016.

[68] Mustacich, *Thirsty Dragon*, p. 172.

[69] "The Little Red Book—A Guide to How China Is Reshaping the Global Wine Industry," *Week in China*, p. 12.

[70] Australian Government, Wine Australia Annual Report 2012–2013, p. 15, http://www.wineaustralia.com/~/media/4AB8FEC66B104E1C91B0F06434380568.ashx, accessed February 2016.

better regulation to improve wine quality as the industry restructured to meet the changing demands. Indeed, a Chinese wine region even created a classification system that mirrored France's.[71]

Regular consumers gradually replaced government employees as the driver of demand as wine transformed from a gift to give to a beverage to drink, particularly among white-collar workers and young people. Consumers started to try a wider variety of wines and in many cases found they preferred the lighter, fruitier wines of the New World to the tannic reds of the Old.[72]

By 2014, entry-level wines accounted for 80% of consumption, primarily made up of domestic wines retailing for under RMB 50 (around €6).[73] Imports, which averaged RMB 150 (around €20) or above, dominated the shrinking top range.[74] Yet following the austerity measures, prices started to drop and high-end consumers traded down. At the same time, entry-level consumers grew more knowledgeable and started looking for more mid-price wines in the premium segment. These changing dynamics opened a new playing field in the mid-level segment (RMB 50 to RMB 150).[75]

Battle Lines Re-Drawn: New Strategies for France and Australia

In the mid-2000s, France's high-end wines remained popular worldwide, while its low- and mid-priced wines were losing share to the New World. In 2008, the French industry launched a five-year industry modernization plan to boost competitiveness with the self-contradictory-sounding goal "to keep tradition in place and at the same time gear the sector towards mass production."[76]

The reform's core element, fully implemented in 2012, was a new French classification system. The essentially unchanged AOC was renamed *Appellation d'Origine Protégée* (AOP). AOP production rules were largely governed by regional committees, while the national government gave marketing support.[77] The next classification level was now called *Indication Géographique Protégée* (IGP), with wines identified by broad regions and made from any varietal. This allowed the employment of New World wine-making techniques, such as using oak chips in place of oak barrel aging or adding powdered tannins.[78] The third level was *vin de France*, wines identified by varietal and blended from grapes across multiple regions. While some in the industry considered the changes "a violation of our wine heritage,"[79] sales of these low- and mid-priced *vin de France* wines were soon on the rise.

In 2010, the Bordeaux wine industry body launched its own three-year revitalization plan with a focus on promoting mid-priced wines to eight key markets, including China.[80] The plan introduced a new price-based segmentation

[71] Mustacich, *Thirsty Dragon*, p. 211.

[72] Wine Intelligence, "Analysis—Wine—China: Life After Bordeaux," *Drinks Global News*, June 20, 2010, via ABI/ProQuest, accessed May 2016.

[73] Larry Gandler and Ben Levin, "Treasury Wine—Middle Wine to the Middle Kingdom," Credit Suisse, December 1, 2015, via Thomson ONE, accessed May 2016.

[74] Gandler and Levin, "Treasury Wine—Middle Wine to the Middle Kingdom."

[75] Gandler and Levin, "Treasury Wine—Middle Wine to the Middle Kingdom."

[76] "French Government Unveils Sweeping Changes to Wine Sector," *Decanter*, May 30, 2008, http://www.decanter.com/wine-news/french-government-unveils-sweeping-changes-to-wine-sector-81950/, accessed March 2016.

[77] Mitch Frank, "France's President Attempts to Reform Wine Industry," *Wine Spectator*, June 18, 2008, http://www.winespectator.com/webfeature/show/id/Frances-President-Attempts-to-Reform-Wine-Industry_4192, accessed January 2016.

[78] Frank, "France's President Attempts to Reform Wine Industry."

[79] James Lawrence, "Vins de France 'Will Be Like Coca-Cola': Anivin," *Decanter*, July 2, 2010, http://www.decanter.com/wine-news/vins-de-france-will-be-like-coca-cola-anivin-54929/, accessed January 2016.

[80] Pierre Mora, "Strategic Thinking for the Future of Bordeaux Wines: An Interview with Bernard Farges," *Wine Economics and Policy* 3 no. 2, (December 2014): 142–146, via ScienceDirect, http://www.sciencedirect.com/science/article/pii/S2212977414000246, accessed March 2016.

system with four tiers: Art (over €20), Exploration (€6 to €20), Fun (€2 to €6), and Basic (under €2). Amid concerns that low-quality wines diminished the Bordeaux image, production of Basic wines would be reduced by 110 million liters.[81]

At the EU level, as exports increased 10% annually from 2010 to 2012, regulators were cautiously optimistic about their own 2008 reforms.[82] But while the vineyard uprooting program had removed 10.2 million hectoliters (hl) of wine by 2012, surplus production—the wine lake—endured.[83] In 2013, the EU doubled its wine promotion budget and introduced reforms to improve marketability through new products, processes, and technologies.[84] But in 2014, the European Court of Auditors criticized that funds had been used to consolidate markets rather than win new ones and had mostly supported large enterprises, not the small and medium-sized ones struggling the most.[85]

In 2013, the EU also proposed loosening restrictions on planting rights to allow vineyards beyond traditional wine regions. Many worried that this would lead to further overproduction, lower quality, lower prices, and the disappearance of family farms.[86] But after much debate,

the EU lifted the restrictions in 2015, but limited the size of new vineyards to 1% of a country's production.[87] Despite the compromise, one French politician opined, "This rule spells the death of the [AOC] system. . . . Terroir, the quality of the earth, exposure to the sun – they will count for nothing."[88]

Australia, meanwhile, focused on its deteriorating image and the declining average price of its wine exports. To provide support, in 2013 the government merged its two wine groups to form a new statuary body known as Wine Australia. In 2015, the new body introduced a strategic plan to boost demand, lift the price premium, and increase the global competitiveness of Australian wine. It focused marketing on the premium segment, promoting wines that reflected Australia's terroir and elevated the image of all wines.[89] The group also expanded growing and winemaking R&D.

Australia's hopes were revived in 2015 as its exports increased by 6.4% in volume and 14.0% by value from 2014, indicating a big rise in its premium wine sales.[90] The average global value of its bottled wine exports reached A$5.50 (€3.70) per liter, the highest price since 2003.[91] And exports of bottles over A$10 (€6.80) per liter grew

81 Suzanne Mustacich, "The Bordeaux Diet," *Wine Spectator*, August 4, 2010, http://www.winespectator .com/webfeature/show/id/43284, accessed March 2016.

82 European Court of Auditors, "Special Report No 7/ 2012—The reform of the common organization of the market in wine: Progress to date," p. 41, http://www .eca.europa.eu/lists/ECADocuments/SR12_07/SR12_ 07_en.pdf, accessed January 2016.

83 European Court of Auditors, "Special Report No 7/ 2012," p. 22.

84 Jancis Robinson, "Subsidising Wine," *Financial Times*, January 2, 2015, http://www.ft.com/intl/cms/s/0/ 982ed0e4-8a1d-11e4-9b5f-00144feabdc0.html, accessed January 2016.

85 European Court of Auditors, "Is the EU investment and promotion support to the wine sector well managed and are its results on the competitiveness of EU wines demonstrated?," Special Report No 09/2014, http:// bookshop.europa.eu/en/is-the-eu-investment-and- promotion-support-to-the-wine-sector-well-managed- and-are-its-results-on-the-competitiveness-of-eu- wines-demonstrated–pbQJAB14005/, accessed January 2016.

86 "The High Level Group on planting rights confirms the disastrous consequences of the liberalisation,"

European Federation of Origin Wines, July 6, 2012, http://efow.eu/the-high-level-group-on-planting- rights-confirms-the-disastrous-consequences-of-the- liberalisation/, accessed February 2016.

87 "Will France's new wine regions threaten Champagne tradition?," BBC News, January 1, 2016, http://www .bbc.com/news/world-europe-35204500, accessed February 2016.

88 "Will France's new wine regions threaten Champagne tradition?," BBC News.

89 Australian Grape and Wine Authority, "Strategic Plan 2015–2020," p. 15, https://www.wineaustralia.com/en/ About%20Us/~/media/AGWA%20Strategic%20Plan% 202015-2020.ashx, accessed January 2016.

90 Wine Australia, "Export Report—Moving Annual Total (MAT) to December 2015," January 21, 2016, p. 4, http://www.wineaustralia.com/en/~/media/0000 Industry%20Site/Documents/Winefacts/Australian% 20Wine%20Export%20Approvals/WEAR/WEAR/ Export%20Report%20%20Dec%2015.ashx, accessed January 2016.

91 Wine Australia, "Export Report—Moving Annual Total (MAT) to December 2015," p. 4.

35% to reach record levels of A$480 million (€330 million).[92]

On the Chinese Battlefield

In 2015, these strategic maneuvers were all playing out in China, the new battlefield in the global wine war. The market had revived somewhat since the austerity measures; Chinese consumers were drinking more frequently and seeking out better value. In 2015, Chinese wine imports reached RMB 12 billion (€1.7 billion),[93] with France leading in value (45% import market share) and volume (43%). But Australia, third in volume (14%) and second in value (23%), was closing the gap.[94]

France could no longer ride on its image to ensure top prices for its fine wines and increasingly promoted its mid-level wines. *Vin de France*'s trade organization launched promotional events, tastings, and educational seminars that helped to boost sales in China by 12% from 2013 to 2014. By 2014, China accounted for 13% (37.9 million bottles) of *vin de France*'s total export volume.[95] Bordeaux producers also decided to back their new mid-range Exploration tier with promotional efforts. A 2014 advertising campaign positioned mid-range "Vins de Bordeaux" as innovative, approachable, and affordable – a shift from its historic reputation.[96] In China, an image of

chopsticks holding a Bordeaux bottle demonstrated that the wines paired well with diverse cuisines.[97]

As Chinese consumers moved to the middle market, Australia's simpler brands and good mid-priced wines became the new favorites.[98] But a declining Australian dollar and a free trade agreement with China also boosted Australia's higher-end prospects. Import tariffs on Australian wine were to be reduced from 2015 levels of 14% for bottles and 20% for bulk to elimination by 2019. In this environment, Wine Australia worked with high-end Chinese retailers to increase the visibility of its premium wines though educational activities and new marketing efforts for premium wines. For example, Treasury Wine Estates, owner of the Penfolds and Wolf Blass brands, responded to Chinese perceptions of quality by replacing screw caps with corks.[99] And to reach the younger generation, in 2015 Wolf Blass became a sponsor of China's National Basketball Association.[100] Treasury then brought its distribution in-house in 2015, reducing the distributor markup to make premium wines more affordable, while also increasing the company's margin.[101]

Together, these factors made 2015 the best year for Australian exports since 2007.[102] From

---

92 Wine Australia, "Export Report—Moving Annual Total (MAT) to December 2015," p. 4.

93 Sylvia Wu, "Chinese Wine Imports Rebound in 2015, Shows Data," *Decanter China*, November 19, 2015, https://www.decanterchina.com/en/news/china-wine-imports-rebound-in-2015-shows-data, accessed January 2016.

94 Wu, "Chinese Wine Imports Rebound in 2015, Shows Data," *Decanter China*.

95 "Vin De France Renews Chinese Trade Tour with Two New Cities," Anivin De France trade blog, July 13, 2016, http://www.vindefrance-cepages.org/blog/en/2015/07/13/vin-de-france-renews-chinese-trade-tour-with-two-new-cities/, accessed March 2016.

96 Geoffrey Dean, "Bordeaux to Launch First Global Marketing Campaign to Address Falling Sales," *Harpers Wine & Spirit*, October 16, 2014, http://www.harpers.co.uk/news/bordeaux-to-launch-first-global-marketing-campaign-to-address-falling-sales/372600.article, accessed March 2016.

97 Dean, "Bordeaux to Launch First Global Marketing Campaign to Address Falling Sales."

98 "Wine in China," June 2015, Euromonitor International, accessed December 2015.

99 Angus Grigg, "Treasury Wine Estates Eyes 'Big' Growth in China," *Australian Financial Review*, June 22, 2015, http://www.afr.com/business/retail/fmcg/treasury-wine-estates-eyes-big-growth-in-china-20150622-ghucat#ixzz41wqOKQ8m, accessed March 2016.

100 Simon Evans, "Booming China Sales Have Corks Popping at Treasury Wines," *Sydney Morning Herald*, February 18, 2016, http://www.smh.com.au/business/retail/booming-china-sales-have-corks-popping-at-treasury-wine-20160217-gmwqng#ixzz41wkiNe8V, accessed March 2016.

101 Grigg, "Treasury Wine Estates Eyes 'Big' Growth in China."

102 Simon Evans, "Optimism Flows as Wine Exports Climb to Best since 2007 on $A Drop," *Sydney Morning Herald*, October 16, 2015, http://www.smh.com.au/business/the-economy/optimism-flows-as-wine-exports-climb-to-best-since-2007-on-a-drop-20151015-gkal2z, accessed March 2016.

2014 to 2015, its wine exports to China grew 66% to reach A$370 million (€250 million), while the value of bottle wine exports averaged A$6.41 (€4.34) per liter.[103] Indeed, some expected it to overtake the UK as Australia's second-largest export market.[104]

In 2015, China also became the top destination of Australia's premium wine exports, confirmed by the fact that Penfold's Bin 407 was vying for top position among China's imports.[105] Compared to France's Lafite, Bin 407 was considered more affordable yet still prestigious and high quality. With new high-status images and portfolios spanning many price segments, Penfolds and its Australian counterparts were poised to battle France for dominance in the large, growing, and fast-changing Chinese market. The global wine wars were entering a new phase.

[103] Wine Australia, "Export Report–Moving Annual Total (MAT) to December 2015," pp. 6, 7.

[104] Chris Mercer, "China Set to Overtake UK for Australian Wine," *Decanter*, February 3, 2016, http://www .decanter.com/wine-news/australian-wine-in-china-exports-2015-289862/, accessed February 2016.

[105] Terry Xu, "The Chinese Distributor's Dilemma," *Decanter China*, May 11, 2016, https://www .decanterchina.com/en/columns/xiao-pi-words-of-wine/the-chinese-distributors-dilemma, accessed May 2016.

IVEY | Publishing

Gordon Institute of Business Science
University of Pretoria

CASE 2.2 MTN AND THE NIGERIAN FINE[1]

On October 26, 2015, South African telecommunications group MTN saw its share price drop by more than 12 per cent after receiving an enormous fine from the Nigerian Communications Commission (NCC). MTN advised shareholders on the Johannesburg Securities Exchange Stock Exchange News Service (SENS):

> The NCC has imposed a fine equivalent to US $5.2 billion[2] on MTN Nigeria. This fine relates to the timing of the disconnection of 5.1 million MTN Nigeria subscribers who were

[1] This case has been written on the basis of published sources only. Consequently, the interpretation and perspectives presented in this case are not necessarily those of MTN or any of its employees.

[2] All currency amounts are in US$ unless otherwise specified.

disconnected in August and September 2015, and is based on a fine of ₦200,000[3] for each unregistered subscriber. MTN Nigeria is currently in discussions with the NCC to resolve the matter in recognition of the circumstances that prevailed with regard to these subscribers. We will continue to update shareholders in this regard.[4]

MTN's subscriber base had been almost entirely prepaid since entering Nigeria in 2001, and about 99 per cent were anonymous until 2011, when Nigerian authorities introduced legislation requiring mobile telecommunications operators to register all users on a central database.

The fine was equivalent to about 20 per cent of MTN's market capitalization and more than MTN's 2014 revenue from its affiliate in Nigeria, which was about $4 billion.[5] Insiders at MTN believed that the fine was less about the regulatory issues than about the Nigerian government's need to raise cash due to falling revenues from oil, as well as security concerns about Boko Haram Islamist militants using the MTN network. The Boko Haram movement had killed more than 30,000 people from 2009 to 2015 through attacks on mosques, churches, political rallies, polling stations, schools, bus stations, and marketplaces.[6]

MTN appeared surprised by the extent of the fine and declared that it had always conducted its business in accordance with established principles related to sound corporate governance. However, its main shareholder, the Public Investment Corporation of South Africa, which managed the state pension funds, did not agree; its chief executive said, "MTN should have handled it better from the outset. I don't expect this to be a surprise. I am worried because there is a lot at stake for shareholders to lose in terms of value."[7] How could MTN, an emerging-market multinational enterprise that operated in some of the riskiest countries, and that had operated in Nigeria since 2001, find itself in this situation? What should it do now?

MTN

MTN was a South African telecommunications company with operations in 22 countries, 21,000 employees, and 232.5 million subscribers in Africa and the Middle East.[8] The company had an annual turnover of $11.55 billion in 2015. In 2015, MTN was the best-known telecommunications brand on the African continent, and was recognized as a best brand in Nigeria, even ahead of Coca-Cola (see Exhibit 1).[9]

Founded in 1994 as one of two mobile telecommunications operator licensees in South Africa, MTN began its first forays into the rest of Africa in 1997, acquiring licences in Uganda, Rwanda, and Swaziland. At the time, MTN was receiving ISO 9001 and 14001 accreditation for its operations in South Africa. In 2000, it acquired a licence in Cameroon (its first non-Anglophone country). In 2001, it expanded into Nigeria. By 2005, MTN had 14 million subscribers, of which 8 million were in South Africa, and in the same year, it acquired a licence to operate in Iran. In 2006, MTN acquired the Investcom LLC group for $5.5 billion, and by 2015, it had subscribers in countries such as

[3] ₦ = NGN = Nigerian naira; US$1 = ₦199.271 on October 26, 2015.

[4] "SENS Note 26 October 2015," www.profile.co.za/irsites/mtngroup/archive/259615.htm.

[5] Andrew England and William Wallis, "MTN Shares Plunge after $5.2bn Fine by Nigerian Regulators," *The Financial Times*, October 26, 2015, accessed February 2, 2017, https://www.ft.com/content/ef26f4b2-7bfd-11e5-98fb-5a6d4728f74e.

[6] "In Figures: All Boko Haram Attacks in 2015," *The Cable*, December 28, 2015, accessed February 2, 2017, https://www.thecable.ng/path-of-a-ruthless-killer-all-boko-haram-deaths-in-2015.

[7] Andrew England, "MTN Hits Back Over $5.2bn Nigeria Fine," *The Financial Times*, November 3, 2015, accessed February 2, 2017, https://www.ft.com/content/fc24c7a6-821b-11e5-8095-ed1a37d1e096.

[8] MTN, *Integrated Report for the Year Ended 31 December 2015*, accessed February 2, 2017, https://www.mtn.com/MTN%20Service%20Detail%20Annual%20Reports/1IAR.pdf.

[9] Andrea Ayemoba, "MTN Nigeria Named Most Valued Brand in the Country," Africa Business Communities, November 22, 2016, accessed February 2, 2017, http://africabusinesscommunities.com/news/mtn-nigeria-named-most-valued-brand-in-the-country.html

Exhibit 1
MTN Subscribers, June 2015

Country	Number of Subscribers (thousands), June 2015	World Economic Forum (WEF) Global Competitiveness Index Ranking, 2016 (out of 138 countries)*
South Africa	28,504	47
Nigeria	62,813	127
Ghana	14,886	114
Cameroon	10,363	119
Ivory Coast	8,488	99
Uganda	11,146	113
Syria	5,765	N/A
Sudan	8,757	N/A
Yemen	5,239	138
Benin	3,913	124
Afghanistan	6,487	N/A
Congo-Brazzaville	2,128	N/A
Rwanda	3,958	52
Zambia	4,901	118
Liberia	1,300	131
Guinea Conakry	3,485	N/A
Cyprus	354	83
Guinea Bissau	705	N/A
South Sudan	982	N/A
Iran	44,146	76
Botswana	1,784	64
Swaziland	892	N/A
Total subscribers	**230,996**	

Note: * Not all countries included in the WEF list.
Source: MTN financial statements for 2015 and WEF Global Competitiveness Index.

Afghanistan, Sudan, Syria, and Yemen. MTN's expansion strategy was to leverage its scale and large footprint across Africa to provide competitive prices and respond to changes in the market through the rapid introduction of new services and products.

MTN's success in Africa and the Middle East was largely attributable to its ability to operate in some of the world's toughest markets. It had a track record of successfully running operations in war-torn countries such as Iran, Afghanistan, Nigeria, Sudan, and Ivory Coast. MTN had managed to be the dominant telecommunications provider in 15 of the 22 countries in which it

operated, and by 2015, its operations were well established and profitable. In some countries, its operations could be regarded as mature, but developing-country challenges remained. In 2015, MTN had to deal with the Ebola crisis in West Africa.[10] The Ebola outbreak and war impacted operations through limiting travel and hindering the ability to repair cellular towers. However, MTN managed to operate through this largely unhindered with the exception of isolated

[10] MTN, *Integrated Report for the Year Ended 31 December 2015*, op. cit.

closures of service centres, and the rerouting of calls and data when cellular tower sites could not be reached.[11]

The success of MTN's approach was dependent on the implementation of a prepaid subscription model. MTN developed the prepaid model during the 1990s to overcome the complexities of billing customers who did not have bank accounts or who did not engage in the formal financial services sector. This led to MTN handling vast amounts of cash in Nigeria, and MTN eventually developed appropriate cash-handling and security abilities that rivalled those of most Nigerian banks.

MTN's operating model evolved over time, as some countries matured quicker than others. When MTN initially entered a market such as Nigeria, it was met with limited competition and the way to gain market share was simply to build a reliable network that covered the whole country as quickly as possible. Customers would use the network if it was reliable and they were willing to pay a premium for services. Early users were predominantly voice users. As the market became more mature, subscribers would begin to use data services more than voice services. Later, data services would be driven by Internet access. The most mature markets (South Africa and Iran) were hardly using voice services, had smartphones, and were using data to access the Internet. In Africa, the use of data was especially prevalent, as a mobile phone was the only way a large number of Africans could access the Internet.

This, in turn, led to customers focusing on network maintenance and quality and putting pressure on MTN's network capacity.[12] These pressures were not unusual for a network provider but were significantly more complex in emerging countries, where infrastructure was not as prevalent as it was in developed countries.

For example, MTN would have to provide electricity-generation capabilities in large parts of its network and also engage with the local communities to protect power generators and electrical equipment from theft by locals who did not have access to these utilities in their homes. MTN's top identified risks recognized this evolving operating environment (see Exhibit 2). MTN's strategy reflected its focus on creating shareholder value through innovation and the sharing of best practices across the Group. Key to achieving this strategy was efficient asset utilization, quality back-office systems and processes, and the sharing of best practices and innovations (see Exhibit 3).

In 2014, the South African and Nigerian operations accounted for almost 65 per cent of MTN's revenues and the chief executive officers (CEOs) of these operations reported directly to Sifiso Dabengwa, the Group CEO. Dabengwa had restructured MTN in line with the strategy. The other country operations were clustered into a large opco (operating company) cluster and a small opco cluster (see Exhibit 4).

MTN in Nigeria

MTN Nigeria was 75.81 per cent owned by MTN International, 18.7 per cent by Nigerian investors, 2.78 per cent by the Mobile Telephone Networks NIC B.V. (an MTN subsidiary in the Netherlands), and 2.71 per cent by Shanduka, a South African investment group founded by Cyril Ramaphosa, who would later become the deputy president of South Africa. MTN entered the Nigerian market in 2001, when it secured one of four licences for $285 million for an initial 15-year period. The first call on the network was made on May 16, 2001, and business operations commenced in August 2001. By February 10, 2003, MTN had 1 million active subscribers in Nigeria. This active subscriber base would eventually exceed 55 million Nigerian users serviced through 15 service centres, 144 MTN Connect Stores, and 247 MTN Connect Points.

MTN had invested more than $15 billion in infrastructure in Nigeria up to 2015 to build a network that covered almost 90 per cent of

[11] "MTN Group Limited Integrated Report 2015," MTN, accessed February 2, 2017, www.mtn-investor.com/mtn_ar2015/ebook/files/assets/basic-html/page-1.html#.

[12] MTN, *Integrated Report for the Year Ended 31 December 2015*, op. cit.

Exhibit 2
MTN's Top Risks and Mitigation Strategies, 2014

Top 5 Identified Risks	Mitigation Strategies
1. Network performance: • Dropped calls due to network constraints • Capital investment does not keep up with demand on the network • Customers migrate to other operators due to dissatisfaction with service quality	• Continuous monitoring of networks for quality, coverage, and demand • Standardization and optimization of systems and processes to reduce costs and focus on core activities • Outsourcing non-core activities • Reducing roll-out costs through the establishment of tower companies • Exploring energy-efficient hybrid power solutions to reduce costs and reliance on grid electricity
2. Create and maintain a competitive advantage: • Changing market conditions threaten market share and revenue streams • Need to provide new services at competitive prices	• Implement a digital strategy with broader service offerings • Effectively manage costs to offset the impact of slowing revenue growth • Build and maintain appropriate skills to roll out new technologies at the correct price
3. Adverse regulatory changes or non-compliance with laws and regulations: • Managing the complexity of 22 jurisdictions • Increased regulatory/legal changes impact negatively on revenues	• Continuous, proactive, and transparent engagement with authorities at Group and country operating company (opco) levels • Closely monitor compliance with the tax risk management framework • Regular review of mitigation strategies developed through tax risk registers at all MTN opcos
4. Financial performance targets: • Changes in the markets are slowing down revenue growth, which threatens earnings before interest, tax, depreciation, and amortization (EBITDA) margins • Lack of operational efficiency as competition intensifies impact on profitability • Currency exposure impacts on reported results and increases costs of servicing foreign denominated obligations	• Cost-saving initiatives and stricter controls on spending • Sale of non-core assets (such as towers) • A local currency funding strategy, which includes principles on gearing and repatriation of cash • Active management of foreign-denominated assets and liabilities to minimize the impact of translation effects
5. Compromised information security: • Increased cyberattacks worldwide • Lack of an effective Group-wide information security program could lead to reputational damage and the loss of customers, in turn impacting revenue and margins	• Establish a security forum with representation from opcos to monitor information security controls • Program and policies to instil ethical behaviour

Source: Adapted from *MTN Integrated Report*, 2014.

Exhibit 3
MTN's Strategy

"MTN's strategy is built around five strategic themes: **Creating and managing stakeholder value** and **innovation and best practice** sharing describe our approach to our work, people and other stakeholders. Tangible priorities under **creating a distinct customer experience**, **driving sustainable growth**, and **transforming our operating model** define how we strive to secure a sustainable competitive advantage and deliver superior shareholder returns."

Strategic Priorities	Target for 2015
Creating and managing stakeholder value: • Sustainable shareholder returns • Responsible corporate citizenship • Creating a great place to work • Sound governance and values	• 5% to 15% dividend growth • Opportunistic share buy-backs • Increase positive media sentiment by 4% from 2014 baseline • Statistical improvement on vital behaviours in the Group culture audit
Creating a distinct customer experience: • Brand leadership • Customer experience • Customer analytics • Network quality and coverage	• Net promoter score improvements • 7.5 million net additions • Implement core-managed services strategy
Driving sustainable growth: • MTN in digital space • Adjacent sectors • Enterprise strategy • Voice and data evolution • Mergers and acquisitions (M&A) and partnerships	• Grow MTN mobile money in smaller markets • Increase new revenue streams—target $2.4 billion • Grow enterprise business unit revenue by 30% year-on-year • M&A and partnerships
Transforming the operating model: • Asset optimization • Supply chain management • Process standardization and optimization	• Group EBITDA margin of 44.6% • Realization of transformation benefits • Improve procurement savings of more than 7% • Improve capital investment efficiency and effectiveness in both South Africa and Nigeria
Innovation and best practices • Innovation • Sharing best practices	• Security framework rolled out and adopted into standard applications • Digital readiness for services migration and deployment

Source: Adapted from *MTN Integrated Report*, 2015.

Nigeria's landmass, including 3,340 cities, towns, and villages across the country. MTN Nigeria had also commissioned the world's largest network switch centre in Lagos in 2010. This expansion was supported by sophisticated marketing campaigns with carefully targeted sponsorships and highly publicized corporate social investment programs. MTN had invested

Exhibit 4 MTN's Organizational Structure, 2014

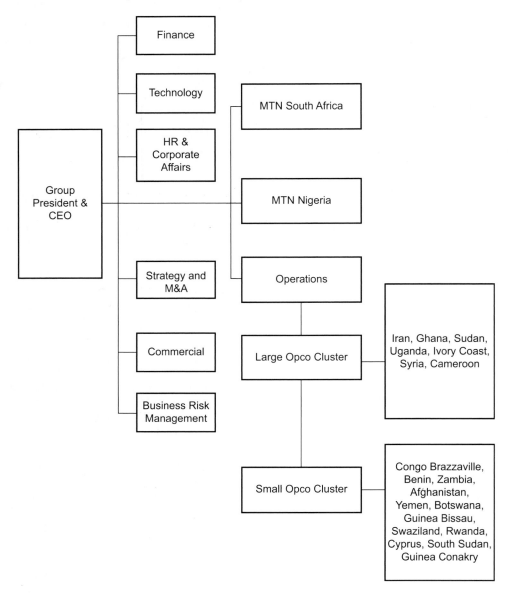

Source: MTN Annual Financial Statement, 2014.

over \$32 million in 338 sustainable projects spanning the education, health, and economic empowerment sectors.[13]

[13] "Corporate Information," MTN, www.mtnonline.com/about-mtn/corporate-information. Note: This citation refers to the previous two paragraphs.

The Nigerian Telecommunications Market

The Nigerian telecommunications sector had been dominated by a state-owned monopoly, Nigerian Telecommunications Limited (NITEL), until 1999, when the government decided to deregulate the sector. Although the Nigerian telecommunications sector had been in existence since the late

1800s, it was characterized by inadequate capacity, an inability to generate much revenue, and poor facility maintenance. As a consequence, NITEL was underfunded and unable to respond quickly to new technologies.[14]

By the mid-1990s, the Nigerian telecommunications sector consisted of 780,000 fixed lines, 10,000 cellular mobile telephones (mostly the outdated code division multiplexing (CDM) technology), and 15,000 voicemail lines. The only digital exchanges in the country were in 47 local government buildings. Nigeria's telephone penetration rate was about eight lines per 1,000 citizens in 1994, and the waiting time for a line was more than 10 years. Cellular telephones were first introduced in 1992, with the formation of Mobile Telecommunications Service (MTS, which would later become MTEL, Mobile Telecommunications Ltd.), a joint venture between NITEL and Digital Communications of Atlanta. MTS had an initial installed capacity of 10,000 lines, but this was exceeded within its first year, and extended to 50,000 lines by the mid-1990s. However, network congestion severely affected the quality of service.[15]

Deregulation

In 1999, the Nigerian government decided to deregulate the telecommunications sector with the auction of three Global System for Mobile Communications (GSM) licences, of which MTN successfully won one. The other two were won by Communications Investments Ltd. (CIL) and Econet Wireless Nigeria. A fourth licence was reserved for MTEL, the mobile arm of the state-owned NITEL.[16]

CIL was a consortium led by Nigerian billionaire Mike Adenuga, but due to a dispute, he was not able to pay the required deposit in time and the licence was revoked. Adenuga would successfully lead another consortium to launch Globacom Limited (Globacom) in 2003, when the Nigerian government conducted a second auction.[17] Globacom would use its Nigerian base to expand into Benin and Ghana, and would become the second-largest operator in Nigeria after MTN.

Econet Wireless Nigeria (ECN) was owned by the Econet Wireless Group, a privately held company with operations in Zimbabwe and Botswana. ECN was a partnership between Econet Wireless Group, Nigerian state government departments, local banks, and wealthy Nigerian investors. Econet Wireless Group was contracted to manage ECN, but this changed when Nigerian shareholders voted it out in 2004. According to the CEO of Econet Wireless Group, this was due to the Group's refusal to pay bribes and facilitation fees to government officials and politically connected individuals.[18] Econet Wireless Group was then replaced by Vodacom from South Africa as the main operator in the consortium. This also lasted a few months, at which time Vodacom abruptly ended its association with the group (later named Vee Networks Limited) amidst rumours of the payment of bribes to Nigerian government officials. Vodacom dismissed its Nigerian CEO and withdrew from Nigeria entirely.[19] Vee Networks was renamed Vmobile and bought by Celtel International in 2006. Celtel was an international company that

14 Nigerian Communications Commission, *Strategic Management Plan (SMP) 2014–2018*, accessed February 2, 2017, www.ncc.gov.ng/docman-main/industry-statistics/research-reports/624-strategic-management-plan-smp-2014-2018/file.

15 "Nigeria: After a Century of Telecommunications Development, What Next?" Chapter 9, in Eli M. Noam, *Telecommunications in Africa* (Oxford: Oxford University Press, 1999).

16 Chris Doyle and Paul McShane, *On the Design and Implementation of the GSM Auction in Nigeria – the World's First Ascending Clock Spectrum Auction* (September 3, 2001), accessed February 2, 2017, https://www.itu.int/osg/spu/ni/3G/resources/licensing_policy/cd_pm-CRA%20UK-2001Aug29.pdf.

17 "I Didn't Default in Payment of 2001 GSM Licence," *Technology Times*, October 7, 2012, accessed February 2, 2017, http://technologytimes.ng/archives-adenuga-i-didnt-default-in-payment-of-2001-gsm-licence.

18 Muyiwa Matuluko, "Econet Founder Reveals Story Behind Company's Downfall in Nigeria," *Techpoint.ng*, October 6, 2015, accessed February 2, 2017, https://techpoint.ng/2015/10/06/econet-founder-reveals-story-behind-companys-downfall-in-nigeria.

19 Rodney Weidemann, "Vodacom Exit 'Not Due to Nigerian Corruption,'" *Web Mobile Business*, June 1, 2004, accessed February 2, 2017, www.itweb.co.za/index.php?option=com_content&view=article&id=14563.

Exhibit 5
Nigerian Telecommunications Usage, 2015

Fixed-telephone subscriptions per 100 inhabitants	0.1
Mobile-cellular subscriptions per 100 inhabitants	82.2
Mobile-broadband subscriptions per 100 inhabitants	21.0
Households with a computer (%)	9.8
Households with Internet access at home (%)	11.4
Individuals using the Internet (%)	47.4

Source: International Telecommunication Union, 2016.

had about 24 million subscribers in 14 countries across Africa at the time. The deal was worth about $1 billion and gave Celtel 65 per cent of the operator. Celtel was later acquired by the Zain Group, and eventually by the Indian company Bharti Airtel, when it became Airtel Nigeria.[20]

MTEL's fortunes were tied to those of its parent firm, NITEL. NITEL was privatized at the same time that the telecommunications industry was deregulated. A series of failed bids by interested outside parties eventually led to Pentascope from the Netherlands taking over NITEL and MTEL. This takeover was unsuccessful and after 23 months, NITEL/MTEL's connected lines dropped from 555,000 to 440,000 and the Nigerian government revoked the privatization deal. The Nigerian government then called for bidders and Transnational Corporation of Nigeria Plc, an investment company from Nigeria, took over NITEL in 2006. The deal was worth $500 million, but also failed to turn the company around. In 2012, the Nigerian government approved the guided liquidation of NITEL.[21]

Dominance of Mobile

The success of deregulating the telecommunications sector was dramatic. In 2016, there were more than 150 million active telephone lines in Nigeria, with mobile lines accounting for more than 99 per cent of those lines. Fixed lines had dropped from a peak of about 1.5 million active lines in 2007 to about 150,000 in 2016 (see Exhibit 5).[22] Mobile lines were almost entirely dominated by the four GSM network operators.[23] MTN was the largest, with an almost 40 per cent market share, and the next largest was Globacom, with an almost 25 per cent market share, followed by Airtel Nigeria and Etisalat Telecommunications Corporation, with roughly 22 per cent and 14 per cent market shares, respectively (see Exhibit 6).

The operators were under continuous pressure to reduce their prices to customers, and had to receive approval from the NCC for pricing and promotions. The average cost per minute for voice calls during peak calling times dropped from an average of ₦34.20 (or $0.27) in 2007 to ₦12.01 (or about $0.05) in 2016. At the same time, the number of Internet subscribers using the GSM network grew from about 28 million in 2012 to about 93 million in 2016.[24]

The Nigerian Economy in 2015

Nigeria was Africa's most populous country, with a population of 183 million and a gross domestic

[20] Ibukun Taiwo, "From Econet to Airtel: How Many Times Has the Telco Changed Hands?," *TechCabal*, October 6, 2015, accessed February 2, 2017, http://techcabal.com/2015/10/06/from-econet-to-airtel-how-many-times-has-the-telco-changed-hands.

[21] Anayo Ezugwu, "New Hope for NITEL/MTEL Survival," *Realnews*, November 25, 2013, accessed February 2, 2017, http://realnewsmagazine.net/business/new-hope-for-nitelmtel-survival.

[22] "Subscriber Statistics," Nigerian Communications Commission, www.ncc.gov.ng/stakeholder/statistics-reports/subscriber-data#annual-subscriber-technology-data.

[23] "Industry Statistics," Nigerian Communications Commission, accessed February 2, 2017, www.ncc.gov.ng/stakeholder/statistics-reports/industry-overview#incoming.

[24] Ibid.

Exhibit 6
Telecommunications Industry in Nigeria in November 2016

	Airtel	Etisalat	Globacom	MTN	Total
Number of subscribers	33,376,556	21,621,832	37,268,483	61,280,293	153,547,164
Market share of GSM (%)	21.74	14.08	24.27	39.91	100
Internet subscribers	19,143,700	14,132,007	27,122,892	32,017,779	92,416,378
Incoming porting*	1,111	13,428	1,381	1,572	17,492
Outgoing porting*	5,770	1,623	3,488	5,746	16,627

Note: * Porting refers to the number of transactions whereby a mobile number is transferred from one operator to another on the request of the subscriber who wishes to retain the same number. Outgoing porting refers to the number of subscribers leaving an operator; incoming are those joining the operator.
Source: Nigerian Communications Commission.

product (GDP) of $485 billion. Nigeria had had a tumultuous political history, but had returned to democracy in 1999, and since then, it had enjoyed relative political stability. Even so, political and security risks remained high, with the emergence of the radical Boko Haram group and Movement for the Emancipation of the Niger Delta (MEND) (see Exhibit 7).

The Nigerian economy was heavily dependent on the export of oil. Its exports were worth $93.55 billion in 2013, of which 95 per cent was in the form of oil and petroleum products. Nigeria's largest export markets were the United States (16.8 per cent of exports in terms of value), India (11.5 per cent), the Netherlands (8.6 per cent), and Brazil (7.6 per cent).[25] Nigeria was the 12th-largest oil producer in the world but the fifth-largest oil exporter. The country produced 2.524 million barrels of oil per day in 2012, but still imported the vast majority of refined petroleum for its economy (see Exhibit 8).[26]

In April 2014, the Nigerian Central Bank published the results of a statistical revision of its economy (a "rebasing"), which led to a redoubling of the calculated value of Nigeria's GDP. This rebasing led to Nigeria supplanting South Africa as Africa's largest economy, and its revised GDP

in 2013 was $510 billion.[27] However, this new status was short lived, and the recalculation was followed by a dramatic decline in the global oil price, from a high of $110 per barrel to less than $30 per barrel in 2015, for an average of below $50 for the year.

The impact of the decline in the oil price on the Nigerian treasury was further complicated by an investigation into billions of dollars of revenues that were unaccounted for from crude sales by the Nigerian state oil company. Nigerian National Petroleum Corporation was reported to have withheld more than $20 billion from the Nigerian government between 2012 and 2013, and there was evidence of further diverting of revenue that should have been remitted to the Nigerian government.[28]

These events were combined with the presidential elections held in March 2015, when Muhammadu Buhari beat outgoing President Goodluck Jonathan by more than 15 million votes. Buhari's campaign was essentially based on fighting corruption, defeating the Boko Haram, and developing a new economic policy that would reduce Nigeria's reliance on oil revenues. Buhari immediately began tackling corruption and dismissed

[25] "General Profile: Nigeria," UNCTAD Stat.
[26] *CIA World Factbook: Nigeria*, accessed December 30, 2016, accessed February 2, 2017, https://www.cia.gov/library/publications/the-world-factbook/geos/ni.html.
[27] "Nigeria's GDP: Step Change," *The Economist*, April 12, 2014.
[28] William Wallis, "Nigerian Audit: State Oil Company Siphoning Oil Revenues," *The Financial Times*, April 28, 2015.

Exhibit 7
Nigeria Worldwide Governance Indicators

	2010		2015	
	Estimate	Ranking	Estimate	Ranking
Voice and accountability (the extent to which a country's citizens are able to participate in selecting their government, as well as freedom of expression, freedom of association, and a free media)	−0.80	27.01	−0.44	33.00
Political stability/no violence (the absence of violence/ terrorism measures, perceptions of the likelihood of political instability, and/or politically motivated violence, including terrorism)	−2.19	3.32	−2.07	5.71
Government effectiveness (the quality of public services, the quality of the civil service and the degree of its independence from political pressures, the quality of policy formulation and implementation, and the credibility of the government's commitment to such policies)	−1.15	10.53	−0.95	16.83
Regulatory quality (the ability of the government to formulate and implement sound policies and regulations that permit and promote private-sector development)	−0.71	26.32	−0.84	21.63
Rule of law (extent to which agents have confidence in and abide by the rules of society—in particular, the quality of contract enforcement, property rights, the police, and the courts, as well as the likelihood of crime and violence)	−1.17	12.32	−1.04	12.98
Control of corruption (the extent to which public power is exercised for private gain, including both petty and grand forms of corruption, as well as "capture" of the state by elites and private interests)	−1.00	15.24	−1.10	11.06

Note: Estimate ranges from −2.5 (weak) to 2.5 (strong); rank is the percentile rank among all countries and ranges from 0 (lowest) to 100 (highest rank).
Source: World Bank Worldwide Governance Indicators.

large numbers of senior public servants, diplomats, and officials in the state oil corporation.[29]

The contribution of the telecommunications industry to the Nigerian economy was not as large as that of the oil industry, but was still significant. During 2012 to 2014, the contribution to GDP was below 8 per cent, but the contribution grew in 2015 to more than 8 per cent, and was almost 10 per cent by 2016.[30] However, the Nigerian economy entered a recession in 2016, with the economy shrinking by 0.4 per cent in the first quarter of 2016, and shrinking a further 2.1 per cent in the second quarter. The International Monetary Fund (IMF) predicted that the Nigerian

[29] "Nigeria's Government: At Work at Last," *The Economist*, November 21, 2015.

[30] "Porting Data–Incoming," Nigerian Communications Commission, accessed February 2, 2017, www.ncc.gov.ng/stakeholder/statistics-reports/ industry-overview#incoming.

Exhibit 8
Nigeria's Economic Trends

Indicator	2010	2011	2012	2013	2014	2015
GDP in millions of US$*	369,062	411,744	460,954	514,965	568,499	525,220
GDP growth rate (%)*	7.84	4.89	4.28	5.39	6.31	2.86
Annualized inflation rate (%)*	13.7	10.8	12.2	8.5	8.1	9
Federal government revenues (₦ in billions)**	2,839	4,628	5,007	4,805	4,714	3,741
Foreign direct investment flow in US$ millions*	6,099	8,915	7,127	5,608	4,694	3,064
Fuel exports (in US$ millions at current prices)***	72,969	87,839	93,492	89,930	77,489	39,318
Annual oil (OPEC Basket Price) US$****	77.45	107.46	109.45	105.87	96.29	49.49
Contribution of telecoms industry to GDP*****	8.9%	8.6%	7.7%	7.4%	7.6%	8.5%

Sources: * UNCTAD; ** Chartered Institute of Management Accountants Nairametrics; *** World Trade Organization; **** Organization of the Petroleum Exporting Countries; ***** Nigerian Communications Commission.

economy would shrink by 1.8 per cent in 2016.[31] The economic crisis caused many multinationals operating in Nigeria to reconsider their investments, and local suppliers were reduced to buying hard currencies at black-market rates when dollars were not available on the official foreign currency market.[32]

The Fine—October 2015

In 2008, the Nigerian security agencies approached the NCC for assistance in dealing with criminals and terrorists who used mobile phones. In response, the NCC launched a registration program in 2010 that ran until 2013 to document and register all existing subscriber identity module (SIM) cards. The GSM required users to use a SIM card in their mobile phones. The SIM card (or subscriber identity module card) was a removable card that stored user-specific data about the network, telephone number, and messages. The SIM registration required biometric information such as photographs and fingerprints, and was supported by a national campaign with the establishment of registration centres in the large cities.[33] The regulations meant that everybody who used a SIM card had to personally register so that their fingerprints and picture could be taken. Fingerprint scanners were not widely available in Nigeria at the time. Many Nigerians preferred not to register their personal details on a national register, or were apathetic about physically visiting a registration centre. Physically capturing subscribers' personal details also required operators to roll out facilities to remote areas that lacked power and infrastructure, and had high levels of social apathy and terrorist activity.[34]

Registrations were confounded by several practices to circumvent the registration by locals. These practices included dealers "pre-registering" SIM cards and then on-selling them at a premium, and agents charging fees for registering customers and network operators registering

[31] Maggie Fick, "IMF Forecasts Nigerian Economy Will Contract by 1.8% This Year," *The Financial Times*, July 19, 2016.
[32] Maggie Fick, "Multinationals Say Nigeria's Dollar Crunch Is Hurting Business," *The Financial Times*, February 29, 2016.

[33] Nigerian Communications Commission Regulations, 2011, Government Notice 229.
[34] MTN, *Integrated Report for the Year Ended 31 December 2015*, op. cit.

users from other networks as their own sub-scribers.[35] Pre-registered SIM cards were difficult to resolve, as network operators had the details of the dealer on their register, but not the end user.

The first registration initiative enjoyed limited success and expired on June 30, 2013. The NCC blamed the lack of success on the network oper-ators and fined them for 146 pre-registered cards that the NCC had acquired in enforcement activ-ities.[36] All four operators were fined, and MTN's fine was ₦29.2 million (or $184,000), with an additional ₦500,000 ($3,100) per day if it failed to settle the penalty within seven days.

The second registration initiative began on June 30, 2013, when the NCC instructed all operators to immediately deactivate all unregistered SIM cards on their networks, including the ability to make and receive calls or send and receive text mes-sages. All operators were to provide the NCC with a summary of registered and active lines on their network as at June 30, 2013 (although the NCC was supposed to already have this information). In addition, operators were instructed to forward the personal details and biometric information of new subscribers weekly so that these could be entered into a central database. The NCC would also begin random checks and test calls on unregistered and deactivated SIM cards to ensure compliance. It would also conduct physical audits of Home Loca-tion Register log files of operators to reconfirm the numbers of active and deactivated lines in the networks based on submissions received from the operators themselves.[37] The second initiative created some confusion, with customers believing that they were correctly registered but finding their lines blocked. Operators were inundated with customers trying to validate their details.

Further fines were imposed on all the network operators for registration-related activities. In June 2015, the NCC fined MTN ₦7 million ($35,000), Airtel ₦5.6 million ($28,000), Globa-com ₦6.4 million ($32,000), and Etisalat ₦6.2 mil-lion ($31,000) for the sale of pre-registered SIM cards. The NCC also instructed the operators to "mop up" all pre-registered SIM cards from the Nigerian market within 21 days, and stipulated that upon expiration of the 21 days, the operators would be fined for every pre-registered SIM card.[38] Mopping up was the process whereby the operator suspended a subscriber's services until they had visited a registration centre and had their correct details registered. The NCC had asked the operators to suspend 37 million SIM cards from their networks after discovering that about 45 per cent of the cards were incorrectly registered and needed revalidation. Of these, 18.6 million were MTN numbers. By the end of August 2015, the NCC claimed that MTN had only removed 1.6 million of those telephone numbers.[39] Operators claimed that they were still in discussions with the NCC about the exact number of unregistered sub-scribers when the deadline passed, and so were under the impression that the matter was still being resolved and that they did not need to take immediate decisive action yet.[40]

In the third quarter of 2015, the NCC advised that the four operators had paid a combined fine amounting to ₦40 million ($200,000) for sales of pre-registered SIM cards. MTN's portion of the fine was ₦21.8 million ($109,000). But it was

[35] Patrick Cairns, "The Background to MTN's Fine in Nigeria," *Moneyweb*, October 29, 2015, accessed February 2, 2017, www.moneyweb.co.za/news/companies-and-deals/the-background-to-mtns-fine-in-nigeria.

[36] Nigerian Communications Commission, *Summary of the Commission's Compliance Monitoring and Enforcement Activities for Quarter 2, 2013*, accessed February 2, 2017, www.ncc.gov.ng/docman-main/legal-regulatory/legal-enforcement/400-enforcement-activities-summary-2013-q2/file.

[37] Ibid.

[38] Nigerian Communications Commission, *Summary of the Commission's Compliance Monitoring and Enforcement Activities for Quarter Two (2), 2015*, accessed February 2, 2017, www.ncc.gov.ng/docman-main/legal-regulatory/legal-enforcement/663-compliance-monitoring-and-enforcement-report-2015-q2/file.

[39] Bankole Orija, "NCC Fines GSM Firms ₦120.4m for Unregistered SIM Cards," *Nigeria Communications Week*, September 1, 2015, accessed February 2, 2017, www.nigeriacommunicationsweek.com.ng/telecom/ncc-fines-gsm-firms-n1204m-for-unregistered-sim-cards.

[40] Patrick Cairns, "The Background to MTN's Fine in Nigeria," *Moneyweb*, October 29, 2015, accessed February 2, 2017, www.moneyweb.co.za/news/companies-and-deals/the-background-to-mtns-fine-in-nigeria.

clear that the NCC was focusing on MTN in the third quarter of 2015, when MTN was fined a further ₦80.4 million ($402,000) for the failure to deactivate 402 registrations that were either incompletely or improperly registered, and none of the other operators were sanctioned.[41] An enforcement team from the NCC visited MTN from September 2 to 4, 2015, at which time MTN admitted that 5.1 million improperly registered SIM cards remained active on its network.[42] The NCC then sent MTN a letter on October 5, giving MTN notice to state why it should not be sanctioned in line with the regulations for failure to deactivate improperly registered SIM cards active at the time of the NCC visit in September. MTN failed to convince the NCC about its reasons for failing to deactivate the SIM cards, and was fined ₦1.4 trillion ($5.2 billion) on October 20.[43] MTN was the only operator that received a fine for pre-registration this time around.[44]

MTN Reacts

Within a month, MTN's long-term credit rating had been downgraded by both Standard & Poor's and Moody's to BBB− and negative Baa2, respectively.[45] This was followed by the resignation of MTN's CEO, Dabengwa, on November 9, 2015, and the appointment of the chairman of the board, Phuthuma Nhleko, as the acting CEO while remaining chairman.[46] Dabengwa had been the head of MTN Nigeria from 2004 to 2006, and later became the chief operating officer of MTN Group, reporting to Nhleko, who was CEO at the time. Dabengwa had succeeded Nhleko as CEO in 2011, when Nhleko became chairman of the MTN Group.

There was speculation that the size of the fine was due to pressure on the Nigerian government to fill a revenue gap left by lower oil prices.[47] The $5.2 billion fine represented 20 per cent of forecasted expenditure and more than 60 per cent of forecast revenues for the Nigerian central government in 2015.[48] The extent of the fine was questioned by many industry analysts, who felt that it was excessive.[49] It was the largest fine any telecommunications company had been fined anywhere in the world at the time. The next-largest fine was the $100 million fine that the U.S. Federal Communications Commission had imposed on AT&T.[50] Concerns were also raised by analysts that the fine had been imposed shortly before MTN was due to negotiate the renewal of its 15-year operating licence. (The NCC did, however, approve the renewal of MTN's licence on November 2, 2015. The extension would allow MTN to operate in Nigeria until August 2021, for $94.2 million.)

Concerns were also raised that the size of the fine would impact MTN's ability to invest in the market and would scare away future investment in Nigeria.[51] However, the NCC defended the fine by stating that MTN had ignored other Nigerian rules and had committed a total of 28 infractions.

[41] "Compliance Monitoring and Enforcement Report 2015 Q3," Nigerian Communications Commission, accessed February 2, 2017, www.ncc.gov.ng/licensing-regulatory/legal/enforcement.

[42] "SIM Deactivation: How MTN Shunned Our 'Small' Fine," The Whistler, November 16, 2015, accessed February 2, 2017, https://thewhistler.ng/story/sim-deactivation-how-mtn-shunned-our-small-fine-ncc.

[43] "Compliance Monitoring and Enforcement Report 2015 Q4," Nigerian Communications Commission, accessed February 2, 2017, www.ncc.gov.ng/licensing-regulatory/legal/enforcement.

[44] Ibid.

[45] "SENS Note 30 October 2015," accessed February 2, 2017, www.profile.co.za/irsites/mtngroup/archive/259932.htm.

[46] "SENS Note 9 November 2015," accessed February 2, 2017, www.profile.co.za/irsites/mtngroup/archive/260485.htm.

[47] Christopher Spillane, James Batty, and Paul Wallace, "Four Charts That Show Why MTN's Nigerian Fine Matters So Much," Bloomberg, November 1, 2015, accessed February 2, 2017, https://www.bloomberg.com/news/articles/2015-11-02/four-charts-that-show-why-mtn-s-nigerian-fine-matters-so-much.

[48] Ibid.

[49] "Nigeria's $5.2bn Fine Against MTN Is 'World's Largest,'" fin24tech, November 20, 2015, accessed February 2, 2017, www.fin24.com/Tech/News/nigerias-52bn-fine-against-mtn-is-worlds-largest-20151120.

[50] Ibid.

[51] Paul Wallace and Yinka Ibukun, "Nigeria Risks Investment It Can't Afford to Lose with MTN Fine," Bloomberg, October 29, 2015, accessed February 2, 2017, https://www.bloomberg.com/news/articles/2015-10-29/nigeria-risks-investment-it-can-t-afford-to-lose-with-mtn-fine.

Tony Ojobo, the spokesperson of the NCC, asked, "Are investors not supposed to respect the laws of the land where they are operating? It is in accordance with our regulations and guidelines that if service providers don't comply they'll face a penalty."[52]

The fine was due on November 16, and MTN's chairman, Nhleko, immediately flew into Nigeria to engage with the Nigerian authorities to reduce the fine or delay its payment. The Nigerian government's response was that it was open to engaging with MTN before the November 16 deadline, but that it was MTN's responsibility to come up with proposals for the Nigerian government to consider. According to the communications minister, the law had to be followed and there had to be consequences, but nobody wanted MTN to leave Nigeria.[53] On November 16, MTN announced that although talks were ongoing, the Nigerian government had agreed, without prejudice, that the fine would not be imposed until talks had been concluded.[54] MTN acknowledged that it should have responded quicker to the regulator but pointed out that compliance with the regulator's conditions meant implementing biometric standards akin to U.S. immigration and Federal Bureau of Investigation standards in a country that had little infrastructure or equipment to do this. MTN spent more than $20 million on equipment and staff to comply. It suffered a further blow when the NCC suspended its regulatory services. This meant that the NCC withdrew approval of new tariff plans and promotions, which were linked to its determination of MTN as a "dominant operator" in the Nigerian market.[55]

---

[52] Ibid.

[53] Julia Payne and Camillus Eboh, "Nigeria Does Not Want MTN 'to Die' from $5.2 Bln Fine," *Yahoo*, November 13, 2015, accessed February 2, 2017, https://www.yahoo.com/news/nigeria-does-not-want-mtn-die-5-2-121103333-finance.html?ref=gs.

[54] "Update to Shareholders and Further Cautionary Announcement," MTN, November 16, 2015, accessed February 2, 2017, https://www.mtn.com/en/mtn-group/press-and-insights/press-releases/Pages/h-press-release-detail.aspx?queryString=67.

[55] MTN, *Integrated Report for the Year Ended 31 December 2015*, op. cit.

⬚IVEY | Publishing

CASE 2.3 IMAX: EXPANSION IN BRIC ECONOMIES[1] (REVISED)

Dwarka Chakravarty wrote this case under the supervision of Professor Paul W. Beamish solely to provide material for class discussion. The authors do not intend to illustrate either effective or ineffective handling of a managerial situation. The authors may have disguised certain names and other identifying information to protect confidentiality.

In September 2013, Richard Gelfond, chief executive officer of IMAX Corporation (IMAX), declared that the route to becoming a billion-dollar company lay in growth markets outside

[1] This case has been written on the basis of published sources only. Consequently, the interpretation and perspectives presented in this case are not necessarily those of IMAX Corporation or any of its employees.

of North America.[2] This was no "blue sky envisioning," but a pragmatic view grounded in facts. These included competition from U.S. exhibitors offering an "IMAX-like" experience, and a flat five year box office trend in North America versus double digit growth in Asia Pacific and Latin America. In 2013, for the first time in four decades, IMAX aggregate revenue from 56 countries outside of the United States and Canada ($151 million,[3] 10 per cent growth from 2012) exceeded North American revenues ($137 million, 6.5 per cent decline from 2012).

Since 2000, emerging markets, led by Brazil, Russia, India and China (the BRIC nations) had fuelled global gross domestic product (GDP) growth. China was foremost on IMAX's radar, with screens growing from one in 2001 to 221 in 2014, making it the second largest IMAX market after the United States (see Exhibit 1). IMAX had far fewer screens in other BRIC countries with 11 in Brazil, 36 in Russia, and eight in India. How should IMAX allocate its future expansion by country in the BRIC economies?

A Brief History of IMAX

Headquartered in Missisauga, Canada, IMAX (an abbreviation of Image Maximum) became synonymous with large-screen, high-quality cinematic experiences. IMAX was conceived during EXPO 1967 in Montreal, Canada, when a small group of Canadian filmmakers developed a method to show a film across multiple screens, using a single powerful projector. The resulting IMAX system revolutionized cinema by projecting movies on a large curved screen, creating an immersive experience. Initial movies were nature documentaries, e.g., *Grand Canyon*—funded by the National Science Foundation and the National Film Board of Canada. These were shot on IMAX cameras, with films 10 times larger than the regular 35mm, and shown on huge

museum screens 20+ metres tall and 30+ metres wide, using special high-intensity projectors. The system was proprietary, capital-intensive, and hard to scale. In the 1990s, IMAX began licensing its technology. Commercial theatres had to pay $2 million for equipment, and spend $3 million to build a screen. The capital cost and difficulty in filming IMAX movies were big barriers to theatre and Hollywood adoption. Burdened by a $200 million debt, IMAX was fighting for survival.[4]

The Breakthrough

In 2001, an IMAX scientist developed a procedure to convert existing 35mm movies into the IMAX format—a patented process called Digital Re-mastering (DMR). The first re-mastered movie was *Apollo 13* in 2002, which took 16 weeks to convert. With experience, the conversion time was reduced to two to three weeks at a cost of only $20,000 to $50,000. Digital movie formats further lowered the cost. Prior to DMR, the only Hollywood films made using IMAX were Disney animations, such as *Fantasia* and *Beauty and the Beast*. The development of DMR was critical since projecting a 35mm film onto an IMAX screen would produce a grainy picture. DMR removed the grain, while preserving image quality. Now, instead of persuading movie studios to film using its cameras, IMAX could convert a movie to its format.

The Business Model

By 2006, IMAX was able to create a near IMAX experience in existing theatres—the new IMAX Digital Theatre, at a fraction of the cost ($150,000). The 70mm projector was replaced with two smaller ones projecting over each other, providing increased resolution relative to standard digital projectors. IMAX also improved the sound system from a regular cinema set up. Importantly, the screen was not altered, but merely moved about 10 meters closer to the

---

[2] Eric Lam, "IMAX CEO Sees $1 Billion Box Office on China," accessed December 20, 2014, www.bloomberg.com/news/2013-09-12/imax-ceo-sees-1-billion-box-office-on-china.html.

[3] All currency amounts are shown in U.S. dollars unless otherwise noted.

[4] Richard Gelfond, "The CEO of IMAX on How It Became a Hollywood Powerhouse," *Harvard Business Review*, July–August 2013, pp. 36–39.

Exhibit 1
IMAX Worldwide: Screens, Box Office, Demographics, and Urbanization

#	Country	Existing Screens (2014)	2013 Box Office ($ million)	Hollywood Box Office Share	Middle and Upper Class Population % Increase (2013–2020)	Urban Population % Increase (2013–2020)
1	ARGENTINA	1	400	76%	32.1	0.4
2	AUSTRALIA	5	1100	95%	3.5	1.6
3	AUSTRIA	5	160	90%	3.5	4.1
4	AZERBAIJAN	2			53.1	6.7
5	BRAZIL	11	900	83%	56.4	2.7
6	BULGARIA	2	25	85%	8.3	4.3
7	CANADA	46	1000	98%	3.5	2.4
8	CHILE	1	130	95%	57.2	1.9
9	CHINA	221	3600	50%	65.8	17.1
10	COLOMBIA	2	230	65%	80	3.5
11	COSTA RICA	1			51.7	7.4
12	CROATIA	1	20	98%	9	7.5
13	CZECH REPUBLIC	1	70	65%	3.5	3.1
14	DENMARK	1	190	60%	3.5	1.1
15	DOMINICAN REPUBLIC	1			96.8	6.7
16	ECUADOR	2	65	95%	71.4	5.5
17	EGYPT	1	120	20%	115.3	13
18	ESTONIA	1	15	95%	3.5	3.1
19	FRANCE	13	1600	54%	3.5	3.3
20	GERMANY	5	1300	64%	3.5	4.2
21	GUATEMALA	2			65.7	11.2
22	HONG KONG	5	210	78%	3.5	0
23	HUNGARY	1	60	91%	12.8	5.7
24	INDIA	8	1500	10%	105.6	17.6
25	INDONESIA	4	195	80%	56.5	14.1
26	ISRAEL	1	115	50%	3.5	0.7
27	ITALY	2	800	53%	3.5	4.5
28	JAPAN	23	2400	39%	3.5	5.2
29	JORDAN	1			24.3	6.4
30	KAZAKHSTAN	2	65	45%	10.5	7.2
31	KENYA	1				24.3
32	KUWAIT	2				0.2
33	MALAYSIA	4	200	82%	29.9	6.7
34	MEXICO	20	900	90%	33.5	3.2
35	MOROCCO	1		44%		14.1
36	NETHERLANDS	6	300	80%	3.5	3.4
37	NEW ZEALAND	1	175	97%	3.5	1.6
38	PHILIPPINES	8	175	80%	55.9	7.8
39	POLAND	5	200	66%	9.3	7.2
40	PORTUGAL	2	85	47%	3.5	8.8

Exhibit 1 (*cont.*)

#	Country	Existing Screens (2014)	2013 Box Office ($ million)	Hollywood Box Office Share	Middle and Upper Class Population % Increase (2013–2020)	Urban Population % Increase (2013–2020)
41	QATAR	2			42.1	0.6
42	ROMANIA	1	45	90%	8.3	7.8
43	RUSSIA	36	1400	83%	16.9	2
44	SAUDI ARABIA	1				1.6
45	SINGAPORE	3	170	90%	3.5	0
46	SOUTH AFRICA	3	90	68%	41.3	7.8
47	SOUTH KOREA	15	1400	46%	4.6	2.7
48	SPAIN	3	700	65%	3.5	2.9
49	SWEDEN	1	200	60%	3.5	-0.9
50	SWITZERLAND	2	200	60%	3.5	6.5
51	TAIWAN	9	300	75%	3.5	3.5
52	THAILAND	5	150	60%	26	17.4
53	TRINIDAD AND TOBAGO	1				
54	TURKEY	4	300	42%	17	5.8
55	UKRAINE	5				5.2
56	UNITED ARAB EMIRATES	1				1.6
57	UNITED KINGDOM	35	1700	60%	3.5	1.2
58	UNITED STATES	385	9900	100%	3.5	2.9

Note: All source data accessed December 26, 2014. For 13 countries, 2013 Box Office is estimated from the average two-year growth rate. For 22 developed nations, a 3.5% European poverty reduction estimate (European Commission, http://ec.europa.eu/eurostat) is used to proxy Middle and Upper Class increase (2013–20).

Sources: for existing screens: IMAX Corporate website, www.imax.com/theatres; for 2013 box office: Motion Picture Association of America Inc., European Audiovisual Observatory, UNESCO Institute of Statistics; for Hollywood box office share: The Hollywood Reporter website, www.hollywoodreporter.com/movies; for middle and upper-class population increase: Asian Development Bank, World Bank, OECD, Ernst and Young; for urban population increase: City Mayors Statistics, "Urban population growth between 1950 and 2030," www.citymayors.com/statistics/urban-population-intro.html.

audience, giving a perception of increased width and height.

Most contracts with exhibitors were revenue-sharing agreements. IMAX would install the digital theatre for free and receive about a third of the box office receipts for IMAX films shown on that screen. Exhibitors and studios typically handed over 20 and 12.5 per cent of the ticket price respectively, excluding taxes. As part of the agreement, IMAX provided advice on theatre design, supervised installation, trained personnel, and performed ongoing maintenance. These agreements were usually non-cancellable for an initial term of 10 to 13 years, after which they could be renewed for one or more terms of 5 to 10 years. Apart from revenue sharing, IMAX also licensed its technology through leases and sales.

The Hollywood Surge

Early IMAX DMR conversions, such as *Apollo 13* and *The Matrix* sequels, were considered

Exhibit 2
IMAX Corporation Balance Sheets, 2010–2013 (in Thousands of $)

Period Ending	2013–12–31	2012–12–31	2011–12–31	2010–12–31
Current Assets				
Cash and Cash Equivalents	29,546	21,336	18,138	30,390
Net Receivables	180,184	136,200	133,373	113,171
Inventory	9,825	15,794	19,747	15,275
Other Current Assets	10,678	7,570	5,514	5,281
Total Current Assets	230,233	180,900	176,772	164,117
Long-Term Assets				
Fixed Assets	132,847	113,610	101,253	74,035
Goodwill	39,027	39,027	39,027	39,027
Intangible Assets	27,745	27,911	24,913	2,437
Other Assets	27,034	23,963	14,238	12,350
Deferred Assets Charges	24,259	36,461	51,046	57,122
Total Assets	**481,145**	**421,872**	**407,249**	**349,088**
Current Liabilities				
Accounts Payable	84,628	83,839	87,840	99,378
Short-Term Debt/Current Portion of Long-Term Debt	0	11,000	55,083	17,500
Other Current Liabilities	76,932	73,954	74,458	73,752
Total Current Liabilities	161,560	168,793	217,381	190,630
Total Liabilities	**161,560**	**168,793**	**217,381**	**190,630**
Stockholders' Equity				
Common Stocks	327,313	313,744	303,395	292,977
Retained Earnings	43,051	87,166	128,503	141,209
Other Equity	35,323	26,501	14,976	6,690
Total Equity	**319,585**	**253,079**	**189,868**	**158,458**
Total Liabilities and Equity	**481,145**	**421,872**	**407,249**	**349,088**

Source: NASDAQ, "IMAX Company Financials," accessed December 21, 2014, www.nasdaq.com/symbol/imax/financials?query=balance-sheet.

successful, but the 2004 computer-animated film *The Polar Express* in IMAX 3D was a game changer. It made cinematic history as the world's first full-length IMAX 3D Hollywood feature, shattering box office records worldwide and becoming the highest grossing DMR release at $60 million on 100 screens. Numerous other Hollywood movies were DMRed and ran successfully on IMAX screens, including the Harry Potter films, *Superman Returns*, *Batman Begins* and *Night at the Museum*.

Since 2002, more than 200 Hollywood films had been digitally re-mastered to IMAX. Of these, about 190 were converted post 2006, once IMAX began retrofitting existing screens. Two notable exceptions to the mass of DMR productions were *The Dark Knight* (2011) and *Mission: Impossible – Ghost Protocol* (2011), both partially filmed using IMAX cameras. Hollywood traction helped IMAX reduce its debt; and, since 2010, it remained debt-free, cash-positive, and profitable (see Exhibits 2 and 3). James Cameron's *Avatar*, released in 2009, grossed $250 million on IMAX screens and represented a financial turning point. From 2008 to 2010, IMAX's stock price increased by over 500 per cent (see Exhibit 4).

Exhibit 3
IMAX Corporation Income Statements, 2010–2013 (in Thousands of $)

Period Ending	2013–12–31	2012–12–31	2011–12–31	2010–12–31
Total Revenue	287,937	282,755	235,098	248,614
Cost of Revenue	123,334	129,510	121,033	110,962
Gross Profit	164,603	153,245	114,065	137,652
Operating Expenses				
Research and Development	14,771	11,411	7,829	6,249
Sales, General and Administrative	82,669	81,560	75,212	78,757
Non-Recurring Items	445	674	1,590	1,488
Other Operating Items	1,618	706	465	513
Operating Income	**65,100**	**58,894**	**28,969**	**50,645**
Additional Income/Expense Items	55	85	57	399
Earnings Before Interest and Tax	65,155	58,979	29,026	51,044
Interest Expense	1,345	689	1,827	1,885
Earnings Before Tax	63,810	58,290	27,199	49,159
Income Tax	16,629	15,079	9,293	(52,574)[5]
Minority Interest	0	0	0	0
Equity Earnings/Loss	2,757	1,362	1,791	493
Net Income-Cont. Operations	44,424	41,849	16,115	101,240
Net Income	**44,115**	**41,337**	**15,260**	**101,240**
Net Income Applicable to Common Shareholders	44,115	41,337	15,260	101,240

Source: NASDAQ, "IMAX Company Financials," accessed December 21,2014, www.nasdaq.com/symbol/imax/financials?query=income-statement.

However, despite Hollywood now actively pursuing IMAX, the company was very selective in the films that it converted to the IMAX format or shot using its cameras. It turned down about five movies for every one it made. It carefully picked blockbuster action-adventure movies that, when rendered in IMAX and projected onto its screens, would provide a truly enriched viewing experience. To further maintain its premium, speciality brand, and ensure adequate profitability per screen, IMAX limited screen numbers and concentrations to ensure reasonable distance between theatres. It was not just the visual enhancements which made filmmakers demand that their movies be shown in IMAX; it was also quality control. From Toronto, IMAX continuously monitored all its locations in 58 countries to ensure volume levels were set correctly,

projector bulbs weren't in danger of burning out and images remained pristine.[6]

Innovation[7]

Despite significant proprietary expertise in projection, sound, and imaging technologies, IMAX did not rest on its laurels. As of December 31, 2013, it held 99 patents in the United States, more

---

[5] This amount includes an income tax benefit of $55 million related to a decrease in the valuation allowance for deferred tax assets and other tax adjustments (from IMAX Corporation Annual Report, 2010).

[6] Brent Lang, "With 'Interstellar,' IMAX Takes Aim at the Bigger Picture," accessed December 24, 2014, http://variety.com/2014/film/features/with-interstellar-imax-hits-hollywoods-bigtime-1201341443/.

[7] IMAX Corporation, Annual Reports, 2013 and 2007.

Exhibit 4 IMAX Corporation Stock Performance, 2008–2013

CUMULATIVE VALUE OF $100 INVESTMENT

Legend:
- IMAX
- NYSE Composite
- S&P/TSX Composite
- Bloomberg Hollywood Reporter

Note: The graph compares the total cumulative shareholder return for $100 invested (assumes that all dividends were reinvested) in common shares of the Company against the cumulative total return of each of the following stock indices—NYSE Composite, S&P/TSX Composite and Bloomberg Hollywood Reporter on December 31, 2008 to December 31, 2013.

Source: IMAX Corporation Annual Report, 2013.

than twice it held six years ago. Corresponding patents were held or had been filed in many other countries, and additional 35 patents were pending. In 2012 and 2013, IMAX significantly increased its level of research and development (R&D) with a focus on developing its next-generation laser projection system. In 2013, IMAX's R&D spend was more than 5 per cent of revenue, with one in six employees (90/541) working on R&D. Other key areas of research activity included improving projector reliability, enhancing 2-D and 3-D image quality, manufacturing digital film cameras, and designing premium home theatre systems.

The Movie Industry[8]

In 2013, more than 7,000 movies were released worldwide, led by India at 1,274. Over 65 per cent of frequent moviegoers were aged 18 to 59. Global box office revenues increased to nearly $36 billion in 2013, a 4 per cent increase over 2012. North America generated the most revenue at $11 billion, growing by 1 per cent over the previous year, followed by China with $3.6 billion and 27 per cent growth. The other BRIC

nations also featured among the top 10 international movie markets, with India at $1.5 billion in revenue; Russia, $1.4 billion and Brazil, $0.9 billion. The U.S. producer Warner Bros. Entertainment Inc. was the highest grossing movie studio with $1.8 billion in revenue. With more than 7,000 screens worldwide, Regal Entertainment Group, a U.S. company, was the world's largest movie exhibitor.

Partnerships with Movie Studios and Exhibitors

IMAX had partnerships with several movie studios to develop IMAX movie versions. These arrangements could be one-off deals for a particular movie, or a broader agreement comprising a number of movies. For instance, in November 2008, IMAX and Disney agreed on a five-picture deal starting with the 2009 release of Disney's *The Jonas Brothers*, followed by the fall 2009 3-D release of Disney's *A Christmas Carol* and *Alice in Wonderland* in spring 2010. Partnerships with studios also extended beyond Hollywood. In June 2009, IMAX and Huayi Bros. Media Corporation Ltd., China's largest privately owned media group, entered a partnership to release up to three mainstream Chinese films to capitalize on the growing size and scope of IMAX in China. Similarly, in March 2013, IMAX announced a partnership with Yash Raj Films Pvt. Ltd. in India

[8] Motion Picture Association of America Inc., *Theatrical Market Statistics*, 2013.

to develop and release three movies in IMAX theatres globally.

IMAX put in place numerous licensing and joint venture agreements with exhibitors in an attempt to build new IMAX theatres or retrofit existing ones. For instance, in December 2007, it entered into a joint venture agreement with AMC Entertainment to install 100 screens equipped with IMAX's digital projection technology at AMC U.S. locations In March 2011, IMAX announced its largest international agreement— a 75 theatre deal in China with Wanda Cinema, Asia's largest cinema operator.

Competition from Exhibitors

In 2014, while 72 premium large format (PLF) brands competed with IMAX, only a few were real threats.[9] Since 2009, North America's five major theatre companies had either retrofitted their theatres or built new ones with oversized screens, adding several dollars to the ticket price. Hence, IMAX faced competition from the very exhibitors it relied on for business. Exhibitor PLF screens were opening at a rapid pace and by December 2014, for every two IMAX screens in North America, there were three such screens. Competing screens usually stretched from floor to ceiling in theatres with enhanced sound and extra-cushy seats, offering what some movie-goers felt was the best viewing experience for Hollywood blockbusters. Exhibitors varied in how aggressively they pursued the PLF strategy. Some stopped adding new IMAX contracts. Others placed their screens near IMAX theatres. Some built new locations that offered both IMAX and their own big-screens under the same roof.

In November 2013, of the $161.1 million grossed during the opening weekend of *The Hunger Games: Catching Fire*, about $9.6 million was collected from U.S. exhibitor PLF screens— only about $3 million less than what IMAX U.S. locations generated. Studios and exhibitors stood to gain millions of dollars by cutting out IMAX.

According to Chris Aronson,[10] president of U.S. distribution at 21st Century Fox Inc., "The distribution and exhibition dynamic is much simpler when there are only two parties involved."

The competition had its roots in the film industry's move to digital distribution. When studios started delivering films digitally rather than in bulky canisters, it became easier to build theatres with sound and lighting for large-format viewing. "There was enough off-the-shelf technology that, if you knew how to put it together, you could create your own PLF experience," said Timothy Warner,[11] chief executive at Cinemark. IMAX retorted that exhibitors were trying to replicate its signature experience without delivering the goods. "It's like putting a Mercedes on a Ford body and saying you have a Mercedes," said Gelfond.[12] A key concern for IMAX was if such exhibitors would renew their IMAX contracts in 2017.

The competition from exhibitors was not limited to North America (see Exhibit 5). In October 2013, Russia's Karo Cinema announced a tie-up with RealD to roll out 10 PLF screens. A year later, China Film Giant Screen (CFGS), a subsidiary of China Film Co. Ltd. entered into a partnership with Deluxe Digital Cinema for subtitling and converting Hollywood films to its PLF format.

Foreign Shores

In 2013, growth markets outside of North America were important to the sustained success of IMAX. In the past few years, domestic ticket sales were flat to down, as more consumers opted to watch movies on home entertainment systems and mobile devices. Internationally though, IMAX movies were becoming increasingly popular, especially in emerging markets. In the United States, the average price of a movie ticket was $8 to $10, but an IMAX ticket ranged from $13 to

[9] Patrick von Sychowski, "IHS: 72 PLF Brands Compete with IMAX," accessed December 26, 2014, http://celluloidjunkie.com/2014/10/31/ihs-72-plf-brands-compete-imax-two-threat/.

[10] Erich Schwartzel, "Movie-Theater Chains Take on IMAX," accessed October 17, 2014, www.wsj.com/articles/SB10001424052702304202204579254453051597642.
[11] Ibid.　[12] Ibid.

Exhibit 5
Exhibitor-Branded Premium Large Format Screens, by Region

Region	PLF Screens	
North America	686	49%
Asia Pacific	378	27%
Central and South America	224	16%
Western Europe	70	5%
Eastern Europe	28	2%
Africa and Middle East	14	1%

Source: Patrick von Sychowski, "IHS: 72 PLF Brands Compete with IMAX," accessed December 26, 2014, http://celluloidjunkie.com/2014/10/31/ihs-72-plf-brands-compete-imax-two-threat/.

$15. Nowhere was the popularity as strong and as price inelastic as in emerging markets. According to Gelfond,[13] an IMAX ticket could cost four times as much as a regular ticket in India, and at least one theatre in Russia charged $80 a ticket and "does very well." He forecasted international ticket receipts to account for 60 per cent of the company's total in the next few years and said "the expanding theatre network around the world, will be a major driver of growth."

The combination of DMR conversions and lower capital cost of retrofitting existing theatres also helped IMAX expand globally. Being debt-free and cash-positive provided IMAX with both investment and licensing options in foreign markets. In most countries, IMAX preferred revenue-sharing agreements, in which it paid for part of the cost of building screens in return for a share of box office revenue. In 2013, IMAX entered into revenue-sharing agreements for 126 screens and licensing agreements for five screens.

The BRIC Countries

In 2001, Jim O'Neill, chief economist at Goldman Sachs, coined the acronym BRIC, which stands for Brazil, Russia, China, and India. He noted that the BRIC countries symbolized a shift in economic power from the developed G7 economies.

From 2003 to 2013, the combined GDP growth of the BRIC nations exceeded by over four times the combined growth of the G7 (Canada, France, Germany, Italy, Japan, the United Kingdom, and the United States). O'Neill estimated that by 2030, the BRIC countries would overtake the G7 in terms of GDP. The key drivers of such economic growth were large urban populations, a high proportion of young people, and increased consumption by a fast-rising middle and upper class (see Exhibits 1, 6, and 11). The rise of the middle classes in BRIC countries, with their willingness and ability to spend, had transformed consumer markets.[14] During a television interview in 2013, Gelfond discussed how this rising middle class, was tipping the scales toward international markets for IMAX.[15] Rapid consumption growth in BRIC nations was prevalent in tier-1 megacities, as well as in several mid-size cities (see Exhibit 7).

---

[13] Lam, op. cit.

[14] Sarah Boumphrey and Eileen Bevis, "Reaching the Emerging Middle Classes beyond BRIC," Euromonitor International, November 12, 2013, accessed December 26, 2015, http://blog.euromonitor.com/2013/11/white-paper-reaching-the-emerging-middle-classes-beyond-bric.html.

[15] Etan Vlessing, "IMAX's International Expansion at Tipping Point," accessed December 21, 2014, www.hollywoodreporter.com/news/imaxs-international-expansion-at-tipping-414859.

Exhibit 6 Economic Comparison of the BRIC Economies

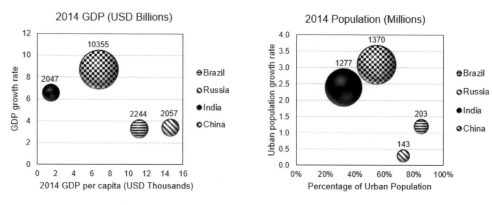

Source: Adapted from Gillaume Corpart, "Assessing the Relative Merits of the BRICS and MIST Economies as Investment Destinations," Americas Market Intelligence, accessed December 21, 2014, http://americasmi.com/en_US/expertise/articles-trends/page/assessing-the-relative-merits-of-the-brics-and-mist-economies-as-investment-destinations.

Brazil

In 2013, Brazil was South America's most populous and influential country, home to more than 200 million people, of which 87 per cent resided in urban areas. Following three centuries of Portuguese colonization, and a fourth century of being ruled by its own monarchs and dictators, Brazil became a democracy in 1985. Exploiting vast agricultural and mineral resources and a large labour pool, it grew steadily over the past three decades to become the world's seventh largest economy. Brazil had also made great strides in reducing social and economic inequality. In 2013, close to 80 per cent of its households were middle class ($15,000 to $30,000 annual income) or upper middle class ($30,000 to $45,000). Nevertheless, wide gaps remained between the rich and the poor. Upper middle class and more affluent households were expected to comprise over 35 per cent of the population by 2020.[16]

Brazil was the only Portuguese-speaking nation in the Americas, giving it a distinct culture from the Spanish-speaking countries. As Portuguese was the official language, it was the only language used for all business and administrative purposes. English, which was often studied in school, was the principal second language among educated Brazilians. Christianity was the dominant faith in Brazil.

Movies released in Brazil generated nearly $1 billion at the box office in 2013, a growth of 14 per cent over 2012, making Brazil the world's 11th largest movie market. Hollywood movies accounted for nearly 83 per cent of revenue. The market for Brazilian movies grew rapidly, with 2013 revenues increasing by more than 80 per cent over 2012. One hundred new cinema screens were added in 2013, increasing the total to more than 2,650 screens. IMAX tied up with UCI (a joint venture between Universal and Paramount), the largest exhibitor in Brazil, and the partnership operated five IMAX theatres in 2013.

[16] Boston Consulting Group Perspectives, "Redefining Brazil's Emerging Middle Class," accessed December 21, 2014, www.bcgperspectives.com/content/articles/center_consumer_customer_insight_globalization_redefining_brazils_emerging_middle_class/?chapter=5.

Russia

In 2013, Russia, home to more than 143 million people, was a developed, high-income country, with an urban population of 72 per cent. Vast oil

Exhibit 7 Population and Average Household Income for 15 Most Affluent Cities

Legend: ▨ 2013 population ■ 2020 population increase (projected) ▨ 2013 household income ■ 2020 household income increase (projected)

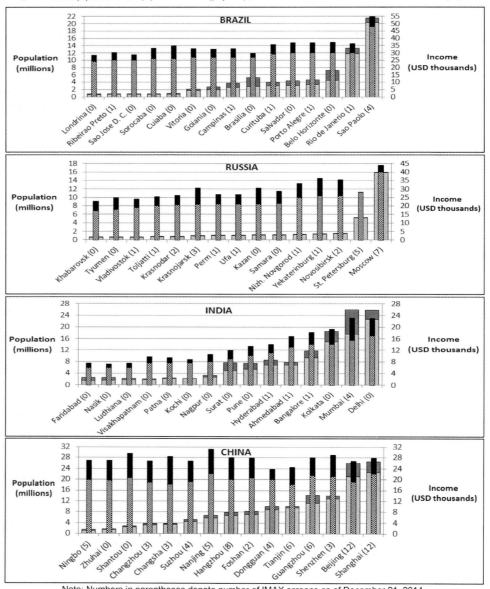

Note: Numbers in parentheses denote number of IMAX screens as of December 21, 2014.

Note: Numbers in parentheses denote number of IMAX screens as of December 21, 2014.

Source: Ugne Saltenyte, "Do Business Opportunities Exist Outside the Largest Cities in BRIC Countries?" accessed December 21, 2014, http://blog.euromonitor.com/2014/04/do-business-opportunities-exist-outside-the-largest-cities-in-bric-countries.html.

and gas resources, helped Russia overcome a late 20th-century economic collapse to become the world's ninth largest economy, and reassert itself as a world power. Economic strength and massive public support, also allowed Vladimir Putin, Russia's dominant political figure since 2000, to enhance state control over political institutions and the media. Approximately 35 per cent of Russia's households were middle class, and some 40 per cent comprised upper middle and more affluent classes. While Russia's population was expected to decline to 140 million by 2020, the middle, upper middle and more affluent households were expected to increase to about 86 per cent.[17]

Russia was a multicultural and multi-ethnic society, with dozens of languages. Russian, the official language, was widely spoken and used for all business and administration. English was the most common second language, but fewer than 10 per cent spoke it fluently. Christianity was Russia's dominant faith.

In 2013, movies released in Russia generated $1.4 billion at the box office, a 13 per cent growth over 2012, making it the world's 7th largest movie market. Hollywood movies accounted for nearly 83 per cent of revenue. Local movie revenues grew more slowly, increasing by 5 per cent over 2012. In June 2014, Russia's minister for culture Vladimir Medinsky spoke in favour of protectionism, hinting at introducing quotas for local films.[18] In September 2014, two top Russian directors argued[19] for restrictions on Hollywood movies. Yuri Kara called for a ban until sanctions imposed against Russia for annexing Crimea from Ukraine were lifted. Stanislav Govorukhin, who had been

Putin's election campaign chief, said, "I believe that it would be good to limit the presence of Hollywood movies on Russian screens."

In October 2013, the World War II epic, *Stalingrad* became the first Russian language IMAX film. It was digitally re-mastered into IMAX 3D and released in Russia, China and several countries in Central and Eastern Europe. The movie was a huge commercial success and became Russia's top grossing local-language film. In the first six months of 2013, 177 new cinema screens were added in Russia, increasing the total to more than 3,200. IMAX had partnerships with Cinema Park and Karo Film, Russia's two largest movie exhibitors, and with several other local exhibitors—Mori Cinema, Kronverk Cinema and Formula Kino. Commenting on the Russian market, in July 2010, Richard Gelfond[20] said, "You have a growing middle class and wealthy class that's seeking premium entertainment." During an interview in July 2012, Andrew Cripps, IMAX President for Europe and Middle East Asia, said,[21] "Russia has been a tremendous market; they embrace technology and the box office has been incredibly strong."

India

In 2013, India was the world's largest democracy, and the second most populous country (at 1.26 billion). From the late 1980s, India initiated reforms that opened up its economy, and encouraged foreign direct investment. Since then, India emerged as a fast-growing and powerful economy, to become the 10th largest in the world. However, India faced huge socio-economic problems. Nearly half of its population was poor and lacked a reasonable level of literacy. Hinduism was the major faith, and Hindi the most widely

[17] Nielsen Newswire, "A Rising Middle Class Will Fuel Growth in Russia," accessed December 21, 2014, www.nielsen.com/us/en/insights/news/2013/a-rising-middle-class-will-fuel-growth-in-russia.html.

[18] Hollie McKay, "Russian Film Industry and Hollywood Uneasy with One Another," accessed November 7, 2014, www.foxnews.com/entertainment/2014/10/14/russian-film-industry-and-hollywood-uneasy-with-one-another/.

[19] Ibid.

[20] "IMAX to Open 10 More Theaters in Russia", *The Moscow Times*, accessed December 21, 2014, www.themoscowtimes.com/business/article/imax-to-open-10-more-theaters-in-russia/411257.html.

[21] Wendy Mitchell, "Andrew Cripps and Richard Gelfond, IMAX," accessed December 21, 2014, www.screendaily.com/andrew-cripps-and-richard-gelfond-imax/5043387.article.

spoken language, although with its many languages, cultures and religions, India was extremely diverse. In 2013, 17 per cent of Indian households belonged to middle, upper middle and affluent classes. These classes were expected to increase to 33 per cent of all households by 2020.[22] By the same year, it was estimated that 40 per cent of Indians would reside in urban areas. Despite gaining independence from Britain in 1947, English remained the language of instruction in most urban schools, and the language of business and administration. India was therefore home to a rapidly expanding urban, English-educated workforce, making it an attractive destination for international business outsourcing.

With $1.5 billion in 2013 box office revenues, India was the world's fifth largest movie market, growing at 11 per cent annually. However, Hollywood's share of India's box office was a mere 10 per cent. Despite producing over 1,000 movies every year, India only had 1,200 multiplex screens—fewer than one per million people. In contrast, the United States had 120 multiplex screens per million. India added over 150 multiplex screens in 2013, but while single-screen cinemas had dwindled from about 13,000 to 10,000 in the past five years, they were still pervasive. Movies in Hindi and many regional languages, collectively known as Bollywood films, dominated the market and were most often shown in small, single-screen cinemas with tickets costing $2 to $3. According to Gelfond, this made it difficult to sell IMAX, a totally different entertainment proposition that cost four times as much or more. In February 2013, commenting on the low penetration of IMAX screens in India, Gelfond said,[23] "It's harder to change people's habits."

December 2013 marked the release of *Dhoom 3*, the first Bollywood movie to be digitally re-mastered by IMAX. Following its success, another Bollywood action thriller, *Bang Bang*, was converted for IMAX and released in October 2014. In India, IMAX had partnerships with Cinepolis, the world's fourth largest exhibitor, and with local exhibitors PVR Films and Sathyam Films.

China

In 2013, China with 1.35 billion people, was the world's most populous country and its fastest-growing economy. In the late 1970s, China's leader, Deng Xiaoping, commenced a process of widespread economic reform. Despite being a communist country, China underwent what has been described as a second industrial revolution. In 2011, fuelled by manufacturing growth, and domestic consumption, China became the world's second-largest economy. In recent decades, many rural dwellers in search of employment moved to the country's eastern cities, which were undergoing a construction boom. In 2013, for the first time, city dwellers outnumbered the rural population. It was estimated that, by 2020, China's population would be 60 per cent urban, with middle and higher classes comprising 700 million people.[24]

China's box offices pulled in $3.6 billion in 2013, a 27 per cent jump from 2012. Hollywood movies enjoyed a one-third market share, and Hollywood box office revenues in China grew by nearly 60 per cent. In February 2013, Gelfond said,[25] "Establishing IMAX in China was aided by the Chinese people's enormous appetite for affordable luxury." He added, "The Chinese have fallen in love with Hollywood movies." China had more than 12,000 multiplex screens, with 10 new screens being added each day. Most of China's 200 IMAX screens were operated by the theatre chain Wanda Cinema, which was China's biggest

[22] Asian Development Bank, *Key Indicators for Asia and the Pacific 2010: The Rise of Asia's Middle Class*, 2010, accessed December 26, 2014, http://digitalcommons.ilr.cornell.edu/cgi/viewcontent.cgi?article=1095&context=intl.

[23] Jorn Madslien, "IMAX Sets Its Sight on Bollywood and India's Audiences," accessed December 20, 2014, www.bbc.com/news/business-21322164.

[24] Asian Development Bank, op. cit.

[25] Madslien, op. cit.

Exhibit 8 Country Culture Comparison of BRIC Countries

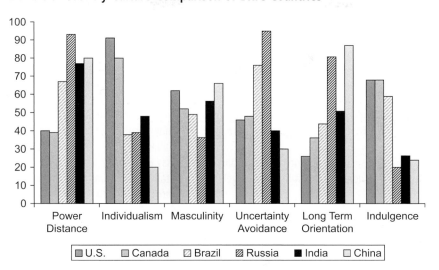

Note: Power Distance (PD) reflects the degree to which hierarchy and unequal distributions of power are accepted. A high PD score implies acceptance of large status differences between superiors and subordinates. Managers tend to be autocratic and paternalistic, while employees tend to do as told.

Individualism (IND) reflects the degree to which personal independence is valued over group membership. A society scoring high on IND values personal goals, initiative, autonomy and privacy. In contrast, a society that scores low values group goals over individual preferences and gives importance to harmony and consensus in decision making.

Masculinity (MAS) reflects the degree to which tough and assertive behaviour is encouraged. Conversely, feminity encourages tender and nurturing behaviour.

Uncertainty Avoidance (UA) reflects the degree of comfort with ambiguous situations and the extent to which efforts have been made to avoid these situations. Managers in high UA cultures tend to depend extensively on systematic rules and regulations. Extensive efforts are made to plan for the future.

Long Term Orientation (LTO) reflects the degree to which short-term pain is accepted for long-term gain. Societies with LTO are less likely to seek out immediate gratification and more likely to plan for and invest in the future.

Source: Geert Hofstede, Gert Jan Hofstede, Michael Minkov, *Cultures and Organizations: Software of the Mind. Revised and Expanded 3rd Edition*. New York: McGraw-Hill USA, 2010.

exhibitor in terms of box office revenue, with more than 15 per cent share of the Chinese market.

The Chinese movie *Aftershock* was the first big non-Hollywood commercial IMAX film. Released in 2010, *Aftershock* was a huge hit, grossing more than $100 million in China. Following its success, additional Chinese IMAX movies were made. In 2014, the digitally re-mastered *Monkey King* became the biggest grossing Chinese film ever, with more than $167 million in global box office receipts. Optimism on China's movie industry growth was, however, tempered by the risk of government interference and protectionism. In June 2014, China Film Bureau chief Zhang Hongsen,[26] claimed the country's film business was at war with Hollywood, and needed

[26] Clifford Coonan, "China Film Bureau Boss Urges Local Industry to Prepare for War With Hollywood," accessed October 19, 2014, www.hollywoodreporter.com/news/china-film-bureau-boss-urges-715332.

Exhibit 9
Risks in the BRIC Economies

BRAZIL	RUSSIA	INDIA	CHINA
High dependence on commodity exports.	High dependence on oil and gas exports.	Current account deficit (foreign investment vital).	High debt levels threatening financial stability.
Current account deficit (foreign investment vital).	Shrinking and ageing population.	Demographic dividend may become liability.	Ageing population and shrinking workforce.
Social pressures impeding structural reform.	Endemic corruption at all societal levels.	Messy democracy stalling structural reform.	Entrenched state enterprises and powerful bureaucracy.
High taxes, red tape, and poor infrastructure.	Crumbling infrastructure eroding competitiveness.	Weak infrastructure crippling manufacturing.	Rising workforce wages burdening economy.

Sources: Adapted from Al Fin, "BRICs: Can the Tail Wag the Dog?" accessed December 21, 2014, http://alfin2100.blogspot.ca/2012/06/brics-can-tail-wag-dog.html; Michael Schuman, "The BRICs have hit a wall" accessed February 16, 2014, http://business.time.com/2014/01/10/brics-in-trouble/; Erich Follath and Martin Hesse "Troubled Times: Developing Economies hit a BRICS Wall", accessed February 16, 2014, www.spiegel.de/international/world/economy-slows-in-brics-countries-as-worries-mount-a-951453.html.

to dramatically up its game to survive when the annual quota for foreign film imports (currently limited to 34) was raised in four years' time. The powerful government regulator urged theatre owners to reduce screen time for Hollywood movies.

Relative Market Emphasis

At the Toronto Film Festival in September 2013, Gelfond said,[27] "We've identified 1,700 target markets to put IMAX theaters into in the world, and about 500 of them are in North America." In the next 14 months, IMAX added 150 new screens worldwide, but only about 25 of them in North America. Hence, as of December 2014, 1,550 screens remained from Gelfond's stated

target. With an estimated investment of $350,000[28] per screen, each one represented a significant commitment. Allocating these by country would convey relative priorities to IMAX and its stakeholders, and enable purposeful implementation. Of the remaining screens, was 475 the right number for North America? If 400 were earmarked for the BRIC economies, how should they be distributed by country? The BRIC nations offered ample business opportunities, but also presented economic, political, and cultural challenges (see Exhibits 8, 9, and 10). What were the country-specific risks for IMAX, and how could they be mitigated?

---

[27] Lam, op. cit.

[28] This estimated investment is based on a capital investment of $23 million for developing 65 theatres under joint revenue-sharing agreements in 2013 (from IMAX Corporation Annual Report 2013).

Exhibit 10 BRIC Countries' Governance Indicators (Percentiles)

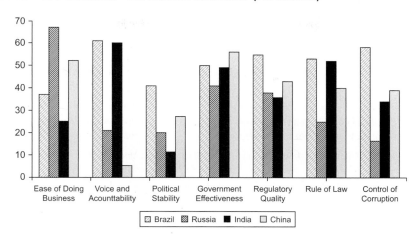

Note: Ease of Doing Business—capturing the conduciveness of the regulatory environment to business operation.

Voice and Accountability—capturing perceptions of the extent to which a country's citizens are able to participate in selecting their government, as well as freedom of expression, freedom of association and a free media.

Political Stability and Absence of Violence/Terrorism—capturing perceptions of the likelihood of political instability and/or politically motivated violence, including terrorism.

Government Effectiveness—capturing perceptions of the quality of public services, the quality of the civil service and the degree of its independence from political pressures, the quality of policy formulation and implementation and the credibility of the government's commitment to such policies.

Regulatory Quality—capturing perceptions of the ability of the government to formulate and implement sound policies and regulations that permit and promote private sector development.

Rule of Law—capturing perceptions of the extent to which agents have confidence in and abide by the rules of society, and in particular the quality of contract enforcement, property rights, the police and the courts, as well as the likelihood of crime and violence.

Control of Corruption—capturing perceptions of the extent to which public power is exercised for private gain, including both petty and grand forms of corruption, as well as "capture" of the state by elites and private interests.

Source: The World Bank, "Data," accessed October 19, 2014, http://data.worldbank.org/indicator/.

Exhibit 11 BRIC Population Age Distribution 2013 and 2020 (Projected)

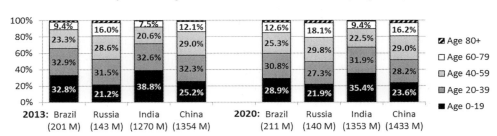

Source: Martin De Wulf, "Population Pyramids of the World from 1950 to 2100," accessed December 20, 2014 http://populationpyramid.net/.

⚜IVEY | Publishing

CASE 2.4 MAHINDRA & MAHINDRA IN SOUTH AFRICA

In May 2011, Pravin Shah, chief executive, International Operations (Automotive and Farm Equipment Sectors) at Mahindra & Mahindra Ltd. (M&M), a leading multinational automotive manufacturer headquartered in Mumbai, India, was weighing his options on the company's growth strategy in the South African market. Shah's dilemma was four-fold. Since 2005, Mahindra & Mahindra South Africa (Proprietary) Ltd. (M&M (SA)), the company's fully owned subsidiary based in Pretoria, South Africa, had grown the market by importing completely built units (CBUs) from its Indian operations. Shah needed to decide whether M&M (SA) should move to the next logical step of an agreement with a local vendor to use the latter's surplus facility for contract assembly of M&M vehicles. Or, M&M (SA) could skip that step altogether and invest in its own manufacturing facility. Alternatively, Shah could wait and watch until the subsidiary logged a critical mass of vehicle sales volumes that would be sustainable in the long term. The fourth option would be to grow the current business model of importing CBUs from India by using South Africa as the hub from which to sell them to other countries in the African continent and, thereby, expand the export market. Said Shah:

> Each option involves tradeoffs. They have to be evaluated in light of M&M (SA)'s long-term

view of the South African automotive market, which, in some ways, is unlike other international markets where we are present. South Africa is clearly a growth market. It is also competitive and fragmented. The basic question is: what is the fit that we want in it? There are issues about how we can build on the competencies we have developed during the last six years and the skills we need to develop, going forward, locally. The larger consideration for whatever call we take in South Africa is the globalization strategy of M&M, which defines the boundary.

Shah needed to present his recommendation to the four-member board of M&M (SA). The board, of which he was himself a member, was chaired by Dr. Pawan Goenka, president (Automotive and Farm Equipment Sectors), M&M. The decision of the board of the South African subsidiary would need to be, in turn, formally approved by the board of M&M, which, as the parent company, had 12 directors, more than half of whom were independent directors. The M&M board was meeting an average of six times in a year to discuss and decide on matters of strategic importance.

Context

M&M, the parent company, had six assembly plants worldwide. One was located in Egypt as part of a non-exclusive arrangement between M&M in India and a contract-manufacturing vendor in Egypt. M&M exported components from India for assembly in Egypt of vehicles intended either for local sales or for export. The Egyptian vendor assembled an average of 200 vehicles per month for M&M when the plant capacity was partially dedicated to M&M, thus proving the basic viability of local assembly as a strategic option for M&M (SA).

South Africa was one of M&M's biggest and most important export markets and was crucial to M&M's strategic growth. M&M had long-term plans to launch a global sport-utility vehicle (SUV) brand from South Africa. It was also planning to launch a new SUV for the South African market built on an altogether new platform. Both plans supported M&M launching its own manufacturing facility.

The wait-and-watch policy was a result of the South African automotive industry having just recovered from a sharp decline in new-vehicle sales in three consecutive years – 2007, 2008 and 2009. In 2010, sales growth had turned positive and was expected to gather momentum. However, the global automotive market had not yet fully recovered from the recession, which had led to the downturn in the South African automotive market. An annual survey of auto executives worldwide, had pointed to over-capacity as the major concern globally during 2011.[1] Over-capacity prevailed in both mature automotive markets (e.g., in the United States, Germany and Japan) and in emerging automotive markets (e.g., China and India). In the automobile industry, which was cyclical in nature, over-capacity was not a unique problem but it always made everyone cautious.

Finally, with the exceptions of Egypt and South Africa, none of the 54 countries in the African continent had a sizeable middle class that

could warrant M&M having a presence along the lines of the inroads M&M had made in South Africa or Egypt. Each individual market needed to be developed over time. In the interim, M&M could cater to the African markets from its South African base, which could be used as a re-export hub. Said Shah:

> Contract assembly is the way to go for companies with low volumes [of less than a few thousand vehicles per annum]. Of late, a growing number of multi-brand assemblers are coming up in Eastern Cape Province. It is also noteworthy that contract manufacturing is common in the industry even between established players who are otherwise competing for market share. Fiat, for example, assembles vehicles for Nissan, which assembles vehicles for Renault. The major factor for consideration is the availability of surplus capacity. On the other hand, it is possible for a company to set up its own manufacturing facility in South Africa once it has reached annual sales of 6,000 units in which a single brand in its portfolio sells approximately 1,500 units annually. It places you firmly on the path of both localization of content and scaling up, which are major issues in auto manufacturing globally. A volume of that order also helps build brand equity in the local market.

South African Automotive Industry

South Africa fared better than its neighbors (both in and out of African continent) in the business environment rankings from 2006 to 2010. The country was expected to retain the lead for the period 2010 to 2015 in several of the 55 parameters used as the basis for rankings (see Exhibit 1).

The South African automotive industry accounted for about 10 per cent of the country's manufacturing exports. Although its annual vehicle production was less than one per cent of global vehicle production, the industry contributed about 7.5 per cent to the gross domestic product (GDP) of South Africa.

The industry was picking up momentum after three consecutive years of negative growth,

[1] Dieter Becker et al., "Global Automotive Executive Survey 2011: Creating a Future Roadmap for the Automotive Industry," pp. 24–26, www.kpmg.com/Global/en/IssuesAndInsights/ArticlesPublications/Documents/Global-Auto-Executive-Survey-2011.pdf, accessed August 25, 2011.

Exhibit 1
South Africa – Business Environment Rankings

#	Indicators	2006–2010		2010–2015	
		South Africa	Regional Average	South Africa	Regional Average
	Political environment				
1	Risk of armed conflict	4	3.2	5	3.4
2	Risk of social unrest	3	2.8	2	2.1
3	Constitutional mechanisms for the orderly transfer of power	3	2.4	3	2.4
4	Government and opposition	4	3.2	3	3.1
5	Threat of politically motivated violence	3	2.6	3	2.7
6	International disputes or tensions	3	2.8	4	2.9
7	Government policy towards business	3	3.1	3	3.1
8	Effectiveness of system in policy formulation and execution	3	2.6	3	2.7
9	Quality of the bureaucracy	3	2.2	2	2.2
10	Transparency and fairness of legal system	2	1.8	4	2.2
11	Efficiency of legal system	4	2.4	4	2.4
12	Corruption	3	2.4	3	2.4
13	Impact of crime	1	3.3	1	3.2
	Taxes				
1	Corporate tax burden	4	3.4	4	3.9
2	Top marginal personal income tax	3	3.9	3	4.0
3	Value-added tax	4	4.2	4	4.1
4	Employers' social security contributions	5	3.7	4	3.9
5	Degree of encouragement for new investment	2	2.5	3	3.0
6	Consistency and fairness of the tax system	2	2.5	3	2.6
7	Tax complexity	4	3.2	4	3.4
	Financing				
1	Openness of the banking sector	3	2.9	3	2.9
2	Stockmarket capitalization	4	2.9	3	3.2
3	Distortions in financial markets	3	3.2	3	3.3
4	Quality of the financial regulatory system	3	2.4	3	2.9
5	Access of foreigners to local capital market	4	2.6	4	2.8
6	Access to medium-term finance for investment	3	2.8	3	2.8
	Labour market				
1	Labour costs adjusted for productivity	3	3.9	3	3.9
2	Availability of skilled labour	2	2.3	3	2.6
3	Quality of workforce	3	2.5	3	2.8
4	Quality of local managers	3	2.5	3	2.6
5	Language skills	4	3.0	4	3.2

Exhibit 1 (*cont.*)

#	Indicators	2006–2010		2010–2015	
		South Africa	Regional Average	South Africa	Regional Average
6	Health of the workforce	1	2.9	1	2.9
7	Level of technical skills	3	2.9	3	2.9
8	Cost of living	4	2.8	4	2.2
9	Incidence of strikes	3	3.5	3	3.3

Notes:
1. Rankings are on a scale from 1 (very bad for business) to 10 (very good for business); 2. Regional average is the total for 17 countries: Algeria, Bahrain, Egypt, Iran, Israel, Jordan, Kuwait, Libya, Morocco, Qatar, Saudi Arabia, Tunisia, UAE, Angola, Kenya, Nigeria and South Africa.
Source: –Pratibha Thaker, ed., *Economist Intelligence Unit – Country Forecast – South Africa*, May 2011, www.eiu.com/countries, accessed November 10, 2011.

which had been preceded by three consecutive years of record-breaking growth. According to the National Association of Automobile Manufacturers of South Africa (NAAMSA), new vehicle sales fell by 5.1 per cent in 2007, 21.1 per cent in 2008 and 25.9 per cent in 2009. The decline was largely due to the global recession, which had reduced the flow of credit in the financial system. Locally, the South African government had passed the National Credit Act[2] in July 2007, which regulated the flow of credit and further limited its availability. In 2010, however, a turnaround began. The industry had grown at 24 per cent over the previous year, exceeding initial projections of a 7 per cent increase. The momentum was expected to be sustainable. The government had targeted a production of 1.2 million vehicles in 2020 from about 0.5 million in 2010 (see Exhibit 2).

South Africa exported vehicles to more than 70 countries, mainly Japan, Australia, the United Kingdom and the United States. African export destinations included Algeria, Botswana, Zambia, Zimbabwe, Lesotho, Mozambique, Namibia and Nigeria.

[2] Republic of South Africa, *National Credit Act, 2005*, www.ncr.org.za/pdfs/NATIONAL_CREDIT_ACT.pdf, accessed August 28, 2011.

South Africans drove 1,390 variants of cars, recreational vehicles and light commercial vehicles. Domestic consumption was limited to well-known brands, such as Toyota, Volkswagen, Ford, Mazda and BMW. These brands together accounted for more than 80 per cent of new-vehicle sales in the country (see Exhibit 3). Present in South Africa were eight of the top 10 global vehicle makers, which sourced components and assembled vehicles for both local and overseas markets. South Africa also had three of the world's largest tire manufacturers. More than 200 automotive component manufacturers were located in South Africa, including several multinationals.

Growth Catalyst

The catalyst for the growth of the South African auto industry had been the government's Motor Industry Development Programme (MIDP). Introduced in 1995, MIDP had been legislated to last until 2009 and was to be phased out by 2012. It would be replaced in 2013 by the Automotive Production and Development Programme (APDP).

Pre-MIDP, the import duty rates for CBUs and completely knocked-down (CKD) components were 115 per cent and 80 per cent, respectively. The high duty rates were aimed at protecting the local industry from global competition. In 1995,

Exhibit 2
South Africa: Total Vehicle Sales, Production, Exports and Imports, 2006–2010

	2010	2009	2008	2007	2006
Cars					
a) Local sales	113,740	94,379	125,454	169,558	215,311
b) Exports (CBUs)	181,654	128,602	195,670	106,460	119,171
c) Total domestic production	295,394	222,981	321,124	276,018	334,482
d) CBU imports	223,390	163,750	203,808	265,095	266,247
e) Total car market (a+d)	337,130	258,129	329,262	434,653	481,558
Light Commercial Vehicles					
a) Local sales	96,823	85,663	118,641	156,626	159,469
b) Exports (CBU)	56,950	45,514	87,314	64,127	60,149
c) Total domestic production	163,773	131,777	205,955	220,763	219,618
d) CBU imports	36,911	32,496	50,825	47,760	40,208
e)Total LCV market (a+d)	133,734	118,159	169,466	204,386	199,677
Medium & Heavy Vehicles					
Sales including imports	22,021	18,934	34,659	37,069	33,080
Exports	861	831	1,227	650	539
Total MCV/HCV market	22,021	18,934	34,659	37,069	33,080
Total Aggregate Market	492,907	395,222	533,387	676,108	714,315
Total Aggregate Exports	239,465	174,947	284,211	171,237	179,859
Total Domestic Production	472,049	373,923	562,965	534,490	587,719
GDP Growth Rate (%)	2.8	(1.7)	3.7	5.5	5.6

Note: CBUs = completely built units; LCV = light commercial vehicle; MCV = medium commercial vehicle; HCV = heavy commercial vehicle; GDP = gross domestic product
Source: National Association of Automobile Manufacturers of South Africa, "New Vehicle Sales Statistics," www.naamsa.co.za/flash/total.asp?/total_market_at_a_glance, accessed August 22, 2011.

Exhibit 3
Mahindra & Mahindra South Africa – Leader Brands' Production

#	Market Segment	Leader Brands	2010	2009	2008	2007	2006
1	Light Commercial Vehicles	Toyota	34,709	29,444	32,273	38,816	28,009
		Isuzu	10,886	10,550	17,191	18,754	22,135
		Nissan	13,082	10,217	12,406	21,102	23,554
		Ford	7,433	7,184	9,938	10,813	12,107
		Mazda	3,835	3,585	4,992	5,097	5,748
2	Sport-Utility Vehicles	Toyota	16,083	10,349	10,362	11,570	10,315
		Land Rover	4,349	3,630	4,363	5,363	4,380
		BMW	4,713	2,831	3,223	3,692	3,050
		Mercedes	3,713	3,070	3,445	5,207	3,970
		Chrysler	2,735	2,299	2,523	3,745	3,583
		M&M	1,555	1,148	1,662	3,160	3,315

Source: Company files.

under the MIDP, the tariffs were reduced to 65 per cent and 49 per cent, respectively. They had continued to decline at a steady rate, reducing year-on-year to 25 per cent for CBUs and 20 per cent for CKDs in 2012.

Several MIDP provisions had helped boost automotive exports from South Africa. For example, the MIDP enabled local vehicle manufacturers to import goods duty-free to the extent of the value of their exports, thus allowing them to concentrate on manufacturing for export. The MIDP also granted vehicle manufacturers a production-asset allowance to invest in new plant and equipment, reimbursing 20 per cent of their capital expenditure in the form of import-duty rebates over a period of five years.

The APDP was meant to create long-term sustainability by concentrating on localization of vehicle content. Meant to last until 2020, the APDP was built around four key elements: tariffs, local assembly allowance, production incentives and automotive investment allowance. The program aimed to create a stable and moderate import tariffs regime from 2013, set at 25 per cent for CBUs and 20 per cent for components. It would also offer a local assembly allowance (LAA), which would enable vehicle manufacturers with a plant volume of at least 50,000 units per annum to import a percentage of their components duty-free. The investment allowance of 20 per cent would also be carried forward from the MIDP regime.

All rebates of import duty were given in the form of certificates that were tradable in the open market and could, therefore, be converted into cash. However, many automotive manufacturers used the certificates themselves to offset the cost of their imports. For example, to reduce the cost of their imports trading companies such as M&M (SA) purchased these certificates, when they were available at low prices in the open market. Said Nico M. Vermeulen, director, NAAMSA:

> A trading company, which imports CBUs at 25 per cent duty and sells them either in the domestic or export markets, will not get any certificate because it is neither manufacturing nor adding value locally. An assembly plant, which imports CKDs at 20 per cent import duty, must meet with three conditions in order to be eligible for a certificate: be registered with the Department of Trade and Industry; assemble a minimum of 50,000 vehicles per annum; and export. The value of the certificate for an assembly plant is linked to the value of export income it generates. A manufacturing company must produce 50,000 vehicles per annum to be eligible for a certificate which is linked, not to exports as in an assembly plant, but to the value added in the form of local content. A manufacturer gets the certificate, irrespective of whether the products are sold locally or exported, as long as it provides evidence of content localization.[3]

MIDP differed from APDP because it incentivized exports of vehicles and components, whereas APDP incentivized value added through local production. Both incentives were in tune with the outcomes the government was seeking at different points of time. The gradual decline in tariff protection was aimed at helping the domestic auto manufacturing companies become efficient in several ways. They could secure economies of scale, rationalize product platforms, focus on exports, compete globally and benchmark their operations against the best in the world. NAAMSA had estimated that the average annual volumes of production per platform would need to increase to a minimum of 80,000 units for a local company to become globally competitive. Similarly, employee productivity would need to improve from 15 vehicles to 30 vehicles per employee per annum.

Consumer Classification

South Africa had a population of 50.6 million, of which the black Africans comprised 40.2 million, white Africans 4.6 million, coloured Africans 4.5 million and Indian/Asian Africans 1.27 million.[4] The South African Advertising Research

---

[3] Interview with case author, September 02, 2011.
[4] South Africa.info, "South Africa's Population," www.southafrica.info/about/people/population.htm, accessed August 18, 2011.

Exhibit 4
South Africa – Customer Segmentation, December 2010

	LSM1	LSM2	LSM3	LSM4	LSM5	LSM6	LSM7	LSM8	LSM9	LSM10
Population ('000s)	808	1,944	2,394	4,744	5,636	6,891	3,621	2,830	3,038	2,114
Population Group (%)										
- Black African	98.4	98.0	98.8	96.8	94.9	82.3	58.7	48.6	34.0	18.9
- Coloured African	1.6	1.9	1.2	3.2	4.3	11.3	18.8	16.1	13.9	6.4
- White African	–	–	–	–	0.2	1.5	4.6	6.7	8.1	9.9
- Indian/Asian African	–	–	–	0.1	0.7	4.9	17.9	28.6	44.0	64.7
Household income (%)										
- >R799	23.1	13.9	12.7	6.8	4.5	1.1	0.3	0.2	0.1	–
- R800 – R1,399	38.0	33.8	28.2	22.1	16.1	6.9	2.2	0.9	0.2	–
- R1,400 – R2,499	28.0	32.9	30.8	23.3	17.2	9.8	3.6	1.8	0.7	0.2
- R2,500 – R4,999	9.7	17.5	23.4	33.4	34.7	25.2	13.3	6.2	2.3	0.6
- R5,000 – R7,999	1.1	1.0	4.4	11.5	18.6	28.0	24.3	16.1	8.9	2.5
- R8,000 – R10,999	0.1	0.6	0.1	2.1	6.0	16.3	25.2	22.0	17.6	7.2
- R11,000 – R19,999	–	0.4	0.5	0.9	2.6	10.6	23.2	31.3	32.2	18.4
- >R20,000	–	–	–	–	0.4	2.1	7.9	21.4	38.1	71.0
Age (% of population)										
- 15–24	30.6	29.5	31.4	32.0	33.9	29.3	25.5	25.9	26.3	26.9
- 25–34	21.2	18.9	20.3	23.1	23.6	26.1	25.7	21.3	19.7	17.2
- 35–49	17.3	22.8	24.7	22.8	23.4	25.1	27.3	28.0	28.8	29.0
- 50 plus	30.8	28.8	23.6	22.1	19.1	19.5	21.5	24.7	25.2	26.9
Community (%)										
- Metro (250,000 plus)	–	29.5	31.4	32.0	33.9	29.3	25.5	25.9	26.3	26.9
- Urban (< 250,000)	–	18.9	20.3	23.1	23.6	26.1	25.7	21.3	19.7	17.2
- Villages (<40,000)	–	22.8	24.7	22.8	23.4	25.1	27.3	28.0	28.8	29.0
- Rural	100	28.8	23.6	22.1	19.1	19.5	21.5	24.7	25.2	26.9

Source: www.saarf.co.za/SAARF_LSM/SAARF_Demographics/Table 40, accessed August 26, 2011.

Foundation (SAARF), an independent trade body, had segmented South African adult consumers (ranging in age from 15 to 50-plus) into 10 categories known as Living Standards Measures (LSMs). The measures graded people from 1 to 10 in an ascending order of their standard of living. Instead of using traditional metrics such as race and income, the SAARF LSM, which had won an award as the "media innovator of the year," grouped people by using such criteria as degree of urbanization and ownership of cars and major appliances. The grading was meant to help marketers and advertisers of goods and services to identify, as accurately as possible, their target markets (see Exhibit 4).

The data for the year ending December 2010 had reiterated a major trend that had long been evident in South African marketing. The buying power of black African consumers, comprising the largest group in the middle-income

(LSM 5–8) market, was rising. Said Ashok Thakur, CEO of M&M (SA):

> The mindset of white African consumers, who have been the bedrock of the vehicles market in South Africa, is similar to the mindset of consumers in the countries of West Europe. They buy well-known brands because they trust them. That explains why there has been a strong influence, for decades, of German brands in the South African automotive market. However, as the percentage of black African consumers entering higher income bands goes up, one would think that black Africans will acquire the buying habits and preferences of white Africans who are already in those bands. But, our experience in South Africa proves the opposite.

The black African consumers were buying Western European brands, and more recently Japanese and Korean brands, not because they trusted them but because they did not trust the local brands. This element of rebound had strategic implications for companies such as M&M (SA). The brand savviness of black Africans provided room for automotive brands other than those from Europe, Japan and Korea to strengthen their brand equity so that they could lock in sales from the growing black African consumers. M&M (SA) saw this situation as an entry-level opportunity.

A June 2010 *McKinsey Quarterly* research article into South African consumer goods had led to similar conclusions. It showed that 49 per cent of middle-income black consumers but only 26 per cent of middle-income white consumers agreed with the statement: "I purchase branded food products because they make me feel good." Among upper-income black Africans, those agreeing with the statement jumped to 65 per cent, while only 22 per cent of upper-income white Africans agreed. Of all black African consumers surveyed, 71 per cent agreed with the statement: "I have to pay careful attention so stores do not cheat me." In electronic goods, more than 60 per cent of black African consumers agreed that "products with no brands or less-known brands might be unsafe to use." In both cases, far fewer white consumers concurred.[5]

According to Thakur, the South African automotive market was also witness to three other trends that contrasted white African and black African consumers. White Africans earned more and also spent more, leaving them with less disposable income to invest in discretionary purchases, such as automobiles. Black Africans earned less but also spent less and seemed to have higher disposable incomes. Second, white Africans were buying used vehicles rather than new vehicles although their brand preferences remained. Black Africans, on the other hand, were buying new vehicles. Third, white Africans preferred functional attributes (such as good mileage), whereas black Africans preferred features, based on aesthetics, design and comfort, in their automobiles.

M&M Company Background

M&M was founded as a steel trading company in Mumbai, India, in 1945, by two brothers, J. C. Mahindra and K. C. Mahindra. Two years later, M&M entered into automotive manufacturing by launching Willys, the iconic World War II jeep, on a franchise from Willys-Overland Motors, the American maker of general purpose utility vehicles (UVs). Willys was the country's first UV. The company began manufacturing farm equipment in 1960. The UV and tractor platform gradually became the company's core competence.

The company had extended its core competence, over time, into the full spectrum of the automotive value chain. By 2011, it was producing two-wheelers at one end, small turbo prop aircraft at the other, and trucks, buses, pickups and cars in between. Positioning itself on the platform of "motorized mobility," the company had also started making powerboats, securing a

[5] Bronwen Chase et al., "A Seismic Shift in South Africa's Consumer Landscape," *McKinsey Quarterly*, June 2010, www.mckinseyquarterly.com/ search.aspx?q=south Africa, accessed August 16, 2011.

Exhibit 5 Mahindra and Mahindra – Business Segments

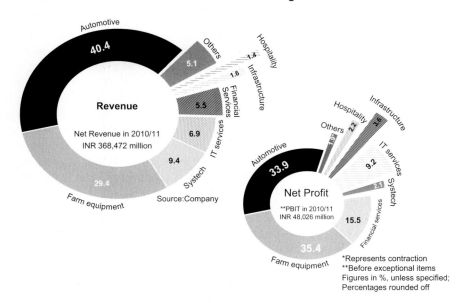

Source:Company

*Represents contraction
**Before exceptional items
Figures in %, unless specified;
Percentages rounded off

Source: Kushan Mitra, "How Anand Mahindra Built His $12.5-Billion Empire," http://businesstoday. intoday.in/story/anand-mahindra-mandm-company-acquisitions/1/18656.html *Business Today*, October 2, 2011, accessed October 20, 2011.

presence in the transportation media across "land, sea and sky."

The mobility platform had generated opportunities for synergies across the company's auto categories. Broadly, they prevailed in sourcing, product development and quality control. Common for all products was the use of raw materials such as steel and aluminum, which were used in castings and forgings. The automotive and tractor divisions had a common engine development team. The processes for quality improvements at the supplier end were uniform across categories. Synergies also prevailed at the level of operations. For example, transmissions and other aggregates were shared between different vehicles.

M&M had also diversified into unrelated areas branching into financial services, information technology (IT), hospitality, infrastructure and other areas. The group was in a total of eight businesses (see Exhibit 5). Each business operated autonomously under its own CEO. Some of the CEOs were members of the Group Executive Board of the parent company. Each was a growing business in an emerging market like India. The group had 45 operating companies, some of which were listed on local stock exchanges.

M&M was one of India's leading multinationals and had 113,000-plus employees, of whom 12 per cent were foreigners and Indian expatriates, located across 79 countries. It had consolidated revenues of ₹[6]370 billion for the year ending March 2011 and profit before tax of ₹45 billion (see Exhibit 6). The group was cash flow positive. It had $650 million surplus and internal accruals were growing every year.

Business Model

The business model followed by M&M was rooted in what the company called "engine theory." The

---

[6] Indian rupee (₹44.9908= 1US$), www.exchange-rates.org/Rate/USD/INR/5-20-2011, accessed November 16, 2011.

Exhibit 6
Mahindra & Mahindra – Consolidated Income Statement

(in million ₹)	2011	2010	2009
Net sales	370,264	316,880	269,198
Less			
- Raw materials	199,970	152,679	130,637
- Personnel	42,183	45,825	42,749
- Interest	9,742	9,798	7,501
- Depreciation	9,724	8,735	7,493
Profit before taxation	45,149	40,328	22,541
Net profit	30,797	24,786	14,054

Note: Net sales includes other income.
Source: Mahindra & Mahindra Annual Report, 2010–11, page 129 and Mahindra & Mahindra Annual Report, 2009–10, page 138.

parent company was viewed as an engine with multiple pistons. Each business vertical was in the nature of a piston. For example, the automotive sector was one piston, IT was another and so on. Each piston was a driver in its own right, focused not only on what it did best but also on improving the performance of the engine. The more verticals the company added, the longer and stronger the crankshaft grew. Each vertical was also receiving the horizontal benefit, or the crankshaft benefit, of group synergies that, in turn, improved its performance. Each vertical was free to form joint ventures to acquire new skills and leverage sourcing, manufacturing and technology of partners outside M&M.

The company had mandated what it called the "50 per cent rule" for each business, wherein even if demand fell by as much as 50 per cent, each business had to remain profitable. The objective was not only to provide enough room for business cycles, global shocks and other external factors but also to create a multiplier effect when volumes grew in times of more consistent activity.

The analyst community was treating M&M as a conglomerate on the ground that it had ventured, over the years, into newer businesses, which they considered to be non-core areas. While valuing the company, analysts were, therefore, giving it a conglomerate discount of 10 to 15 per cent. But the management of M&M saw the group as a federation of independent companies, benefiting from both business focus and group synergies. It was of the view that unlike a conglomerate, M&M provided an opportunity for investors in the parent company to participate in the equity of distinctive businesses that were creating shareholder value. Thus, according to the management, M&M should have received a federation premium, instead of a conglomerate discount.

The parent company saw its role as an allocator of capital. The group was trying to find a sweet spot between being a private equity firm (which juggled a diverse portfolio of investments and used leverage to create short-term value for each investment) and a family-run conglomerate (which focused on skill development and took a longer-term view of business).

Automotive Products

In addition to the production facilities that had become part of M&M as a result of acquisitions over the years, both in India and overseas, M&M had six assembly plants outside of India and nine manufacturing plants of its own within India. The company had an 88,000 square foot assembly unit in Houston, Texas, and one smaller unit each in Red Bluff, California, and in Chattanooga, Tennessee. These units were assembling

Exhibit 7
Mahindra & Mahindra – Indian Domestic Market Shares by Volume

Category	2011			2010		
	Total Domestic Sales	M&M Sales	M&M Share (%)	Total Domestic Sales	M&M Sales	M&M Share (%)
Utility Vehicles	323,896	169,205	52.2	272,741	150,726	55.2
Light Commercial Vehicles	353,621	114,856	32.4	287,777	86,217	–
Three-wheelers	526,022	62,142	11.8	440,392	44,438	3.0
Two-wheelers	11,790,305	163,914	1.4	9,371,231	70,008	0.7
Cars	1,982,990	10,009	0.5	1,528,337	5,332	0.3
Medium/Heavy Commercial Vehicles	322,749	843	0.4	244,944	–	–
Multi Purpose Vehicles	213,507	966	0.4	150,256	–	–
Total Auto Products	15,513,090	521,935		12,295,678	356,721	
Tractors	480,377	-	-	400,203	-	-

Note: Industry sales attributed in the report to the Society of Indian Automotive Manufacturers (SIAM).
Source: Mahindra & Mahindra Annual Report, 2010–11 pages 28 and 29 of 172.

tractors from completely knocked down (CKD) kits imported from India. M&M also had one assembly facility each in Brazil, Australia and Egypt. These units were assembling commercial vehicles and pickups from CKDs imported from India.

M&M had entered the India urban UV segment in 2002 with the launch of the Scorpio. The UV segment was small in India and growing at about 14 per cent per annum. Although the Scorpio was a UV, it was billed as "more than a car" (or "car plus") – a new segment M&M had created on a price-value proposition (of between ₹500,000 and ₹700,000) aimed at both the B segment (cars selling up to ₹500,000) and the C segment (cars selling at ₹700,000). By positioning the Scorpio as a mid-size car competing with car makers in B and C segments rather than with UV makers, M&M was able to grow the Scorpio sales in India at 30 per cent.

M&M had a 60 per cent share of the domestic UV market by value and 52 per cent by volume (see Exhibit 7). Its UV products consisted of multi-purpose vehicles, sport-utility vehicles (SUV) and pickup trucks characterized by ruggedness and reliability. The company's long-term goal was to build a global brand in the SUV and pickups segment. M&M was also the largest producer of tractors in the world by volume.

Globalization

A global perspective was a hallmark at M&M from the beginning. The company had entered into a series of joint ventures with overseas companies. The launch of economic reforms by the federal government of India in July 1991 had given the ongoing perspective a new push. M&M was of the view that each of its businesses would be facing new competition from international companies entering India; consequently, it had to prepare to defend its turf on the home ground. Said Shah:

> The anchor of our globalization strategy is that competing with multinational companies in overseas markets helps us compete with them better in India. Globalization gives us access to new technologies, new markets and new skill sets. It makes us competitive in emerging markets like Brazil, Russia, India

and China and, of late, South Africa, which will be the growth markets of the future. M&M believes in the Africa story. South Africa, in particular, is of interest to us not just because it is one of the most important export markets for M&M but because it is a springboard for the larger African market. South Africa is also where there is a good fit between what the customers need and what we can provide and between the price we offer and the value perceived by the customer.

The long-term aspiration of M&M was to be recognized as a global SUV brand. In line with that aspiration, M&M had acquired a majority stake in SsangYong Motor Company (SsangYong) of Korea in February 2011. SsangYong was a major SUV manufacturer and a natural fit for M&M. The product range, the markets and the price range created a continuum for M&M, opening up new markets for M&M's SUV brands in Russia, China and Korea.[7]

M&M in South Africa

M&M formally entered the South African market in February 2005, by setting up a 51 per cent subsidiary, Mahindra & Mahindra SA (M&M (SA)). The balance of 49 per cent was held by a local partner whose investment wing of the business had helped finance the venture. M&M had been exporting its automobiles to South Africa since October 2004 and had appointed dealers in all nine provinces of South Africa. M&M (SA) had also created a network of customer service outlets and collaborated with a local logistics company to ensure distribution of spare parts to service outlets countrywide within 24 hours.

By October 2004, M&M (SA) started importing two of its leading Indian brands – Bolero and Scorpio – both SUVs, in five models, fully assembled. Subsequently, it was importing two other SUV brands, Xylo and Thar, from M&M's plants

in India. Before being launched in South Africa, all models had been tested in the hazardous terrains of Australia and Europe, in high altitudes, low levels, deserts and cold conditions, in addition to being tested in the local terrain by local testing agencies. Said Thakur:

> Our entry strategy into South Africa was two-fold. First, we wanted a niche in the SUV segment straddling both cargo and passenger traffic. We did not want to play in the mass market. We identified four-wheeler passenger vehicles and pickups and delivery vehicles carrying cargo as our market segments. Second, we offered a value proposition by pricing Bolero, our launch vehicle, at between 20 per cent and 30 per cent lower than the prevailing competition. Bolero caught up with farming and small business segments and did very well with customers in semi-urban and rural areas and in villages where it was identified with "toughness" – an attribute which is valued in an African terrain. Scorpio reinforced it. We now need to build on it in the urban markets.

The global launch of the Scorpio pickup range of vehicles was held in South Africa in 2006, highlighting the strategic importance of South Africa as a market in the company's global growth plans. The company was making new brands available in South Africa, around the same time it launched the brands in India. For example, Xylo, a multi-purpose vehicle, was launched in India in January 2009 and in South Africa in March 2009.

M&M (SA) bought out its local partner's stake in August 2009, with a view to fully control and manage the business. It had the mission of "providing world-class products and services, at an unbeatable all round value to the customer, by unleashing the power of our people to benefit both partner countries and the communities we serve."[8] In five years of doing business in South Africa, M&M (SA) had sold a total of 11,000 vehicles. By 2011, it had a turnover of $40.3

---

[7] Mahindra & Mahindra, "Inside an International Acquisition," video clip, http://rise.mahindra.com/rise_topics/inside-an-international-acquisition, between 3:11 and 4:35 of 7:45-minute video, accessed September 1, 2011.

[8] www.mahindra.com/spotlight, accessed September 10, 2011.

Exhibit 8
Mahindra & Mahindra South Africa – Income Statement

Year ending March	2011	2010	2009
in South African Rand (ZAR)			
Sale of Vehicles	235,876,218	161,563,355	157,855,190
Sales of Spares	34,448,679	29,318,826	30,217,514
Sale of Tractors	273,000	1,511,999	9,483,660
Sale of Accessories	169,051	69,583	176,020
Sale of Services	–	–	952,766
Total Revenue	**270,766,948**	**192,463,763**	**198,685,150**
Less Cost of Sales	221,703,228	166,470,257	199,642,431
Gross Profit	49,063,720	25,993,506	(957,281)
Add Other Income	138,082	1,653,520	369,597
Add Investment Revenue	3,145,901	2,970,225	1,138,512
Less Finance Cost	2,409,208	4,518,481	11,985,817
Less Operating Expenses	23,900,437	22,425,423	41,954,297
Profit Before Tax	**26,038,058**	**3,673,347**	**(53,389,286)**
Tax	**7,293,834**	**1,044,461**	**14,664,466**
Profit After Tax	**18,744,224**	**2,628,886**	**(38,724,820)**

Note: 1 ZAR = US$ 0.148954.

Source: www.mahindra.com/investors/mahindra&mahindra/resources/2010-11/ subsidiary_ annual_ report_part_2 and www.mahindra.com?investors/mahindra &mahindra/resources/2009–10 /subsidiary _ annual_report, p. 6 and p. 13 of the Subsidiary Annual Report, 2010–11 Part 2 and p. 746 of the Subsidiary Annual Report, 2009–10, accessed October 01, 2011.

million for the year ending March 2010 (see Exhibit 8). It had secured a market share of about 1.2 per cent in the pickup market and in the low to medium range SUV markets, and the goal was to increase these markets to 5 per cent (see Exhibit 9).

The Mahindra brand in South Africa used different SUVs to target different segments – individuals, families, mining companies and farmers. It competed with Kia, Hyundai and Nissan for SUVs and with Toyota for pickups. Soon, M&M (SA) was a player of choice in the used-car market. Many local customers were becoming second-time buyers, indicating a strong loyalty for the Mahindra brand.

The medium to long-term plan was to make M&M (SA) the entry point into Africa. A major constraint M&M (SA) faced in this regard was the vehicle ordering cycle from India, which took more than two months. This long cycle was a limitation when bidding for contracts from the African governments, particularly those in the sub-Sahara region, which were the single largest buyers of new vehicles. A short lead time was often a competitive advantage in winning those contracts.

Issues Before Shah

Contract Assembly

M&M (SA) had been in talks with a few vendors in South Africa regarding the assembly of pickup vehicles, which were being shipped out of India to countries in West Africa. Local assembly would improve margins by reducing, by about 25 per cent, the cost of shipping CBUs from India to African destinations. The vehicles could be assembled in South Africa for export to African destinations. Costs could be further reduced by launching variants that were in demand and by locally sourcing some of the components and

Exhibit 9
Mahindra & Mahindra South Africa – Sales Volume

#	M&M Models	Models	Year of Launch	Main Attributes	Target Customer Segments	2010	2009	2008	2007	2006	2005
1	Bolero	S/Cab D/Cab	2004	Tough Durable Work and play	Contractors Farmers Service providers	387	342	725	1,429	1,442	579
2	Scorpio	Manual Auto Petrol Diesel	2004	7-8 seater Off-road use Safety features	Urban consumers	211	267	355	810	1,128	366
3	Scorpio Pickup	S/Cab D/Cab 2-Wheel 4-Wheel	2006	Multi-Utility Vehicle	Contractors Farmers Small businesses	612	375	582	921	745	-
4	Mahindra Thar	4 by 4	2010	Sports Utility Vehicle	Outdoor customers Off-roaders Retro-look seekers	107	-	-	-	-	-
5	Mahindra Xylo	E8 E2	2009 2009	Luxury People mover	Taxi operators Ferry owners Shuttle providers	238	164	-	-	-	-
	Total					1,555	1,148	1,662	3,160	3,315	945

Source: Company files.

extra fitments. Once M&M (SA) made the decision to assemble the vehicles locally, only three-months lead time would be needed to commence operations. Local assembly also meant that M&M (SA) would not need to make any major upfront investment in the vendor's facilities.

Brand equity was a major driver in the South African automobile market, where consumers bought cars and trucks on the basis of brand recall. Consumers preferred global brands because South Africa had no home-grown automobile brands. In spite of more than five years of presence in South Africa, M&M (SA)'s volume of sales was not comparable to global players operating in South Africa. Its brand equity was also not comparable with such global competitors as Toyota, Nissan and others.

M&M was accustomed to occupying the driver's seat. The mindset of being in charge prevailed throughout the organization, from the way it structured joint ventures (in which it invariably held the majority shareholding), to its staffing of key positions at the top with its own people. As a result, a contract assembly, in which the vendor ruled, particularly in mobilizing and deploying resources, would be a difficult proposition for M&M managers.

For the past two years, the company had contracted an assembly plant in Egypt for the Scorpio vehicle and another in Brazil for a pickup vehicle. When using local assembly, the vehicle ordering cycle would be about 10 days. The choice of contract assembly depended upon the availability of surplus capacity, the ability of the vendor to ramp up capacity consistent with changing needs and the vendor's knowledge and technical know-how, financial capability and management bandwidth.

Certification of the locally assembled vehicles local agencies was an area in which M&M (SA) did not have competence since it was only importing CBUs from its Indian operations. The certification could be outsourced in South Africa; however, doing so would be a departure from the norm at M&M, which typically retained all critical business processes under its control.

Own Manufacturing

Setting up a manufacturing plant in South Africa would be consistent with M&M's mission of being a long-term player. It would also demonstrate to customers its commitment to the local market, which would be a major factor in an industry where after-sales service, such as a warranty, was a crucial factor in attracting sales. Setting up its own manufacturing plant would also present an opportunity to lock in customers at the beginning of the growth curve in the South African market, which was the biggest export market for the parent company M&M. Raising funds in this option was not an area of concern because M&M had always operated as a cash surplus company.

Manufacturing was the easier part in automobiles. The real challenge, particularly in South Africa, was localization of content. Gross margins in the automobile industry fluctuated with production volume because many of the costs related to vehicle production were fixed. Once M&M (SA) got into manufacturing, it would be under pressure to sustain high production levels just to break even. Beyond the break-even point, fixed costs could be spread over more units, opening the doors for profitability.

Wait and Watch

M&M (SA) sales had suffered during the downturn but the confidence levels of the subsidiary had been high. The subsidiary had used the recessionary period to reduce fixed costs (through outsourcing, among other solutions), streamline operations (particularly for shipping and port-related work), improve its business processes and enlarge the reach and quality of its dealer network so that when the recession ended, M&M (SA) could become stronger and would be better prepared to face competition.

M&M (SA) could continue its prevailing business model of importing automotive products from India and exporting them from South Africa. This approach would help the company tide over the recession from which it was only mid-way to recovery. However, it would need to bear the higher rate of import duty of 25 per cent compared with local assemblers and manufacturers.

Use South Africa as a Hub

M&M (SA) had an opportunity to develop markets in the 54 countries on the African continent, which were just opening up. Africa and Asia (with the exception of Japan) were the only continents that grew during the recession years of 2007 to 2009. Africa's GDP growth slowed to 2 per cent in 2009 but recovered to 4.7 per cent in 2010 and was expected to move upward. Companies entering the African continent at the beginning of the new growth period could take the lead in shaping industry structures, segmenting markets and establishing brands.

The boom in commodity prices in early 2007 had led global companies to show interest in the African region, which, in addition to having rich deposits of minerals and metals, had 10 per cent of the world's oil reserves. But many companies were guarded in developing entry strategies for the region because of the ongoing recession. The political turmoil in countries such as Algeria, Egypt, Libya, Morocco and Tunisia added to the uncertainty. The paradox for a multinational was that the fastest growing economies in the region also carried the highest macro-economic risks.

In a study entitled "Lions on the Move" published in June 2010, McKinsey Global Institute had categorized the African economies into four buckets: oil exporters, diversified economies, transition economies and pre-transition economies. It had further categorized the African economies on the basis of GDP per capita. Algeria, Botswana, Equatorial Guinea, Gabon, Libya and Mauritius ranked first with South Africa, with per capita GDP in excess of $5,000 per annum. Congo Republic, Morocco, Namibia and Tunisia ranked second with GDP per capita ranging between $2,000 and $5,000. Cameroon, Côte d'Ivoire, Egypt, Nigeria, Sudan, Senegal and Zambia ranked third with GDP per capita ranging between $1,000 and $2,000.[9] These 17 countries together comprised the first line of target for re-exports from South Africa. Said Shah:

> The board would be interested in understanding the trade-offs involved in each of the four options. The members would, of course, want to know the level of investment and the expected return. These are quantitative and it would not take long to reach a consensus on them. The litmus test would be qualitative; it will be about the growth potential of the South African market. Their question would be something like, "Where will our decision now take M&M (SA) by 2015?"

[9] McKinsey Global Institute, *Lions on the Move: The Progress and Potential of African Economies*, www.mckinsey.com/mgi/publications/progress_and_potential_of_african_economies/index.asp, p.5, accessed September 12, 2011.

Chapter 2   Recommended Practitioner Readings

- Ezra Greenberg, Martin Hirt, and Sven Smit, "The global forces inspiring a new narrative of progress," *McKinsey Quarterly*, April (2017).

    In "The global forces inspiring a new narrative of progress," Greenberg, Hirt, and Smit discuss how growth is shifting, disruption is accelerating, and societal tensions are rising. Confronting these dynamics will help companies to craft a better strategy. To help leaders spot opportunities the authors clarify nine major global forces and their interactions. They characterize the forces as crucibles.

- Michael F. Porter, "Clusters and the new economics of competition," *Harvard Business Review*, 76:6 (1998), 77–90.

In "Clusters and the new economics of competition," Porter details how clusters – critical masses in one place of unusual success in a particular field – influence competitiveness. By co-locating in near proximity, companies, customers, and suppliers are better able to innovate, thereby creating a competitive advantage within the particular country.

- Ian Bremmer, "The new rules of globalization," *Harvard Business Review*, 92:1/2 (2014), 103–7.

  In "The new rules of globalization," Bremmer notes that until 2008 going global seemed to make sense for just about every company in the world. Since then, we've entered a different phase, one of guarded globalization. Governments of developing nations have become wary of opening more industries to MNCs. They are defining national security more broadly and perceiving more sectors to be of strategic importance, taking active steps to deter foreign companies from entering them and promoting domestic, often state-owned enterprises. Executives must now consider their industry's strategic importance to the host government and their home government. They can then choose among various approaches: strike alliances with local players, look for new ways to add value abroad, enter multiple sectors, or stay home.

- Pankaj Ghemawat, "The cosmopolitan corporation," *Harvard Business Review*, 89:5 (2011), 92–9.

  In "The cosmopolitan corporation," Ghemawat notes that today's global landscape is marked by unbalanced growth, protectionism, and ethnic, religious, and linguistic divides. Differences still matter. The ideal of a truly global, stateless corporation has become popular, but it simply isn't possible to achieve. Crafting a global strategy and organization is possible, but you must focus on understanding the differences among people, cultures, and places – not on eliminating them. One tool that can help you get a handle on the most critical differences is a rooted map, which sizes countries according to measures that reflect a particular nation's perspective, such as the amount of industry services they purchase from domestic companies. A cosmopolitan approach may lead firms, at least in the midterm, to concentrate more on adaptation to local markets than on aggregation or arbitrage.

- Pankaj Ghemawat, "Even in a digital world, globalization is not inevitable," *Harvard Business Review*, February 1 (2017).

  In "Even in a digital world, globalization is not inevitable," Ghemawat provides eight reasons why he is not convinced that digital technologies are sufficient to drive globalization forward.

These readings all elaborate on the environmental forces facing MNEs and reinforce how they need to respond to their often conflicting demands.

3 Developing Transnational Strategies
Building Layers of Competitive Advantage

In this chapter, we discuss how the numerous conflicting demands and pressures described in the first two chapters shape the strategic choices that MNEs must make. In this complex situation, an MNE determines strategy by balancing the motivations for its own international expansion with the economic imperatives of its industry structure and competitive dynamics, the social and cultural forces of the markets it has entered worldwide, and the political demands of its home- and host-country governments. To frame this complex analysis, this chapter examines how MNEs balance strategic means and ends to build the three required capabilities: global-scale efficiency and competitiveness, multinational flexibility and responsiveness, and worldwide innovation and learning. After defining each of the dominant historic strategic approaches – what we term classic multinational, international, and global strategies – we explore the emerging transnational strategic model that most MNEs must adopt today. Finally, we describe not only how companies can develop this approach themselves but also how they can defend against transnational competitors.

The strategies of MNEs at the start of the twenty-first century were shaped by the turbulent international environment that redefined global competition in the closing decades of the twentieth century. It was during that turmoil that a number of different perspectives and prescriptions emerged about how companies could create strategic advantage in their worldwide businesses.

Consider, for example, three of the most influential articles on global strategy published during the 1980s – the decade in which many new trends first emerged.[1] Each is reasonable and intuitively appealing. What soon becomes clear, however, is that their prescriptions are very different and often contradictory, a reality that highlights not only the complexity of the strategic challenge that faced managers in large, worldwide companies but also the confusion of advice being offered to them.

- Theodore Levitt argued that effective global strategy was not a bag of many tricks but the successful practice of just one: product standardization. Here the core of a

---

[1] See Theodeore Levitt, "The globalization of markets," *Harvard Business Review*, 61:3 (1983), 92–102; Thomas Hout, Michael E. Porter, and Eileen Rudden, "How global companies win out," *Harvard Business Review*, 60:5 (1982), 98–109; Gary Hamel and C. K. Prahalad, "Do you really have a global strategy?" *Harvard Business Review*, 63:4 (1985), 139–49.

global strategy lay in developing a standardized product to be produced and sold the same way throughout the world.

- In contrast, an article by Michael Porter and his colleagues suggested that effective global strategy required the approach not of a hedgehog, who knows only one trick, but that of a fox, who knows many. These "tricks" include exploiting economies of scale through global volume, taking preemptive positions through quick and large investments, and managing interdependently to achieve synergies across different activities.

- Gary Hamel and C. K. Prahalad's prescription for a global strategy contradicted Levitt's even more sharply. Instead of a single standardized product, they recommended a broad product portfolio, with many product varieties, so that investments in technologies and distribution channels could be shared. Cross-subsidization across products and markets, and the development of a strong worldwide distribution system were at the center of these authors' view of how to succeed in the game of global chess.

As we described in the preceding chapter, what was becoming increasingly clear during the next two decades was that to achieve sustainable competitive advantage, MNEs needed to develop layers of competitive advantage – global-scale efficiency, multinational flexibility, and the ability to develop innovations and leverage knowledge on a worldwide basis. And although each of the different prescriptions focuses on one or another of these different strategic objectives, the challenge for most companies today is to achieve all of them simultaneously.

Worldwide Competitive Advantage: Goals and Means

Competitive advantage is developed by taking strategic actions that optimize a company's achievement of these three different and, at times, conflicting goals. In developing each of these capabilities, the MNE can utilize three very different tools and approaches, which we described briefly in Chapter 1 as the main forces motivating companies to internationalize. It can leverage the scale economies that are potentially available in its different worldwide activities, it can exploit the differences in sourcing and market opportunities among the many countries in which it operates, and it can capitalize on the diversity of its activities and operations to create synergies or develop economies of scope.

The MNE's strategic challenge therefore is to exploit all three sources of global competitive advantage – scale economies, national differences, and scope economies – to optimize global efficiencies, multinational flexibility, and worldwide learning. And thus the key to worldwide competitive advantage lies in managing the interactions between the different goals and the different means.

The Goals: Efficiency, Flexibility, and Learning

Let us now consider each of these strategic goals in a little more detail.

Global Efficiency

Viewing an MNE as an input–output system, we can think of its overall efficiency as the ratio of the value of its outputs to the value of its inputs. In this simplified view of the firm, its efficiency could be enhanced by increasing the value of outputs (i.e., securing higher revenues), lowering the value of its inputs (i.e., lowering costs), or doing both. This is a simple point but one that is often overlooked: efficiency improvement is not just cost reduction but also revenue enhancement.

To help understand the concept of global efficiency, we use the global integration–national responsiveness framework first developed by C. K. Prahalad (see Figure 3.1).[2] The vertical axis represents the potential benefits from the global integration of activities – benefits that largely translate into lower costs through scale and scope economies. The horizontal axis represents the benefits of national responsiveness – those that result from the country-by-country differentiation of product, strategies, and activities. These benefits essentially translate into better revenues from more effective differentiation in response to national differences in tastes, industry structures, distribution systems, and government regulations.

The framework can be used to understand differences in the benefits of integration and responsiveness at the aggregate level of industries, as well as to identify and describe differences in the strategic approaches of companies competing in the same industry. Also, as Figure 3.1 indicates, industry characteristics alone do not determine company strategies. In automobiles, for example, Fiat historically pursued a classical multinational strategy, helping establish national auto industries through its joint venture partnerships and host government support in Spain, Poland, and many other countries with state-sponsored auto industries. Toyota, by contrast, succeeded originally by developing products and manufacturing them in centralized, globally scaled facilities in Japan. A "regional" strategy becomes feasible when geographic regions or groups of countries are sufficiently large and internally homogeneous markets but differ substantially from other regions or groups. Honda has implemented such an approach by dividing its organization into six autonomous geographical regions – North America, Japan, Europe, China, Asia, and the Middle East. In addition to manufacturing and marketing global models such as the Civic and the Accord, each region manages the full value chain for specific regional models such as the Pilot in North America and the Brio series in Asia. This sort of strategic choice to focus on the objective of global efficiency (rather than local responsiveness) creates vulnerabilities and challenges as well as clear benefits.

Multinational Flexibility

A worldwide company faces an operating environment characterized by diversity and volatility. Some opportunities and risks generated by this environment are

---

[2] For a detailed exposition of this framework, see C. K. Prahalad and Yves Doz, *The Multinational Mission* (New York: The Free Press, 1987).

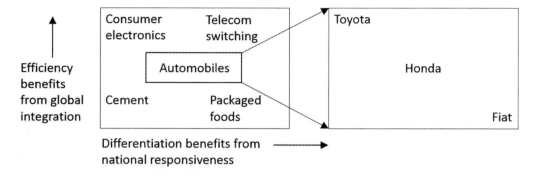

Figure 3.1 The integration–responsiveness framework
Christopher A. Bartlett and Sumantra Ghoshal, *Managing Across Borders: The Transnational Solution* (Boston: Harvard Business School Press, 1989).

endemic to all firms; others, however, are unique to companies operating across national borders. A key element of worldwide competitiveness therefore is multinational flexibility – the ability of a company to manage the risks and exploit the opportunities that arise from the diversity and volatility of the global environment.[3]

Although there are many sources of diversity and volatility, it is worth highlighting four that we regard as particularly important. First, there are *macroeconomic risks* that are completely outside the control of the MNE, such as changes in prices, factor costs, or exchange rates caused by wars, natural calamities, or economic cycles. Second, there are *political risks* that arise from policy actions of national governments, such as managed changes in exchange rates or interest rate adjustments, or events that are related to political instability. Third, there are *competitive risks* arising from the uncertainties of competitors' responses to the MNE's own strategies. And fourth, there are *resource risks,* such as the availability of raw materials, capital, or managerial talent. In all four categories, the common characteristic of the various types of risks is that they vary across countries and change over time. This variance makes flexibility the key strategic management requirement, because diversity and volatility create attendant opportunities that must be considered jointly.

In general, multinational flexibility requires management to scan its broad environment to detect changes and discontinuities and then respond to the new situation in the context of the worldwide business. MNEs following this approach exploit their exposure to diverse and dynamic environments to develop strategies – and structures – in more general and more flexible terms so as to be robust to different international environmental scenarios. For example, having a network of affiliated subsidiaries that emphasize global exports rather than individual local

[3] This issue of multinational flexibility is discussed more fully in Bruce Kogut, "Designing global strategies: profiting from operating flexibility," *Sloan Management Review*, Fall (1985), 27–38.

markets provides a flexibility to shift production when a particular national market faces an economic crisis.[4]

Worldwide Learning

Most existing theories of the MNE view it as an instrument to extract additional revenues from internalized capabilities. The assumption is that the firm goes abroad to make more profits by exploiting its technology, brand name, or management capabilities in different countries around the world. And most traditional theory assumes that the key competencies reside at the MNE's center.

Although the search for additional profits or the desire to protect existing revenues may explain why MNEs come to exist, it does not provide a complete explanation of why some of them continue to grow and flourish. As we suggested in Chapter 1, an alternative view may well be that a key asset of the multinational is the diversity of environments in which it operates. This diversity exposes the MNE to multiple stimuli, allows it to develop diverse capabilities, and provides it with broader learning opportunities than are available to a purely domestic firm. Furthermore, its initial stock of knowledge provides the MNE with strength that allows it to create organizational diversity in the first place. In Chapter 5, we engage in a detailed discussion of the approaches that MNEs use to deliver on the objective of worldwide learning.

The Means: National Differences, Scale, and Scope Economies

There are three fundamental tools for building worldwide competitive advantage: exploiting differences in sourcing and market potential across countries, exploiting economies of scope, and exploiting economies of scale. In this section, we explore each of them in more depth.

National Differences

In the absence of efficient markets, the fact that different nations have different factor endowments (e.g., an abundance of labor, land, materials) leads to inter-country differences in factor costs. Because different activities of the firm, such as R&D, production, or marketing, use various factors to different degrees, a firm can gain cost advantages by configuring its value chain so that each activity is located in the country that has the least cost for its most intensively used factor. For example, R&D facilities may be placed in the UK because of the available supply of high-quality, yet relatively modestly paid, scientists; manufacturing of labor-intensive components may be undertaken in Malaysia to capitalize on the lower cost, efficient labor force; and software development could concentrate in India,

---

[4] Additional examples of multinational flexibility are discussed in Tony Tong and Jeffrey Reuer, "Real options in multinational corporations: organizational challenges and risk implications," *Journal of International Business Studies*, 38:2 (2007), 215–30.

where skilled software engineers are paid a fraction of Western salaries. Initially, General Electric's "global product concept" was set up to concentrate manufacturing wherever it could be implemented in the most cost-effective way (while still retaining quality). Over time, however, changes in cost structures, the threat of imitators, and the pursuit of control over the supply chain eventually led the company to move back some of the manufacturing sites to the United States.[5] This highlights the fact that global situations are rarely stable over long periods of time, and that MNE strategy must above all be flexible and responsive to changing differences in home- and host-country environments.

Market potential varies across countries

In the October 2016 World Economic Outlook (WEO) by the International Monetary Fund (IMF), growth in emerging market and developing economies was expected to account for more than three-quarters of projected world growth. In January 2017, the IMF released an updated WEO, which projected emerging market and developing economies growth at 4.5% in 2017. PwC predicts that the E7 economies (China, India, Indonesia, Russia, Brazil, Turkey, and Mexico) could be double the size of the G7 by 2050 in terms of purchasing power parity.[6]

National differences may also exist in output markets. As we have discussed, distribution systems, government regulations, the effectiveness of different promotion strategies, and customer tastes and preferences may vary in different countries.

In order to exploit national differences, companies may need to reshuffle their business models. For example, the growing middle classes in emerging markets will have different needs and priorities than those that most of the current business models address.[7] They may still have very basic unmet needs (e.g., refrigeration and clothes washing) that require a different value proposition versus the business model existing in advanced markets. Much more of the average household income in emerging markets is spent on food and transportation whereas this figure in the United States is 25%. For companies operating in emerging economies, addressing such needs is not a matter of transferring their existing business models and adjusting them with small tweaks. Instead, MNEs will sometimes need to rethink their business models, so as to solve problems such as accessibility and affordability. To illustrate, consider whether consumer needs in emerging economies are basically local or global. Fashion products and personal banking are examples of global needs, while economy cars and basic and affordable home appliances are exemplars of local needs in these markets. Depending on each of the four categories of the needs and consumer combinations shown in Figure 3.2, companies can develop strategies to better serve middle-class consumers there.

---

[5] Jeffrey R. Immelt, "The CEO of General Electric on sparking an American manufacturing renewal," *Harvard Business Review*, 90 (2012), 43–6.

[6] John Hawksworth, Hannah Audino, Rob Clarry, and Duncan McKellar, "The long view: how will the global economic order change by 2050?" in *The World in 2050* (PwC, 2017), p. 54.

[7] David Court and Laxman Narasimhan, "Capturing the world's emerging middle class," *McKinsey Quarterly*, 3 (2010), 12–17.

Middle-class consumers' needs

		Local	Global
Middle-class consumers' ability to buy	High	Shape or localize	Create a platform
	Low	Reinvent business model	Target niche

Figure 3.2 Category-specific strategies to help companies serve middle-class consumers in emerging economies
Source: Condensed from David Court and Laxman Narasimhan, "Capturing the world's emerging middle class," *McKinsey Quarterly,* 3 (2010), 12–17.

As we will also see in many case examples, a firm can obtain higher prices for its output by tailoring its offerings to fit the unique requirements in each national market.

Scale Economies

Microeconomic theory provides a strong basis for evaluating the effect of scale on cost reduction, and the use of scale as a competitive tool is common in industries ranging from roller bearings to semiconductors. Whereas scale, by itself, is a static concept, there may be dynamic benefits of scale through what has been variously described as the experience or learning effect. The higher volume that helps a firm to exploit scale benefits also allows it to accumulate learning,[8] which leads to progressive cost reduction as the firm moves down its learning curve. So although emerging Korean electronics firms were able to match the scale of experienced Japanese competitors, it took them many years before they could finally compensate for the innumerable process-related efficiencies the Japanese had learned after decades of operating their global-scale plants.

Scope Economies

The concept of scope economies is based on the notion that certain economies arise from the fact that the cost of the joint production (or development or distribution) of two or more products can be less than the cost of producing them separately.[9] Such cost reductions may take place for many reasons – for example, resources such as information or technologies, once acquired for use in producing one item (television sets, for example), are available without cost for production of other items (video players, for instance).

---

[8] For an understanding that accumulation of learning may differ across different firms, see Jaeyong Song, "Subsidiary absorptive capacity and knowledge transfer within multinational corporations," *Journal of International Business Studies*, 45:1 (2014), 73–84.

[9] For a detailed exposition of scope economies, see David J. Teece, "Economies of scope and the scope of the enterprise," *Journal of Economic Behavior and Organization*, 1:3 (1980), 223–47.

Table 3.1 Scope economies in product and market diversification

	Sources of scope economics	
	Product diversification	Market diversification
Shared physical assets	Factory automation with flexibility to produce multiple products (Ford)	Global brand name (Apple)
Shared external relations	Using common distribution channels for multiple products (Samsung)	Servicing multinational customers worldwide (Citibank)
Shared learning	Shared R&D in computer and communications business (NEC)	Pooling knowledge developed in different markets (P&G)

Source: Adapted from Prahalad (1987).

The strategic importance of scope economies arises from a diversified firm's ability to share investments and costs across the same or different value chains – a source of economies that competitors without such internal and external diversity cannot match. Such sharing can take place across segments, products, or markets and may involve the joint use of different kinds of assets (see Table 3.1).

Implicit with each of these tools is the ability to develop an organizational infrastructure that supports it. As we discuss in later chapters, the organizational ability to leverage a global network and value chain will differentiate the winners and losers.

Mapping Ends and Means: Building Blocks for Worldwide Advantage

Table 3.2 shows a mapping of the different goals and means for achieving worldwide competitiveness. Each goals–means intersection suggests some of the factors that may enhance a company's strategic position. Although the factors are only illustrative, it may be useful to study them carefully and compare them against the proposals of the three academic articles mentioned at the beginning of the chapter. It will become apparent that each author focuses on a specific subset of factors – essentially, some different goals–means combinations – and the differences among their prescriptions can be understood in terms of the differences in the particular aspect of worldwide competitive advantage on which they focus.

International, Multinational, Global, and Transnational Strategies

In Chapter 2, we described how environmental forces in different industries shaped alternative approaches to managing worldwide operations that we described as international, multinational, global, and transnational. We now elaborate on the

Table 3.2 Worldwide advantage: goals and means

	Sources of competitive advantage		
Strategic objectives	National differences	Scale economies	Scope economies
Achieving efficiency in current operations	Benefiting from differences in factor costs – wages and cost of capital	Expanding and exploiting potential scale economies in each activity	Sharing of investments and costs across markets and businesses
Managing risks through multinational flexibility	Managing different kinds of risks arising from market- or policy-induced changes in comparative advantages of different countries	Balancing scale with strategic and operational flexibility	Portfolio diversification of risks and creation of options and side bets
Innovation, learning, and adaptation	Learning from societal differences in organizational and managerial processes and systems	Benefiting from experience – cost reduction and innovation	Shared learning across organizational components in different products, markets, or businesses

distinctions among these different approaches, as well as their respective strengths and vulnerabilities in terms of the different goals–means combinations we have just described.

International Strategy

Companies adopting this broad approach focus on creating and exploiting innovations on a worldwide basis, using all the different means to achieve this end. MNEs headquartered in technologically advanced countries with sophisticated markets often adopted this strategic approach but limited it primarily to exploiting home-country innovations to develop their competitive positions abroad. The international product cycle theory we described in Chapter 1 encompasses both the strategic motivation and competitive posture of these companies: at least initially, their internationalization process relied heavily on transferring new products, processes, or strategies developed in the home country to less advanced overseas markets.

This approach was common among US-based MNEs such as Kraft, Pfizer, P&G, and General Electric. Although these companies built considerable strength out of their ability to create and leverage innovation, many suffered from deficiencies of both efficiency and flexibility because they did not develop either the centralized and high-scale operations of companies adopting global strategies or the very high degree of local responsiveness that multinational companies could muster through their autonomous, self-sufficient, and entrepreneurial local operations. This deficiency has led some of the companies in this category to change. Kraft, for example, in an effort to leverage its iconic North American brands in the global snack business, created a new subsidiary Mondelez International Inc. – hence its efficiency stand. At the same time, its North America-focused grocery business aims to have flexibility and local responsiveness in this line of business.

Johnnie Walkers in turn, pursued both a global and local (glocal) advertising strategy with their "Keep Walking" campaign. The elements of the campaign were slightly modified depending on the culture and market it appeared in; however, the underlying message was retained. They have more than doubled their global business in ten years and have changed the Johnnie Walker and Scotch whisky business globally.[10]

Multinational Strategy

The multinational strategic approach focuses primarily on one means (national differences) to achieve most of its strategic objectives. Companies adopting this approach tend to focus on the revenue side, usually by differentiating their products and services in response to national differences in customer preferences, industry characteristics, and government regulations. This approach leads most multinational companies to depend on local-for-local innovations, a process requiring the subsidiary to not only identify local needs but also use its own local resources to respond to those needs. Carrying out most activities within each country on a local-for-local basis also allows those adopting a multinational strategy to match costs and revenues on a currency-by-currency basis.

Historically, many European companies, such as Unilever, ICI, Philips, and Nestlé, followed this strategic model. In these companies, assets and resources historically were widely dispersed, allowing overseas subsidiaries to carry out a wide range of activities from development and production to sales and services. Their self-sufficiency was typically accompanied by considerable local autonomy. But, although such independent national units were unusually flexible and responsive to their local environments, they inevitably suffered problems of inefficiencies and an inability to exploit the knowledge and competencies of other national units. These inefficiencies have led some of these companies to change. The CEO of Unilever, for example, in its 2011 annual report expressed that: "We are changing the organization. Today we are more agile, more consumer responsive and better able to leverage global scale." Yet by 2017, the same CEO said, "it has seen the world become more 'multipolar' with local tastes and nationalism playing a bigger role in consumers' lives."

Global Strategy

Companies adopting the classic global strategic approach, as we have defined it, depend primarily on developing global efficiency. They use all the different means to achieve the best cost and quality positions for their products.

---

[10] Jerry Wind, Stan Sthanunathan, and Rob Malcolm, "Great advertising is both local and global," *Harvard Business Review*, March 29 (2013). Accessed March 13, 2017, https://hbr.org/2013/03/great-advertising-is-both-loca.

This means has been the classic approach of many Japanese companies such as Toyota, Canon, Komatsu, and Matsushita (Panasonic). As these and other similar companies have found, however, such efficiency comes with some compromises of both flexibility and learning. For example, concentrating manufacturing to capture global scale may also result in a high level of intercountry product shipments that can raise risks of policy intervention, particularly by host governments in major importer countries. Similarly, companies that centralize R&D for efficiency reasons often find they are constrained in their ability to capture new developments in countries outside their home markets or to leverage innovations created by foreign subsidiaries in the rest of their worldwide operations. And, finally, the concentration (most often through centralization) of activities such as R&D and manufacturing to achieve a global scale exposes such companies to high sourcing risks, particularly in exchange rate exposure. As an example, the 2011 earthquake in Japan was so harmful to Canon that it announced it was pursuing a new regional headquarters management system (one headquarters each in the United States, Europe, and Japan) to manage its local product developments. Each has the authority to roll out businesses globally.

The descriptions we have presented to this point regarding multinational versus global strategies have been mostly described in their pure forms. In practice, of course, many firms do adopt a regional strategy, focusing much of their international expansion on the home region, plus perhaps one or two other regions. Ford Motor Company, for example, operates two manufacturing plants in India and has invested over \$2 billion since 1995. The Ford Next-Gen Figo, Aspire, and EcoSport models are exported to over 40 markets.

Transnational Strategy

Beneath each of these three traditional strategic approaches lies some implicit assumptions about how best to build worldwide competitive advantage. The global company assumes that the best cost position is the key source of competitiveness; the multinational company sees differentiation as the primary way to enhance performance; and the international company expects to use innovations to reduce costs, enhance revenues, or both. Companies adopting the transnational strategy recognize that each of these traditional approaches is partial, that each has its own merits, but none represents the whole truth.

To achieve worldwide competitive advantage, costs and revenues have to be managed simultaneously, both efficiency and innovation are important, and innovations can arise in many different parts of the organization. Therefore instead of focusing on any subpart of the set of issues shown in Table 3.2, the transnational company focuses on exploiting each and every goals–means combination to develop layers of competitive advantage by exploiting efficiency, flexibility, and learning simultaneously.

To achieve this ambitious strategic approach, however, the transnational company must develop a very different configuration of assets and capabilities than is typical of traditional multinational, international, and global company structures. The global company tends to concentrate all its resources – either in its home country or in low-cost overseas locations – to exploit the scale economies available in each activity. The multinational company typically disperses its resources among its different national operations to be able to respond to local needs. And the international company tends to centralize those resources that are key to developing innovations but decentralize others to allow its innovations to be adapted worldwide.

The transnational, however, must develop a more sophisticated and differentiated configuration of assets and capabilities. It first decides which key resources and capabilities are best centralized within the home-country operation, not only to realize scale economies but also to protect certain core competencies and provide the necessary supervision of corporate management. Basic research, for example, is often viewed as such a capability, with core technologies kept at home for reasons of strategic security as well as competence concentration.

Certain other resources may be concentrated but not necessarily at home – a configuration that might be termed "ex-centralization" rather than decentralization. World-scale production plants for labor-intensive products may be built in a low-wage country such as Mexico or Bangladesh. The advanced state of a particular technology may demand concentration of relevant R&D resources and activities in Japan, Germany, or the United States. Such flexible specialization – or ex-centralization – complements the benefits of scale economies with the flexibility of accessing low input costs or scarce resources and the responsiveness of accommodating national political interests. This approach can also apply to specific functional activities. For example, McDonald's moved its international tax base to Britain. This holding company would receive royalties from licensing deals outside the United States. Earlier, Amsterdam-based software company Irdeto opened a second headquarters in Beijing to enhance the influence of its managers in the fast-growing Chinese market on the company's decision-making processes. To underscore the commitment, the CEO and his family moved to China in 2007.

Some other resources may best be decentralized on a regional or local basis because either potential economies of scale are small or there is a need to create flexibility by avoiding exclusive dependence on a single facility. Local or regional facilities may not only afford protection against exchange rate shifts, strikes, natural disasters, and other disruptions, but also reduce logistical and coordination costs. An important side benefit provided by such facilities is the impact they can have in building the motivation and capability of national subsidiaries, an impact that can easily make small efficiency sacrifices worthwhile.

Table 3.3 summarizes the differences in the asset configurations that support the different strategic approaches of the various MNE models. We explore these strategy–organizational linkages in more detail in Chapter 4.

Worldwide Competitive Advantage: The Strategic Tasks

In the final section of this chapter, we look at how a company can respond to the strategic challenges we have described. The task will clearly be very different

Table 3.3 Strategic orientation and configuration of assets and capabilities in international, multinational, global, and transnational companies

	International	Multinational	Global	Transnational
Strategic orientation	Exploiting parent-company knowledge and capabilities through worldwide diffusion and adaptation	Building flexibility to respond to national differences through strong, resourceful, and entrepreneurial national operations	Building cost advantages through centralized, global-scale operations	Developing global efficiency, flexibility, and worldwide learning capability simultaneously
Configuration of assets and capabilities	Sources of core competencies centralized, others decentralized	Decentralized and nationally self-sufficient	Centralized and globally scaled	Dispersed, interdependent, and specialized

depending on the company's international posture and history. Companies that are among the major worldwide players in their businesses must focus on defending their dominance while also building new sources of advantage. For companies that are smaller, but aspire to worldwide competitiveness, the task is one of building the resources and capabilities needed to challenge the entrenched leaders. And for companies that are focused on their national markets and lack either the resources or the motivation for international expansion, the challenge is to protect their domestic positions from others that have the advantage of being MNEs.

Defending Worldwide Dominance

In recent decades, the shifting external forces we have described have resulted in severe difficulties – even for those MNEs that had enjoyed strong historical positions in their businesses worldwide.

Typically, most of these companies pursued traditional multinational, international, or global strategies, and their past successes were built on the fit between their specific strategic capability and the dominant environmental force in their industries. In multinational industries such as branded packaged products, in which forces for national responsiveness were dominant, companies such as Unilever developed strong worldwide positions by adopting multinational strategies. In contrast, in global industries such as consumer electronics or semiconductor chips, companies such as Panasonic or Hitachi built leadership positions by adopting global strategies.

In the emerging competitive environment, however, these companies could no longer rely on their historic ability to exploit global efficiency, multinational flexibility, or worldwide learning. As an increasing number of industries developed what we have termed transnational characteristics, companies faced the need to master all three strategic capabilities simultaneously.

The challenge for the leading companies was to protect and enhance the particular strength they had while simultaneously building the other capabilities.

For many MNEs, the initial response to this new strategic challenge was to try to restructure the configuration of their assets and activities to develop the capabilities they lacked. For example, global companies with highly centralized resources sought to develop flexibility by dispersing resources among their national subsidiaries; multinational companies, in contrast, tried to emulate their global competitors by centralizing R&D, manufacturing, and other scale-intensive activities. In essence, these companies tried to find a new "fit" configuration through drastic restructuring of their existing configuration.

Such a zero-based search for the ideal configuration not only led to external problems, such as conflict with host governments over issues like plant closures, but also resulted in trauma inside the company's own organization. The greatest problem with such an approach, however, was that it tended to erode the particular competency the company already had without effectively adding the new strengths it sought.[11]

The complex balancing act of protecting existing advantages while building new ones required companies to follow two fairly simple principles. First, they had to concentrate at least as much on defending and reinforcing their existing assets and capabilities as on developing new ones. Their approach tended to be one of building on – and eventually modifying – their existing infrastructure instead of radical restructuring. To the extent possible, they relied on modernizing existing facilities rather than dismantling the old and creating new ones.

Second, most successful adaptors looked for ways to compensate for their deficiency or approximate a competitor's source of advantage, rather than trying to imitate its asset structure or task configuration. In searching for efficiency, multinational companies with a decentralized and dispersed resource structure found it easier to develop efficiency by adopting new flexible manufacturing technologies in some of their existing plants and upgrading others to become global or regional sources, rather than to close those plants and shift production to lower cost countries to match the structure of competitive global companies.

Similarly, successful global companies found it more effective to develop responsiveness and flexibility by creating internal linkages between their national sales subsidiaries and their centralized development or manufacturing units, rather than trying to mimic multinational companies by dispersing their resources to each country operation and, in the process, undermining their core strength of efficiency.

Challenging the Global Leader

A number of companies have managed to evolve from relatively small national players to major worldwide competitors, challenging the dominance of traditional

[11] For a discussion about the dynamic capabilities perspective, see John Cantwell, "Revisiting international business theory: a capabilities-based theory of the MNE," *Journal of International Business Studies*, 45:1 (2014), 1–7.

leaders in their businesses. Dell in the computer industry, Magna in auto parts, Electrolux in the domestic appliances business, and CEMEX in the cement industry are examples of companies that have evolved from relative obscurity to global visibility within relatively short periods of time.

The actual processes adopted to manage such dramatic transformations vary widely from company to company. Electrolux, for example, grew almost exclusively through acquisitions, whereas Dell built capabilities largely through internal development, and Magna and CEMEX used a mix of greenfield investments and acquisitions. Similarly, whereas Dell built its growth on the basis of cost advantages and logistics capabilities, it expanded internationally because of its direct sales business model and its ability to react quickly to changes in customer demand.

Despite wide differences in their specific approaches, however, most of these new champions appear to have followed a similar step-by-step approach to building their competitive positions.

Each developed an initial toehold in the market by focusing on a narrow niche – often one specific product within one specific market – and developing a strong competitive position within that niche. That competitive position was built on multiple sources of competitive advantage rather than on a single strategic capability.

Next, they expanded their toehold to a foothold by limited and carefully selected expansion along both product and geographic dimensions and by extending the step-by-step improvement of both cost and quality to this expanded portfolio. Such expansion was sometimes focused on products and markets that were not of central importance to the established leaders in the business. By staying outside the range of the leaders' peripheral vision, the challenger could remain relatively invisible, thereby building up its strength and infrastructure without incurring direct retaliation from competitors with far greater resources. For example, emerging companies often focused initially on relatively low-margin products such as small-screen TV sets or subcompact cars.

While developing their own product portfolio, technological capabilities, geographic scope, and marketing expertise, challengers were often able to build up manufacturing volume and its resulting cost efficiencies by becoming original equipment manufacturer suppliers to their larger competitors. Although this supply allowed the larger competitor to benefit from the challenger's cost advantages, it also developed the supplying company's understanding of customer needs and marketing strategies in the advanced markets served by the leading companies.

Once these building blocks for worldwide advantage were in place, the challenger typically moved rapidly to convert its low-profile foothold into a strong permanent position in the worldwide business. Dramatic scaling up of production facilities typically preceded a wave of new product introductions and expansion into the key markets through multiple channels and their own brand names.

Another way a challenger may pursue rapid transition into a strong international presence is through acquisitions, as Shuanghui International did in 2013 with the acquisition of Smithfield Foods or as Qingdao Haier Company did in 2016 with the acquisition of General Electric's appliance business. These deals were valued at $7.1 billion and $5.4 billion respectively.

Protecting Domestic Niches

For reasons of limited resources or other constraints, some national companies may not be able to aspire to such worldwide expansion, although they are not insulated from the impact of global competition. Their major challenge is to protect their domestic niches from worldwide players with superior resources and multiple sources of competitive advantage.[12] This concern is particularly an issue in developing markets such as India and China, where local companies face much larger, more aggressive, and deeper pocketed competitors.

There are three broad alternative courses of action that can be pursued by such national competitors. The first approach is to defend against the competitor's global advantage. Just as MNE managers can act to facilitate the globalization of industry structure, so their counterparts in national companies can use their influence in the opposite direction. An astute manager of a national company might be able to foil the attempts of a global competitor by taking action to influence industry structure or market conditions to the national company's advantage. These actions might involve influencing consumer preference to demand a more locally adapted or service-intensive product; it could imply tying up key distribution channels; or it might mean preempting local sources of critical supplies. Many companies trying to enter the Japanese market claim to have faced this type of defensive strategy by local firms.

A second strategic option would be to offset the competitor's global advantage. The simplest way to do this is to lobby for government assistance in the form of tariff protections. However, in an era of declining tariffs, this is increasingly unsuccessful. A more ambitious approach is to gain government sponsorship to develop equivalent global capabilities through funding of R&D, subsidizing exports, and financing capital investments. As a "national champion," the company would theoretically be able to compete globally. However, in reality, it is very unusual for such a company to prosper. Airbus Industrie, which now shares the global market for large commercial airplanes with Boeing, is one of the few exceptions – rising from the ashes of other attempts by European governments to sponsor a viable computer company in the 1970s and then to promote a European electronics industry a decade later. Also, General Electric's lobbying activities in 2009 led to its inclusion in the bailout program of the US government.

The third alternative is to approximate the competitors' global advantages by linking up in some form of alliance or coalition with a viable global company. Numerous such linkages have been formed with the purpose of sharing the risks and costs of operating in a high-risk global environment. By pooling or exchanging market access, technology, and production capability, smaller competitors can gain some measure of defense against global giants. For example, in March 2017, a memorandum of understanding was signed between Volkswagen and India's Tata Motors. This agreement will allow them to explore a partnership of developing auto components and vehicles for the Indian market and more. Both companies have

---

[12] For a detailed discussion, see Niraj Dawar and Tony Frost, "Competing with giants: survival strategies for local companies competing in emerging markets," *Harvard Business Review*, 77:2 (1999), 119–30.

fallen behind in the Indian market against competitors such as Hyundai and Maruti Suzuki. Similarly, the Indian telecom company Bharti has established a variety of inbound alliances with foreign firms to create a winning strategy for the Indian market and is now one of the top telecom companies in the world.

CONCLUDING COMMENTS

Although these three strategic responses obviously do not cover every possible scenario, they highlight two important points from this chapter. First, the MNE faces a complex set of options in terms of the strategic levers it can pull to achieve competitive advantage, and the framework in Table 3.2 helps make sense of those options by separating out means and ends. Second, the competitive intensity in most industries is such that a company cannot solely afford to do something different from what other companies do. Rather, it is necessary to gain competitive parity on all relevant dimensions (efficiency, flexibility, learning) while also achieving differentiation on one. To be sure, the ability to achieve multiple competitive objectives at the same time is far from straightforward and, as a result, we see many MNEs experimenting with new ways of organizing their worldwide activities. And this organization will be the core issue we will address in the next chapter.

HARVARD | BUSINESS | SCHOOL

REV. NOVEMBER 23, 2015

BRIEF CASES

Christopher A. Bartlett and Carole Carlson

CASE 3.1 UNITED CEREAL: LORA BRILL'S EUROBRAND CHALLENGE

Lora Brill, United Cereal's European vice president, was alone in her office early on a cold March morning in 2010. "I've given approval to a dozen big product launches in my career," she thought. "But the implications that this one has for our European strategy and organization make it by far the most difficult I've had to make."

The decision related to Healthy Berry Crunch, a new breakfast cereal that the French subsidiary wanted to launch. But Europe's changing market and competitive conditions had led Brill to consider making this the company's first coordinated multimarket Eurobrand launch. It was a possibility that had surfaced some equally challenging organizational questions. "Well it's only 7 AM," Brill thought to herself, smiling. "I have until my lunch appointment to decide!"

United Cereal: Breakfast Cereal Pioneer

In 2010, United Cereal celebrated its 100th birthday. Established in 1910 by Jed Thomas, an immigrant grocer from England, the company's first product was a packaged mix of cracked wheat, rolled oats, and malt flakes that Thomas sold in his Kalamazoo, Michigan, grocery store. UC, as it was known in the industry, eventually diversified into snack foods, dairy products, drinks and beverages, frozen foods, and baked goods. By 2010 UC was a $9 billion business, but breakfast cereals still accounted for one-third of its revenues and even more of its profits.

UC's Corporate Values, Policies, and Practices

Thomas grew the company with a strong set of values that endured through its history, and "commitment, diligence, and loyalty" were watchwords in UC. As a result, it attracted people who wanted to make a career with the company, and it promoted managers from within.

Among its managers United Cereal instilled a strong commitment to "The UC Way," a set of time-tested policies, processes, and practices embedded in iconic company phrases. For example, "Listen to the customer" was a deeply rooted belief that led UC to become a pioneer in the use of consumer research and focus groups. "Spot the trend, make the market" was another iconic phrase reflecting the high value placed on extensive market testing prior to launching new products. Finally, the value of "Honoring the past while embracing the future" led UC to reject the conventional wisdom that processed food brands had fixed life cycles. Through continuous innovation in marketing and product development, many of its products remained market leaders despite being more than half a century old.

United Cereal had a well-earned reputation as an innovator. During its 100-year history, its R&D labs had secured more product and process patents than any other competitor. The company had also pioneered the "brand management" system in the food industry, giving brand managers leadership of cross-functional teams that included manufacturing, marketing, and other functions. Each brand was managed as a profit center and was constantly measured against other brands. Brand managers also competed for R&D and product development resources.

Although this system reduced lateral communication, vertical communication was strong, and top managers were very involved in seemingly mundane brand decisions. For example, advertising copy and label changes could require up to a dozen sign-offs before obtaining final approval at the corporate VP level. "It's due to the high value we attach to our brands and our image," explained a senior executive. "But it's also because we give our brand managers responsibility at a very young age." While the company took few risks (a failed launch could cost millions even in small markets), it balanced deliberate cautiousness with a willingness to invest in products it decided to support. "The competitors can see us coming months ahead and miles away," the senior executives said. "But they know that when we get there, we'll bet the farm."

The Breakfast Cereal Market

Breakfast cereal was in its infancy when UC was founded, but it soon grew to be one of the great food commercialization successes of the 20th century. From the 1890s when Keith Kellogg created corn flakes in his attempt to improve the diet of hospital patients, the industry had grown to achieve worldwide revenues exceeding $21 billion in 2009. The U.S. industry included more than 30 companies with combined annual revenues of $12 billion. But just five players accounted for 80% of sales.

The industry recognized two categories of cereals–hot and ready-to-eat. The latter accounted for 90% of sales in both the United States and Europe. In this highly competitive industry, more than 10% of revenues was spent on advertising and marketing. Profitability also depended on operating efficiently, managing materials costs, and maximizing retail shelf space. Larger companies had significant advantages in purchasing, distribution, and marketing.

In the fight for share, several new product introductions typically occurred each year. Developing a new brand was time-intensive and expensive, typically taking two to four years. Brand extensions–for example, General Mills's creation of Honey Nut Cheerios–were generally less expensive and less risky due to scale economies that could be leveraged in both production and marketing. But for most U.S. cereal companies, growth was increasingly coming from expansion into new offshore markets, and UC was no exception.

UC's European Operations

United Cereal entered European markets in 1952 by acquiring an English baked goods company. (Its European offices were still in London.) Over the next 30 years, UC expanded its European presence, typically by acquiring an established company with local market distribution, and then growing it by introducing products from the U.S. line. By 2009, Europe accounted for 20% of United Cereal's worldwide sales.

European Industry and Competitive Structure

Europe's $7 billion breakfast cereal market in 2010 had been overlaid on a variety of national tastes and breakfast traditions–cold meats and cheese in the Netherlands, pastries in Greece, bacon and eggs in Britain, and croissants in France. As a result, per capita consumption of cereals varied significantly across markets from 8 kg. a year in the United Kingdom to 0.5 kg. a year in Italy. Channels also varied widely by country, with supermarkets and hypermarkets accounting for more than 80% of grocery sales in Germany, 37% in France, and only 17% in Italy.

U.S.-based companies Kellogg and United Cereal were the largest two competitors in the European market with 26% and 20% share respectively. Cereal Partners, a joint venture between General Mills and Nestlé, ranked third with 17%, and U.K.-based Weetabix trailed these leaders with 7%. Numerous smaller manufacturers divided the remaining 30% of the market.

United Cereal regarded Kellogg as its toughest competitor. Operating through strong national subsidiaries, Kellogg used its volume to lower operating costs and to establish and maintain shelf space. Cereal Partners sold brands that included Cheerios and Shredded Wheat, and leveraged Nestlé's technical expertise and its European retailer relationships to compete. Although Weetabix was a smaller private company, like the bigger competitors, it also relied on strong branding and promotions to gain market share. Smaller competitors tended to hold niche market positions, but often challenged larger players with targeted price promotions.

UC's Europe Strategy and Organization

Major differences across European markets had led United Cereal to establish national subsidiaries, each led by a country manager (CM) who operated with wide latitude to make product and marketing decisions that would maximize the subsidiary's local profit. Based on their market understanding, these CMs usually selected from United Cereal's stable of more than 100 branded products, adapting them to the local situation.

Expecting its CMs to conform to its embedded values, policies, and procedures, United Cereal built its subsidiaries as "mini UC's"–exact replicas of the parent organization staffed by managers well-versed in UC's corporate values and practices. So while CMs were able to customize products, adjust manufacturing processes, and adapt advertising and promotions, they had to do so while respecting the "UC Way."

This approach unleashed CMs' entrepreneurial instincts and led to strong penetration in most national markets. While many products flourished through such local customization, over time, wide differences in product profiles and market strategies became problematic. For example, in the U.K., the Wake Up! instant coffee brand was formulated as a mild to medium roast beverage promoted as "the perfect milk coffee." But in France and Italy it was sold as a dark roast product and advertised as "the instant espresso." And differences in the positioning of Mother Hubbard's Pies resulted in it being offered as a high-end dessert in Germany, while in the U.K. it was priced aggressively and positioned as "a convenient everyday treat."

Increasing Price and Profit Pressure

Over the preceding decade, the cereal market in Europe had become increasingly competitive. While total grocery sales had remained remarkably stable through the 2008–09 global recession, all manufacturers had seen their product mix shift toward their lower-priced offerings. Market growth slowed to less than 1% annually, and UC experienced growing price and promotion pressure from Kellogg and Cereal Partners in virtually every country in which it operated. As margins came under pressure, achieving lower costs and implementing more efficient processes became vital. (See **Exhibits 1** and **2** for financial performance.)

In this changing landscape, some of UC's historical policies came under the microscope. The company's focus on local products and markets, with its need for significant marketing and product development teams in each country, had led to a situation where sales, general and administrative (SG&A) expenses were 25% higher than in the U.S. operations. Furthermore, due to the high costs of developing and launching new products for single country markets, the pace of major new product introductions had slowed considerably in recent years. Lacking the resources for either large-scale market testing or new product launches, most CMs now favored product extensions over new product introductions, and many increasingly relied on cost reductions in their existing portfolios to maintain profits. It was a situation that raised concerns.

United Cereal Response

The earliest response to these problems had been initiated by Arne Olsen, a Norwegian appointed as UC's European VP in 2002 with a mandate to invigorate the product portfolio and reverse declining profitability. Olsen quickly reorganized R&D, reinforcing the European research facility near UC Europe's headquarters in London. To link these food scientists working on basic issues with the subsidiary-based technologists refining and testing products in local markets, Olsen created a European Technical Team (ETT) for each major product group. Each ETT was composed of the strongest local product development technologists teamed with central R&D scientists to provide

Exhibit 1
United Cereal Selected Financial Results (USD in 000s)

	2007	2008	2009
Sales	8,993,204	9,069,242	9,254,329
COGS	4,226,806	4,271,613	4,445,671
SG&A	2,787,893	2,856,811	2,868,842
Depreciation and Amortization	362,500	375,000	370,173
Operating Income	1,616,005	1,565,818	1,569,643
Interest Expense	44,120	45,667	46,271
Other Income	19,653	22,500	18,508
Income Before Taxes	1,591,538	1,542,651	1,541,880
Income Taxes	410,232	415,450	420,000
Net Income	1,181,306	1,127,201	1,121,880
Total Assets	6,313,000	6,215,890	6,300,000
Long-term Debt	1,021,300	998,100	1,050,000
Shareholder's Equity	1,722,900	1,786,200	1,751,400

Exhibit 2
United Cereal SG&A by Market (USD in 000s)

2009 Sales and SG&A Expense			
	United Cereal	**Europe**	**France**
Sales	9,254,329	1,850,866	388,682
SG&A			
Advertising and Other Marketing	1,526,964	378,687	75,737
Product Development	188,815	54,701	5,553
Other SG&A	1,153,063	216,263	46,071
SG&A subtotal	2,868,842	649,651	127,361
SG&A as a % of Sales	31.00%	35.10%	32.77%

overall direction on European product development. To facilitate collaboration, Olsen encouraged transfers between the London team and the country offices, and also strengthened relationships with the R&D labs in Kalamazoo.

In 2004, Olsen expanded this technical program into what he called the "Europeanization Initiative," aimed squarely at product market strategies. His first test was UC's frozen fruit juice line, which had languished for years. He was convinced that there was little difference in tastes for fruit juice across markets, and that there were significant benefits in standardizing the products as well as their marketing, promotion, and advertising. He transferred a senior manager from Germany to the European headquarters and gave him responsibility to standardize products, develop a coordinated Europewide strategy, and oversee implementation across subsidiaries.

The experiment was a disaster. Local CMs perceived the initiative as a direct challenge to their local autonomy–a belief made worse by the domineering personality of the individual they called the "European Juice Nazi." While they reluctantly implemented his imposed product positioning and advertising directives, they provided minimal support from the local sales forces that remained under their control. Unsurprisingly, the frozen juice category stagnated, and eventually responsibility for juice products was returned to the countries.

In 2006, Olsen was transferred to Kalamazoo in a senior marketing role, and Lora Brill, former UK country manager, became the new European vice president. In the aftermath of the 2008/2009 recession, with continuing pressure on margins, Brill needed to leverage marketing resources–the largest controllable expense in subsidiary budgets. Eventually, she too became convinced that the coordinated European approach that had succeeded in product development could be adapted for product marketing. It was in this context that she began to pursue an idea she referred to as the "Eurobrand" concept. And in 2010, a proposal by the French subsidiary to launch Healthy Berry Crunch offered the possibility of a first test case.

The Healthy Berry Crunch Project

In the late 1990s, aging baby boomers took an increased interest in natural, healthy foods in both the United States and Europe. This created a challenge for cereal companies whose highly processed products were typically high in sugar. In response, some felt that the addition of fruit could provide "a halo of health." The main technical problem was that fruit's moisture content made it difficult to maintain the crispness and shelf life of cereal. But a solution was found in the use of freeze-dried fruits, which also retained their color and shape in a cereal mix.

The French Opportunity

In 2003, Kellogg introduced Special K with freeze-dried strawberries in the U.K., and in

2007 Cereal Partners launched Berry Burst Cheerios. Seeing interest in healthy breakfast foods growing in France, UC's French country manager Jean-Luc Michel felt there could be a market for an organic fruit-based cereal in his market. Although Kellogg's Special K with Strawberries had been launched in France in 2006, to date it was alone in this new segment.

In 2008, Michel started initial product development and testing in France, later involving the ETT to develop detailed specifications. He recommended an organic blueberry-based cereal as a product extension of Healthy Crunch–a UC cereal already positioned in the health-conscious adult segment but experiencing no growth in recent years. He felt the use of blueberries, with their well-known antioxidant qualities, would reinforce the positioning.

In keeping with UC policy, as soon as the product was ready, Michel implemented a full-scale test market in Lyon. (See **Exhibit 3** for test market results.) Results were mixed, with some consumers finding the berries too tart. With the "intention to repurchase" rate below UC's 60%

Exhibit 3
Test Market and Consumer Panel Results
Lyon Test Market: September–November 2009

	Shipments in Stock Taking Units (000s) (volume index)			Share %	
Month	**Actual**	**Target**		**Actual**	**Target**
September	4.6	1.9		1.5	0.6
October	4.0	2.5		1.3	0.8
November	3.1	4.0		1.0	1.3

Use and Awareness (After 3 months, 188 responses)	
Ever consumed	14
Consumed in past 4 weeks	4
Ever purchased[a]	3
Purchased past 4 weeks	2
Advertising awareness	19
Brand awareness	28

Attitude Data (After 3 months, 126 responses: Free sample and purchase users)	
Taste: cereal	65/11[b]
Taste: fruit	49/19
Health aspect	37/4
Form, consistency	13/6

Intent to Repurchase (After 3 months: 126 responses from free and sample purchase users)	%
"I plan to repurchase the product in the next three months"	56/26/18[c]

[a] Difference between consumed and purchased data due to free sampling.

[b] Number of unsolicited and unduplicated comments Favorable/Unfavorable in user interviews (e.g., among 126 consumers interviewed, 65 commented favorably on the cereal taste and 11 commented negatively).

[c] Percentage split Yes/No/Unsure.

minimum target, an alternate raspberry-based product was developed but proved too expensive to manufacture. So a sweeter blueberry version was taste-tested with focus groups in six French cities. While lacking the validated full test-market data UC policy required, Michel felt focus group data indicating a 64% intention to repurchase was very promising. He was ready to launch:

> It's clearly a big improvement on our initial test market data. But this is a new product concept, so any test only provides a general indication. In a fast-growing category like this, we need to launch now before competitors preempt us ... We've been in development and testing for more than a year. We can't wait three months more to mount another full-scale test market. Besides, my budget won't support the $2 million it would cost.

The European Debate

Even before Michel set about obtaining launch approval, Brill was aware of his intention and had begun exploring the idea of launching Healthy Berry Crunch Europewide to test her nascent Eurobrand concept. Her director of finance had estimated that implementing coordinated European product market strategies could result in staff reductions and other savings that would cut product development and marketing costs by 10% to 15% over three years. Since these costs were running above 23% of sales in Europe, the savings could be very significant.

Brill next met with Kurt Jaeger, her Division VP responsible for Northern Europe and the person she regarded as Europe's most knowledgeable about breakfast cereal strategy. He was strongly in favor of a coordinated European rollout:

> Our strategy of responding to local market differences was right for its time, but not necessarily today. Consumer tastes are converging, old cultural habits are disappearing, and EU regulation of labeling, advertising, and general marketing practices is eroding market differences ... I've had my CMs in Germany and Benelux conduct consumer panels on Healthy Berry Crunch. The samples are small,

but it's encouraging that their results are similar to the French panel findings...Our biggest risk is the competition. The PodCafé debacle shows that they are way ahead of us in coordinating European strategy.

The "PodCafé debacle" to which Jaeger referred had occurred following UC's introduction of its innovative PodCafé single-serve coffee pods for home espresso machines in Germany in 2003. But by the time the French subsidiary decided to launch its version in 2006, and Italy the following year, the coffee pod market had become crowded with copycat products, and United Cereal's product was relegated to a third-place share in both of those key markets.

But Jorge Sanchez, the Division VP for Southern Europe to whom Jean-Luc Michel reported, was less enthusiastic about the Eurobrand idea. He told Brill:

> Although Jean-Luc has only been in his CM role for 18 months, I think his enthusiasm for Healthy Berry Crunch is just the kind of entrepreneurial initiative we want from our CM's. But a launch like this will cost at least $20 million in France–10 times my approval level, and twice yours. Frankly, I have real concerns about whether his budget can support it ... Even if France goes ahead, my Italian CM tells me he doesn't think he could get shelf space for a specialty cereal. And our struggling Spanish subsidiary is still in recovery from the recession. There's no way they have a budget for a new launch now.

Brill also heard from her old boss, Arne Olsen, who told her that word of the proposed French launch had already reached to Kalamazoo. Olsen thought she should know about a conversation he recently had with the company's executive vice president:

> Lou's an old traditionalist who has spent his whole career here in corporate headquarters, and sees himself as a guardian of the company's values. He told me over lunch that he's worried that Europe is rushing into this launch, shortcutting the product, consumer, and market research that has ensured UC's past successes. His is one of the signatures

you'll need to authorize the launch, so I thought you should know his views.

The Organizational Challenge

As she listened to this different advice, Brill was also aware that her decision would be based on organizational as well as strategic considerations. Having witnessed the disastrous European fruit juice strategy years earlier, she was determined to learn from its failure. In meetings with her HR director, she began to develop some alternative organizational proposals.

For some time, she had been planning to expand the responsibilities of her three regional vice presidents. In addition to their current roles supervising subsidiaries by region, she proposed giving each of them Europewide coordinating responsibility for several products. For example, Kurt Jaeger, who was responsible for UC's subsidiaries in Germany, Austria, Switzerland, and Benelux, would also oversee the cross-market coordination of strategy for cereals, snacks, and baked goods. For the first time, the structure would introduce a European perspective to product strategy. But Brill was conscious that she did not want to dilute the responsibility of CMs and clearly described the VPs' new product roles as advisory. She hoped that the status, position, and experience of these senior managers would ensure that their input would be carefully considered. (**Exhibit 4** shows the proposed organization.)

Conscious that these changes would not be sufficient to implement her Eurobrand concept, Brill began to explore the idea of creating Eurobrand Teams modeled on the European Technical Teams that had proved so effective. The proposed teams would be composed of brand managers from each country subsidiary that sold the product, representatives of the European central functional departments including manufacturing, R&D, purchasing and logistics, and a representative from the appropriate regional division VP's office. They would be chaired by the brand manager of an assigned "lead country," selected based on the individual's experience and the subsidiary's resources, expertise, and strong market position in the brand.

Brill envisioned that European brand strategies would be developed by the relevant Eurobrand Teams rather than by someone at European headquarters. This meant that these teams would decide product formulation, market positioning, packaging, advertising, pricing, and promotions. In her vision, the teams would also be responsible for finding ways to reduce costs and increase brand profitability.

As she tested these ideas with her HR director and others in the London office, the European VP received some positive feedback but also heard some criticisms and concerns. Some wondered whether the CMs might still see this as a challenge to their local authority; others raised the question of whether the allocation of "lead country" roles might not concentrate power in a few large subsidiaries like Germany; and still others questioned whether teams with a dozen or more members would function effectively.

But the strongest pushback Brill received was from James Miller, the Division VP responsible for U.K. and Scandinavian countries. "This all sounds far too complex for me," he told her. "If we're serious about competing as one company in Europe, let's forget about all these teams and just move to a European product structure with someone clearly in charge."

Decision Time

On a cold March morning, Brill arrived in her office at 7 AM and began checking her e-mail. At the top of the inbox was a message from Jean-Luc Michel to Jorge Sanchez with a copy to Brill: "Jorge: One of my sales reps just heard a rumor that Cereal Partners is planning to launch Berry Burst Cheerios in France. It's now two weeks since I submitted my Healthy Berry Crunch launch request. Can you advise when I might expect a decision? Regards, Jean-Luc."

Brill nodded silently as she checked her appointment schedule for the day and saw that Kurt Jaeger had set up a lunch meeting with her for noon. Her assistant had noted on the calendar entry: "Re. Eurobrand launch decision."

Exhibit 4 Organization Chart

United Cereal Europe Organization

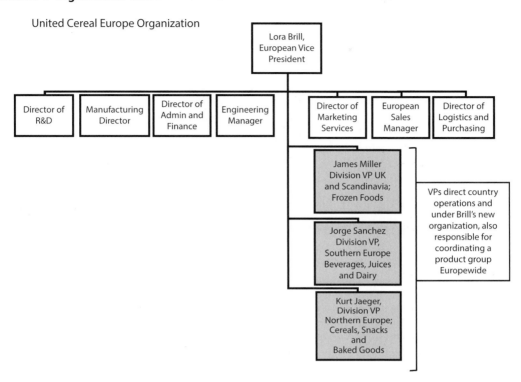

United Cereal Country Organization

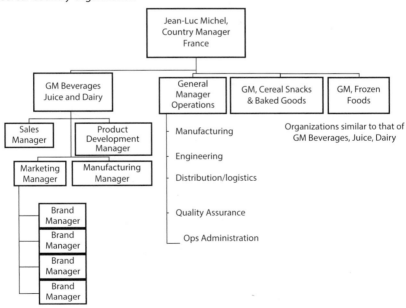

It was clear that both men quite reasonably would be looking for answers today. Should she authorize the launch in France? Should Healthy Berry Crunch become UC's first Eurobrand? And if so, what kind of organization did she need to put in place to ensure its effective implementation? These were big questions, and the stakes were high for both United Cereal and for her career. But Brill realized she had all the information. Now it was decision time.

HARVARD | BUSINESS | SCHOOL

APRIL 21, 2017

BRIEF CASES

Christopher A. Bartlett and Paul S. Myers

CASE 3.2 YUSHAN BICYCLES: LEARNING TO RIDE ABROAD

HBS Professor Emeritus Christopher A. Bartlett and Paul S. Myers, Lecturer at Simmons School of Management, prepared this case solely as a basis for class discussion and not as an endorsement, a source of primary data, or an illustration of effective or ineffective management. Many thanks to Kuan-Feng Ko (MBA 2000) of Klever Mobility for his assistance. Although based on real events and despite occasional references to actual companies, this case is fictitious and any resemblance to actual persons or entities is coincidental.

In March 2016, the growing tension between senior management at Yushan Bicycles (Yushan) and the general manager of its Australian subsidiary came to a head at a management meeting in Taiwan. An unexpectedly large quarterly loss at Yushan Australia (YA) led Chih-hao Zonghan, Yushan's director of global sales operations, to consider exercising tighter control over YA. Zonghan was even more concerned about the unconventional strategy that YA's general manager, James Hamilton, was pursuing.

Hamilton, on the other hand, felt he was responding appropriately to Australian consumer preferences and distribution channel prospects, and was unhappy with what he saw as interference in his operations. He felt the parent company had contributed significantly to his subsidiary's setback due to its problems supplying products and transfer pricing issues. He was looking for a quick resolution.

Company Background and Expansion

Yan-Ting Hsieh and Zhiwen Tseng, both semi-professional cyclists, started Yushan Bicycles in 1985, naming their company after Taiwan's highest mountain. Yushan's headquarters and manufacturing operations were in Taichung, Taiwan, home to almost 600 bicycle companies, which created a close-knit supply chain, from component makers to distributors. China led the world in bicycle production, but Taiwanese manufacturers generally made midrange to high-end products of superior quality.

Yushan was the seventh-largest bike manufacturer in Taiwan, producing 200,000 bicycles a year. It fabricated frames from aluminum, titanium, and carbon fiber, and it sourced components such as drivetrains, brakes, seats, wheels, handlebars, and pedals from local suppliers. Its 25,000-square-foot factory employed 260 people. Unlike most other Taiwanese bicycle companies, Yushan had from the outset designed, produced, and branded its own product line, selling through specialty bicycle stores throughout Taiwan. Its bikes emphasized comfort and performance and were distinguished by their streamlined shapes and distinctive colors.

The company's product line included road bikes designed to be ridden on smooth pavement; touring bikes suited to long-distance rides; mountain bikes intended for rugged terrain; aerodynamic sport/performance bikes; and hybrids that combined features of road and mountain bikes and were well-suited for commuting. Within each bicycle type, Yushan offered several models that were differentiated by frame design and size, handlebar style, number of gears, and saddle.

Yushan targeted a wide range of consumers, from those seeking basic bicycles at a reasonable price to experienced cyclists willing to pay more for additional attributes and performance. In recent years, it had shifted its product mix to favor the latter category of buyer and thereby capture the larger margins this segment offered.

In 2007, Yushan introduced its first electric bicycle. With their rechargeable battery–powered motors, electric bikes enabled riders to maintain a constant speed on flat or inclined roads at speeds of up to 28 miles per hour, although local speed limits were often lower. Unlike a traditional motorbike or moped, the e-bike motor engaged only when the rider was pedaling. An e-bike could travel 40 miles or more on one charge. To produce its e-bikes, Yushan used similar frames and many of the same components as it did for its conventional bicycles. Liu Chen, who oversaw the company's manufacturing operations, believed that as production of e-bikes reached scale, their profit margins would be at least double those of Yushan's conventional bikes.

Yushan's International Strategy

With growth in its domestic market slowing and local demand concentrated on Yushan's less expensive models, Hsieh and Tseng decided to expand internationally not only to capture production scale economies, but also to upgrade the product mix. Yushan's first overseas foray came in 2006, when it began exporting to Singapore. Two years later, it successfully entered the Japanese market, where, just as in Taiwan, the distribution channels were dominated by specialty retailers. Sales in the Asia Group built steadily, but there was increasing demand for higher-end models. Zonghan, a hard-driving executive with a lifetime of sales experience in the Taiwanese bicycle industry, was particularly pleased with Japanese e-bike sales. Since their introduction in the 1990s, e-bikes had proved extremely popular with Japanese women.

The second phase of Yushan's international thrust came with the creation of the Europe Group, one of Taiwan's largest bicycle export markets. Approximately 10% of the 20 million bicycles sold across Europe annually were imported from Taiwan, the highest demand coming from consumers seeking higher-end models. Hsieh and Tseng believed that, in addition to providing increased volume, Yushan needed to learn from more sophisticated European consumers.

Specialty bicycle retailers represented the dominant channel in most European countries, ranging from a 43% market share in France to a 72% share in the Netherlands. At the same time, e-bikes were gaining popularity: sales were growing by more than 20% per annum. Demand came not only from affluent, environmentally conscious commuters but also increasingly from commercial users for tasks such as package delivery. In 2010, in anticipation of expanded demand, the company expanded its factory capacity and increased the proportion of space used to produce the titanium and carbon-fiber frames used in higher-priced bicycles. It also increased its production capacity for e-bikes.

Competitors in the European market were well entrenched, and it was difficult for newcomers like Yushan to gain share. While trying to build its share through traditional distribution strategies, the company also began pursuing a parallel strategy. Following a chance meeting between Hsieh and a trade minister from Poland, Yushan's Europe Group also started to focus opportunistically on contracts for large-volume sales in Eastern Europe, particularly new urban bike-share programs.

In 2013, Yushan launched the third leg of its international expansion strategy by establishing sales subsidiaries in Australia, New Zealand, and Indonesia. Chen suggested the seasonal peaks in demand in the Southern Hemisphere would help him balance production schedules. Furthermore, because penetration of the European market was slow and difficult, Zonghan believed the Australian and New Zealand markets could provide knowledge and experience that would be valuable in Yushan's eventual planned entry into the United States.

As the international strategy evolved, so did the company's organizational structure (see **Exhibit 1**). Manufacturing operations were centralized and operated as a profit center. Functional departments such as engineering, personnel, and marketing were also located in Taichung and were designated as cost centers.

To manage the scope and complexity of the unfamiliar international operations, Zonghan appointed three regional group managers to oversee subsidiaries in Asia, Europe, and Oceania.

Subsidiaries in Australia, New Zealand, and Indonesia reported to Zonghan through the Oceania Group, led by Wei Yeh, a 40-year-old manager newly recruited from a Taiwanese export company. All subsidiaries were autonomous profit centers reporting to the group managers, all located at Yushan's headquarters. Country subsidiary managers had considerable freedom to adapt approaches for their local markets. They were also required to propose annual sales and profit objectives.

By late 2015, the Asia Group (including domestic Taiwan sales) accounted for 70% of revenue, the Europe Group provided 22%, and the Oceania Group contributed the remaining 8%. Profitability varied even more widely by group. **Exhibit 2** provides selected financial information.

Yushan in Australia

Australia was one of the top-ten destinations for Taiwan bicycle exports. Although the market for

Exhibit 1 Yushan Bicycles Organizational Structure

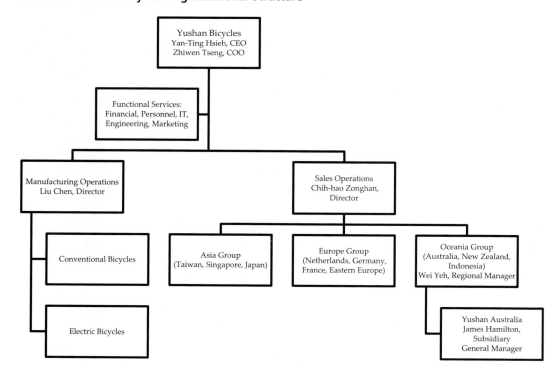

Exhibit 2
Yushan Bicycles Selected Financial Data, 2015 (NT$)

	Asia Group	Europe Group	Oceania Group
Revenue	1,611,850,128	506,581,469	184,211,443
Cost of Goods Sold	983,228,578	283,685,623	119,737,438
Marketing and Distribution	117,665,059	43,059,425	14,184,281
Warehouse and Inventory Management	48,355,504	18,743,514	5,894,766
Sales, General, and Administrative	322,370,026	126,645,367	40,526,518
Operating Income (Loss)	140,230,961	34,447,540	3,868,440

less expensive models was larger in Indonesia, Zonghan believed YA was Yushan's strategically most important subsidiary in Oceania. He was aware that 17% of Australia's 23 million people–21% of males and 12% of females–rode a bike at least weekly. Although the e-bike market was still in its infancy, he believed that the country's pleasant climate, outdoor lifestyle, and large cities with many commuters would make Australia a natural fit for this product.

Australian Market Structure

In Australia, around 1,000 independent specialty bicycle retail shops were the primary channels serving the needs of cyclists. They stocked a range of bike types, styles, and price points to cater not only to bike enthusiasts but also to quality-oriented casual riders; these outlets had an estimated 45% share of the bicycle market. At the other end of the spectrum, mass merchandisers such as Big W, Kmart, and Target sold lower-priced bicycles, including children's models, sourced mostly from China. They were estimated to have less than 10% of the market.

In contrast to most other countries where Yushan operated, Australia had another important channel positioned between these traditional retailers. Sporting-goods chains like Rebel and Amart Sports carried a focused array of midrange and higher-end bikes and were estimated to have 35% of the market. In these stores, bicycles from Taiwan typically sold for 10% to 15% more than lower-quality models produced in China did. It was predicted this segment would be disrupted by

the arrival of French-based Decathlon. As the world's largest sporting-goods retailer, Decathlon planned to open 35 warehouse-style stores in Australia by 2020.

In the e-bike segment, Australia was in the early stages of adoption, with low volume and low consumer awareness. In contrast to the Japanese market, early adopters in Australia seemed to be primarily male commuters. As the market developed, a 2012 federal government regulation increased its attractiveness. E-bikes with a power output of 250 watts or less were now classified as bicycles and therefore did not require a license or registration, as motorbikes did. Priced between A$2,000 and A$3,000, e-bikes were more expensive than the A$400 to A$1,300 cost of most traditional bikes. High-end bicycles, however, sold for as much as A$8,500. Australian sales of e-bikes were estimated at under 15,000 units in 2014. Several e-bike makers from Europe were exporting into the Australian market, but none had established itself as a market leader.

Startup: Strategy and Organization

James Hamilton was named general manager of YA in April 2013. Although he lacked familiarity with bicycles or sporting goods, he had 25 years of experience leading high-performance sales and marketing teams in several successful Australian consumer-goods companies. Like all Yushan's subsidiaries, YA was expected to become financially self-sufficient as quickly as possible. Hamilton lost little time building YA's operation from the ground up, while simultaneously developing a local strategy that fit into Yushan's objectives.

Hamilton's first priorities were to hire staff, lease office and warehouse space, and develop relationships with distributors. By late 2013, he had begun to implement a strategy aimed at building volume quickly with the company's most popular road and touring bikes. Because he did not have the staff to penetrate Australia's multiplicity of widely dispersed independent specialty bicycle stores, he decided initially to target sporting-goods chains. In another deviation from the company's normal practice, Hamilton set prices at the lower end of the range for similar-quality bicycles on the market to build volume quickly.

Once a sales threshold of 10,000 units was met–something he hoped to achieve within two to three years–Hamilton planned to raise prices, hoping to self-fund investment in the next phase of his strategy. This second stage would involve advertising to build Yushan's brand image, expanding distribution to specialty bicycle shops, and providing the service levels required to support its higher-end, higher-margin bicycles. He observed, "Until we build our brand and product reputation, the specialty retailers won't have any interest in us."

Within his first four months, YA's new leader had built a staff of 15, comprising sales reps, marketing specialists, warehouse workers, and administrative personnel. The subsidiary was based in Melbourne, but, recognizing the country's large geographic expanse, Hamilton had begun opening sales offices in Sydney, Brisbane, and Perth. Because of his reputation and track record, as well as Taiwanese management's lack of familiarity with the Australian market, Yushan gave Hamilton considerable autonomy in both strategic and operational matters.

2016: Problems and Conflicts

By December 2015, Yushan's bicycle sales in Australia had reached 5,960 units, and Hamilton felt he was making solid progress toward the 10,000-unit target he had set before he increased prices and upgraded the product mix. In the last quarter of 2015, however, YA reported results significantly below budget. See **Exhibit 3** for YA's financial information. The unanticipated loss led to tensions between Yushan's headquarters and YA. Each offered different explanations for the poor results and different proposals for action needed.

Transfer Pricing Conflicts

Hamilton felt YA's losses were due in part to Yushan's transfer pricing policies, which were based on direct manufacturing costs, overhead allocation, a finance charge, and a markup to cover centralized services such as marketing and research and development. Hamilton and several of Yushan's other subsidiary managers felt that Yushan put the profitability of its Taiwan-based operations ahead of that of off-shore subsidiaries. He felt subsidiaries were carrying a burden of factory costs they could not control and headquarters overhead from which they did not benefit. He had also heard that when big opportunities came up–such as

Exhibit 3
Yushan Bicycles Australia Subsidiary Selected Financial Data, 2015 (NT$)

Revenue	80,471,443
Cost of Goods Sold	54,720,581
Marketing and Distribution	5,713,472
Warehouse and Inventory Management	2,575,086
Sales, General, and Administrative	21,727,290
Operating Income (Loss)	(4,264,986)

Note: A$1 = NT$24.04 on December 31, 2015.

bike-share contracts in large European cities–some subsidiaries had negotiated transfer prices that excluded overhead, thereby increasing the burden on other subsidiaries. Headquarters managers countered that transfer prices to Oceania were insufficient to cover even their share of marketing costs and technical expenditures from which they benefited.

Equally frustrating to Hamilton was the unpredictability of transfer prices, which were adjusted quarterly to reflect increases in manufacturing costs. Zonghan defended the practice, explaining that Yushan was financially stretched by its international expansion and required subsidiaries to recoup cost increases. But the policy created difficulties in YA. When transfer prices rose sharply in the third quarter of 2015, YA had been unable to raise its local prices on a very large order accepted in May but scheduled for delivery over the following six months. This price increase ate up YA's margin on the sale. Hamilton particularly resented headquarters' managers regarding this as his own error because he did not account for a possible increase in transfer prices during negotiations.

Currency fluctuations posed another problem. For example, between January 2015 and September 2015, the Australian dollar (A$) lost 15% against the New Taiwan Dollar (NT$). Because transfer prices were stated in NT$, the subsidiary bore the costs of this weakening of the local currency, which significantly increased actual product costs above their budgeted cost of goods.

Information Systems Problems

Hamilton also pointed to problems with the company's new enterprise resource planning system, introduced in early 2015, to support Yushan's sales, distribution, and accounting functions. The system had incorrectly reported stock availability on several occasions, leading sales staff to make unrealistic delivery commitments. In one case the mistake led a new customer to cancel the order rather than accept the expected delay. Furthermore, owing to problems integrating cost data into the new database, subsidiary sales prices that the system generated by adding a margin to total cost per unit markup were inaccurate, often falling below the transfer price.

Because the new system significantly increased the amount of time it took for YA sales staff to record orders, they saw it as unnecessarily complicated. During implementation, they made several mistakes that resulted in subsequent order corrections that disrupted plant production schedules. Hamilton blamed poor documentation and insufficient training for these errors, but Zonghan and Yeh felt the disruption was due to a lack of effort and poor attitude on the part of the Australian staff.

Delivery Delays

Hamilton also believed Yushan gave priority to deliveries to its established subsidiaries in Asia, which led him to question the company's commitment to Oceania. In June, for example, stock destined for Australia was diverted to fill a large order from Singapore's biggest customer. Expected shipments often arrived late, which Hamilton said made delivery commitments nearly impossible to keep. He worried YA would gain a reputation as an unreliable supplier, which would damage its ability to grow.

Zonghan and Yeh saw the matter differently. Both were increasingly skeptical of YA's forecasts, and had developed a bias toward confirmed commitments from established markets over questionable assurances from a hopeful one. They also acknowledged that in times of product shortage, the rational corporate decision was to assign priority to sales to Japan, which provided more accurate forecasts and offered much higher margins than YA, which was budgeted to operate at breakeven.

Headquarters' Response

In late January 2016, after seeing YA's fourth-quarter results for 2015, Zonghan instructed Yeh to report on the causes of the unexpected losses in YA and to recommend changes to stop the financial bleeding. Following his scheduled quarterly trip to Melbourne in February, Yeh reported he was increasingly concerned that Hamilton had invested too quickly in staff and organization in the expectation that volume growth would absorb the fixed costs built into his strategic plan. Yeh confirmed he would ask Hamilton to commit to a 10% increase in profitability through a combination of a price hike and a reduction in fixed costs. Specifically, he wanted Hamilton to review the need for regional sales offices.

When he reviewed Yeh's report, Hamilton saw it as another example of distant Taiwanese management intervening in decisions when they had very little knowledge of the local situation. He pointed out that the increase from 6,000 to 10,000 units annually would require no additional staff or warehouse space. Even as volume approached 15,000 units annually, he estimated he would need to add only two additional staff. Regarding the price increase proposal, he cited an analysis his sales force had prepared following the recent transfer price problems. It concluded that intense competition from new branded imports was limiting the market's willingness to accept price increases.

Meanwhile, Yeh also supported Chen's request for YA to update its forecasts weekly rather than monthly. Although YA's forecasts had been correct in the aggregate, estimates for specific models had not been reliable. This had created stock-outs, which led customers to question the company's supply reliability. It had also created a surplus of some models, which had to be sold at reduced prices to create warehouse space for arrivals of more popular stock items. Chen convinced Yeh more frequent updates would allow inventory to be managed more effectively. Hamilton viewed this change as an indication of a lack of trust in his judgment. He argued that YA was new to this market and was beginning only now to get a good sense of how to assess demand.

The biggest issue worrying Zonghan was Hamilton's market-entry strategy, which seemed to be building share more slowly and less profitably than expected. Worse still, he had heard a rumor that a major Chinese e-bike competitor was planning to enter the Australian market. He was concerned that the longer YA waited to launch, the more likely it could be shut out altogether. Due to Yushan's experience in Japan and Singapore, Zonghan believed the established marketing approach for targeting potential e-bike buyers would work in Australia.

Chen supported Zonghan, pointing to excess plant capacity as an opportunity to produce a larger number of e-bikes.

Following discussions at headquarters, Zonghan and Yeh urged Hamilton to accelerate his plans to expand the product line to include higher-end models, particularly e-bikes. Hamilton responded that in his sales team's experience, retailers would carry only a limited range of bikes from each supplier. Overall, he felt headquarters' increasing controls and its proposals on product strategy were taking away important elements of the autonomy he believed he needed to succeed.

Meeting at Headquarters

In March, Yushan had its annual management meeting in Taiwan, which it held in conjunction with the Taipei International Cycle Show. The meeting gave Hsieh and Tseng a platform for reiterating their goal of becoming one of the world's most respected bicycle brands. Yushan's senior managers, including Zonghan, Chen, and Yeh, attended, as did the heads of all overseas subsidiaries.

Hsieh and Tseng opened the meeting by reaffirming each geographic group's role in Yushan's emerging strategy. Asia, which included the domestic market, would continue to be the largest source of sales and profit. Europe was to be managed opportunistically, gradually establishing a foothold at the high end while bidding on large contracts for urban bike-share programs to exploit factory capacity. Oceania represented Yushan's growth opportunity. Key objectives were to build distribution strength, upgrade the product mix, and learn from the new market experiences.

As the meeting progressed through a review of 2015's results, each subsidiary manager was invited to comment on his or her unit's performance. In his introductory remarks, Zonghan identified YA as a concern, but said he expected additional controls and a change in strategy to correct the problem. When Hsieh asked Hamilton to comment, the Australian executive decided this request gave him an opportunity to express his concerns.

After briefly outlining his strategy, Hamilton acknowledged YA had not yet achieved the volume and market penetration he was seeking. He argued, however, it was inappropriate and premature to cut sales offices, raise prices, or shift product strategy because his team needed more time to deliver on his plan. He believed attempting to upgrade the product focus or engage specialty bicycle retailers without sufficient resources to establish the brand or provide strong support risked failure. He also touched on the delivery and transfer pricing problems and suggested a lack of support from the administrative departments was also a concern. His proposed solution was to ask for another year to pursue his original strategy, as he was confident YA would achieve its objectives in that time.

When Hamilton sat down, the silence was deafening. With the lunch break approaching, Hsieh suggested that Hamilton and Zonghan use that time to resolve their differences. When they reconvened after lunch, he expected to hear how they planned to move forward.

♛IVEY | Publishing

Gordon Institute of Business Science
University of Pretoria

CASE 3.3 BEER FOR ALL: SABMILLER IN MOZAMBIQUE

Professor Margie Sutherland and Dr. Tashmia Ismail wrote this case solely to provide material for class discussion. The authors do not intend to illustrate either effective or ineffective handling of a managerial situation. The authors may have disguised certain names and other identifying information to protect confidentiality.

This publication may not be transmitted, photocopied, digitized or otherwise reproduced in any form or by any means without the permission of the copyright holder. Reproduction of this material is not covered under authorization by any reproduction rights organization. To order copies or request permission to reproduce materials, contact Ivey Publishing, Ivey Business School, Western University, London, Ontario, Canada, N6G 0N1; (t) 519.661.3208; (e) cases@ivey.ca; www.iveycases.com.

Copyright © 2014, Richard Ivey School of Business Foundation

Version: 2014–05–12

Gerry van den Houten, SABMiller Africa's director of Enterprise Development, sat in his Johannesburg office reading a Reuters website describing the rollout of cassava beer into Ghana. A quote about a customer caught his eye:

Eugene admits he is no beer expert, but he'll tell you the bottle of Eagle lager he treats himself to every week is a step up from the murky homebrew that had been his preferred tipple. He now saves so on Saturdays he has the 61 cents[1] for an Eagle. "Eagle is my first experience with beers," he says as he settles into a plastic chair at a roadside bar in Sogakape, a dusty town 150 kilometres from the Ghanaian capital Accra. "I really like this drink."[2]

Van den Houten reflected on the journey SABMiller had taken since unveiling its first cassava-based beer in Mozambique 18 months earlier. He wondered how many times SABMiller could replicate this business innovation and whether a product and process could be too successful.

---

[1] All currency is shown in US$, as at July 2013.

[2] Ekow Dontoh and Janice Kew, "SABMiller Sells Cassava Beer to Woo African Drinkers," *Business Week*, May 23, 2013, www.businessweek.com/articles/2013-05-23/sabmiller-sells-cassava-beer-to-woo-african-drinkers, accessed August 10, 2013.

Mozambique

In 2012, Mozambique, a long thin country on the Indian Ocean coastline of Southern Africa, had a population of 24 million and a per capita gross domestic product (GDP) of $583 per person.[3] The Global Competitiveness Index 2012/13 ranked it 138th overall out of 144 countries[4]: 101st for domestic market size[5] and 41st for foreign direct investment (FDI) and technology transfer.[6] Mozambique's official language was Portuguese, a remnant from its colonial era, and its median population age was 16.8 years with an adult literacy rate of 56 per cent.[7] When Mozambique was granted its independence from Portugal in 1975, it was rated as one of the world's poorest countries. Within a year of gaining its independence, almost all 250,000 Portuguese had left the country. For the next 15 years, an intense and destructive civil war ensued, lasting from 1977 to 1992.

The return of political stability brought with it a turnaround in the country's economic trajectory. Between 1997 and 2007, Mozambique had one of the fastest growing economies on the continent, with a growth rate of 9 per cent per annum, after dipping to a very low base. Despite impressive growth in 2008, half of the country's population continued to live below the poverty line, and more than half of the country's annual budget came from foreign assistance.[8]

Since 2008, Mozambique's economy had continued to grow at 7 per cent annually, but despite having one of the world's fastest growing GDPs, the country remained very poor, as evidenced by its minimum legal salary of $78 per month.[9] The economy was also not immune to inflation: in 2008, bread prices rose by 50 per cent; and, after a further 17 per cent price rise was announced in 2010, riots broke out across the country.[10] The bulk of the economy's annual growth rate stemmed from natural resource extraction by foreign organizations with the resource being exported and turned into manufactured products in other countries and thus had little direct benefit for the average Mozambican.[11] Subsistence agriculture employed 81 per cent of the population and nearly 90 per cent of arable land was still undeveloped; however, one of the main crops grown in Mozambique was cassava.

Cassava

Cassava is a drought-resistant, starch-rich root vegetable that was introduced to Africa by the Portuguese who brought it from Brazil about 400 years ago. Cassava, known as a "rough and ready" crop, had long been the foundation of food security in Africa. Among its unique properties were its ability to thrive in marginal soils, its being a non-seasonal crop (it could be planted at any time of the year and, depending on climate, would be ready for harvest 12 to 16 months later) and its ability to survive intact in long-term underground storage before being harvested. The downside of cassava is the need to process it within a day or two of harvesting; otherwise, the tuber turns black and becomes unpalatable and useless for processing.

In Africa, 500 million people eat cassava every day, each consuming, on average, 80 kilograms of cassava annually.[12] The tubers are high

---

[3] World Economic Forum, *The Global Competitiveness Report 2012–2013*, p. 266, www.reports.weforum.org/global-competitiveness-report-2012-2013/, accessed February 15, 2014.

[4] Ibid.

[5] Ibid.; Domestic market size = gross domestic product + value of imported goods and services.

[6] Ibid., p. 267; FDI and technology transfer were measured as an opinion to the question "To what extent does foreign direct investment (FDI) bring new technology into your country?"

[7] The World Fact Book, "Mozambique," https://www.cia.gov/library/publications/the-world-factbook/geos/mz.html, accessed July 9, 2013.

[8] Ibid.

[9] Wageindicator Foundation, www.wageindicator.org/main/salary/minimum, accessed March 1, 2014.

[10] "Cassava Revolution Takes off in Mozambique," www.freshfruitportal.com/2013/07/04/cassava-revolution-takes-off-in-mozambique/, accessed July 9, 2013.

[11] *Mozambique Food and Drink Report Q1 2013*, www.marketresearch.com/Business-Monitor-International –v304/ Mozambique – Food-Drink – Q1-7264790/, accessed March 1, 2014.

[12] International Institute of Tropical Agriculture, "Cassava," www.iita.org/cassava, accessed July 9, 2013.

in starch, and the protein-rich leaves, a spinach-like vegetable, are also eaten by farmers' families. Mozambique's agricultural census of 2010 indicated 2.3 million cassava farms, with the majority of the farmers never taking their products to market,[13] as very few had any method of transportation besides walking. The average farm size was two hectares, and the working tools were simple and of little value. The farmers' homes were built from adobe brick with leaf, grass or straw roofs.[14] Compared with other crops, cassava required little labour to plant and grow but was extremely labour-intensive in the post-harvest stage to make it consumable. Of the total domestically produced cassava, nearly one-third was estimated to be lost through waste.[15] According to van den Houten, "Cassava is the biggest crop in Africa but the least commercialized."[16] The lack of commercialization was probably due to the severe logistical challenges in collecting the roots for commercial use: firstly, the smallholder farmers were very widely dispersed; secondly, cassava was subject to rapid perishability; thirdly, the irregular sizes and shapes of the large tubers and fourthly their high water content, and thus their weight, made them unsuitable for transporting over long distances, especially on the rutted roads of rural Africa. The launch of SABMiller's beer in Mozambique marked the first time that cassava had been used to brew beer on a commercial scale, despite cassava having been used by generations of home brewers in Africa.

SABMiller

SABMiller, one of the world's largest brewers, was listed on both the London and Johannesburg stock exchanges and had more than 200 beer brands and 70,000 employees in over 75 countries. In the financial year ending March 31, 2013, international revenue was $31.3 billion with SABMiller paying 77 per cent of its taxes to governments in emerging and developing economies. The group's portfolio included both global brands, such as Pilsner Urquell, Peroni, Miller Genuine Draft and Grolsch, and the leading local brands in many countries, such as Castle in South Africa, Snow in China and Aguila in Colombia. Beer was a local product the world over – typically brewed, sold and consumed in the same community. SABMiller was also one of the world's largest bottlers of Coca-Cola products.

SABMiller generated two-thirds of its worldwide profits in emerging markets; in Africa, the group operated in 37 countries.[17] Sustainability was one of SABMiller's four global strategic priorities. As explained by then chief executive, Graham Mackay, in the company's 2012 annual Sustainable Development Report,[18] SABMiller integrated sustainable development into its business: "The greatest contribution we can make to the economies in which we operate is to run successful, profitable businesses that create jobs, pay taxes and stimulate local enterprise while making efficient use of limited resources." One of the three global focus areas within the strategic priority of sustainability was "local enterprise development in the value chain," and, as stated by the company, "By sharing knowledge and working collaboratively with our stakeholders, we are confident that we can deliver innovative solutions at a local level." SABMiller was also determined to ensure its "licence to trade" by implementing its 10 pillars of sustainability,

[13] "Cassava Revolution Takes off in Mozambique," op. cit.
[14] International Fertilizer Development Center, "Commercialized Cassava Production in Mozambique Helps Farmers," *FDC Report*, vol. 37, no. 2, 2012, www.ifdc.org/Nations/Mozambique/Articles/ Commercialized-Cassava-Production-in-Mozambique-He/, accessed July 9, 2013.
[15] FAOSTAT, 2007, http://faostat.fao.org/agp/agpc/gcds/ en/strategy, accessed March 2014.
[16] David Smith, "Cassava Beer Debuts as Commercial Brew in African Bars," *The Guardian*, November 1, 2011, www.theguardian.com/world/2011/nov/01/ cassava-beer-commercial-brew-africa, accessed July 9, 2013.

[17] Ekow Dontoh and Janice Kew, "SABMiller Sells Cassava Beer to Woo African Drinkers," *Business Week*, May 23, 2013, www.businessweek.com/search?q=sells +beer+to+woo, accessed August 10, 2013.
[18] www.sabmiller.com/files/reports/2012_SD_report.pdf, accessed March 1, 2014.

which included sourcing locally grown inputs into brewing and nurturing its relationships with all its stakeholders. SABMiller considered a good corporate reputation to be fundamental to its business success.

SABMiller invested in Mozambique in 1995, acquiring two breweries, one in the south, in the capital Maputo, and one in the centre of the country, in Beira. In 2010, the local subsidiary, known as Cervejas de Moçambique (CDM), built a new brewery in Nampula, in the rural north of the country, home to nearly half of the country's population. Nampula had grown from a population of 126,000 in 1970 to 478,000 in 2007.[19] It had few Western-style hotels, restaurants or shopping malls. In 2012, CDM employed 1,100 people and had a 92 per cent share of the national beer market, where the average beer consumption was nine litres per capita per year.[20]

The Beer Market in Africa

Africans had traditionally drunk mainly home-brewed beer made from a wide range of fermentable ingredients, such as sorghum, millet and bananas, with the homebrew market being four times the size of the formal beer market, as measured by volume.[21] The main reason for the greater homebrew market was that homebrew was considerably less costly than commercially brewed beer. On a continent where so many people were living in poverty, price often determined their choice. Another feature of the alcohol industry in Africa was the prevalence of "informal" commercial spirits and the illicit alcohol market. These sectors were unregulated, untaxed and often had poor if any quality controls. Thus, homebrew was often viewed as

posing health risks to consumers and leading to a range of social problems. The commercial beer market in Africa, home to 16 per cent of the world's population, represented only 5 per cent of worldwide volumes, with four players controlling 80 per cent of the market. Two of those players were SABMiller and Diageo.[22] SABMiller regarded its biggest competitors in Africa as "the guy or gal" who made beer at home[23] and the commercial illicit alcohol producers and retailers. On most of the continent, commercial beer was an aspirational product to the many who could not afford it.

An article in the *Economist* noted, "Brewers are betting that Africa's fast-growing middle class will want to trade up. Homebrew can be excellent, but it is highly variable, sometimes lumpy and lacks a certain cachet."[24] A *Wall Street Journal* article noted that the idea was "to create a ladder for Africans to climb as their disposable incomes rise."[25] They might start by drinking Chibuku (a milkshake-like opaque "homebrew beer" that SABMiller sold at 50 cents per serving in 12 countries), then later trade up to low-price lagers made from local ingredients and, ultimately, they might be able to purchase and drink premium beers. The extent of this challenge, however, was evidenced by the fact that to afford a commercial beer an African needed to work, on average, three hours, compared with 12 minutes of work for a European.[26] Africans drank, on average, eight litres of commercially brewed beer

[19] Agencia of Informacao de Mocambicue – Mozambique census, http://allafrica.com/stories/200911240886.html, accessed January 3, 2014.

[20] SABMiller, "Where We Operate: Mozambique," www.sabmiller.com/index.asp?pageid=1161, accessed July 9, 2013.

[21] "From Lumps to Lager," *The Economist*, March 24, 2013, www.economist.com/node/21551092, accessed July 9, 2013.

[22] https://www.moodys.com/research/Moodys alcoholic beverage companies to benefit from growing consumer market. PR_245336, accessed March 18, 2013.

[23] Marc Gunther, "SABMiller: Beer at the Bottom of the Pyramid," January 12, 2012, www.marcgunther.com/sabmiller-beer-at-the-bottom-of-the-pyramid/, accessed July 9, 2013.

[24] "From Lumps to Lager," March 24, 2013, op.cit.

[25] Paul Sonne, Devon Maylie and Drew Hinshaw, "With West Flat, Big Brewers Peddle Cheap Beer in Africa," *Wall Street Journal*, March 19, 2013, http://online.wsj.com/news/articles/SB10001424127887324034804578348533702226420, accessed February 17, 2014.

[26] Reuters, "Africa's Beer Thirst," *Fin24*, June 19, 2012, www.fin24.com/Companies/Industrial/Africas-beers-thirst - 20120619, accessed July 9, 2013.

a year, compared with the average American's annual consumption of 70 litres.[27]

Africa's economic outlook was rapidly changing, and the continent's real GDP grew an average of 4.7 per cent per year between 2000 and 2010, a rate double that of the 1980s and 1990s.[28] As a result of a host of opportunities being created, Africa was "open for business" and was one of the last remaining frontiers for beer,[29] where volumes were expected to grow at double the global rate. Africa's population of more than one billion was set to double by 2050,[30] sparking the interest of global beer producers who were keen to expand into Africa as they sought growth markets to compensate for flat and falling beer sales in the rich developed world.[31] One strategy behind successfully tapping into these opportunities was to become a dominant player by being the first to market and entrench a brand.[32] According to Bernstein Research, Africa was probably the most attractive region for long-term profit growth for global brewers.[33] Diageo and SABMiller were in a race, targeting low-income earners, those who earned as little as $2 or $3 a day.[34]

One of SABMiller's main African strategies was to make beer more affordable and less of a luxury product. "We are looking at sub-inflation pricing," said Mark Bowman, Africa's regional managing director.[35] The group aimed for annual growth in Africa at a rate of 6 to 8 per cent by volume and to increase its earnings by 10 per cent. Key to this strategy was using locally grown crops as a brewing ingredient to create a portfolio of high-quality, affordable beers for local lower-income customers.[36] The success of this strategy had been demonstrated in Uganda, where SABMiller had sold a sorghum-based beer since 2002. There, its sales constituted 50 per cent of its 55 per cent beer market share, with the sorghum being sourced from 9,000 small-scale farmers.[37]

Impala Beer

In November 2011, CDM launched the first-ever commercial-scale, cassava-based clear beer, Impala,[38] named after the widespread African antelope. The beer was made at the Nampula brewery using 70 per cent locally grown cassava in place of expensive imported malted barley. The beer, bottled in 550-ml bottles, contained 6.5 per cent alcohol and sold at two thirds the price of mainstream commercial beers,[39] but double the price of homebrew. Impala offered low-income earners a high-quality, affordable local beer and aimed to attract customers in the vicinity who had traditionally drunk homebrews and illicit commercial spirits. Mackay said, "Very often illicit alcohol is positively dangerous. What we are doing is offering a legal alternative to that large percentage of alcohol that is homemade and for which governments get no taxes."[40]

When asked how the beer tasted, Andy Wales, SABMiller's global head of sustainability, replied, "It's excellent, not too dissimilar from a regular lager. It looks like any other beer – golden and sparkling with a foam head."[41] Bowman commented, "The cassava beers are more bitter

[27] "From Lumps to Lager," March 24, 2013, op.cit.
[28] Mutsa Chironga, Acha Leke, Susan Lund and Arend van Wamelen, "Cracking the Next Growth Market: Africa," *Harvard Business Review*, May 2011, pp. 117–122.
[29] Matt Clinch, "Beer and Africa: A Recipe for Profit?" March 25, 2013, www.cnbc.com/id/100587943, accessed July 9, 2013.
[30] Reuters, "Africa's Beer Thirst," *Fin24*, June 19, 2012.
[31] "From Lumps to Lager," March 24, 2013, op.cit.
[32] Ekow Dontoh and Janice Kew, May 23, 2013.
[33] Clinch, "Beer and Africa: A Recipe for Profit?," March 25, 2013, op.cit.
[34] Sonne, Maylie and Hinshaw, March 19, 2013, op.cit.
[35] David Jones, "SABMiller Strives to Make Beer Affordable in Africa," March 13, 2012, www.reuters.com/article/2012/03/13/sabmiller-africa-idUSL5E8EC4UZ20120313, accessed July 9, 2013.

[36] Dutch Agricultural Development and Trading Company, "SABMiller," www.dadtco.nl/sabmiller, accessed July 9, 2013.
[37] Gunther, "SABMiller: Beer at the Bottom of the Pyramid," January 12, 2012, op.cit.
[38] www.sabmiller.com/files/reports/2012_SD_report.pdf, op. cit.
[39] Ibid.   [40] Smith, November 1, 2011, op.cit.
[41] Gunther, January 12, 2012, op.cit.

than the barley lagers," adding that the new beers were "not supposed to be quite the same as mainstream beers, in terms of taste. The difference could be a turnoff for some drinkers accustomed to smoother, more expensive quaffs."[42] Bowman further said that "low cost, locally sourced beers could double or triple the size of the beer market as people move away from homebrew. Those beers are a clear way to reach a market that wants to drink beer but can't afford to."[43]

But it had been a complex journey. Van den Houten had conceived of the idea of making beer from cassava 20 years previously but had been assured by SAB technical researchers that doing so would be impossible. In recent years, however, SABMiller had run trials in Swaziland and Nigeria on producing beer from cassava but a fundamental problem had been getting a reliable supply of the crop to a centralized factory: "I had done the economics for that and whichever way you looked at it, it just didn't work out." On his many business trips in rural Africa, van den Houten had been frustrated by the glaring poverty and suffering of rural farmers. In late 2010, a chance discussion with a colleague in Kenya, who worked for the Africa Enterprise Challenge Fund (AECF), had led to van den Houten becoming aware of the breakthrough cassava technology of the Dutch Agricultural Development and Trading Company (DADTCO), one of the companies the AECF was sponsoring. A few months of email correspondence ensued, and then van den Houten visited a DADTCO site in Nigeria to see the technology at work.

DADTCO's innovative solution was a mobile processing unit called the Autonomous Mobile Processing Unit (AMPU), which was taken from one farming area to another. DADTCO's trademark saying was "If the farmer can't come to the factory; let's bring the factory to the farmer."[44]

The units were housed in modified 40-foot (12-metre) containers that had self-contained power supplies, but required water on site from either a borehole or river. The unit processed cassava tubers by chopping and rasping them into a slurry that was turned into a plastic-wrapped, easy-to-transport "cake" that could be stored for at least six months.[45] The AMPU could process 3.8 metric tons (MT) of cassava roots into two MT of cake within an hour.[46] The AMPU produced very little effluent (which was pumped onto neighbouring farming land as free irrigation), and the peels of the cassava were turned into compost for the farmers.

At the outset, DADTCO provided SABMiller with cassava cake for brewing trials, information on cassava's particular starch characteristics and advice on managing the supply chain from smallholder farmers. DADTCO had a spare AMPU in Nigeria, and SABMiller initially considered buying it but that was not the arrangement DADTCO wanted. A joint venture was then considered but had many complexities. In April 2011, the project was given the go-ahead, and an Africa-wide framework agreement was drawn up between the two organizations. SABMiller agreed to invest in cassava beer projects and to supply a low-cost loan to DADTCO, which was in need of financing. In return, DADTCO agreed to exclusively provide SABMiller with product and value chain know-how for brewing-related endeavours and to provide a team to manage the farmers and the technology.[47]

SABMiller chose Mozambique after also considering South Sudan, Nigeria and Angola. The deciding factors included proximity to the regional head office in Johannesburg in South

---

[42] Ekow Dontoh and Janice Kew, May 23, 2013, op.cit.

[43] Ibid.

[44] Dutch Agricultural Development and Trading Company, "AMPU," www.dadtco.nl/ampu, accessed October 15, 2013.

[45] Melissa Rudd, "SABMiller's Cassava Beer Aims to Win over Home Brewers," www.africanbusinessreview.co.za/money_matters/sabmiller-aims-to-win-over-home-brewers-with-cassava-beer, accessed September 1, 2013.

[46] "Cassava Revolution Takes off in Mozambique," www.freshfruitportal.com/2013/07/04/cassava-revolution-takes-off-in-mozambique/, accessed July 9, 2013.

[47] Email from Peter Bolt to one of the case writers, August 9, 2013.

Africa, the excitement and support of the project expressed by the CDM managing director and the ready support of the Mozambican government for the project.

The Underpinning Networks

Cassava+ was a public private partnership in Mozambique comprising three partners: DADTCO, the International Fertilizer Development Center (IFDC) and the Dutch government's Directorate General for International Cooperation, the latter providing substantial funding for the project. Drawing on the expertise of each partner, Cassava+ aimed to turn a subsistence crop into a cash crop and to double Mozambique's cassava yield. IFDC, a non-profit organization working in more than 100 countries, assisted farmers to develop upstream components of a value chain, by giving them access to improved varieties of seed, fertilizer and training on appropriate crop practices via their field extension officers.[48] It was also working with Mozambique's government-funded National Institute of Agricultural Research to introduce new disease-free cassava planting materials. DADTCO, a small private sector company, had 30 years' experience working with farmers in the developing world, creating innovative technologies and business models.[49] The vision of DADTCO's chief executive officer, Peter Bolt, was to decrease African countries' dependency on food imports and to give farmers realistic, competitive markets for their products.[50] Other stakeholders in the system included Corridor Agro Limited that multiplied the improved varieties developed by the National Institute. ORAM, a local non-governmental

organization (NGO), organized the information-sharing events where DADTCO staff explained to the farmers the process of selling their cassava roots to them. According to an estimate by van den Houten, $2 million in donor funds was needed per year, for three years, to develop the smallholder farmer model and to maintain the cassava supply chain in Mozambique.

As van den Houten had learned, "the best knowledge sharing in Africa comes from being part of informal networks." The project was founded on a new approach involving multiple stakeholder relationships. The public sector involvement came through developing close relationships with Mozambique's government ministers of agriculture, finance (responsible for excise taxes) and trade and industry, and by taking time to understand the government's national agenda and then respond to it. The government had previously commissioned consultants to produce a two-volume report on how to develop the cassava industry, but was under-resourced to implement the plan. Providing a plan to help impoverished farmers was a national imperative. Van den Houten noted that business leaders in multinationals were not usually skilled in engaging government to achieve mutually beneficial goals. For example, SABMiller had to learn how to engage with the Mozambican government by first learning "the language" of the government and then, over time, building trust with government officials. Equally, governments in Africa had to learn how to engage with multinationals to assist them in development. The Mozambican government had at first worried about what the project would mean for food security – would the farmers sell their subsistence crop for cash and leave their families hungry? However Cassava+ had placated their concerns by illustrating how easy it was to double the cassava yield per hectare.[51] Van den Houten had found it important to build

[48] www.dadtco.nl/sabmiller-dadtco, accessed July 9, 2013.

[49] SABMiller, "SABMiller Launches First Ever Cassava Lager in Mozambique," www.sabmiller.com/index.asp?pageid=149&newsid=1748, accessed July 9, 2013.

[50] Rockefeller Foundation, *Catalytic Innovations in African Agriculture, Innovation for the Next 100 Years*, Centennial series, Mobile Cassava, DADTCO, Mozambique.

[51] Gerry van den Houten, presentation at Gordon Institute of Business Science, Pretoria, South Africa, July 18, 2013.

a compelling case for government to utilize excise rates as one of the tools for addressing socio-economic issues including the abuse of illicit alcohol in unregulated (and untaxed) markets.

The next stakeholder group was the private sector, represented by SABMiller and DADTCO, which worked closely together despite the significant differences in their scales of operation. The final stakeholder group had two components: the small-scale farmers themselves and the NGOs, which "helped keep all parties honest," through their close relationships with, and unique sensitivity to the dynamics of, people living in these remote communities. DADTCO and some NGOs conducted baseline measures before the project was rolled out so that the socio-economic impact of the project could be assessed over a few years.

Van den Houten had learned it was imperative for all stakeholders' roles to be specified, recognized and adhered to. He felt that one of the program's success factors was that it worked from only a framework agreement and had no legal contracts between the parties. He believed that the win–win partnerships with government, NGOs, DADTCO and the farmers had led to stronger and more effective relationships than those governed by legal ties. He also believed that to be sustainable, the projects needed to deliver satisfaction to all the partners not only to the customers.

The Implementation

The drivers for the project were business imperatives: recent commodity price fluctuations, exchange rate volatility and, in some global markets, shortages of supplies of key materials, such as hops. As a result of these effects, SABMiller was vulnerable to factors beyond its control. Thus, SABMiller's strategy was to drive down costs and waste by collapsing the supply chain, which, in rural Africa, was often very long and expensive because of the continent's poor infrastructure. This strategy was a business necessity, but the process was "stumbled into" rather than the result of a planned process of innovation. Van den Houten commented, "It's important to recognize possibilities – to see potential in mistakes."

SABMiller also wanted to enhance its perceived "license to trade" in Africa. In line with the enterprise development principles of its sustainability strategy, SABMiller saw an opportunity to create a new market for subsistence farmers in Mozambique and to help them earn an income, often for the first time, by guaranteeing them a market for their crops.[52] The farmers in this extremely poor area had previously struggled to sell more than one bag of cassava every two weeks.[53]

DADTCO managed the cassava production value chain, and IFDC provided agricultural extension services. Farmers sold their surplus cassava roots for cash to DADTCO, which offered a ready, accessible market and a purchase guarantee in a one-page contract. The farmers were paid different rates, depending on whether they delivered their crop to the AMPU or whether DADTCO collected the crop. The contract scheme provided great opportunities for farmers to increase their income with little risk.[54] DADTCO produced the cassava cake at the AMPU, then sold the cakes to CDM, which, in turn, used the cakes for the brewing of Impala beer at the Nampula factory.

In recognition of the contribution of cassava-based beer to the country's agricultural and economic development, the Mozambican government introduced, in 2011, a new excise category for beer made from cassava that was sold and consumed in the same community. Whereas producers of malt-based beers paid a 40 per cent tax rate, the tax rate on Impala beer was set at 10 per cent.[55] In 2011, CDM received

---

[52] www.sabmiller.com/files/reports/2012_SD_report.pdf, op. cit.

[53] Dutch Agricultural Development and Trading Company, "SABMiller," www.dadtco.nl/sabmiller, accessed July 9, 2013.

[54] Rockefeller Foundation, op. cit.

[55] Paul Sonne, Devon Maylie and Drew Hinshaw, March 19, 2013.

the Best Taxpayer of the Year award from the Mozambican Revenue Authority for the second consecutive year.[56] CDM was by far the biggest taxpayer in Mozambique, paying 7.2 per cent of the total taxes collected in 2010 and generating 2.4 per cent of GDP.[57] SABMiller had guaranteed that if the tax amount payable decreased, it would pay the government the difference, but no decrease had occurred because of the volumes that were sold.[58] Mackay, referring to developing these low-cost beers, said, "You can't do this without hemorrhaging your margins – unless you can get the government to come to the party."[59] Government officials acknowledged that cutting such deals had led to some benefits. "Alcohol and beer aren't good for health, but at the same time they bring revenue," said Herminio Sueia, director general of Mozambique's revenue authority.[60]

The implementation process had been complex. Bolt recalled,

> SABMillers' strength has been built on repeating well-known processes worldwide using global supply chains. The global scale and mindset were not compatible at the start with a new raw material, which is bought locally from many, many smallholder farmers. Personal relationships and the enormous drive of van den Houten and Bowman and other managers made the organization capable of surmounting this incompatibility. Brewers are a traditional and conservative group and they battled to understand the need for change. We see, albeit very slowly, SABMiller better understanding that this needs a completely different approach. There is an endless list of advantages which outweigh, in a large way, the challenges encountered to build a completely new supply chain. But there was

a tough struggle with the naysayers in SABMiller, day after day.[61]

Coordination presented some challenges because farmers had limited access to phones, and some farmers, unaware that they needed to communicate with the company to arrange for pick up of their crops, had experienced crop spoilage.[62] Other challenges were transporting crops on very poor roads and the high fuel costs required to move the AMPU. In response, DADTCO decided to establish regular pickups at collection sites and to strategically rotate the AMPU to new areas to minimize transportation costs throughout the year.

Van den Houten added, "Africa is no place for sissies. It was difficult for a successful, huge company, such as SABMiller, to shift its mindset. The route to market – that is, getting previously illicit liquor drinkers to change their habits to include a mainstream local beer – was unknown and difficult to navigate. And with a global organization's high level of bureaucratic governance controls, policies and procedures, it was a difficult task to get SABMiller to lend money to a financially unsound organization."[63]

Bolt reflected on the critical success factors in the project, specifying the following:

> The drive, commitment and vision of a few senior managers at SABMiller: The short command lines and personal relationships between these senior managers allowed for quick decisions and forging ahead at great speed. The fact that SABMiller has great financial muscle while DADTCO had the technology innovation and know-how needed, but was cash strapped, made it necessary for both companies to become partners and be bound to each other with "mutually financial chains." Both partners needed each other and had a mutual interest to make the project a success. The understanding on both sides that

[56] www.sabmiller.com/files/reprts/ar2011/CDMa CDM annual report for 2011, accessed March 1, 2014.

[57] "Mozambique: CDM Planning Two New Breweries," *All Africa*, April 5, 2012, www.allafrica.com/stories/201204051178.html, accessed July 9, 2013.

[58] Sonne, Maylie and Hinshaw March 19, 2013, op.cit.

[59] Ibid.   [60] Ibid.

[61] Email from Peter Bolt to case writer, August 9, 2013.

[62] Rockefeller Foundation, op. cit.

[63] van den Houten, July 18, 2013, op.cit.

creating such a complete new raw material will have many challenges and that a process of change takes time was most important.

Bolt's experience was that, at the level of the smallholder farmers, change could take decades; and, in a multinational company, it could take at least five years. He concluded, "A process of change needs and takes a long time. If senior management fails to grasp that and only looks at the short-term profits, the change is doomed to fail."[64]

Outcomes

Within two months of its launch, Impala had taken 1.7 per cent of Mozambique's beer market and had boosted output of the Nampula factory. Five months after the launch of Impala, the Nampula brewery had produced three million bottles of Impala, which were sold through 400 retailers, most of which were located in remote rural areas.[65] In April 2012, CDM announced it was building two new breweries, in Tete and Sofala provinces, both of which would produce Impala alongside other brands. By December 2012, 12.5 million bottles of Impala had been produced using 3,800 tons of cassava root bought from nearly 1,000 farmers who had been paid a total of $220,000. In 2012, the Impala brand won the prestigious SABMiller Mercatus Global Marketing Award.[66] By June 2013, 18.5 million bottles of Impala had been sold, and van den Houten attested that "Impala has been an extremely profitable initiative."[67]

The project led to many spin-offs. For example, DADTCO was developing two new cassava-based products: flour made from cassava, which could replace expensive imported wheat products in Nigeria, and a cassava-based bio-ethanol for use in ethanol cooking stoves, which would replace charcoal-based stoves. The bio-ethanol could have far-reaching environmental implications, as local wood supplies were being decimated by charcoal production.[68] Farmers in Nampula were working in a new hub-and-spoke system, whereby newly developed commercial farmers assisted nearby subsistence farmers.

Bolt commented, "By creating a sustainable, vibrant market for their crops, buying from them directly, helping them improve their yield, there is no doubt that this project will have a significant impact on the farmers' lives and the local economy."[69] He recalled an elderly woman walking 15 kilometres to the AMPU with a bundle of roots on her head. On receiving her cash payment, she burst into tears – it was the first money she had ever earned. Ernesto Sebastian, one of the farmers in the Nampula district who sold cassava to DADTCO, told interviewers: "I have been able to buy a bike, clothes for the children and school supplies."[70] He had previously occasionally sold dried cassava he had processed laboriously by hand to iterant traders but was now receiving the same price for heavy unprocessed cassava and, through the input of the Cassava + consortium, he had doubled his cassava yield per hectare.

Van den Houten, who retired from SABMiller in September 2012 after more than 30 years' service, was re-engaged to continue to drive the roll-out of the strategically important cassava initiative across SABMiller's African businesses. He felt deep personal satisfaction from the project as it "has a very, very strong business case, and a very strong socio-economic case. It's very satisfying being able to put something back in to Africa and at the same time it is very much a game-changer for our company: It has opened up a whole new market." But van den Houten also wondered how all the stakeholders would react if the process and product proved to be "too successful"?

---

[64] Email from Peter Bolt to case writer, August 9, 2013.

[65] van den Houten, July 18, 2013, op.cit.

[66] www.dadtco.nl/sabmiller-dadtco, accessed July 9, 2013.

[67] van den Houten, July 18, 2013, op.cit.

[68] Dutch Agricultural Development and Trading Company, "Ethanol Production," www.dadtco.nl/ethanol-production, accessed October 15, 2013.

[69] Dutch Agricultural Development and Trading Company, "SABMiller," op. cit.

[70] Rockefeller Foundation, op. cit.

HARVARD | BUSINESS | SCHOOL   REV: JUNE 30, 2008

Christopher A. Bartlett, Brian J. Hall, and Nicole S. Bennett

CASE 3.4 GE'S IMAGINATION BREAKTHROUGHS: THE EVO PROJECT

Professors Christopher A. Bartlett and Brian J. Hall and Research Associate Nicole S. Bennett prepared this case. Some company information and data have been disguised for confidentiality. HBS cases are developed solely as the basis for class discussion. Cases are not intended to serve as endorsements, sources of primary data, or illustrations of effective or ineffective management.

As he prepared for the December 2006 meeting with GE's CEO Jeff Immelt, Pierre Comte faced some difficult decisions. Only eight months into his job as chief marketing officer (CMO) of GE's Transportation business, Comte would be presenting Transportation's recommendations on some of the most visible growth initiatives in its locomotive business–projects that had been designated "Imagination Breakthroughs." IBs, as they were called within GE, were new projects with the potential to generate $100 million in new business within two to three years, and were a key part of Immelt's organic growth strategy. At the IB Review, Immelt expected to hear how Transportation was progressing with each of its locomotive IBs and what plans they had for their future.

Within GE Transportation, however, the future of several IBs had been a source of considerable debate, with none more sensitive than the Hybrid locomotive. Launched two years earlier in the belief that it could become a disruptive technology that could redefine the industry, the Hybrid had struggled to develop cost-effective performance, and some of its key sponsors were beginning to wonder if resources should continue to be committed to it. The ongoing debate had resurfaced in November at a growth review meeting in Erie, Pennsylvania, where Transportation's CEO John Dineen asked Comte and Brett BeGole, head of Transportation's Locomotive P&L unit, to describe how they planned to update Immelt on the Hybrid IB. BeGole, an experienced and effective business leader, explained that problems with the cost and performance of batteries had made the project's future highly uncertain. Feeling it was sapping resources from more profitable growth opportunities, he wondered whether it should be sidelined until the technology was further developed.

Comte was uncomfortable with that proposition. He felt that the Hybrid represented a real opportunity for GE to lead fundamental market change, and that sidelining the project could cause it to lose the resources and attention it needed at this critical stage of its development. He also worried about Immelt's reaction, especially since the Hybrid was one of his favorite IB projects. But while he knew that the IB process was designed to encourage risk-taking, Comte also realized that at the end of the day, it had to be commercially viable. In GE, the bottom line always mattered.

As Dineen listened to his direct reports, he understood the source of their differences. BeGole was responsible for the profitability and growth of the Locomotive P&L unit, and would be held accountable for its bottom-line results. But Comte, with his mandate to develop market knowledge and competitive intelligence, had been asked to challenge and stretch the existing organization. Indeed, Dineen recalled telling his new CMO, "Pierre, your job is to make marketing 'the point of the spear'; to take us to places we don't want to go." Now, after listening to the debate, Dineen wondered what Transportation's position on the Hybrid should be in its upcoming IB Review with Immelt.

Immelt Takes Charge: New Demands, New Responses[1]

On Friday, September 7, 2001, 43-year-old Jeff Immelt became GE's ninth CEO in its 109-year history. Four days later, two planes crashed into the World Trade Center towers. In the turmoil that followed, an already fragile post-Internet bubble stock market dropped further, and the subsequent downturn in the economy resulted in a drop in confidence that spread rapidly around the globe.

Despite his many efforts to tighten operations while continuing to grow the business, the new CEO did not have an easy initiation as he tried to deal with the resulting economic downturn, the post-Enron suspicions of large corporations, and the growing global political instability. In 2002, after promising that earnings would grow by double digits, Immelt had to report a modest 7% increase in GE's profits on revenues that were up only 5% on the 2001 sales, which had declined 3% from the prior year. (See **Exhibit 1** for GE financials, 1995–2006.) By the end of 2002, GE's stock was trading at $24, down 39% from a year earlier and 60% from its all-time high of $60 in August 2000. With considerable understatement, Immelt said, "This was not a great year to be a rookie CEO."[2]

Driving Growth: The Strategic Priority

Beyond this immediate market pressure, Immelt was acutely aware that he stood in the very long

shadow cast by his predecessor, Jack Welch, under whose leadership GE had generated a total return to shareholders of 23% per annum for 20 years, representing an astonishing $380 billion increase in shareholder wealth over his two decades as CEO. Much of the company's stock price premium was due to the fact that Welch had built GE into a disciplined, efficient machine that delivered on its promise of consistent growth in sales and earnings. The results were achieved in part through effective operations management that drove a 4% per annum organic growth rate (much of it productivity driven), but primarily through a continuous stream of timely acquisitions and clever deal making. This two-pronged approach had resulted in double-digit revenue and profit increases through most of the 1990s.

But Immelt knew that he could not hope to replicate such a performance by simply continuing the same strategy. The environment in the new millennium had changed too much. The new CEO wanted to use GE's size and diversity as sources of strength and to drive growth by investing in places and in ways that others could not easily follow. He began to articulate a strategy that would rely on technology leadership, commercial excellence, and global expansion to build new business bases that would capitalize on what he described as "unstoppable trends."

Beginning in 2002, he challenged his business leaders to identify these new "growth platforms" with the potential to generate $1 billion in operating profit within the next few years. In response, several opportunities emerged, and the company soon began engaging in new fields such as oil and gas technology, securities and sensors, water technology, Hispanic broadcasting, and consumer finance, all of which were growing at a 15% annual rate. "The growth platforms we have identified are in markets that have above average growth rates and can uniquely benefit from GE's capabilities," said Immelt. "Growth is *the* initiative, *the* core competency that we are building in GE."[3]

---

[1] This section summarizes "GE's Growth Strategy: The Immelt Initiative," Harvard Business School Case No. 306–087.

[2] GE 2002 Annual Report, p. 5.

[3] GE 2003 Annual Report, p. 9.

Exhibit 1
GE Financial Performance, 1995–2006 ($ millions)

	2006	2005	2004	2003	2002	2001	2000	1995
General Electric Company & Consolidated Affiliates								
Revenues	163,391	147,956	134,291	113,421	132,226	125,913	129,853	70,028
Earnings from continuing operations	20,666	18,631	16,601	15,589	15,133	14,128	12,735	6,573
Loss from discontinued operations	163	(1,922)	559	2,057	(616)	(444)	0	
Net earnings	20,829	16,711	17,160	14,091	14,629	13,684	12,735	6,573
Dividends declared	10,675	9,647	8,594	7,759	7,266	6,555	5,647	2,838
Earned on average shareowner's equity	19.5%	17.8%	17.9%	20%	25.2%	27.1%	27.5%	23.5%
Per share:								
Net earnings	1.99	1.76	1.59	1.4	1.46	1.41	3.87	3.90
Net earnings–diluted	1.99	1.76	1.59	1.4	1.52	1.37	3.81	
Dividends declared	1.03	0.91	0.82	0.77	0.73	0.66	1.71	1.69
Stock price range[a]	38.49–32.06	37.34–32.67	37.75–28.88	32.43–21.30	41.84–21.40	52.90–28.25	60.5–41.66	73.13–49.88
Total assets of continuing operations	697,239	673,321	750,617	647,834	575,018	495,023	437,006	228,035
Long-term borrowings	260,804	212,281	207,871	170,309	138,570	79,806	82,132	51,027
Shares outstanding–average (in thousands)	10,359,320	10,569,805	10,399,629	10,018,587	9,947,113	9,932,245	3,299,037	1,683,812
Employees at year-end:								
United States	155,000	161,000	165,000	155,000	161,000	158,000	168,000	150,000
Other countries	165,000	155,000	142,000	150,000	154,000	152,000	145,000	72,000
Total employees	319,000	316,000	307,000	305,000	315,000	310,000	313,000	222,000

Source: Compiled from GE annual reports, various years.
[a] Stock price adjusted for stock split in 2000.

Building New Capabilities: Investing in Technology and Marketing

To reposition GE's portfolio to leverage growth, Immelt's team lost little time in acquiring companies such as Telemundo to build a base in Hispanic broadcasting, Interlogix in security systems, BetzDearborn in water-processing services, and Enron Wind in renewable energy. After completing $35 billion worth of acquisitions in 2001 and 2002, GE completed the biggest acquisition year in its history in 2003, including two megadeals: $14 billion for media giant Vivendi Universal Entertainment (VUE), and $10 billion for UK-based Amersham, a leader in biosciences.

But Immelt also recognized that he would have to make equally significant internal investments to ensure that his strategy of technology-driven, commercially-oriented global expansion could build on this new growth platform. Within his first six months, he had committed $100 million to upgrade GE's major R&D facility at Niskayuna in upstate New York. Then, in 2002, he authorized a new Global Research Center (GRC) in Shanghai, and in 2003 agreed to build another GRC in Munich, investments involving another $100 million. And despite the slowing economy, he upped the R&D budget 14% to $359 million in 2003. When asked about the increase in spending during such a difficult time for the company, he said, "Organic growth is the driver. Acquisitions are secondary to that. I can't see us go out and pay a start-up $100 million for technology that, if we had just spent $2 million a year for 10 years, we could have done a better job at it. I hate that, I just hate that."[4]

Rather than concentrating primarily on short-term product development as it had in the past, the GRCs' agenda become more oriented toward the long term. R&D also became more focused, with more than 1,000 projects slashed to just 100. Furthermore, the research group identified five very long-term technology areas for special attention, in fields as diverse as nanotechnology,

advanced propulsion, and biotechnology. It was a longer-term R&D focus than GE had seen for many years.

The other core competency Immelt wanted to use to drive organic growth was marketing. As an ex-salesman, he had always focused on the customer and felt that an unintended by-product of Welch's obsession with operating efficiency and cost-cutting had been the development of a culture that was too internally focused. He wanted the organization to turn its attention to the marketplace and to bring in a more commercially oriented perspective to its decisions.

In one of Immelt's first appointments, Beth Comstock was named GE's chief marketing officer, a position Welch had abolished decades earlier. (See **Exhibit 2** for the GE's corporate organization chart.) Immelt also redeployed most of GE's large acquisition-oriented corporate business development staff into marketing roles, and asked each of GE's businesses to appoint a VP-level marketing head to develop that capability in the business. Because of the shortage of internal talent, many of these marketing leaders had to be recruited from outside, an uncommon practice at GE.

To provide a forum for these new leaders to monitor and drive the change Immelt wanted, in 2003 he formed a Commercial Council made up of 20 respected commercial leaders drawn from a diverse range of GE businesses. Not all members were corporate officers, or even among the top 600 in GE's Senior Executive Band, but all shared the distinction of being personally selected by the CEO for their innovative thinking. Meeting monthly by phone and quarterly in person, the group used this forum to discuss mega-trends, to identify broad strategies for international growth, and to diffuse best marketing practices rapidly throughout GE. To underline its importance, Immelt chaired the council.

Realigning Personal Competencies: Developing "Growth Leaders"

The investment in new capabilities had an immediate impact on GE's management profile. Within Immelt's first two years, the company recruited over 5000 engineers, and among the

[4] Robert Buderi, "GE Finds Its Inner Edison," *Technology Review*, October, 2003, pp. 46–50.

Exhibit 2 GE Corporate Structure

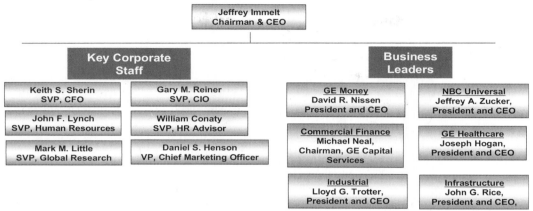

GE Corporate Structure

Jeffrey Immelt
Chairman & CEO

Key Corporate Staff

Keith S. Sherin SVP, CFO	Gary M. Reiner SVP, CIO
John F. Lynch SVP, Human Resources	William Conaty SVP, HR Advisor
Mark M. Little SVP, Global Research	Daniel S. Henson VP, Chief Marketing Officer

Business Leaders

GE Money David R. Nissen President and CEO	NBC Universal Jeffrey A. Zucker, President and CEO
Commercial Finance Michael Neal, Chairman, GE Capital Services	GE Healthcare Joseph Hogan, President and CEO
Industrial Lloyd G. Trotter, President and CEO	Infrastructure John G. Rice, President and CEO,

Source: GE Annual Report, 2006, pp. 114–115.

175 corporate officers, the number of engineers grew from seven to 21. The same dramatic change was occurring in sales and marketing, and in 2003, the company began a process to increase GE's under-resourced marketing staff by 2000 over the next two years. To help integrate this influx of senior-level marketers into GE's culture and systems, the Experienced Commercial Leadership Program was created.

As big a task as it was, recruiting top talent into these growth-driving functions was less of a concern to the CEO than the challenge of developing new capabilities in his current management team. While strong in operations and finance, some lacked the skills Immelt felt they would need to succeed in the more entrepreneurial, risk-taking environment he wanted to create. To help define the leadership behaviors that would be required to drive organic growth, the human resources staff researched the competency profiles at 15 large, fast-growth global companies such as Toyota, P&G, and Dell. They concluded that five leadership traits would be key to driving organic growth in GE:

- An external focus
- An ability to think clearly
- Imagination and courage
- Inclusiveness and connection with people
- In-depth expertise

Soon, all courses at GE's Crotonville education center focused on developing these characteristics, and Immelt made it clear that unless managers had these traits or were developing them, they would not be likely to succeed at GE regardless of their past track record. And to underline his commitment to supporting a new generation of "growth leaders," he began making changes to some of GE's well-established norms and practices. For example, to develop leaders with more in-depth market and technological knowledge and domain expertise, Immelt decided to slow the job rotations that had long been central to management development at GE; to build new technological and marketing capabilities rapidly, he accepted the need to recruit from the outside; and to encourage individuals to take risks, and even to fail, Immelt adjusted the evaluation and reward processes that previously had been tied to flawless execution of short-term budget objectives.

Embedding Growth in Processes and Metrics

In classic GE form, all elements of the new organic growth initiative were soon being reinforced in metrics, systems, and processes to ensure that the new objectives received the disciplined follow-up that characterized GE's management style. It was this cycle of tightly

Exhibit 3 GE's Operating System

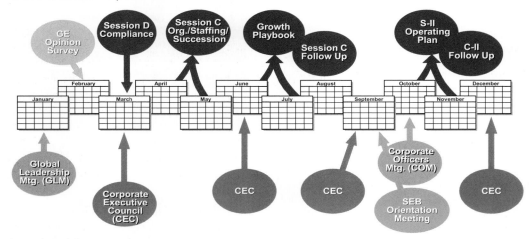

GE Operating System
Annual Integrated Business and Leadership Processes
Core business processes

Leadership meetings

imagination at work

Source: GE internal documents.

linked and mutually supportive systems and processes, that were the backbone of the company's Operating System, that supported GE's reputation for clear strategy and a disciplined implementation.

At the heart of the Operating System were three core processes that had framed management reviews over many decades–Session C, Session I, and Session II. (See **Exhibit 3** for a graphic representation.) Each was now harnessed to drive the growth agenda. For example, the Session C organization, staffing, and succession reviews each May became a powerful tool to reinforce the recruitment, promotion, and deployment of technological and marketing talent, as well as the development of a new generation of "growth leaders" willing to take risks to build new businesses. Next, in July, Session I (GE's strategy review process that Immelt renamed the Growth Playbook) required each business to drill down on how market trends and customer needs provided

opportunities for them to grow their business organically. And in November's Session II, discussions of the operating budget (driven in the GE model by stretch targets rather than line item expense reviews) made sure that each business's commitments to invest in and deliver on growth projects were not cut back in order to meet short-term performance objectives.

Further, the metrics used in the implementation of each of these systems were also changed to reflect the new growth objectives. For example, individual development reviews and performance evaluations leading up to Session C now evaluated managers against the new growth traits. In the first year, only corporate officers were evaluated; the following year, the metrics were extended to the 600 in the Senior Executive Band; and by year three, the top 7000 executives were getting feedback and development support around the required growth traits. New metrics in the Session I/Growth Playbook review required managers to develop and defend strategies to achieve Immelt's objective organic growth rate of 5% above GDP growth by doubling GE's organic growth from 4% to 8% annually. And in Session II, a new Net Promoter Score was added to hold managers accountable for a demanding measure of customer loyalty and repurchase.

Imagination Breakthroughs: Engine of Organic Growth

By the end of 2003, Immelt told investors that he had now completed the big investments needed to re-position the company's business platforms for the future. But results were still disappointing, and with both income and revenue barely above the levels of 2000, some observers were beginning to question whether the GE's greatest growth was behind it. Immelt rejected that notion, and saw no reason for GE to slow down as long as it was able to change its approach and emphasize organic growth. "In the late 1990s, we became business traders not business growers," he said. "Today, organic growth is absolutely the biggest task in every one of our companies."[5]

Having spent his first two years repositioning the business portfolio and investing in new organizational capabilities, Immelt now wanted to drive the pursuit of organic growth much deeper into the company. In September 2003, he convened a meeting of marketing directors from each of GE's businesses and challenged to develop by November five proposals for new growth businesses—"Imagination Breakthroughs" he called them, or IBs as they quickly became known. "We have to put growth on steroids," he said. "I want game changers. Take a big swing."[6]

Over the next two months, the marketing leaders engaged management of all of GE's businesses to respond to Immelt's challenge. In November, they presented 50 IB proposals to the CEO and a small group of corporate marketing staff who now became the IB Review Committee. Of this initial portfolio, the CEO green-lighted 35,

which the businesses were then expected to fund, adapt, and pursue. And Immelt indicated that he intended to monitor progress–personally and closely.

GE Transportation's First IB: The Evo Story

In September 2003, in response to Immelt's request, GE Transportation identified its five potential IBs. Perhaps the most exciting was the Evolution Locomotive, a product already on the shelf as a planned new product introduction, but struggling to get support due to challenges in both its technical development and its market acceptance. The designation of this project as an IB turned a corporate spotlight on its funding and put a supercharger on its commercialization.

Origins of the Evolution Locomotive

GE began serving the North American rail market in 1918, and through numerous cycles over the better part of the next century, the company steadily built a good business selling to North America's six large rail companies. By the mid-1990s, with revenues approaching $2 billion, GE had built a dominant market share, and its AC4400 long-haul locomotive was recognized as the most successful engine on the market. But it was a mature and conservative industry, and an unlikely place to jumpstart an initiative that called for cutting-edge technology, innovation, and risk taking.

In a rare innovative move in the industry, in 1995 GE introduced its much anticipated "super-loco," the AC6000. Touted as the most powerful locomotive on the market, its size and hauling capability were impressive. But within a year of its launch, North American customers were reporting that most of the AC6000's new capabilities were unnecessary or uneconomical. This unfortunate misreading of market needs led to only 207 units of the 6000 being sold over the next five years compared with more than 3,000 classic AC4400 locomotives in the same period.[7]

---

[5] Jeffrey R. Immelt, "Growth As a Process," *Harvard Business Review*, June 2006, p. 64.

[6] Erick Schonfeld, "GE Sees the Light," *Business 2.0*, July 2004, Vol. 5, Iss. 6, pp. 80–86.

[7] "US loco market still a two-horse race," *Railway Gazette International*, July 1, 2006.

Worse, many of those that were sold either failed to deliver on their promised cost-benefit performance or had reliability problems. The AC6000 locomotive was eventually discontinued and became a black eye on GE's otherwise strong record in the industry.

Meanwhile, in December 1997, Environmental Protection Agency (EPA) upset the predictable rail market by announcing strict emissions requirements for all new locomotives to be put in service after January 1, 2005. The regulations posed serious engineering challenges and a major commercial risk for locomotive manufacturers whose safest response was to modify existing models to meet the new standards. While most companies chose to follow this conservative strategy, GE engineers committed to a riskier and more expensive approach of designing a completely new platform able to meet future emissions standards while also keeping fuel costs down.

Over the following three years, engineers in Erie and at the Global Research Center in Niskayuna worked to redefine the paradigm of locomotive design by eliminating the traditional tradeoff between fuel efficiency and emissions. The result was the Evolution Locomotive (quickly dubbed the Evo) which used a revolutionary engine combined with a patented cooling system to achieve 3% to 5% fuel savings while generating 40% less emissions than the previous generation. It also incorporated a locomotive control system enhancement that managed the speed and throttle settings to minimize fuel consumption and/or emissions, taking into account train composition, terrain, track conditions, train dynamics, and weather, without negatively impacting the train's arrival time.

Although this radical new engine represented a clear technical advancement, the decision to take it from design to production was a gamble. Because locomotives delivered before January 1, 2005 were exempt from the new regulations, some predicted that there would be a spike in demand for old models in 2004, leaving little market for the Evo in 2005. Indeed, the sales force reported that most customers were wary about making early commitments to meet the new requirements. But the believers on the GE team argued that the Evo could deliver real savings in fuel and labor, areas in which costs were mounting rapidly in the industry. In a major bet, in 2002 GE committed to building its Evolution locomotive. (See **Exhibit 4** for a photo and basic specifications for the Evo.)

Evo Becomes an IB

The earlier AC6000 product failure coupled with the looming change in environmental regulations in the industry put the locomotive business leaders in Erie under intense pressure to prove to the CEO that they could grow their mature business organically. When Immelt announced his quest for $100 million Imagination Breakthroughs, it was clear that the Evo would be a "make or break" project. Despite the continuing uncertainty around its market potential, the Evo became the centerpiece of Transportation's presentation in its first IB Review with Immelt. The CEO was immediately taken by the project's potential and told the sponsoring managers that he would be monitoring progress in regular review meetings that he planned to conduct monthly with those responsible for IBs.

True to his word, Immelt conducted reviews of several businesses' IBs every month. This meant that every six months or so, those directly responsible for Evo–the P&L leader, the technology leader, and/or the marketing leader–met with him to describe progress and outline next steps for their project. As the team soon learned, PowerPoint presentations were strictly prohibited in these meetings. To encourage an atmosphere of discussion and debate, presenters were allowed no more than one page of documentation for each IB. Although the meetings were small and informal, the managers were not necessarily relaxed. They knew that questioning would be intense, and were advised to be prepared to discuss a range of sample questions. (See **Exhibit 5** for a preparatory list.) So meeting the CEO (supported by just a few of his corporate marketing staff), created some nervous tension. As one manager reflected, "Do you really want to be the only business that shows no imagination or, compared to other business's IBs being presented, has no breakthrough?"

Exhibit 4 Evolution Locomotive Product Specifications

EVOLUTION SERIES TECHNOLOGY BEARS CLOSE INSPECTION, BY ACCOUNTING AS WELL AS ENGINEERING.

Overcoming obstacles with technological innovation is meaningless if that technology isn't economically viable for everyday use. That's why every component in an Evolution Series locomotive is proven to meet the demands of those who operate them as well as those who pay for them.

Nowhere is this more evident than with the GEVO-12 engine. The heart of the Evolution Series locomotives, the 45-degree, 12-cylinder, 4-stroke, turbocharged GEVO-12 engine produces the same 4,400 HP as its 16-cylinder predecessor. And it does it with greater fuel efficiency, lower emissions, and extended overhaul intervals. Enhanced cooling and higher-strength materials dramatically improve reliability and allow for future increases in power and efficiency.

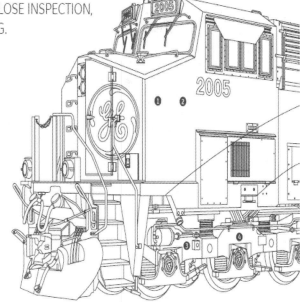

❶ Smart Displays
Several add-on black boxes are eliminated with a new computer display combination, enhancing both reliability and operator ergonomics.

❷ Enhanced Microprocessor Controls
Upgraded components and software improve wheel slip/slide control and reliability while providing more comprehensive and simplified diagnostics. Open architecture enables easier integration of software and third-party devices.

❸ HiAd™ Trucks
Low weight transfer, an improved microprocessor wheel slip/slide system, and a single inverter per motor, combine to optimize adhesion under all rail conditions. Design simplicity and 10-year overhaul intervals significantly reduce maintenance costs.

❹ Low-Slip, High-Performance AC Traction Motors
Get a full 166,000 lbs. (AC) of continuous tractive effort and up to 198,000 lbs. (AC) starting tractive effort from a 6-axle locomotive. Integral pinion design eliminates slippage, extending pinion life to 2 million miles. Million-mile motor overhaul intervals further reduce maintenance costs.

❺ Superior Dynamic Braking
Evolution Series locomotives feature up to 117,000 lbs. (AC) of braking effort, utilizing the proven grids and blowers from our current production AC 4400 & Dash 9. Braking grids are also completely isolated for greater reliability and simplified maintenance.

❻ Air-Cooled Inverters
No coolant. No environmental concerns. A single air-cooled inverter per traction motor provides individual axle control that improves wheel slip/slide, increases mission reliability, maximizes tractive effort, and improves transmission efficiency.

Source: Evolution Locomotive brochure, GE Transportation website: http://www.getransportation.com/na/en/evolution.html.

Managers came to IB Review meetings armed with extensive market information, the result of a rigorous analytical process called CECOR that was being rolled out by the corporate marketing group to help business-level marketing teams systematize analysis to support the IB process.[8]

(See **Exhibit 6** for an outline of the CECOR process and tools.) Because of Immelt's understanding of the issues and his direct, in-depth questioning, some began calling the IB Review meetings the "Committee of One."

In the glare of the IB spotlight, the Evo product management and sales team found themselves

---

[8] CECOR stood for Calibrate, Explore, Create, Organize, and Realize, an analytical process that the corporate marketing group had developed. It was supported by a portfolio of tools borrowed from a variety of sources including the consulting groups Bain and McKinsey, which had proved helpful in doing market segmentation, customer analysis, competitive analysis, etc.

Exhibit 4 (*cont.*)

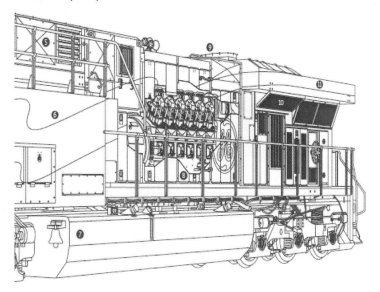

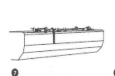

7
High-Impact Fuel Tank
This tank exceeds AAR S-5506 with thickened, reinforced walls and baffles for even greater puncture resistance.

8
Isolation Mounts
Smoother. Quieter. New isolation mounts on the engine and alternator significantly improve operator environment with reduced cab noise and vibration.

EPA
United States
Environmental Protection
Agency

9
Emissions
"Environmentally compatible" is more than a buzzword for Evolution Series locomotives. Advanced electronic fuel injection, air-to-air cooling, adaptive controls, and GEVO-12 engine technology combine to reduce emissions by over 40 percent.

10
Air-To-Air Intercooler
Manifold Air Temperature (MAT) is greatly reduced with the new hybrid cooling system and air-to-air intercooler. The lower MAT enables emissions compliance while simultaneously improving fuel efficiency.

11
Split Cooling
The proven Split Cooling radiator system reduces engine-air-inlet temperatures and cools the engine oil for increased reliability and longer engine-bearing life.

under increased pressure to perform. But discussions with customers revealed that GE was still "paying for sins of the past," as one salesman put it, and the team concluded that it would not be able to sell the Evo's value proposition from a piece of paper and a set of specifications. After the failure of the AC6000, customers wanted solid evidence of the benefits being promised.

In a leap of faith, GE Transportation took the financial risk of committing $100 million to build 50 Evo units, which they then planned to lease to customers for a nominal fee. The locomotives were to be carried on GE's books, but would be operated by customers and used on their North American lines. The goal was to log five million miles before the 2005 launch, thereby regaining customers' trust by proving the engine's reliability and the value of the technological advancements.

Preparing to Launch: The Agony …

In early 2004, vague concerns about Evo began turning to panic. A year into the leasing plan, the sales team did not have a single firm order. Sales reps were getting positive feedback about performance of the leased Evos, but customers were still reluctant to make the capital expenditure. Transportation's November SII Budget Review for Evo had been grim: worst-case scenarios projected sales of only 30 or 50 locomotives out of a

Exhibit 5
IB Review Preparation: Sample Questions

The following are a few of the questions given to IB teams to help them prepare for reviews:

Market Opportunity
- Can you start with the answer: Where would you like to be and why?
- How does this fit in your strategy?
- What does it take to be good at this?
- How does technology play a role here? Does it give us an advantage?

Competition
- Is anyone else doing this? Who is best at this?
- How we placed vis-à-vis the competition?
- How many others have tried this? Have they succeeded or failed?
- Do our competitors make money at this?

Pricing
- How much would we make on this product?
- How much would the customer pay for this product?
- How do we price it correctly?
- Why aren't we charging a higher price?

Resources
- Where do we have in-house expertise?
- Are you working with any other GE business on this?
- How do we use GE Financial Services as a weapon?
- What resources do we need to hit the growth target? A doubling/tripling of resources?

Go to Market
- What is standing in our way in order to execute this well?
- Is there a way to tap into global suppliers to fill the global pipeline?
- What is the value proposition? How would you differentiate?
- How will you build capability?

Source: GE internal documents.

total 2005 capacity of 600 Evos. It was a performance that would result in significant losses. While some felt that GE might have to offer the Evo at an attractive initial price to attract sales, Immelt challenged that assumption. At IB Review meetings, he was pushing the team in the opposite direction, urging them to focus on how to price the soon-to-be-launched product to capture its full value.

Because the Evo offered significant economic savings to the railroads over its lifecycle, Immelt asked why it could not be sold at a premium over the previous model. Discussion about the impact of rising energy costs in the IB Review meetings spilled over into detailed market and product analysis in Growth Playbook sessions. These meetings with Immelt were very different from the Session I strategy reviews over which Welch had presided. Where Welch had been cost and efficiency-driven, Immelt was focused on the market value of technological advancements like the Evo. "In a deflationary world, you could get margin by working productivity," Immelt said. "Now you need marketing to get a price."[9]

___

[9] Jeffrey R. Immelt, "Growth As a Process," *Harvard Business Review*, June 2006, p. 64.

Exhibit 6 CECOR Tool Kit

CECOR Framework
Identifying questions to ask and tools to apply

C CALIBRATE	E EXPLORE	C CREATE	O ORGANIZE	R REALIZE
▶ What industry are you in? ▶ Who are the customers and what do they need?	▶ What are our potential avenues of growth? ▶ Which ones will you target?	▶ What are our best ideas? ▶ What is the customer value?	▶ Is the go-to-market plan aligned with the value proposition? ▶ Are you prepared to implement?	▶ Will you meet your revenue and income plans? ▶ How will you measure customer and GE impact?

Tools

•Five Forces •Market Maps •Profit Pools •Value Chain	•Customer Experience Grid •Segmentation •Competitive Assessment •Targeting	•Capability Assessment • Ideation Sessions • Positioning	•Conjoint Analysis •Value Proposition •Value Based Pricing •Branding	•Go-to-Market Plan •Continuous Feedback (VoC) •Impact Metrics

GE *imagination at work*

CECOR's fit in GE's operating rigor

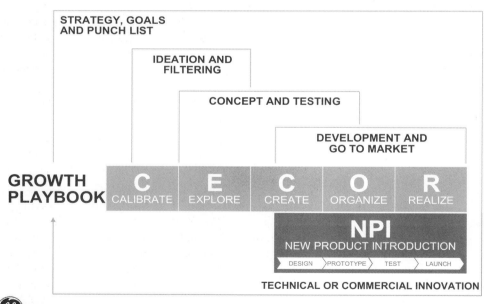

Source: GE internal documents.

As a result of these discussions, the IB team refined Evo's value story to focus on its lifecycle costs, and decided to reflect the Evo's significant performance improvements in a 10% price premium. Knowing that this decision would cause anxiety within the sales ranks, Dave Tucker, Transportation's VP of Global Sales, turned the annual January sales meeting in Coco Beach, Florida into a call to arms for the Evo. Despite having a single firm order, in the opening session he announced that by June the sales team needed to sell out the factory–and at a significant price premium over the previous model. "It scared the hell out of the sales force," Tucker recalled. "Frankly, we had never had a step-function increase in pricing like that."

Tucker challenged his sales force to come up with the means to implement the plan. In addition to worries about the expected customer reaction, some expressed concerns about the likely response of a key competitor who had not made the same upfront investment. But the marketing group's analysis suggested that rising oil prices, increased rail traffic, and tightening emission standards could make customers more open to Evo's benefits. After several days of joint discussions with marketing and product management, the sales force hit the streets committed to booking orders at the new price.

Implementing the Launch: ... The Ecstasy

Over the following months, the sales team went back to its customers, emphasizing value to convince them that Evo was worth its price premium. As if responding to a cue, oil prices continued to rise – from $32 a barrel in January 2004, to $40 by June, and $50 by October. At the same time, driven by surging Chinese imports entering the U.S. on the West Coast, transcontinental rail traffic was booming. And state regulatory bodies' demands were making emissions an industry-wide concern. The marketing analyses had proved correct: customers were ready for the Evo.

By the launch date on January 1, 2005, not only was Evo's entire 2005 production sold out, product was on backorder through much of 2006. Despite earlier concerns about a risk of a temporary drop in market share, industry experts estimated that GE maintained or increased its 70% share through the launch and outsold its competition by three to one in the U.S. market during 2005.[8] By mid-2006, there was a backlog of 1500 locomotives, representing two years of production capacity. The early success of the Evo continued into 2007, with all-time highs in deliveries surpassing records set just one year earlier. The Evo had become a poster-child IB success story.

Managing the IB Lifecycle: Raising the Evo Babies

When John Dineen became CEO of GE Transportation in the summer of 2005, Evo was well on its way to being one of the outstanding IB successes. But Dineen made it clear that he wanted to drive even more growth from this old-line, mature portfolio of businesses. To emphasize that objective, he reinforced Immelt's annual corporate Growth Playbook process by creating a Growth Council, to which he invited his entire management team to engage in a monthly review of growth initiatives in each of Transportation's businesses. His objective was to build a growth agenda into the pulse of the business and make it part of the ongoing management discussion.

Birth of an Evo Baby: The Global Modular Locomotive

Acknowledging that the slow-growth domestic markets already dominated by GE were unlikely to be the major source of new business, Dineen emphasized the opportunities for international expansion. Responding to that challenge, Tim Schweikert, general manager of the Locomotive P&L unit, began to explore with his team the challenge of breaking into the global locomotive market. They soon identified the hurdles they would have to clear in order to sell internationally. First, because railway gauge width, weight limits, and clearance requirements varied widely by country, the team decided that there could be no standardized "global locomotive." Furthermore, the number of locomotives called for in most international tenders (as few as 10 or 15) made the huge upfront investment in engineering a major cost barrier. And finally, because governments were typically the operators of railways, the selling process usually involved complex political negotiations.

Recognizing all of these constraints, Schweikert and his team developed a product concept that it termed the Global Modular Locomotive (GML), a design developed around a set of standard components that could be built to different national requirements using a Lego-like construction approach. With great excitement, they took their idea to Dineen's monthly Growth Council where it was endorsed as a candidate for Immelt's IB Review. Presenting their ideas in this forum in September 2005, the locomotive team preempted Immelt's opening question by identifying GML's three value-creating objectives: to reduce the response time in international tender processing, to reduce the amount spent on nonrecurring engineering, and to reduce the time between the order and the sale. After further probing questions, Immelt congratulated them and approved GML as an IB.

To help Schweikert implement the new IB project, Dineen assigned Gokhan Bayhan to the role of marketing leader for the Locomotive P&L unit. The move was part of a larger strategy of transferring recognized talent into the fledgling business marketing roles. "We took some of our best people from our commercial and engineering organization and put them into these roles," said Dineen. "As soon as you start doing that, the rest of the organization realizes it's important. Initially, we had to draft people and assure them that the move was going to be good for their careers. But it was hard. Every bone in their body was telling them not to do it because there was no track record." (See **Exhibit 7** for GE Transportation's organization chart.)

Because Bayhan had earlier worked on a locomotive modernization contract that GE had won to overhaul and rebuild 400 locomotives for the state-owned railway in Kazakhstan, he decided this was a perfect place to explore GML's potential. Soon, he and the sales team were talking to government contacts about the new concept and about the opportunity for GE to help them expand and modernize their railway system to meet the needs of Kazakhstan's fast-growing China trade.

The disciplined process of analyzing the market opportunities and customer needs was part of the marketing group's responsibility. But because this analysis was a new element in the existing process of bringing a product to market, gaining acceptance was not always easy, as Bayhan explained:

> The relationships between product management, sales, and engineering were well established, so a lot of marketing team members had difficulty breaking into that process, and taking on a role that didn't exist before. It was hardest for those from the outside, and they were the majority. It helped that I'd been in the organization in various product management and finance roles because it allowed me to use my access and credibility to contribute a marketing point of view. But lots of others had a hard time with it.

Meanwhile, as sales, engineering, and marketing worked together to test and approve the GML concept, a major boost to the effort occurred in December 2005 when the company announced that it had received an order for 300 GML locomotives from the Chinese railway. In October, Schweikert, who had been close to the Chinese negotiations, was transferred from his position in Erie to become head of GE transportation in China, not only to oversee this important contract, but to use it to expand GE's penetration into this huge market.

Making Marketing Mainstream

As the role and impact of the marketing function grew within Transportation, Dineen accelerated his efforts to find a head of marketing who could not only accelerate existing marketing efforts, but could also provide the function with greater access and influence at the most senior levels of discussion in the company. Finally, in early 2006, he found the person he felt could fill the role. Pierre Comte became chief marketing officer of GE Transportation in May 2006. Surprisingly, although he had a strong commercial background built up through an international career,

Exhibit 7 GE Transportation Organizational Chart

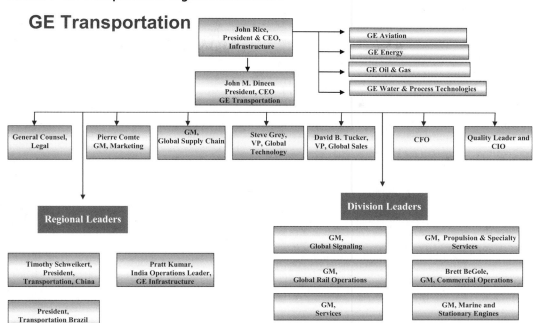

Source: GE internal documents.

he did not come from a traditional marketing background. Most recently he had run the rail signaling business at a major European transportation company. But to Dineen, he seemed an ideal fit–someone with relevant industry expertise, good frontline experience, and a strong enough personality to deal credibly with his P&L leaders, and understand their pressures and constraints.

In his first meeting with his new CMO, Dineen told Comte to "create a crisis around growth." But Comte realized he would first have to convince his bottom-line-driven peers that he could help them:

> When you run a $2 billion Locomotive P&L that's doing great, you don't have a pressing need to reinvent yourself and your business. The role of the marketing group is to push the P&L leaders to revisit their portfolios. But they won't listen to chart makers or theoreticians. So I spent three months telling them, "I'm like you, I'm a business guy; I've lived in Asia and Europe. I've run a P&L with a couple of

thousand people reporting to me. I know that the last thing you want is another headquarters guy giving you more work to do. I'm not going to do that. I'm here to help you make your P&Ls bigger, stronger."

Under Comte, the new marketing team began to take a more active role in the business, a role that became more and more evident as the Evo offshoot businesses started to grow. The contributions that Gokhan Bayhan made to the redefinition of GML provided a classic example.

The Baby Grows into a Family

In April 2006, as members of the locomotive management team sat down to prepare for their presentation to Immelt at Transportation's Growth Playbook/Session I review in June, some of the initial ideas behind the GML concept were beginning to seem questionable. Doubts were being expressed by people from project management, marketing, and engineering about whether the GML's Lego design would work in practice.

To resolve the concerns, Brett BeGole, Schweikert's replacement as global operations general manager for the Locomotive P&L unit, commissioned a "Tiger Team" of six people from engineering, product management, and marketing and gave them two weeks to recommend what changes, if any, should be made to the GML concept.

Much of the team's work was based on a rigorous analysis of a rich set of data on customers, competitors, and market trends that Gokhan Bayhan had assembled. Using CECOR tools including a customer needs analysis, a competitive response analysis, and a market segmentation map, Bayhan presented Steve Gray, his engineering counterpart on the Tiger Team, a rich picture of the critical technical and quality elements that customers were demanding.

After an intense two weeks of analysis, the team came to the conclusion that the GML concept was too complex and too expensive to serve the market efficiently. Instead, they proposed that GML's modular approach be replaced by a platform concept that defined five different families of locomotives, which together would serve 85% to 90% of the global market demand. Three of the five platforms to be developed were based on the Evo engine, while the two other family members would use another engine still under development.

The Tiger Team's recommendations were presented at Transportation's Growth Council in May, where Dineen backed their recommendation by committing to invest in the development engineering required for the Global Locomotive Families (GLF) ahead of any orders being received. It was a major change in practice for the business. With strong analysis and data to support the team's proposal and a clear commitment to invest in it, the new GLF concept was quickly accepted and supported in July's Growth Playbook/Session I review with Immelt and became one of Transportation's official IBs.

The concept was soon validated when, in September of 2006, the Kazakhstan Railway placed an order for 310 locomotives; soon after, GE received an additional large order from a mining company in Australia; and before year's end it won a tender for 40 more locomotives in Egypt. Bayhan described it as the industry's "perfect storm":

> The big driver was what we call the "China Effect." Our analysis showed how increased trade with China is driving a big surge in demand for all forms of transportation. Around the world, GDP is growing, industrialization is happening, and the China Effect is spreading to other countries. And we were right there when it happened with a good understanding of the customers' needs and the newest technology to meet them. So we were able to respond to the perfect storm with a great product, the right commercial strategy, and perfect market timing.

Like the China order nine months earlier, the big Kazakhstan order came with a condition that after building the first 10 locomotives in Erie, GE would commit to transferring the assembly operation to Kazakhstan in the second half of 2008. The facility would assemble kits shipped from Erie and would become the regional source for locomotives sold to other countries in the CIS (the Commonwealth of Independent States, consisting of 11 former Soviet Republics in Eurasia). It was part of GE's "In Country, For Country" international strategy, and a matter of great pride for the country's prime minister, who proudly announced that Kazakhstan had locomotives with the same technology as the U.S. models.

The Morphing Continues: The New Regional Strategy

As the locomotive contract negotiations were being finalized, they provided a convenient market entrée to other parts of GE's transportation business. In particular, the sales and marketing people from the Services and Signaling P&Ls began using the Locomotive team's contacts to introduce their own products and services. For example, Transportation's Service P&L planned to link any new locomotive sales with a service contract to renew and refurbish worn components locally rather than replacing them with imported new parts. Not only could they promise to save the customer money, they could offer to transfer technology and bring employment to the country.

Exhibit 8 Comte's Marketing Organization

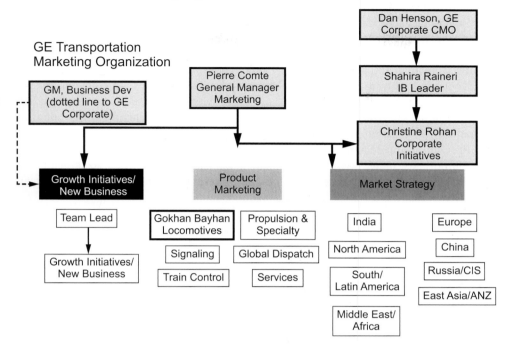

Source: Casewriter, based on GE internal documents.

As initiatives such as this became the norm in markets where locomotive contracts had been signed, the management team of the Locomotive P&L began to explore whether an integrated regional approach to growth might be a more effective business model than the product-based Global Families approach. It was an approach that Comte believed had great value. As he grew the Transportation marketing staff from 14 people to 32, he began moving a significant number of them out of Erie and into the field where they could be closer to the customer. As part of a new geographic-based capability, he deployed seven Regional Marketing Strategists, each of whom built his own local capabilities to support Transportation's regional general managers. (See **Exhibit 8** for Transportation's marketing organization.)

In December 2006, when the message came down that the Commercial Council would like to see businesses submitting more IB proposals for new emerging countries, it gave support to the growing notion that there was a need to

reconfigure the global locomotive IB project once again. One proposal was to morph the major thrust of the GLF project into three integrated regional IBs–one for China, one for Russia/CIS, and one for India–each responsible for driving growth by developing its market for an integrated package of GE locomotives, signals, services, etc. It was an intriguing idea with the potential to roll out to other regions, but would mark the third iteration of this IB in its young, less than 18 month life. Some were concerned that it might seem like project churning.

The Hybrid Engine Dilemma: To Be or Not to Be?

At the same December IB Review, the Transportation business was also scheduled to present its latest plans for the Hybrid Locomotive IB. As the entire management team understood, almost three years earlier the Hybrid had captured Immelt's attention as a perfect candidate to fit into the company's just-announced Ecomagination program committed to environmentally responsive innovation. Indeed, it had been the CEO's suggestion to elevate the research on the Hybrid engine and to give it IB status. As he had publicly stated, the Hybrid Locomotive represented "the right solution for the customer, for the market, for the environment, and for GE."

The plans for the Hybrid were centered on a diesel-electric engine that would capture the energy generated during braking and store it in a series of sophisticated batteries. That stored energy could then be used on demand, reducing fuel consumption by as much as 15% and emissions by as much as 50% compared with freight locomotives already in service.[10] But as the concept was translated into a product, it became clear that the battery technology at the core of its design was not able to achieve the proposed customer benefits or provide them at a cost that would make the project economical. As a result, three years into the program, there was no clear evidence that the Hybrid IB would be able to meet any of its original stated objectives–to add value to the customer, to provide returns to GE, and to allow access to new markets. This led some to suggest that the Hybrid should join of the lapsed IBs that had been declared "worthwhile experiments that did not work out."

At Transportation's monthly Growth Council preparing for Immelt's December IB Review, Dineen, BeGole, and Comte explored the options. BeGole argued that with all the opportunities available in other product-line extensions and geographic expansions, the opportunity cost of the Hybrid project was very high. Specifically, he explained that because of his limited finances and engineering resources (particularly the latter), committing to this option would mean postponing the rollout of some of the promising new international regional platforms for Evo.

On the other hand, as Compte reminded the team, the long-term trend away from fossil fuels and toward alternative energy meant that eventually GE would have to develop hybrid technology. Knowing Immelt's commitment to the

Hybrid project, Compte asked whether the team had done enough to understand how customer value could be created in different segments, to explore alternative technological solutions, or to pursue other sources of funding. On the last point, he explained that while his marketing organization had located some potential government funding for hybrid development, they had not applied for funds since this was not GE's normal approach to project financing. In response to questioning, however, Compte acknowledge that even with such additional funds, investing in the Hybrid would mean diverting resources from other growth prospects that seemed more immediately promising.

As Dineen summarized the discussions, he posed three alternative scenarios that could be presented at the December IB Review:

- The first option would be to explain that while the project as currently defined appeared to have very limited to short- to medium-term commercial viability, the business would commit to it as an IB and continue to explore alternative ways to make it successful.
- The second approach would be to acknowledge the Hybrid's long-term potential, but suggest that it be placed on hold as an IB, perhaps by transferring primary responsibility to the Global Research Center to work on the battery technology in collaboration with various GE businesses–including Transportation–that had an interest in its development.
- The final alternative would be to recommend that the company acknowledge the fact that after three years of hard work on Hybrid, neither the technology development nor the market acceptance of the concept had indicated that it could be a viable commercial proposition in the foreseeable future, and therefore that it be dropped as an IB.

As the management team talked through these options, they tried to balance the best interest of the business with what Immelt was likely to believe was in the best interests of the company. With 83 IBs now approved, and 35 already launched and generating more than $2 billion in additional revenues, the CEO felt that the process of generating organic growth was

---

[10] From GE press documents. "Ecomagination: The Hybrid Locomotive," www.ge.com.

established. But that did not mean that he was becoming less involved. He personally tracked every IB, and focused even more intently on those that had caught his attention–like the Hybrid Locomotive. But in true GE fashion, he also held each business responsible for its current performance. As Transportation's management team realized, determining the Hybrid's future was a tough and vital decision that it must now make.

Chapter 3 Recommended Practitioner Readings

- Pankaj Ghemawat, "Managing differences: the central challenge of global strategy," *Harvard Business Review*, 85 (2007), 58–68.

  In "Managing differences: the central challenge of global strategy," Ghemawat introduces a framework to help managers think through their options. The three broad strategies available are: aggregation – achieving economies of scale by standardizing regional or global operations; adaptation – boosting market share by customizing processes and offerings to meet local markets' unique needs; and arbitrage – exploiting difference, by such activities as offshoring certain processes to countries with cheaper labor. Each strategy is considered against seven questions.

- David Court and Laxman Narasimhan, "Capturing the world's emerging middle class," *McKinsey Quarterly*, July (2010), 12–17.

  In "Capturing the world's emerging middle class," Court and Narasimhan emphasize the importance of the emergence of the middle class in emerging economies, a population of close to 2 billion. This group create a great opportunity for MNEs to gain advantage by addressing their needs. The needs of this group are different, and so too are their priorities. After understanding the idiosyncrasies of the middle class, companies will have to introduce new business models to address their specific needs. The types of need (global or local) and consumer characteristics are discussed, and the appropriate strategies are introduced.

- Matthew J. Eyring, Mark W. Johnson, and Hari Nair, "New business models in emerging markets," *Harvard Business Review*, 89 (2011), 88–95.

  In "New business models in emerging markets," Eyring, Johnson, and Nair argue for the need to rethink the business models for emerging markets. A better way to tap these markets is to consider the existing unmet needs, some of them very basic. Affordability and accessibility for consumers in the middle class is key for the success of new business models in these markets. Depending on the basis on which firms compete (differentiation or price), the article explains the sequence through which business models are developed. Examples of such business models are presented.

- William R. Kerr, "Harnessing the best of globalization," *MIT Sloan Management Review*, 58:1 (2016), 59–69.

  In "Harnessing the best of globalization," Kerr notes that the opportunities for global businesses are expanding thanks to rapidly emerging product markets, the worldwide race for talent, and the widening impact of digitization. The traditional route to becoming a global company involves taking existing products or services to new markets. In contrast to traditional efforts by mature businesses to exploit international differences for internal cost advantages or incremental sales, innovative global models use market differences (be they costs, skill levels, or resource availability) as part of their value proposition and construct businesses that take advantage of the opportunities globalization offers. Most companies approach globalization from the perspective of taking their best products or resources to overseas markets. However, some global ventures seek to harness the best the world has to offer.

- Marcus Alexander and Harry Korine, "When you shouldn't go global," *Harvard Business Review*, 86:12 (2008), 70–7.

  In "When you shouldn't go global," Alexander and Korine say firms with ill-considered globalization strategies are poised to become targets for break-up or overhaul by activist share owners. Yet many businesses (particularly in deregulated, service, and manufacturing industries) have made complacent assumptions about the need to go global and moved full steam ahead toward failure. If they had paused to answer three simple questions, they might well have avoided their missteps. Are there potential benefits for our company? Moves that make sense for some firms won't necessarily work for others. Do we have the necessary management skills? Even if potential benefits do exist for a company, it may not be in a position to realize them. Will the costs outweigh the benefits? Global efforts can be rendered counterproductive through unanticipated collateral damage.

While all five recommended readings for this chapter highlight that although the general concepts of how to build competitive advantage are constant, situations of time and space evolve such that companies need to heed them while developing their strategies. That MNEs should build their capabilities, layer by layer, however, holds in all contexts.

Part II
The Organizational Challenge

4 Developing a Transnational Organization
Managing Integration, Responsiveness, and Flexibility

In preceding chapters, we described how changes in the international operating environment have forced MNEs to simultaneously respond to the strategic need for global efficiency, national responsiveness, and worldwide learning. Implementing such a complex, three-pronged strategic objective would be difficult under any circumstances, but the very act of "going international" multiplies a company's organizational complexity.

Most domestic companies find it difficult enough to balance business units with corporate staff functions, so the thought of adding a geographically oriented management dimension to the organization can be daunting. It implies maintaining a three-way balance of perspectives and capabilities among organizational units responsible for the MNE's businesses, functions, and regions. The difficulty is further increased because the resolution of the inevitable tensions must be accomplished in an organization whose operating units are divided by distance and time, and whose key members are separated by barriers of culture and language.

Beyond Structural Fit

Because the choice of a basic organizational structure has such a powerful influence on the management process in an MNE, much of the attention of managers and researchers alike was historically focused on trying to find which formal structure provided the right "fit" in various conditions. The most widely recognized early study on this issue was Stopford and Wells' research on the 187 largest US-based MNEs. Their work resulted in a "stages model" of international organization structure that defined two variables to capture the strategic and administrative complexity most companies faced as they expanded abroad: the number of products sold internationally ("foreign product diversity" in Figure 4.1) and the importance of international sales to the company ("foreign sales as a percentage of total sales"). Plotting the structural changes made by the sample companies, they found that these MNEs adopted different organizational structures at different stages of international expansion. This led Stopford and Wells to develop their international structural stages model.

According to this model, in the early stages of foreign expansion, MNEs typically managed their overseas operations by creating a separate international division.

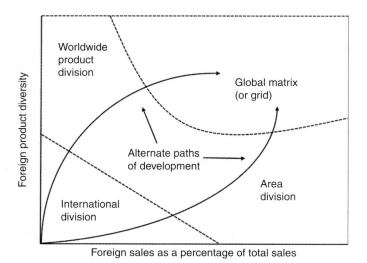

Figure 4.1 Stopford and Wells' international structural stages model
Source: Adapted from John M. Stopford and Louis T. Wells, *Strategy and Structure of the Multinational Enterprise* (New York: Basic Books, 1972).

Subsequently, those companies that expanded further by entering more countries with a limited range of products typically adopted an area structure (e.g., European region, Asia–Pacific region). Other MNEs that chose to grow overseas by increasing their foreign product diversity in fewer countries tended to adopt a worldwide product division structure (e.g., chemicals division, plastics division). Finally, when both foreign sales and foreign product diversity were high, companies were likely to organize around some form of global matrix in which, for example, the manager of the chemicals business in France might report simultaneously to the company's European regional head as well as the global chemicals division president.

Despite the fact that these ideas were presented as a descriptive/explanatory model rather than a normative ideal, consultants and managers soon began to apply the model prescriptively and a new generation of international organizations was created. In the process, the debate was often reduced to generalized discussions of the comparative value of product- versus geography-based structures and to simplistic choices between "centralization" and "decentralization."

Confronted with increasing complexity, diversity, and change in the 1980s and 1990s, managers in many worldwide companies looked for an ideal structure that would allow them to manage their large, complex international operations. And even though the global matrix was a new structural form that had been adopted by relatively few companies, conventional wisdom suggested it was an organizational solution to the complexity of international management. For a while it seemed as if the old adage "structure follows strategy" had been replaced by "structure follows fashion." But for most companies, the results of the serial restructurings were disappointing. In particular, the promised land of the global matrix turned out to be an organizational quagmire from which they were forced to retreat.

Challenges of the Matrix

In theory, the matrix solution should have worked. Having frontline managers report simultaneously to different organizational groups (e.g., the French chemicals manager in the preceding example) should have enabled companies to resolve the conflict built into MNEs' strategy and operations. Theoretically, such dual reporting relationships should have allowed companies to maintain a balance between centralized efficiency and local responsiveness. Further, the matrix's multiple channels of communication and control promised the ability to transmit and resolve diverse management perspectives. The reality turned out to be otherwise, however, and the history of numerous companies that built formal global matrix structures – Citibank, Nestlé, Xerox, IBM, Shell, and ABB among the most prominent – was an unhappy one.[1]

Dow Chemical, a pioneer of the global matrix organization, was also one of the first to abandon it, returning clear lines of responsibility to its geographic managers. And after spending more than a decade serving as the classic example of a global matrix through the 1990s, ABB abandoned the structure in 2002. So too did scores of other companies that tried to manage their worldwide activities through a structure that often seemed to result in complex, bureaucratic processes and relationships.

Dual reporting led to conflict and confusion on many levels: the proliferation of channels created informational logjams, conflicts could be resolved only by escalation, and overlapping responsibilities resulted in turf battles and a loss of accountability. In short, by forcing all issues through the dual chains of command, the global matrix amplified the differences in perspectives and interests so that even a minor difference could become the subject of heated disagreement and debate. Separated by barriers of distance, time, language, and culture, managers found it virtually impossible to clarify the resulting confusion and resolve the conflicts. As a result, in company after company, the initial appeal of the global matrix structure quickly faded into the recognition that a different solution was required.

Building Organizational Capability

The basic problem underlying a company's search for a structural fit was that it focused on only one organizational variable – formal structure. This single tool proved unequal to the job of capturing and managing the complexity of the strategic tasks facing most MNEs.

First, the emphasis on making either/or choices between product versus geographically based structures often forced managers to ignore the multiple demands in their external environment. Second, the focus on structure led to the definition of a *static* set of roles, responsibilities, and relationships in a strategic task

---

[1] This is not to say that all global matrix organizations failed. Currently, several MNEs such as Starbucks, IBM, and Microsoft have matrix structures that they have learned to manage successfully.

environment that was highly *dynamic*. And, third, restructuring efforts often proved harmful, with organizations often traumatized by a major overnight realignment of roles, responsibilities, and relationships.

As MNE managers found it increasingly difficult to define structures that reflected their more complex strategies, they recognized that formal structure was a powerful but blunt instrument of strategic change. To develop the vital multidimensional and flexible capabilities required by today's MNE, there was a growing realization that a company must reorient its managers' thinking and reshape its core decision-making capabilities. In doing so, the company's entire management process – its administrative systems, communication channels, decision-making forums, and interpersonal relationships – becomes the means for managing such change. In short, rather than imposing a structure that defines formal responsibilities, the challenge facing MNEs today is to develop an organization with an appropriate internal network of relationships.

In exploring some of the more subtle and sophisticated tools required to bring about such a change, we first must examine how an MNE's *administrative heritage* – its history and embedded management culture – influences its ability and willingness to change. It is a concept to which we have already alluded in previous chapters when we acknowledged how an MNE's management mentality and strategic posture may have been shaped by different motivations for international expansion, different historical and cultural factors, and different external industry forces. History matters – even in shaping how MNEs think about their organizations.

Administrative Heritage

Whereas industry analysis can reveal a company's *external* competitive challenges and market needs, the MNE's ability to meet those external opportunities and threats will be greatly influenced – sometimes positively, sometimes negatively – by its existing *internal* world. Its ability to respond will be shaped by its in-place configuration of assets and resources, its historical definition of management responsibilities, and its ingrained organizational norms. In short, a company's organization is shaped not only by current external task demands but also by past internal structures and management biases. Each company is influenced by the path by which it developed (its organizational history) and the values, norms, and practices of its management (its management culture). Collectively, these factors constitute what we call a company's *administrative heritage.*

Administrative heritage can be one of the company's greatest assets providing the underlying source of its core competencies. At the same time, it can also be a significant liability, because it embeds attitudes that may resist change and thereby prevents realignment. Unlike strategic plans that can be scrapped and redrawn overnight, there is no such thing as a zero-based organization. Companies are, to a significant extent, captives of their past, and any organizational transformation must focus at least as much on where the company is coming from – its administrative heritage – as on where it wants to go.

In the following sections, we will illustrate the importance of a company's administrative heritage by contrasting the development of a typical European MNE whose major international expansion occurred in the decades of the 1920s and 1930s, a typical American MNE that expanded abroad in the 1950s and 1960s, and a typical Japanese company that made its main overseas thrust in the 1970s and 1980s. Even when these companies were in the same industry, their different heritages usually led them to adopt very different strategic and organizational models.

This is also proving to be true of a new generation of MNEs that are now expanding from developing countries such as China, India, Mexico, and Brazil. Their strategic posture, their organizational framework, and their management mentalities are being shaped by the cultural norms of their home countries in addition to the global environment into which they are expanding. Like the current generation of MNEs described in the following paragraphs, the unique administrative heritage of these emerging market multinationals will shape the way they operate for decades to come.

Decentralized Federation

Focusing first on the European companies that dominated international foreign direct investment in the pre-World War II era, these MNEs expanded abroad in a period of rising tariffs and discriminatory legislation. As they expanded abroad, they were forced to build local production facilities to compete effectively with national competitors. These local plants were run by the national subsidiaries of MNEs allowing them to modify products and marketing approaches to meet widely differing local market needs. The increasing independence of these self-sufficient national units was reinforced by the high international communication barriers that existed in that era, limiting headquarters' ability to intervene in the management of the company's spreading worldwide operations.

This configuration of widely distributed assets and delegated responsibility fit well with management norms and practices that existed in many European companies at that time. Many European companies, particularly those from the UK, the Netherlands, and France, had developed management practices that emphasized personal relationships (an "old boys' network") rather than formal structures, and financial controls more than operational controls. These internal cultural norms reinforced these European companies' willingness to delegate more operating independence and strategic freedom to their foreign subsidiaries. Highly autonomous national companies were often managed more as a portfolio of offshore investments rather than a single international business.

The resulting organization pattern was a loose federation of independent national subsidiaries, each focused primarily on its local market. As a result, many of these companies, including classic European MNEs such as Philips, Unilever, and Nestlé, adopted what we have described in previous chapters as the *multinational strategy* and managed it through a *decentralized federation* organization model, as represented in Figure 4.2(a).

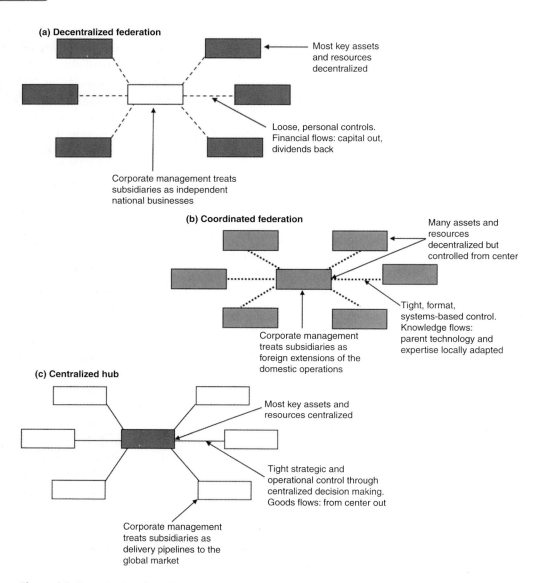

Figure 4.2 Organizational configuration models
Source: Christopher A. Bartlett and Sumatra Ghoshal, *Managing Across Borders: The Transnational Solution* (Boston: Harvard Business School Press, 1989).

Coordinated Federation

American companies, many of which enjoyed their fastest international expansion in the 1950s and 1960s, developed in very different circumstances. The strength of companies such as GE, Pfizer, and P&G lay in the new technologies and management processes they had developed through being in the United States – at that time, the world's largest, richest, and most technologically advanced market. After World War II, their foreign expansion focused primarily on leveraging this strength, giving rise to the international product cycle theory referred to in Chapter 1.

Reinforcing this strategy was a "professional" managerial culture that contrasted with the "old boys' network" that typified the European companies' processes. The US management approach was built on a willingness to delegate responsibility while retaining overall control through sophisticated management systems and specialist corporate staffs. Foreign subsidiaries were often free to adapt products or strategies to reflect market differences, but their dependence on the parent company for new products, processes, and ideas dictated a great deal more coordination and control by headquarters than did the classic European decentralized federation organization. This relationship was facilitated by the existence of formal systems and controls in the US-based companies' headquarters–subsidiary link.

The main handicap such MNEs faced was that the parent company management often adopted a parochial and even superior attitude toward international operations, perhaps because of the assumption that new ideas and developments came predominantly from the parent. Despite corporate management's increased understanding of its overseas markets, it often seemed to view foreign operations as appendages whose principal purpose was to leverage the capabilities and resources developed in the home market.

Nonetheless, the approach was highly successful in the postwar decades, and many US-based companies adopted what we have described as the *international strategy* and a *coordinated federation* organizational model shown in Figure 4.2(b).

Centralized Hub

In contrast to both the European and the American models, the Japanese companies that made their major impact on the international economy in the 1970s and 1980s faced a greatly altered external environment and operated with very different internal norms and values. With limited prior overseas exposure, Japanese MNEs such as Sony, Toyota, and Komatsu typically chose not to match the well-established local marketing capabilities and facilities of their European and US competitors. (Indeed, well-established Japanese trading companies often provided them an easier means of entering foreign markets by exporting.) However, the rapid postwar growth of their domestic economy gave the Japanese MNEs new, efficient, scale-intensive plants that became major assets as they expanded into a global environment of declining trade barriers.

These factors gave these companies the incentive to develop a competitive advantage at the upstream end of the value-added chain. Their competitive strategy emphasized cost advantages and quality assurance, both of which demanded tight control over product development, procurement, and manufacturing. When forced by political pressure or regulation will, these Japanese-based MNEs moved some assembly operations offshore, but most kept the major value-adding and strategic activities at home. This centrally controlled, export-based internationalization strategy represented a perfect fit with the external environment and companies' competitive capabilities.

Such an approach also fit the cultural background and organizational values that were part of the deeply embedded administrative heritage of these emerging

Japanese MNEs. At the foundation were strong national cultural norms that emphasized group behavior and valued interpersonal harmony as reflected in management practices such as *nemawashi* (consensus building) and *ringi* (shared decision making).

By keeping primary decision making and control at the center, the Japanese company could retain its culturally dependent management system that was so communications intensive and people dependent. In addition, international growth that kept key operations at home made it possible for Japanese MNEs to retain their system of lifetime employment. Because of these internal and external factors, these companies adopted what we have described as a *global strategy*, which they managed through a *centralized hub* organizational model, as we show in Figure 4.2(c).

Administrative Heritage Meets Transnational Challenge

In Chapters 2 and 3 we suggested that over the past couple of decades, many worldwide industries have been transformed from traditional multinational, international, and global forms into transnational forms. Instead of demanding efficiency *or* responsiveness *or* learning as the key capability for success, to remain competitive in these businesses participating firms must now achieve some degree of all those strategic capabilities simultaneously. In this new environment, all three organization models described above were being challenged.

Table 4.1 summarizes the key characteristics of the decentralized federation, coordinated federation, and centralized hub organizations – the structures and

Table 4.1 Organizational characteristics of decentralized federation, coordinated federation, and centralized hub organizations

	Decentralized federation	Coordinated federation	Centralized hub
Strategic approach	Multinational	International	Global
Key strategic capability	National responsiveness	Transfer abroad home-country innovations	Global-scale efficiency
Configuration of key assets and capabilities	Predominantly decentralized and nationally self-sufficient	Core innovative capabilities centralized; adaptive capabilities decentralized	Predominantly centralized and globally scaled
Role of overseas operations	Sensing and exploiting local opportunities	Adapting and leveraging parent company competencies	Implementing parent company strategies
Development and diffusion of most key knowledge	Developed and retained within each unit	Developed at the center and transferred to overseas units	Developed and retained at the center

processes that supported companies pursuing multinational, international, and global strategies respectively. A review of these characteristics immediately reveals the problems each of the three archetypal company models might face in responding to the transnational challenge.

With its centralized hub organization designed to concentrate key resources and capabilities at the center, the *global* company achieves efficiency primarily by exploiting potential scale economies in all its activities. But the central groups often lack the understanding to respond to local market needs, while its national subsidiaries lack the resources, capabilities, or authority to do so. The problem is that a global organization cannot overcome such problems without jeopardizing its core advantage of global efficiency.

The classic decentralized federation organizational form of the *multinational* company suffers from other limitations. Although its dispersed resources and decentralized decision-making authority allow its national subsidiaries to respond to local needs, the resulting fragmentation of activities leads to inefficiency. Worldwide learning also suffers, because knowledge is not consolidated and does not flow freely across national boundaries. So local innovations often represent little more than the efforts of subsidiary management to protect its turf and autonomy, or reinventions of the wheel caused by blocked communication or the not-invented-here (NIH) syndrome.[2]

And while the *international* company's coordinated federation organization is designed to allow it to leverage the knowledge and capabilities of the parent company, its resource configuration and operating systems make it less efficient than the global company and less responsive than the multinational company.

The Transnational Organization

As MNEs recognized these limitations imposed by their administrative heritage, many began trying to match the capabilities of their competitors while simultaneously protecting their existing sources of competitive advantage. Those that succeeded gradually developed the characteristics of what we describe as transnational organizations.

Three important organizational characteristics characterize this emerging form of cross-border organization and distinguish it from its multinational, international, or global counterparts: transnational organizations have decision-making roles and

---

[2] See K. E. Meyer, R. Mudambi, and R. Narula, "Multinational enterprises and local contexts: the opportunities and challenges of multiple embeddedness," *Journal of Management Studies*, 48:2 (2011), 235–52.

Despite the increased frequency and intensity of interactions across local contexts, local contexts continue to retain their distinctive differences. MNEs must organize their networks to exploit effectively both the differences and similarities of their multiple host locations. At the subsidiary level, they must balance "internal" embeddedness within the MNE network, with their "external" embeddedness in the host milieu.

responsibilities that legitimize multiple diverse management perspectives; their structure is based on assets and capabilities that are both distributed and interdependent; and they have built internal integrative processes that are robust and flexible. In this section, we will describe and illustrate each of these vital, core organizational characteristics.

Multidimensional Perspectives

An MNE cannot respond effectively to strategic demands that are diverse and changeable if it is constrained by an organization that is one-dimensional and static. The transnational company must create the multidimensional ability to sense and analyze these diverse and often conflicting opportunities, pressures, and demands. Strong *national subsidiary management* is needed to sense and represent the changing needs of local consumers and the increasing pressures from host governments; capable *global business management* is required to track the strategy of global competitors and provide the coordination necessary to respond appropriately; and influential *worldwide functional management* is needed to concentrate corporate knowledge, information, and expertise, and facilitate its transfer among organizational units.

Unfortunately, in many companies, power is concentrated with the management group that has historically had responsibility for the company's principal critical strategic task – often at the cost of the influence of groups representing other needs. For example, in companies pursuing a *multinational* strategy, key decisions were usually dominated by the country management, the group that made the most critical contribution to achieving national responsiveness. In *global* companies, managers running the worldwide business divisions were typically the most influential, because they played the key role in the company's efforts to seek global efficiency. And in *international* companies, functional management groups often came to assume this position of dominance because of their roles in building, accumulating, and transferring the company's knowledge and capabilities in technology, marketing, and other specialist fields.

In *transnational* companies, however, such biases in the decision-making process are offset through a conscious effort to build up the capability, credibility, and influence of the less powerful management groups while protecting the morale and expertise of the dominant group. The objective is to create a multidimensional organization in which all three management groups have a voice in the discussion.[3]

---

[3] See C. Bouquet and J. Birkinshaw, "Managing power in the multinational corporation: how low-power actors gain influence," *Journal of Management*, 34:3 (2008), 477–508.

This article provides a conceptual integration and synthesis of the literature on power and influence in MNCs. The focus is on those within the MNC network who are currently in weak or low-status positions vis-à-vis others. The authors distinguish between ends and means: between the objectives pursued by low-power actors (their ends) and the strategies or tactics they pursue to achieve these objectives (their means).

Companies that are born into today's environment of multiple conflicting demands – new web-based firms like Amazon, for example, or MNEs launching into the world from emerging economies like the Chinese appliance company Haier – typically are creating such organizations from the beginning. But as the Philips versus Matsushita case that follows this chapter will show, existing MNEs with deeply embedded administrative heritages can spend decades struggling to develop such balanced multidimensional management perspectives.

Distributed, Interdependent Capabilities

It's one thing to ensure that multidimensional management perspectives are represented in key decisions, but quite another to be able to respond to the diverse opportunities and demands they bring to their input. To do so requires an organizational model where the assets, resources, and capabilities are arranged in ways quite different from the global organization's centralized hub configuration or the multinational organization's decentralized federation of independent operations.

Recognizing that centralization is not the only way to achieve efficiency, transnational organizations ensure that key operations are located wherever they have the greatest strategic advantage – whether in the home country or abroad. And recognizing that scale is achieved by specialization rather than by centralization, they identify their most effective manufacturing operations and make them the company's regional or global source for a given product or expertise. Similarly, key R&D and marketing activities tap into important technological advances and market developments wherever they occur, engaging and harnessing the most effective product development and marketing groups in national units to become centers of excellence or lead country marketing operations.

One major consequence of such a distribution of specialized assets and responsibilities is that the relationship across organizational units changes from dependence or independence to interdependence. For example, in an evolved transnational organization such as GE, a new opportunity for a diesel engine targeted at a specialized mining application may first be sensed by the company's Australian subsidiary, developed through a collaboration between corporate R&D and GE's German technical group, jointly produced by the South Korean and Mexican manufacturing operations, and rolled out into the global marketplace through the company's subsidiaries worldwide.

In such an organization, simple structural configurations like the decentralized federation, coordinated federation, or centralized hub are inadequate for the task facing the transnational corporation. What is needed is a structure we term the "integrated network" (see Figure 4.3). In this structure, management regards each of the worldwide units as a source of ideas, skills, capabilities, knowledge, and expertise that can be harnessed for the benefit of the total organization. Efficient local plants may be converted into regional or global production centers; innovative national or regional development labs may be designated the company's "centers of excellence" for a particular product or process development; and creative

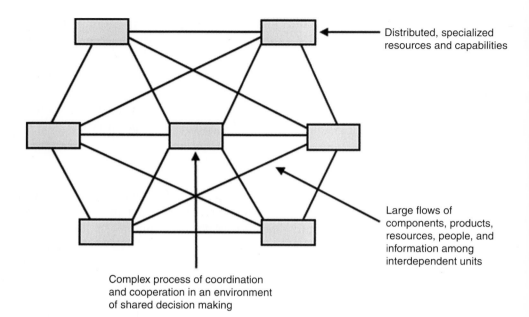

Distributed, specialized resources and capabilities

Large flows of components, products, resources, people, and information among interdependent units

Complex process of coordination and cooperation in an environment of shared decision making

Figure 4.3 Integrated network model
Source: Christopher A. Bartlett and Sumatra Ghoshal, *Managing Across Borders: The Transnational Solution* (Boston: Harvard Business School Press, 1989).

subsidiary marketing groups may be given a lead role in developing worldwide marketing strategies for certain products or businesses.

Flexible Integrative Process

Finally, the transnational organization requires a management process that can resolve tensions across the diversity of interests and integrate the dispersed assets and resources described above. In doing so, such an organization cannot be bound by a single dominant process that defines the task in such traditionally simplistic terms as centralization versus decentralization. The reason is simple: the strategic benefits of centralizing worldwide research will typically exceed the benefits to be gained by centralizing the sales and service functions. Similarly, the need for centralized coordination for control will also vary by business and by geographic area. Aircraft engine companies clearly need central control of more decisions than multinational food packagers, and an MNE's operations in developing countries may need more support from the center than those in advanced countries. Furthermore, all such central coordination and control will probably change over time.

In short, the transnational organization recognizes that there is not a single static management model that it can apply universally. It acknowledges that the management process must be able to change from product to product, from country to country, and even from decision to decision. Elaborating on the integration-responsiveness framework we developed in Chapter 3, we illustrate such a distribution of roles and responsibilities in Figure 4.4 with an example from Unilever. As the

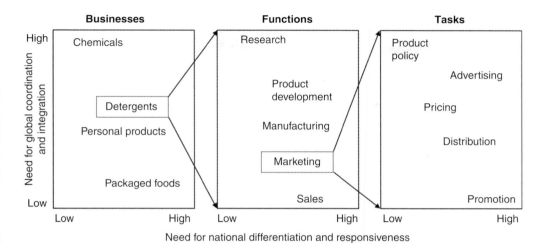

Figure 4.4 Integration and differentiation needs at Unilever
Source: Christopher A. Bartlett and Sumatra Ghoshal, *Managing Across Borders: The Transnational Solution* (Boston: Harvard Business School Press, 1989).

figure represents, Unilever's chemicals business is managed in a much more globally integrated way than its packaged food business. And even within the detergent business, R&D is managed more centrally than marketing, which in turn manages its product policy decisions more centrally that its promotions policies.

The implied distribution of roles and responsibilities requires the development of rather sophisticated and subtle decision-making machinery based on three interdependent management processes. The first is a focused and constrained escalation process that allows top management to intervene directly in key decision content. This carefully managed form of *centralization* may be appropriate for major resource allocation commitments, for example. The second is a process in which management structures individual roles and administrative systems to influence specific decisions. This *formalization* process is typically used for decisions involving repetitive or routine activities such as setting transfer prices. The third is a self-regulatory capability in which top management's role is to establish a broad culture and set of relationships that provide a supportive organizational context for delegated decisions. This is a sophisticated management process driven by *socialization* and is most useful in decisions that require the effective use of the large amounts of information, knowledge, and expertise that resides in the dispersed activities of the transnational organization.

Building a Transnational Organization: Beyond Structure

The kind of organization we have described as a transnational clearly represents something quite different from its predecessors – the multinational, international, and global organizations. Building a transnational organization requires much more than choosing between a product or a geographic organization structure; and managing it implies much more than centralizing or decentralizing decisions. So what exactly is involved in building a transnational organization?

At the beginning of this chapter, we saw that the classic structural stages model no longer provides a helpful description of international organization development. To describe the transnational organization, we need a different way to frame the more complex and subtle array of characteristics and capabilities that we have described in the preceding paragraphs. The simple framework we adopt here describes the organization in terms of a physiological model. This allows us to hypothesize that any effective organization must be framed by a strong anatomy (the formal structure of its assets, resources, and responsibilities) complemented by a robust, functioning physiology (the systems and decision processes) and an appropriate, healthy psychology (the culture and management mentality).

Using this model, we will now describe the different tools and processes used to build and manage the transnational organization.

Structuring the Organizational Anatomy

As we have seen, the traditional approach to MNE organization problems has been defined in macro-structural terms that focused on simple but rather superficial choices, such as the classic "product versus geography" structural debate. In a transnational organization, however, managers avoid such simple dichotomies. Their focus is more on how to supplement and counterbalance the embedded power of their dominant line managers.

Having carefully defined the roles and responsibilities of geographic, functional, and product management groups (recognizing that those may vary business by business as illustrated in Figure 4.4), the next challenge is to ensure that those without line authority also have appropriate access to and influence in the management process. Rather than achieving this through macro structure, this typically requires the use of micro-structural tools such as cross-unit teams, task forces, or committees. These subtler mechanisms can create supplemental decision-making forums that allow non-line managers to have significant influence and even to assume responsibility in a way that is not possible in classic unidimensional organizations. So, in the example illustrated in Figure 4.4, while the detergent product manager may have formal line authority for worldwide pricing, those decisions may be set in consultation with geographic managers who may negotiate flexibility for their regions or countries based on local competitive situations.

Where task forces and consultative committees were once considered ad hoc, quick-fix devices, companies building transnational organizations use them as legitimate, ongoing micro-structural tools through which top management can fine-tune or rebalance the basic macro structure. To stretch our anatomical analogy, if the formal line structure is the organization's backbone, the non-line groups represent its rib cage, and these micro-structural overlays, such as teams and task forces, provide the muscle, tendons, and cartilage that give the organizational skeleton its flexibility.

Building the Organizational Physiology

One of the key roles of management is to develop the communication channels through which the organization's decision-making process operates. By adapting the organization's various administrative systems and informal relationships, management can shape the volume, content, and direction of information flows that provide the lifeblood of all management processes. It is this flow of information that defines the organizational physiology – its veins, arteries, and airways.

Many researchers have shown the strong link between the complexity and uncertainty of the tasks to be performed and the need for information. In an integrated network configuration, task complexity and uncertainty are very high. Operating in such a multidimensional, interdependent system requires large volumes of information to be gathered, exchanged, and processed, so the role of formal systems – including information, planning, reporting, and control systems – is vital. But formal systems alone cannot support the huge information processing needs, and companies are forced to look beyond their traditional tools and conventional systems.

For years, managers have recognized that a great deal of information exchange and even decision making occurs through the organization's innumerable informal channels and relationships. Yet this part of the management process has often been dismissed as either unimportant ("office gossip" or "rumor mill") or unmanageable ("disruptive cliques" or "unholy alliances"). In the management of transnational organizations, such biases need to be reexamined. Because organizational units are widely separated and information is scarce, it is even more important for managers of these units to exert some control and influence over informal systems.

Getting started is often remarkably easy, requiring managers to do little more than use their daily involvement in the ongoing management processes to shape the nature and quality of communications patterns and relationships. The easiest place to start is to recognize, legitimize, and reinforce existing informal relationships that have the potential to contribute to the corporate objective. These can then be consciously influenced by adjusting the frequency and agenda of management trips and corporate meetings (a good way to focus and diffuse information), the pattern of committee assignments (an effective way of building relationships and shaping decisions), and the track of people's career development (a powerful way to reinforce and reward flexibility and collaboration).

Developing the Organizational Psychology

In addition to an anatomy and a physiology, each organization also has a psychology – a set of explicit or implicit corporate values and shared beliefs – that greatly influences the way its members act. Particularly when employees come from a variety of different national backgrounds, management cannot assume that all will share common values and relate to common norms. Furthermore, in an operating environment in which managers are separated by distance, language, and time barriers, shared management understanding is often a much more powerful tool than formal structures and systems for coordinating diverse activities.

Of the numerous tools and techniques that can affect an organization's psychology, our review of transnational organizations has highlighted three that are particularly important. The first is the need for a clear, shared understanding of the company's mission and objectives. Classic models range from Google's mission "to organize the world's information and make it universally accessible and useful" to Panasonic founder, Konasuke Matsushita's mission "to create material abundance by providing goods as plentiful and inexpensive as tap water" – a mission he translated into a 250-year plan broken into ten 25-year goals!

The second important tool is the visible behavior and public actions of senior management. Particularly in a transnational organization in which other signals may be diluted or distorted, top management's actions speak louder than words and tend to have a powerful influence on the company's culture. They represent the clearest role model of behavior and a signal of the company's strategic and organizational priorities. For example, Amazon CEO Jeff Bezos did not want a repeat of the company's disastrous entry into the China market where it was lagging far behind Alibaba. Wanting to send a strong signal about Amazon's commitment to India, he traveled to Bangalore to give his top Indian executive a giant check made out for $2 billion. The publicity that surrounded the elaborate check presentation ceremony ensured that everyone, both inside and outside the company, understood that Amazon would spend whatever was necessary to dominate the Indian market. Bezos subsequently doubled down on his funding commitment by pledging an additional $3 billion to its Indian operations.

The third and most commonly used set of tools for modifying organizational psychology in the transnational organization is nested in the company's personnel policies, practices, and systems. A company can develop a multidimensional and flexible organization process only if its personnel systems develop and reinforce the appropriate kinds of people.[4] At Eli Lilly, the recruiting and promotion policies emphasize the importance of good interpersonal skills and flexible, non-parochial personalities; its career path management is used not only to develop necessary management skills and expertise but also to broaden individual perspectives and interpersonal relationships; and its measurement and reward systems are explicitly designed to reinforce the thrust of organization-building efforts and cultural values.

Although the process of adapting an organization's culture, values, or beliefs is slow and the techniques are subtle, this tool plays a particularly important role in the development of a transnational organization, because change in the

---

[4] See P. Caligiuri, "Many moving parts: factors influencing the effectiveness of HRM practices designed to improve knowledge transfer within MNCs," *Journal of International Business Studies*, 45:1 (2014), 63–72.

Mentoring, training and development, performance management and rewards, and job design are considered among the "moving parts" in the relationship between HRM and employees' knowledge transfer behavior. Also discussed are individual differences, cultural differences, and comparative HR systems, and the effectiveness of HRM practices in knowledge transfer.

organizational anatomy and physiology without complementary modifications to its psychology can lead to severe organizational problems.

Managing the Process of Change

As they adapted their worldwide operations, managers in some companies assumed that organizational change could be driven by changes in the formal structure. One of the most dramatic examples was Westinghouse's reorganization of its operations. Dissatisfied with its worldwide product organization, top management assigned a team of executives to study the company's international organization problems for 90 days. Its proposal that Westinghouse adopt a global matrix was accepted, and the team was then given three months to "install the new structure." We saw a similar approach at P&G when it adopted its "Organization 2005" and then with little input or discussion, rolled out the radical structural change worldwide. Within two years of the program's introduction, the sponsoring CEO had been replaced.

Such examples are far from unusual – literally hundreds of other companies have done something similar. The managers involved seemed to assume that by announcing changes in formal roles and reporting relationships (the organization's anatomy) they would force changes in the organizational relationships and decision processes (its physiology), which in turn would reshape the way individual managers think and act (its psychology). This model of the process of organizational change is illustrated in Figure 4.5.

But such an approach loses sight of the real organization behind the boxes and lines on the chart. The boxes that are casually shifted around represent people with abilities, motivations, beliefs, and interests, not just formal positions with specified roles. The lines that are redrawn are not just formal reporting channels but interpersonal relationships that may have taken years to develop. The new relationships defined in the reorganized structure will often take months to establish at the most basic level, and a year or more to become truly effective. And developing new individual attitudes and behaviors will take even longer, because many employees will be frustrated, alienated, or simply unequal to the new job requirements.

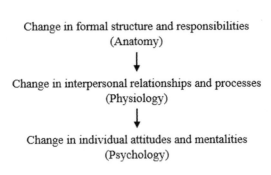

Change in formal structure and responsibilities
(Anatomy)

↓

Change in interpersonal relationships and processes
(Physiology)

↓

Change in individual attitudes and mentalities
(Psychology)

Figure 4.5 Model I: the traditional change process

Change in individual attitudes and mentalities

↓

Change in interpersonal relationships and processes

↓

Change in formal structure and responsibilities

Figure 4.6 Model II: the emerging change process

More sophisticated MNEs tend to adopt a very different approach that relies more on the micro-structures and informal processes we discussed earlier. For example, these companies often use new assignments and key personnel transfers to forge interpersonal links, build organizational cohesion, and develop policy consistency. And in some companies (particularly those in high-tech industries) emphasis is often placed on socializing the individual into the organization and shaping his or her attitudes to conform with overall corporate values. In such instances, organizational change is typically driven more by intensive education and mentoring programs than by reconfigurations of the structure or systems.

Although the specific change process and sequence varies significantly from one company to the next, the overall change process adopted in these MNEs is very different from the process driven by structural realignment. Indeed, the sequence is often the reverse. The first objective is to influence the understanding and perceptions of key individuals. Then follows a series of changes aimed to modify the communication flows and decision-making processes. Only in a final stage are the changes consolidated and confirmed by structural realignment. This process is represented by the model in Figure 4.6.

Of course, these two models of organizational change are both gross oversimplifications of the process. But they do serve to highlight the key message that organizations are shaped and defined by more than their formal structures, and therefore that organizational change must involve more than simply redrawing the organization chart.

All change processes inevitably involve substantial overlap of changes to the organizational anatomy, physiology, and psychology; the two sequences merely reflect differences in the relative emphasis on each set of tools during the process. Although the more gradual change process is much less organizationally traumatic, in times of crisis – chronic poor performance, a badly misaligned structure, or a major structural change in the environment, for example – radical restructuring may be necessary to achieve rapid and sweeping change. For most organizations, however, dramatic structural change is highly traumatic and can distract managers from their external tasks as they focus on the internal realignment. Fortunately, most change processes can be managed in a more evolutionary manner, focusing first on the modification of individual perspectives and interpersonal relationships before tackling the formal redistribution of responsibilities and power.

The Transnational Organization in Transition

During the past decade or so, political, competitive, and social pressures have reinforced the need for MNEs to create organizations that can sense and respond to complex yet often conflicting demands. So as more and more companies confront the need to build worldwide organizations that are both multidimensional and flexible, the form of the transnational organization they are creating continues to adapt. While many adaptations have occurred, in the following paragraphs we will highlight three of the most widespread transnational organizational trends we have observed in recent years: a disenchantment with formal matrix structures, the redefinition of primary organizational dimensions, and the changing role of functional management.

Disenchantment with Formal Matrix Structures

As an increasing number of managers recognized the need to develop the multidimensional organizational capabilities that characterize a transnational organization, the initial reaction of many was to impose the new model through a global matrix structure.

Widespread press coverage of ABB's decade-long global expansion through such an organization encouraged some to believe that this structure was the key to exploiting global-scale efficiencies while responding to local market needs. But as many soon discovered, the strategic benefits provided by such a complex organization came at an organizational cost.

Although some companies were able to create the culture and process vital to the success of the matrix structure – in ABB's case, they supported the company's ambitious global expansion for more than a decade – others were much less successful. One such failure was P&G's much publicized "Organization 2005" referred to briefly above. This radical structural change boldly imposed a global product structure over the company's historically successful geographic organization. The resulting global matrix was installed worldwide, creating problems that eventually cost CEO Durk Jager his job.

But despite continuing nervousness about the global matrix structure, most MNEs still recognize the need to create multidimensional and flexible organizations. The big lesson of the 2000s was that such organizations are best built by developing overlaid processes and supportive cultures, not just by formalizing multiple reporting relationships. A. G. Lafley, P&G's CEO who succeeded Jager, put it well when he said, "We built this new house, then moved in before the plumbing and wiring were connected. You cannot change organization with structure alone." Or in the terms we have used, changes in an organization's anatomy must be supplemented with changes to its physiology and psychology.

Redefinition of Key Organization Dimensions

Historically, the dominant dimensions around which most MNEs built their worldwide operations had business management on one side and country management on the other. But in the past decade or so, the global customer dimension is becoming increasingly important in many worldwide organizations.

The pressure to create such customer-driven organizations grew gradually in the new millennium. First, as global customers began demanding uniform prices and service levels from their suppliers, MNEs were forced to respond by creating dedicated global account managers who would take responsibility for all sales to customers around the world.[5] Then, as customers expected increasing levels of value-added services, companies began to shift from "selling products" to "providing solutions."

These and similar forces led to the creation of transnational organizations in which front-end, customer-facing units bundled products from back-end, product-driven units. A good example of this was IBM's Global Services Organization, one of the most successful customer-facing organizations, which grew rapidly because of its ability to supply customers whose operations often spread around the globe with a combination of IBM's products, consulting services, and often an additional package of related, outsourced products and services.

Changing the Functional Management Role

In transnational organizations built around business, geography, and, more recently, the customer, functional managers responsible for finance, human resources, logistics, and other cross-business and cross-organizational specialties were often relegated to secondary staff roles. However, with the expansion of the information-based, knowledge-intensive service economy, the resources and expertise that resided in these specialized functions became increasingly important sources of competitive advantage. As a result, in recent years their roles have become progressively more central in many transnational organizations.

Managers of finance, HR, and IT functions gained importance because of their control of the scarce strategic resources of information and knowledge that were so critical to capture and leverage on a worldwide basis. With the globalization of financial markets in the global financial crisis of 2008 to 2009, the finance function was often able to play a critically important role in lowering the cost of capital and managing-border risk exposure. Just as dramatic has been the role of the HR experts as MNEs tapped into scarce knowledge and expertise outside the home country and leveraged it for global competitive advantage. Similarly, the

---

[5] See L. H. Shi, J. C. White, S. Zou, and S. T. Cavusgil, "Global account management strategies: drivers and outcomes," *Journal of International Business Studies*, 41:4 (2010), 620–38.
   This study finds that: (1) global strategic priority and globalization are significant drivers of four global account management (GAM) strategies – intercountry coordination, inter-organizational coordination, marketing activities' standardization, and global integration; (2) intercountry and inter-organizational coordination have significant effects on GAM performance; and (3) GAM performance significantly influences relationship continuity. Implications for theory are discussed.

emergence of the chief knowledge officer role reflects the importance that many companies are placing on the organization's ability to capture and leverage valuable information, best practices, and scarce knowledge and expertise wherever it exists in the company.

Again, this trend is creating a need for transnational companies to create organizational overlays supplemented by new channels of communication and forums of decision making that enable managers to develop and leverage the company's competitive advantage through its sophisticated organizational capabilities. The form and function of the transnational organization continues to adapt as MNE managers seek new ways to develop and deliver layers of competitive advantage.

CONCLUDING COMMENTS

In this chapter, we have looked at the organizational capabilities that the MNE must build to operate effectively in today's fast-changing global business environment. The strategic challenge, as we have described it, requires the MNE to capture and enhance global efficiency, national responsiveness, and worldwide learning simultaneously. To deliver on this complex and conflicting set of demands, a new form of organization is required – one that we call the transnational. The transnational organization is defined by its several core characteristics: its ability to legitimize multidimensional perspectives, its distributed and interdependent capabilities, and its flexible integrative processes. It is an organizational model that is becoming increasingly mainstream in today's complex and dynamic global strategic environment.

HARVARD | BUSINESS | SCHOOL   FEBRUARY 23, 2012

BRIEF CASES

Christopher A. Bartlett and Laura Winig

CASE 4.1 KENT CHEMICAL: ORGANIZING FOR INTERNATIONAL GROWTH

HBS Professor Christopher A. Bartlett and writer Laura Winig prepared this case solely as a basis for class discussion and not as a source of primary data, an endorsement, or an illustration of effective or ineffective management. This case, though based on real events, is fictionalized, and any resemblance to actual persons or entities is coincidental. There are occasional references to actual companies in the narration.

In July 2008, Luis Morales, president of Kent Chemical International (KCI), the international arm of Kent Chemical Products (KCP), balanced a computer on his lap, trying to merge the organizational charts of his KCI worldwide operations with KCP's domestic businesses. After his third attempt, the two charts finally shared the screen. He had achieved digital success, but as he looked at a chart that reminded him of a multiheaded hydra, Morales was not convinced he had found a real-life solution.

Over the past two years, the KCI president had been searching for a way to better coordinate his fast-growing international operations with Kent's domestic core. Two previous reorganizations had not achieved that objective, and now the global economy looked as if it were headed for a recession. If he was to recommend another restructuring, Morales knew it would have to be successful.

Kent Chemical Products: The Company and Its Businesses

Kent was established in 1917 as a rubber producer, and its historical roots were still evident. The founding Fisher family owned 10% of the stock and was still the largest stockholder, family members held a few key positions, and corporate headquarters remained in Kent, Ohio, a town outside Akron.

During the 1940s, Kent had diversified into plastics and, as that market soared, expanded through acquisitions to become one of the country's largest producers and marketers of plastic additives and other specialty chemicals. Responding to postwar opportunities, KCP opened a research laboratory in 1953, harnessing technology-based research to drive product development. By the 2000s, Kent had become a leading global specialty-chemical company, with 2007 revenues of $2.2 billion. (See Exhibit 1 for summary financials.) It held minority and majority stakes in more than two dozen businesses in the U.S. and overseas, employed 4,200 people including 1,200 offshore, operated 30 manufacturing facilities in 13 countries, and sold its products in almost 100 countries.

Kent offered a wide range of products from specialty lubricants to polymer additives, focusing on niche-market needs in the construction, electronics, medical products, and consumer industries. The range was managed through six business divisions, three of which had significant international sales.

Consumer Products

Grease-B-Gone, the company's first major consumer product, was introduced in 1966 and became the leading de-greaser in the U.S. First targeted at the auto engine market, the brand had expanded into a range of specially formulated products designed for high-margin niche household applications such as oven, barbeque, and stainless steel cleaners. KCP subsequently introduced other specialty household products including drain openers, rust removers, and eco-friendly surface cleaners.

In the U.S., these products were distributed primarily through independent retailers and buying groups in the hardware and do-it-yourself sectors. Outside the U.S., consumer sales outlets and retail distribution channels varied by country. In Brazil, for example, Kent sold through distributors to small independent outlets; in France a direct sales force sold to national chains. And while consumer preferences in the U.S. were largely homogeneous, overseas the product's packaging, container size, aesthetics (scent, color, etc.), and even active ingredients could vary from one country to the next.

About one-third of this business's $522 million worldwide sales were outside the U.S., with strong local and regional competitors in each offshore market. General household products were produced in the company's large, multiproduct mixing and packing plants in markets from France to Brazil to New Zealand. However, the only non-U.S. facility able to produce the specially formulated, aerosol-packaged *Grease-B-Gone* line was in France, in a single-product plant built in 1990.

Fire Protection Products

Kent entered the fire protection business in the 1950s by acquiring a company that had developed fire retardant chemicals for the apparel industry. Subsequently, Kent's R&D lab developed other fire retardants for the electronics, building, and transport industries. Then, following the 1967 fire that claimed the lives of three Apollo astronauts, government-funded research led Kent to develop a line of foams, chemicals, and gases, thereby allowing it to enter the larger fire control market segment.

Exhibit 1
Kent Chemical: Summary of Financial Data, 2003–2007 ($ millions)

	2007	2006	2005	2004	2003
Consolidated Statements of Income					
Net sales	$2,238	$2,072	$1,937	$1,810	$1,628
Cost of sales	1,700	1,440	1,339	1277	1,150
	538	632	598	533	478
Selling, general, and administrative expenses	320	305	295	263	248
Research and development expenses	90	84	82	77	68
	410	389	377	340	316
Income from operations	128	243	221	193	162
Royalty, interest, and dividend income	33	51	44	49	47
Interest expense	−38	−44	−23	−30	−22
Other income (deductions)	−2	−20	−3	−3	−1
Taxes on income	−50	−110	−115	−96	−88
Income before minority interest and equity earnings	71	120	124	113	98
Minority interest earnings (losses) of subsidiaries	5	−1	−3	6	0
Earnings of associated companies	20	21	28	34	40
Net income	$ 96	$ 140	$ 149	$ 154	$ 128
Kent Chemical International contributions to corporate results (Unaudited)					
Net sales	$ 598	$ 578	$ 466	$ 402	$ 322
Net income	$ 24	$ 38	$ 37	$ 33	$ 23

By 2008, fire retardants were mature commodities, but the fire control segment was a large, fast-growing and increasingly specialized field, requiring big investments in R&D to keep pace. The latter product line was sold to both fire control systems companies and original equipment manufacturers (OEMs) in the electronics, building, and oil refining industries. Intense price competition particularly in the retardant segment, caused Kent to focus on reducing production costs.

Outside the U.S., fire retardants were produced by former Kent licensees, FireGard plc in England and SicherFeuer AG in Germany, both with long histories in the industry. Fire protection regulations varied by country, so the chemical agents Kent produced in its four plants around the world often had to be adapted to local markets. A few multinational customers accounted for the majority of Kent's $210 million in worldwide sales, 45% of which came from international markets. As the number-three competitor worldwide, Kent faced pressure from both local and global companies.

Medical Plastics

In the 1960s, Kent collaborated with a major hospital supply company to develop a non-leaching, sterilizable plastic that won the U.S. Food and Drug Administration approval to hold intravenous solutions. That partnership created plastic IV bags that gradually replaced the ubiquitous glass bottles hanging over hospital beds around the world. Building on that reputation, Kent became a leading supplier of plastics for medical applications. Over subsequent decades it developed special formulations for everything from surgical instruments to implantable devices to replacement joints.

Its customers were large global hospital supply and medical device companies with which it worked in partnership to develop specialized plastics for targeted applications. In addition to properties such as biocompatibility, self-lubrication, and non-toxicity, these plastics also had to retain those characteristics under sterilization-imposed conditions of extreme temperature and moisture.

The company's growing line of medical products all were developed in the company's Ohio R&D labs and manufactured in one of two specialized plants in California and the Netherlands. Overseas sales accounted for about 35% of the business's $625 million global revenue.

Kent Chemical International: Going Global for Growth

For many years, Kent's overseas operations were seen as a source of incremental sales through exports, licensing agreements, and minority joint ventures (JVs). That view changed in 1998, when Ben Fisher, KCP's newly appointed CEO, announced that a more strategic approach to global expansion would be his top priority: "Our goal is to remake Kent from a U.S. company dabbling in international markets to one that develops, manufactures, and sells worldwide."

Old Root Stock, New Growth

To implement his vision of a global integrated company, Fisher named Luis Morales to head the revitalized international division. Morales was a 22-year Kent veteran who had joined its Mexican subsidiary in sales, risen to become country manager, then moved to Ohio to run KCP's Consumer Products division. He had a reputation as a smart, hardworking team player who liked to win.

Morales began implementing the global integration strategy by taking majority interests in Kent's 15 offshore JVs, acquiring other overseas companies, and generally expanding global presence. The subsequent rapid international sales growth—from $139 million in 1999 (11% of total revenue) to $598 million in 2007 (27% of revenue)—was managed through Kent's International division. That division reported to Morales through three regional directors—for Europe, Middle East, and Africa (EMEA); Central and South America; and Asia-Pacific—all located in Kent, Ohio. (See Exhibit 2.)

Historically, regional directors had managed subsidiary and JV managers in 22 countries with a light touch encouraging them to optimize their local positions. Because Kent was a minority shareholder of many of these companies, its financial and operating control were often limited. But strong informal links ensured the necessary financial and technological support. "For decades we'd provided them support, and they had sent us dividends," Morales said.

The entrepreneurial independence of offshore entities was often complicated by long competitive histories. Morales acknowledged that the regional directors' post-acquisition task of coordinating activities and integrating operations was extremely difficult. "For example, FireGard and SicherFeuer had been competitors for decades," he said. "Even after we took minority positions, they refused to cooperate or even to coordinate activities. In fact, it's only in the last couple of years that we've finally begun to get many of our own subsidiaries to stop exporting into each other's markets."

Exhibit 2 KCP International Division Organizational Chart, 2000

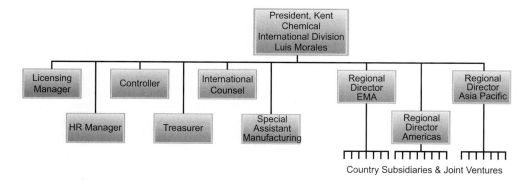

Country Subsidiaries & Joint Ventures

Even after Kent took majority positions, establishing control often proved to be difficult. In 2000, the EMEA regional manager relocated his staff to Hamburg. "We needed to work more closely with local companies to rationalize overlapping activities and duplicative operations," he said. "But relocating didn't solve the problem. When my staff tried to consolidate redundant European manufacturing, for example, local managers with 20 or 30 years' experience in their markets ran circles around them. It soon became clear that most of the regional staff simply lacked the market knowledge and detailed technical expertise to counter the country subsidiaries' strong pushback."

New Strategies, New Stresses

As overseas operations grew, Morales became concerned that his organization was not adapting well to changing pressures and demands. His first concern was the impact of new systems. As Kent acquired majority positions, corporate reporting systems had been added to allow operations to be controlled and financial reports consolidated. But these changes had caused strains. "Having the data sometimes tempted my staff to second-guess local country managers," admitted Morales. "The subsidiaries felt that we set arbitrary financial targets that were out of touch with their market realities. Despite our good intentions, I think the country managers were often right."

Capital allocation had also become more complex. Subsidiaries now had to complete capital requests that were first reviewed by a regional manager, then by Morales, and often at the corporate level. In the process, relations between subsidiaries and their U.S. technical contacts shifted. A country manager explained: "Our U.S. colleagues used to consult with us on our projects, but once they were involved in the funding decisions, they became more critical and less collaborative."

Morales's second concern was that overseas subsidiaries' long history of independence led managers to protect their self-interests. "When the Korean subsidiary wanted to manufacture fire retardants for its electronics customers, its plans challenged the German subsidiary that had been exporting retardants to Korea for years," he said.

"When we began trying to integrate the strategies of our overseas operations, conflicts like this regularly reached my desk for resolution."

Parochial attitudes also blocked technology transfer when the informal relationships that had long linked offshore operations with U.S. technical experts were replaced by the more-formal structures that growth had required. Berthold Hugel, SicherFeuer's general manager, explained:

> As we grew, a U.S.-based technical manager was appointed to the regional director's staff as our liaison with domestic divisions. Perhaps he just lacked good contacts, but we were never properly connected. So I sent an English-speaking SicherFeuer employee to Ohio to serve as our technical link. But he had no clout, so that didn't work either. Finally, I decided that the only way to get technical help and to learn what new products were being developed was for me personally to travel to Kent headquarters every 60 days. So that's what I did.

Frustration about links between geographic and product organizations also existed in the U.S. divisions, as reflected in the comments of Jack Davies, the VP responsible for Fire Protection:

> We had developed this great new halogenated flame retardant product that was selling great in the U.S., but it was stalled in Europe. The U.K. subsidiary told me that their project-appropriation request had been blocked by corporate. I discovered that someone in the controller's office was withholding approval as a lever to force the U.K. to bring its receivables under control. It wasn't my responsibility, but I stepped in to put a stop to it.

The third problem worrying Morales was that even within his international division, the regional organization had difficulty coordinating issues with global implications. In the Medical Plastics business for example, most of KCP's customers were multinational hospital supply and medical device companies. So when the Brazilian subsidiary unilaterally reduced prices on its line of general purpose polycarbonates as a loss leader to sell more of the expensive, technical medical products, the pricing impact was felt throughout Kent's worldwide medical plastics business.

The issue highlighted the fact that nobody was coordinating price, product, or sourcing decisions globally. "Worse still, because the international division had a regional rather than a product-based structure, our global product-development needs and priorities were seldom communicated to the research group," said Morales. "And since our R&D efforts respond to specific problems or identified applications, they rarely focused on offshore opportunities or needs."

The 2006 Reorganization: Bridging Gaps with GBDs

In June 2006, when CEO Ben Fisher also became Kent's board chairman, he used the occasion to announce a major reorganization. Angela Perri, who had joined KCP 20 years earlier as a PhD scientist in the R&D lab, was named president of the U.S. businesses. Perri was a capable, hard-driving, ambitious executive who most recently had run the U.S. Medical Plastics division.

Simultaneously, Peter Fisher, Ben's 35-year-old son was named vice chairman with responsibility for all corporate staffs and the international operations. Peter had joined Kent in sales before heading the Consumer Products division for the past four years. Under the new organization, the International division became Kent Chemical International (KCI), a separate legal entity structured as

a subsidiary of KCP. Both Angela Perri and Peter Fisher reported to the chairman. (See Exhibit 3.)

Morales hoped the reorganization would improve domestic/international relations. "Historically, all vital communication between us occurred either at top levels or on the front lines," he said. "At my level, I'd negotiate funding decisions, and in the trenches relationships between U.S.-based technical experts and international plant managers got things done." But as overseas operations grew, Morales had become stretched thin as KCI's principal top-level contact. And the advice and support that had long flowed freely to the front lines was now provided slowly, reluctantly, and often accompanied by an invoice for intercompany charges. "The regional directors should have provided the extra link with the domestic divisions. But they never had the status or power of product division managers, who were all KCP vice presidents," said Morales.

To respond to these problems, Morales in 2006 appointed three global business directors (GBDs), each with a long, successful U.S. career before moving to KCI. The GBDs would be responsible for the three lines of business within KCI, and although the new roles were not well defined, they were announced as VP-level positions reporting directly to Morales. Each GBD assembled a staff of 3 to 6 product or project managers and began defining their roles and setting priorities.

Exhibit 3 Kent Chemical Products Organizational Chart, 2006

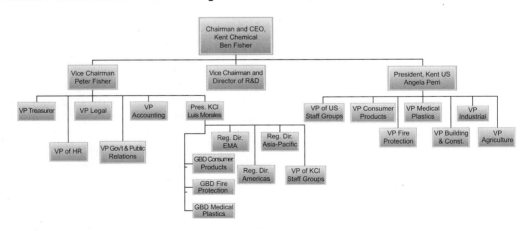

The consumer-products GBD was a 25-year Kent veteran of senior sales management in KCP's Consumer Products division. Before this appointment, he had run a small domestic JV. He explained his understanding of the new role: "I'm trying to inject consumer-oriented thinking into our overseas subsidiaries. I don't care if they see my role as advisory or directive, as long as they do what needs to be done. They have to realize they're part of a global company now." Responding to his mandate to "sort things out," particularly within EMEA, he saw his first priority as determining why the *Grease-B-Gone* line had not sold as well in Europe as it had in the U.S.–and then to fix it.

A second GBD was given responsibility for fire protection products. He had 10 years of international sales experience and four as manager of market planning in the Fire Protection division. "I'll need to assume worldwide technology control and marketing responsibility," he said. "The way I see it, regional managers should be mainly responsible for production and government relations."

The third GBD, an engineer and 15-year KCP veteran, was assigned to medical plastics. She saw her role as a strategic planner linking the U.S., regional, and subsidiary managers. "To be effective, the regional managers will have to maintain authority over their operations," she said. "I can be most useful by helping to integrate the international and domestic parts of our operation."

After just a few months, the GBDs were faltering. "The subsidiaries saw GBDs as interlopers, but some more than others," said Morales. "The medical-plastics GBD was appreciated because she provided useful worldwide business coordination. But the consumer-products GBD was a disaster. Subsidiaries felt he interfered in local issues where he had neither experience nor understanding."

Many reasons were offered for KCI's post-reorganization problems. The EMEA regional director thought the new structure just strained the existing organization's time and resources. "We wanted to integrate our businesses globally, but the GBDs didn't know what their role was, and as regional directors, we weren't clear about how to work with them," he said. "So we ended up in a lot of meetings that took us away from dealing with important day-to-day matters."

Morales felt the main problem was the GBDs' inability to provide a link to the domestic product divisions and assume the conflict-resolution roles he had been playing. "Despite years of service, the GBDs lacked the credibility and power to get things done. And some of the domestic managers didn't help. They just seemed to want control over the fast growth overseas businesses," he said.

Jack Davies, the VP responsible for the Fire Protection division had a different view. He felt the problem lay in the people appointed as GBDs. "I don't think there was a single vice president in the domestic corporation who saw them as equals," he said.

The 2007 Adaptation: World Boards

By mid-2007, it was clear that the GBD concept was struggling. After long discussions with Morales about more-effective means to integrate KCI with KCP, Peter Fisher developed the idea to support GBDs with world boards. They would be composed of managers from the domestic and international organizations, with geographic, product, and functional expertise all represented. These boards would be responsible for developing strategies for the global businesses.

In June 2007, Peter Fisher presented the concept to a meeting of the company's top 150 managers:

> The GBDs are serving an important function linking our U.S. and international operations. But they can't manage this vital role by themselves. To provide support, we are introducing world boards to help each business advance its global strategy and integrate its worldwide operations. They are not meant to replace local management. Their role will be as planners, reviewers, and communicators, not managers or controllers. They offer us an opportunity to work together and share responsibility for ensuring that our global businesses succeed.

A world board was formed for each of the company's three major worldwide businesses. Each was instructed to provide worldwide marketing and operations planning, optimize global sourcing, develop technology on a global scale, make investment recommendations, and build international management capabilities. Although they determined their own membership, they typically included the head of the U.S. product division, the division's technical and marketing staff members, key country general managers, and their appropriate product managers. The GBD served as board chair, providing him or her with a forum to involve the domestic division managers in the international business, and to give regional and subsidiary managers a link to the parent company.

The fire protection world board got off to a strong start and generally met the stated objectives. "It works because the business has opportunities and problems with worldwide implications," said Berthold Hugel, the former German subsidiary general manager who was named Fire Protection GBD in 2007. "Also, before each board meeting, Jack Davies (the domestic division VP) and I sit down and work through all the issues so that the discussions never become politicized."

The other two world boards did not fare as well. The medical plastics board became a platform for discussion but rarely reached agreement or decided on action. And despite Peter Fisher's personal intervention, the consumer products board met only twice, then quietly disbanded. "We couldn't even agree on what issues needed to be managed locally or globally," said the new Consumer GBD.

Reflecting on the experience, Morales felt that the negative reaction to the 2006 GBD concept had made managers hesitate to embrace the world boards. "Some of my country and regional managers felt threatened and thought this was the first step in dismantling the regional organizations. And many domestic managers thought it was just a way to give our struggling GBDs more power," he said. He also noted that in order to succeed, all board members–GBDs, domestic division managers and country managers–had to be open, cooperative, rational team players, even when their interests were not being served. "The model requires practically perfect managers," he said.

Peter Fisher had a different view. "To accommodate all interests, some world boards had more than 20 members. They had just become too large and unwieldy. There were too many competing priorities, so the big issues were never addressed. And, frankly, many domestic division managers were blocking progress and trying to control the global business directly," he said.

From Perri's point of view, the domestic organization would have been more supportive if key managers had been consulted when the world boards were formed. "Peter and Luis expected the division managers to be involved and supportive. But I was never asked my opinion about the world boards' structure or activities, and frankly I didn't altogether agree with the concept," she said.

Back to the Drawing Board: Another Change?

In March 2008, with the world boards concept struggling and strains in international/domestic relationships, Perri met with Morales and Peter Fisher to discuss possible solutions. Perri was blunt. "We're a science-based company," she said. "Our competitive advantage is in using our scientific expertise to develop products. So it's a real problem that we have barriers between the scientific resources that I manage and the international markets that you control. We really need to fix this."

Peter Fisher responded. "I agree that our technological capability is a huge asset, Angela," he said. "But let's acknowledge that Kent's domestic growth has plateaued. So the company's future relies on our ability to expand into international markets. We need an organizational solution that empowers rather than subjugates our international presence."

The Consultants' Proposal

Recognizing the need to find a solution, the three senior executives contacted Sterling Partners, a respected international management consulting firm, to help them sort through the issue. For a fee of $1.8 million, a team of four consultants worked with four Kent managers to gather information on the industry context, Kent's competitive position, and the strategic objectives of each of its global businesses. After analyzing these data, they prepared recommendations that they hoped would convince Kent chairman Ben Fisher, a longtime skeptic of both outside consultants and complex organizational structures.

The consultants concluded that one of the company's main problems was that it had been imposing uniform organizational solutions on a strategically diverse portfolio. Because each business had a different mix of global imperatives and local demands, they suggested taking a more tailored approach. In summary, their detailed report of analysis and conclusions found:

- The consumer product line's key strategic need was for locally adapted marketing programs to respond to local consumer needs, distribution channel differences, and competition that varied by country. While the aerosol-based *Grease-B-Gone* line was sourced regionally, locally tailored general household products were usually produced in national mixing plants. The report suggested a business that should be predominantly managed locally and regionally.
- The consultants placed the medical plastics business at the other end of the local–global spectrum. Here the key success factor was the central R&D input required to develop new products and technologies. Manufacturing occurred in two specialized globally scaled plants where quality was tightly controlled. Customers were primarily multinational companies with worldwide operations. These factors indicated a business that needed global control.
- Fire control products fell between these extremes. Because R&D was important for innovation, global coordination was critical. But fire prevention was a highly regulated industry in which relationships with national regulatory bodies and control agencies were critical. While some customers were multinational corporations, many smaller national and regional customers (and competitors) were also significant. Product sourcing was largely regional.

Under the Fisher family's mandate that Kent not be broken up, the consultants recommended that the company evolve to a more differentiated organization using a tool they termed "decision matrix." The tool's purpose was to expand on their analysis by defining core decisions business by business and then creating a process to analyze how they should be decided. This process would involve assembling the key business, geographic, and functional managers from each business and engaging them in discussions about the decisions. The discussions would be facilitated by a consultant.

As a model, the consultants had prepared a set of blank fire protection decision-matrix forms. The one for resource-allocation decisions for the European fire protection business is shown in Exhibit 4. This completed form identifies that multiple players would be responsible to provide input (IP), offer business or technical concurrence (BC or TC), and make recommendations (R). But it clarifies that the final decision (D) on product development would be made by the Fire Protection division VP.

Ten similar sheets listed decisions relating to strategy development, budget preparation, marketing decisions, etc. In all, 62 European fire protection decisions were identified for review. As the next step, the consultants proposed that the executive team authorize a trial run of facilitated discussions with European fire protection managers to complete these forms.

A Brewing Storm, A Key Decision

Although many senior Kent managers found the report convincing, others were worried it was too complex. Some regional managers argued that the company should just revert to the geographic structure that had allowed it to grow. But several domestic managers felt the time had come to simplify the structure by giving them worldwide business responsibility.

While digesting the Sterling report, top management was also focused on the global economy. Its 2007 results had been down 30% from the previous year, and 2008 was beginning to look worse. With an ongoing subprime mortgage crisis in the U.S., some felt a global economic downturn was brewing.

Morales knew that the time had come to make his recommendation. Conscious he had two strikes against him on organizational change, he knew that his proposal not only had to resolve the company's organizational problems, but it also had to do so within a skeptical organization operating in a threatening global economic environment. It was probably the biggest decision of his career.

Exhibit 4   Decision Matrix for Resource-Allocation Decisions on the European Fire Protection Business

Resource Allocation

	KCI: Fire Protection					European Fire Protection — Firegard plc						European Fire Protection — SicherFeuer AG					KCP Fire Protection Division (Ohio)				Corporate Staffs						
	Regional Director EMEA	GBD Fire Protection	Controller	Special Asst. Manufacturing	Human Resources Manager	Firesafe GM	Division Manager, Fire Protection	Plant Controller	Production Manager	Sales and Marketing Manager	Technical Director	Sicher-Feuer General Manager	Production Manager	Technical Manager	Financial Manager	General Sales Manager	KCP VP Fire Protection	Business Development Manager	Manufacturing/Engineering Manager	Controller	Treasurer	Controller	Manufacturing	Industrial Relations	Human Resources	Government & Public Relations	Legal
1. Recommend allocation of resources to major new product development programs	R	R	IP	R	R	BC	R	IP	R	R	IP	BC	R	C		IP	D	R	IP	IP		TC	R/TC		IP/TC		TC
2. Recommend allocation of resources to major process development programs	R	IP	IP	RJ	IP	BC	R	IP	R	IP	IP	BC	R	C			D	IP	R	IP		TC	R/TC		IP/TC		C
3. Recommend allocation of resources for major cost reduction programs	R	IP	IP	R		BC	R	IP	R	IP	R	BC	R	C			D	IP	R	IP		TC	R/TC		IP/TC		
4. Determine need, location, and timing for adding or reducing manufacturing capacity	D*	IP	IP	R		D*	R	IP	R	IP	IP	D*	R	R	IP	IP	D*	IP	R	IP		TC	R	IP/TC	C IP/TC	C**	TC
5. Decide management of production workforce (expansion, contraction, assignment)	C	IP		D		D	R		R			D	R				C		R				R			C**	TC**
6. Decide on inter-region sourcing	R	IP	IP	R		BC	R	IP	R	IP	IP	R	IP	R	IP	IP	D	IP	IP	R	TC	TC	IP			C	C
7. Decide who maintains existing technologies	R	IP		R		BC	R		R	IP	IP	BC	R	R			D	IP	R	IP			R/TC				

* Joint decision

** For U.S. decisions only

D = Decides; A = Approves; R = Recommends; BC = Business concurrence; TC = Technical concurrence; C = Concurs; I = Initiates; IP = Inputs.

⊛IVEY | Publishing

CASE 4.2 LUNDBECK KOREA: MANAGING AN INTERNATIONAL GROWTH ENGINE

Michael Roberts wrote this case under the supervision of Professor Paul Beamish solely to provide material for class discussion. The authors do not intend to illustrate either effective or ineffective handling of a managerial situation. The authors may have disguised certain names and other identifying information to protect confidentiality.

Copyright © 2010, Richard Ivey School of Business Foundation   Version: 2012–02–14

Early in 2005, Michael Andersen, vice president of Lundbeck – a leading central nervous system (CNS) pharmaceutical company in Denmark, questioned whether he should rethink Lundbeck's reporting structure in Asia. In particular, the Korean subsidiary was experiencing very strong growth and Andersen wondered whether Lundbeck Korea would achieve its full potential if it remained part of Lundbeck Asia, the regional group, or whether it would be better to have the managers at Lundbeck Korea report directly to him in Copenhagen.

Korea had proven itself to be a rising star among Lundbeck's overseas subsidiaries, and the staff in Korea, led by country manager Jin-Ho Jun (Jun), wanted more independence to chart their own path. The Korean subsidiary's performance had far exceeded what was projected in the original business plan. It had grown from one employee in 2002 to over 50 employees in 2005, and had sales of KRW25 billion (approximately US$22 million). Given the current success, Andersen wondered whether the current reporting structure was still appropriate.

The decision was not to be taken lightly; while the Korean division, under the leadership of Jun, was experiencing enormous growth, it was only barely three years in the making. In addition, while normal and expected in a recently established subsidiary, Lundbeck Korea was still not a profitable business unit. Since most of the other Asian countries were part of the Asia division, Andersen also had to think about how this would affect Lundbeck's regional and worldwide organizational reporting norms; in particular, he was concerned about the Chinese subsidiary. While making adjustments to reporting structures was a normal part of doing business for Lundbeck, Andersen had not anticipated that he would be considering this decision so soon for Korea.

The CNS Landscape

However, these markets were fairly stable and generally experienced low single-digit growth. Exhibit 1 is a list of the top pharmaceutical markets. The major CNS pharmaceutical markets by country were: United States, 59%; Germany, 5%; Japan, 4%; France, 4%; United Kingdom, 4%; Spain, 3%; Italy, 2%; South Korea, 1.5%. The bulk of the remaining 19 per cent of the CNS market came from emerging economies such as Brazil, China, India, and South Korea. While the market for CNS drugs in these emerging

Exhibit 1
Top Pharmaceutical Markets, 2005

Country	Pharmaceutical Market Size (billions USD)	Population (millions USD)	Lundbeck Functions
United States	270.2	307.2	Sales/Research
Japan	76.2	127.1	—
Germany	43.9	82.3	Sales
France	39.1	64.1	Sales
United Kingdom	31.3	61.1	Sales
Italy	24.3	58.1	Sales/Research
China	20.4	1,338.6	Sales
Canada	16.3	33.5	Sales
India	9.3	1,166.1	Sales
South Korea	7.9	48.5	Sales
Russia	7.9	140.0	Sales
Turkey	7.5	76.8	Sales
. . .	. . .	. . .	. . .
Denmark	2.6	5.5	Sales/Research/Production

Source: *Business Monitor International*, "Pharmaceutical Market Statistics: Statistics for 2005," London, United Kingdom, 2009.

economies was much smaller, the rate of growth in many of these countries was in excess of 15 per cent per year.[1]

The global industry for CNS pharmaceuticals was about $93 billion in 2005. CNS diseases are serious and life-threatening and affect the quality of life of patients as well as of their relatives. Over the past 50 years, new pharmaceuticals had revolutionized treatment options, but there remained a large unmet need for new and innovative therapeutics.

Overall, the industry was marked by intense competition from both rival branded pharmaceutical firms and generic competitors. In most markets, branded pharmaceuticals were given a number of years of exclusivity – a period in which no generic version of the drug can be sold. However, these periods of exclusivity varied greatly by country. Patent protection could range from no protection to 20 years of exclusivity. In

most developed markets, for example the United States, exclusivity began at the time the drug was patented; in other markets, for instance South Korea, it began when the drug was launched. The laws and regulations around granting exclusivity also varied by country, and were often heavily influenced by political concerns. Regardless of the region, when the exclusivity periods run out, the price of a drug drops dramatically. The revenues from Eli Lilly's anti-depressant drug Prozac, for example, fell by over 80 per cent following the loss of its patent protection at the end of the 1990s.[2] While the decrease in revenues from this drug could also be attributed to new branded pharmaceuticals entering the anti-depressant market, the significance of loss of patent protection cannot be overstated.

Almost 60 per cent of the total market sales in the CNS industry came from the nine largest firms (Johnson & Johnson, 11%; Glaxo Smith

[1] B. Nehru, *The CNS Market Outlook to 2012*, Business Insights Ltd, London, United Kingdom, 2007, p. 59.

[2] B. Massingham, *CNS Market Outlook to 2000*, Business Insights Ltd, London, United Kingdom, 2000.

Kline, or GSK, 9%; Pfizer, 8%; Lilly, 7%; Sanofi-Aventis, 5%; Novartis, 5%; Astra Zeneca, 5%; Wyeth, 5%; Forest Labs, 3%). Lundbeck held 2%. In this industry, sales growth was highly dependent on the successful introduction of a new patented drug, and sales declines were most often a result of a patent expiration. A firm's revenue was often disproportionally dominated by one blockbuster drug – a drug that dominates a class of drugs. For example, Johnson & Johnson generated 41 per cent of its revenue from the blockbuster schizophrenia drug Risperdal.[3]

Depending on the country, buyers of pharmaceuticals could be national health services, private insurance companies, or individuals. However, in general, decisions about prescribing drugs were made by practitioners (i.e. doctors, etc.).[4] Psychiatrists represented the largest group of practitioners in the CNS industry. Since doctors were the ultimate decision makers, the buyer had little direct product choice. However, the type of buyer system greatly affected the potential market size and price that could be charged for the product. The presence of a national health service that covered prescription drugs, for example, could greatly expand the market, but government pressure could potentially lower prices per unit.

Key Products

The largest class of drugs in the CNS market was comprised of anti-depressants, which represented almost 20 per cent of the total market. Depression is a genuine physical condition and affects approximately 10 per cent of the global population.[5] "Bad" mood, loss of energy, feelings of worthlessness, difficulty concentrating, and even thoughts of suicide are just some of the many symptoms.

The market for anti-depressants was $19 billion in 2005 (see Exhibit 2). However, the market segment was due to have very poor growth rates

over the next several years because of the large influx of generic drugs in selective serotonin reuptake inhibitors (SSRIs), the largest class of anti-depressant drugs. SSRIs, which made up more than 50 per cent of the anti-depressant market segment, were a class of compounds typically used in the treatment of depression, anxiety disorders, personality disorders, and some cases of insomnia. In particular, sales of Zoloft by Pfizer were expected to decrease by one third in 2006 due to the expiration of its patent in the U.S. market. This left only three products with patent protection: Effexor by Wyeth, Lexapro by Lundbeck, and Yentreve by Lilly.[6] Overall, this class of drugs was only forecasted to growth by 1.5 per cent a year until 2012.

New growth in the CNS market was driven by drugs for Alzheimer's disease (AD). Over the last few years, this class of drugs experienced growth rates upwards of 15 per cent per year.[7] The market for AD medications was $4 billion in 2005, and was expected to see growth of more than 15 per cent in 2006. Exhibit 2 gives an overview of the AD medication market. The future of AD medication was in the NMDA receptor antagonist class of drugs, which was expected to grow by over 30 per cent in 2006. The drugs in this class were all derivates of memantine. There were three memantine-based drugs on the market; however, they were not in direct competition with each other as they were a result of shared development and licensing. Forest Labs marketed Namenda in the United States; Merz sold Axura in Germany; and Lundbeck marketed Ebixa in the rest of Europe. Memantine was an important medication because it was the only pharmaceutical available for moderate and severe forms of AD. Since most AD patients lived long enough to experience all stages of the disease, memantine filled a crucial role in AD therapy. There were no threats of generics to memantine until after 2008. Overall, this class of drugs was forecasted to grow by 13.1 per cent a year until 2012.[8]

---

[3] B. Nehru, op.cit., p. 15.

[4] *Datamonitor*, "Global Pharmaceuticals, Biotechnology & Life Sciences: Industry Profile," New York, 2009.

[5] B. Nehru, op.cit., p. 33.

[6] Ibid., p. 53.   [7] Ibid., pp. 58–60.

[8] Ibid., pp. 94–98.

Exhibit 2

Leading Anti-Depressants and Alzheimer's Disease Medications in the Global CNS Market, 2005

Brand	Company	Generic	Class	Sales (millions USD)	Share (%)	Expected Growth (% per yr.) 2006	2012	Patent Expiry
Anti-Depressants								
Effexor	Wyeth	venlafaxine	SNRI	3,830	20.1	3.0	-20.4	2007
Lexapro	Lundbeck/ Forest	escitalopram	SSRI	2,455**	12.9	19.0	8.4	2011
Zoloft	Pfizer	sertraline	SSRI	3,641	19.2	-34.0	-32.6	expired
Wellbutrin	GSK	bupropion	Other	1,605	8.4	22.0	-*	-
Yentreve	Lilly	duloxetine	SNRI	684	3.6	95.0	23.9	2013
Seroxat	GSK	paroxetine	SSRI	819	4.3	-13.0	-28.3	expired
Prozac	Lilly	fluoxetine	SSRI	408	2.1	-21.0	-34.7	expired
Remeron	Organon	mirtazapine	Other	351	1.8	-15.0	-	-
Others				5,220	27.5	-3.0	-2.7	
Total				19,013	100.0	3.5	1.5	
Alzheimer's Medications								
Aricept	Pfizer	donepezil	CI	2,215	54.9	13.5	-5.5	2010
Namenda	Forest	memantine	NMDAA	482	11.9	35.7	24.6	2014
Exelon	Novartis	rivastigmine	CI	496	12.3	5.6	-0.9	2012
Reminyl	J&J	galantamine	CI	490	12.1	6.7	-16.7	2008
Ebixa	Lundbeck	memantine	NMDAA	189	4.7	29.7	0.6	2010
Akatinol	Lundbeck	memantine	NMDAA	60	1.5	13.2	-11.5	2008
Axura	Merz	memantine	NMDAA	22	0.5	35.6	7.2	2008
Prometax	Novartis	rivastigmine	CI	25	0.6	5.3	4.0	2012
Other				57	1.4	29.1	98	
Total				4,036	100	15.4	13.1	

* - is used to indicate that no information is available

** of which Lundbeck is 863

Source: Modified from B. Nehru, *The CNS Market Outlook to 2012*, Business Insights Ltd, London, United Kingdom, 2007.

The Asian Market

At $97.4 billion in 2005, the pharmaceutical market in Asia represented approximately 20 per cent of the global pharmaceutical industry. The Asia pharmaceutical market had a growth rate of about 6.4 per cent a year which was forecasted to remain steady for the next several years. However, some markets throughout Asia were vastly different from others. For example, the largest market in Asia was Japan, which accounted for 55 per cent of the entire market but only had a growth rate of 2.4 per cent a year. China, on the other hand, accounted for 17.5 per cent of the pharmaceutical market, with a growth rate in excess of 20 per cent per year. The other major markets in Asia were South Korea and India, representing 8.3 per cent and 8.1 per cent of the market, respectively. Excluding Japan, the other Asian markets grew at an average rate of 11.3 per cent per year. The CNS market represented nine per cent of the total pharmaceutical market in Asia for a total of $8.7 billion.[9]

The payer systems also varied greatly throughout Asia. Japan had a combination of government insurance and private employer-based insurance. Hong Kong and Singapore had a combination of private pay and private insurance programs. South Korea had a fully government-funded national insurance for pharmaceutical prescriptions. China, Thailand, and Malaysia had virtually no group or collective programs and most costs for pharmaceuticals were paid by individuals.

Lundbeck

Lundbeck was an international CNS pharmaceutical company headquartered in Denmark. Founded as a trading company in 1915 by Hans Lundbeck, the company had evolved into a global CNS pharmaceutical firm. In 2005, Lundbeck earned over $240 million in operating profits from over $1.5 billion in sales. Lundbeck conducted research on, developed, manufactured, marketed, sold, and distributed pharmaceuticals for the treatment of neurological disorders, including depression, schizophrenia, Alzheimer's disease, Parkinson's disease and insomnia.

Lundbeck employed 5,500 people worldwide, 2,100 of whom were based in Denmark. It manufactured its products in Denmark and Italy, and had research facilities in Denmark and the United States. Lundbeck's drugs were registered for sale in more than 90 countries, and it had its own independent sales forces in 55 countries. For Lundbeck's financial highlights in 2005 (see Exhibit 3).

Lundbeck was a research-intensive company, structured to be constantly producing the next generation of drugs. The primary mission of the company was to undertake the tasks of improving the quality of life for persons with a psychiatric or neurological disorder, and to work intensely to find and develop new and improved drugs. It employed a total of 1,100 specialists in its R&D units, which consumed more than 20 per cent of annual revenues.

Strategic Drivers

Lundbeck's strategy was driven by four principles: specialization, speed, integration, and results.[10]

Specialization: Unlike many of its competitors, Lundbeck specialized exclusively in the CNS pharmaceutical area. Moreover, the strategy of specialization had been extended to include all aspects of its business. Thus, Lundbeck's goal was to focus and streamline its key products, simplify its processes and business procedures, and focus on long-term growth in the CNS industry. To do this, Lundbeck focused on marketing and distributing its new and innovative products. Lundbeck tried to balance innovative activities while maintaining a competitive cost structure.

Speed: Lundbeck's strategy was to use its small size as an advantage. The goal was to maintain short decision-making processes in order to respond quickly to the demands of a highly competitive market. That being said, Lundbeck set up strong control systems to ensure that the company was able to balance its results-focused mindset with exposure to risk and the need to maintain ethical business practices. Lundbeck used its small size to flexibly respond to risks at all stages in the value chain. Some of the key risks that it identified at the sales and marketing level included generic competition; adherence to ethical sales and marketing practices; and risks associated with product liability. Its intention was to structure its organization to control and respond quickly to any new threat.

Integration: Lundbeck's goal was to continue to become a global pharmaceutical firm. In order

[9] *Datamonitor*, "Pharmaceuticals in Asia-Pacific," New York, New York, 2008, p. 9.

[10] Company documents.

Exhibit 3
Lundbeck Financial Highlights, 2005

	DKK millions	USD millions
Revenue	9,070	1,513
Profit from operations	2,174	363
Finance income, net	17	3
Profit before tax	2,156	360
Net profit	1,457	243
		0
Cash flows from operating activities	2,074	346
		0
Total assets	11,560	1,928
Capital and reserves	7,437	1,240
EBIT margin (%)	24	
Return on equity (%)	19.3	
Earnings per share (EPS)	6.52	1.1
Earnings per share - diluted (DEPS)	6.5	1.1
Cash flow per share	9.2	1.5

Revenue By Product and Region	Product	Region	Product	Region
Europe		4,680		781
Cipralex®/Lexapro®	1,963		327	
Ebixa®	933		156	
Azilect®	6		1	
Other pharmaceuticals	1,777		296	
United States		2,618		437
Income from Cipralex®/Lexapro®	2,552		426	
Other pharmaceuticals	66		11	
International Markets*		1,539		257
Cipralex®/Lexapro®	662		110	
Ebixa®	172		29	
Azilect®	0		0	
Other pharmaceuticals	706		118	
Other revenue		232		39
Total group revenue		9,070		1,513

* Asia, Australia, Africa, Americas, Canada, Middle East
* Estimated on the 2005 annual DKK/USD exchange rate of 5.996475
Source: Company documents.

to achieve that, it sought to continue to develop strong competencies through the entire value chain of the pharmaceuticals market, from knowledge and control of research to the development of new pharmaceuticals, production, marketing and sales. However, it did not believe that it had to do everything in-house or at home in Denmark. As the firm grew in its global competency, it planned to seek new locations and partners for any aspect of the value chain that could offer better value in terms of quality, price, commodities, and labour.

Results: Lundbeck intended to provide continuous short-term and long-term value to its shareholders. In 1999, Lundbeck's shares were listed on the Copenhagen Stock Exchange. The Lundbeck Foundation, which distributed $40 million to $50 million each year in grants to the scientific community for various types of research, owned about 70 per cent of the shares in Lundbeck, while the remaining 30 per cent were traded on the stock exchange. Lundbeck's semi-private ownership by the Lundbeck Foundation was a long-term strength for the company because this ownership structure gave the firm greater flexibility than most of its competitors to re-invest its current profits for long-term growth.[11]

Lundbeck's leading products were Lexapro and Ebixa. Lexapro represented 57.1 per cent of Lundbeck's revenues and Ebixa represented 12.2 per cent. Lexapro was one of the world's most often prescribed SSRIs for the treatment of depression and anxiety disorders. Lexapro was launched in 2002 and was marketed globally by Lundbeck and its partners. Unlike most other SSRIs on the market, which had lost patent protection or would lose protection over the next year or two, Lexapro would have patent protection until 2011. Lexapro could expect growth of more than 20 per cent per year until 2011, when its sales would drop off dramatically. Lexapro was a next-generation drug launched to replace the drug Cipram (citalopram), which had lost its

patent protection in major markets. However, Lexapro had proven to be superior to Cipram in controlling many disorders.

Ebixa was Lundbeck's memantine drug for the treatment of AD. This drug was certain to be a major growth engine for Lundbeck. However, due to licensing agreements with Merz and Forest, Lundbeck was prohibited from marketing the drug in Germany or the United States. Lundbeck anticipated that growth in 2006 would be in excess of 25 per cent. Ebixa was forecasted to have strong growth until 2010, when it would lose patent protection.

Lundbeck Asia

Lundbeck products had been available in many Asian countries since the early 1990s. In the past, Lundbeck chose to licence its product for sales and distribution by local pharmaceutical firms. As a result, several of Lundbeck's key products for depression and Alzheimer's had become well known throughout Asia, and had been used as primary psychiatric medications. Seeing the importance of Asia for its long-term growth, Lundbeck decided in the late 1990s to set up wholly owned subsidiaries in each of its markets in Asia and gradually retake its licences. Before this time, Lundbeck had no standalone subsidiaries in Asia. So, controlling its own distribution, sales, and marketing would allow Lundbeck to integrate the Asian markets into the Lundbeck strategy of specialization, speed, integration, and results. By the early 2000s, Lundbeck had established subsidiaries in most Asian markets.

The Asian subsidiaries were joined together as part of a regional group headquartered in Hong Kong, called Lundbeck Asia. In total, Lundbeck Asia consisted of eight country subsidiaries: China, Hong Kong, Indonesia, Malaysia, Pakistan, the Philippines, Singapore, and Thailand. Due to unfavourable market conditions, Lundbeck did not initially establish any successful distribution channels in South Korea.

Lundbeck established a subsidiary in Japan, but had not been able to generate any sales there. The complexity of the regulations surrounding exclusivity rights in Japan made it very difficult

[11] *Datamonitor*, "H. Lundbeck A/S," New York, 2009, p. 16.

for Lundbeck to market its drugs in the Japanese market. One of the biggest hurdles was that Japanese regulators required that the data used in the application documentation for exclusivity be gathered in Japan.

The purpose of Lundbeck Asia was to provide control, support, guidance, and direction for the Lundbeck subsidiaries in the region. The management team consisted of regional vice president Asif Rajar, plus a regional product manager, a regional finance officer, and a regional regulatory affairs officer. The management at Lundbeck Asia was tasked with implementing Lundbeck's strategy in Asia and ensuring that it be executed appropriately in each country. Since Lundbeck was just entering these markets, the regional management was also charged with developing a sense of corporate identity and pride.

The Korean Pharmaceutical Market

In 2005, the South Korean pharmaceutical market was the 11th largest in the world (see Exhibit 1). The past 10 years had been revolutionary for the Korean pharmaceutical market because the prescription drug market in Korea was quite underdeveloped prior to 2001. Without a doctor's prescription, pharmacists were able to dispense any medicine that was legal for sale. Thus, existing medications were available from pharmacists upon request. However, beginning in 2001, Korea divided pharmaceuticals into prescription only and over-the-counter (OTC) medication. This caused a surge in the prescription drug market.

After the Asian financial meltdown in 1997 (known in Korea as the IMF crisis – because the Korean government needed to secure large loan agreements from the International Monetary Fund), the Korean government began a process of opening up markets to foreign multinational enterprises (MNEs). Before 2000, any MNE wishing to enter the Korean pharmaceutical market needed to have a joint venture with a Korean company. In addition, prior to 2000, it would have been very difficult for a pharmaceutical firm to establish a subsidiary in Korea unless it was prepared to establish production facilities. While not an absolute legal requirement, a firm that was trying to sell imported medicine could expect to receive very unfair treatment from regulators, price boards, and practitioners.

CNS Pharmaceuticals in Korea

Even though the market share for treatment of CNS disorders was growing fast, it was still quite small compared to the rest of the Korean pharmaceutical market. This was because mental disorders were not given high legitimacy in Asian societies like Korea; thus, there were limited resources for treating people who suffered from mental illness. Instead, Korean society gave priority and medical resources to physically life-threatening diseases such as cancer and heart disease.

There were stigmas surrounding mental disorders everywhere in the world, but in South Korea these were very pronounced. Only a few years earlier, anyone with depression would have tried to conceal it. However, this had begun to change in 2005 after the son of a well-known businessman committed suicide and it was publicly announced that he had suffered from depression. The situation repeated itself soon after, when a very popular Korean film actress committed suicide. These incidents sent shock waves through society. The Korean people simply could not comprehend how someone with so much success could possibly take their own life. However, these unfortunate situations led to a greater public discourse on, and improved understanding of, mental illness. As such, Korean society had begun to experience greater openness around depression during the last five years.

In 2001, when the Korean pharmaceutical market was divided into prescription only and over-the-counter (OTC) medication, the government insurance policy began to pay for CNS prescription medication. The CNS industry began to see market increases of 30 to 40 per cent per year, making CNS medications a nearly three quarters of a billion dollar industry by 2005.[12] Growth estimations were projected to continue at the same pace for the next several years. In an

---

[12] Calculated based on available data.

established market, such as the United States or Western Europe, sales had the potential for growing at one or two per cent per year.

Lundbeck Korea

While many of the big pharmaceutical companies had entered the Korean market, to Lundbeck, Korea did not seem like a significant market in the 1990s. Moreover, Lundbeck had centralized production, and it was not prepared to allow production outside of Denmark or Italy just to enter a very small market. In fact, in 1996, one of Lundbeck's key drugs, Cipram, was licensed to a Korean firm and registered for sale; however, it was never marketed because of the requirement to have the drug manufactured in Korea.

Lundbeck Korea was established in March 2002, after Lundbeck could justify the establishment of a subsidiary based on developments in the Korean market. The original plan was to establish the Korean and Japanese subsidiaries as one unit separate from the rest of Asia. However, immediately after Lundbeck Korea was established, the executives in Copenhagen chose to have the managers in Lundbeck Korea report to Lundbeck Asia, the regional headquarters. Jin-Ho Jun was hired as the country manager of Korea. Jun reported directly to Rajar in Hong Kong, who reported to Andersen in Copenhagen.

Even though Lundbeck was a small actor in the South Korean market, it quickly established a strong reputation. Lundbeck worked primarily with the hospitals because Koreans generally preferred to seek treatment at hospitals rather than private clinics. They considered the medical staff to be more competent at major hospitals and saw major hospitals as having superior facilities and equipment. With a few exceptions, major hospitals were generally part of large university systems.

Jin-Ho Jun

Jun had the two essential qualities that Lundbeck needed to help establish its subsidiary in this unfamiliar market: he had almost fifteen years of experience in the CNS market in Korea, which made him a local expert; and he had spent most of his career working for multi-national pharmaceutical companies. This gave him the global mindset needed to carry out Lundbeck's strategies and corporate policies. Jun began working for the German multinational pharmaceutical company Bayer in 1990 as a CNS product manager. He was quite successful and was promoted to strategic product manager in 1996. In 1999, he left Bayer to work at an American MNE, Eli Lilly, as its product manager of neuroscience and eventually as its senior product manager. At Bayer and Lilly, Jun developed a deep and rich knowledge of the Korean CNS pharmaceutical market.

Perhaps even more importantly, especially in Korea, Jun developed a very good network of relationships with the top Korean psychiatrists. He devoted considerable time and effort to ensuring high-quality relationships with these important opinion leaders. This was not an easy or painless endeavour. In Korea, good relationships were built up over time, and involved numerous hours eating and socializing during evening social gatherings. To establish the quality of network that Jun had achieved, a person must be willing to sacrifice a great deal of family time. These social meetings were a very important forum for professional discussions and sales pitches.

The State of Local Management

To Jun's mind, choosing how much control and supervision to place on local managers was always tricky in Korea. Sitting in on meetings as a junior manager, he repeatedly heard the Korean managers explain with great frustration to the regional and headquarters managers that the non-Korean managers did not understand the uniqueness of the Korean market. On the other hand, it was difficult for the parent company managers to trust the Korean managers: the educational backgrounds, communication skills, and global knowledge of the Korean managers were usually inferior to those of their foreign counterparts. While their local knowledge was essential, they did not have the necessary management skills. However, because of foreign managers' imperfect knowledge of the Korean market, they were apt to make strategic miscalculations.

In 2005, Jun knew that the Korean pharmaceutical market had become similar to markets in other developed nations. Local knowledge and skills, while still important, were not quite as important as they were 20 years earlier. Meanwhile, Korean managers' communication skills, management skills, and global knowledge needed to succeed in an MNE were much more sophisticated than they were 20 years ago. As a consequence, Jun believed that Korean subsidiaries now required less supervision and control.

Asif Rajar

Being part of Lundbeck Asia had advantages for Lundbeck Korea. Asif Rajar helped establish Lundbeck Korea. Located in Hong Kong, he could easily maintain tight control over the Asian operation. Rajar had extensive experience with Lundbeck throughout Asia, spending many years with Lundbeck in Thailand, Indonesia and other Southeast Asian countries. Though he was a Swiss citizen through marriage, Rajar was originally from Pakistan, giving him a background with both a European and Asian mindset. He was bright and well educated, having achieved his MBA from a top business school in the United States, where he was now often invited to give guest lectures.

Rajar was very active in helping the Asian country managers run their businesses, and was enjoying very good success. He involved himself in all areas of planning and even took the time to interview candidates for important staff positions before the country manager hired them. Rajar requested that all decisions be cleared with him, and involved himself quite heavily in the strategic plans of the subsidiaries under his control. As regional vice president, Rajar was focused on implementing Lundbeck's strategy in Asia. His success was measured on how well he was able to execute that strategy and grow the Asia region.

Rajar's goals were to launch and market Lundbeck's newest and most innovative products; to control costs and preserve resources; to create effective communication channels between the corporate office and Lundbeck's customers (doctors, regulators, and patients) in order to respond quickly to their needs; to reduce risks by ensuring that all ethical standards were being followed; and to have an understanding of the strengths and weaknesses of each of his markets.

Rajar was a very direct communicator and provided very clear guidelines to Jun. His expectations were unambiguous and he was able to illustrate a comprehensible path for Lundbeck Korea that followed the Lundbeck strategy. Before Jun sent any report or proposal to the head office, Rajar took the time to review the reports and provide Jun with feedback and suggestions. Rajar provided active assistance to Jun on how to communicate with the management team in Copenhagen. Because Rajar had extensive experience in management, his guidance was indispensible. He was also adept at paying attention to the details of local business. Rajar also organized extremely helpful meetings and conferences for the Asian country managers. Rajar facilitated meetings where country managers could share their best practices and discuss ways of developing local programs and handling difficult situations. Through these meetings, the Lundbeck Asia managers gained a sense of association and pride in being part of Lundbeck. Overall, Rajar was a good coach and mentor and was a significant player in the creation and execution of the business plan for Lundbeck Korea.

The First Lundbeck Product in Korea: Cipram

Lundbeck began by marketing Cipram, the forerunner of Lexapro, in the newly established Korean subsidiary in 2002. For the purpose of distributing and marketing Cipram, Lundbeck entered into a sales alliance with Whanin, a local Korean firm, by establishing a separate business unit. Each firm agreed to invest an increasing number of resources into the Cipram business unit each year. However, this business unit was only established for the marketing of Cipram. If Lundbeck were to launch a different class of drugs, it would do so on its own or under a separate arrangement.

The launching of Cipram was Lundbeck Korea's first of many successful attempts to debunk local myths. Initially, many industry leaders doubted the success of Cipram, as it would be the fifth SSRI in the market. Since the other four products were well established and better priced, there was little chance for the launch of Cipram to be successful. However, within three years, Lundbeck was able to capture almost 8.3 per cent of the highly competitive and generic-filled market with Cipram, thereby making Lundbeck Korea a major market player. As a comparison, the other major anti-depressant medications in the Korean market in 2005 were Seroxat (12 per cent of market share), Effexor (11 per cent), and Paxil CR (five per cent). The rest of the market was dominated by generics. This initial success allowed Jun to gain an upper hand that gave Lundbeck an advantage in future contract negotiations with the local partner.

The Launch of Ebixa

Ebixa was the only medication available for the treatment of severe stages of Alzheimer's. All other drugs on the market only targeted mild and moderate cases. Since most Alzheimer's patients would enter the severe stage long before they died of the disease, Ebixa was an important medication. In most markets, Lundbeck sold Ebixa as a new product; and in fact, Ebixa had been registered many years ago by a Korean pharmaceutical firm, but unfortunately it was poorly promoted in the Korean market.

Since Ebixa had been registered many years earlier, the price set by the government insurance regulator was very low, in fact well below the current production cost. Jun and his staff combined Lundbeck's competencies with their understanding of the local market. The normal way to convince the insurance regulator to increase the price of a drug was to hire a large law firm and have lawyers present clear and convincing arguments. However, this rarely worked, and so after consultation with an old colleague who was familiar with the politics of medical insurance pricing, Jun chose a different approach. He decided to put Lundbeck's highly specialized knowledge and small size to work by developing personal contacts with members of the regulatory body to win over both their hearts and their

minds. Though, of course, Jun and his staff needed to provide persuasive evidence, they decided that they would also try to win the members over with emotional arguments. Jun argued that:

> Since Korean society is still a Confucian society, we have a very high regard for elder members of society. So, we met the key people and told them that this is the only medicine that can help severe Alzheimer patients. We asked them to imagine if their mother, father or close relative had Alzheimer's. Would you want them to be without medication when they entered the severe state? In this way, we convinced them that the product was necessary, and since it was the only available product on the market, it should have a price equal to other Alzheimer medications.

In the end, they were able to successfully argue for a substantially greater price for Ebixa. By opening up this new market, the Ebixa case demonstrated to Jun that local expertise played a significant role in achieving an unprecedented success in the industry.

The Lexapro Launch: A Conflict of Strategy

Lundbeck focused on streamlining its key products, and on long-term growth in the CNS industry. This included marketing the new and most innovative products. As part of bringing Lundbeck Asia into step with the rest of the Lundbeck group, Rajar believed that it was important that all the subsidiaries kept up to date with Lundbeck's product offerings. Jun's position was somewhat different; he believed that Lundbeck Korea should simply pursue the path that maximized revenue in Korea.

These diverging perspectives became apparent when Lundbeck introduced Lexapro to replace Cipram. The corporate strategy was to launch a switch-over campaign, which involved convincing doctors to stop prescribing a particular drug and switch to that drug's "next generation" product. By 2005, Rajar felt that Lundbeck Asia was ready to participate in this switch-over campaign. Since Cipram had been launched and promoted by local firms for several years in most of the other countries in the Asia region, the brand was well known.

In contrast, Cipram had only just been introduced in Korea. Thus, in the Korean market it was a new drug, which made the Korean situation different in two ways. First, Lundbeck Korea was just beginning to build the brand awareness in Korea; and second, since Cipram had just been launched in Korea, Cipram still had four years in which generic copies could not be introduced into the market. To avoid sending confusing signals to doctors, sales reps and other stakeholders, and to capture the benefits from the exclusivity period, Jun proposed a special Korea strategy. He believed Lundbeck Korea should continue to sell Cipram until the brand was fully established and then introduce Lexapro.

Rajar disagreed. He argued that a generic company might register a generic version of Lexapro. If it did, the generic brand would be the original and Lexapro would become the generic in the Korean market. Jun's team argued that such a possibility would be highly improbable in Korea due to the data that would have to be gathered and presented to the regulatory board. Rajar retorted that while it might be improbable, it was not impossible. As long as any possibility remained, he would not allow it.

Jun, rightly or wrongly, felt that Rajar was using the possibility of a generic brand entering the market as an excuse not to allow Korea to pursue an independent strategy. According to Jun, what Rajar really seemed to be saying was that Korea was part of Lundbeck and the launching of Lexapro was part of the corporate strategy. Lundbeck's strategy of specialization was to promote its newest and most innovative drugs. The tension was clear; Rajar, as regional vice president, was focused on developing a strong Asia market that was integrated into the Lundbeck strategy. Jun, as the country manager of Korea, wanted to build Lundbeck Korea and maximize long-term growth and profits in Korea.

Rajar was the regional boss, and his preference was to put Lexapro on the market as soon as possible. Thus, assuming Lexapro passed all government regulations in a timely manner, it would be launched in Korea in early 2006. The result would be that Jun would face an uphill battle in his switch-over campaign. Since they had only been prescribing it for a few years, many Korean psychiatrists were still very happy with Cipram. The Whanin representatives were upset because they saw Cipram as having good margins and consistent sales. They were not interested in introducing an entirely new product when they were making money on the old one. However, the decision was made final. While this may have been the most visible sign of conflict between Jun and Rajar, there was a growing number of issues that Jun felt Lundbeck Asia was not handling in the best interests of Korea. He felt strongly that Korea was quite different from other countries in the region.

Conflict in the Placement of Marketing Resources

Jun had dedicated an enormous amount of his staff's time and energy on building relationships with the country's top psychiatrists in the CNS industry rather than the more common approach of marketing to a broader base of practitioners. In Jun's opinion, the management of these key opinion leaders was quite important. "Korea is a very hierarchical society. Also, since we only have one culture, we have very strong barriers to becoming influential and powerful; however, once you overcome those barriers you gain extremely high credibility and power in the market." He felt that there was no sense targeting the lower tier of doctors until he had the support of the opinion leaders. A positive endorsement from these doctors would be more effective than any other marketing campaign.

Rajar was keen to make certain that resources were not wasted, costs were controlled and that marketing and business practices were perceived to be beyond reproach. Thus, Rajar believed that this type of selective marketing was risky. A broader marketing approach had worked well in the other Asian markets, and Rajar was not convinced that Korea was much different because other Asian societies were also quite hierarchal. Rajar continued to ask Jun how Lundbeck could justify spending significant amounts of money to target so few individuals. Rajar insisted that Jun should use these resources to fund other programs. He wanted Jun to integrate his approach into the established Lundbeck approach.

In addition, Rajar felt that the client entertainment that occurred in the Korean subsidiary was excessive, and as such a poor business practice. He certainly did not feel that there was a need to spend so much time eating, drinking, and going to karaoke bars with the top doctors. In contrast, Jun felt that Rajar needed to be more open-minded to the Korean situation:

> Rajar didn't understand the importance of our entertainment culture. In Korea, social events generally consist of a main meal in a restaurant, followed by drinking in a bar or pub, and then topped off with a visit to the karaoke bar. Usually when he was in town, he went home after dinner. However, this is our culture and he needed to understand it. When he went home early, it made a poor impression on the people with whom I was trying to build relationships. In Korean culture, togetherness and harmony are very important, but I don't think he understood this.

In terms of cultural understanding, Jun recalled giving a doctor a few small gifts with the Lundbeck logo imprinted on them. The doctor thanked him and told him that the current sales representatives from other foreign companies were so restricted by their global ethical regulations that they could not even bring small gifts. Jun and the doctor agreed that these regulations reflected a poor appreciation for the Korean culture, where it is expected and customary to bring gifts.

Jun's Car and its Effect on Lundbeck's Image

Jun also recalled a story that to him represented the cultural tension that existed with his relationship with Lundbeck Asia and Rajar. For Jun, this was a microcosm of how difficult it was being controlled by the regional office.

> When I first started as Lundbeck Korea country manager, the person who hired me asked me what kind of car I wanted. I thought about

it carefully because it is very important in Korea to match your car with your status – too low of a car and you will not be respected, too high of a car and you will look arrogant. Since I was young and the country manager of a newly established subsidiary, I felt that I needed to be quite modest. The original boss allowed me enough budget to get a stylish midsize car with a 2.5 litre engine. However, I thought that was a little too much for me, so I got one with a smaller engine on a three year lease. Then, in 2005, I had to renew the car. So, I proposed to Rajar that I get a car that was not too high end, but something better than I had been driving. I didn't want anything too fancy; however, as an important symbol to show that our company was growing, I believed that I should have a car of above average status. The symbolism is quite important – my customers really notice this type of thing, so it is important for doing business. So, I proposed that I get a full-size sedan. But he thought that was unnecessary and told me that status is not important and that I should break that type of thinking; however, I cannot change the importance that Koreans place on symbolism. He wanted me to provide him every detail on the cars that I was considering and then insisted I buy a car of similar status as the one I had been driving. When I went out to entertain the opinion leaders, they commented on my car. This was not good for our business. It made it harder for me to gain their respect. Everyone might think this is a small thing, but it is not. It really discourages the local manager and is bad for the company's image.

Lundbeck's Strategy Interpreted by Jun for Korea

Jun believed that he had a very clear understanding of Lundbeck's core strategy. Integrating the uniqueness of Korea with the global beliefs of Lundbeck had always been his goal. In every room in the Lundbeck Korea office was a poster from headquarters that highlighted the strategy of Lundbeck. Jun's goal was to find a balance between integrating local expertise with the overall strategy of Lundbeck.

Jun believed that in order to convince the Korean medical profession and government regulators that Lundbeck's products were substantially more valuable than the products offered by the general pharmaceutical firms and the generic producers, the staff would have to mirror the specialization of the company. So, from the beginning, all key people in Lundbeck Korea were required to have a CNS background. This gave Lundbeck instant credibility and allowed it to quickly establish a foundation in the CNS field. Jun believed that this expertise was the basis for Lundbeck Korea's major achievements.

In respect to speed, he understood that in the Korean market, response times were important. Abandoning the traditional hierarchical organizational structures that were prevalent in Korean firms, Lundbeck Korea established a lean organization with straight reporting lines. Jun believed that this agility in the market was one of Lundbeck's advantages over bigger competitors. It allowed Lundbeck to hear customer demand quickly, discuss options immediately, and implement decisions swiftly.

In respect to integration, Lundbeck's Korean partner Whanin had a very different set of competencies, organizational structure, and business philosophy. As such, it would have been very easy for Lundbeck Korea and Whanin to be constantly butting heads. Do they follow the Lundbeck way or the Whanin way? Using a spirit of integration, Jun chose to avoid this conflict by having each group focus its energies where it had a competitive advantage.

In respect to results, by maintaining focus on the results, Lundbeck Korea easily surpassed the business case set for it. Jun argued that Lundbeck Korea "have been able to constantly add value every year. The key is that we generate better results and add value in everything we do." Lundbeck Korea focused its energies on projects and activities that generated the most income.

The Decision

The question for Andersen, vice president for Lundbeck, was how to move Lundbeck Korea forward. He believed that Rajar had done a very good job implementing Lundbeck's strategy in the Asian markets. In fact, under Rajar's leadership Korea had emerged, in Andersen's opinion, as the market with the most potential. Lundbeck Korea had good protection from generics, a strong government insurance program for reimbursement, decent pricing on its products, a large and growing market, and a highly innovative staff. Rajar had done a very good job at running a tight ship – he focused on control, cost effectiveness, knowledge transfer, and instilling ethical business practices, which are all important roles for a regional manager. However, Andersen wondered if Rajar was putting too little emphasis on developing new and unique opportunities. The question for Andersen was whether Jun would blossom without the controls or whether the lack of guidance would hinder his development. In addition, as the goal was to integrate all aspects of the value chain, Andersen certainly did not want Korea to be off in its own little world.

In addition, there seemed to be a conflict of personalities. In several meetings, Andersen had sensed poor chemistry between Jun and Rajar. He could not exactly put his finger on it, and it was impossible for him to get Jun to open up about this. Andersen believed that an individual's strengths and weaknesses were part of the strategic decision process. Moreover, he wondered whether Lundbeck Korea might blossom under less strict management and at the same time benefit from a direct relationship with the headquarters functions in Copenhagen. Finally, Andersen wanted to find a way to create more focus on Korea in headquarters.

Of course, no decision is made in a vacuum. The Chinese subsidiary, which had been part of the Lundbeck Asia division for many years, was also growing rapidly. Even though China was in a different position than Korea, would the Chinese managers expect the same treatment? And should they receive it? Also, Andersen had to consider his key person in Asia, Asif Rajar. How would he react to having one of his fastest growing units taken away from him?

HARVARD | BUSINESS | SCHOOL

DECEMBER 11, 2009

Christopher A. Bartlett

CASE 4.3 PHILIPS VERSUS MATSUSHITA: THE COMPETITIVE BATTLE CONTINUES

Professor Christopher A. Bartlett prepared the original version of this case, "Philips versus Matsushita: A Portrait of Two Evolving Companies," HBS No. 392-156. This version was prepared by the same author and is a continuation of a series of earlier cases by Professor Bartlett including "Philips versus Matsushita: Preparing for a New Round," HBS No. 399-102, "Philips and Matsushita: A New Century, A New Round", HBS No. 302-049, and "Matsushita Electric Industrial (MEI) in 1987," HBS No. 388-144. HBS cases are developed solely as the basis for class discussion. Cases are not intended to serve as endorsements, sources of primary data, or illustrations of effective or ineffective management.

Throughout their long histories, N.V. Philips (Netherlands) and Matsushita Electric (Japan) had followed very different strategies and emerged with very different organizational capabilities. Philips built its success on a worldwide portfolio of responsive national organizations while Matsushita based its global competitiveness on its centralized, highly efficient operations in Japan.

During the first decade of the 21st century, however, both companies experienced major challenges to their historic competitive positions and organizational models. Implementing yet another round of strategic initiatives and organizational restructurings, the CEOs at both companies were taking their respective organizations in very different directions. At the end of the decade, observers wondered how the changes would affect their long-running competitive battle.

Philips: Background

In 1892, Gerard Philips and his father opened a small light-bulb factory in Eindhoven, Holland. When their venture almost failed, they recruited Gerard's brother, Anton, an excellent salesman and manager. By 1900, Philips was the third largest light-bulb producer in Europe.

Technological Competence and Geographic Expansion

While larger electrical products companies were racing to diversify, Philips made only light-bulbs. This one-product focus and Gerard's technological prowess enabled the company to create significant innovations. Company policy was to scrap old plants and use new machines or factories whenever advances were made in new production technology. Anton wrote down assets rapidly and set aside substantial reserves for replacing outdated equipment. Philips also became a leader in industrial research, creating physics and chemistry labs to address production problems as well as more abstract scientific ones. The labs developed a tungsten metal filament bulb that was a great commercial success and gave Philips the financial strength to compete against its giant rivals.

Holland's small size soon forced Philips to look aboard for enough volume to mass produce. In 1899, Anton hired the company's first export manager, and soon the company was selling into such diverse markets as Japan, Australia, Canada, Brazil, and Russia. In 1912, as the electric lamp industry began to show signs of overcapacity, Philips started building sales organizations in the United States, Canada, and France. All other functions remained highly centralized in Eindhoven. In many foreign countries Philips created local joint ventures to gain market acceptance.

In 1919, Philips entered into the Principal Agreement with General Electric, giving each company the use of the other's patents, while simultaneously dividing the world into "three spheres of influence." After this time, Philips began evolving from a highly centralized company, whose sales were conducted through third parties, to a decentralized sales organization with autonomous marketing companies in 14 European countries, China, Brazil, and Australia.

During this period, the company also broadened its product line significantly. In 1918, it began producing electronic vacuum tubes; eight years later its first radios appeared, capturing a 20% world market share within a decade; and during the 1930s, Philips began producing X-ray tubes. The Great Depression brought with it trade barriers and high tariffs, and Philips was forced to build local production facilities to protect its foreign sales of these products.

Philips: Organizational Development

One of the earliest traditions at Philips was a shared but competitive leadership by the commercial and technical functions. Gerard, an engineer, and Anton, a businessman, began a subtle competition where Gerard would try to produce more than Anton could sell and vice versa. Nevertheless, the two agreed that strong research was vital to Philips' survival.

During the late 1930s, in anticipation of the impending war, Philips transferred its overseas assets to two trusts, British Philips and the North American Philips Corporation; it also moved most of its vital research laboratories to Redhill in Surrey, England, and its top management to the United States. Supported by the assets and resources transferred abroad, and isolated from

their parent, the individual country organizations became more independent during the war.

Because waves of Allied and German bombing had pummeled most of Philips' industrial plant in the Netherlands, the management board decided to build the postwar organization on the strengths of the national organizations (NOs). Their greatly increased self-sufficiency during the war had allowed most to become adept at responding to country-specific market conditions–a capability that became a valuable asset in the postwar era. For example, when international wrangling precluded any agreement on three competing television transmission standards (PAL, SECAM, and NTSC), each nation decided which to adopt. Furthermore, consumer preferences and economic conditions varied: in some countries, rich, furniture-encased TV sets were the norm; in others, sleek, contemporary models dominated the market. In the United Kingdom, the only way to penetrate the market was to establish a rental business; in richer countries, a major marketing challenge was overcoming elitist prejudice against television. In this environment, the independent NOs had a great advantage in being able to sense and respond to the differences.

Eventually, responsiveness extended beyond adaptive marketing. As NOs built their own technical capabilities, product development often became a function of local market conditions. For example, Philips of Canada created the company's first color TV; Philips of Australia created the first stereo TV; and Philips of the United Kingdom created the first TVs with teletext.

While NOs took major responsibility for financial, legal, and administrative matters, fourteen product divisions (PDs), located in Eindhoven, were formally responsible for development, production, and global distribution. (In reality, the NOs' control of assets and the PDs' distance from the operations often undercut this formal role.) The research function remained independent and, with continued strong funding, set up eight separate laboratories in Europe and the United States.

While the formal corporate-level structure was represented as a type of geographic/product matrix, it was clear that NOs had the real power. They reported directly to the management board, which Philips enlarged from four members to 10 to ensure that top management remained in contact with the highly autonomous NOs. Each NO also regularly sent envoys to Eindhoven to represent its interests. Top management, most of whom had careers that included multiple foreign tours of duty, made frequent overseas visits to the NOs. In 1954, the board established the International Concern Council to formalize regular meetings with the heads of all major NOs.

Within the NOs, management structure mimicked the legendary joint technical and commercial leadership of the two Philips brothers. Most were led by a technical manager and a commercial manager. In some locations, a finance manager filled out the top management triad that typically reached key decisions collectively. This cross-functional coordination capability was reflected down through the NOs in front-line product teams, product-group-level management teams, and at the senior management committee of the NOs' top commercial, technical, and financial managers.

The overwhelming importance of foreign operations to Philips, the commensurate status of the NOs within the corporate hierarchy, and even the cosmopolitan appeal of many of the offshore subsidiaries' locations encouraged many Philips managers to take extended foreign tours of duty, working in a series of two- or three-year posts. This elite group of expatriate managers identified strongly with each other and with the NOs as a group and had no difficulty representing their strong, country-oriented views to corporate management.

Philips: Attempts at Reorganization

In the late 1960s, the creation of the European Common Market eroded trade barriers and diluted the rationale for independent country subsidiaries. New transistor-based technologies demanded larger production runs than most national plants could justify, and many of Philips' competitors were moving production of electronics to new facilities in low-wage areas in Asia and South America.

Simultaneously, Philips' ability to bring its innovative products to market began to falter, and in the 1960s it watched Japanese competitors capture the mass market for audiocassettes and microwave ovens, two technologies it had invented. A decade later, it had to abandon its V2000 videocassette format–superior technically to Sony's Beta or Matsushita's VHS–when North American Philips decided to outsource a VHS product which it manufactured under license from Matsushita.

Over the next four decades, seven chairmen experimented with reorganizing the company to deal with its growing problems. Yet, in 2009, Philips' financial performance remained poor and its global competitiveness was still in question. (See Exhibits 1 and 2.)

Van Reimsdijk and the Yellow Booklet

Concerned about what one magazine described as "continued profitless progress," newly appointed CEO Hendrick van Riemsdijk created an organization committee to prepare a policy paper on the division of responsibilities between the PDs and the NOs. In 1971, their report, dubbed the "Yellow Booklet," outlined the disadvantages of Philips' matrix organization in 1971: "Without an agreement [defining the relationship between national organizations and product divisions], it is impossible to determine in any given situation which of the two parties is responsible.... As operations become increasingly complex, an organizational form of this type will only lower the speed of reaction of an enterprise."

On the basis of this report, van Reimsdijk proposed rebalancing the managerial relationships between PDs and NOs–"tilting the matrix towards the PDs" in his words–to allow Philips to decrease the number of products marketed, build scale by concentrating production, and increase the product flows across NOs. He proposed closing the least efficient local plants and converting the best into International Production Centers (IPCs), each supplying many NOs. In so doing, van Reimsdijk hoped that PD managers would gain control over manufacturing operations. Due to the political and organizational

Exhibit 1
Philips Group Summary Financial Data, 1970–2008 (Reported in millions of Dutch Guilders (F) to 1996; Euros (€) after 1997

	2008	2000	1990	1980	1970
Net sales	€26,385	€37,862	F55,764	F36,536	F15,070
Income from operations (excluding restructuring)	N/A	N/A	2,260	1,577	1,280
Income from operations (including restructuring)	551	3,022	-2,389	N/A	N/A
As a percentage of net sales	2.1%	8.0%	-4.3%	4.3%	8.5%
Income after taxes	N/A	N/A	F-4,447	F532	F446
Net income from normal business operations	(178)	9,577	-4,526	328	435
Stockholders' equity (common)	16,267	15,847	11,165	12,996	6,324
Return on stockholders' equity	-1.0%	60.4%	-30.2%	2.7%	7.3%
Distribution per common share, par value F10 (in guilders)	€0.7	€0.36	F0.0	F1.80	F1.70
Total assets	33,048	38,541	51,595	39,647	19,088
Inventories as a percentage of net sales	12.8%	13.9%	20.7%	32.8%	35.2%
Outstanding trade receivables in month's sales	1.9	1.6	1.6	3.0	2.8
Current ratio	1.2	1.2	1.4	1.7	1.7
Employees at year-end (in thousands)	121	219	273	373	359
Selected data in millions of dollars:					
Sales	$36,868	$35,564	$33,018	$16,993	$4,163
Operating profit	770	2,838	1,247	734	N/A
Pretax income	155	9,587	-2,380	364	N/A
Net income	(260)	9,078	-2,510	153	120
Total assets	46,169	35,885	30,549	18,440	5,273
Shareholders' equity (common)	22,697	20,238	6,611	6,044	1,747

Source: Annual reports; Standard & Poor's Compustat®; Moody's Industrial and International Manuals.
Note: Exchange rate

Guilder/Dollar	1970	3.62
	1980	2.15
	1990	1.68
Euro/Dollar	2000	0.94
	2008	1.40

difficulty of closing local plants, however, implementation was slow.

Rodenberg and Dekker: "Tilting the Matrix"

In the late 1970s, van Riemsdijk's successor, Dr. Rodenburg, continued his thrust. Several IPCs were established, but the NOs seemed as powerful and independent as ever. He furthered matrix simplification by replacing the dual commercial and technical leadership with single management at both the corporate and national organizational levels. Yet the power struggles continued.

Upon becoming CEO in 1982, Wisse Dekker outlined a new initiative. Aware of the cost advantage of Philips' Japanese counterparts, he closed inefficient operations–particularly in Europe where 40 of the company's more than 200 plants were shut. He focused on core operations by selling peripheral businesses such

Exhibit 2
Philips Group, Sales by Product and Geographic Segment, 1985–2003 (Reported in millions of Dutch Guilders (F) to 1996; Euros (€) after 1997)

	2003		2000		1995		1990		1985	
Net Sales by Product Segment:										
Lighting	€4,634	16%	€5,051	13%	F8,353	13%	F7,026	13%	F7,976	12%
Consumer electronics	9,415	33	14,681	39	22,027	34	25,400	46	16,906	26
Domestic appliances	2,183	7	2,107	6	–		–		6,664	10
Professional products/Systems	–		–		11,562	18	13,059	23	17,850	28
Components/Semiconductors	3,984	14%	10,440	28	10,714	17	8,161	15	11,620	18
Software/Services	–		–		9,425	15	–		–	
Medical systems/Health care	6,138	21	3,030	8	–		–		–	
Origin	–		716	2	–		–		–	
Miscellaneous	4,455	15	1,831	5	2,381	4	2,118	4	3,272	5
Total	28,627		37,862	100%	64,462	100%	F55,764	100%	F64,266	100%
Operating Income by Sector:										
Lighting	591		668	16%	983	24%	419	18%	F910	30%
Consumer electronics	254		374	9	167	4	1,499	66	34	1
Domestic appliances	407		287	7	–		–		397	13
Professional products/Systems	–		–		157	4	189	8	1,484	48
Components/Semiconductors	-336		1,915	45	2,233	55	-43	-2	44	1
Software/Services	–		–		886	22	–		–	
Medical systems	441		169	4	–		–		–	
Origin	–		1,063	25	–		–		–	
Miscellaneous	-845		-113	-3	423	10	218	10	200	7
Increase not attributable to a sector	–		-82	-2	(805)	(20)	-22	-1	6	0
Total	513		4,280	100%	4,044	100%	2,260	100%	F3,074	100%

Source: Annual reports.

Notes:

Totals may not add due to rounding.

Product sector sales after 1988 are external sales only; therefore, no eliminations are made; sector sales before 1988 include sales to other sectors; therefore, eliminations are made.

Data are not comparable to consolidated financial summary due to restating.

welding, energy cables, and furniture making, while simultaneously acquiring an interest in Grundig and Westinghouse's North American lamp activities.

He also continued to "tilt the matrix," giving PDs product management responsibility, but leaving NOs responsible for local profits. And he allowed NOs to input into product planning, but gave global PDs the final decision on long-range direction. Still sales declined and profits stagnated.

Van der Klug's Radical Restructuring

When Cor van der Klugt succeeded Dekker as chairman in 1987, Philips had lost its long-held consumer electronics leadership position to Matsushita, and was one of only two non-Japanese companies in the world's top ten. Its net profit margins of 1% to 2% not only lagged behind General Electric's 9%, but even its highly aggressive Japanese competitors' slim 4%. Van der Klugt set a profit objective of 3% to 4% and made beating the Japanese companies a top priority.

As van der Klugt reviewed Philips' strategy, he designated various businesses as core (those that shared related technologies, had strategic importance, or were technical leaders) and non-core (stand-alone businesses that were not targets for world leadership and could eventually be sold if required). Of the four businesses defined as core, three were strategically linked: components, consumer electronics, and telecommunications and data systems. The fourth, lighting, was regarded as strategically vital because its cash flow funded development. The non-core businesses included domestic appliances and medical systems which van der Klugt spun off into joint ventures with Whirlpool and GE, respectively.

In continuing efforts to strengthen the PDs relative to the NOs, van der Klugt restructured Philips around the four core global divisions rather than the former 14 PDs. This allowed him to trim the management board, appointing the displaced board members to a new policy-making Group Management Committee. Consisting primarily of PD heads and functional chiefs, this

body replaced the old NO-dominated International Concern Council. Finally, he sharply reduced the 3,000-strong headquarters staff, reallocating many of them to the PDs.

To link PDs more directly to markets, van der Klugt dispatched many experienced product-line managers to Philips' most competitive markets. For example, management of the digital audio tape and electric-shaver product lines were relocated to Japan, while the medical technology and domestic appliances lines were moved to the United States.

Such moves, along with continued efforts at globalizing product development and production efforts, required that the parent company gain firmer control over NOs, especially the giant North American Philips Corp. (NAPC). Although Philips had obtained a majority equity interest after World War II, it was not always able to make the U.S. company respond to directives from the center, as the V2000 VCR incident showed. To prevent replays of such experiences, in 1987 van der Klugt repurchased publicly owned NAPC shares for $700 million.

Reflecting the growing sentiment among some managers that R&D was not market oriented enough, van der Klugt halved spending on basic research to about 10% of total R&D. To manage what he described as "R&D's tendency to ponder the fundamental laws of nature," he made the R&D budget the direct responsibility of the businesses being supported by the research. This required that each research lab become focused on specific business areas (see Exhibit 3).

Finally, van der Klugt continued the effort to build efficient, specialized, multi-market production facilities by closing 75 of the company's 420 remaining plants worldwide. He also eliminated 38,000 of its 344,000 employees–21,000 through divesting businesses, shaking up the myth of lifetime employment at the company. He anticipated that all these restructurings would lead to a financial recovery by 1990. Unanticipated losses for that year, however–more than 4.5 billion Dutch guilders ($2.5 billion)–provoked a class-action law suit by angry American investors, who alleged that positive projections by the company had been misleading. In a surprise

Exhibit 3
Philips Research Labs by Location and Specialty, 1987

Location	Size (staff)	Specialty
Eindhoven, The Netherlands	2,000	Basic research, electronics, manufacturing technology
Redhill, Surrey, England	450	Microelectronics, television, defense
Hamburg, Germany	350	Communications, office equipment, medical imaging
Aachen, W. Germany	250	Fiber optics, X-ray systems
Paris, France	350	Microprocessors, chip materials, design
Brussels	50	Artificial intelligence
Briarcliff Manor, New York	35	Optical systems, television, superconductivity, defense
Sunnyvale, California	150	Integrated circuits

Source: Philips, in *Business Week*, March 21, 1988, p. 156.

move, on May 14, 1990, van der Klugt and half of the management board were replaced.

Timmer's "Operation Centurion"

The new president, Jan Timmer, had spent most of his 35-year Philips career turning around unprofitable businesses. Under the banner "Operation Centurion," he lost no time in launching an initiative that cut headcount by 68,000 or 22% over the next 18 months, earning Timmer the nickname "The Butcher of Eindhoven." Because European laws required substantial compensation for layoffs–Eindhoven workers received 15 months' pay, for example–the first round of 10,000 layoffs alone cost Philips $700 million. To spread the burden around the globe, Timmer asked his PD managers to negotiate cuts with NO managers. But according to one report, country managers were "digging in their heels to save local jobs." Nonetheless, cuts came–many from overseas operations.

To focus resources further, Timmer sold off various businesses including integrated circuits to Matsushita, minicomputers to Digital, defense electronics to Thomson and the remaining 53% of appliances to Whirlpool. Yet profitability was still well below the modest 4% on sales he promised. In particular, consumer electronics lagged with slow growth in a price-competitive market. The core problem was identified by a 1994 McKinsey study that estimated that value added

per hour in Japanese consumer electronic factories was still 68% above that of European plants.

After three years of cost-cutting, in early 1994 Timmer finally presented a new growth strategy to the board. His plan was to expand software, services, and multimedia to become 40% of revenues by 2000. He was betting on Philips' legendary innovative capability to restart the growth engines. He hired Hewlett-Packard's director of research and encouraged him to focus on developing 15 core technologies. The list, which included interactive compact disc (CD-i), digital compact cassettes (DCC), high definition television (HDTV), and multimedia software, was soon dubbed "the president's projects." Over the next few years, Philips invested over $2.5 billion in these technologies. But the earlier divestment of some of the company's truly high-tech businesses and a 37% cut in R&D personnel left it with few who understood the technology of the new priority businesses.

By 1996, it was clear that Philips' analog HDTV technology would not become industry standard, that its DCC gamble had lost out to Sony's Minidisc, and that CD-i was a marketing failure. And while costs in Philips were lower, so too was morale, particularly among middle management. Critics claimed that the company's drive for cost-cutting and standardization had led it to ignore new worldwide market demands for more segmented products and higher consumer service.

Boonstra's Reorganization

When Timmer stepped down in October 1996, the board replaced him with a radical choice for Philips–an outsider whose expertise was in marketing and Asia rather than technology and Europe. Cor Boonstra was a 58-year-old Dutchman whose years as CEO of Sara Lee, the U.S. consumer products firm, had earned him a reputation as a hard-driving marketing genius. Joining Philips in 1994, he headed the Asia Pacific region and the lighting division before being tapped as CEO.

Unencumbered by tradition, he announced strategic sweeping changes designed to reach his goal of increasing return on net assets from 17% to 24% by 1999. "There are no taboos, no sacred cows," he said. "The bleeders must be turned around, sold, or closed." Within three years, he had sold off 40 of Philips' 120 major businesses–including such well known units as Polygram and Grundig.

Promising to transform a structure he described as "a plate of spaghetti" into "a neat row of asparagus," he then initiated a major worldwide restructuring. "How can we compete with the Koreans?" he asked. "They don't have 350 companies all over the world. Their factory in Ireland covers Europe and their manufacturing facility in Mexico serves North America. We need a more structured and simpler manufacturing and marketing organization to achieve a cost pattern in line with those who do not have our heritage. This is still one of the biggest issues facing Philips."

Within a year, 3,100 jobs were eliminated in North America and 3,000 employees were added in Asia Pacific, emphasizing Boonstra's determination to shift production to low-wage countries and his broader commitment to Asia. And after three years, he had closed 100 of the company's 356 factories worldwide. At the same time, he replaced the company's 21 PDs with 7 divisions, but shifted day-to-day operating responsibility to 100 business units, each responsible for its profits worldwide. It was a move designed to finally eliminate the old PD/NO matrix. Finally, in a move that shocked most employees, he announced that the 100-year-old Eindhoven headquarters would be relocated to Amsterdam with only 400 of the 3000 corporate positions remaining.

By early 1998, he was ready to announce his new strategy. Despite early speculation that he might abandon consumer electronics, he proclaimed it as the center of Philips' future. Betting on the "digital revolution," he planned to focus on established technologies such as cellular phones (through a joint venture with Lucent), digital TV, digital videodisc, and web TV. Furthermore, he committed major resources to marketing, including a 40% increase in advertising to raise awareness and image of the Philips brand and de-emphasize most of the 150 other brands it supported worldwide–from Magnavox TVs to Norelco shavers to Marantz stereos.

While not everything succeeded (the Lucent cell phone JV collapsed after nine months, for example), overall performance improved significantly in the late 1990s. By 2000, Boonstra was able to announce that he had achieved his objective of a 24% return on net assets.

Kleisterlee's Refocusing

By the time the Boonstra stepped down in May 2001, however, a global "tech wreck" recession had begun, resulting in what Fortune described as "a tidal wave of red ink" to greet the new CEO, Gerard Kleisterlee, a 54-year-old career Philips man. With the share price in free fall from $60 in $2001 to $13 in 2002, Kleisterlee faced what he described as "the biggest losses in the history of the company."

Moving quickly, the new CEO began restructuring the company, announcing the outsourcing of Philips mobile phone production to CEC of China, and the production of VCRs to Japan's Funai Electric. But it was not sufficient to prevent a 2001 loss of €2.6 billion compared to a €9.6 billion profit in 2000. So, over the next few years, he continued to outsource production of TVs, CD players, and components, while simultaneously moving the remaining in-house production to low-cost countries like China, Poland, or Mexico. He also sold off several businesses including most components, mobile phones, audio, and even the core semiconductor business. Within four years he had removed more than one in four Philips employees, reducing headcount by 60,000.

But Kleisterlee felt he faced a bigger challenge. "Phillips never really had any kind of strategy," he conceded. "If our engineers could make it, we would try to sell it... In 2001, we were still focused on a broad range of volatile, high-volume products like consumer electronics, semi-conductors, and components. Now we are trying to create a company that generates value in a more predictable way with a portfolio that is less volatile."

The shape of that new portfolio soon became clear. Using funds generated by selling businesses, Kleisterlee began acquiring companies in the high-growth medical and lighting segments, and began referring to Philips as "a lifestyle company" centered on health and well-being. "We came to the conclusion that the thing that holds everything together is not the fact that we made our own components and semiconductors. It's the fact that we have a common mission," he said.

A business once at the center of Philips portfolio now had a new role. "Consumer electronics is a very, very small leftover part in our lifestyle portfolio," he explained. "That business is too big a battle to fight now. We plan to be the Dell of consumer electronics, making less and marketing more. That means that we will be focused on product development, brand, and channel management."

So while Phillips continued to create innovations for its TVs, it focused them on its high-definition plasma and LCD sets with breakthroughs like Pixel Plus 2, a digital technology that refined the incoming signal to produce sharper pictures with more vivid color. But in addition to technological breakthroughs, R&D was also focused on more basic products for developing markets – hand-crank radios, high powered mixers designed for exotic foods, and irons with dust tolerant thermostats.

Phillips approach to marketing was also changing. In the developed world, it slashed the number of retail chains it serviced from 600 to 200, focusing particularly on seven giants like Wal-Mart, Tesco, and Carrefour. But in developing countries, it took a different approach. For example in India, its strategy was to sell its adapted low-end products through 35,000 village stores.

Kleisterlee explained how his adaptive product-market strategy worked: "In India, we have vans with diagnostic and lab equipment, equipped with a satellite video link to a top hospital. Instead of making long trips to a city hospital, people can now get cheaper, more convenient treatment where they live." With 700 million people in rural India, the company felt it had a great opportunity.

By 2008, Kleisterlee was ready to confirm his new focused strategy in the organization structure. Having earlier cut the number of divisions to five (there have been 14 as recently as 1995), in early 2008, he defined just three – healthcare, lighting, and consumer lifestyle. "We have to organize around markets," he said. "We're going to organize from the outside in."

But competition in consumer electronics remained brutal, especially in a growing global recession. In late 2008, Philips licensed Funai to make and market TVs under the Philips name in North America. A few months later, it extended that license to cover other markets as well as products such as DVDs, home theater, Blu-Ray, and other products. "We spent the 1980s and 1990s restructuring and trying to find our way," Kleisterlee said. "My goal is to leave behind a company on a successful part to steady, profitable growth." Some wondered whether he had found that path.

Matsushita: Background

In 1918, 23 year old Konosuke Matsushita (or "KM" as he was affectionately known), invested ¥100 to start production of double-ended sockets in his modest home. The company grew rapidly, expanding into battery-powered lamps, electric irons, and radios. On May 5, 1932, Matsushita's 14th anniversary, KM announced to his 162 employees a 250-year corporate plan, broken into 25-year sections, each to be carried out by successive generations. His plan was codified in a company creed and in the "Seven Spirits of Matsushita" (see Exhibit 4), which provided the basis

Exhibit 4
Matsushita Creed and Philosophy (Excerpts)

Creed
Through our industrial activities, we strive to foster progress, to promote the general welfare of society, and to
   devote ourselves to furthering the development of world culture.

Seven Spirits of Matsushita
> Service through Industry
> Fairness
> Harmony and Cooperation
> Struggle for Progress
> Courtesy and Humility
> Adjustment and Assimilation
> Gratitude

KM's Business Philosophy (Selected Quotations)
"The purpose of an enterprise is to contribute to society by supplying goods of high quality at low prices in
   ample quantity."

"Profit comes in compensation for contribution to society.... [It] is a result rather than a goal."

"The responsibility of the manufacturer cannot be relieved until its product is disposed of by the end user."

"Unsuccessful business employs a wrong management. You should not find its causes in bad fortune,
   unfavorable surroundings or wrong timing."

"Business appetite has no self-restraining mechanism.... When you notice you have gone too far, you must
   have the courage to come back."

Source: Christopher A. Bartlett, *Matsushita Electric Industrial (MEI) in 1987*, HBS No. 388–144 (Boston: Harvard
Business School Publishing, 1988) p. 17.

of the "cultural and spiritual training" all new employees received on joining the company.

In the post-war boom, Matsushita introduced a flood of new products: TV sets in 1952; transistor radios in 1958; color TVs, dishwashers, and electric ovens in 1960. Capitalizing on its broad line of 5,000 products, the company opened 25,000 domestic retail outlets – 40% of appliance stores in Japan in the late 1960s. These not only assured sales volume, but also gave the company direct access to market trends. When post-war growth slowed, however, product line expansion and an excellent distribution system no longer insured growth, and the company looked to export markets.

The Organization's Foundation: Divisional Structure

Plagued by ill health, KM began to delegate more than was typical in Japanese companies. In 1933, Matsushita became the first Japanese company to adopt a divisional structure. In addition to creating a "small business" environment, the structure generated internal competition that spurred each business to drive growth by leveraging its technology to develop new products. But after the innovating division had earned substantial profits on its new product, the "one-product-one-division" policy was to spin it off as a new division to maintain the "hungry spirit."

Management provided each division with funds to establish largely self-sufficient development, production, and marketing capabilities. Corporate treasury operated like a commercial bank, reviewing divisions' loan requests for which it charged slightly higher-than-market interest, and accepting interest-bearing deposits on their excess funds. Divisional profitability was determined after deductions for central services and interest on internal borrowings. Each division paid 60% of earnings to headquarters and financed working capital and fixed asset needs from the retained 40%. Transfer prices were based on the market and settled through the treasury on normal commercial terms. KM expected uniform performance across the company's 36 divisions, and division managers whose operating profits fell below 4% of sales for two successive years were replaced.

While basic technology was developed in a central research laboratory (CRL), product development and engineering occurred in each of the product divisions. Matsushita intentionally under-funded the CRL, forcing it to compete for additional funding from the divisions. Annually, the CRL publicized its major research projects to the product divisions, which then provided funding for CRL to develop technology for marketable applications. Rarely the innovator, Matsushita was usually very fast to market–earning it the nickname "Manishita," or copycat.

Matsushita: Internationalization

Although the establishment of overseas markets was a major thrust of the second 25 years in the 250-year plan, in an overseas trip in 1951 KM had been unable to find any American company willing to collaborate with Matsushita. The best he could do was a technology exchange and licensing agreement with Philips. Nonetheless, the push to internationalize continued.

Expanding Through Color TV

In the 1950s and 1960s, trade liberalization and lower shipping allowed Matsushita to build a healthy export business with its black and white TV sets. In 1953, the company opened its first overseas branch office–the Matsushita Electric Corporation of America (MECA). With neither a distribution network nor a strong brand, the company had to resort to selling through mass merchandisers and discounters under their private brands.

During the 1960s, pressure from national governments in developing countries led Matsushita to open plants Southeast Asia and Central and South America. As manufacturing costs in Japan rose, the company shifted more basic production to these low-wage countries, but almost all high-value components and subassemblies remained in its scale-intensive Japanese plants. By the 1970s, political pressure forced Matsushita to establish assembly operations in the Americas and Europe. In 1972, it opened a plant in Canada; in 1974, it bought Motorola's TV business in the United States; and in 1976, it for him built a plant in Wales to supply the European Common Market.

Building Global Leadership Through VCRs

The birth of the videocassette recorder (VCR) propelled Matsushita into first place in the consumer electronics industry during the 1980s. Recognizing the potential mass-market appeal of the professional broadcast VCR first developed in 1956 by Californian company Ampex, Matsushita began developing the technology. It launched its commercial broadcast video recorder in 1964, and two years later, introduced a consumer version.

Subsequently, a battle over VCR format developed. In 1975, Sony introduced the technically superior "Betamax" format, and in 1976, JVC launched a competing "VHS" format. Under pressure from MITI, Japan's industrial planning ministry, Matsushita agreed to give up its own format and adopt the VHS standard. During its 20 years of development, Matsushita's research team lived the VCR product cycle, moving from CRL to the product division's development labs, and eventually to the plants producing VCRs.

Between 1977 and 1985, Matsushita increased VCR capacity 33-fold to 6.8 million units, not only to meet its own needs, but also those of OEM customers like GE, RCA, Philips, and Zenith, who decided to forego self-manufacture and outsource to the low-cost Japanese. Increased volume enabled Matsushita to slash prices 50% within five years of launch. In parallel, the company licensed the VHS format to other manufacturers, including Hitachi, Sharp, Mitsubishi and, eventually, Philips. By the mid-1980s, VCRs accounted for 30% of Matsushita's sales and 45% of its profits.

Changing Systems and Controls

In the mid-1980s, Matsushita's growing number of overseas companies reported to the parent in one of two ways: wholly owned, single-product global plants reported directly to the appropriate product division, while overseas sales and marketing subsidiaries and overseas companies producing a broad product line for local markets reported to Matsushita Electric Trading Company (METC), a separate legal entity. (See Exhibit 5 for METC's organization.)

Throughout the 1970s, product divisions maintained strong operating control over their offshore operations. They had plant and equipment designed by the parent company, followed manufacturing procedures dictated by the center, and used materials from Matsushita's domestic plants. By the 1980s, increased local sourcing gradually weakened the divisions' direct control, so instead of controlling inputs, they began to monitor output – quality and productivity levels for example.

Headquarters-Subsidiary Relations

Although METC and the product divisions set detailed sales and profits targets for their overseas subsidiaries, they told local managers they had autonomy on how to achieve them. But as "Mike" Matsuoko, president of the European source in Cardiff, Wales emphasized, failure forfeited freedom: "Losses show bad health and invite many doctors from Japan who provide advice and support."

Exhibit 5 Organization of METC, 1985

1985 Organization:

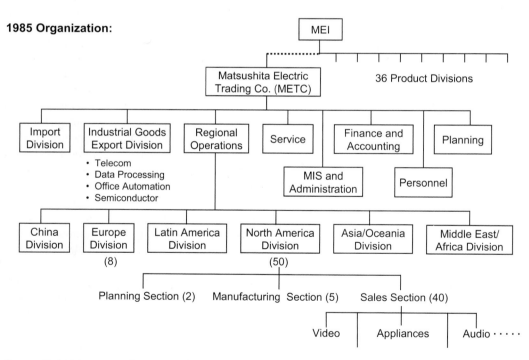

Source: Christopher A. Bartlett, *Matsushita Electric Industrial (MEI) in 1987*, HBS No. 388–144 (Boston: Harvard Business School Publishing, 1988) p. 23.
Note: ( ) = number of people.

In the mid-1980s, Matsushita had over 700 expatriate Japanese managers and technicians on foreign assignment for four to eight years, primarily to play a "vital communication role." Explained one senior executive, "Even if a local manager speaks Japanese, he would not have the long experience that is needed to build relationships and understand our management processes."

Expatriate managers were located throughout foreign subsidiaries, but there were a few positions that were almost always reserved for them. The most visible were subsidiary general managers whose main role was to translate Matsushita philosophy abroad. Expatriate accounting managers were expected to "mercilessly expose the truth" to corporate headquarters; and Japanese technical managers were sent to transfer product and process technologies and provide headquarters with local market information. These expatriates maintained relationships with senior colleagues in their divisions, who acted as career mentors, evaluated performance (with some input from local managers), and provided expatriates with information about parent company developments.

Subsidiary general managers visited Osaka at least two or three times each year–some as often as every month. Corporate managers reciprocated these visits, and on average, major operations hosted a headquarters manager each day of the year. Face-to-face meetings were considered vital: "Figures are important," said one manager, "but the meetings are necessary to develop judgment." Daily faxes and nightly phone calls from headquarters to offshore expatriates were considered vital.

Yamashita's "Operation Localization"

Although international sales kept rising, growing host country pressures caused concern about the company's highly centralized operations. In 1982, Matsushita's newly appointed president Toshihiko Yamashita launched "Operation Localization" to boost offshore production from less than 10% of value-added to 25%, or half of overseas sales, by 1990. To support the target,

he set out a program of four localizations–personnel, technology, material, and capital.

Over the next few years, Matsushita increased the number of local nationals in key positions. In the United States, for example, American became presidents of three of six local companies, while in Taiwan the majority of division heads were replaced by Chinese managers. In each case, however, local national managers were supported by Japanese advisors who maintained direct links with the parent company. To localize technology and materials, the company developed local subsidiaries' expertise in sourcing equipment locally, modifying designs to local requirements, incorporating local components, and adapting corporate processes and technologies to accommodate the changes. And by the mid-1980s, offshore production subsidiaries were free to buy minor supplies from local vendors, but still had to buy key components from internal sources.

One of the most successful innovations was to give overseas sales subsidiaries more choice over the products they sold. Each year the company held a two-week internal merchandising show and product planning meeting where product divisions exhibited the new lines. Here, foreign subsidiary managers negotiated for changes in product features, quantities, and even prices for products they felt would better meet their local needs. Product division managers, however, could overrule the sales subsidiary if they thought introduction of a particular product was of strategic importance.

President Yamashita's hope was that Operation Localization would help Matsushita's overseas companies develop the innovative capability and entrepreneurial initiatives that he had long admired in the NOs of rival Philips.[1] Yet despite his four localizations, overseas companies continued to act primarily as the implementation

---

[1] Past efforts to develop such capabilities abroad had failed. For example, when Matsushita acquired Motorola's TV business in the United States, the U.S. company's highly innovative technology group atrophied as American engineers resigned in response to what they felt to be excessive control from Japan's highly centralized R&D operations.

arms of Japanese-based product divisions. Unusually for a Japanese CEO, Yamashita publicly expressed his unhappiness with the lack of initiative at the TV plant in Cardiff. Despite the transfer of substantial resources and the delegation of many responsibilities, he felt that the plant remained too dependent on the center.

Tanii's Integration and Expansion

Yamashita's successor, Akio Tanii, expanded on his predecessor's initiatives. In 1986, in an effort to integrate domestic and overseas operations, he brought all foreign subsidiaries under the control of METC, then merged METC into the parent company. Then, to shift operational control nearer to local markets, he relocated major regional headquarters functions from Japan to North America, Europe, and Southeast Asia. Yet still he was frustrated that the overseas subsidiary companies acted as little more than the implementing agents of the Osaka-based product divisions.

Through all these changes, however, Matsushita's worldwide growth continued, generating huge reserves. With $17.5 billion in liquid financial assets at the end of 1989, the company was referred to as the "Matsushita Bank." Frustrated by their inability to develop innovative overseas companies, top management decided to buy them. To obtain a software source for its hardware businesses, in 1991 the company acquired MCA, the U.S. entertainment giant, for $6.1 billion. Within a year, however, Japan's bubble economy had burst, and almost overnight, Tanii had to shift the focus from expansion to cost containment. Despite his best efforts, the problems ran too deep. With 1992 profits less than half their 1991 level, the board took the unusual move of forcing Tanii to resign in February 1993.

Morishita's Challenge and Response

At 56, Yoichi Morishita was the most junior of the company's executive vice presidents when he was tapped as the new president. In a major strategic reversal, he sold 80% of MCI to Seagram, booking a $1.2 billion loss on the transaction. Over the following 18 months, under the slogan "simple, small, speedy and strategic," he then moved 6,000 staff to operating jobs.

Yet the company continued to struggle. Japan's domestic market for consumer electronics collapsed–from $42 billion in 1989 to $21 billion in 1999. And the rise of new competition– from Korea, then China–created a global glut, then a price collapse. With a strong yen making its exports uncompetitive, Matsushita's product divisions shifted production offshore, mostly to low-cost countries like China and Malaysia. By the end of the decade, its 160 factories outside Japan employed 140,000 people–about the same number of employees as in its 133 plants in Japan. Yet management seemed unwilling to close inefficient Japanese plans or lay off staff with the commitment of lifetime employment. Despite Morishita's promises, internal resistance prevented his implementation of much of the promised radical change.

In the closing years of the decade, Morishita began emphasizing the need to develop technology and innovation offshore. Concerned that only 250 of the company's 3,000 R&D scientists and engineers were located outside Japan, he began investing in R&D partnerships and technical exchanges, particularly in emerging fields. For example, an 1998, he signed a joint R&D agreement with the Chinese Academy of Sciences, China's leading research organization. Later that year, he announced the establishment of the Panasonic Digital Concepts Center in California. Its mission was to act as a venture fund and an incubation center for the new ideas and technologies emerging in Silicon Valley. To some it was an indication that Matsushita had given up trying to generate new technology and business initiatives from its own overseas companies.

Nakamura's Transformation

In June 2000, Kunio Nakamura, the 38-year veteran who had headed MEI's North American operations was named president. Operating profits were 2.2% of sales, with consumer electronics generating only 0.4% due to losses in the

TV and VCR divisions. Just as Morishita had promised seven years earlier, the new CEO vowed to raise operating margins to 5% in three years.

By December, Nakamura was ready to announce his first three-year plan dubbed "Value Creation 21" or VC 21. Its main objective was to build a "super manufacturing company" on three foundations: a strong technology-based components business, a flexible and responsive manufacturing capability, and customer-oriented, solutions-based businesses. The new CEO emphasized the need to retain Matsushita's fully integrated value chain, justifying it with a "smile curve" which promised high returns in both upstream components and downstream services and solutions to offset lower returns in the highly competitive consumer electronics products in the middle of the value chain.

At the core of VC 21 was a plan to close inefficient scale-driven plants and concentrate production in Manufacturing Centers, facilities transformed from old mass production assembly lines to modern flexible manufacturing cells. The transformation would be implemented first in Japanese mother plants, and then rolled out to the 170 plants it had worldwide.

Furthermore, as part of a plan to replace Matsushita's historic fragmented and compartmentalized structure with a "flat web-based organization", Nakamura separated plants from product divisions which now had to source their products from non-captive and non-exclusive Manufacturing Centers. Sales and marketing was also stripped from the once powerful product divisions, and absorbed in one of two global marketing organizations, one for appliances and the other for consumer electronics. "It was a cultural revolution," said one manager.

But the strong financial performance Nakamura had assumed would support his plan, disappeared with the "tech wreck" recession of 2001, resulting in Matsushita's first quarterly loss in its history. The CEO and immediately announced five emergency measures to reverse the situation. In one bold move, the company dropped its lifetime employment practice and offered early retirement to 18,000 employees.

Over 13,000 accepted, not only reducing costs, but also allowing a new generation of managers to emerge. In total, the domestic workforce was cut by 25,000, and 30 inefficient plants were closed.

Despite these efforts, in March 2002 Matsushita announced an operating loss of ¥199 billion ($1.7 billion), and an even more shocking loss of ¥428 billion ($3.7 billion) including restructuring charges. Calling the situation "an intolerable social evil", Nakamura committed to delivering profit of ¥100 billion the next year. He told his executives that because implementation of his emergency measures had not been satisfactory, he was launching a management improvement initiative. He challenged them to deliver "a V-shaped recovery" driven by V-Products – innovative, customer-focused products launched rapidly into global markets, at competitive prices. He focused 70% of investments on consumer electronics and semiconductors, urging his managers to move past Matsushita's reputation for slow innovation and imitation. "In the digital age, there is no room for imitators," he said.

To eliminate the internal competitiveness he felt that had constrained the turnaround, he grouped all businesses into one of three closely linked domains – Digital Networks (primarily consumer electronics, mobile phones, and telecom), Home Appliances (including lighting and environmental systems), and Components (with semiconductors, batteries, and motors.)

In March 2004, at the end of the three year "VC 21" plan, the company reported a profit of ¥185 billion ($1.9 billion) on sales of ¥7,500 billion ($72 billion). As impressive as the result was, it was still less than half of the promised 5% operating margin. So Nakamura announced a new three-year plan called "Leap Ahead 21" with a 5% objective for 2007 as an interim step on the way to 10% by 2010.

Ohtsubo's Inheritance

In April 2006, after announcing operating profits of $3.6 billion, Nakamura announced that he would step down as CEO in June. Spontaneously,

Exhibit 6
Matsushita, Summary Financial Data, 1970–2000[a]

	2008	2000	1995	1990	1985	1980	1975	1970
In billions of yen and percent:								
Sales	¥9,069	¥7,299	¥6,948	¥6,003	¥5,291	¥2,916	¥1,385	¥932
Income before tax	527	219	232	572	723	324	83	147
As % of sales	5.8%	3.0%	3.3%	9.5%	13.7%	11.1%	6.0%	15.8%
Net income	¥282	¥100	¥90	¥236	¥216	¥125	¥32	¥70
As % of sales	3.1%	1.4%	1.3%	3.9%	4.1%	4.3%	2.3%	7.6%
Cash dividends (per share)	¥35.00	¥14.00	¥13.50	¥10.00	¥ 9.52	¥7.51	¥6.82	¥6.21
Total assets	7,443	7,955	8,202	7,851	5,076	2,479	1,274	735
Stockholders' equity	3,742	3,684	3,255	3,201	2,084	1,092	573	324
Capital investment	503	355	316	355	288	NA	NA	NA
Depreciation	320	343	296	238	227	65	28	23
R&D	554	526	378	346	248	102	51	NA
Employees (units)	305,828	290,448	265,397	198,299	175,828	107,057	82,869	78,924
Overseas employees	170,265	143,773	112,314	59,216	38,380	NA	NA	NA
As % of total employees	56%	50%	42%	30%	22%	NA	NA	NA
Exchange rate (fiscal period end; ¥/$)	100	103	89	159	213	213	303	360
In millions of dollars:								
Sales	$90,949	$68,862	$78,069	$37,753	$24,890	$13,690	$4,572	$2,588
Operating income before depreciation	8,424	4,944	6,250	4,343	3,682	1,606	317	NA
Operating income after depreciation	NA	1,501	2,609	2,847	2,764	1,301	224	NA
Pretax income	4,263	2,224	2,678	3,667	3,396	1,520	273	408
Net income	2,827	941	1,017	1,482	1,214	584	105	195
Total assets	74,648	77,233	92,159	49,379	21,499	11,636	4,206	2,042
Total equity	37,530	35,767	36,575	20,131	10,153	5,129	1,890	900

Source: Annual reports; Standard & Poor's Compustat®; Moody's Industrial and International Manuals.
[a] Data prior to 1987 are for the fiscal year ending November 20; data 1988 and after are for the fiscal year ending March 31.

analysts at the presentation gave him a standing ovation, a unique event in reserved Japan. His successor, Eumio Ohtsubo, previously head the consumer electronics business, embraced Naka-mura's commitment to surpass Samsung's 9.4% operating margin by 2010.

Having led effort making Matsushita the world's leading plasma TV maker, Ohtsubo committed to dominating the fast-growing flatscreen market by investing Its $1.3 billion cash balance in focused R&D and more efficient global production. He wanted to build an ability to develop, manufacture, and launch superior new products twice a year, globally. "We will absolutely not be beaten in the flat-panel TV business," he said.

Exhibit 7
Matsushita, Sales by Product and Geographic Segment, 1985–2000 (billion yen)

	2008	2000		1995		FY 1990		FY 1985	
By Product Segment:									
Audio, Video, Communications Networks	¥4,319	–	–	–		–		–	–
Video and Audio Equipment	–	¥1,706	23%	¥1,827	26%	¥2,159	36%	¥2,517	48%
Electronic components	–	–	–	893	13	781	13	573	11
Home appliances and household equipment	1,316	1,306	18	–	–	–	–	–	–
Home appliances	–	–	–	916	13	802	13	763	14
Communication and industrial equipment		–	–	1,797	26	1,375	23	849	16
Batteries and kitchen-related equipment	–	–	–	374	4	312	5	217	4
Information and communications equipment	–	2,175	28	–	–	–	–	–	–
Industrial equipment	–	817	11	–	–	–	–	–	–
Components	1,399	1,618	21	–	–	–	–	–	–
Others	123	–	–	530	8	573	10	372	7
Total	¥9,069	¥7,682	100%	¥6,948	100%	¥6,003	100%	¥5,291	100%
By Geographic Segment:									
Domestic	¥6,789	¥3,698	51%	¥3,455	50%	¥3,382	56%	¥2,659	50%
Overseas	5,404	3,601	49	3,493	50	2,621	44	2,632	50
Corporate	(3,120)								

Source: Annual reports.
Notes: Total may not add due to rounding.

In January 2008, he surprised many when he announced the change in the company's name from Matsushita to Panasonic, reflecting the name of the company's best-known brand. It was part of Ohtsubo's efforts to grow overseas revenues from less than 50% to 60% by 2010. Still, with Panasonic in 78th place on the Interbrand survey of the world brand recognition, he had a way to go.

But any talk about foreign sales growth evaporated when the global financial crisis struck in 2008. In the December quarter, company sales slid 20%, while operating profit plunged 84%.

Immediately Ohtsubo initiated a review of the company's 170 overseas plants, vowing to shut down any with operating profit of less than 3%, or declining sales over three years. The review resulted in the closure of 27 plants, and the lay off 15,000 workers. But the global crisis hit hard, and with restructuring charges and write-offs, the company projected a $4.2 billion loss for the full year ending in March 2009. The carefully laid plans for $90 billion in revenues and 10% operating margin by 2010 were vanishing dreams.

⚜IVEY | Publishing

CASE 4.4 BEIERSDORF AG: EXPANDING NIVEA'S GLOBAL REACH[1]

On April 26, 2012, Stefan F. Heidenreich walked into the conference center in Hamburg, Germany, for Beiersdorf's annual stockholder meeting. There, he would officially be introduced as the new chief executive of the NIVEA producer and take the reins in a time of transition and complex challenges. His predecessor, Thomas-Bernd Quaas, was to give his farewell speech in front of 800 shareholders. Quaas had been the CEO for the past seven years and had led the company's international expansion. The company's flagship brand, NIVEA, had turned 100 years old last year and consumers around the world were familiar with the cream in the signature blue tin. The expansion was not only geographical but also categorical: a number of innovations had resulted in a broad product range under the NIVEA brand.

However, this expansion was hurting profitability. While competitors like Henkel, Unilever, and Procter & Gamble had recovered from the economic recession and were expanding rapidly, Beiersdorf's revenues were still lagging expectations. As a consequence, the company had announced a major restructuring project costing €270 million in March 2010. Under the slogan "Focus on skin care. Closer to markets," Beiersdorf aimed at reorganizing its consumer division to boost revenues again. The objective was to increase profitability by downsizing structures and streamlining the expansive product range, while remaining responsive to local tastes by granting foreign subsidiaries more responsibility.

As Quaas spoke about the progress of the restructuring project, it became clear that it was far from complete. Although most measures were on target, operating margins were still not satisfactory.[2] Just a few months earlier, Beiersdorf had announced a plan to cut up to 1,000 jobs worldwide. The progress of restructuring had been slower than planned because the challenges

---

[1] This case has been written on the basis of published sources only. The interpretation and perspectives presented in this case are not necessarily those of Beiersdorf or any of its employees.

[2] Daniela Stürmlinger, "Hamburger Nivea-Hersteller: Aktionäre kritisieren Beiersdorf-Vorstand," *Hamburger Abendblatt*, www.abendblatt.de/ hamburg/article2259390/Aktionaere-kritisieren-Beiersdorf-Vorstand.html, accessed September 15, 2012.

had been bigger than expected.[3] In fact, the last quarter of 2011 had ended with a loss. Thus, an investor at the annual stockholder meeting voiced his opinion: "The management has been asleep for the past few years instead of setting the course for the company's future!"[4] This outcry raised numerous questions: Was Beiersdorf's restructuring approach the right way to get back on track? Would the company be able to compete against the big players in the industry again? And was downsizing really the right path to international growth? Heidenreich had certainly taken on a major task.

Background

In 1882, Paul C. Beiersdorf, owner of a pharmacy in Hamburg, Germany, filed a patent for the manufacturing process of medical sticking plasters, which he had developed in collaboration with leading dermatologists. Through academic publications, the company acquired popularity among doctors and pharmacists, which helped to increase revenues. In 1890, the associated laboratory was sold to the pharmacist Dr. Oscar Troplowitz, who turned the small enterprise into a rapidly growing consumer products manufacturer with a consumer care and a sticking plasters/adhesives division. In accordance with the company's medical and academic background, Dr. Troplowitz continued to focus on a highly scientific research and development process.

Around 1900, a chemist at Beiersdorf discovered the emulsifying agent *Eucerit*, which allowed for a stable combination of oil and water. This discovery laid the foundation for the unique skin moisturizing formula of the NIVEA cream. The first NIVEA cream tin was sold in 1911. It provided good results at low cost and quickly became popular among a broad range of consumers. Beiersdorf was quick to continue to deliver innovations such as Labello, a creamy colorless lipstick, and other care products. The sticking plasters segment grew as well, with innovations such as Hansaplast and Leukoplast.

In 1922, Beiersdorf was turned into a public company. The success of the young company's brands, especially NIVEA, gave it the opportunity to expand internationally. By the beginning of World War II, Beiersdorf had 34 representative offices abroad (in countries including the United States, Mexico, Brazil, and Thailand) and subsidiaries in England and Austria. As a result of the war, the trademark rights for NIVEA in these international locations were confiscated by the respective countries. It took years for Beiersdorf to regain all the rights, a process that ended in 1997 with the repurchase of the rights in Poland.

These setbacks, however, did not stop Beiersdorf from expanding internationally again after the war. By the end of the fiscal year 2011, the company employed 17,666 people, owned more than 150 subsidiaries worldwide, and earned 85 per cent of its total revenues (€4.75 out of €5.6 billion) outside of Germany.

Throughout its 130-year history, Beiersdorf repeatedly emphasized traditional values such as trust, reliability, and quality. This was in accordance with the tradition of the "Hanseatic merchant" – in the old trading town of Hamburg, businessmen took pride in the fact that they concluded reliable contracts with a simple handshake. Thus, the company built on its traditional foundations and continuous innovations to attain its vision: "To become the best skin care company in the world."

---

[3] "Gewinnrueckgang: Konzernumbau lastet schwer auf Beiersdorf," *Financial Times Deutschland*, www.ftd.de/unternehmen/industrie/:gewinnrueckgang-konzernumbau-lastet-schwer-auf-beiersdorf/60159302.html, accessed September 21, 2012.

[4] Translation. Daniela Stürmlinger, "Hamburger Nivea-Hersteller: Aktionäre kritisieren Beiersdorf-Vorstand," op. cit.

Company Structure

Divisions/Regions

Due to its origins, Beiersdorf was divided into two rather unrelated divisions. The main division, *consumer*, generated the lion's share of the company's revenues at 84 per cent, or €4.73 billion,

Exhibit 1
Beiersdorf Subsidiaries

Region	Countries with subsidiaries
North America	United States, Canada
South America	Argentina, Bolivia, Brazil, British Virgin Islands, Chile, Costa Rica, Dominican Republic, Ecuador, El Salvador, Guatemala, Colombia, Mexico, Panama, Paraguay, Peru, Uruguay, Venezuela
Europe	Belgium, Bulgaria, Denmark, Germany, Estonia, Finland, France, Greece, United Kingdom, Ireland, Iceland, Italy, Croatia, Latvia, Lithuania, Macedonia, Netherlands, Norway, Austria, Poland, Portugal, Serbia, Romania, Russia, Sweden, Slovakia, Slovenia, Spain, Czech Republic, Turkey, Ukraine, Hungary
Africa	Ghana, Kenya, Morocco, South Africa
Asia	China, India, Indonesia, Japan, Kazakhstan, South Korea, Malaysia, Singapore, Thailand, United Arab Emirates, Vietnam
Australia	Australia, New Zealand

Source: www.beiersdorf.de.

in 2011. In this division, about 13,870 employees worked to serve three segments: the mass market, the dermo-cosmetic segment, which offered medical care products, and the premium segment. Each segment had very successful brands: the leading global brands were NIVEA for the mass market, Eucerin for the dermo-cosmetic segment, and La Prairie for the premium segment.

The other division, *tesa*, was named after its main brand and became a legally independent subsidiary in 2001. About 3,795 employees developed adhesives for industrial and consumer clients. In 2011, the tesa division contributed 16 per cent of Beiersdorf's total revenue. After major restructuring efforts, which ended in 2010, as well as the recovery of the auto industry, which was one of the main buyers of adhesives, the tesa division outperformed the consumer division in terms of growth rates: while the consumer division grew by 1.1 per cent in 2011, tesa reported growth of 7.9 per cent.

In 2011, the consumer division generated 59 per cent of its revenue in Europe (of which 15 per cent came from Germany), 12 per cent in Latin America, 7 per cent in North America, and 22 per cent in Africa, Asia, and Australia combined. A network of more than 150 subsidiaries ensured that these markets were served reliably

(see Exhibit 1). Moreover, Beiersdorf exported to 200 countries, making it a company with a truly global reach.

In an earlier effort to reduce costs and become more profitable, Beiersdorf closed many of its 20 European facilities between 2006 and 2008.[5] By 2012, Beiersdorf owned 16 production facilities including locations in Germany, Spain, Poland, Argentina, Chile, Brazil, Mexico, Indonesia, India, China, Thailand, and Kenya. Throughout Beiersdorf's current restructuring project, even more production facilities were either closed (e.g. in Germany and the United States) or put up for sale (e.g. in Switzerland).

For years, much of Beiersdorf's internationalization strategy focused on securing profits in mature markets such as Europe. Among these, Germany continued to be one of Beiersdorf's most important. In 2011, sales within the consumer division were €717 million, which accounted for 34 per cent of all sales in the European market. At the same time, Beiersdorf invested in exploring new opportunities for

[5] "Beiersdorf strafft seine Produktion," *Financial Times Deutschland*, www.ftd.de/unternehmen/industrie/: beiersdorf-strafft-die-produktion/31664.html, accessed September 17, 2012.

growth in some of the BRIC nations (Brazil, Russia, India, and China). In fact, between 2010 and 2011, consumer sales in Latin America and Eastern Europe (including Russia) grew by 15.2 and 5.2 per cent, respectively – as opposed to a 3.7 per cent decrease in Western European sales (excluding Germany, which decreased by 3.2 per cent).

However, not all of the internationalization strategy worked as smoothly as Beiersdorf had hoped. Despite its long experience with international expansion, Beiersdorf faced difficulties, especially with regards to entering new emerging countries. In 2007, the company acquired 85 per cent of the shares of C-Bons, China's third-largest hair care producer, for €269 million. The objective was to enhance awareness of the NIVEA brand in the Chinese market by benefiting from C-Bons's distribution and sales network. However, the returns on this investment were slow in coming. In 2011, the investment resulted in a €50 million loss because the Chinese brand could not prevail over international competitors who had entered the Chinese market. As a result, unsold products filled C-Bons's warehouses. Moreover, the distribution and sales network turned out to be heavily focused on non-target areas, whereas Beiersdorf's initial intention was to use C-Bons's network to distribute the NIVEA brand throughout the large Chinese market, mostly to metropolises. As a consequence of this unsuccessful acquisition, Beiersdorf had to lay off about 4,000 Chinese workers and report massive write-offs, and the newly appointed executive board member James C. Wei left the company by the end of 2011.[6]

The U.S. market was identified as another area with major potential for growth. Despite intensive marketing efforts, profits remained sluggish[7] and revenues increased by a meager 2.1 per cent in 2011. After pursuing a strategy of deemphasizing non-focus brands, a process which had started in 2007, Beiersdorf remained present in the U.S. market with its core skin care brands like Eucerin and NIVEA. Since then, Beiersdorf outperformed its closest category competitors in terms of sales growth by at least 5.2 percentage points.[8] In total, however, the North American market accounted for only 6 per cent (€300 million) of Beiersdorf's total revenues.[9]

Management and Ownership

In accordance with German corporate governance law, the management of Beiersdorf was divided into two distinct committees. While the executive board was in charge of developing a company strategy and putting it into action, the supervisory board's task was to assist the executive board in developing the strategy while taking the interests of various stakeholders (e.g. employees, investors) into consideration.

Until April 26, 2012, the *executive board* (composed of Peter Feld, Ralph Gusko, Dr. Ulrich Schmidt, and Ümit Subaşi) was chaired by the CEO Thomas-Bernd Quaas. Quaas was born in 1952 and entered the company in 1979 as a trainee. He worked his way up through a sales/marketing career until he ascended to the CEO position in 2005. He was described as a manager who was so enthusiastic about Beiersdorf's brands that he preferred them over any other brands, even in his personal life.[10] When Quaas became the CEO, subordinates and employee representatives described him as "smart and very

---

[6] Christoph Kapalschinski, "Beiersdorf und sein Ringen um den Klassenerhalt," *Handelsblatt*, www.handelsblatt.com/unternehmen/industrie/hauptversammlung-beiersdorf-und-sein-ringen-um-den-klassenerhalt/6555266.html, accessed September 16, 2012.

[7] Ibid.

[8] "Kalender & Präsentationen - Investorenkonferenz German Investment Seminar (New York)," Beiersdorf AG, www.beiersdorf.de/Investoren/Kalender_Pr%C3%A4sentationen/2010.html, accessed September 29, 2012.

[9] Birger Nicolai, "Beiersdorf steht in China vor einem Scherbenhaufen," *Die Welt*, www.welt.de/wirtschaft/article13898137/Beiersdorf-steht-in-China-vor-einem-Scherbenhaufen.html, accessed September 29, 2012.

[10] Thiemo Heeg, "Porträt: Der Nivea-Mann," *Frankfurter Allgemeine Zeitung*, www.faz.net/aktuell/wirtschaft/portraet-der-nivea-mann-1233868.html, accessed October 1, 2012.

warm in interaction." "He is a very open, team-minded, communicative person. And he is one of us."[11]

Heidenreich's appointment as CEO came as a surprise to shareholders and employees[12] and marked a major change from the company's previous tradition of appointing CEOs from within the company. Heidenreich came from the food producer Hero as a replacement for Quaas. There had been an internal heir apparent for the CEO position for years, the former board member Markus Pinger (responsible for brands & supply chain), but he surprisingly announced he would leave the company by June 30, 2011 in the midst of the restructuring process. Pinger knew the company inside out and Quaas had been hopeful that Pinger would put it back on track and lead it to its former success. Pinger's departure thus left Beiersdorf in a state of shock and uncertainty. Rumor had it that disagreements about the strategic direction of the repositioning were the reason for the sudden falling out.[13]

Stefan F. Heidenreich, born in 1962, became a member of the executive board on January 1, 2012, before his official appointment as CEO of Beiersdorf on April 26, 2012. In his previous position at Hero, where he had been the CEO for seven years, Heidenreich convinced many investors of his ability to generate continuous profits and grow share prices. Employees at Beiersdorf, however, were skeptical of the company outsider, especially during a time of economic and cultural turmoil.[14] Heidenreich had strong supporters though, including the head of the supervisory board, Dr. Reinhard Pöllath, who had met Heidenreich during an investor meeting and who was the driving force behind convincing him to join Beiersdorf.[15] Like Beiersdorf, Heidenreich's former employer Hero had undergone major restructuring efforts and was controlled in part by a major blockholder. Heidenreich had been especially efficient in managing the blockholder's influence and leading Hero to continuous growth and increased share prices.[16]

Heidenreich was described as strong-willed and dynamic but also risk-seeking and aggressive.[17] He held the title of Vice European Champion in windsurfing[18] and sometimes participated in races with his cross-country motorcycles.[19] In the company's newsletter to employees, he gave a glimpse of what to expect from him: "I know what I want... You have to act – not just react."[20]

The *supervisory board* of Beiersdorf, on the other hand, was composed of twelve members and chaired by Pöllath. Three of the twelve board members represented Beiersdorf's work council,

[11] Translation. "Beiersdorf: 'Mr Nivea' geht - Quaas übernimmt," *Hamburger Morgenpost*, www.mopo.de/news/beiersdorf-mr-nivea-geht—quaas-uebernimmt,5066732,5792958.html, accessed October 1, 2012.

[12] Daniela Stürmlinger, "Nivea-Hersteller Beiersdorf: Thomas B. Quaas: 'Endlich mehr Zeit für die Familie,'" *Hamburger Abendblatt*, www.abendblatt.de/wirtschaft/article2081992/Thomas-B-Quaas-Endlich-mehr-Zeit-fuer-die-Familie.html, accessed October 1, 2012.

[13] "Wechsel im Topmanagement: Beiersdorf beruft Ersatz für Kronprinzen," *Financial Times Deutschland*, www.ftd.de/karriere/management/:wechsel-im-topmanagement-beiersdorf-beruft-ersatz-fuer-kronprinzen/60068592.html, accessed October 1, 2012.

[14] Sven Oliver Clausen, "Kopf des Tages: Stefan Heidenreich - Blaue Hoffnung," *Financial Times Deutschland*, www.ftd.de/unternehmen/industrie/:kopf-des-tages-stefan-heidenreich-blaue-hoffnung/60176444.html, accessed October 1, 2012.

[15] Johannes Ritter and Jürgen Dunsch, "Heidenreich neuer Vorstandsvorsitzender: Ein Frühstücksdirektor für Beiersdorf," *Frankfurter Allgemeine Zeitung*, www.faz.net/aktuell/wirtschaft/unternehmen/heidenreich-neuer-vorstandsvorsitzender-ein-fruehstuecksdirektor-fuer-beiersdorf-11484569.html, accessed September 30, 2012.

[16] Sven Oliver Clausen, "Kopf des Tages: Stefan Heidenreich - Blaue Hoffnung," op. cit.

[17] Mario Brück, "Das neue Gesicht des Nivea-Konzerns," *Wirtschaftswoche*, www.wiwo.de/unternehmen/industrie/beiersdorf-heidenreich-im-profil/5965848-2.html, accessed September 30, 2012.

[18] Translation. Sven Oliver Clausen, "Kopf des Tages: Stefan Heidenreich - Blaue Hoffnung," op. cit.

[19] Mario Brück, "Das neue Gesicht des Nivea-Konzerns," op. cit.

[20] Translation. Sven Oliver Clausen, "Kopf des Tages: Stefan Heidenreich - Blaue Hoffnung," op. cit.

whereas another three members were associated with the investment firm Maxinvest AG, including Pöllath. Maxinvest AG was owned by the Herz family and owned a total of 50.89 per cent of Beiersdorf's shares. This gave the family, and Michael Herz as the CEO of Maxinvest AG especially, major voting right privileges and influence over the executive board members' decisions.

After Quaas's resignation as a member of the executive board, he would be appointed a new member of the supervisory board. This was an uncommon procedure and some felt that it would have been better corporate governance to allow for the usual two-year cooling-off period. Such a period was usually imposed on CEOs after resignation to make sure that they did not hinder the correction of mistakes they had made during their time as executive board members.[21]

Apart from the 50.89 per cent held by the Herz family, Beiersdorf itself owned 9.99 per cent of its shares and had 39.12 per cent in free float. It was listed in the Deutscher Aktien Index (DAX), a German stock exchange index of the country's 30 biggest public companies in terms of market capitalization and order volume.

Research and Development (R&D)

Beiersdorf's commitment to rigorous skin research became apparent when it opened its extended Hamburg-based Global Research Center in 2004. In the 16,000-square-meter (172,222 square foot) building complex, researchers from all over the world collaborated with universities and dermatological institutes to not only work on product innovations but also advance basic skin research. The center was considered one of the biggest and most modern skin research facilities in Europe and one of its highlights was the auditorium: a room with the architectonic shape of a cell. Researchers at Beiersdorf called it the "philosopher's stone" because it housed research efforts that aimed at discovering ingredients that had rejuvenating effects on the skin.

Another feature of the center was its capacity to simulate the climatic conditions of other regions such as Asia or Latin America. Thus, the majority of consumer tests were conducted there, with an annual total of about 1,500 tests with 21,000 test persons to ensure that products met quality standards as well as consumer needs. About 1,000 studies were carried out in countries other than Germany to respond to local consumer preferences. For this purpose of local adaptation, Beiersdorf collaborated with approximately 50 institutes from around the world. This was in accordance with an important part of Beiersdorf's innovation philosophy, especially with regards to NIVEA: "to offer the best skin care for every age, skin type, culture, and location."[22]

For example, in 2008 Beiersdorf launched a product called "Whitening Oil Control" – a whitening cream specifically designed for male Indian consumers with oily skin. A similar product line, Nivea Body Natural Tone, was popular in Latin America, where it helped consumers even their skin tone as a response to sun damage. The local adaptation strategy was so pervasive that many of Beiersdorf's international customers considered NIVEA a local brand.

As a result of this heavy emphasis on innovation and local adaptation, the NIVEA brand had proliferated from its humble beginnings to become the largest skin care brand in the world, incorporating more than 500 products and a variety of product lines (see Exhibit 2). This innovation intensity was also reflected in the fact that about 30 per cent of Beiersdorf's revenue was generated with products that were less than five years old.[23] In 2011 alone, Beiersdorf filed for

---

[21] Sven Oliver Clausen, "Neuer Vorstandschef. Beiersdorf holt Schwartau-Chef," *Financial Times Deutschland*, www.ftd.de/unternehmen/industrie/:neuer-vorstandschef-beiersdorf-holt-schwartau-chef/60112470.html, accessed September 30, 2012.

[22] Translation. "Verschiedene Hauttypen: Verschiedene Bedürfnisse," NIVEA, www.nivea.de/Unser-Unternehmen/beiersdorf/NIVEAHistory#!stories/story02, accessed October 1, 2012.

[23] Thomas Schönen (Beiersdorf AG), "NIVEA," www.beiersdorf.de/GetFile.ashx?id=3061, accessed October 9, 2012.

Exhibit 2
Major Innovations under the Nivea Brand Umbrella

Date of introduction	Product
Dec. 1911	Original NIVEA cream
1919	NIVEA soap
1920	NIVEA hair milk (hair care product line)
1922	NIVEA shaving soap for men
1927	NIVEA bleaching cream
1960	NIVEA baby line
1986	NIVEA for men
1991	NIVEA hair care, NIVEA deodorant
1992	NIVEA body
1993	NIVEA sun, NIVEA visage
1994	NIVEA vital for mature skin
1996	NIVEA bath care
1997	NIVEA beauté
1998	NIVEA visage anti-wrinkle cream Q10, NIVEA hand
. . .	. . .
by 2012	More than 500 products in various product lines

Sources: NIVEA, http://www.nivea.de/Unser-Unternehmen/beiersdorf/NIVEAHistory#!stories/story02, accessed September 17, 2012; Thomas Schönen (Beiersdorf AG), "NIVEA," www.beiersdorf.de/GetFile.ashx?id=3061, accessed October 9, 2012.

81 new product-related patents. R&D expenses were €163 million in 2011 (as opposed to €152 million in 2010) and 967 employees worldwide worked in this area (out of which 564 were in the consumer division and 403 were in the tesa division).

In 2011, Beiersdorf intensified its innovation efforts by launching a web-based open innovation platform called *Pearlfinder*. It enabled external researchers from all over the world to collaborate with Beiersdorf on creative ideas and research proposals with regards to products and packaging. The purpose of this platform was to generate innovative concepts early on in the research process.

Despite this vast research effort and emphasis on innovation, there were some trends that Beiersdorf addressed relatively late. For instance, the first product that responded to consumer preferences towards more natural products was introduced in 2011 – many years after

competitors had already established themselves in the natural cosmetics realm.[24]

Brands

Beiersdorf's portfolio encompassed a total of nine brand families: NIVEA, Eucerin, La Prairie, Labello, Florena, 8&4, Hansaplast, SLEK, and tesa. Of these, the first three were Beiersdorf's global brands.

NIVEA

NIVEA was Beiersdorf's most important brand by revenue and brand awareness. The first NIVEA tin was sold in 1911, which made it almost as

---

[24] "Nivea: Beiersdorf liftet seine Kultmarke," *Wirtschaftswoche*, www.wiwo.de/unternehmen/nivea-beiersdorf-liftet-seine-kultmarke/5262218.html, accessed September 25, 2012.

time-honored a brand as Campbell Soup or Coca
Cola. The brand's name was derived from the
Latin word for snow (nix, nivis) because of the
cream's pure white color. NIVEA soon became a
household brand for many families in booming
post-war economies and the ritual of using the
cream was passed down from parents to children.
Many consumers had childhood memories that
involved the NIVEA brand – for instance, when
families started to have disposable income again
after World War II, they went on vacation and
the preferred choice for sunscreen was NIVEA.
Beiersdorf fostered the connection between its
products and the beach by releasing the now-
famous inflatable NIVEA beach ball – a
marketing strategy so successful that NIVEA distributed about 20 million of these balls due to
popular demand within the past 40 years alone.
The profoundness of such a generation-spanning
product might be reflected in the fact that consumers associated the brand with core values like
trust, honesty, reliability, family, and quality,
even in 2011.

Over the decades, a variety of categories
evolved under the NIVEA brand umbrella, including products for babies, body hygiene, body care,
deodorants, facial care, hair care & styling, care
for men, moisturizers (NIVEA soft), sun screen,
and make-up. All of these categories again had
specific product types subsumed underneath
them; for instance, the *deodorants* category was
divided into spray, roll-on, diffuser, stick, and
cream. However, not only did the products themselves change, but also their design. While the
original NIVEA cream was sold in a tin with a
simple white and blue design, the new products
were now packaged in fashionable designs like
curvy bottles with a color palette ranging from
white to beige, light blue, dark blue, and purple.

In 2011, the brand celebrated its 100th birthday with a major worldwide marketing campaign
"NIVEA – 100 Years Skin Care for Life." In an
effort to bridge the historical origins of the brand
with modern consumer tastes, Beiersdorf initiated
a massive social network campaign with American singer Rihanna as the voice of the anniversary campaign. By the end of 2011, the brand's
Facebook page had 2.7 million fans.

Eucerin

Eucerin was based on the same chemical innovation as NIVEA, the emulsifier *Eucerit*. While
NIVEA's main focus was on personal care, the
Eucerin product line was intended for medical
use. Thus, the first products of the line were soap,
cream, and powder for the treatment of wounds,
and were often recommended by dermatologists.
Beiersdorf's main focus with the Eucerin brand
was on providing the basic ingredients for oint-
ments to pharmacies. This changed in 1950,
when Beiersdorf launched yet another innovation
based on scientific research: the ointment
Eucerin-ph5, which protected the natural acid
mantle of the skin. This was significant because
it marked Beiersdorf's entry into selling ready-
made products to consumers through pharmacies
as the preferred distribution channel.

During the 1960s, the Eucerin product line
evolved from a brand with predominantly medical use to one that could also be applied to more
common issues such as rough skin on hands or
feet. Like NIVEA, the Eucerin brand incorporated
a wide range of innovations, from products for
extra dry skin or atopic eczema to sun protection
and anti-aging. That it was recommended by
dermatologists and sold in pharmacies gave it a
considerable amount of credibility.

In 2011, Eucerin celebrated its 111th birthday
with a global marketing campaign that aimed at
direct interaction with the consumer at the point
of sale. By that time, the brand included eight
product lines, which covered medically relevant
skin issues from head to toe. It was available in
41 countries on four continents and generated
4.8 per cent growth in 2011 compared to the
previous year.

La Prairie

In 1991, Beiersdorf acquired the Laboratoires La
Prairie, a Swiss research company that had
evolved from the renowned Clinique La Prairie
in Montreux. Laboratoires La Prairie was focused
on developing high-end anti-aging skin care
products with ingredients such as caviar and a
substance called Exclusive Cellular Complex.
Soon after the acquisition, Beiersdorf integrated

other high-end brands into the La Prairie group, including Juvena and Marlies Möller beauty hair care. By the end of 2011, the La Prairie brand was available in 17 countries on three continents and reported growth of 3.4 per cent in 2011.

Financial Situation

At the beginning of the global financial crisis in 2008, Beiersdorf reported the best results in its history with €5,971 million in revenues (an 8.4 per cent increase compared to 2007) and earnings before interest and taxes (EBIT) of €797 million (including special items) (see Exhibits 3–4). The consumer division contributed €5,125 million (85.83 per cent) to the company's revenues, while the tesa division reported €846 million (14.17 per cent). This success culminated in Beiersdorf's inclusion in the DAX, Germany's index of the country's top 30 companies in terms of book value and market capitalization, on December 22, 2008.

Just a year later, Quaas started his *Letter to Investors* in the annual report with the statement that "2009 was a difficult year."[25] Although revenues were still at a relatively high level at €5,748 million, the company's growth rates had declined to -0.7 per cent.

By 2012, Beiersdorf had still not returned to its previous strength. At the annual stockholder meeting, the company reported €5,633 million in revenues, less than in 2008. Unlike in previous years, the tesa division was the main driver of growth. Another reason for the delayed recovery was identified in the massive write-downs in the context of the acquisition of C-Bons. These impairment losses accumulated to €213 million between 2010 and 2011. Moreover, the restructuring project not only increased one-time costs by €213 million in 2011 alone, but also led to a decrease in sales in affected countries.

Despite these sobering figures, Beiersdorf was not a poor company by any means. In fact, it enjoyed a comfortable cushion of reserves worth about €2.2 billion.[26] The continuous flow of profits from the NIVEA brand kept the company liquid.

Market Environment and Competition

Beiersdorf was operating in an industry with very strong global competitors, the closest of which were Procter & Gamble, Unilever, L'Oreal, Henkel, and Johnson & Johnson (see Exhibits 5 to 7). The effects of such strong competition were especially apparent in the Western European market, where market saturation was high. Here, Beiersdorf competed for limited shelf space in an economic environment of decreasing market size. In many cases, innovations such as stain-free deodorants were merely designed as a substitute for a competitor's product on the shelves. Thus, Quaas identified "maintaining the current position" as a priority.[27]

The European Union's economic downturn, with Greece announcing its bankruptcy and other countries being on the verge of it, did not help matters. The inflation rate in the European Union grew by 2.7 per cent, while consumer spending practically stagnated at 0.5 per cent in 2011. This economic environment was especially distressing because the European market was where Beiersdorf earned most of its profits. Here, Beiersdorf earned 92 per cent of its EBIT, with 59 per cent of its revenue in the consumer division. Thus, any losses in European market share were especially painful.

At the same time, Beiersdorf was still able to defend the NIVEA product family's position as the biggest skin care brand in the world,[28] with 166 category leadership positions worldwide.[29]

---

[25] Translation. "Finanzberichte - Geschäftsbericht 2009," Beiersdorf AG, www.beiersdorf.de/Investoren/ Finanzberichte/Gesch%C3%A4ftsberichte.html, accessed September 15, 2012.

[26] Christoph Kapalschinski, "Beiersdorf und sein Ringen um den Klassenerhalt," op. cit.

[27] Birger Nicolai, "Beiersdorf steht in China vor einem Scherbenhaufen," op. cit.

[28] Jens Bergmann, "Die Vernuenftige," Brand Eins Online, www.brandeins.de/magazin/qualitaet-ist-was-geht/ die-vernuenftige.html, accessed September 30, 2012.

[29] "Kalender & Präsentationen - Investorenkonferenz German Investment Seminar (New York)," Beiersdorf AG, op. cit.

Exhibit 3
Beiersdorf Balance Sheet 2008–2011

[in million €]	2008	2009	2010	2011
ASSETS				
Intangible assets	398	382	306	172
Property, plant, and equipment	727	725	716	635
Non-current financial assets/securities	11	10	438	686
Other non-current assets	4	2	2	3
Deferred tax assets	36	58	76	87
Non-current assets	**1,176**	**1,177**	**1,538**	**1,583**
Inventories	634	561	632	699
Trade receivables	894	906	1,001	1,019
Other current financial assets	128	91	72	113
Income tax receivables	45	41	63	73
Other current assets	81	96	112	115
Securities	897	955	704	712
Cash and cash equivalents	613	767	973	941
Non-current assets and disposal groups held for sale	-	-	-	20
Current assets	**3,292**	**3,417**	**3,557**	**3,692**
	4,468	**4,594**	**5,095**	**5,275**
LIABILITIES				
Share capital	252	252	252	252
Additional paid-in capital	47	47	47	47
Retained earnings	2,280	2,450	2,609	2,700
Accumulated other consolidated income	-129	-123	-1	3
Equity attributable to equity holders of Beiersdorf AG	**2,450**	**2,626**	**2,907**	**3,002**
Non-controlling interests	10	10	13	14
Equity	**2,460**	**2,636**	**2,920**	**3,016**
Provisions for pensions and other post-employment benefits	235	221	209	190
Other non-current provisions	131	138	117	107
Non-current financial liabilities	72	7	8	5
Other non-current liabilities	6	5	5	4
Deferred tax liabilities	164	161	155	148
Non-current liabilities	**608**	**532**	**494**	**454**
Other current provisions	363	391	486	527
Income tax liabilities	99	107	126	82
Trade payables	690	699	863	946
Other current financial liabilities	174	158	135	172
Other current liabilities	74	71	71	78
Current liabilities	**1,400**	**1,426**	**1,681**	**1,805**
	4,468	**4,594**	**5,095**	**5,275**

Sources: "Finanzberichte - Geschäftsberichte - Ausgewählte Kennzahlen 2009," Beiersdorf AG, www.beiersdorf.de/Investoren/Finanzberichte/Gesch%C3%A4ftsberichte.html, accessed October 20, 2012; "Finanzberichte - Geschäftsberichte - Ausgewählte Kennzahlen 2011," Beiersdorf AG, www.beiersdorf.de/Investoren/Finanzberichte/Aktuelle_Finanzberichte.html, accessed September 30, 2012.

Exhibit 4
Beiersdorf Income Statement and Additional Financials 2008–2011

[in million €]	2008	2009	2010	2011
INCOME STATEMENT*				
Sales	**5,971**	**5,748**	**5,571**	**5,633**
Change against prior year (in %)	8.4	-3.7	7.8	1.1
Consumer	5,125	5,011	4,698	4,696
Tesa	846	737	873	937
Europe	4,090	3,767	3,450	3,414
America	832	851	932	993
Africa/Asia/Australia	1,049	1,130	1,189	1,226
Cost of goods sold	-1,979	-1,882	-2,016	-2,077
Gross profit	**3,992**	**3,866**	**3,555**	**3,556**
Marketing and selling expenses	-2,874	-2,766	-2,336	-2,454
Research and development expenses	-149	-149	-152	-163
General and administrative expenses	-292	-283	-278	-291
Other operating income	108	94	86	158
Other operating expenses	-89	-175	-292	-375
Special factors relating to divestments	96	-	-	-
Special factors relating to the realignment of the consumer supply chain	5	-	-	-
Operating result (EBIT)	**797**	**587**	**583**	**431**
Interest income	47	21	19	31
Interest expense	-14	-15	-13	-19
Net pension result	8	-2	-6	-2
Other financial result	-16	-8	-30	-1
Financial result	**25**	**-4**	**-30**	**9**
Profit before tax	**822**	**583**	**553**	**440**
Taxes on income	-255	-203	-227	-181
Profit after tax	**567**	**380**	**326**	**259**
Profit attributable to equity holders at Beiersdorf AG	562	374	318	250
Profit attributable to non-controlling interests	5	6	8	9
ADDITIONAL FINANCIALS				
Cost of materials**	**1,453**	**1,199**	**1,370**	**1,437**
Personnel expenses**	**922**	**947**	**974**	**1,000**
Basic/diluted earnings per share (in €)	2.48	1.65	1.40	1.10
Dividend per share (in €)	0.90	0.70	0.70	0.70
Beiersdorf's shares – year-end closing price	**42.00**	**45.93**	**41.53**	**43.82**
Market capitalization as of Dec. 31	10,584	11,574	10,466	11,043
Employees as of Dec. 31	**21,766**	**20,346**	**19,128**	**17,666**

* The income statement was prepared according to the cost of sales approach.
** The cost of materials and personnel expenses are included but not explicated in the income calculation and are therefore listed here for transparency purposes.
Sources: "Finanzberichte - Geschäftsberichte - Ausgewählte Kennzahlen 2009," Beiersdorf AG, op. cit.; "Finanzberichte - Geschäftsberichte - Ausgewählte Kennzahlen 2011," Beiersdorf AG, op. cit.

Exhibit 5
Biggest Global Competitors (Overview)

	Location of HQ	Employees	Revenue [in million US $]	Revenue growth to previous year [%]	Net profit [in million US $]	Most similar product to NIVEA
Beiersdorf	**Hamburg, Germany**	**17,666 (in 2011)**	**7,843.4 (FY* 2011)**	**1.1**	**348.1**	-
Unilever	London, U.K.	171,000 (in 2011)	64,700.7 (FY 2011)	5.0	5,920.5	Dove, Vaseline, St. Ives
Procter & Gamble	Cincinnati, U.S.A.	126,000 (in 2012)	83,680 (FY 2012)	3.2	10,756	Olay
Johnson & Johnson	New Brunswick, U.S.A.	117,900 (in 2012)	65,030 (FY 2011)	5.6	9,672	Aveeno, Clean & Clear
L'Oreal S.A.	Clichy, France	68,900 (in 2011)	28,325.7 (FY 2011)	4.3	3,395.2	L'Oreal Paris, Garnier
Henkel AG & Co KGaA	Düsseldorf, Germany	47,265	21,728.4 (FY 2011)	3.4	1,744.7	Aok, Schwarzkopf, Diadermine
Avon Products, Inc.	New York City, U.S.A.	40,600 (in 2011)	11,291.6 (FY 2011)	3.9	513.6	Avon
Estee Lauder Companies	New York City, U.S.A.	32,300 (in 2011)	8,810 (FY 2011)	13.0	700.8	Estee Lauder, Clinique, Aveda
Clarins S.A.	Neuilly-sur-Seine, France	6,100		Not published		Clarins

* FY: Fiscal Year

Note: In order to allow for better comparability, all figures were converted into U.S. dollars.

Source: Marketline Database, Company Reports 2011–2012.

Exhibit 6
Global Market Segmentation, 2010

Industry	Global market value [in million $]	Regional share [%]			
		Asia-Pacific	Europe	Americas	Middle East & Africa
Global facial care	50,891.9	51.0	30.1	17.1	1.7
Global sun care	7,326.1	29.5	39.8	28.9	1.8
Global hand & body care	18,049.7	41.1	31.2	25.8	1.8
Global hair care	49,515.7	30.8	35.0	30.9	3.3

Source: Marketline Database, Industry Reports 2011.

Clearly, the value of the NIVEA brand did not go unnoticed by Beiersdorf's competitors. Procter & Gamble expressed its continued interest in the company. In 2003, a takeover by the U.S.-based company was prevented with the help of the Herz family and the Hanseatic City of Hamburg. In 2010, Procter & Gamble's CEO Robert McDonald renewed interest in an acquisition.[30]

The Restructuring Project

The overarching vision for the restructuring process was for Beiersdorf to get closer to becoming the world's best skin care company. The slogan "Focus on Skin Care. Closer to Markets" was the means through which this vision was to be attained.

Focus on Skin Care

A core element of the restructuring strategy was for Beiersdorf to remember its core competence – excellence in skin and body care – and refocus its resources accordingly. This entailed an emphasis on core products lines. For instance, the NIVEA brand was heavily advertised with a new marketing platform of integrated 360-degree channels (including radio, TV, and cruise ships).

Moreover, non-core product lines were deemphasized. In Europe alone, Beiersdorf removed about 1,000 products from shelves (19 per cent of the European assortment). Beiersdorf not only sold regionally distributed brands like Juvena and Marlies Möeller, but also exited the makeup category.

Closer to Markets

One of the first measures after the restructuring project was announced in 2010 was the rearrangement of responsibilities in the top management team. In 2009, the members of the executive board were associated with corporate functions such as finance, law, logistics, sustainability, communication, and marketing. In March 2010, Beiersdorf announced the introduction of two functional (finance/HR and brands/supply chain) and three regional areas of responsibility (Europe/North America, Asia/Australia, and emerging markets). Each member of the board was responsible for either a function or a region.

Since the beginning of this rearrangement within the top management team in 2010, all of the members of the executive board had left the company. Quaas's resignation marked the departure of the last member who had also been on the board in 2009, before the rearrangement. Thus, in 2012 the functions and regional responsibilities were divided such that Peter Feld was responsible for Europe/North America, Ralph Gusko for brands and supply chain (as a replacement for Markus Pinger), and Dr. Ulrich Schmidt

---

[30] Birger Nicolai, "Nivea macht Sorgenfalten," *Die Welt*, www.welt.de/print/die_welt/wirtschaft/article12101352/Nivea-macht-Sorgenfalten.html, accessed October 2, 2012.

Exhibit 7
Competitors (Overview of Selected Market Shares)

	Market Value in 2010 [million US $]	Market Growth in 2010 [%]	1st Position	[%]	2nd Position	[%]	3rd Position	[%]	Rest [%]
FACIAL CARE INDUSTRY									
Global	50,891.9	4.6	L'Oreal S.A.	13.6	Unilever	7.8	Beiersdorf AG	7.5	71.0
Europe	15,335.3	3.6	L'Oreal S.A.	23.8	Beiersdorf AG	16.3	Estée Lauder	6.1	53.8
Germany	2,229.2	2.1	Beiersdorf AG	22.5	L'Oreal S.A.	20.6	Reckitt Benckiser PLC	8.0	48.9
Asia-Pac.	25,953.1	5.4	Kao Corporation	10.1	Unilever	10.1	Shiseido	9.1	70.7
China	7,703.4	10.0	L'Oreal S.A.	16.6	Procter & Gamble	12.5	Cheng Ming Ming	12.0	58.9
U.S.	5,012.5	3.3	Procter & Gamble	20.9	Johnson & Johnson	14.2	Unilever	12.4	52.5
Canada	821.5	3.3	Unilever	35.8	Johnson & Johnson	18.2	Beiersdorf AG	11.2	34.8
SUN CARE INDUSTRY									
Global	7,326.1	5.1	L'Oreal S.A.	14.0	Beiersdorf AG	13.5	Johnson & Johnson	9.8	62.7
Europe	2,919.0	3.4	L'Oreal S.A.	26.0	Beiersdorf AG	23.0	Johnson & Johnson	6.3	44.7
Germany	200.6	0.8	Beiersdorf AG	29.8	L'Oreal S.A.	20.0	Coty Inc	12.3	38.0
Asia-Pac.	2,161.2	5.4	Kao Corporation	14.3	Beiersdorf AG	7.9	Shiseido	6.4	71.5
China	762.7	5.8	Kao Corporation	29.9	Procter & Gamble	9.3	Johnson & Johnson	8.3	52.6
U.S.	1,155.6	4.3	Merck & Co., Inc.	23.8	Johnson & Johnson	18.2	Energizer Holdings	18.1	39.9
Canada	172.6	3.6	L'Oreal S.A.	17.5	Schering-Plough	12.2	Johnson & Johnson	9.4	60.8
HAND & BODY CARE INDUSTRY									
Global	18,049.7	3.8	Beiersdorf AG	13.0	Unilever	9.5	L'Oreal S.A.	7.3	70.2
Europe	5,632.3	2.5	Beiersdorf AG	24.0	L'Oreal S.A.	11.8	Unilever	10.6	53.5

(Continued)

Exhibit 7 (*cont.*)

	Market Value in 2010	Market Growth in 2010	1st Position		2nd Position		3rd Position		Rest
Germany	1,216.7	0.7	Beiersdorf AG	39.6	Unilever	12.9	L'Oreal S.A.	6.9	40.6
Asia-Pac.	7,420.1	3.7	Shiseido	16.0	Kao Corporation	10.7	Beiersdorf AG	5.8	67.5
China					no data				
U.S.	2,374.1	3.3	Unilever	13.0	Kao Corporation	11.4	Avon Products	8.7	66.8
Canada					no data				
HAIR CARE INDUSTRY									
Global	49,515.7	3.1	Procter & Gamble	24.1	L'Oreal S.A.	16.7	Unilever	11.7	47.4
Europe	17,326.0	2.0	Procter & Gamble	32.5	Henkel KGaA	17.0	-	-	50.5
Germany	2,473.9	0.3	Henkel KGaA	31.5	L'Oreal S.A.	26.6	P&G	18.7	23.2
Asia-Pac.	15,266.1	4.5	Procter & Gamble	22.0	Unilever	15.2	Kao Corporation	11.4	51.4
China	3,767.1	5.4	Procter & Gamble	39.4	Unilever	14.1	Beiersdorf AG	7.9	38.6
U.S.	7,232.3	-1.6	Procter & Gamble	28.2	L'Oreal S.A.	20.1	Unilever	9.6	42.1
Canada	1,116.0	2.3	Procter & Gamble	30.4	Unilever	15.7	L'Oreal S.A.	13.7	40.2

Source: Marketline Database, Industry Reports 2011.

for finance/HR. Ümit Subaşi was appointed a new member of the board in March 2011 and given the responsibility to develop the emerging markets area.

Beiersdorf also realigned its corporate structures in an effort to grant regional subsidiaries more decision-making authority. Only the broad corporate strategy was to be provided by the headquarters. This led to an overall thinning of structures with an accompanying cost savings of an estimated €90 million per year, predicted to be in full effect by 2014. In 2011, Beiersdorf cut about 1,000 jobs in the consumer division worldwide (almost 7 per cent of the division's workforce),[31] with most of them at the German headquarters.

Challenges

On April 26, 2012, all of these measures were still very fresh in the minds of many of Beiersdorf's shareholders and employees. Just a year ago, at the 2011 annual shareholder meeting, employees were standing outside of the conference center, protesting against the job cuts.[32] The company, founded on traditional values like trust and consistency, was deeply shaken to the core of its cultural identity. Within just a few years, Beiersdorf had evolved from a company with stable management and solid profitability to one with high volatility in the top management team and sobering year-end accounts, as well as ever-growing competitors. Employees were confused and anxious; shareholders were starting to become impatient.

Had Beiersdorf taken too big a bite of the world's consumer market? Was Beiersdorf big enough to take on its major competitors? Had it made the right choice of strategy and was it the right timing for its implementation? And how could it balance profitability while maintaining local responsiveness? On April 27, 2012, Heidenreich's first day as new CEO, he would have to be ready to deliver.

[31]   Daniela Stürmlinger, "Nivea-Konzern: Beiersdorf baut 1000 Arbeitsplätze ab," *Hamburger Abendblatt*, www.abendblatt.de/wirtschaft/article2111611/ Beiersdorf-baut-1000-Arbeitsplaetze-ab.html, accessed September 15, 2012.

[32]   Daniela Stuermlinger, "Angst vor Arbeitslosigkeit: Beiersdorf schminkt sich ab - Protest auf Hauptversammlung," *Hamburger Abendblatt*, www.abendblatt.de/wirtschaft/article1865982/ Beiersdorf-schminkt-sich-ab-Protest-auf-Hauptversammlung.html, accessed October 8, 2012.

Chapter 4   Recommended Practitioner Readings

- John Rice, "How GE is becoming a truly global network," *McKinsey Quarterly*, April (2017).

    In "How GE is becoming a truly global network," GE's vice-chairman describes their efforts to bust silos, boost collaboration, and build an internal marketplace of ideas and solutions. GE's challenge has been how to connect more than 300,000 people, operating in over 180 countries, in a dynamic and practical way without adding more process and bureaucracy that slows them down. The five steps GE is taking to create a new team culture and establish a new way of working are discussed.

- Tony Gibbs, Suzanne Heywood, and Leigh Weiss. "Organizations for an emerging world," *McKinsey Quarterly*, June (2012), 81–91.

    "Organizing for an emerging world" draws on the lessons learned by McKinsey organizational consultants as they worked with companies expanding into emerging markets. They address questions of how to adjust structure to support growth in emerging markets, how to find a productive balance between standardized global and diverse local processes, where to locate the corporate center and what to do there, and how to deploy knowledge and skills effectively around the world by getting the right people to communicate with each other.

- Nirmalya Kumar and Phanish Puranam, "Have you restructured for global success?" *Harvard Business Review*, 89:10 (2011), 123–30.

  In "Have you restructured for global success?" Kumar and Puranam emphasize the importance of creating organizations that are not only able to manage existing operations in developed countries, but also have the ability to capture the energy, ambition, and optimism that they often unleash in the developing world. They propose the creation of a T-shaped organization that allows the MNE to "walk the tightrope" between these different organizational needs.

- Cyril Bouquet, Julian Birkinshaw, and Jean-Louis Barsoux, "Fighting the 'headquarters knows best' syndrome," *MIT Sloan Management Review*, 57:2 (2016), 59–66.

  "Fighting the 'headquarters knows best' syndrome' examines how many executives believe their companies suffer from "headquarters knows best syndrome." This syndrome can hinder a company's global competitiveness. Bouquet, Birkinshaw, and Barsoux explain how Irdeto achieved a change in mindset by establishing two headquarters, one in the Netherlands and the other in China. This provided an effective way to realign the focus of the company, and it had significant positive effects on Irdeto's performance. A broad set of recommendations are provided.

- Erin Meyer, "When culture doesn't translate," *Harvard Business Review*, 93:10 (2015), 66–72.

  In "When culture doesn't translate," Meyer argues that as companies internationalize, their employees lose shared assumptions and norms. Organically grown corporate cultures begin to break down; miscommunication becomes more frequent, and trust erodes, especially between the head office and the regional units. To fix these problems, companies risk compromising attributes that underlie their commercial success. Five principles are presented that can prevent disintegration. Managers should: (1) identify the dimensions of difference between the corporate culture and local ones; (2) make sure every cultural group has a voice; (3) protect the most creative units, letting communication and job descriptions remain more ambiguous; (4) train everyone in key norms; (5) ensure diversity in every location.

In different ways, each of these readings underscores the need to build an organization that balances global integration, national responsiveness, and worldwide learning.

5 Creating Worldwide Innovation and Learning
Exploiting Cross-Border Knowledge Management

In the information-based, knowledge-intensive economy of the twenty-first century, MNEs are not competing only on the basis of their traditional ability to access new markets and arbitrage factor costs. Today the challenge is to build transnational organizations that can sense an emerging consumer trend in one country, link it to a new technology or capability it has in another, develop a creative new product or service in a third, and then diffuse that innovation rapidly around the world. This transnational innovation process is much more sophisticated than the more traditional "center-for-global" and "local-to-local" approaches that have been the dominant form of cross-border innovation in the past. In this chapter, we describe the traditional and the emerging models of cross-border innovation as well as the nature of the organizational capabilities that must be developed to make them effective. The chapter concludes with a closer examination of the characteristics of the transnational organization that allows the MNE to develop and manage cross-border flows of human and intellectual capital supplement with the same facility it has traditionally managed its international flows of financial capital.

In Chapter 3 we described how MNEs competing in today's global competitive environment are required to build layers of competitive advantage – the ability to capture global-scale efficiencies, local market responsiveness, and worldwide learning capability. As many of these companies found ways to match one another in the more familiar attributes of global-scale efficiency and local responsiveness, they had to find new ways to gain competitive advantage. In this process, competitive battles among leading-edge MNEs (particularly those in knowledge-intensive industries such as telecommunications, biotechnology, pharmaceuticals, etc.) have shifted to their ability to link and leverage their worldwide resources and capabilities to develop and diffuse innovation.[1]

The trend is reflected in the fact that R&D expenditure globally more than doubled in real terms between 1992 and 2010. Unsurprisingly, worldwide patent applications grew from 922,000 in 1985 to almost 2 million in 2010. In the same period, trademark applications also increased worldwide from about 1 million in 1985 to 3.6 million in 2010.

---

[1] Throughout this chapter, when we talk about innovation we are not only referring to the creation of technology-based new products or services but also to innovations that come from organizational effectiveness breakthroughs, pioneering marketing strategies, state-of-the-art manufacturing processes, or logistical innovations.

Among US companies, this fast-growing investment in knowledge-based assets is reflected in the value of intangible assets (i.e., *not* fixed assets such as plant and equipment or current assets like inventory) of the average S&P 500 company, which has risen from 32% of the total value in 1985, to 68% in 1995, and to over 84% by 2015.

All of this is changing the way companies regard their international operations. In the early decades of internationalization, many MNEs regarded their stock of domestically accumulated knowledge and expertise as an asset they could sell into foreign markets. This was particularly true of the US-based MNEs that followed the "international" strategy we described in Chapter 3. For example, in the 1960s RCA decided that its most appropriate strategy of international expansion was to license its leading-edge technology. But the strategy came with risks. By treating the global market simply as an opportunity to generate incremental revenue and not as a source of innovation and learning, the company soon found that after its licensees had learned what they could, they quickly caught up with and then overtook RCA in creating new innovative products more adapted to the global market.

In today's competitive environment, no company can assume that it can accumulate world-class knowledge and expertise by focusing only on its home-country environment, or that it can succeed just by tweaking its domestic product line. So while Qualcomm, the world leader in mobile and wireless technologies, may appear to be like RCA in licensing its technology as a core element of its international expansion, its strategy is very different. By licensing essentially every company in the telecom industry worldwide, Qualcomm generates over a third of its total revenue from royalty-based licensing agreements. But almost a quarter of its total revenue is plowed back into R&D at its major research centers in the United States, Germany, China, India, Korea, and the UK. In each of these countries, the company actively recruits the brightest technologists, monitors technological and competitive developments, collaborates with leading university researchers, and develops products in partnership with its global customers. In short, Qualcomm is using its worldwide presence to maintain and expand its innovative lead.

The MNE's ability to develop and rapidly diffuse innovations around the world is vital, and in this challenge overseas operations need to take on important new responsibilities. In addition to their traditional roles, the offshore sales subsidiaries, manufacturing operations, and R&D centers also must now become the sensors of new market trends or technological developments; they must be able to attract scarce talent and expertise; and they must be able to act collectively with the parent company and other offshore units to exploit the resulting innovations worldwide, regardless of where they originated.[2]

---

[2] See A. Y. Lewin, S. Massini, and C. Peeters, "Why are companies offshoring innovation? The emerging global race for talent,"*Journal of International Business Studies*, 40:6 (2009), 901–25.

    The emerging shortage of highly skilled science and engineering talent in the United States and, more generally, the need to access qualified personnel, are important explanatory factors for offshoring innovation decisions. Contrary to drivers of many other functions, labor arbitrage is less important than other forms of cost savings. The changing dynamics underlying the offshoring of innovation activities suggest that companies are entering a global race for talent.

Yet developing this capability to create, leverage, and apply knowledge worldwide is not a simple task organizationally. Although people are innately curious and naturally motivated to learn from one another, most modern corporations are constructed in a way that constrains and sometimes kills this natural human instinct. In this chapter, we focus on one of the most important current challenges facing MNE management: how to capture, develop, leverage, and exploit knowledge to support effective worldwide innovation and learning.

Traditional Innovation: Central and Local Models

Traditionally, MNEs' innovative capabilities were dominated by one of two classic processes. In what we describe as the *center-for-global* innovation model, the new opportunity was sensed in the home country; the parent company then used its centralized resources and capabilities to create the new product or process, usually in the main R&D center; and implementation internationally involved driving the innovation through subsidiaries whose role it was to introduce that innovation to their local market. Classic examples of this model would be Pfizer's R&D that led to the development and eventual worldwide introduction of Viagra®, or Komatsu's international roll-out of its line of heavy construction equipment designed and developed in Japan.

In contrast, what we call *local-for-local* innovation relies on subsidiary-based knowledge development. Responding to perceived local opportunities, subsidiaries use their own resources and capabilities to create innovative responses that are then implemented in the local market. Unilever's development of a detergent bar in response to the Indian market's need for a product suitable for stream washing is a good illustration of the process, as is Philippines-based Jollibee's strategy of adapting its fast-food products to the local market structures and taste preferences in each country it entered.

As MNEs relying on each of these sources of innovation competed for market share, the more sophisticated among them tried to develop elements of both models. But the tension between the knowledge-management processes supporting each model usually meant that one philosophy and set of practices ended up dominating. Not surprisingly, center-for-global innovation tends to dominate in companies we describe as "global" or "international," whereas local-for-local processes fit more easily into the "multinational" strategic model.

Regardless of which model dominated, the first challenge facing all these companies was to overcome the limitations and vulnerabilities built into their dominant process of cross-border innovation. In the following paragraphs, we will outline how the most effective MNEs did so. But, as we will see in a later section of the chapter, even the best managed central and local innovation processes were rarely sufficient, particularly for companies in fast-changing, knowledge-intensive industries like electronics, biotechnology, and communications. These MNEs required an entirely different set of skills to master what we will call transnational innovation capability. First, however, let's review how companies learned to make their traditional models of cross-border innovation effective.

Making Central Innovations Effective

The key strength on which many Japanese companies built their global leadership positions in a range of businesses from automobiles to zippers lay in the effectiveness of their center-for-global innovations. This is not to say that many did not use some other modes but, in general, the Japanese became the champion managers of centralized innovation – indeed, many have remained so. This process not only supported the Japanese juggernaut of international expansion in the 1980s and 1990s, in the twenty-first century this innovation model powered the success of many Korean MNEs as they expanded abroad.

Over time, many of these companies learned that the greatest risk of center-for-global innovation is market insensitivity, often accompanied by the resistance of local subsidiary management to new centrally developed products and processes that they view as inappropriate. But some MNEs learned how to adapt to these problems. The most successful in making their center-for-global process more effective developed three important capabilities: gaining the input of subsidiaries into centralized activities; ensuring that all functional tasks are linked to market needs; and integrating value-chain functions by managing the transfer of responsibilities across development, production, and marketing.

Gaining Subsidiary Input: Multiple Linkages

The most important problems facing a company with highly centralized operations are that, on the one hand, those at the center may not understand the needs of distant markets, and on the other, those in the subsidiaries may not be committed to the central innovation that they are required to implement. Both problems are best addressed by building multiple linkages between headquarters and overseas subsidiaries. Such linkages not only give headquarters managers a better understanding of country-level needs and opportunities, they also offer subsidiary managers greater access to and involvement in centralized decisions and tasks.

When Microsoft recognized that its strong, formal linkages between its headquarters and its subsidiaries were not as strong in developing countries, it created a dedicated Emerging Markets Development team at its headquarters. The team immediately began focusing on how it could get more input from its subsidiaries in China and India to deal with the major challenge of software piracy rampant in these countries. Working intensively with its local managers, the company introduced lower price point versions of its products, subscription-based offerings, and extensive student discounts to combat piracy. The impact was immediate, and industry analysts estimate that Microsoft revenues now exceed $1 billion in India and $2 billion from China – a tenfold increase in both countries over the last decade.

Responding to National Needs: Market Mechanisms

Like many other MNEs, 3M has developed several integrative processes to ensure that headquarters managers responsible for R&D, manufacturing, and marketing are not sheltered from the constraints and demands felt by managers on the frontlines of the operations. A key element in achieving this difficult organizational task is the company's use of internal "market mechanisms" to direct and regulate central activities.

Long known as one of the world's most innovative companies, 3M is committed to achieve 40% of annual sales from products that did not exist five years earlier. As one of many mechanisms driving this ambitious innovation objective, the company has created 50 customer innovation centers around the world. In these centers, 3M marketing and sales employees facilitate meetings between customers, 3M technical staff, and business decision makers, connecting consumer demand directly to technological innovation. By providing a platform for cross-functional teams to understand customer issues and opportunities, and exposing them to the full range of current, future, and potential 3M products, these innovation centers have proved to be a powerful way of sharing ideas and best practice, solving technical and business issues, and making decisions on innovation projects.

Managing Responsibility Transfer: Personnel Flow

When parent company units take the lead role in the development and manufacture of new products and processes, it is much more difficult to achieve the essential integration of research, manufacturing, and marketing than in the local-for-local innovation processes. This is because local-for-local innovation processes are greatly facilitated by the smaller size and closer proximity of the various units responsible for the cross-functional coordination. In contrast, centralized organizations must create alternative means to integrate the research, manufacturing, and marketing functions.

At the Japanese electronics company Panasonic, the integrative systems rely heavily on the transfer of people. The career paths of research engineers are structured to ensure that many of them spend about five to eight years in the central research laboratories engaged in pure research before moving on to the product divisions, typically in applied R&D. In a later stage of their careers, many move into a direct operational function, such as production or marketing, where they often take line management positions. Typically, an engineer will make the transition from one department to the next coincident with the transfer of the major project on which he or she has been working, thereby ensuring that specific knowledge about the project moves with the individual.

Another mechanism for cross-functional integration in Panasonic works in the opposite direction. Wherever possible, the company tries to identify the manager who will head the production task for a new product under development and makes that person a full-time member of the R&D team from the initial stage of the product development process. This system not only injects direct production expertise into the development team but also facilitates the transfer of the project after the design is completed.

Making Local Innovations Efficient

If the classic global companies are the champion managers of central innovation, the archetypal multinational companies are typically masters at managing local innovations. But these companies must deal with the fact that local-for-local innovations often suffer from needless differentiation and "reinvention of the wheel" caused by resource-rich subsidiaries trying to protect their independence and autonomy.

Of the many ways such companies have successfully dealt with these problems, three abilities proved to be the most effective: to empower local management in national subsidiaries, to establish mechanisms to link these local managers into corporate decision-making processes, and to force tight cross-functional integration within each subsidiary.

Empowering Local Management

Perhaps the most important factor supporting local innovation is through the dispersal of organizational assets and resources and the delegation of authority to accompany that process. These twin prerequisites provide the tools for country-level organizations to take the initiative in creating new products or processes. Companies like Unilever and Philips with their well-established decentralized federation organizations had little difficulty in creating local-for-local innovation. (Recall Hindustan Unilever's detergent bar for stream washing cited previously.) But many other MNEs struggled, and had to jumpstart this process by transferring assets and resources and empowering their subsidiary operations.

When US agricultural machinery manufacturer John Deere found its significant market position in India being challenged by local competitor Mahindra Mahindra, management decided it needed a more locally tailored product line. The company created a technology center in Pune, India, staffed by 2,000 technical employees and focused on the needs of cost-conscious Indian farmers. The subsequent creation of the simpler 55 to 75 horse power John Deere 5003 series tractor, developed specifically for those local needs, resulted in the turnaround of their share of this large and important agricultural equipment market.

Linking Local Managers to Corporate Decision-Making Processes

Whereas local resources and local autonomy make it feasible for overseas subsidiary managers to be creative and entrepreneurial, to make such local-for-local tasks effective for the company as a whole, the MNE must link those local entrepreneurs to corporate decision-making processes. That certainly was true for John Deere's Indian technology group, which was closely linked to the company's main technical center in Moline, Illinois, through the many development teams on which they worked collaboratively.

In many European companies, a cadre of entrepreneurial expatriates has long played a key role in developing and maintaining such linkages to the corporate center. At Dutch-based Philips, for example, many of the best managers from that home country spend much of their careers in overseas operations, working for three to four years in a series of national subsidiaries – jobs that are often much larger than those available in the small home-country market of the Netherlands. Not surprisingly, such a career assignment pattern has an important influence on managerial attitudes and organizational relationships. The expatriate managers typically tend to identify with the perspective of their assigned national organization, and it is this shared identity that creates a strong bond and distinct subculture among subsidiary managers within the company.[3] In contrast, Panasonic has been able to generate very little interaction among its expatriate managers, who tend to regard themselves as parent company executives temporarily on assignment in a foreign company.

Integrating Subsidiary Functions

Finally, the local innovativeness of decentralized federation organizations is enhanced when there is strong cross-functional integration within each national operation. Most Philips' subsidiaries use integration mechanisms at three organizational levels. For each project in a local subsidiary (e.g., to adapt a new food-processor model for the local market) Philips creates what it calls an "article team." This consists of relatively junior managers from both the commercial and the technical functions who are given responsibility to propose product policies and prepare annual sales plans and budgets.

Then, at the subsidiary product level (e.g., all Brazilian home appliances), cross-functional coordination is accomplished through a product group team of technical and commercial representatives. This team meets to review results, suggest corrective actions, and resolve any interfunctional differences. Keeping control and conflict resolution at this level facilitates sensitive and rapid responses to initiatives and ideas generated at the local level.

Finally, the highest subsidiary-level coordination forum is the senior management committee (SMC), which consists of the top commercial, technical, and financial managers in the subsidiary. Acting essentially as a local board, the SMC coordinates efforts among the functional groups and ensures that the national operation retains primary responsibility for its own strategies and priorities. Each

---

[3] See J. B. Hocking, M. Brown, and A. W. Harzing, "Balancing global and local strategic contexts: expatriate knowledge transfer, applications, and learning within a transnational organization," *Human Resource Management*, 46:4 (2007), 513–33.

The authors find that expatriate knowledge applications result from frequent knowledge access and communication with the corporate headquarters and other global units of the firm. In contrast, experiential learning derives from frequent access to host-country (local) knowledge that subsequently is adapted to the global corporate context.

of these three forums facilitates local initiative by ensuring that issues are resolved without escalation for approval or arbitration.

Transnational Innovation: Locally Leveraged, Globally Linked

In recent years, however, it has become clear that no matter how effectively companies implement the traditional local-for-local and center-for-global models, they are no longer sufficient in today's fast-moving, knowledge-intensive global environment. In that context, these two traditional processes increasingly are being supplemented by two new transnational innovation models that we have dubbed "locally leveraged" and "globally linked."

Locally leveraged innovation involves ensuring that the special resources and capabilities of each national subsidiary are available not only to that local entity but also to other MNE units worldwide. For example, in 2009, Cisco's R&D center in India undertook the development of a mobile backhaul router to provide "last mile" linkage from consumers' phones to cell towers into the telecom network. Because they understood the telecommunications needs of developing countries, within a couple of years of the product's introduction in 2011, it had been sold to more than 100 customers in 46 countries worldwide.

Globally linked innovations are a little more complex. They are created by pooling the resources and capabilities of many different units – typically at both the parent company and the subsidiary level – to create and manage an activity jointly. Such innovations allow the company to take market intelligence developed in one part of the organization, perhaps link it to specialized expertise located in a second entity and a scarce resource in a third, and then eventually diffuse the new product, service, or activity worldwide.

An example of globally linked innovation occurred when P&G wanted to launch an improved liquid laundry detergent and deliberately decide to draw on the diverse technological capabilities being applied separately to products it sold in Europe, Japan, and the United States. Because laundry in Japan is often done in cold water, researchers in that country had developed a more robust surfactant, the key ingredient that removes greasy stains. Meanwhile, the Europeans had been working on a liquid detergent with bleach substitutes, water softeners, and enzymes that would work in their high-temperature frontloading washers. These innovations were combined with a new generation of detergent builders that had been developed in the United States to prevent the redisposition of dirt. The result was a global heavy-duty liquid detergent, introduced as Improved Liquid Tide in the United States, Liquid Ariel in Europe, and Liquid Cheer in Japan.

Although these two transnational innovation processes are becoming more widespread, they have supplemented rather than replaced the traditional center-for-global and local-for-local innovation processes that are so well embedded in many MNEs. In a competitive environment, most companies recognize the need to engage their resources and capabilities in as many ways as they can. The challenge is to build an organization that can simultaneously facilitate all four processes of cross-border innovation and learning. This requires an understanding not only of the power of each process but also their limitations.[4]

Making Transnational Processes Feasible

Building a portfolio of processes to drive worldwide innovation and learning requires that companies overcome two related problems: they must avoid the pitfalls associated with each separate innovation process, while simultaneously finding ways to overcome the organizational contradictions among them.

In many MNEs, the drive to reduce complexity has led management to make the following simplifying assumptions that block its ability to create multifaceted and often contradictory innovation processes:

- an assumption, often implicit, that roles of organizational units responsible for very different businesses, functions, and national operations should be defined symmetrically
- an assumption, conscious or unconscious, that headquarters–subsidiary relationships should be based on clear and unambiguous patterns of dependence or independence
- an assumption that corporate management has a responsibility to exercise decision making and control uniformly.

Companies that are most successful in developing transnational innovations challenge these assumptions. Instead of treating all businesses, functions, and subsidiaries the same way, they systematically differentiate tasks and responsibilities. Instead of seeking organizational clarity by basing relationships on dependence or independence, they build and manage interdependence among the different units. And instead of considering control their key task, corporate managers search for subtle mechanisms to coordinate the worldwide resources and activities, co-opting the dispersed units into sharing a vision of the company's strategic tasks.

From Symmetry to Differentiation

Like many other companies, Unilever built its international operations with an implicit assumption of organizational symmetry. Managers of diverse local *businesses*, with products ranging from packaged foods to chemicals and detergents, all reported to strongly independent national subsidiary managers, who in turn reported through regional directors to the board. But as senior management began to recognize the need to capture potential economies across national boundaries and

---

[4] See M. Von Zedtwitz, O. Gassmann, and R. Boutellier, "Organizing global R&D: challenges and dilemmas," *Journal of International Management*, 10:1 (2004), 21–49.

Top managers in MNCs take decentralized competencies for granted. The authors identify six fundamental dilemmas that make it difficult even for companies with carefully managed distributed R&D networks to exploit the full potential of global innovation.

transfer learning worldwide, product coordination groups were formed at the corporate center, and soon encompassed all businesses.

As this change progressed, however, there was a recognition that different businesses faced different demands for global integration and local responsiveness. While considerable benefits accrued to cross-country standardization, coordination, and integration in the chemical and detergent businesses, for example, important differences in local tastes and national market structures impeded the same degree of standardization, coordination, and integration in its branded packaged-foods business.

As Unilever tackled the challenge of managing some businesses in a more globally (or at least regionally) coordinated manner, it was also confronted with the question of what *functions* to coordinate. Historically, national subsidiaries had typically developed, manufactured, and marketed products they thought appropriate. Over time, however, decentralization of all functional responsibilities became increasingly difficult to support. For the sake of cost control and competitive effectiveness, Unilever recognized it needed to break with tradition and begin centralizing European product development and purchasing, for example, but was less compelled to pull local sales and promotional responsibilities to the center.

Finally, in addition to differentiating the way they managed their various businesses and functions, most companies eventually recognized the importance of differentiating the management of diverse *geographic* operations. Even though national subsidiaries in a single geographic region often operated with very different external environments and internal constraints, in many MNEs, they were typically managed through the same organizational structure. For example, country operations in Sydney, Singapore, and Shanghai might all report through the same channels, share a common set of generalized subsidiary mandates, and be subject to a single, standard planning and control system.

Recognizing that such symmetrical treatment could constrain strategic capabilities, more sophisticated MNEs eventually made changes. At Unilever, for example, Europe's highly competitive markets and closely linked economies led management to increase the role of product coordinators until they eventually had direct line responsibility for all operating companies in their European businesses. In Latin America, however, national subsidiary managers maintained their historic line-management role, and product coordinators acted only as advisers. Unilever has thus moved in sequence from a symmetrical organization managed through a uniformly decentralized federation to a much more differentiated one: differentiating first by product, then by function, and finally by geography.

From Dependence or Independence to Interdependence

As we described in Chapter 4, national subsidiaries in decentralized federation organizations enjoyed considerable independence from the headquarters, whereas those in centralized hub organizations remained strongly dependent on the parent company for resources and capabilities. But the emerging strategic demands – including the need to develop transnational innovation and learning capabilities – make organizational models based on such simple interunit dependence or independence inappropriate. Increasingly, they find they must build the interdependent relationships that are at the heart of the transnational integrated network organization.

Yet it is not easy to change relationships that have been developed over a long history. Many MNEs initially tried to improve interunit collaboration by adding layer upon layer of administrative mechanisms, before recognizing that such means of fostering cooperation generally failed. The typical response was that independent units feigned compliance while fiercely protecting their independence, while dependent units often discovered that the newly enforced cooperative mechanisms bestowed little more than the right to agree with those on whom they had previously depended.

To create an effective interdependent organization, two requirements must be met. First, the company must develop the configuration of dispersed and specialized resources that we described as an integrated network in Chapter 4. Because it is explicitly based on interdependent relationships, such an organization model can frame the new roles and responsibilities necessary for worldwide innovation and learning. In this organization, all country subsidiary companies take on sensing and scanning roles to detect the consumer trends, technological advances, or competitive activities that may trigger a new opportunity or threat. Typically, such information is fed to those units in the network with primary responsibility for that particular product or technology – a global product manager, a lead country subsidiary, or a regional development lab designated a center-of-excellence, for example.

Beyond creating a configuration of interdependent specialized operations, the innovative transnational organization must build interunit integration mechanisms to ensure that task interdependencies lead to the benefits of synergy rather than the paralysis of conflict. Above all else, interunit cooperation requires good interpersonal relations among managers in different units: the headquarters-based business manager must work effectively with the center-of-excellence technician, and the lead country marketing specialist, for example.[5]

The experiences of Ericsson, the Swedish telecommunications company, suggest that the movement of people is one of the strongest mechanisms for breaking down local dogmas. Ericsson achieved this with a long-standing policy of transferring large numbers of people back and forth between headquarters and subsidiaries. Whereas its Japanese competitor NEC may transfer a new technology through a few key managers sent on temporary assignment, Ericsson will send a team of 50 or 100 engineers and managers for a year or two; whereas NEC's flow is primarily from headquarters to subsidiary, Ericsson's is a balanced two-way flow in which people come to the parent company to both learn and provide their expertise; and whereas

[5] See M. Kotabe, D. Dunlap-Hinkler, R. Parente, and H. A. Mishra, "Determinants of cross-national knowledge transfer and its effect on firm innovation," *Journal of International Business Studies*, 38:2 (2007), 259–82.

From a resource-based view, this study evaluates the impact of cross-national knowledge transfer on firm innovative performance. (1) At low and moderate levels of international-knowledge content, a firm's strategy to transfer international knowledge improves its innovative performance; (2) at higher levels of international-knowledge content, there are diminishing marginal returns to transferring knowledge from overseas.

NEC's transfers are predominantly Japanese, Ericsson's multidirectional process involves all nationalities.

However, any organization in which there are shared tasks and joint responsibilities requires additional decision-making and conflict-resolution forums. In Ericsson, the often-divergent objectives and interests of the parent company and the local subsidiary are exchanged in the national company's board meetings. Unlike many companies whose local boards are designed solely to satisfy national legal requirements, Ericsson uses its local boards as legitimate forums for communicating objectives, resolving differences, and making decisions.

From Simple Control to Flexible Coordination

With the simplifying assumptions of organizational symmetry supported by equally simplified relationships defined by dependence or independence, management processes tended to be dominated by simple control: tight operational controls in subsidiaries that depended on the center, or looser administrative coordination processes in decentralized units. But when subsidiaries began to take innovative roles that required more collaborative behavior, they had to challenge the assumptions underlying those more complex organizational roles and relationships. The growing interdependence of organizational units strained the simple control-dominated systems and underscored the need to supplement existing processes with more subtle and sophisticated ones.

As MNEs began exploring transnational innovation opportunities, they found that there was an explosion in the number of issues that had to be linked or integrated. Eventually, the additional coordination needs forced many MNEs to develop new processes adapted to fit the needs of various functions and tasks.

This involved the recognition that three flows are the lifeblood of any organization but are of particular importance in a transnational company. The first is the *flow of goods*: the complex interconnections through which companies source their raw materials and other supplies, link the flows of components and subassemblies, and distribute finished goods. The second is the *flow of resources*, which encompasses not only the allocation of capital and repatriation of dividends but also the movement of personnel and technological resources throughout the system. The third is the *flow of information and knowledge* – from raw data and analyzed information to accrued knowledge and embedded expertise – that an MNE must diffuse throughout its worldwide network if it is to create transnational innovations.

It can be very difficult to coordinate the flows of *goods* in a complex, integrated network of interdependent operations. But, in most companies, this coordination process can be managed effectively at lower levels of the organization through clear procedures and strong systems. In other words, the flow of goods is best achieved through the *formalization* of management processes.

Coordinating flows of financial, human, and technological *resources* can be more difficult. Allocation of these scarce resources represents the major strategic choices the company makes and must therefore be controlled at the corporate level. We have described the transnational company as an organization of diverse needs and perspectives, many of which are in conflict and all of which are changing. In such an organization, only managers with an overview of the total situation can make critical decisions about the funding of projects, the sharing of scarce technological resources, and the allocation of organizational skills and capabilities. Managing the flow of resources is a classic example of the need for coordination by *centralization*.

Perhaps the most difficult task is to coordinate the huge flow of strategic information and proprietary *knowledge* required to operate a transnational organization. Much of the most valuable parts of this increasingly vital asset exist in the form of tacit knowledge and embedded expertise. This makes it impossible to coordinate through formal systems or centralized controls. The most effective way to ensure that worldwide organizational units analyze their diverse environments appropriately is to sensitize local managers to broader corporate objectives and priorities ensuring that they are exposed to the relevant knowledge of values through frequent contacts, or by creating organizational forums that allow for the free exchange of information and foster cross-unit learning. In short, the *socialization* process is the classic solution for the coordination of information flows.

Naturally, none of these broad characterizations of the fit between flows and processes is absolute, and companies use a variety of coordinative mechanisms to manage all three flows. For example, goods flows may be centrally coordinated for products under allocation, when several plants operate at less than capacity, or if the cost structures or host government demand change. And as information flows become routine, they can be coordinated through formalization if appropriate management information systems have been installed.

Realistically, a one-size-fits-all approach to capturing the benefits of innovation will not work in a large MNE. As Figure 5.1 suggests, the most effective way to

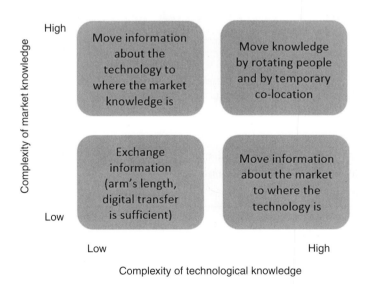

Figure 5.1 Mobilizing knowledge.
Source: Jose Santos, Yves Doz, and Peter Williamson, "Is your innovation process global?" *MIT Sloan Management Review*, 45:4 (2005), 36.

exploit the knowledge within an organization depends on the complexity of the technology itself and the understanding of the focal market. In practice, the best way to capture innovation will sometimes be to move people and sometimes to move or exchange the information.

CONCLUDING COMMENTS

The innovation processes in MNEs have changed considerably. Whereas once MNEs relied on simple models of centralized or localized innovation, the majority now find it necessary to build such activities around multiple operating units and geographically disparate sources of knowledge. In this chapter, we identified three generic approaches to innovation and, for each, we identified its typical limitations and the approaches MNEs can use to overcome them. To be clear, there is no single right way of managing the innovation process in an MNE, because each company has its own unique administrative heritage that it cannot and should not disavow. Nonetheless, it is possible to identify certain principles – around the differentiation of roles, interdependence of units, and modes of control – that underpin the development of an effective transnational organization.

HARVARD | BUSINESS | SCHOOL   REV: MARCH 3, 2004

Christopher A. Bartlett

CASE 5.1 P&G JAPAN: THE SK-II GLOBALIZATION PROJECT

In November 1999, Paolo de Cesare was preparing for a meeting with the Global Leadership Team (GLT) of P&G's Beauty Care Global Business Unit (GBU) to present his analysis of whether SK-II, a prestige skin care line from Japan, should become a global P&G brand.

As president of Max Factor Japan, the hub of P&G's fast-growing cosmetics business in Asia, and previous head of its European skin care business, de Cesare had considerable credibility with the GLT. Yet, as he readily acknowledged, there were significant risks

Exhibit 1
P&G's Internationalization Timetable

Year	Markets Entered
1837–1930	United States and Canada
1930–1940	United Kingdom, Philippines
1940–1950	Puerto Rico, Venezuela, Mexico
1950–1960	Switzerland, France, Belgium, Italy, Peru, Saudi Arabia, Morocco
1960–1970	Germany, Greece, Spain, Netherlands, Sweden, Austria, Indonesia, Malaysia, Hong Kong, Singapore, Japan
1970–1980	Ireland
1980–1990	Colombia, Chile, Caribbean, Guatemala, Kenya, Egypt, Thailand, Australia, New Zealand, India, Taiwan, South Korea, Pakistan, Turkey, Brazil, El Salvador
1990–2000	Russia, China, Czech Republic, Hungary, Poland, Slovak Republic, Bulgaria, Belarus, Latvia, Estonia, Romania, Lithuania, Kazakhstan, Yugoslavia, Croatia, Uzbekistan, Ukraine, Slovenia, Nigeria, South Africa, Denmark, Portugal, Norway, Argentina, Yemen, Sri Lanka, Vietnam, Bangladesh, Costa Rica, Turkmenistan

Source: Company records.

in his proposal to expand SK-II into China and Europe.

Chairing the GLT meeting was Alan ("A. G.") Lafley, head of P&G's Beauty Care GBU, to which de Cesare reported. In the end, it was his organization–and his budget–that would support such a global expansion. Although he had been an early champion of SK-II in Japan, Lafley would need strong evidence to support P&G's first-ever proposal to expand a Japanese brand worldwide. After all, SK-II's success had been achieved in a culture where the consumers, distribution channels, and competitors were vastly different from those in most other countries.

Another constraint facing de Cesare was that P&G's global organization was in the midst of the bold but disruptive Organization 2005 restructuring program. As GBUs took over profit responsibility historically held by P&G's country-based organizations, management was still trying to negotiate their new working relationships. In this context, de Cesare, Lafley, and other GLT members struggled to answer some key questions: Did SK-II have the potential to develop into a major global brand? If so, which markets were the most important to enter now? And how should this be implemented in P&G's newly reorganized global operations?

P&G's Internationalization: Engine of Growth

De Cesare's expansion plans for a Japanese product was just the latest step in a process of internationalization that had begun three-quarters of a century earlier. But it was the creation of the Overseas Division in 1948 that drove three decades of rapid expansion. Growing first in Europe, then Latin America and Asia, by 1980 P&G's operations in 27 overseas countries accounted for over 25% of its $11 billion worldwide sales. (Exhibit 1 summarizes P&G's international expansion.)

Local Adaptiveness Meets Cross-Market Integration

Throughout its early expansion, the company adhered to a set of principles set down by Walter Lingle, the first vice president of overseas operations. "We must tailor our products to meet consumer demands in each nation," he said. "But we must create local country subsidiaries whose structure, policies, and practices are as exact a replica of the U.S. Procter & Gamble organization as it is possible to create." Under the Lingle principles, the company soon built a portfolio of self-sufficient subsidiaries run by

Exhibit 2 P&G European Organization, 1986

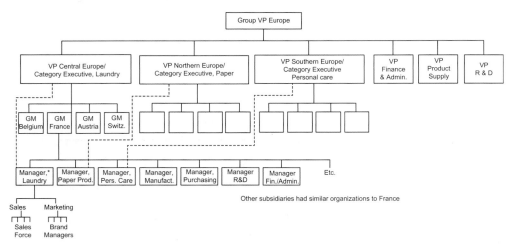

*Managers of Laundry Products in all subsidiaries had a similar dotted line relationship to the European Category Executive for Laundry.

Source: Company records.

country general managers (GMs) who grew their companies by adapting P&G technology and marketing expertise to their knowledge of their local markets.

Yet, by the 1980s, two problems emerged. First, the cost of running all the local product development labs and manufacturing plants was limiting profits. And second, the ferocious autonomy of national subsidiaries was preventing the global rollout of new products and technology improvements. Local GMs often resisted such initiatives due to the negative impact they had on local profits, for which the country subsidiaries were held accountable. As a result, new products could take a decade or more to be introduced worldwide.

Consequently, during the 1980s, P&G's historically "hands-off" regional headquarters became more active. In Europe, for example, Euro Technical Teams were formed to eliminate needless country-by-country product differences, reduce duplicated development efforts, and gain consensus on new-technology diffusion. Subsequently, regionwide coordination spread to purchasing, finance, and even marketing. In particular, the formation of Euro Brand Teams became an effective forum for marketing managers to coordinate regionwide product strategy and new product rollouts.

By the mid-1980s, these overlaid coordinating processes were formalized when each of the three European regional vice presidents was also given coordinative responsibility for a product category. While these individuals clearly had organizational influence, profit responsibility remained with the country subsidiary GMs. (See Exhibit 2 for the 1986 European organization.)

Birth of Global Management

In 1986, P&G's seven divisions in the U.S. organization were broken into 26 product categories, each with its own product development, product supply, and sales and marketing capabilities. Given the parallel development of a European category management structure, it was not a big leap to appoint the first global category executives in 1989. These new roles were given significant responsibility for developing global strategy, managing the technology program, and qualifying expansion markets–but not profit responsibility, which still rested with the country subsidiary GMs.

Then, building on the success of the strong regional organization in Europe, P&G replaced its International Division with four regional entities–for North America, Europe, Latin America, and

Exhibit 3 P&G's Worldwide Organizational Structure, 1990

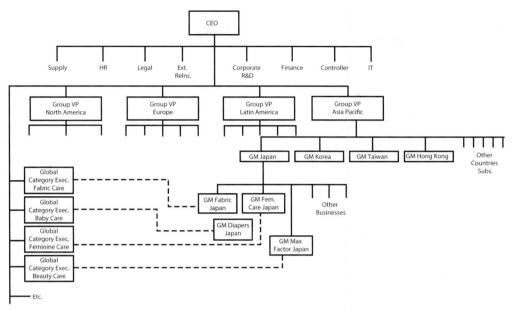

Source: Company records.

Asia–each assuming primary responsibility for profitability. (See Exhibit 3 for P&G's structure in 1990.) A significant boost in the company's overseas growth followed, particularly in opening the untapped markets of Eastern Europe and China.

By the mid-1990s, with operations in over 75 countries, major new expansion opportunities were shrinking and growth was slowing. Furthermore, while global category management had improved cross-market coordination, innovative new products such as two-in-one shampoo and compact detergent were still being developed very slowly – particularly if they originated overseas. And even when they did, they were taking years to roll out worldwide. To many in the organization, the matrix structure seemed an impediment to entrepreneurship and flexibility.

P&G Japan: Difficult Childhood, Struggling Adolescence

Up to the mid-1980s, P&G Japan had been a minor contributor to P&G's international growth. Indeed, the start-up had been so difficult that, in 1984, 12 years after entering the Japan market, P&G's board reviewed the accumulated losses of $200 million, the ongoing negative operating margins of 75%, and the eroding sales base– decreasing from 44 billion yen (¥) in 1979 to ¥26 billion in 1984–and wondered if it was time to exit this market. But CEO Ed Artzt convinced the board that Japan was strategically important, that the organization had learned from its mistakes–and that Durk Jager, the energetic new country GM, could turn things around.

The Turnaround

In 1985, as the first step in developing a program he called "Ichidai Hiyaku" ("The Great Flying Leap"), Jager analyzed the causes of P&G's spectacular failure in Japan. One of his key findings was that the company had not recognized the distinctive needs and habits of the very demanding Japanese consumer. (For instance, P&G Japan had built its laundry-detergent business around All Temperature Cheer, a product that ignored the Japanese practice of doing the laundry in tap water, not a range of water temperatures.) Furthermore, he found that the company had not respected the innovative capability of Japanese companies such as Kao and Lion, which turned out to be among the world's toughest competitors. (After creating the market for disposable diapers in Japan, for example, P&G Japan watched Pampers' market share drop from 100% in 1979 to 8% in 1985 as local competitors introduced similar products with major improvements.) And Jager concluded that P&G Japan had not adapted to the complex Japanese distribution system. (For instance, after realizing that its 3,000 wholesalers were providing little promotional support for its products, the company resorted to aggressive discounting that triggered several years of distributor disengagement and competitive price wars.)

Jager argued that without a major in-country product development capability, P&G could never respond to the demanding Japanese consumer and the tough, technology-driven local competitors. Envisioning a technology center that would support product development throughout Asia and even take a worldwide leadership role, he persuaded his superiors to grow P&G's 60-person research and development (R&D) team into an organization that could compete with competitor Kao's 2,000-strong R&D operation.

Over the next four years, radical change in market research, advertising, and distribution resulted in a 270% increase in sales that, in turn, reduced unit production costs by 62%. In 1988, with laundry detergents again profitable and Pampers and Whisper (the Japanese version of P&G's Always feminine napkin) achieving market leadership, Jager began to emphasize expansion. In particular, he promoted more product introductions and a bold expansion into the beauty products category. When P&G implemented its new region-based reorganization in 1990, Jager became the logical candidate to assume the newly created position of group vice president for Asia, a position he held until 1991, when he left to run the huge U.S. business.

The Relapse

In the early 1990s, however, P&G Japan's strong performance began eroding. The problems began when Japan's "bubble economy" burst in 1991. More troubling, however, was the fact that, even within this stagnating market, P&G was losing share. Between 1992 and 1996 its yen sales fell 3% to 4% annually for a cumulative 20% total decline, while in the same period competitor Unicharm's annual growth was 13% and Kao's was 3%.

Even P&G's entry into the new category of beauty care worsened rather than improved the situation. The parent company's 1991 acquisition of Max Factor gave P&G Japan a foothold in the $10 billion Japanese cosmetics market. But in Japan, sales of only $300 million made it a distant number-five competitor, its 3% market share dwarfed by Shiseido's 20% plus. Then, in 1992 P&G's global beauty care category executive announced the global launch of Max Factor Blue, a top-end, self-select color cosmetic line to be sold through general merchandise and drug stores. But in Japan, over 80% of the market was sold by trained beauty counselors in specialty stores or department store cosmetics counters. The new self-select strategy, coupled with a decision to cut costs in the expensive beauty-counselor distribution channel, led to a 15% decline in sales in the Japanese cosmetics business. The previous break-even performance became a negative operating margin of 10% in 1993. Things became even worse the following year, with losses running at $1 million per week.

In 1994, the Japanese beauty care business lost $50 million on sales of less than $300 million. Among the scores of businesses in the 15 countries reporting to him, A. G. Lafley, the newly arrived vice president of the Asian region, quickly zeroed in on Max Factor Japan as a priority problem area. "We first had to clean up the Max Factor Blue mass-market mess then review our basic strategy," he said. Over the next three years, the local organization worked hard to make Max Factor Japan profitable. Its product line was rationalized from 1,400 SKUs (or stockkeeping units) to 500, distribution support was focused on 4,000 sales outlets as opposed to the previous 10,000, and sales and marketing staff was cut from 600 to 150. It was a trying time for Max Factor Japan.

Organization 2005: Blueprint for Global Growth

In 1996 Jager, now promoted to chief operating officer under CEO John Pepper, signaled that he saw the development of new products as the key to P&G's future growth. While supporting Pepper's emphasis on expanding into emerging markets, he voiced concern that the company would "start running out of white space towards the end of the decade." To emphasize the importance of creating new businesses, he became the champion of a Leadership Innovation Team to identify and support major companywide innovations.

When he succeeded Pepper as CEO in January 1999, Jager continued his mission. Citing P&G breakthroughs such as the first synthetic detergent in the 1930s, the introduction of fluoride toothpaste in the 1950s, and the development of the first disposable diaper in the 1960s, he said, "Almost without exception, we've won biggest on the strength of superior product technology. . . . But frankly, we've come nowhere near exploiting its full potential." Backing this belief, in 1999 he increased the budget for R&D by 12% while cutting marketing expenditures by 9%.

If P&G's growth would now depend on its ability to develop new products and roll them out rapidly worldwide, Jager believed his new strategic thrust had to be implemented through a radically different organization. Since early 1998 he and Pepper had been planning Organization 2005, an initiative he felt represented "the most dramatic change to P&G's structure, processes, and culture in the company's history." Implementing O2005, as it came to be called, he promised would bring 13% to 15% annual earnings growth and would result in $900 million in annual savings starting in 2004. Implementation would be painful, he warned; in the first five years, it called for the closing of 10 plants and the loss of 15,000 jobs–13% of the worldwide workforce. The cost of the restructuring was estimated at $1.9 billion, with $1 billion of that total forecast for 1999 and 2000.

Changing the Culture

During the three months prior to assuming the CEO role, Jager toured company facilities worldwide. He concluded that P&G's sluggish 2% annual volume growth and its loss of global market share was due to a culture he saw as slow, conformist, and risk averse. (See Exhibit 4 for P&G's financial performance.) In his view, employees were wasting half their time on "non-value-added work" such as memo writing, form filling, or chart preparation, slowing down decisions and making the company vulnerable to more nimble competition. (One observer described P&G's product development model as "ready, aim, aim, aim, aim, fire.") He concluded that any organizational change would have to be built on a cultural revolution.

With "stretch, innovation, and speed" as his watchwords, Jager signaled his intent to shake up norms and practices that had shaped generations of highly disciplined, intensely loyal managers often referred to within the industry as "Proctoids." "Great ideas come from conflict and dissatisfaction with the status quo," he said. "I'd like an organization where there are rebels." To signal the importance of risk taking and speed, Jager gave a green light to the Leadership Innovation Team to implement a global rollout of two radically new products: Dryel, a home dry-cleaning kit; and Swiffer, an electrostatically charged dust mop. Just 18 months after entering their first test market, they were on sale in the United States, Europe, Latin America, and Asia. Jager promised 20 more new products over the next 18 months. "And if you are worried about oversight," he said, "I am the portfolio manager."

Changing the Processes

Reinforcing the new culture were some major changes to P&G's traditional systems and processes. To emphasize the need for greater risk taking, Jager leveraged the performance-based component of compensation so that, for example, the variability of a vice president's annual pay package increased from a traditional range of 20% (10% up or down) to 80% (40% up or down). And to motivate people and align them with the overall success of the company, he extended the reach of the stock option plan from senior management to virtually all employees. Even outsiders were involved, and P&G's advertising agencies soon found their compensation linked to sales increases per dollar spent.

Exhibit 4
P&G Select Financial Performance Data, 1980–1999

Annual Income Statement ($ millions)	June 1999	June 1998	June 1997	June 1996	June 1995	June 1990	June 1985	June 1980
Sales	38,125	37,154	35,764	35,284	33,434	24,081	13,552	10,772
Cost of Goods Sold	18,615	19,466	18,829	19,404	18,370	14,658	9,099	7,471
Gross Profit	19,510	17,688	16,935	15,880	15,064	9,423	4,453	3,301
Selling, General, and Administrative Expense	10,628	10,035	9,960	9,707	9,632	6,262	3,099	1,977
of which:								
Research and Development Expense	1,726	1,546	1,469	1,399	1,148	693	400	228
Advertising Expense	3,538	3,704	3,466	3,254	3,284	2,059	1,105	621
Depreciation, Depletion, and Amortization	2,148	1,598	1,487	1,358	1,253	859	378	196
Operating Profit	6,734	6,055	5,488	4,815	4,179	2,302	976	1,128
Interest Expense	650	548	457	493	511	395	165	97
Non-Operating Income/Expense	235	201	218	272	409	561	193	51
Special Items	-481	0	0	75	-77	0	0	0
Total Income Taxes	2,075	1,928	1,834	1,623	1,355	914	369	440
Net Income	3,763	3,780	3,415	3,046	2,645	1,554	635	642
Geographic Breakdown: Net Sales								
Americas	58.4%	54.7%	53.8%	52.9%	55.1%			
United States						62.5%	75.4%	80.9%
Europe, Middle East, and Africa	31.9%	35.1%	35.3%	35.2%	32.9%			
International						39.9%	22.3%	22.4%
Asia	9.7%	10.2%	10.9%	11.9%	10.8%			
Corporate					1.2%	-2.1%	2.3%	-3.3%
Number of Employees	110,000	110,000	106,000	103,000	99,200	94,000	62,000	59,000

Abbreviated Balance Sheet ($ millions)	June 1999	June 1998	June 1997	June 1996	June 1995	June 1990	June 1985	June 1980
ASSETS								
Total Current Assets	11,358	10,577	10,786	10,807	10,842	7,644	3,816	3,007
Plant, Property & Equipment, net	12,626	12,180	11,376	11,118	11,026	7,436	5,292	3,237
Other Assets	8,129	8,209	5,382	5,805	6,257	3,407	575	309
TOTAL ASSETS	32,113	30,966	27,544	27,730	28,125	18,487	9,683	6,553

Exhibit 4 (*cont.*)

Abbreviated Balance Sheet ($ millions)	June 1999	June 1998	June 1997	June 1996	June 1995	June 1990	June 1985	June 1980
LIABILITIES								
Total Current Liabilities	10,761	9,250	7,798	7,825	8,648	5,417	2,589	1,670
Long-Term Debt	6,231	5,765	4,143	4,670	5,161	3,588	877	835
Deferred Taxes	362	428	559	638	531	1,258	945	445
Other Liabilities	2,701	3,287	2,998	2,875	3,196	706	0	0
TOTAL LIABILITIES	20,055	18,730	15,498	16,008	17,536	10,969	4,411	2,950
TOTAL EQUITY	12,058	12,236	12,046	11,722	10,589	7,518	5,272	3,603
TOTAL LIABILITIES & EQUITY	32,113	30,966	27,544	27,730	28,125	18,487	9,683	6,553

Source: SEC filings, Standard & Poor's Research Insight.

Another major systems shift occurred in the area of budgets. Jager felt that the annual ritual of preparing, negotiating, and revising line item sales and expenses by product and country was enormously time wasting and energy sapping. In future, they would be encouraged to propose ambitious stretch objectives. And going forward, Jager also argued to replace the episodic nature of separate marketing, payroll, and initiative budgets with an integrated business planning process where all budget elements of the operating plan could be reviewed and approved together.

Changing the Structure

In perhaps the most drastic change introduced in O2005, primary profit responsibility shifted from P&G's four regional organizations to seven global business units (GBUs) that would now manage product development, manufacturing, and marketing of their respective categories worldwide. The old regional organizations were reconstituted into seven market development organizations (MDOs) that assumed responsibility for local implementation of the GBUs' global strategies.[1] And transactional activities such as accounting, human resources, payroll, and much of IT were coordinated through a global business service unit (GBS). (See Exhibit 5 for a representation of the new structure.)

Beyond their clear responsibility for developing and rolling out new products, the GBUs were also charged with the task of increasing efficiency by standardizing manufacturing processes, simplifying brand portfolios, and coordinating marketing activities. For example, by reducing the company's 12 different diaper-manufacturing processes to one standard production model, Jager believed that P&G could not only reap economies but might also remove a major barrier to rapid new-product rollouts. And by axing some of its 300 brands and evaluating the core group with global potential, he felt the company could exploit its resources more efficiently.

The restructuring also aimed to eliminate bureaucracy and increase accountability. Overall, six management layers were stripped out, reducing the levels between the chairman and the front line from 13 to 7. Furthermore, numerous committee responsibilities were transferred to individuals. For example, the final sign-off on new advertising copy was given to individual executives, not approval boards, cutting the time it took to get out ads from months to days.

---

[1] In an exception to the shift of profit responsibility to the GBUs, the MDOs responsible for developing countries were treated as profit centers.

Exhibit 5 P&G Organization, 1999 (Post O2005 Implementation)

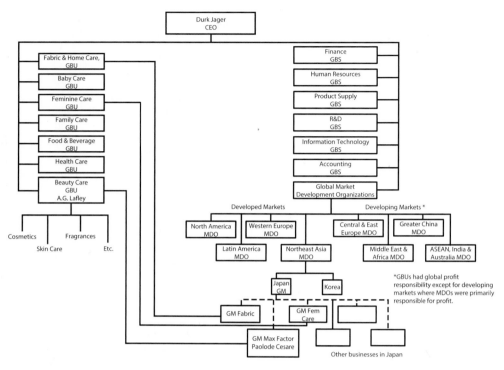

Source: Company records.

New Corporate Priorities Meet Old Japanese Problems

The seeds of Jager's strategic and organizational initiatives began sprouting long before he assumed the CEO role in January 1999. For years, he had been pushing his belief in growth through innovation, urging businesses to invest in new products and technologies. Even the organizational review that resulted in the O2005 blueprint had begun a year before he took over. These winds of change blew through all parts of the company, including the long-suffering Japanese company's beauty care business, which was finally emerging from years of problems.

Building the Base: From Mass to Class

By 1997 the Japanese cosmetics business had broken even. With guidance and support from Lafley, the vice president for the Asian region, the Japanese team had focused its advertising investment on just two brands–Max Factor Color, and a prestige skin care brand called SK-II.[2] "Poring through the Japanese business, we found this little jewel called SK-II," recalled Lafley. "To those of us familiar with rich Western facial creams and lotions, this clear, unperfumed liquid with a distinctive odor seemed very different. But the discriminating Japanese consumer

---

[2] SK-II was an obscure skin care product that had not even been recognized, much less evaluated, in the Max Factor acquisition. Containing Pitera, a secret yeast-based ingredient supposedly developed by a Japanese monk who noticed how the hands of workers in sake breweries kept young looking, SK-II had a small but extremely loyal following. Priced at ¥15,000 ($120) or more per bottle, it clearly was at the top of the skin care range.

Exhibit 6 Beauty Counselor Work Flow

Skin Care Counseling

Skin Diagnosis

↓

Skin Care Regimen Recommendation

↓

Product Demonstration
Plus
Skin Care Service (i.e., facial/massage)

↓

Make-up Service

↓

Record Consumer's Purchase

Make-up Counseling

Color Counseling
(Consumer Color-tone Analysis)

↓

Product Demonstration

↓

Make-up Service

↓

Record Consumer's Purchase

Source: Company documents.

loved it, and it became the cornerstone of our new focus on the prestige beauty-counselor segment."

Max Factor Japan began rebuilding its beauty-counselor channels, which involved significant investments in training as well as counter design and installation (see Exhibits 6 and 7). And because SK-II was such a high margin item, management launched a bold experiment in TV advertising featuring a well-respected Japanese actress in her late 30s. In three years SK-II's awareness ratings rose from around 20% to over 70%, while sales in the same period more than doubled.

Building on this success, management adapted the ad campaign for Hong Kong and Taiwan, where SK-II had quietly built a loyal following among the many women who took their fashion cues from Tokyo. In both markets, sales rocketed, and by 1997, export sales of $68 million represented about 30% of the brand's total sales. More important, SK-II was now generating significant operating profits. Yet within P&G, this high-end product had little visibility outside Japan. Paolo de Cesare, general manager of P&G's European skin care business in the mid-1990s, felt that, because the company's skin care experience came

from the highly successful mass-market Olay brand, few outside Japan understood SK-II. "I remember some people saying that SK-II was like Olay for Japan," he recalled. "People outside Japan just didn't know what to make of it."

Responding to the Innovation Push

Meanwhile, Jager had begun his push for more innovation. Given his firmly held belief that Japan's demanding consumers and tough competitors made it an important source of leading-edge ideas, it was not surprising that more innovative ideas and initiatives from Japan began finding their way through the company. For example, an electrostatically charged cleaning cloth developed by a Japanese competitor became the genesis of P&G's global rollout of Swiffer dry mops; rising Japanese sensitivity to hygiene and sanitation spawned worldwide application in products such as Ariel Pure Clean ("beyond whiteness, it washes away germs"); and dozens of other ideas from Japan–from a waterless car-washing cloth to a disposable stain-removing pad to a washing machine-based dry-cleaning product–were all put into P&G's product development pipeline.

Exhibit 7 In-Store SK-II Counter Space

 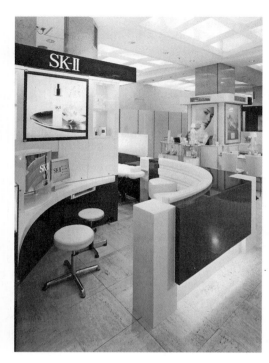

Source: Company documents.

Because Japanese women had by far the highest use of beauty care products in the world, it was natural that the global beauty care category management started to regard Max Factor Japan as a potential source of innovation. One of the first worldwide development projects on which Japan played a key role was Lipfinity, a long-lasting lipstick that was felt to have global potential.

In the mid-1990s, the impressive but short-lived success of long-lasting lipsticks introduced in Japan by Shiseido and Kenebo reinforced P&G's own consumer research, which had long indicated the potential for such a product. Working with R&D labs in Cincinnati and the United Kingdom, several Japanese technologists participated on a global team that developed a new product involving a durable color base and a renewable moisturizing second coat. Recognizing that this two-stage application would result in a more expensive product that involved basic habit changes, the global cosmetics category executive asked Max Factor Japan to be the new brand's global lead market.

Viewing their task as "translating the breakthrough technology invention into a market-sensitive product innovation," the Japanese product management team developed the marketing approach–concept, packaging, positioning, communications strategy, and so on–that led to the new brand, Lipfinity, becoming Japan's best-selling lipstick. The Japanese innovations were then transferred worldwide, as Lipfinity rolled out in Europe and the United States within six months of the Japanese launch.

O2005 Rolls Out

Soon after O2005 was first announced in September 1998, massive management changes began. By the time of its formal implementation in July 1999, half the top 30 managers and a third of the top 300 were new to their jobs. For example, Lafley, who had just returned from Asia to head the North American region, was asked to prepare to hand off that role and take over as head of the Beauty Care GBU. "It was a crazy year," recalled Lafley. "There was so much to build, but beyond the grand design, we were not clear about how it should operate."

In another of the hundreds of O2005 senior management changes, de Cesare, head of P&G's European skin care business, was promoted to vice president and asked to move to Osaka and head up Max Factor Japan. Under the new structure he would report directly to Lafley's Beauty Care GBU and on a dotted-line basis to the head of the MDO for Northeast Asia.

In addition to adjusting to this new complexity where responsibilities and relationships were still being defined, de Cesare found himself in a new global role. As president of Max Factor Japan he became a member of the Beauty Care Global Leadership Team (GLT), a group comprised of the business GMs from three key MDOs, representatives from key functions such as R&D, consumer research, product supply, HR, and finance, and chaired by Lafley as GBU head. These meetings became vital forums for implementing Lafley's charge "to review P&G's huge beauty care portfolio and focus investment on the top brands with the potential to become global assets." The question took on new importance for de Cesare when he was named global franchise leader for SK-II and asked to explore its potential as a global brand.

A New Global Product Development Process

Soon after arriving in Japan, de Cesare discovered that the Japanese Max Factor organization was increasingly involved in new global product development activities following its successful Lipfinity role. This process began under the leadership of the Beauty Care GLT when consumer research identified an unmet consumer need worldwide. A lead research center then developed a technical model of how P&G could respond to the need. Next, the GLT process brought in marketing expertise from lead markets to expand that technology "chassis" to a holistic new product concept. Finally, contributing technologists and marketers were designated to work on the variations in ingredients or aesthetics necessary to adapt the core technology or product concept to local markets.

This global product development process was set in motion when consumer researchers found

that, despite regional differences, there was a worldwide opportunity in facial cleansing. The research showed that, although U.S. women were satisfied with the clean feeling they got using bar soaps, it left their skin tight and dry; in Europe, women applied a cleansing milk with a cotton pad that left their skin moisturized and conditioned but not as clean as they wanted; and in Japan, the habit of using foaming facial cleansers left women satisfied with skin conditioning but not with moisturizing. Globally, however, the unmet need was to achieve soft, moisturized, clean-feeling skin, and herein the GBU saw the product opportunity–and the technological challenge.

A technology team was assembled at an R&D facility in Cincinnati, drawing on the most qualified technologists from its P&G's labs worldwide. For example, because the average Japanese woman spent 4.5 minutes on her face-cleansing regime compared with 1.7 minutes for the typical American woman, Japanese technologists were sought for their refined expertise in the cleansing processes and their particular understanding of how to develop a product with the rich, creamy lather.

Working with a woven substrate technology developed by P&G's paper business, the core technology team found that a 10-micron fiber, when woven into a mesh, was effective in trapping and absorbing dirt and impurities. By impregnating this substrate with a dry-sprayed formula of cleansers and moisturizers activated at different times in the cleansing process, team members felt they could develop a disposable cleansing cloth that would respond to the identified consumer need. After this technology "chassis" had been developed, a technology team in Japan adapted it to allow the cloth to be impregnated with a different cleanser formulation that included the SK-II ingredient, Pitera. (See Exhibit 8 for an overview of the development process.)

A U.S.-based marketing team took on the task of developing the Olay version. Identifying its consumers' view of a multistep salon facial as the ultimate cleansing experience, this team came up with the concept of a one-step routine that offered the benefits of cleansing, conditioning, and toning–"just like a daily facial." Meanwhile, another team had the same assignment in Japan, which became the lead market for the

Exhibit 8 Representation of Global Cleansing Cloth Development Program

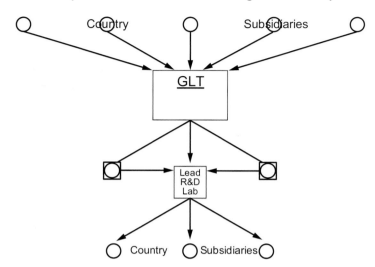

1. Consumer research on facial cleansing needs by country.

2. Identification of an unmet worldwide consumer need for cleansing that resulted in "soft, moisturized clean-feeling skin."

3. Technologists and marketers from key labs and markets are assembled in a lead R&D lab to develop a technology "chassis" and a core product concept.

4. Local technologists and marketers adapt the core technology and product concept to fit local needs and opportunities.

Source: Casewriter's interpretation.

SK-II version. Because women already had a five- or six-step cleansing routine, the SK-II version was positioned not as a "daily facial" but as a "foaming massage cloth" that built on the ritual experience of increasing skin circulation through a massage while boosting skin clarity due to the microfibers' ability to clean pores and trap dirt. (See Exhibit 9 for illustration of the Foaming Massage Cloth with other core SK-II products.)

Because of its premium pricing strategy, the SK-II Foaming Massage Cloth was packaged in a much more elegant dispensing box and was priced at ¥6,000 ($50), compared to $7 for the Olay Facial Cloth in the United States. And Japan assigned several technologists to the task of developing detailed product performance data that Japanese beauty magazines required for the much more scientific product reviews they published compared to their Western counterparts. In the end, each market ended up with a distinct

product built on a common technology platform. Marketing expertise was also shared–some Japanese performance analysis and data were also relevant for the Olay version and were used in Europe, for example–allowing the organization to leverage its local learning.

The SK-II Decision: A Global Brand?

After barely six months in Japan, de Cesare recognized that he now had three different roles in the new organization. As president of Max Factor Japan, he was impressed by the turnaround this local company had pulled off and was optimistic about its ability to grow significantly in the large Japanese beauty market. As GLT member on the Beauty Care GBU, he was proud of his organization's contribution to the GBU-sponsored global new product innovation process and was convinced that Japan could continue to contribute to

Exhibit 9 Illustration of Part of SK-II Product Line

pitera soak

FACIAL TREATMENT ESSENCE
Skin Balancing Essence

The heart of the SK-II range, the revolutionary **Facial Treatment Essence** is the second point in your Ritual. This unique Pitera-rich product helps boost moisture levels to improve texture and clarity for a more beautiful, glowing complexion.

Women are so passionate about **Facial Treatment Essence** that they describe it as their 'holy' water. It contains the most concentrated amount of Pitera of all our skincare products — around 90% pure SK-II Pitera. It absorbs easily and leaves your skin looking radiant, with a supple, smooth feel.

FOAMING MASSAGE CLOTH
Purifying Cleansing Cloth

These innovative **Foaming Massage Cloths** leave your skin feeling smooth and velvety. A single sheet offers the outstanding effects of a cleanser, facial wash and massage. It gently washes away impurities, excess oil and non-waterproof eye make-up, leaving your skin clean, pure and refreshed.

FACIAL TREATMENT CLEAR LOTION
Clear Purifying Lotion

For a perfectly conditioned and ultra-fresh skin, use the **Facial Treatment Clear Lotion** morning and evening after cleansing your face and neck. The final part of your cleansing process, this Lotion helps remove residual impurities and dead skin cells.

Source: Company brochure.

and learn from P&G's impressive technology base. And now as global franchise leader for SK-II, he was excited by the opportunity to explore whether the brand could break into the $9 billion worldwide prestige skin care market. (See Exhibit 10 for prestige market data.)

When he arrived in Japan, de Cesare found that SK-II's success in Taiwan and Hong Kong (by 1999, 45% of total SK-II sales) had already encouraged management to begin expansion into three other regional markets–Singapore, Malaysia, and South Korea. But these were relatively small markets, and as he reviewed data on the global skin care and prestige beauty markets, he wondered if the time was right to make a bold entry into one or more major markets. (See Exhibits 11 and 12 for global skin-care market and consumer data.)

As he reviewed the opportunities, three alternatives presented themselves. First, the beauty care management team for Greater China was interested in expanding on SK-II's success in

Taiwan and Hong Kong by introducing the brand into mainland China. Next, at GLT meetings de Cesare had discussed with the head of beauty care in Europe the possibilities of bringing SK-II into that large Western market. His third possibility–really his first option, he realized–was to build on the brand's success in SK-II's rich and proven home Japanese market.

The Japanese Opportunity

Japanese women were among the most sophisticated users of beauty products in the world, and per capita they were the world's leading consumers of these products. Despite its improved performance in recent years, Max Factor Japan claimed less than a 3% share of this $10 billion beauty product market. "It's huge," boasted one local manager. "Larger than the U.S. laundry market."

Although SK-II had sales of more than $150 million in Japan in 1999, de Cesare was also

Exhibit 10
Global Prestige Market: Size and Geographic Split

- **Global Prestige Market: 1999**
  (Fragrances, Cosmetics, Skin) = $15 billion at retail level
  (of which approximately 60% is skin care)

United States	26%
Canada	2
Asia/Pacific[a]	25
United Kingdom	5
France	5
Germany	5
Rest of Europe	16
Rest of World	16

Source: Company data.

[a] Japan represented over 80% of the Asia/Pacific total.

Exhibit 11
Global Skin Care Market Size: 1999

Skin Care (Main market and prestige)

Region/Country	Retail Sales ($ million)	Two-Year Growth Rate
Western Europe	8,736	7%
France	2,019	7
Germany	1,839	14
United Kingdom	1,052	17
North America	6,059	18
United States	5,603	18
Asia/Pacific	11,220	2
China	1,022	28
Japan	6,869	6
South Korea	1,895	9
Taiwan	532	18
Hong Kong	266	6

Source: Company data.

aware that in recent years its home market growth had slowed. This was something the new manager felt he could change by tapping into P&G's extensive technological resources. The successful experience of the foaming massage cloth convinced him that there was a significant opportunity to expand sales by extending the SK-II line beyond its traditional product offerings. For example, he could see an immediate opportunity to move into new segments by adding anti-aging and skin-whitening products to the SK-II range. Although this would take a considerable amount of time and effort, it would exploit internal capabilities and external brand

Exhibit 12
Skin Care and Cosmetics Habits and Practices: Selected Countries

Product Usage (% Past 7 Days)	United States[a]	Japan[a]	China[b]	United Kingdom[a]
Facial Moisturizer–Lotion	45%	95%	26%	37%
Facial Moisturizer–Cream	25	28	52	45
Facial Cleansers (excluding Family Bar Soap)	51	90	57	41
Foundation	70	85	35	57
Lipstick	84	97	75	85
Mascara	76	27	13	75

Source: Company data.

[a] Based on broad, representative sample of consumers.

[b] Based on upper-income consumers in Beijing City.

image. Compared to the new-market entry options, investment would be quite low.

An exciting development that would support this home market thrust emerged when he discovered that his SK-II technology and marketing teams had come together to develop an innovative beauty imaging system (BIS). Using the Japanese technicians' skills in miniaturization and software development, they were working to create a simplified version of scientific equipment used by P&G lab technicians to qualify new skin care products by measuring improvements in skin condition. The plan was to install the modified BIS at SK-II counters and have beauty consultants use it to boost the accuracy and credibility of their skin diagnosis. The project fit perfectly with de Cesare's vision for SK-II to become the brand that solved individual skin care problems. He felt it could build significant loyalty in the analytically inclined Japanese consumer.

With the company's having such a small share of such a rich market, de Cesare felt that a strategy of product innovation and superior in-store service had the potential to accelerate a growth rate that had slowed to 5% per annum over the past three years. Although Shiseido could be expected to put up a good fight, he felt SK-II should double sales in Japan over the next six or seven years. In short, de Cesare was extremely excited about SK-II's potential for growth in its home market. He said: "It's a fabulous opportunity. One loyal SK-II customer in Japan already spends about $1,000 a year on the

brand. Even a regular consumer of all P&G's other products–from toothpaste and deodorant to shampoo and detergent–all together spends nowhere near that amount annually."

The Chinese Puzzle

A very different opportunity existed in China, where P&G had been operating only since 1988. Because of the extraordinarily low prices of Chinese laundry products, the company had uncharacteristically led with beauty products when it entered this huge market. Olay was launched in 1989 and, after early problems, eventually became highly successful by adopting a nontraditional marketing strategy. To justify its price premium–its price was 20 to 30 times the price of local skin care products–Shivesh Ram, the entrepreneurial beauty care manager in China, decided to add a service component to Olay's superior product formulation. Borrowing from the Max Factor Japan model, he began selling through counters in the state-owned department stores staffed by beauty counselors. By 1999, Olay had almost 1,000 such counters in China and was a huge success.

As the Chinese market opened to international retailers, department stores from Taiwan, Hong Kong, and Singapore began opening in Beijing and Shanghai. Familiar with Olay as a mass-market brand, they questioned allocating it scarce beauty counter space alongside Estee Lauder, Lancôme, Shiseido, and other premium brands that had already claimed the prime locations critical to success in this business. It was at this point that Ram began exploring the possibility of introducing SK-II, allowing Olay to move more deeply into second-tier department stores, stores in smaller cities, and to "second-floor" cosmetics locations in large stores. "China is widely predicted to become the second-largest market in the world," said Ram. "The prestige beauty segment is growing at 30 to 40% a year, and virtually every major competitor in that space is already here."

Counterbalancing Ram's enthusiastic proposals, de Cesare also heard voices of concern. Beyond the potential impact on a successful Olay market position, some were worried that SK-II would be a distraction to P&G's strategy of becoming a mainstream Chinese company and to its competitive goal of entering 600 Chinese cities ahead of Unilever, Kao, and other global players. They argued that targeting an elite consumer group with a niche product was not in keeping with the objective of reaching the 1.2 billion population with laundry, hair care, oral care, diapers, and other basics. After all, even with SK-II's basic four-step regimen, a three-month supply could cost more than one month's salary for the average woman working in a major Chinese city.

Furthermore, the skeptics wondered if the Chinese consumer was ready for SK-II. Olay had succeeded only by the company's educating its customers to move from a one-step skin care process–washing with bar soap and water–to a three-step cleansing and moisturizing process.

SK-II relied on women developing at least a four-to six-step regimen, something the doubters felt was unrealistic. But as Ram and others argued, within the target market, skin care practices were quite developed, and penetration of skin care products was higher than in many developed markets.

Finally, the Chinese market presented numerous other risks, from the widespread existence of counterfeit prestige products to the bureaucracy attached to a one-year import-registration process. But the biggest concern was the likelihood that SK-II would attract import duties of 35% to 40%. This meant that even if P&G squeezed its margin in China, SK-II would have to be priced significantly above the retail level in other markets. Still, the China team calculated that because of the lower cost of beauty consultants, the product could still be profitable. (See Exhibit 13 for cost estimates.)

Despite the critics, Ram was eager to try, and he responded to their concerns: "There are three Chinas–rural China, low-income urban China, and sophisticated, wealthy China concentrated in Shanghai, Beijing, and Guangzhou. The third group is as big a target consumer group as in many developed markets. If we don't move soon, the battle for that elite will be lost to the global beauty care powerhouses that have been here for three years or more."

Ram was strongly supported by his regional beauty care manager and by the Greater China MDO president. Together, they were willing to experiment with a few counters in Shanghai, and if successful, to expand to more counters in other

Exhibit 13
Global SK-II Cost Structure (% of net sales)[a]

FY1999/2000	Japan	Taiwan/ Hong Kong	PR China Expected	United Kingdom Expected
Net sales	100%	100%	100%	100%
Cost of products sold	22	26	45	29
Marketing, research, and selling/ administrative expense	67	58	44	63
Operating income	11	16	11	8

Source: Company estimates.

[a] Data disguised.

major cities. Over the first three years, they expected to generate $10 million to $15 million in sales, by which time they expected the brand to break even. They estimated the initial investment to build counters, train beauty consultants, and support the introduction would probably mean losses of about 10% of sales over that three-year period.

The European Question

As he explored global opportunities for SK-II, de Cesare's mind kept returning to the European market he knew so well. Unlike China, Europe had a relatively large and sophisticated group of beauty-conscious consumers who already practiced a multistep regimen using various specialized skin care products. What he was unsure of was whether there was a significant group willing to adopt the disciplined six- to eight-step ritual that the most devoted Japanese SK-II users followed.

The bigger challenge, in his view, would be introducing a totally new brand into an already crowded field of high-profile, well-respected competitors including Estee Lauder, Clinique, Lancôme, Chanel, and Dior. While TV advertising had proven highly effective in raising SK-II's awareness and sales in Japan, Taiwan, and Hong Kong, the cost of television–or even print–ads in Europe made such an approach there prohibitive. And without any real brand awareness or heritage, he wondered if SK-II's mystique would transfer to a Western market.

As he thought through these issues, de Cesare spoke with his old boss, Mike Thompson, the head of P&G's beauty business in Europe. Because the Max Faxtor sales force sold primarily to mass-distribution outlets, Thompson did not think it provided SK-II the appropriate access to the European market. However, he explained that the fine-fragrance business was beginning to do quite well. In the United Kingdom, for example, its 25-person sales force was on track in 1999 to book $1 million in after-tax profit on sales of $12 million. Because it sold brands such as Hugo Boss, Giorgio, and Beverly Hills to department stores and Boots, the major pharmacy chain, its sales approach and trade relationship was different from the SK-II model in Japan. Nevertheless, Thompson felt it was a major asset that could be exploited.

Furthermore, Thompson told de Cesare that his wife was a loyal SK-II user and reasoned that since she was a critical judge of products, other women would discover the same benefits in the product she did. He believed that SK-II provided the fine-fragrance business a way to extend its line in the few department stores that dominated U.K. distribution in the prestige business. He thought they would be willing to give SK-II a try. (He was less optimistic about countries such as France and Germany, however, where prestige products were sold through thousands of perfumeries, making it impossible to justify the SK-II consultants who would be vital to the sales model.)

Initial consumer research in the United Kingdom had provided mixed results. But de Cesare felt that while this kind of blind testing could provide useful data on detergents, it was less helpful in this case. The consumers tested the product blind for one week, then were interviewed about their impressions. But because they lacked the beauty counselors' analysis and advice and had not practiced the full skin care regimen, he felt the results did not adequately predict SK-II's potential.

In discussions with Thompson, de Cesare concluded that he could hope to achieve sales of $10 million by the fourth year in the U.K. market. Given the intense competition, he recognized that he would have to absorb losses of $1 million to $2 million annually over that period as the startup investment.

The Organizational Constraint

While the strategic opportunities were clear, de Cesare also recognized that his decision needed to comply with the organizational reality in which it would be implemented. While GBU head Lafley was an early champion and continuing supporter of SK-II, his boss, Jager, was less committed. Jager was among those in P&G who openly questioned how well some of the products in the beauty care business–particularly some of the acquired brands–fit in the P&G portfolio. While he was comfortable with high-volume products like shampoo, he was more skeptical of the upper end of the line, particularly fine fragrances. In his view, the fashion-linked and promotion-driven sales models of luxury products neither played well to P&G's "stack it high, sell it cheap" marketing skills nor leveraged its superior technologies.

The other organizational reality was that the implementation of O2005 was causing a good deal of organizational disruption and management distraction. This was particularly true in Europe, as Thompson explained:

> We swung the pendulum 180 degrees, from a local to a global focus. Marketing plans and budgets had previously been developed locally, strongly debated with European managers, then rolled up. Now they were developed globally–or at least regionally–by new people who often did not understand the competitive and trade differences across markets. We began to standardize and centralize our policies and practices out of Geneva. Not surprisingly, a lot of our best local managers left the company.

One result of the O2005 change was that country subsidiary GMs now focused more on maximizing sales volume than profits, and this had put the beauty care business under significant budget pressure. Thompson explained the situation in Europe in 1999:

One thing became clear very quickly: It was a lot easier to sell cases of Ariel [detergent] or Pampers [diapers] than cases of cosmetics, so guess where the sales force effort went? At the same time, the new product pipeline was resulting in almost a "launch of the month," and with the introduction of new products like Swiffer and Febreze, it was hard for the MDOs to manage all of these corporate priorities. . . . Finally, because cosmetics sales required more time and effort from local sales forces, more local costs were assigned to that business, and that has added to profit pressures.

Framing the Proposal

It was in this context that de Cesare was framing his proposal based on the global potential of SK-II as a brand and his plans to exploit the opportunities he saw. But he knew Lafley's long ties and positive feelings towards SK-II would not be sufficient to convince him. The GBU head was committed to focusing beauty care on the core brands that could be developed as a global franchise, and his questions would likely zero in on whether de Cesare could build SK-II into such a brand.

HARVARD | BUSINESS | SCHOOL

FEBRUARY 19, 2010

BRIEF CASES

Christopher A. Bartlett and Heather Beckham
CASE 5.2 APPLIED RESEARCH TECHNOLOGIES, INC.: GLOBAL INNOVATION'S CHALLENGES

On June 5, 2006, Peter Vyas paced his office as he grappled with a request for $2 million to relaunch a mini water-oxidation product. Despite two failures to bring this product to market over the past three years, his team was confident this latest iteration was a winner.

For Vyas, general manager of the Filtration Unit of Applied Research Technologies (ART), the request presented a major challenge. He recognized that his team had worked tirelessly to make this project a reality and strongly believed they were now headed in the right direction. But he also understood that the Filtration Unit's track record of failure during this product's development had hurt its credibility. If he supported the proposal, he knew he would be putting on the line not only his own personal credibility but also that of the entire unit.

Due to the project's size, final approval would be made by Vyas's boss, Cynthia Jackson–the newly appointed vice president of ART's Water Management Division. Jackson was acutely aware of the mounting losses in the Filtration Unit, and she had already devoted a significant amount of time trying to get them back on track. She had confided to one of her colleagues:

> When I took on this assignment, I was told my first task was to "fix" the Filtration Unit. The unit only had one revenue-generating product line and had failed to bring a profitable new product to market in five years. It was clear that I was expected to either turn it around or shut it down.
>
> I'm trying to protect them and ensure they get support, but my initial feeling is if they are to survive, they must become much more disciplined. They seem to be making progress on that front, but in all honesty, I sometimes wonder if it is time to cut our losses and initiate a harvest strategy for the unit.

Applied Research Technologies, Inc.

ART was one of the technology world's emerging giants. The company had grown through the merger and acquisition of numerous technology-based industrial companies, acquired in the LBO buyout waves of the 1980s and 1990s.

By 2006, ART consisted of a portfolio of about 60 business units, each of which operated as a profit center. Total corporate revenue was $11 billion in 2006.[1] Major divisions in the corporation included Healthcare (medical diagnostic equipment), Industrial Automation (robotics), Energy (extraction, conversion, and transportation solutions for the oil and gas industry–including the Water Management Division), and HVAC (Heating Ventilation and Air Conditioning, including climate control solutions for residential, commercial, and industrial markets). Exhibit 1 shows the organization structure of the company.

The company's success had been built on its innovative and entrepreneurial culture, coupled with a decentralized management philosophy. ART's vision statement, proudly displayed in almost every office and cubicle, stated: "We aim to change the world through innovation, and to grow our place in it through entrepreneurship."

Culture and Practices

ART was dedicated to supporting innovation not only with funding (the company's R&D spending was double the rate for U.S. industrial companies), but also in its practices, several of which were deeply embedded in the company's culture. ART encouraged employees to spend a half day each week "experimenting, brainstorming, and thinking outside the box." It was a practice that the company's visionary founder and current CEO, David Hall, referred to as "tinker time." He explained the concept:

> Innovation and entrepreneurship are the twin engines driving this company. It's the reason we've ingrained "tinker time" in our culture... I expect all our managers, and particularly those on the front line, to create, promote, and back promising ideas. But we understand that when you go for the big leap, you won't always clear the bar. So there is no shame in failure when you are stretching for big

---

[1] Of that total, Water Management Division sales were $560 million and Filtration Unit sales were $38 million

Exhibit 1 ART Organization with Filtration Unit Detail

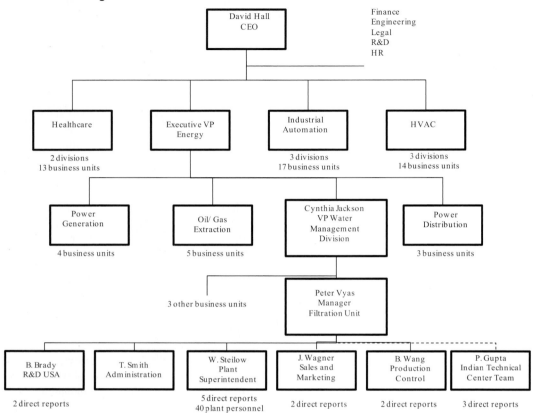

objectives. Around here we routinely celebrate what we call "worthy attempts"–even when they are unsuccessful.

Knowledge sharing and dissemination was another key part of ART's business philosophy, and despite the high level of decentralization and profit accountability, technology and human capital were both widely shared among divisions. For example, experts in one division routinely served as advisors on project committees for other divisions, and it was not uncommon for employees to go "on loan" to help another unit with a promising product idea or technology.

The company also moved quickly to bring products to market. If an idea showed promise, funding was usually available for small "beta batch" productions, which often allowed market testing to achieve what was called "proof of concept" within ART. Once an innovation was proven, significant investment was quickly put behind it.

Objectives and Priorities

To infuse discipline into its decentralized organization, ART's top management set highly aggressive performance objectives and tied executive compensation tightly to them. In 2006, as in any other year, each division was expected to deliver sales growth of 10%, pretax margins of 15%, and return on invested capital of 20%, referred to as the "10/15/20 Target." The belief that innovative products were the source of the company's ongoing competitive advantage was reflected in a companywide metric requiring

30% of each division's total sales come from products developed in the last four years.[2]

Hall also continually emphasized that to be competitive, ART had to shorten the life cycle between a new technology's conception and its commercialization. In response, the company had introduced the "Fast Track Pipeline," a program that focused on the highest priority projects by providing them with additional resources and management attention. ART currently had 67 such projects in the pipeline, six in the Water Division, but none in the Filtration Unit. (The mini oxidation unit had not been identified as a "Fast Track" project).

In the late 1990s, Hall began pushing to grow ART's global presence. "It's important not just to expand our market access, but also to broaden our talent access," he insisted. "Innovation and entrepreneurship know no national boundaries." In the quest to meet this challenge "to attract the best and the brightest wherever they live," in 2000, the corporate R&D group opened the India Technical Center (ITC)–a substantial operation that Hall hoped would become a model for other R&D centers he planned to open up around the globe.

The Filtration Business Unit

The Filtration Unit was part of a business ART acquired from an oil and gas services company in 1996. Its core product line was in mobile water treatment that allowed oil and gas exploration companies to meet government water recycling requirements at well heads and drilling sites. These products were still the unit's core line, but in the late 1990s, new competition from Chinese manufacturers had led to a commoditization of the business and an erosion of margins. ART's newly acquired filtration business had tried to develop the next generation of products and technologies, but after two high-profile new product failures, the unit had lost confidence. By 2006, it was losing about $6 million annually.

---

[2] Hall had recently increased this target from 25% of each unit's sales from products developed in the last five years.

New Management, New Energy

In a promotion from his role as a lab manager in the HVAC Division, the 32-year-old Vyas had assumed the role of business manager for the Filtration Unit in June 2001. He immediately confronted the unit's twin organizational problems of low morale and growing turnover, and in his first year, rebuilt the team by carefully selecting entrepreneurial-minded individuals to fill the vacancies left by turnover in the unit. One of his key recruits was Janice Wagner, whom he knew from her five years as a marketing manager in the HVAC Division. She was excited to join a unit that had an opportunity to develop a new business from scratch.

Convinced that survival depended on innovative growth, Vyas appointed a technology evaluation team early in his tenure, charging them with the responsibility to focus on technologies with the potential to turn the unit around. In one of his first reviews with that team, Vyas learned that for almost a year, the filtration unit had been working with ITC technicians on an exciting new technology the young Indian team had developed based on a license obtained from a Delhi-based start-up company. Developed as a potential solution to the widespread Third World problem of obtaining clean water in remote regions, this small-scale oxidation system was thought to have application in many less-developed markets. But in an effort to cut costs, the filtration unit's previous management had decided to abandon the collaboration a year earlier.

After reviewing the technology, Vyas became convinced that this had been a mistake and encouraged his evaluation team to pursue the project. Working closely with the ITC technologists, the team concluded that the oxidation technology was the most promising opportunity in their portfolio, and recommended developing a small-scale oxidation system that enabled waste-water disinfection in small batches. "We were so excited by that decision," said Div Verma, the ITC technologist in charge of the project. "We believe this project can make a huge difference to the lives of millions."

Motivated by the support they received, the ITC technicians developed a promising initial design. Without bulky equipment (the equipment was a 26-inch cube) or an electrical power source (it utilized battery power), this small system could transform waste water into potable water without chemicals in minutes. A single unit had the capacity to process approximately 2,000 liters of contaminated water per day. With pride, they took their design to Vyas.

But Vyas wanted to understand the business opportunity and asked Wagner to prepare a brief overview. Wagner learned that only about 2.5% of the world's water was fresh, and most of that was frozen. Population growth, industrial development, and agricultural expansion were all putting pressure on fresh-water supplies in both developed and developing countries. Indeed, the World Resources Institute found that demand for water was growing at twice the rate of the population. As a result, the World Health Organization estimated that over 1.1 billion people lacked access to clean water, and that 2.4 billion lacked access to basic sanitation. The research also revealed that water-borne diseases accounted for 80% of infections in the developing world, and in 2002, 3.1 million deaths occurred (90% children) as a result of diarrheal diseases and malaria. As countries such as India and China industrialized, they used more fresh water and added more pollution to existing water sources.

Wagner concluded that the scarcity of clean water was reaching crisis levels in developing nations, and that the mini-oxidation system could help avert some of the catastrophic effects. But she also reported comparable R&D efforts also underway in the government and private sectors in China and Europe, and that several companies in the United States and Canada were researching the technology. Nevertheless, her analysis suggested the ITC team's product was further along and probably superior to anything else in the space.

New Opportunities, New Initiatives

Vyas decided to pursue the project and convinced the VP of Corporate R&D who had ITC oversight to allow the three ITC technologists working on it to become members of his technical team–a move that would allow them to focus on developing commercial designs for the oxidation technology. Simultaneously, he asked Wagner to do a first-cut market assessment to identify potential opportunities for the technology. Over the next few weeks, through focus groups and interviews with potential customers, she uncovered several promising applications. (See Exhibit 2).

Exhibit 2
Wagner's List of Potential Markets

Developing Nations
- Provide potable water solutions for areas with unsafe drinking water

U.S. Residential
- Landscape irrigation
- Pools
- In-house water recirculation for non-drinking purposes (e.g., laundry, dishwashers, etc.)

U.S. Commercial
- Restaurants
- Grocery stores
- Laundromats
- Linen/Uniform companies
- Farms
- Landscape irrigation

U.S. and Overseas Emergency Units
- Disaster relief
- Military

But while the market research was exciting, progress in bringing a product to market proved to be slow and difficult. From January 2003 to February 2006, the technology team coordinated with separate manufacturing and marketing teams located in the United States to work through two complete cycles of product development, beta batch productions, and test marketing of two different versions of the mini-oxidation system. Both failed due to what were subsequently revealed to be defects in the design and lack of interest in the marketplace.

The first-generation product was aimed at the application for which the technology was originally developed–to provide developing nations with safe drinking water. Largely supported by foreign aid, the mini-oxidation system was field-tested by representatives from funding agencies. Unfortunately, the output water had a detectable odor which the funders found unacceptable. Despite assurances that ITC technicians could fix the problem, the trials failed to convert into orders.

The team decided to refocus a second-generation product on specialized applications in Western countries where funding was more available. The plan was to develop a slightly modified version of the product and aim it at a potential market for military use and NGO disaster relief activities that Wagner had identified in her initial analysis. This decision was enormously disappointing to the Indian technologists who had developed the initial prototypes, and Vyas had to work hard to keep them on board. The second-generation product fixed the odor problem, but field trials showed that the solution caused the unit to consume too much power, requiring frequent battery replacement. Once again, no orders were forthcoming.

While these trials were occurring, the filtration unit's small R&D team in the United States persuaded Vyas to allow them to work with corporate R&D on an entirely new version of the product that would utilize ultrasound waves for water disinfection. High frequency vibrations were shown to control the growth of algae, organic waste, and bacteria such as E. coli. Market applications for this technology included treatment for clean water storage receptacles,

public/private ponds, fish tanks, and ballast water. However, in 2006 this technology was still in the earliest stages of research and testing.

New Oversight, New Discipline

In January 2006, just as Vyas and the rest of the mini-oxidation team were launching their second-generation system, Cynthia Jackson was appointed vice president of the Water Management Division. Jackson's attention was soon drawn to the troubled Filtration Unit which she felt needed to put much more rigor into the planning and analysis that supported their product development activities. According to Jackson:

> Peter Vyas seems to be an excellent talent manager. He was able to recruit and retain good people to his unit, and then build them into highly motivated teams on two different continents. He's also shown himself to be an outstanding advocate for the group's ideas–skilled at managing upward, gaining support, and running interference so his team can concentrate on the task at hand. And I'm aware that the company has high hopes for the Filtration Unit, but the results just are not there.
>
> In my view, the unit lacks discipline. They had a promising technology that was in search of a market, but had not done the work to nail down either. In the first meeting I had with them I explained that they would be developing any future proposals using a rigorous three-phase process linking market analysis and technological development to business planning.

In her first meeting with Vyas, Jackson also made it clear that the unit's continued existence was in jeopardy if they did not turn things around.

Mini-Oxidation's Third Launch Attempt

To coordinate the third launch of the mini-oxidation system, Vyas assembled a single six-person development team with representatives from various functions located in the United States and India. Because Janice Wagner had demonstrated strong project management skills,

Exhibit 3

ART Mini Water Oxidation System–Development Committee Team Structure

New Product Introduction Team Members	
D. Verma	Laboratory Leader–Indian Technical Center
R. Patel	Product Development–Indian Technical Center
B. Wang	Manufacturing
H. Lewis	Quality Assurance
J. Wagner	Marketing (TEAM LEADER)
T. Smith	Project Administration
C. Cortez[a]	HVAC Division Representative
G. Steinberg[a]	Healthcare Division Representative

[a] Member from another unit of ART added in Phase 2.

Vyas named her as the team leader. (Exhibit 3 details committee membership.) From the outset, the team was highly committed to the product and worked tirelessly to complete Jackson's three-phase process.

Phase 1: General Product Concept and Market Analysis

Wagner took the lead in preparing the Phase 1 requirement "to develop a general product concept supported by market research." Having learned that the unit lacked the expertise to sell to developing markets, governments, and NGOs, she decided to focus additional research on U.S. data that seemed to indicate strong potential for a residential water purification system. She also decided to see if opportunities might exist in domestic agricultural applications.

According to the Palmer Drought Index from April of 2006, 26% of the United States was considered in moderate to extreme drought conditions, and Wagner's research showed that low rainfall, high wind, and rapid population growth in the Western and Southeastern regions of the country caused a major water scarcity problem for these areas. The resulting government-imposed water restrictions often led to severe limitations or outright bans of water used in residential landscape irrigation. Because re-use of waste water would serve conservation efforts while preserving residential landscaping, Wagner

felt that the mini-oxidation system offered a perfect solution for the needs of homeowners in these drought-stricken areas. In addition, since the product would be used for irrigation and not for drinking water, the disinfection quality could be lowered and energy consumption would therefore be reduced compared to past product iterations.

Wagner's research on the U.S. water industry indicated that the domestic water-treatment equipment market generated sales of over $9 billion. (Exhibit 4 provides selected data from the research.) Residential water treatment products ranged from water filters that reduced sediment, rust, and chlorine odor (average retail price $50) to systems that provided more comprehensive household water purification (retail price $1,500 to $3,000). The research also showed that in-ground sprinkler systems cost between $1,800 and $4,000, and after conducting some industry interviews and focus groups, Wagner felt this was a good barometer of what a homeowner was willing to pay for a lush, green lawn.

After discussing the product concept with the development committee members, the team decided to recommend a retail price of $2,000 ($1,000 wholesale price) for a residential irrigation mini-oxidation system (RIMOS) capable of supporting a 10,000 square-foot lawn. Pricing for an agricultural irrigation large oxidation system (AILOS) would be significantly less on a per-acre basis, with details to be developed only after

Exhibit 4
Market Research: Summary Data

The U.S. Water Industry (Revenues in millions)[a]	
Water Treatment Equipment	$9,110
Delivery Equipment	$11,660
Chemicals	$4,020
Contract Operations	$2,350
Consulting/Engineering	$7,460
Maintenance Services	$1,780
Instruments and Testing	$1,400
Wastewater Utilities	$34,130
Drinking Water Utilities s	$35,070
Total U.S. Water Industry	**$106,980**
U.S. Residences (2000 Census)	
Total Housing Units	116 million
Single-Family Detached Homes	70 million
Drought Indicators (Palmer Drought Index 4/10/2006)	
% of the contiguous U.S. in severe to extreme drought	13%
% of the contiguous U.S. in moderate to extreme drought	26%

NOTE: Mini-Oxidation Systems are a "new-to-the-world" product with unknown market potential.
[a] *Source:* Adapted from the *Environmental Business Journal*, 2006

further research had been done. Wagner and Vyas compiled the data and product concept information in a formal proposal for Jackson to approve.

Jackson responded to the team's Phase 1 proposal with a flurry of questions and challenges. She highlighted the sparseness of concrete market numbers and their lack of data on target markets. And when the team floated the idea of designing a larger-scale agricultural version of the system, she asked them to think about whether that would stretch resources too thin. With the whole company under pressure to trim budgets, Jackson asked the team to consider reducing the project's costs by eliminating either the RIMOS or AILOS product. After some discussion, Vyas and his team agreed to focus future product development and marketing efforts on the RIMOS product for the U.S. market.

Phase 2: Technical Specifications and Prototype

Having won the approval of Phase 1, the team was now ready to begin the second phase of Jackson's product development process. This involved designing actual product specifications and determining how to do this within the $1,000 wholesale price point that the group had determined was appropriate. A working prototype was also to be created as part of this phase.

The team relied heavily on ITC expertise to adapt the existing product originally designed to provide potable water in remote locations, to one capable of processing wastewater for lawn irrigation. During this phase, several misunderstandings surfaced between team members in the United States and India. For example, Wagner became concerned when the Indian team repeatedly missed design deadlines she had requested. When she confronted Div Verma, the lab leader responsible for the project, he responded tersely:

Peter told us he wanted the new design to be flawless. I take that as my number one priority. We can't meet this deliverable without proper testing. Why is everything so rushed with you? If we don't have a perfect design,

Exhibit 5
Summary Sales and Profit Forecast for RIMOS

	2007	2008	2009	2010	2011
Forecast Sales ($ millions)	$ 5.45	$ 7.08	$ 8.86	$ 10.89	$ 13.07
Forecast Operating Income (%)	10%	15%	20%	20%	20%

then we run the risk of failing a third time and that is not acceptable. My team will not provide designs for a prototype until we are sure that all the bugs have been worked out. We don't want to be involved in another failure.

Emphasizing the mandate to move quickly while ensuring product quality, Vyas mediated the disagreement by crafting a compromise that gave the Indian technical team a formal schedule allowing them two weeks of extra testing time. "I felt there was a mix of disappointment and pride that had to be dealt with," said Vias. "I also told Div that this third generation product would give us the credibility to return to the developing world project." Once the prototype was finished, the final designs and specs were again submitted for review.

Jackson was impressed by the attention to detail in this latest iteration, but wanted to ensure that the team was fully utilizing the internal expertise available at ART. With Jackson's help, Vyas tapped engineers and manufacturing managers from the HVAC and Healthcare Divisions who had expertise his team was lacking. He invited them to join his development team, and they quickly became deeply engaged in the project. They identified several design changes and production specifications that increased efficiency and lowered manufacturing costs.

Phase 3: Business Plan

The development of the business plan was the most difficult phase for Vyas and his team. They were unaccustomed to creating complex sales forecast models and cost estimates. But eventually they developed a detailed product concept, marketing approach, and manufacturing strategy for RIMOS, as well as sales forecasts, cost

projections, and expense estimates. They also acknowledged that they still believed there was a significant market in water treatment for the developing world and in emergency relief work, but these future options had not been included in the current forecasts or business plan. They hoped to explore these with the help of the Oil and Gas Division which had excellent international contacts.

Jackson challenged the team's pro forma financials which she felt lacked the data to support their assumptions. She asked the team to perform additional due diligence and to justify their assumptions. She also pushed back on the projected sales assumptions and suggested that the pro forma financials needed to be stress-tested. But after testing the analysis, Wagner felt her research was sound and was adamant about the size of the opportunity and their ability to capture the market. Vyas stood by Wagner and also defended the financial data which he felt had been carefully developed by the manufacturing and technology experts. Exhibit 5 summarizes the team's sales and operating margin forecasts.

The team acknowledged that its assumptions relied on the ability to gain access to the HVAC Group's Residential Market Division. As Wagner pointed out, ART's norms encouraged them to take advantage of these types of synergies, and they had good contacts in the division. However, the HVAC Residential Market Division's senior executives had full discretion regarding the products distributed through its channels, and they had not yet made a formal decision about RIMOS.

Jackson also expressed her concerns with the $2,000 retail price point and pushed Vyas to clearly identify the risks associated with the plan.

Exhibit 6
Summary Risk Analysis and Risk Mitigation for RIMOS

Risk	Level	Plan
May not gain market acceptance	High	– Ensure HVAC distribution support – Highlight ART name – Supplement marketing budget for product launch
Product design flaws	Medium	– Monitor beta batch closely
Price point too high	Medium	– Quantify customer savings from increased water efficiency – Provide sales training to distributors
Emerging competition	Low	– Get to market first – Leverage ART global presence, technical support, supplier relationships, and distribution network

After further consideration, the team developed a risk assessment and response matrix, which they included in the business plan (Exhibit 6). The business plan revealed the need for $2 million in funding for beta batch production of RIMOS and the marketing budget to support its distribution and promotion.

Toward a Decision: Go or No Go?

An hour after receiving the investment proposal from his team, Vyas was still pacing back and forth trying to decide whether to support or reject their request for the $2 million in funding for RIMOS. He knew his development team was absolutely convinced it could succeed, but he also realized that the unit's existence and even his own career were being openly questioned.

Two floors above Vyas's office, Jackson was also contemplating the RIMOS project. Having heard through the company grapevine that a funding request had been submitted to Vyas, she began to think about how she would handle the request if it was sent up to her. She had heard rumblings from other managers in her division that the Filtration Unit was a drain on division resources and that it was time to pull the plug on any additional funding.

As a newly promoted division VP, Jackson understood that her actions would be closely watched. She wanted to make sure she did not drop the ball.

IMD

CASE 5.3 CISCO INDIA (A): INNOVATION IN EMERGING MARKETS

Professor Srivardhini K. Jha (IIM Bangalore), Professor Rishikesha T. Krishnan (IIM Indore), Professor Charles Dhanaraj (IMD) and Research Associate Ivy Buche (IMD) prepared this case as a basis for class discussion rather than to illustrate either effective or ineffective handling of a business situation.

Dr Ishwardutt Parulkar, principal architect at Cisco's Indian subsidiary at Bangalore, was on his way to the office one early morning in July 2010. His team had held weeks of detailed discussions with major Indian telecom operators such as Airtel, Reliance and Vodafone on business needs and technology requirements for building their next generation networks. The broad contour of a product – a router developed in India for India – addressing the specific needs of telecom networks in emerging markets was taking shape in Parulkar's mind.[1] After working for Apple, Sun Microsystems and Cisco for 15 years in the US, he had recently moved to India for such an opportunity.

Given the value consciousness of emerging market customers, the lack of significant revenue in the short term and little precedence for such products in emerging markets, the business case for such a router was far from compelling. Parulkar realized that selling the idea internally would be an uphill task:

> Basically, we know that our product idea fills a gap in our emerging market offering, and the feedback from customers is also encouraging. But, in the absence of a strong business case – in the traditional sense of a high, predictable ROI in the short-term – it will be difficult to get approval and funding to develop the product through the established processes and criteria in the company. Further, the Indian ecosystem is not fully mature in terms of partners and skills required to develop such a product, such as tier-1 chip vendors, senior engineering talent in specific areas, labs that can test and certify telecom-grade equipment to global standards, manufacturing capability for complex hardware and so on.

Parulkar and his team were scheduled to meet Wim Elfrink, chief globalization officer, and Pankaj Patel, senior vice president and general manager, service provider business unit, to table their new product development proposal for his approval. They had to put forward a strong rationale!

Cisco Systems, Inc.

Cisco was founded in 1984 by Stanford University computer scientists Len Bosack and Sandy Lemer who named it after the city of San Francisco. Cisco pioneered the development of Internet Protocol (IP)-based networking technologies with the invention of the first multi-protocol router. Over the next 25 years, the tradition for innovation continued with the development of routing, switching and other network-based technologies such as application networking services, collaboration, home networking, security, storage area networking, TelePresence systems, unified communications, unified computing, video systems and wireless. Cisco's strategy centered on leveraging the network as a platform, to expand its share of customers' information technology spending. In fiscal year ending 31 July 2010, Cisco employed over 70,000 people in more than 150 countries and recorded annual revenues of $40 billion with a net income of $7.8 billion.[2] Despite the ongoing economic downturn, the company achieved revenue growth from both product and service segments across all geographic regions (*refer to Exhibit 1 for a revenue breakdown by product and geography*).

Cisco focused on its core networking capabilities while continuing to expand and transition into adjacent products and markets. The company sought to take advantage of virtualization and cloud-driven transitions (brought about by the convergence of networking, computing, storage and software technologies) in the enterprise data center market through its Unified Computing System platform and Nexus product families, which were designed to integrate the previously siloed technologies in the enterprise data center with a unified architecture.[3] In addition, Cisco aimed to apply this architectural approach to market adjacencies such as mobility, the consumer and electrical services infrastructure. With regard to mobility, the growth of IP traffic on handheld devices was driving the need for more robust architectures, equipment and services in order to accommodate not only an increasing

---

[1] These events have been dramatized for the purpose of the case.

[2] Cisco Systems Inc., Annual Report 2010.   [3] Ibid.

Exhibit 1
Cisco Revenue Breakdown by Product and Geography
Revenue by product

Year	2010	2009	2008
Net Sales	40,040	36,117	39,540
Product	32,420	29,131	33,099
% of Net sales	*81.0%*	*80.7%*	*83.7%*
Routers	6,574	6,311	7,940
Switches	13,568	12,119	13,538
Advanced Technologies	9,639	9,093	9,446
Others	2,639	1,608	2,175
Service	7,620	6,986	6,441
% of net sales	*19.0%*	*19.3%*	*16.3%*
Net income	7,767	6,134	8,052

Revenue by geography

Year	2010	2009	2008
Net Sales	40,040	36,117	39,540
United States and Canada	21,740	19,345	21,242
% of net sales	*54.3%*	*53.5%*	*53.7%*
European markets	8,048	7,683	8,123
% of net sales	*20.1%*	*21.3%*	*20.5%*
Emerging markets	4,367	3,999	4,530
% of net sales	*10.9%*	*10.3%*	*11.5%*
Asia Pacific	4,359	3,718	4,276
% of net sales	*10.9%*	*10.3%*	*10.8%*
Japan	1,526	1,372	2,175
% of net sales	*3.8%*	*3.8%*	*3.5%*

Source: Cisco Systems, Inc. Annual report 2010.

number of worldwide mobile device users but also increased user demand for broadband-quality business network and consumer web applications to be seamlessly delivered on such devices.

Globally, Cisco employed over 20,000 engineers and invested more than $5 billion or 13% of its annual revenues in R&D. Some of Cisco's prominent R&D units were located in San Jose, Boston, Raleigh, Shanghai, Durham and Tel Aviv. The company held a portfolio of over 15,000 patents. In 2009 it won 913 patents, a 30% increase over the previous year, securing 18th position among the top 50 patent winners in the US.[4]

Cisco in India

Cisco commenced its India operations in 1995 with a sales presence, followed by an R&D center

---

[4] U.S. patents awarded in 2009: IBM (4,914), Samsung Electronics (3,611) and Microsoft (2,906) occupied the top three spots.

in 1998 in Bangalore with 10 engineers working for a couple of business units in "extension" mode, i.e. they worked as an offshore team of Cisco, San Jose, executing specific tasks. The primary drivers for setting up the R&D center were availability of a large pool of English-speaking engineering talent and lower R&D costs. In the initial years, the charter of the India team included engineering functions such as testing support and sustenance that supported the core development activities undertaken in the US.

Over the next decade, the India center enhanced its capability by continuously learning from its interaction with headquarters. The ability of the India team to meet delivery and quality targets created good momentum, and several benefits accrued for the India center. First, it created an environment for more business units to set up teams in India. Second, the size of the India teams rapidly increased, not only because of cost efficiencies but also because of the capabilities at the center. Third, the India teams took on more responsibility and moved toward a model of greater ownership, taking complete responsibility for future development, support and services of certain protocols/components for Cisco's worldwide market. This shift to owning pockets of technology moved the center toward engineering leadership driven from India. In 2005 Cisco headquarters supported the growth of the India center by announcing a $1 billion direct investment in R&D, leasing and finance, sales and support and venture capital.[5] At this point, Cisco India typically focused on developing products for developed countries and then customized them for sale in emerging markets.

India's Growing Importance within Cisco

In December 2006 Cisco CEO and chairman John Chambers articulated that his strategic focus for India was to target emerging market businesses and customers. He announced the selection of India as the site for its globalization center, setting the stage of the company's globalization policy for talent, innovation and growth. He stated:

I don't make my decisions based on a quarter or a year. You are going to see us increase our investments in India, partnering with Indian companies and with the government. We invested in India looking at where we want to be in five, 10, 20 years. I am an optimist on India from a market perspective.[6]

In tandem, Cisco sought to decentralize 20% of the company's top executives over the following three to five years. To begin with, Elfrink, executive vice president, Cisco Services, was given additional responsibility as Cisco's first chief globalization officer. He relocated to India in January 2007 and became the first direct report of Chambers to live outside of California. Elfrink also brought 20 executives with him to kick-start the new globalization center. In October 2007, the Globalisation Centre East (GCE) was launched in Bangalore as Cisco's second largest R&D center aimed at developing products from concept to completion in India *(refer to Exhibit 2 for Cisco India R&D evolution)*. The company also announced an additional $100 million venture capital funding to expand investments in early-stage Indian companies. Elfrink stated:

This [GCE] has been set up as our second headquarters throughout this region and for the world as a whole. . . you can think about it as "Cisco East." The GCE is much more than a sales center or an R&D center. Every function at Cisco is represented here [sales, business development and manufacturing], at every level, from individual contributor to executive vice president. Working in the developing world first hand, I am able to understand and shape our strategy, so that we do not approach globalization by "selling what we have" but rather by "creating what we need" – or rather, what our customers need.[7]

Chambers had set a target of growing the headcount from 1,700 in 2007 to 10,000 over the

---

[5] "Cisco to invest over US$1 billion in India over next three years." Cisco Press Release, 19 October 2005.

[6] "Our growth is way above the industry average." *Business Today*, 29 April 2012.

[7] "Cisco's Wim Elfrink: 'Today, we are seeing what I call the globalization of the corporate brain.'" Knowledge@Wharton, Wharton University of Pennsylvania, 16 July 2009.

Exhibit 2 Cisco India R&D Evolution

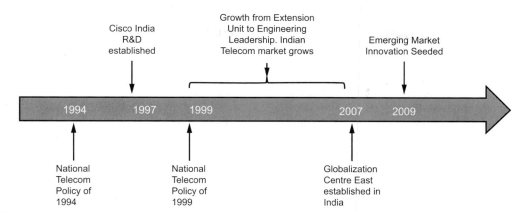

Source: Author.

following five years. In line with these manpower targets, Cisco recruited engineers on a large scale and by 2010 had about 4,700 people in its R&D center in Bangalore. Cisco India also opened 170 academies across the country, training about 8,600 students to overcome the talent crunch.[8]

Furthermore, the company set about expanding its innovation network by systematically developing an ecosystem of about 2,500 partners beyond firm boundaries. R&D work was almost equally divided between its captive R&D center and the partners, which included Infosys, TCS and Wipro.[9] By 2010 GCE had incubated and piloted several initiatives such as smart connected communities and smart connected healthcare[10] and education from India. According to Cisco, Smart +Connected Communities was perhaps the most significant new global initiative that GCE launched to help cities use the network as the next utility for integrated city management,

better quality of life for citizens and economic development. Although just about 2% of the company's global revenues came from India in 2014, Cisco remained confident that this share would grow to 5% in the next five years.[11]

Seeding Innovation in India

India saw a major transformation in the telecommunication sector, beginning with the National Telecom Policy of 1994 and followed by the National Telecom Policy of 1999. These policy initiatives opened up all segments of the telecom sector for participation from the private sector and cleared the path for foreign direct investment (FDI). As a result of the deregulation, a number of domestic and foreign telecom service providers entered the Indian market. Consequently, telecom equipment manufacturers, who supplied equipment to the service providers, followed suit. The Indian telecom industry grew over 20 times in just 10 years, from 28.5 million subscribers in 2000 to over 621 million in 2010 (refer to Exhibit 3 for Indian telecom industry growth).[12] The mobile subscriber base stood at 584 million, registering an annual growth rate of 49%, and India was primed to become the world's second-largest mobile phone user base

---

[8] Sharma, M. "Cisco bullish over R&D growth in India." CXOtoday.com, 28 May 2009. http://www.cxotoday.com/story/cisco-bullish-over-rd-growth-in-india/ (retrieved 5 March 2015).

[9] Kedia B.L and S.C. Jain. Restoring America's Global Competitiveness through Innovation. Cheltenham, UK and Northampton, MA: Edward Elgar Publishing, 2013.

[10] The smart connected healthcare initiative being piloted with Apollo Hospitals aims to drive down healthcare costs to one dollar a month and increase reach in rural areas through use of tele-medicine.

[11] "India to contribute 5% of Cisco's global revenue: CEO." The Times of India, 26 March 2014.

[12] Telecom Regulatory Authority of India, Annual Report 2009–10.

Exhibit 3   Indian Telecom Industry
Growth in subscriber base (in millions)

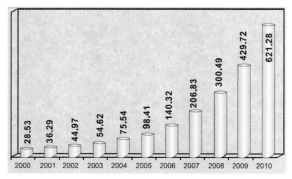

Subscriber base of wireless operators

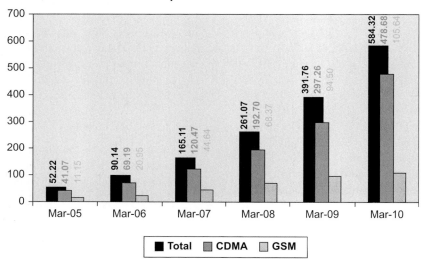

Note: Financial year ending in March.
Source: Telecom Regulatory Authority of India. Annual report 2009/10.

by 2012. To keep pace with this growth, telecom service provider investments in network infrastructure also grew sharply in India, increasing from $60.8 billion in 2007 to $89.6 billion in 2010, at a time when capital investments stayed flat in developed markets.[13]

Within this context, Elfrink's mandate was two-pronged: (1) to develop innovative products with strong local appeal and (2) to grow the leadership bench strength in India. He achieved some success in growing the India site talent pool as the number of vice presidents increased from 1 in 2007 to 14 in 2010, while the number of directors increased from 8 to 80 over the same period. Elfrink highlighted:

> We have been able to attract over 60 families to India from around the world, and at all levels of the organization and all functions across the company. The type of employee who comes here is an entrepreneurial one,

[13] Joint report by Department of Telecommunication (DoT), KPMG and FICCI titled "m-Powering India," 2011.

people who are motivated by the opportunity to create, pioneer, innovate.[14]

The increasing capability of Cisco India had sufficiently increased the credibility of the site in the eyes of the headquarters for the latter to raise the initial funding to set up a new business unit called "Emerging Country Solutions and Services" (ECSS). Cisco leadership, led by Patel based at San Jose and supported by Elfrink and Aravind Sitaraman, the India R&D site leader, set up a seed fund for building the new product development team. To jump start the innovation process, they recruited Ishwardutt Parulkar, a senior technology architect, and Mahesh Raghava, as a product manager, thereby filling two critical skill gaps for product development at the India R&D center.

Parulkar had 15 years of industry experience in the US at Apple, Sun Microsystems and Cisco. He returned to India in early 2010 with the goal of connecting emerging markets with the developed ones using innovative and cost-effective products. According to him, India could offer a whole new range of products at different price points. Raghava, a Cisco India veteran who was extremely familiar with the Indian telecom ecosystem, took on the product management role. Parulkar and Raghava were the only members of ECSS and they directly reported to Sitaraman. The broad charter of ECSS was to assess the needs of emerging market customers and build products and solutions to address those needs. Parulkar explained that creating a separate business unit was beneficial in several ways:

> First, it gave the team a separate identity and a sense of purpose. Second, it ensured that the team was not burdened by the procedural overheads normally associated with being affiliated to a larger business unit. It helped the team work in a startup mode within a large company. Third, the team had easy access to the site leadership, which was helpful in getting quick resolutions on issues and challenges.

When Parulkar joined, he realized that the India center had evolved from a predominantly engineering organization to incorporate other strong functions such as Cisco services (comprising both technical and advanced services), sales, marketing and IT. Such growth on multiple functional dimensions improved dialogue between R&D and customer-facing teams. The R&D center started receiving feedback on the lack of certain products for the local market and the high price points of existing products, allowing them to gain a better understanding of unmet needs as well as the opportunities and challenges in the local market. This created the business case to innovate – a product conceptualized and executed from India for India and India-like markets. Defining the right product that would find traction with customers was going to be critical!

Product Conceptualization

The explosion in the number of mobile subscribers in India was fueling the rapid capacity expansion of service providers, and the number of cell sites was growing fast (*refer to Exhibit 4 for typical telecom network structure*). ABI research predicted that by 2014, 39% of all cell towers would be located in the Asia-Pacific region. In 2009 India was adding about 15 million new mobile subscribers a month. Parulkar and his team realized that building telecom products out of India made sense as capital expenditure on telecom was increasing at the rate of 15% per year in the developing world – i.e. double the growth rate in the developed world. According to industry sources, the enterprise and service providers' routing market in India was estimated to be approximately $300 million in 2012. India was one of the fastest-growing telecom markets in the world, and some of the largest Indian telecom companies such as Airtel, Vodafone and Reliance had more than 100 million subscribers each. The team embarked on a six-month journey to meet these major mobile operators. Raghava explained:

> We had to basically go and meet the customers and their CTOs, understand the products and come up with common definitions in terms of what is required for this region. Meetings were

[14] "Cisco's Wim Elfrink: 'Today, we are seeing what I call the globalization of the corporate brain.'" Knowledge@Wharton, Wharton University of Pennsylvania, 16 July 2009.

Exhibit 4 Telecom Network Structure

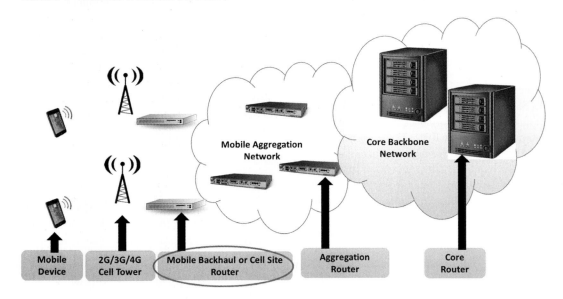

Mobile Aggregation Network

Core Backbone Network

| Mobile Device | 2G/3G/4G Cell Tower | Mobile Backhaul or Cell Site Router | Aggregation Router | Core Router |

Source: Cisco India.

open-ended and often lasted all day as we tried to understand customers' current and anticipated challenges, and identify a common set of requirements that would guide a new product offering.

As they brainstormed, the team posed five basic questions for each innovative idea that they came up with:

1. Does it address a real pain point?
2. Will it appeal to a big enough market?
3. Is the timing right?
4. If we pursue the idea, will we be good at it? Can we convince the headquarters to invest in developing the product?
5. Can we exploit the opportunity for the long term, or will this market commoditize so quickly that we would not be able to stay profitable?

Ultimately, Parulkar's team identified a mobile backhaul cell site router for mobile network operators (MNOs) as a suitable product/product category to develop in India, because it was not only relevant for the local market but also a segment that Cisco could do better in.

Challenges

As Parulkar and Raghava proceeded to the prototype development phase, several challenges came to the fore.

Funding

There was lack of visibility on funding for the next stage. It was not clear whether the next level of funding would come through to fund a larger team. According to Parulkar, it was similar to a start-up running out of seed funding while uncertainty loomed in terms of getting round-A funding.

Talent Gaps

Availability of the right type and level of talent was critical as prototype development involved working across the entire stack of technologies: silicon chips, platform hardware, platform software, network operating system and network management. This required adequate staffing across technology layers along with close interaction between experts from various technologies. First, the engineering team had to be strengthened with senior engineers who could implement the complex technical pieces and provide technical direction to the rest of the engineering team. Second, there was a serious shortage of domain experts, especially in some of the advanced networking protocols and Cisco's proprietary operating system IOS, which made it difficult to hire from outside. However, with minimal seed funding, increasing the staff was not possible.

Lack of a Mature Local Ecosystem

The complex nature of the product required physical proximity and the involvement of silicon vendors and third-party laboratories. For this, Parulkar's team had to bank on the local ecosystem. However, they found that the local ecosystem was not mature enough and lacking in several areas. The Cisco team decided to leverage their long-standing relationships with various partners and support them via co-development. They also had to persuade vendors to enhance their local capabilities as well as transfer knowledge and best practices to them in areas like global certifications. Parulkar elaborated:

> To be more specific, the pieces in the ecosystem of silicon vendors, the companies that develop silicon chips, service engineering partners, manufacturing partners… not all of these have the same level of maturity. Most of these tend to be MNCs with a presence in India. Not all of them have invested enough and developed the same level of expertise. There are some who are leading edge. For instance, Texas Instruments has been around for a long time, but if I pick some of the other companies, they just have a handful of application engineers, without a lot of depth in terms of products. When you are working on an "end-to-end" solution, you require a lot of capabilities, which the ecosystem limits.[15]

Design Tradeoffs

The router had to be reasonably complex but possible to develop within a relatively short period of time. A product of low complexity

would not make a substantial technical and business contribution and would be regarded as trivial. But a very complex product would take too long and test the patience of the headquarters. The team might run out of steam before it had established its development capability. Therefore, the right balance of product complexity and time taken for development was important in defining the product features.

Price Sensitivity and Power Requirements

The new router had to straddle seemingly irreconcilable requirements by being simultaneously low cost and feature rich. It had to meet the critical requirements of telecom companies in developing countries in terms of low up-front capital costs and operating expenses while protecting their existing investments in earlier technologies. This translated into three primary requirements: (1) very low power consumption to reduce the cost of operating the network; (2) high reliability in harsh operating environments; and (3) ease of manageability to save installation, configuration, repair and upgrade costs to build next generation service networks. These features would help operators reduce backhaul operating costs, simplify and converge their radio-access networks (RAN) and Ethernet access networks, and enhance operators profit opportunities with mobile and premium Ethernet services.

Bridging Legacy and Advanced 4G Systems

India was witnessing the advent and rapid adoption of mobile devices like smartphones and tablets at the user end and rich content at the content creation end. To meet these demands, the next generation internet had to be: (1) more mobile; (2) more visual; (3) more virtual; and (4) simpler. Therefore, cellular backhaul in India was moving from the previously prevalent TDM technology[16] to packet-based technology, driven by the rollout of 3G/4G.

---

[15] "All pieces of the ecosystem are not mature enough." *Business and Economy*, 30 May 2012.

[16] Time Division Multiplexing (TDM) is used in traditional circuit switched networks where a dedicated channel is established between two communicating nodes.

Exhibit 5 Cisco's R&D Project Approval Process

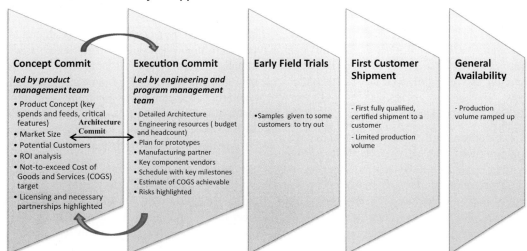

Concept Commit	Execution Commit	Early Field Trials	First Customer Shipment	General Availability
led by product management team	*Led by engineering and program management team*			

Concept Commit

led by product management team

- Product Concept (key spends and feeds, critical features)
- Market Size
- Potential Customers
- ROI analysis
- Not-to-exceed Cost of Goods and Services (COGS) target
- Licensing and necessary partnerships highlighted

Architecture Commit

Execution Commit

Led by engineering and program management team

- Detailed Architecture
- Engineering resources (budget and headcount)
- Plan for prototypes
- Manufacturing partner
- Key component vendors
- Schedule with key milestones
- Estimate of COGS achievable
- Risks highlighted

Early Field Trials

•Samples given to some customers to try out

First Customer Shipment

- First fully qualified, certified shipment to a customer
- Limited production volume

General Availability

- Production volume ramped up

If there was a major change during development, either in requirement of features or COGS exceeding target or a change in schedule, a quick execution commit was repeated and the program was recommitted.
Source: Created by author based on information provided by the company.

However, despite the deployment of 3G/4G, legacy 2G systems persisted. Therefore, the new router had to be versatile to handle rapid scalability in bandwidth, ranging from legacy 2G standards to the next generation 4G/LTE[17] cell mobile backhaul and Carrier Ethernet technology with advanced features to support the exponential growth of mobile internet traffic over the coming years.

The Next Phase

Parulkar and his team were excited as they prepared their business case for review by Elfrink and Patel. Patel's directive was clear:

We had decided to design products in India for footprint, energy consumption and scalability.[18]

Approval would hinge primarily on convincing them about the long-term market opportunity and capability of the team[19] (*refer to Exhibit 5 for Cisco's R&D project approval process*). Looking ahead, Parulkar knew that within the next 18 months they would have to launch the first Cisco product developed end-to-end at the India site, from conception, architecture, development of the hardware and software, testing and qualification to manufacturing and marketing. The success of the new router would mark a milestone in Cisco's journey of evolution of engineering capability in emerging countries into the next phase of innovation and thought leadership.

---

[17] 4G/LTE: 4G refers to the fourth generation of data technology for cellular networks following 3G, the third generation. 4G technologies are designed to provide IP-based voice, data and multimedia streaming at speeds of at least 100 Mbps and up to as fast as 1 Gbps. LTE, an acronym for Long Term Evolution, is a 4G wireless communications standard designed to provide up to 10x the speeds of 3G networks for mobile devices.

[18] "Bangalore R&D unit key to us; has filed 800-plus patents: Cisco." *Economic Times.* 8 February 2015.

[19] This was different from the usual approval process.

Chapter 5 Recommended Practitioner Readings

- Morten T. Hansen and Nitin Nohria, "How to build collaborative advantage," *MIT Sloan Management Review*, 46:1 (2004), 22–30.

  In "How to build collaborative advantage," Hansen and Nohria propose that collaboration can be an MNC's source of competitive advantage, especially in an environment where new economies of scope are based on the ability of business units, subsidiaries, and functional departments within the company to collaborate by sharing knowledge and jointly developing new products and services.

- Jeffrey R. Immelt, Vijay Govindarajan, and Chris Trimble, "How GE is disrupting itself," *Harvard Business Review*, 87:10 (2009), 56–65.

  In "How GE is disrupting itself," General Electric (GE) CEO Jeff Immelt, along with academics Govindarajan and Trimble, describe how GE has learned to master a process of reverse innovation that allows it to bring low-end products created for emerging markets into wealthy markets. It is an innovation process that is increasingly necessary to compete against the emerging giants from developing countries.

- Srivardhini K. Jha, Ishwardutt Parulkar, Rishikesha T. Krishnan, and Charles Dhanaraj, "Developing new products in emerging markets," *MIT Sloan Management Review*, 57:3 (2016), 55–62.

  In "Developing new products in emerging markets," Jha, Parulkar, Krishnan, and Dhanaraj note that MNEs from developed countries are now moving a substantial part of their R&D activity to emerging markets such as India and China. The location of R&D in developing countries has been driven largely by the availability of skilled staff at low cost. R&D subsidiaries in emerging markets are uniquely positioned to play an important role in multinational companies' innovation strategies. A large market opportunity combined with unique customer requirements is a key enabler of innovation for emerging markets. While most emerging markets do present a sizable market opportunity, it is the uniqueness of customer requirements that creates a compelling need to innovate.

- Hae-Jung Hong and Yves Doz, "L'Oréal masters multiculturalism," *Harvard Business Review*, 91:6 (2013), 114–18.

  In "L'Oréal masters multiculturalism," Hong and Doz discuss how L'Oréal transformed itself from a very French business into a global leader. It grappled with the global integration versus national responsiveness tension that is at the heart of every global enterprise. L'Oréal dealt with that tension by nurturing a pool of managers with mixed cultural backgrounds, placing them at the center of knowledge-based interactions in the company's most critical activity: new product development. L'Oréal built product development teams around these managers, who, by virtue of their upbringing and experiences, have gained familiarity with the norms and behaviors of multiple cultures and can switch easily among them. They are uniquely qualified to: spot new product opportunities, facilitate communication across cultural boundaries, assimilate newcomers, and serve as a cultural buffer between executives and their direct reports and between subsidiaries and headquarters.

- Keeley Wilson and Yves Doz, "Ten rules for managing global innovation," *Harvard Business Review*, 90:10 (2012), 84–90.

  In "Ten rules for managing global innovation," Wilson and Doz examine how companies recognize that their dispersed global operations are a treasure trove of ideas and capabilities for innovation. But it is proving hard to unearth those ideas or exploit those capabilities. Part of the problem is that companies manage global innovation the same way they manage traditional, single-location projects. Single-location projects draw on a large reservoir of tacit knowledge, shared context, and trust that global projects lack. The management challenge is to replicate the positive aspects of co-location while harnessing the opportunities of dispersion. Guidelines are presented for setting up and managing global innovation. They explain how the challenges of global projects can be overcome by applying superior project management skills across teams, fostering a strong collaborative culture, and using a robust array of communications tools.

All of these readings underscore the value in exploiting cross-border knowledge management to create worldwide innovation and learning for competitive advantage.

6 Engaging in Cross-Border Collaboration
Managing Across Corporate Boundaries

As we saw in the last chapter, in the international business environment of the twenty-first century, few companies have all the resources and capabilities they need to develop the kind of multidimensional strategies and adaptive organizational capabilities we have described. Increasingly, they must collaborate not only for research purposes, but also with their suppliers, distributors, customers, agents, licensors, joint venture partners, and others to meet the needs of the increasingly complex global environment. This requirement implies that today's MNEs must develop the skills to not only manage assets and resources under their own direct control but also span their corporate boundaries and capture vital capabilities in the partnerships and alliances that are central to the strategic response capability of so many companies. After exploring the motivation for entering into such partnerships, we examine some of the costs and risks of collaboration before discussing the organizational and managerial skills required to build and manage these boundary-spanning relationships effectively.

Historically, the strategic challenge for a company has been viewed primarily as one of protecting potential profits from erosion through either competition or bargaining. Such erosion of profits could be caused not only by the actions of competitors but also by the bargaining powers of customers, suppliers, and governments. The key challenge facing a company was assumed to be its ability to maintain its independence by maintaining strong control over its activities. Furthermore, this strategic approach emphasized the defensive value of making other entities depend on it by capturing critical resources, building switching costs, and exploiting other vulnerabilities.[1]

This view of strategy subsequently underwent a sea change. The need to pursue multiple sources of competitive advantage simultaneously (as we discussed in detail in Chapter 3) led to the need to build both an interdependent and integrated network organization within the company (Chapter 4) but also collaborative relationships externally with other firms, be they competitors, customers, suppliers, or other institutions.

This important shift in strategic perspective was triggered by a variety of factors, including rising R&D costs, shortened product life cycles, growing barriers to market

---

[1] For the most influential exposition of this view, see Michael E. Porter, *Competitive Strategy* (New York: Free Press, 1980).

entry, increasing needs for global-scale economies, and the expanding importance of global standards. Such dramatic changes led managers to recognize that many of the human, financial, and technological resources they required to compete effectively lay beyond their boundaries, and were sometimes – for political or regulatory reasons – not for sale. In response, many shifted their strategic focus away from an all-encompassing obsession with preempting competition to a broader view of building competitive advantage through selective, often simultaneous, reliance on both collaboration and competition.

The previously dominant focus on value appropriation that characterized all dealings across a company's organizational boundary changed to the simultaneous consideration of both value creation and value appropriation. Instead of trying to enhance their bargaining power over customers, companies began to build partnerships with them, thereby bolstering the customer's competitive position and, at the same time, leveraging their own competitiveness and innovative capabilities.

However, perhaps the most visible manifestation of this growing role of collaborative strategies appears in the phenomenon often described as strategic alliances: the increasing propensity of MNEs to form cooperative relationships with their competitors. The Strategic Alliance Program implemented by Unisys provides a good illustration. Unisys is a global information technology company whose Strategic Alliance Program has positioned the company to develop strategic relationships with other global leaders in the information technology industry, including Microsoft, SAP, Oracle, BMC, Cisco, Dell, Intel, Amazon Web Services, Google, Salesforce, and IBM. As the company describes it, "Our alliances allow us to innovate, develop new technologies, and offer clients cutting-edge products and services."

Although our analysis of the causes and consequences of such collaborative strategies in this chapter focuses on the phenomenon of strategic alliances among global companies, some of our arguments can be applied to a broader range of cooperative relations, including those with customers, suppliers, and governments. We begin with a discussion of the key motivations for forming strategic alliances.

Why Strategic Alliances?

The term strategic alliance currently is widely used to describe a variety of interfirm cooperation agreements, ranging from shared research to formal joint ventures and minority equity participation[2] (see Figure 6.1).

---

[2] In "Cooperative strategies in international business and management," Beamish and Lupton trace the history of research regarding the successful management of cross-border, interfirm collaboration. They highlight the evolution of interest in different contexts, phenomena, theories, and methodologies, along with the factors that have driven interest in these topics.

Paul W. Beamish and Nathaniel C. Lupton, "Cooperative strategies in international business and management: reflections on the past 50 years and future directions," *Journal of World Business*, 51:1 (2016), 163–75.

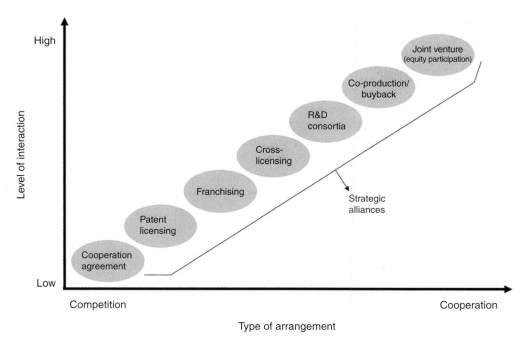

Figure 6.1 Range of strategic alliances

The key challenges surrounding the management of the various types of alliances detailed in Figure 6.1 will vary. In some they may relate to the "fairness" of management or technology payments; in others, they may be related to where the organizational problems typically will arise. Every form of alliance has predictable strengths and weaknesses, because each form is intended for particular circumstances.

Large numbers of firms worldwide, including many industry leaders, are increasingly involved in strategic alliances. International joint ventures (IJVs) continue to be a primary means to enter foreign markets. A PwC survey of 1,409 global CEOs in 83 countries reported that nearly half (49%) planned to enter into a new joint venture or strategic alliance in 2016.[3] Furthermore, several surveys suggest that such partnerships may be distinguished from traditional foreign investment joint ventures in important ways.

Classically, traditional joint ventures were formed between a senior multinational headquartered in an industrialized country and a junior local partner in a less developed or less industrialized country. The primary goal that dominated their formation was to gain new market access for existing products. In this classic contractual agreement, the senior partner provided existing products while the junior partner provided the local marketing expertise, the means to overcome any

---

[3] Valerie Demont and Soumya Sharma, "How to reduce international joint venture risk," *CFO.com*. Accessed August 30, 2017, http://ww2.cfo.com/global-business/2016/03/overcome-international-joint-venture-risk/.

protectionist barriers, and the governmental contacts to deal with national regulations. Both partners benefited: the multinational achieved increased sales volume, and the local firm gained access to new products and often learned important new skills from its partner.

In contrast, the scope and motivations for the modern form of strategic alliance are clearly broadening. There are three trends that are particularly noteworthy. First, present-day strategic alliances are frequently between firms in industrialized countries. Second, the focus is often on the creation of new products and technologies rather than the distribution of existing ones. And, third, present-day strategic alliances are often forged for only short durations.

All of these characteristics mean the new forms of strategic alliances considerably expand the strategic importance of cooperation beyond that which existed for classic joint ventures, and today the opportunity for competitive gain and loss through partnering is substantial. In the following sections, we discuss in more detail why this form of business relationship has become so important by focusing on five key motivations that are driving the formation of strategic alliances: technology exchange, global competition, industry convergence, economies of scale, and alliances as an alternative to merger.

Technology Exchange

As we discussed in some detail in Chapter 5, technology transfer or R&D collaboration is a major objective of many strategic alliances. The reason that technological exchange is such a strong driver of alliances is simple: as more and more breakthroughs and major innovations are based on interdisciplinary and inter-industry advances, the formerly clear boundaries between different industrial sectors and technologies become blurred. As a result, the necessary capabilities and resources are often beyond the scope of a single firm, making it increasingly difficult to compete effectively on the strength of one's own internal R&D efforts. The need to collaborate is further intensified by shorter product life cycles that increase both the time pressure and risk exposures while reducing the potential payback of massive R&D investments.

Not surprisingly, technology-intensive sectors such as telecommunications, information technology, electronics, pharmaceuticals, and specialty chemicals have become the central arenas for major and extensive cooperative agreements. Companies in these industries face an environment of accelerating change, short product life cycles, small market windows, and multiple vertical and lateral dependencies in their value chains. Because interfirm cooperation has provided solutions to many of these strategic challenges, much of the technological development in these industries is being driven by some form of R&D partnership.

Even mainstream industrial MNEs have employed strategic alliances to meet the challenge of coordinating and deploying discrete pools of technological resources without sacrificing R&D and commercialization scale advantages. For example, in 2016, SEAT, Samsung Electronics, and SAP formed a partnership to develop solutions for the connected car. The alliance will combine their innovation and industry-leading expertise. They have already presented their first couple of concepts: an app that can reserve a parking spot and pay for it without leaving one's car; and digitally sharing one's car with anyone, anywhere using fingertip authorization. SEAT Executive Committee President Luca de Meo commented, "For SEAT, connectivity is a key factor. This technological alliance with Samsung and SAP strengthens SEAT's aim of becoming a reference in the field of connectivity, and above all, of allying with the best partners to implement new mobility ecosystems business."

Global Competition

A widespread perception has emerged that global competitive battles will increasingly be fought between teams of players aligned in strategic partnerships. In 2017, the triumvirate of major airline alliances (Star Alliance, Sky Team, and OneWorld) provided over 60% of worldwide revenue passenger miles.

Particularly in industries in which there is a dominant worldwide market leader, joint ventures, strategic alliances, and networks allow coalitions of smaller partners to compete more effectively against a global "common enemy" rather than one another. For example, Ola (India), Lyft (United States), Didi Kuaidi (China), and GrabTaxi (Malaysia, Singapore, Indonesia, Philippines, Vietnam, and Thailand) have created a partnership to compete with Uber in the ride-hailing sector. The new partnership covers countries making up almost 50% of the world's population and allows customers to use whichever app they are familiar with, no matter their location.

Industry Convergence

Many high-technology industries are converging and overlapping in a way that seems destined to create a huge competitive traffic jam. Producers of computers, telecommunications, and components are merging; biological and chip technologies are intersecting; and advanced materials applications are creating greater overlaps in diverse applications from the aerospace to the automotive industry. Again, the preferred solution has been to create cross-industry alliances.

Furthermore, strategic alliances are sometimes the only way to develop the complex and interdisciplinary skills necessary in the time frame required. Alliances become a way of shaping competition by reducing competitive intensity, excluding potential entrants and isolating particular players, and building complex integrated value chains that can act as barriers to those who choose to go it alone.

Nowhere are the implications of this cross-industry convergence and broad-based collaboration clearer than in the hydrogen fuel cell technology for automobiles. Three distinct joint ventures have emerged in the automobile industry: the Fuel Cell System Manufacturing joint venture between GM and Honda; the AFCC joint venture with Daimler and Ford; and the BMW–Toyota joint venture. While these different partnerships compete with each other, there is convergence regarding industry-wide commitment to the technology. A hydrogen alliance comprising auto manufacturers, as well as energy and engineering companies, has been established to foster broad-based commitment to the technology, such as development of a standard (re)fueling network, market promotion, and mobilizing government support across countries.

Economies of Scale and Reduction of Risk

There are several ways strategic alliances and networks allow participating firms to reap the benefits of scale economies or learning – advantages that are particularly interesting to smaller companies trying to match the economic benefits that accrue to the largest MNEs. First, partners can pool their resources and concentrate their activities not only to raise the scale of activity, but also to raise the rate of learning within the alliance over that of each firm operating separately. Second, alliances enable partners to share and leverage the specific strengths and capabilities of each of the other participating firms. Third, trading different or complementary resources among companies can result in mutual gains and save each partner the high cost of duplication.

While partnering has proven to be particularly useful for smaller firms that pursue rapid growth with limited resources, even the very largest MNEs have recognized the investment and growth benefits associated with partnering rather than "going it alone." For example, as part of Dow Chemical's effort to shift its focus toward the Middle East, the company implemented its "asset-light strategy," which resulted in the firm divesting many capital-intensive operations in favor of investing in a greater number of joint ventures with chemical firms situated in the growing emerging markets of the Middle East. David Kepler, Dow's chief information officer, commented that "we are doing much more partnering because of the large capital size of these investments." One industry analyst who agrees with Dow's strategy noted that "the projects are so big and capital intensive that even Dow... doesn't have the capital to undertake them on its own," while another analyst observed that "by splitting the investment cost with a partner, Dow can invest in larger projects than it could alone, thereby adding shareholder value... the risk of the investment is shared and Dow can achieve quicker growth."

One company activity that is particularly motivated by the risk-sharing opportunities of such partnerships is R&D, where product life cycles are shortening and technological complexity is increasing. At the same time, R&D expenses are being driven sharply higher by personnel and capital costs. Because none of the participating firms bears the full risk and cost of the joint activity, alliances are often seen as an attractive risk-hedging mechanism.

One alliance driven by these motivations is the Renault–Nissan partnership. These two companies came together in 1999, with Renault taking a 36% share in Nissan and installing Carlos Ghosn as its chief operating officer. Although Nissan's perilous financial position was evidently a key factor in the decision to bring in a foreign partner, the underlying driver of the alliance was the need – on both sides – for greater economies of scale and scope to achieve competitive parity with General Motors (GM), Ford, and Toyota. The alliance led to a surprisingly fast turnaround of Nissan's fortunes, largely through Ghosn's decisive leadership, and subsequently to a broad set of projects to deliver synergies in product development, manufacturing, and distribution. The Renault–Nissan alliance was in 2016 the fastest growing of the top four players in the global automobile industry. Its global car sales were very close to that of GM, and within striking distance of Toyota and Volkswagen Group.

General Motors and South Korea's LG Corp. created a joint venture for the production of GM's electric and hybrid vehicles by combining GM's auto making strength with LG's leadership in electronics and lithium-ion battery technologies. The partnership is one of the most extensive between a US automaker and an overseas supplier. General Motors will shift more of the development and production costs to LG, which has considerable technical expertise, while LG can leverage this supply agreement to enhance LG Electronics' auto business.

Another instance is Magna International Inc., who in 2015 announced a 50/50 joint venture with Changan Ford and other Chinese clients to supply seating components and complete seating systems. Magna has over 285 manufacturing operations, which are a mix of wholly owned subsidiaries and joint ventures.

Alliance as an Alternative to Merger

Finally, there remain industry sectors in which political, regulatory, and legal constraints limit the extent of cross-border mergers and acquisitions. In such cases, companies often create alliances not because they are inherently the most attractive organizational form but because they represent the best available alternative to a merger.

The classic examples of this phenomenon occur in the airline and telecommunications industries. Many countries still preclude foreign ownership in these industries. But a simple analysis of the economics of the industry – in terms of potential economies of scale, concentration of suppliers, opportunities for standardization of services, and competitive dynamics – would highlight the availability of substantial benefits from global integration. So, as a means of generating at least some of the benefits of global integration but not breaking the rules against foreign ownership, most major airlines have formed themselves into marketing and code-sharing partnerships, including Star Alliance and OneWorld, and many telecom companies have formed telecommunications alliances.

Alliances of this type often lead to full-scale global integration if restrictions on foreign ownership are lifted. For example, as the telecommunications industry was gradually deregulated during the 1990s, alliances such as Concert and Unisource gave way to the emergence of true multinational players such as Verizon, Vodafone, Telefonica, AT&T, China Mobile, and Deutsche Telekom. Firms may prefer to engage in longer term partnership relationships rather than merge.

The Risks and Costs of Collaboration

Because of these different motivations, there was an initial period of euphoria during which partnerships were seen as the panacea for most of the MNEs' global strategic problems and opportunities. The euphoria of the 1980s to form relationships was fueled by two fashionable management concepts of the period: triad power[4] and stick to your knitting.[5]

The triad-power concept emphasized the need to develop significant positions in the three key markets of the United States, Western Europe, and Japan as a prerequisite for competing in global industries. Given the enormous costs and difficulties of accessing any one of these developed and highly competitive markets independently, many companies with unequal legs on their geographic stool regarded alliances as the only feasible way to develop this triadic position.

The stick-to-your-knitting prescription in essence urged managers to disaggregate the value chain and focus their investments, efforts, and attention on only those tasks in which the company had a significant competitive advantage. Other operations were to be externalized through outsourcing or alliances. The seductive logic of both arguments, coupled with rapidly evolving environmental demands, led to an explosion in the formation of such alliances.

Since then, the experience that companies gathered through such collaborative ventures has highlighted some of the costs and risks of such partnerships. Some risks arise from the simultaneous presence of both collaborative and competitive aspects in the relationships. Others arise from the higher levels of strategic and organizational complexity involved in managing cooperative relationships outside the company's own boundaries.

The Risks of Competitive Collaboration

Some strategic alliances – including some of the most visible – involve partners who are fierce competitors outside the specific scope of the cooperative venture. Such relationships create the possibility that the collaborative venture might be used by one or both partners to develop a competitive edge over the other, or at least that the benefits from the partnership will be asymmetrical for the two parties, which might change their relative competitive positions. There are several factors that might cause such asymmetry.

A partnership is often motivated by the desire to join and leverage complementary skills and resources. The partners may have access to very different resources and capabilities that could be combined to create new businesses or products. For example, TelkomTelstra Indonesia is a JV between Telstra of Australia

---

[4] See Kenichi Ohmae, *Triad Power* (New York: Free Press, 1985).

[5] This idea is one of the lessons developed in the highly influential book by Thomas Peters and Robert Waterman, *In Search of Excellence* (New York: Harper & Row, 1982).

and PT Telkom of Indonesia to provide cloud-based network services to Indonesian enterprises, MNEs, and Australian companies operating in Indonesia. The goal of the JV is to utilize the Australian carrier's advanced enterprise cloud-computing services with the Indonesian's knowledge of the local market. Such an arrangement for competency pooling inevitably entails the possibility that, in the course of the partnership, one of the partners will learn and internalize the other's skills while carefully protecting its own, thereby creating the option of discarding the partner and appropriating all the benefits created by the partnership.[6] This possibility becomes particularly salient when the skills and competencies of one partner are tacit and deeply embedded in complex organizational processes (and thereby difficult to learn or emulate), whereas those of the other partner are explicit and embodied in specific individual machines or drawings (and thereby liable to relatively easy observation and emulation).

When General Foods entered into a partnership with Ajinomoto, the Japanese food giant, it agreed to make available its advanced processing technology for products such as freeze-dried coffee. In return, its Japanese partner would contribute its marketing expertise to launch the new products on the Japanese market. After several years, however, the collaboration deteriorated and was eventually dissolved when Ajinomoto had absorbed the technology transfer and management felt it was no longer learning from its American partner. Unfortunately, General Foods had not done such a good job in learning about the Japanese market and left the alliance with some bitterness.

Another predatory tactic might involve using the partnership to erode the other's competitive position. In this scenario, the company ensures that it, rather than the partner, makes and keeps control over the critical investments. Such investments can be in the domain of product development, manufacturing, marketing, or wherever the most strategically vital part of the business value chain is located. Through these tactics, the aggressive company can strip its partner of the necessary infrastructure for competing independently and create one-way dependence in the collaboration that can be exploited at will.

Although they provide lively copy for magazine articles, such Machiavellian intentions and actions remain the exception, and the vast majority of cross-company collaborations are founded and maintained on a basis of mutual trust and shared commitment. Yet even the most carefully constructed strategic alliances can become problematic. Although many provide short-term solutions to some strategic problems, they also serve to hide the deeper and more fundamental

---

[6] In "Strategic alliance structuring: a game theoretic and transaction cost examination of interfirm cooperation," Parkhe discusses how maintaining robust cooperation in interfirm strategic alliances poses special problems. Research grounded in game theory has suggested that some alliance structures are inherently more likely than others to be associated with high opportunity to cheat, high behavioral uncertainty, and poor stability, longevity, and performance. Findings suggested the need for a greater focus on game-theoretic structural dimensions and institutional responses to perceived opportunism in the study of voluntary interfirm cooperation.

Arvind Parkhe, "Strategic alliance structuring: a game theoretic and transaction cost examination of interfirm cooperation," *Academy of Management Journal*, 36:4 (1993), 794–829.

deficiencies that cause those problems. The short-term solution takes the pressure off the problem without solving it and makes the company highly vulnerable when the problem finally resurfaces, usually in a more extreme and immediate form.

Furthermore, because such alliances typically involve task sharing, each company almost inevitably trades off some of the benefits of "learning by doing" the tasks that it externalizes to its partner. Thus even in the best case scenario of a partnership that fully meets all expectations, the very success of the partnership leads to some benefits for each partner and therefore to some strengthening of a competitor. Behind the success of the alliance, therefore, lies the ever-present possibility that a competitor's newly acquired strength will be used against its alliance partner in some future competitive battle.[7] Consider the example of Shanghai Automotive Industry Corp. (SAIC), one of China's larger state-owned enterprises. In April 2006, it announced that it was going to start producing a car under its own name. Up to that time, Shanghai Automotive had been operating large joint ventures for many years with both Volkswagen and GM for the Chinese market; under Chinese law, foreign companies wishing to produce automobiles in China must have a local partner who owns at least 50% of the business. Henceforth, the technology-intensive Volkswagen and GM joint ventures with Shanghai Automotive would be competing with Shanghai Automotive's wholly owned subsidiary. The good news for SAIC was that, by 2016, it was the leading China-based automaker in terms of output volume. The bad news for its own-brand aspirations was that most of these sales were via their joint venture partners.

Finally, there is the risk that collaborating with a competitor might be a precursor to a takeover by one of the firms. Carlsberg's Baltic Beverages joint venture with Scottish & Newcastle (S&N) was created in 2002 to target the Russian and other emerging Eastern European beer markets. Eventually, Carlsberg sought to pursue these markets without its joint venture partner. However, a "shotgun clause" in the joint venture agreement required either partner to offer its shares in Baltic Beverages to the other partner in the event that either partner wanted to exit the joint venture. In court filings, S&N alleged that Carlsberg was attempting to circumvent the clause in 2007 when Carlsberg announced the formation of a consortium with Heineken in order to finance the hostile acquisition of S&N. Ultimately, Carlsberg's attempted acquisition of S&N was successful, and Carlsberg assumed ownership over S&N's share.

The Cost of Strategic and Organizational Complexity

Cooperation is difficult to attain even in the best of circumstances. One of the strongest forces facilitating such behavior within a single company's internal operations is the understanding that the risks and rewards ultimately accrue to the company's own accounts and therefore, either directly or indirectly, to the cooperating participants. This basic motivation is diluted in strategic alliances. Furthermore, the scope of most alliances and the environmental uncertainties they

---

[7] These potential risks of competitive collaboration are discussed in Gary Hamel, Yves L. Doz, and C. K. Prahalad, "Collaborate with your competitor – and win," *Harvard Business Review*, January/February (1989).

inevitably face often prevent a clear understanding of the risks that might be incurred or rewards that might accrue in the course of the partnership's evolution. As a result, cooperation in the context of allocated risks and rewards and divided loyalties inevitably creates additional strategic and organizational complexity that in turn involves additional costs to manage.

International partnerships bring together companies that are often products of different economic, political, social, and cultural systems. Such differences in the administrative heritages of the partner companies, each of which brings its own strategic mentality and managerial practices to the venture, further exacerbate the organizational challenge. For example, tensions between Xerox and Fuji Xerox – a successful but often troubled relationship – were as much an outgrowth of the differences in the business systems in which each was located as of the differences in the corporate culture between the US company and its Japanese joint venture. Similarly, the tumultuous eight-year joint venture relationship between Italy's Fiat and China's Nanjing Automotive was presided over by no fewer than four different CEOs who terminated seven different sales and marketing heads before the joint venture was dissolved.

Organizational complexity, due to the very broad scope of operations typical of many strategic alliances, also contributes to added difficulties. As we have described, one of the distinguishing characteristics of present-day alliances is that they often cover a broad range of activities. This expansion of scope requires partners not only to manage the many areas of contact within the alliance but also to coordinate the different alliance-related tasks within their own organizations. And the goals, tasks, and management processes for the alliance must be constantly monitored and adapted to changing conditions.

Building and Managing Collaborative Ventures

As we have described in the preceding sections, alliances are neither conventional organizations with fully internalized activities nor well-specified transaction relationships through which externalized activities may be linked by market-based contracts. Instead, they combine elements of both. The participating companies retain their own competitive strategies and performance expectations, as well as their national, ideological, and administrative identities. Yet to obtain the required benefits of a partnership, diverse organizational units in different companies and different countries must effectively and flexibly coordinate their activities.

There are numerous reasons why such collaborative ventures inevitably present some significant management challenges: strategic and environmental disparities among the partners, lack of a common experience and perception base, difficulties in interfirm communication, conflicts of interest and priorities, and inevitable personal differences among the individuals who manage the interface. As a result, though it is clear to most managers that strategic alliances can provide great benefits, they also realize that there is a big difference between establishing alliances and making them work.

The challenge can be considered in two parts, reflecting the pre-alliance tasks of analysis, negotiation, and decision making, and the post-alliance tasks of coordination, integration, and adaptation.

Building Cooperative Ventures

The quality of the pre-alliance processes of partner selection and negotiation influence the clarity and reciprocity of mutual expectations from the alliance. There are three aspects of the pre-alliance process to which managers must pay close attention if the alliance is to have the best possible chance of success: partner selection, escalating commitment, and alliance scope.[8]

Partner Selection: Strategic and Organizational Analysis

The process of analyzing a potential partner's strategic and organizational capabilities is an important, yet difficult, pre-alliance task. Several factors impede the quality of the choice-making process.

The most important constraint lies in the availability of information required for an effective evaluation of the potential partner. Effective pre-alliance analysis needs data about the partner's relevant physical assets (e.g., the condition and productivity of plants and equipment), as well as less tangible assets (e.g., strength of brands, quality of customer relationships, level of technological expertise) and organizational capabilities (e.g., managerial competence, employee loyalty, shared values). The difficulty of obtaining such information in the short time limits in which most alliances are finalized is further complicated by the barriers of cultural and physical distance that MNEs must also overcome.[9]

---

[8] The pre-alliance process is in many ways similar to a pre-acquisition process and shares the same needs. See David B. Jemison and Sim B. Sitkin, "Acquisitions: the process can be a problem," *Harvard Business Review*, 2 (1986), 107–14.

[9] The paper "Signals and international alliance formation: the roles of affiliations and international activities" extends signaling theory to the study of firms' international alliances. Signals reduce the risk of adverse partner selection. The authors find that the signaling benefits of these affiliations diminish with the firm's engagement in international activities, which can function as alternative signals by which firms convey the quality of their resources and prospects. Examining firms' cross-border activities helps to identify new and important signals that are unique to the international setting. The authors contrast some of the main arguments and predictions of signaling theory with other theories used in international business.

Jeffrey J. Reuer and Roberto Ragozzino, "Signals and international alliance formation: the roles of affiliations and international activities" *Journal of International Business Studies*, 45:3 (2014), 321–37.

"The influence of top management team international exposure on international alliance formation" develops arguments based on relational capital theory to suggest that top executives with international exposure are critical to firms' international alliance formation. Supporting this view, the authors find that top management team international exposure is positively associated with the formation of international alliances.

Ho-Uk Lee and Jong-Hun Park, "The influence of top management team international exposure on international alliance formation," *Journal of Management Studies*, 45:5 (2008), 961–81.

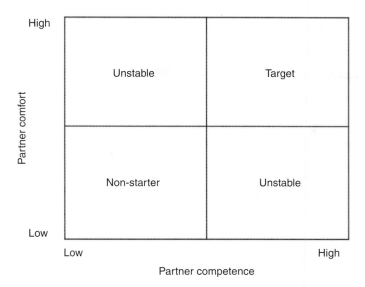

Figure 6.2 Partner selection: comfort vs. competence

The pressures of time and distance sometimes result in suboptimal partner selection. As Figure 6.2 suggests, there is no real upside to selecting a partner who is competent but with whom you may not be comfortable working. Partners should not be selected on the basis of comfort rather than competence.

A key lesson emerging from the experience of most strategic alliances is that changes in each partner's competitive positions and strategic priorities have crucial impacts on the viability of the alliance over time. Even if the strategic trajectories of two companies cross at a particular point of time, creating complementarities and the potential for a partnership, their paths may be so divergent as to make such complementarities too transient for the alliance to have any lasting value. The Eli Lilly in India case example explores whether the Eli Lilly–Ranbaxy joint venture still meets each partner's strategic objectives, 15 years after it was established.

Although it is difficult enough to make a static assessment of a potential partner's strategic and organizational capabilities, it is almost impossible to make an effective pre-alliance analysis of how those capabilities are likely to evolve over time. This challenge may be more pronounced where partnerships are formed between developed market and developing market firms. For example, John Hopkins Medicine International, a non-profit organization, partners with governments, insurance firms, other charitable foundations, and health, care companies to develop and operate state-of-the-art medical facilities worldwide.[10] Hopkins' CEO,

---

[10] Steven J. Thompson, "The perils of partnering in developing markets," *Harvard Business Review*, June (2012).

Steven J. Thompson, has suggested that partnering with developing market firms poses a unique set of challenges, including the incessant conflict between a partner's local market culture and best practices in Western medicine, as well as the risk that developing market partners are more concerned with securing healthy financial returns than with being committed to the goal of delivering sustainable quality in developing market medical services. To mitigate against these risks, Thompson advises firms that seek to engage with developing market partners to assess their potential partner's willingness to commit resources, to work with the partner through a project or business planning process, and to ensure that both partners can reach a clear understanding of the potential project, as well as agreeing to realistic expectations for the project.

There probably is no solution to this problem of how a potential partner's capabilities are likely to evolve over time, but companies that recognize alliances as a permanent and important part of their future organization have made monitoring their partners an ongoing rather than an ad hoc process. Some have linked such activities to their integrated business intelligence system, which was set up to monitor competitors. By having this group not only analyze competitors' potential strategies but also assess their value as acquisition or alliance candidates, these companies find themselves much better prepared when a specific alliance opportunity arises.

Escalating Commitment: Thrill of the Chase

The very process of alliance planning and negotiations can cause unrealistic expectations and wrong choices. In particular, some managers involved in the process can build up a great deal of personal enthusiasm and expectations in trying to sell the idea of the alliance within their own organization. This escalation process is similar to a process observed in many acquisition decisions where, in one manager's words, "The thrill of the chase blinds pursuers to the consequences of the catch." Because the champions of the idea – those most often caught in a spiral of escalating commitment – may not be the operational managers who are later given responsibility for making the alliance work, major problems arise when the latter are confronted with inevitable pitfalls and less visible problems.

The most effective way to control this escalation process is to ensure that at least the key operating managers likely to be involved in the implementation stage of the alliance are involved in the pre-decision negotiation process. Their involvement not only ensures greater commitment but also creates continuity between pre- and post-alliance actions. But the greatest benefit accrues to the long-term understanding that must develop between the partners. By ensuring that the broader strategic goals that motivate the alliance are related to specific operational details in the negotiation stage, the companies can enhance the clarity and consistency of both the definition and the understanding of the alliance's goals and tasks. The Nora-Sakari case example considers in detail the challenges of negotiating such a venture.

Alliance Scope: Striving for Simplicity and Flexibility

All too often, in an effort to show commitment at the time of the agreement, partners press for broad and all-encompassing corporate partnerships and equity participation or exchange. Yet a key to successful alliance building lies in defining as simple and focused a scope for the partnership as is adequate to get the job done, but to retain at the same time the possibility to redefine and broaden the scope if needed. Alliances that are more complex also require more management attention to succeed and tend to be more difficult to manage.

Three factors add to the management complexity of a partnership: complicated cross-holdings of ownership or equity, the need for cross-functional coordination or integration, and breadth in the number and scope of joint activities. Before involving any alliance in such potentially complicated arrangements, management should ask: "Are these conditions absolutely necessary, given our objectives?" If a simple OEM (original equipment manufacturer) arrangement can suffice, it is not only unnecessary to enter into a more committed alliance relationship but also is undesirable because the added complexity will increase the likelihood of problems and difficulties in achieving the objectives of the partnership.

At the same time, it might be useful to provide some flexibility in the terms of the alliance for renegotiating and changing the scope, if and when necessary. Even when a broad-based and multifaceted alliance represents the ultimate goal, many companies have found it preferable to start with a relatively simple and limited partnership whose scope is expanded gradually as both partners develop a better understanding of and greater trust in each other's motives, capabilities, and expectations.

Multinationals are increasingly relying upon highly flexible and globally oriented inter-organizational networks to supplement their more traditional dyadic alliances and partnerships. As an example, P&G recognized that it was unable to sustain high revenue growth by continuing to rely on an innovation model that depended on internally networking its business units. As a result, the firm shifted its R&D model and mandated that 50% of its innovations should be acquired from a worldwide network of external engineers and scientists. Larry Huston, P&G's vice-president for innovation and knowledge, and Nabil Sakkab, the firm's president for corporate R&D, acknowledged that "we needed to change how we defined, and perceived, our R&D organization – from 7,500 people inside to 7,500 plus 1.5 million (P&G's estimate of the number) qualified scientists and engineers worldwide, with a permeable boundary between them. It was against this backdrop that we created our 'connect and develop' innovation model. With a clear sense of consumers' needs, we could identify promising ideas throughout the world and apply our own R&D, manufacturing, marketing, and purchasing capabilities to them to create better and cheaper products, faster."[11]

[11] Larry Huston and Nabil Sakkab, "Connect and develop: inside Procter & Gamble's new model for innovation," *Harvard Business Review*, March (2006), 59–60.

Managing Cooperative Ventures

Although the pre-alliance analysis and negotiation processes are important, a company's ability to manage an ongoing relationship also tends to be a key determining factor for the success or failure of an alliance. Among the numerous issues that influence a company's ability to manage a cooperative venture, there are three that appear to present the greatest challenges: managing the boundary, managing knowledge flows, and providing strategic directions.

Managing the Boundary: Structuring the Interface

There are many different ways in which the partners can structure the boundary of an alliance and manage the interface between this boundary and their own organizations. At one extreme, an independent legal organization can be created and given complete freedom to manage the alliance tasks. Alternatively, the alliance's operations can be managed by one or both parents with more substantial strategic, operational, or administrative controls. In many cases, however, the creation of such a distinct entity is not necessary, and simpler, less bureaucratic governance mechanisms such as joint committees may be enough to guide and supervise shared tasks. Also, given the potentially enormous breadth in the scope of activities (see Table 6.1), it may be more practical to start with a limited agreement. It is always easier to gain a partner's agreement to expand than to contract an alliance's terms of reference.

The choice among alternative boundary structures depends largely on the scope of the alliance. When the alliance's tasks are characterized by extensive functional interdependencies, there is a need for a high level of integration in the decision-making process related to those shared tasks. In such circumstances, the creation of a separate entity is often the only effective way to manage such dense interlinkages. In contrast, an alliance between two companies with the objective of marketing each other's existing products in non-competitive markets may need only a few simple rules that govern marketing parameters and financial arrangements, and a single joint committee to review the outcomes periodically.

Table 6.1 Scope of activity

Narrow	vs.	Wide
Single, geographic market	vs.	Multi-country
Single function	vs.	Complete value chain
Single industry/customer group	vs.	Multi-industry
Modest investment	vs.	Large scale
Existing business	vs.	New business
Limited term	vs.	Forever

Following the growing prominence and regulation pertaining to corporate governance in the domain of publicly traded firms, issues of governance have begun to attract increased attention within the realm of joint ventures.[12] Governance processes are particularly important in alliances characterized by a high level of integration. Consultants at McKinsey have recommended that parent companies should strive to focus their active participation on the joint venture or alliance's board to three areas that are directly related to the new entity's financial performance and the protection of shareholder interests – capital allocation, risk management, and performance management.[13] Additionally, they recommend that the parent companies restrict their involvement in operational processes because the failure to do so can impinge upon the joint venture or alliance's ability to remain competitive and responsive to changing market forces. Ultimately, an alliance's governance structure must include clear rules pertaining to decision making among the entity's partners and its general manager.[14]

Managing Knowledge Flows: Integrating the Interface

Irrespective of the specific objectives of any alliance, the very process of collaboration creates flows of information across the boundaries of the participating companies and creates the potential for learning from each other. Managing these knowledge flows involves two kinds of tasks for the participating companies. First, they must ensure full exploitation of the created learning potential. Second, they must prevent the outflow of any information or knowledge they do not wish to share with their alliance partners.

In terms of the first point, the key problem is that the individuals managing the interface may not be the best users of such knowledge. To maximize its learning from a partnership, a company must effectively integrate its interface managers into the rest of its organization. The gatekeepers must have knowledge of and access to the different individuals and management groups within the company that are likely to benefit most from the diverse kinds of information that flow through an alliance boundary. Managers familiar with the difficulties of managing information flows within the company's boundaries will readily realize that such cross-boundary learning is unlikely to occur unless specific mechanisms are in place to make it happen.

The selection of appropriate interface managers is perhaps the single most important factor for facilitating such learning. Interface managers should have at least three key attributes: they must be well versed in the company's internal organizational process; they must have the personal credibility and status necessary to access key managers in different parts of the organization; and they must

[12] Jeffrey J. Reuer, Elko Klijn, Frans A. J. van den Bosch, and Henk W. Volberda, "Building corporate governance to international joint ventures," *Global Strategy Journal*, 1 (2011), 54–66.

[13] James Bamford, David Ernst, and David G. Fubini, "Launching a world-class joint venture," *Harvard Business Review*, 82 (2004), 91–100.

[14] Paul W. Beamish, *Joint Venturing* (Charlotte, NC: Information Age Publishing, 2008).

have a sufficiently broad understanding of the company's business and strategies to be able to recognize useful information and knowledge that might cross their path.

Merely placing the right managers at the interface is not sufficient to ensure effective learning, however. Supportive administrative processes must also be developed to facilitate the systematic transfer of information and monitor the effectiveness of those transfers. Such support is often achieved most effectively through simple systems and mechanisms, such as task forces or periodic review meetings.

While exploiting the alliance's learning potential, however, each company must also manage the interface to prevent unintended flows of information to its partner. It is a delicate balancing task for the gatekeepers to ensure the free flow of information across the organizational boundaries while effectively regulating the flow of people and data to ensure that sensitive or proprietary knowledge is appropriately protected.

Providing Strategic Direction: The Governance Structure

The key to providing leadership and direction, ensuring strategic control, and resolving inter-organizational conflicts is an effective governance structure. Unlike acquisitions, alliances are often premised on the equality of both partners, but an obsession to protect such equality can prevent companies from creating an effective governance structure for the partnership. Committees consisting of an equal number of participants from both companies and operating under strict norms of equality are often incapable of providing clear directions or forcing conflict resolution at lower levels. Indeed, many otherwise well-conceived alliances have floundered because of their dependence on such committees for their leadership and control.

To find their way around such problems, partners must negotiate on the basis of "integrative" rather than "distributive" equality. With such an agreement, each committee is structured with clear, single-handed leadership, but each company takes the responsibility for different tasks. However, such delicately balanced arrangements can work only if the partners can agree on specific individuals, delegate the overall responsibility for the alliance to these individuals, and protect their ability to work in the best interests of the alliance itself rather than those of the parents.

CONCLUDING COMMENTS

Perspectives on strategic alliances have oscillated between the extremes of euphoria and disillusionment. Finally, however, there seems to be some recognition that although such partnerships may not represent perfect solutions, they are often the best solution available to a particular company at a particular point in time.

Easy – But Sometimes Not the Best Solution

Perhaps the biggest danger for many companies is to pretend that the "quick and easy" option of a strategic alliance is also the best or only option available. Cooperative arrangements are perhaps too tempting in catch-up situations in which the partnership might provide a façade of recovery that masks serious problems.

Yet although going it alone may well be the most desirable option for a specific objective or task in the long term, almost no company can afford to meet all of its objectives in this way. When complete independence and self-sufficiency are not possible because of resource scarcity, lack of expertise, or time – or any other such constraint – strategic alliances often become the most realistic option.

Alliances Need Not Be Permanent

Another important factor commonly misunderstood is that the dissolution of a partnership is not synonymous with failure. Many companies appear to have suffered because of their unwillingness or inability to terminate partnership arrangements when changing circumstances made those arrangements inappropriate or because they failed to discuss upfront with their partner whether the alliance should have a sunset clause. All organizations create internal pressures for their own perpetuation, and an alliance is no exception to this enduring reality. One important task for senior managers of the participating companies is to ask periodically why the alliance should not be terminated and then continue with the arrangement only if they find compelling reasons to do so.

Flexibility is Key

The original agreement for a partnership typically is based on limited information and unrealistic expectations. Experience gained from the actual process of working together provides the opportunity for fine-tuning and often finding better ways to achieve higher levels of joint value creation. In such circumstances, the flexibility to adapt the goals, scope, and management of the alliance to changing conditions is essential. In addition, changing environmental conditions may make original intentions and plans obsolete. Effective partnering requires the ability to monitor such changes and allow the partnership to evolve in response.

An Internal Knowledge Network: Basis for Learning

Finally, learning is one of the main benefits that a company can derive from a partnership, irrespective of whether it represents one of the formal goals. For such learning to occur, however, a company must be receptive to the knowledge and skills available from the partner and have an organization able to diffuse and leverage such learning. In the absence of an internal knowledge network, information obtained from the partner cannot be transferred and applied, regardless of its potential value. Thus building and managing an integrated network organization, as described in Chapter 4, is an essential prerequisite for not only effective internal processes but also effective management across organizational boundaries.

⚐IVEY | Publishing

CASE 6.1 NORA-SAKARI: A PROPOSED JV IN MALAYSIA (REVISED)

R. Azimah Ainuddin wrote this case under the supervision of Professor Paul Beamish solely to provide material for class discussion. Revised (2015) with the assistance of Dwarka Chakravarty. The authors do not intend to illustrate either effective or ineffective handling of a managerial situation. The authors may have disguised certain names and other identifying information to protect confidentiality.

Copyright © 2015, Richard Ivey School of Business Foundation   Version: 2017–02–22

On Monday, March 11, 2013, Zainal Hashim, vice-chairman of Nora Holdings Sdn Bhd[1] (Nora), was thinking about the Friday evening reception that he had hosted at his home in Kuala Lumpur (KL), Malaysia, for a team of negotiators from Sakari Oy[2] (Sakari) of Finland. Nora was a leading supplier of telecommunications (telecom) equipment in Malaysia while Sakari, a Finnish conglomerate, was a leader in the manufacture and deployment of mobile broadband network infrastructure. The team from Sakari was in KL to negotiate with Nora the formation of a joint-venture (JV) between the two telecom companies.

This final negotiation would determine whether a JV agreement would materialize.

The negotiation had ended late Friday afternoon, having lasted for five consecutive days. The JV, if established, would be set up in Malaysia to manufacture and commission 4G (fourth generation) mobile network equipment to meet the needs of the telecom industry in Malaysia and in neighbouring countries, particularly Indonesia and Thailand. While Nora would benefit in terms of technology transfer, the venture would pave the way for Sakari to acquire knowledge and gain access to the markets of Southeast Asia.

The opportunity emerged two and half years earlier when Peter Mattsson, president of Sakari's Asian regional office in Singapore, approached Zainal[3] to explore the possibility of forming a

[1] Sdn Bhd is an abbreviation for Sendirian Berhad, which means private limited company in Malaysia.

[2] Oy is an abbreviation for Osakeyhtiot, which means private limited company in Finland.

[3] The first name is used because the Malay name does not carry a family name. The first and/or middle names belong to the individual and the last name is his/her father's name.

cooperative venture between Nora and Sakari. Mattsson said:

> In the next five years, we expect over 100 per cent mobile network infrastructure growth in Asia, compared to worldwide growth of about 60 per cent a year. We expect mobile broadband (4G) to be the fastest growing segment in Asia, accounting for 40 per cent of all mobile network traffic by 2015. Mobile broadband network project revenues can range from a hundred million to several billion euros. In Malaysia, Thailand, Indonesia, and China, such projects are currently approaching contract stage. Thus it is imperative that Sakari establish its presence in this region to capture a share in the market.

The large potential for mobile broadband networks was also evidenced in the low penetration rates for most Southeast Asian countries. In 2011, mobile broadband penetration rates for Indonesia, Thailand, Malaysia and the Philippines ranged from three to 30 connections per 100 people compared to the rates in Japan, Finland, United States and Sweden, which exceeded 75 connections per 100 people.

The Telecom Industry in Malaysia

Telekom Malaysia Bhd (TMB), the national telecom company, was given the authority by the Malaysian government to develop the country's telecom infrastructure. With a paid-up capital of RM2.4 billion,[4] it was also given the mandate to provide telecom services that were on par with those available in developed countries. In 2013, Malaysia had one dominant fixed line operator – TMB and three major mobile operators – Maxis, Celcom, and DiGi, all three of whom had been awarded 1800 MHz (Mega Hertz) wireless 4G spectrum licenses by the government. Maxis was the first to launch its 4G LTE (Long Term Evolution) service in 2013, followed by Celcom, and DiGi. TMB was also

looking to move into the wireless 4G LTE space in order to increase coverage and quality of its nationwide broadband service. It planned to use a block of 850 MHz spectrum that it had licensed in 1998 and aimed to have one million subscribers on its wireless LTE network by 2017. Use of the lower frequency 850 MHz band would improve geographic coverage, and entail reduced TMB investment in cell sites relative to the competition.

As the nation's largest telecom company, TMB's operations were regulated through a 20-year license issued by the Ministry of Energy, Telecommunications and Posts. In line with the government's Vision 2020 program, which targeted Malaysia to become a developed nation by the year 2020, there was a strong need for upgrading the telecom infrastructure in rural areas. In his statement in TMB's 2013 Annual Report, the Group CEO said:

> 2014 will also see TM moving into the LTE space as the Group continues with its plan to expand its wireless broadband services, especially in under-served areas, and complementing TM's existing suite of fixed broadband services. Providing mobility solutions to TM customers is a natural progression and is in line with the industry evolution towards true convergence, not just from a technology or device perspective, but more importantly from a customer experience point of view, in the delivery of end-to-end broadband and data services.

Although TMB had become a large national telecom company, it often lacked the expertise and technology to undertake massive infrastructure projects. In several cases, local telecom companies would be invited to submit their bids for a particular contract. It was also common for these local companies to form partnerships with large multinational corporations (MNCs), mainly for technological support. For example, Pernas-NEC, a JV company between Pernas Holdings and NEC, was one of the companies that had been successful in securing large telecom contracts from the Malaysian authorities.

---

[4] RM is Ringgit Malaysia, the Malaysian currency. As at March 11, 2013, US$1 = RM3.11.

Exhibit 1 How 4G LTE (And Mobile Broadband) Works: A Simplified Network Representation

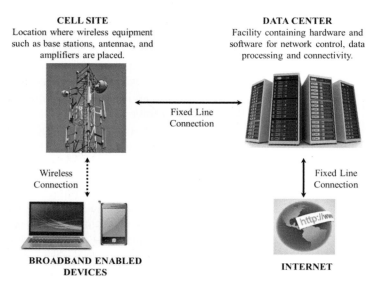

CELL SITE
Location where wireless equipment such as base stations, antennae, and amplifiers are placed.

DATA CENTER
Facility containing hardware and software for network control, data processing and connectivity.

Fixed Line Connection

Wireless Connection

Fixed Line Connection

BROADBAND ENABLED DEVICES

INTERNET

Source: Dwarka Chakravarty.

Exhibit 2
Mobile Networks: Evolution and Comparison

GENERATION	1G	2G	3G	4G LTE
Introduced	1980s	1990s	2000s	2010s
Peak Data Rate	2 KBps	0.5 MBps	63 MBps	300 MBps
Services	Voice	Voice, Text	Voice, Video, Data	Voice, Video, Data
Signal	Analog	Digital	Digital	Digital
Network	PSTN	PSTN	PSTN and Internet	Internet

Note: KBps/MBps = Kilo/Mega Bytes per second; PSTN = Public Switched Telephone Network.
Source: Qualcomm, "The Evolution of Mobile Technologies," www.qualcomm.com/media/documents/files/the-evolution-of-mobile-technologies-1g-to-2g-to-3g-to-4g-lte.pdf, accessed June 16, 2015.

Nora's Search for a JV Partner

In August 2012, TMB called for tenders to bid on a two-year project worth RM1 billion for building an LTE radio access network in various parts of the country. The project involved deploying cell sites (towers) comprising antennae, amplifiers, LTE base stations and switches, laying fiber optic cable to connect cell sites with the fixed broadband network, and implementing network planning and optimization software. See Exhibit 1 for a simplified representation of a 4G LTE (and mobile broadband) network.

With peak speeds of up to 300 MBps (Mega Bytes per second), 4G LTE networks were about five times faster than 3G networks. (See Exhibit 2 for a comparison of 1G, 2G, 3G, and 4G LTE mobile networks). Each LTE cell tower could potentially support twice as many simultaneous network users (64 to 128) as a 3G tower (32 to 64).

Nora was interested in securing a share of the RM1 billion contract from TMB and more importantly, in acquiring the knowledge in LTE technology from its partnership with a telecom MNC. During the initial stages, when Nora first began to consider potential partners in the bid for this contract, MNCs such as Samsung and NEC seemed appropriate candidates. Nora also had the experience of long-term working relationships with Japanese partners, including a fiber optic joint venture with NEC, and a five-year technical assistance agreement with Samsung to manufacture telephone handsets. Alcatel-Lucent and Ericsson were not considered, as they were already involved with other local competitors.

Subsequent to Zainal's meeting with Mattsson, he decided to consider Sakari as a serious potential partner. He was briefed about Sakari's SK4LTE, a 4G LTE platform that was based on an open IP (Internet Protocol) centric and technology neutral architecture, which enabled the use of standard components, standard software development tools, and standard software languages. The core of its platform – the SK10 base station–was an industry benchmark in size, spectrum flexibility, data capacity, and energy consumption. The system was modular, and its software could be upgraded to provide new services and applications and could interface easily with new network equipment, thus providing the assurance of "future proofing." This was a very attractive feature of the SK4LTE as it would facilitate development and implementation of advanced wireless systems.

Mattsson had also convinced Zainal and other Nora managers that although Sakari was a relatively large player in mobile broadband networks, these networks were easily adaptable, and could cater to densely populated urban areas as well as geographically dispersed rural needs. Nora was also concerned that Sakari would be less willing to provide custom-made products and would tend to offer standard products that, in some aspects, were not consistent with the needs of the customer. Apparently, despite

Sakari's larger size and global 4G LTE footprint, compared to that of some of the other MNCs, Sakari was prepared to work out customized products according to TMB and Nora's needs. Mattson pointed to the mobile network equipment JV manufacturing facility that Sakari had established in Brazil to cater to the needs of the local market and other Latin American countries, as an exemplar of what could be done in Malaysia.

Prior to the March 2013 meeting, 20 meetings had been held in KL or Helsinki to establish relationships between the two companies. Each side had invested no less than RM4 million in promoting the relationship. Mattsson and Ilkka Junttila, Sakari's representative in KL, were the key people in bringing the companies together. (See Exhibits 3 and 4 for brief backgrounds on Malaysia and Finland respectively.)

Nora Holdings Sdn Bhd

Nora was one of the leading companies in the telecom industry in Malaysia. It was established in 1975 with a paid-up capital of RM2 million. Last year, the company recorded a turnover of RM640 million. Nora Holdings consisted of 35 subsidiaries, including two publicly listed companies: Multiphone Bhd, and Nora Telecommunications Bhd. Nora had 5,545 employees, of which 923 were categorized as managerial (including 440 engineers) and 4,622 as non-managerial (including 484 engineers and technicians).

Since the inception of the company, Nora had secured two cable-laying projects. For the latter project worth RM500 million, Nora formed a JV with two Japanese companies, Sumitomo Electric Industries Ltd. (held 10 per cent equity share) and Marubeni Corporation (held five per cent equity share). Nora also acquired a 63 per cent stake in a local cable-laying company, Selangor Cables Sdn Bhd.

Nora had become a household name in Malaysia as a telephone manufacturer. It started in 1980 when the company obtained a contract to supply telephone sets to the government-owned Telecom authority, TMB. The RM130 million contract lasted for 15 years. In 1985 Nora secured

Exhibit 3
Malaysia: Background Information

Malaysia is centrally located in Southeast Asia. It consists of Peninsular Malaysia, and the states of Sabah and Sarawak on the island of Borneo. Malaysia has a total land area of about 330,000 square kilometres, of which 80 per cent is covered with tropical rainforest.

In 2013, Malaysia's population was 30 million, with approximately 13 million in the labour force. The population was relatively young, with 40 per cent between the ages of 15 and 39. The average household size was four, but extended families were common. Kuala Lumpur had close to 1.5 million inhabitants.

The population is multiracial; the largest ethnic group is the Bumiputeras (the Malays and other indigenous groups such as the Ibans in Sarawak and Kadazans in Sabah), followed by the Chinese and Indians. Bahasa Malaysia is the national language but English is widely used in business circles.

Islam is the official religion but other religions (mainly Christianity, Buddhism and Hinduism) are widely practised. All Malays are Muslims, followers of the Islamic faith. During the period of British rule, secularism was introduced to the country, which led to the separation of the Islamic religion from daily life. In the late 1970s and 1980s, several groups of devout Muslims undertook efforts to reverse the process, emphasizing a dynamic and progressive approach to Islam. As a result, changes were made to meet daily religious needs. Islamic banking and insurance facilities were introduced and prayer rooms were provided in government offices, private companies, factories, and even in shopping complexes.

Malaysia is a parliamentary democracy under a constitutional monarchy. In 2013, the Barisan Nasional, a coalition of several political parties representing various ethnic groups, was the ruling political party. Its predominance had contributed to political stability and economic progress in the last two decades.

The recession of the mid 1980s led to structural changes in the Malaysian economy, which had been too dependent on primary commodities (rubber, tin, palm oil and timber) and had a very narrow export base. To promote the establishment of export-oriented industries, the government directed resources to the manufacturing sector, introduced generous incentives and relaxed foreign equity restrictions. Heavy investments were made to modernize the country's infrastructure. This led to rapid economic growth in the late 1980s and early 1990s. The growth had been mostly driven by exports, particularly of electronics.

From 2003 to 2008, Malaysia's GDP grew at an average rate of 6.5% per year. Malaysia was severely affected by the global financial crisis of 2008–2009, given its economic exposure to the U.S. and Japan – top export destinations and key sources of foreign investment. In 2010, the government launched its New Economic Model (NEM) comprising a number of reforms to boost private sector driven, inclusive economic growth to enable Malaysia to achieve developed nation status by 2020.

From 2011 to 2013, GDP grew at an average of 5% per year. Consumer price inflation averaged 2.3% and the unemployment rate was 3%. In 2013, the services sector accounted for over 50% of GDP, with manufacturing making up 25% of the economy. Malaysia had also succeeded in nearly eradicating poverty. Malaysia had a GDP per capita of US$10,500 and was ranked 18th among all countries in terms of ease of doing business by the World Bank.

Sources: Ernst and Young, "Doing Business in Malaysia", 1997, Ernst and Young International, New York. The World Bank, http://data.worldbank.org/indicator/, accessed April 29, 2015. Other online sources.

Exhibit 4
Finland: Background Information

Finland is situated in the north-east of Europe, sharing borders with Sweden, Norway and the former Soviet Union. About 65 per cent of its area of 338,000 square kilometres is covered with forest, about 15 per cent lakes and about 10 per cent arable land. Finland has a temperate climate with four distinct seasons.

In 2013, Finland was one of the most sparsely populated countries in Europe with a population of 5.4 million, 80 per cent of whom lived in the urban areas. Helsinki had a population of about 590,000. Finland had a well-educated work force of about 2.7 million. About half of the work force was engaged in providing services, 25 per cent in manufacturing and construction, and four per cent in agricultural production. The small size of the population and an ageing demographic (33 per cent of the population above the age of 55 and only about 30% in the age group 15 to 39), led to scarce and expensive labour. Thus Finland had to compete by exploiting its lead in high-tech industries.

Finland's official languages are Finnish and Swedish, but only about five per cent of Finns speak Swedish. English is the most widely spoken foreign language. About 75 per cent of Finns are Lutheran Christians and about one per cent are Orthodox Christians. Finland has been an independent republic since 1917. A President and a 200-member single-chamber parliament are elected every six and four years, respectively.

Since the mid-1990s, the Finnish growth has mainly been bolstered by intense growth in telecommunications equipment manufacturing. The Finnish economy grew at an average of nearly 5% per year from 1994 to 2000. Finland was one of the 11 countries that joined the Economic and Monetary Union (EMU) on January 1, 1999. Finland has been experiencing a rapidly increasing integration with Western Europe. Membership in the EMU provides the Finnish economy with an array of benefits, such as lower and stable interest rates, elimination of foreign currency risk within the Euro area, reduction of transaction costs of business and travel, and so forth. The EMU did pose structural risks in regard to monetary interconnectedness of stronger and weaker economies without a corresponding fiscal union.

The IT sector slump in 2001 and 2002 had its impact on the Finnish economy, which for the years 2001 to 2003 registered an average growth of 2.1 per cent. The economy rebounded from 2004 onwards, achieving a growth of 5.2 per cent in 2007, but was hit hard by the global financial crisis of 2008–2009. A feeble recovery in 2010 and 2011 was stymied by the debt crisis and economic downturn in Europe and Finland's economy declined in 2012 and 2013. The GDP in 2013 still languished at about 5 per cent below its 2008 level. In the period from 2011 to 2013, Finland's average consumer price inflation and unemployment rate were 2.6 per cent and 7.9 per cent, respectively. Finland's 2013 GDP per capita was US$39,000 and it was ranked 8th among all countries in terms of ease of doing business by the World Bank.

Finland is a developed nation and its standard of living is among the highest in the world. The Finns have small families with an average household size of two. For long, the stable trading relationship with the former Soviet Union and other Scandinavian countries led to few interactions between the Finns and people in other parts of the world. The Finns are described as rather reserved, obstinate, and serious people. A Finn commented, "We do not engage easily in small talk with strangers. Furthermore, we have a strong love for nature and we have the tendency to be silent as we observe our surroundings. Unfortunately, others tend to view such behaviour as cold and serious."

Sources: Ernst and Young, "Doing Business in Finland", 1997, Ernst and Young International, New York. The World Bank, http://data.worldbank.org/indicator/, accessed April 29, 2015.
Other online sources.

licenses from Siemens and Nortel to manufacture telephone handsets and subsequently developed its own telephone sets – the N300S (single line), N300M (micro-computer controlled), and N300V (hands-free, voice-activated) models.

Upon expiry of the contract as a supplier of telephone sets to TMB, Nora suffered a major setback when it lost a RM32 million contract to supply 600,000 N300S telephones. The contract was instead given to a Taiwanese manufacturer that quoted a lower price. Subsequently, Nora moved towards the high-end feature phone domestic market, selling about 6,000 high-end sets per month, in Malaysia. Nora had also ventured into the export market with its feature phones. The foreign markets were very competitive and many manufacturers already had well-established brands. With the rise in mobile telephone usage, sales of fixed-line phones were stagnating and Nora expected the business to slowly decline in the coming years.

Nora had also secured a 15-year TMB contract to install, operate and maintain payphones in Malaysia. In 1997, Nora started to manufacture card payphones under a license from GEC Plessey Telecommunications (GPT) of the United Kingdom. The agreement also permitted Nora to sell the products to several countries in Southeast Asia. While payphone revenues were as high as RM120 million a year, profit margins were only about 10 per cent because of high investment and maintenance costs. With growing telephone ownership across Southeast Asia, particularly of mobile phones, growth in the payphone business had steadily declined since 2008. Demand for and installation of new payphones was largely confined to poor and/or rural areas. Payphone companies were going out of business in the developed nations and Nora was concerned about long-term viability.

In 2011, Nora acquired S&B Telecom's business for RM80 million, with the intent of securing a foothold into the fast growing and higher margin mobile network services business. S&B Telecom's work involved installation, commissioning, and maintenance of mobile cell tower equipment, and laying fiber optic cables to connect the cell towers with fixed networks. Nora saw this line of business as crucial for winning the TMB 4G LTE contract and establishing a successful JV with a MNC network equipment provider.

The Management

When Nora was established, its founder, Osman Jaafar, managed the company with his wife, Nora Asyikin Yusof, and seven employees. Osman was known as a conservative businessman who did not like to dabble in acquisitions and mergers to make quick capital gains. He was formerly an electrical engineer who was trained in the United Kingdom and had held several senior positions at the national Telecom Department in Malaysia.

Osman subsequently recruited Zainal Hashim for the position of deputy managing director at Nora. Zainal held a master's degree in microwave communications from a British university and had experience as a production engineer at Pernas-NEC Sdn Bhd, a manufacturer of transmission equipment. Zainal was later promoted to the position of managing director and six years later, the vice-chairman.

Industry analysts observed that Nora's success was attributed to the complementary roles, trust, and mutual understanding between Osman and Zainal. While Osman "likes to fight for new business opportunities," Zainal preferred a low profile and concentrated on managing Nora's operations. Industry observers also speculated that Osman, a former civil servant and an entrepreneur, was close to Malaysian politicians, notably the Prime Minister, while Zainal had been a close friend of the Finance Minister. Zainal disagreed with allegations that Nora had succeeded due to its close relationships with Malaysian politicians. However, he acknowledged that such perceptions in the industry had been beneficial to the company.

Osman and Zainal had an obsession for high-tech and made the development of research and development (R&D) skills and resources a priority in the company. About two per cent of Nora's earnings was reinvested into R&D activities. Although this amount was considered small by international standards, Nora planned to increase it gradually to 5 to 6 per cent over the next two to three years. Zainal said:

> We believe in making improvements in small steps, similar to the Japanese *kaizen* principle. Over time, each small improvement could lead to a major creation. To be able to make improvements, we must learn from others. Thus, we would borrow a technology from others, but eventually, we must be able to develop our own to sustain our industry competitiveness.

To further enhance R&D activities at Nora, Nora Research Sdn Bhd (NRSB) formed a wholly owned subsidiary (WOS) with a staff of 60 technicians/engineers. NRSB operated as an independent company undertaking R&D activities for Nora as well as private clients in related fields. The company facilitated R&D activities with other companies as well as government organizations, research institutions, and universities.

Sakari Oy

Sakari was established in 1865 as a pulp and paper mill northwest of Helsinki. In the 1960s, Sakari started to expand into the rubber and cable industries when it merged with the Finnish Rubber Works and Finnish Cable Works. In 1975, Aatos Olkkola took over as Sakari's president and led it into businesses such as computers, consumer electronics, and cellular phones via a series of acquisitions, mergers and alliances.

In 1979, a JV between Sakari and Vantala, Sakari-Vantala, was set up to develop and manufacture mobile telephones. Sakari-Vantala had captured about 14 per cent of the world's market share for mobile phones and held a 20 per cent market share in Europe for its mobile phone handsets. Outside Europe, a 50–50 JV was formed with Tandy Corporation, which had made significant sales in the United States, Malaysia and Thailand.

Sakari first edged into the telecom market by selling switching systems licensed from France's Alcatel and by developing the software and systems to suit the needs of small Finnish phone companies. Sakari avoided head-on competition with Siemens and Ericsson by not trying to enter the market for large telephone networks. Instead, Sakari concentrated on developing dedicated telecom networks for large private users, such as utility and railway companies. In Finland, Sakari held 40 per cent of the market for telecom infrastructure, versus Ericsson (34 per cent), Siemens (25 per cent), and Alcatel (1 per cent).

In 1989 Mikko Koskinen took over as president of Sakari. He announced that telecommunications, computers, and consumer electronics would be maintained as Sakari's core business, and that he would continue efforts in expanding the company overseas. To do so, he envisaged the setting up of several alliances, each designed for a specific purpose. He said, "Sakari has become an interesting partner with which to cooperate on an equal footing in the areas of R&D, manufacturing and marketing."

Due to the recession in Finland, which began in 1990, Sakari began divesting its less profitable companies within the basic industries (metal, rubber, and paper), as well as leaving the troubled European computer market with the sale of its computer subsidiary, Sakari Macro. The company's new strategy was to focus on two main areas: telecom systems and mobile phones globally, and consumer electronic products in Europe. The company's divestment strategy led to a reduction of Sakari's employees from about 41,000 in 1989 to 29,000 in 1991.

The Finnish economy went through a rapid revival in 1993, followed by a new period of intense growth. Since the mid-1990s the Finnish growth had been bolstered by intense growth in telecommunications equipment manufacturing as a result of an exploding global telecommunications market. Sakari capitalized on this opportunity and played a major role in the telecommunications equipment manufacturing sector.

In 1998, despite having nearly $15 billion in telecom equipment sales, and being the world leader in mobile phones, Sakari was still a small company by international standards. There were six larger competitors headquartered respectively in the United States (2), Sweden, France, Canada and Germany. Sakari lacked a strong marketing capability and had to rely on JVs to enter the world market, particularly the United States. In its efforts to develop market position quickly, Sakari had to accept lower margins for its products, and often the Sakari name was not revealed on the product.

In 2001, Sakari was Finland's largest publicly-traded industrial company and derived the majority of its total sales from exports and overseas operations. The company had succeeded in globalizing and diversifying its operations to make the most of its high-tech capabilities. Sakari had also started marketing under its own name. As a result, Sakari emerged as a more influential player in international markets and had gained international brand recognition.

In 2007, Sakari combined its telecoms infrastructure operations with those of Magma to form a JV named Sakari-Magma (SM). The plan was to reduce cost, identify product and service complementarities, and provide a superior market alternative to both Ericsson's high-end offerings and Huawei's low cost solutions. SM became a leading global provider of both wireless and landline telecom infrastructure equipment to telecom operators around the world. However, the JV struggled to support existing customers of Magma and work effectively with services partners. In 2011, SM announced that it would cut 17,000 jobs over the next two years and restructure its business to focus on mobile broadband solutions.

By January 2013, SM had secured 75 LTE network infrastructure contracts worldwide and had an LTE contract share of 18 per cent behind Ericsson at 38 per cent and Huawei at 32 per cent. Its SK4LTE platform had sold well in developed nations such as Canada, Germany, and South Korea, as well as in developing countries such as China, Brazil, and India. In the first quarter of 2013, Sakari purchased Magma's stake in SM for $2 billion, and announced the sale of its devices business to Oscorp for $7 billion.

Sakari attributed its success in the telecom industry to R&D. Strong in-house R&D in core competence areas enabled the company to develop technology platforms, such as its SK4LTE system, that were reliable, flexible, widely compatible and economical. About 20 per cent of its annual sales revenue was invested into R&D and

product development units in Finland, the United States, Germany, China, and India. Sakari's current strategy entailed global operations in production and R&D. It planned to set up additional R&D centres in leading markets, as well as in Southeast Asia – a region where it had no business experience.

The Nora-Sakari Negotiation

Nora and Sakari had discussed the potential of forming a JV in Malaysia for more than two years. Nora engineers went to Helsinki to assess SK4LTE technology in terms of its compatibility with Malaysian requirements, while Sakari managers travelled to KL to assess Nora's capability in manufacturing and installing 4G LTE equipment and the feasibility of gaining access to the Malaysian market.

In October 2012, Nora submitted its bid for TMB's RM1 billion contract to supply and install 4G LTE equipment supporting 1200 cell sites. Assuming the Nora-Sakari JV would materialize, Nora based its bid on supplying Sakari's 4G LTE technology. Nora competed with five other companies shortlisted by TMB, all offering their partners' technology – Alcatel-Lucent, Ericsson, Huawei, NEC, and Samsung. In mid-January 2013, TMB announced three successful companies in the bid. They were companies using technology from Alcatel-Lucent, Ericsson, and Sakari. Each was awarded a one-third share of the RM1 billion contract and would be responsible for delivering 400 cell sites over a period of two years. Industry observers were critical of TMB's decision to select Sakari and Ericsson, despite both being market leaders in 4G LTE products and services. Sakari's SK4LTE platform was criticized for failing to make any impact in the United States, one of the world's largest and most important mobile markets. Ericsson was criticized for lacking flexibility in adapting its solutions and delivery priorities to align with customer needs.

The February 4 Meeting

Following the successful bid and ignoring the criticisms against Sakari, Nora and Sakari held a major meeting in Helsinki on February 4 to finalize the formation of the JV. Zainal led Nora's five-member negotiation team, which comprised Nora's general manager for corporate planning division, an accountant, two engineers, and Marina Mohamed, a lawyer. One of the engineers was Salleh Lindstrom who was of Swedish origin, a Muslim and had worked for Nora for almost 10 years.

Sakari's team was led by Kuusisto, Sakari's vice-president. His team comprised Junttila, Hussein Ghazi, Aziz Majid, three engineers, and Julia Ruola, a lawyer. Ghazi was Sakari's senior manager who was of Egyptian origin and also a Muslim who had worked for Sakari for more than 20 years, while Aziz, a Malay, had been Sakari's manager for more than 12 years.

The meeting went on for several days. The main issue raised at the meeting was Nora's capability in penetrating the Southeast Asian market. Other issues included Sakari's concerns over the efficiency of Malaysian workers in manufacturing, maintaining product quality and ensuring prompt deliveries.

Zainal said that this was the most difficult negotiation he had ever experienced. Zainal was Nora's most experienced negotiator and had single-handedly represented Nora in several major negotiations for the past 10 years. In the negotiation with Sakari, Zainal admitted making the mistake of applying the approach he often used when negotiating with companies based in North America or the United Kingdom. He said:

> Negotiators from the U.S. tend to be very open and often state their positions early and definitively. They are highly verbal and usually prepare well-planned presentations. They also often engage in small talk and 'joke around' with us at the end of a negotiation. In contrast, the Sakari negotiators are serious, reserved and 'cold.' They are also relatively less verbal and do not convey much through their facial expressions. As a result, it was difficult to determine whether they are really interested in the deal or not.

Zainal said that the negotiation on February 4 turned out to be particularly difficult when

Sakari became interested in bidding on a recently-announced tender for a major telecom contract in the United Kingdom. Internal politics within Sakari led to the formation of two opposing "camps." One "camp" held a strong belief that there would be very high growth in the Asia-Pacific region and that the JV in Malaysia was seen as a hub to enter these markets. Although the government had liberalized equity ownership restrictions and allowed the formation of WOS's, JVs were still an efficient way to enter the Malaysian market for a company that lacked local knowledge. This group was represented mostly by Sakari's managers positioned in Asia and engineers who had made several trips to Malaysia, which usually included visits to Nora's facilities. It also had the support of Sakari's vice-president, Kuusisto, who was involved in most of the meetings with Nora, particularly when Zainal was present. Kuusisto had also made efforts to be present at meetings held in KL. This group also argued that Nora had secured the contract in Malaysia whereas the chance of getting the United Kingdom contract was low in view of the intense competition prevailing in that market.

The "camp" not in favour of the JV believed that Sakari should focus its resources on entering the United Kingdom, which could be used as a hub to penetrate the European Union (EU) market. There was also the belief that Europe was closer to home, making management easier, and that problems arising from cultural differences would be minimized. This group was also particularly concerned that Nora had the potential of copying Sakari's technology and eventually becoming a strong regional competitor. Also, because the United Kingdom market was relatively "familiar" and Sakari had local knowledge, it could set up a WOS instead of a JV and avoid JV-related problems, such as joint control, joint profits, and technology leakage.

Zainal felt that the lack of full support from Sakari's management led to a difficult negotiation when new misgivings arose concerning Nora's capability to deliver its part of the deal. It was apparent that the group in favour of the Nora-Sakari JV was under pressure to further justify its proposal and provide counterarguments against the United Kingdom proposal. A Sakari manager explained, "We are tempted to pursue both proposals, but our current resources are limited. Thus, a choice has to made, and soon."

The March 4 Meeting

Another meeting to negotiate the JV agreement was scheduled for March 4. Sakari's eight-member team arrived in KL on Sunday afternoon of March 3, and was met at the airport by the key Nora managers involved in the negotiation. Kuusisto did not accompany the Sakari team to this meeting.

The negotiation started early Monday morning at Nora's headquarters and continued for the next five days, with each day's meeting ending late in the evening. Members of the Nora team were the same members who had attended the February 4 meeting in Finland, except Zainal, who did not participate. The Sakari team was also represented by the same members in attendance at the previous meeting plus a new member, Solail Pekkarinen, Sakari's senior accountant. On the third day, the Nora team requested that Sakari ask Pekkarinen to leave the negotiation. He was perceived as extremely arrogant and insensitive to the local culture, which tended to value modesty and diplomacy. Pekkarinen left for Helsinki the following morning.

Although Zainal had decided not to participate actively in the negotiations, he followed the process closely and was briefed by his negotiators regularly. Some of the issues that they complained were difficult to resolve had often led to heated arguments between the two negotiating teams. These included:

1. Equity Ownership

In previous meetings, both companies agreed to form the JV with a paid-up capital of RM8 million. However, they disagreed on the equity share proposed by each side. Sakari proposed an equity split of 49 per cent for Sakari and 51 per cent for Nora. Nora, on the other hand, proposed a 30 per cent Sakari and 70 per cent Nora split. Nora's proposal was based on the common practice in Malaysia as a result of historical foreign equity regulations set by the Malaysian government that allowed a maximum of 30 per cent foreign equity ownership unless the company would export a certain percentage of its products. Though these regulations were liberalized by the Malaysian government effective July 1998 and new regulations had replaced the old ones, the 30–70 foreign-Malaysian ownership divide was still commonly observed.

Equity ownership became a major issue as it was associated with control. Sakari was concerned about its ability to control the accessibility of its technology to Nora and about decisions concerning the activities of the JV as a whole. The lack of control was perceived by Sakari as an obstacle to protecting its interests. Nora had concerns about its ability to exert control over the JV because it was intended as a key part of its long-term strategy to develop its own mobile broadband equipment and related high-tech products.

2. Technology Transfer

Sakari proposed to provide the JV with the basic structure of the SK10 base station. The JV company would assemble the base stations at the JV plant and subsequently install the exchanges in designated locations identified by TMB. By offering Nora only the basic structure of the SK10, the core of Sakari's 4G LTE platform would still be well-protected.

On the other hand, Nora proposed that the basic structure of the SK10 base station be developed at the JV company. Based on Sakari's proposal, Nora felt that only the technical aspects in assembling and installing the SK10 would be obtained. This was perceived as another "screwdriver" form of technology transfer while the core technology associated with making the base stations would still be unknown.

3. Royalty Payment

Closely related to the issue of technology transfer was the payment of a royalty for the technology used in building the base stations. Sakari proposed a royalty payment of 5 per cent of the JV gross sales while Nora proposed a payment of 2 per cent of net sales. (Net sales were overall sales minus returns, allowances for damaged or missing goods, plus any discounts.)

Nora considered the royalty rate of 5 per cent too high because it would affect Nora's financial situation. Financial simulations prepared by Nora's managers indicated that its return on investment would be less than the desired 10 per cent if royalty rates exceeded three per cent of net sales. This was because Nora had already agreed to make large additional investments in support of the JV. Nora would invest in a building to be rented to the JV company to accommodate an office and the base station plant. Nora would also invest in another plant to supply the JV with antennae and amplifiers required for the cell sites.

An added argument raised by the Nora negotiators in support of a two per cent royalty was that Sakari would receive benefits from the JV's access to Japanese technology used in manufacturing antennae and amplifiers. Apparently the Japanese technology was more advanced than Sakari's present technology.

4. Expatriates' Salaries and Perks

To allay Sakari's concerns over Nora's level of efficiency, Nora suggested that Sakari provide the necessary training for the JV technical employees. Subsequently, Sakari had agreed to provide eight engineering experts for the JV company on two types of contracts, short-term and long-term. Experts employed on a short-term basis would be paid a daily rate of US$1640 plus travel/accommodation. The permanent experts would be paid a monthly salary of US$26,000. Three permanent experts would be attached to the JV and the number would gradually be reduced to one, after a year. Five experts would be available on a short-term basis of less than three months each year to provide specific training.

The Nora negotiation team was appalled at the exorbitant amount proposed by the Sakari negotiators. They were surprised that the Sakari team had not surveyed the industry rates, as the Japanese and other western negotiators would normally have done. In response to Sakari's proposal, Nora negotiators adopted an unusual "take-it or leave-it" stance. They deemed the following proposal reasonable in view of the comparisons made with other JVs that Nora had entered into with other foreign parties:

Permanent experts' monthly salary ranges to be paid by the JV company were as follows:

(1) Senior expert (seven to 10 years' experience). RM32,800–RM37,700
(2) Expert (four to six years' experience). RM30,300–RM34,100
(3) Junior expert (two to three years' experience). RM27,900–RM31,600
(4) Any Malaysian income taxes payable would be added to the salaries.
(5) A car for personal use.
(6) Annual paid vacation of five weeks.
(7) Return flight tickets to home country twice a year for singles and once a year for families.
(8) Any expenses incurred during official travelling.

Temporary experts invited by the JV for technical assistance would be paid the following fees:

(1) Senior expert. . . . . . RM1,800 per working day
(2) Expert. . . . . RM1,600 per working day
(3) The JV company would not reimburse the following:
   • Flight tickets between Finland (or any other country) and Malaysia.
   • Hotel or any other form of accommodation.
   • Local transportation.

In defense of their proposed rates, Sakari's negotiators argued that the rates presented by Nora were too low. Sakari suggested that Nora's negotiators take into consideration the fact that Sakari would have to subsidize the difference between the experts' present salaries and the amount paid by the JV company. A large difference would require that large amounts of subsidy payments be made to the affected employees.

5. Arbitration

Another major issue discussed in the negotiation was related to arbitration. While both parties agreed to an arbitration process in the event of future disputes, they disagreed on the location for dispute resolution. Because Nora would be the majority stakeholder in the JV, Nora insisted that any arbitration should take place in KL. Sakari, however, insisted on Helsinki, following its commonly practised norm. At the end of the five-day negotiation, many issues could not be resolved. While Nora could agree on certain matters after consulting Zainal, the Sakari team had to refer contentious items to its board before making any decision.

The Decision

Zainal read through the minutes of the negotiation and was disappointed that an agreement had not yet been reached. He was concerned about the contractual commitment Nora had made to TMB. Nora would be expected to fulfill the contract soon but had yet to find a partner to provide the technology. Companies such as NEC and Samsung, which had failed in the bid, could still be potential partners. However, Zainal had also not rejected the possibility of a reconciliation with Sakari. He could start by contacting Kuusisto in Helsinki. But should he?

🛡️**IVEY** | Publishing

CASE 6.2 ELI LILLY IN INDIA: RETHINKING THE JOINT VENTURE STRATEGY

Nikhil Celly prepared this case under the supervision of Professors Charles Dhanaraj and Paul W. Beamish solely to provide material for class discussion. The authors do not intend to illustrate either effective or ineffective handling of a managerial situation. The authors may have disguised certain names and other identifying information to protect confidentiality.

Version: (A) 2017–03–13

In August 2001, Dr. Lorenzo Tallarigo, president of Intercontinental Operations, Eli Lilly and Company (Lilly), a leading pharmaceutical firm based in the United States, was getting ready for a meeting in New York with D. S. Brar, chairman and chief executive officer (CEO) of Ranbaxy Laboratories Limited (Ranbaxy), India. Lilly and Ranbaxy had started a joint venture (JV) in India, Eli Lilly-Ranbaxy Private Limited (ELR), that was incorporated in March 1993. The JV had steadily grown to a full-fledged organization employing more than 500 people in 2001. However, in recent months Lilly was re-evaluating the directions for the JV, with Ranbaxy signaling an intention to sell its stake. Tallarigo was scheduled to meet with Brar to decide on the next steps.

The Global Pharmaceutical Industry in the 1990s

The pharmaceutical industry had come about through both forward integration from the

Exhibit 1
World Pharmaceutical Suppliers 1992 and 2001 (US$ millions)

Company	Origin	1992 Sales*	Company	Origin	2001 Sales**
Glaxo	US	8,704	Pfizer	USA	25,500
Merck	UK	8,214	GlaxoSmithKline	UK	24,800
Bristol-Myers Squibb	US	6,313	Merck & Co	USA	21,350
Hoechst	GER	6,042	AstraZeneca	UK	16,480
Ciba-Geigy	SWI	5,192	Bristol-Myers Squibb	USA	15,600
SmithKline Beecham	US	5,100	Aventis	FRA	15,350
Roche	SWI	4,897	Johnson & Johnson	USA	14,900
Sandoz	SWI	4,886	Novartis	SWI	14,500
Bayer	GER	4,670	Pharmacia Corp	USA	11,970
American Home	US	4,589	Eli Lilly	USA	11,540
Pfizer	US	4,558	Wyeth	USA	11,710
Eli Lilly	US	4,537	Roche	SWI	8,530
Johnson & Johnson	US	4,340	Schering-Plough	USA	8,360
Rhone Poulenc Rorer	US	4,096	Abbott Laboratories	USA	8,170
Abbott	US	4,025	Takeda	JAP	7,770
			Sanofi-Synthélabo	FRA	5,700
			Boehringer Ingelheim	GER	5,600
			Bayer	GER	5,040
			Schering AG	GER	3,900
			Akzo Nobel	NTH	3,550

* *Market Share Reporter*, 1993.
** *Pharmaceutical Executive*, May 2002.

manufacture of organic chemicals and a backward integration from druggist-supply houses. The industry's rapid growth was aided by increasing worldwide incomes and a universal demand for better health care; however, most of the world market for pharmaceuticals was concentrated in North America, Europe and Japan. Typically, the largest four firms claimed 20 per cent of sales, the top 20 firms claimed 50 to 60 per cent, and the 50 largest companies accounted for 65 to 75 per cent of sales (see Exhibit 1). Drug discovery was an expensive process, with leading firms spending more than 20 per cent of their sales on research and development (R&D). Developing a drug, from discovery to launch in a major market, took 10 to 12 years and typically cost US$500 million to US$800 million (in 1992). Bulk production of active ingredients was the norm, along with the ability to decentralize manufacturing and packaging to adapt to particular market needs. Marketing was usually equally targeted to physicians and the paying customers. Increasingly, government agencies, such as Medicare, and health management organizations (HMOs) in the United States, were gaining influence in the buying processes. In most countries, all activities related to drug research and manufacturing were strictly controlled by government agencies, such as the Food and Drug Administration (FDA) in the United States, the Committee on Proprietary Medicinal Products (CPMP) in Europe, and the Ministry of Health and Welfare (MHW) in Japan.

Patents were the essential means by which a firm protected its proprietary knowledge. The safety provided by the patents allowed firms to price their products appropriately in order to accumulate funds for future research. The basic reason to patent a new drug was to guarantee the exclusive legal right to profit from its innovation for a certain number of years, typically 20 years for a product patent. There was usually a time lag of about eight to 10 years from the time the patent was obtained and the time of regulatory approval to first launch in the United States or Europe. Time lags for emerging markets and in Japan were longer. The "product patent" covered the chemical substance itself, while a "process patent" covered the method of processing or manufacture. Both patents guaranteed the inventor a 20-year monopoly on the innovation, but the process patent offered much less protection, since it was fairly easy to modify a chemical process. It was also very difficult to legally prove that a process patent had been created to manufacture a product identical to that of a competitor. Most countries relied solely on process patents until the mid-1950s, although many countries had since recognized the product patent in law. While companies used the global market to amortize the huge investments required to produce a new drug, they were hesitant to invest in countries where the intellectual property regime was weak.

As health care costs soared in the 1990s, the pharmaceutical industry in developed countries began coming under increased scrutiny. Although patent protection was strong in developed countries, there were various types of price controls. Prices for the same drugs varied between the United States and Canada by a factor of 1.2 to 2.5.[1] Parallel trade or trade by independent firms taking advantage of such differentials represented a serious threat to pharmaceutical suppliers, especially in Europe. Also, the rise of generics, unbranded drugs of comparable efficacy in treating the disease but available at a fraction of the cost of the branded drugs, were challenging the pricing power of the pharmaceutical companies. Manufacturers of generic drugs had no expense for drug research and development of new compounds and only had limited budgets for popularizing the compound with the medical community. The generic companies made their money by copying what other pharmaceutical companies discovered, developed and created a market for. Health management organizations (HMOs) were growing and consolidating their drug purchases. In the United States, the administration under President Clinton, which took office in 1992, investigated the possibility of a comprehensive health plan, which, among other things, would have allowed an increased use of generics and laid down some form of regulatory pressure on pharmaceutical profits.

The Indian Pharmaceutical Industry in the 1990s

Developing countries, such as India, although large by population, were characterized by low per capita gross domestic product (GDP). Typically, healthcare expenditures accounted for a very small share of GDP, and health insurance was not commonly available. The 1990 figures for per capita annual expenditure on drugs in India were estimated at US$3, compared to US$412 in Japan, US$222 in Germany and US$191 in the United Kingdom.[2] Governments and large corporations extended health coverage, including prescription drug coverage, to their workers.

In the years before and following India's independence in 1947, the country had no indigenous capability to produce pharmaceuticals, and was dependent on imports. The Patent and Designs Act of 1911, an extension of the British colonial rule, enforced adherence to the international patent law, and gave rise to a number of

---

[1] Estimates of industry average wholesale price levels in Europe (with Spanish levels indexed at 100 in 1989) were: Spain 100; Portugal 107; France 113; Italy 118; Belgium 131: United Kingdom 201; The Netherlands 229; West Germany 251. Source: Thomas Malnight, "Globalization of an Ethnocentric Firm: An Evolutionary Perspective," *Strategic Management Journal*, 1995, Vol. 16 p. 128.

[2] Organization of Pharmaceutical Producers of India Report.

multinational firms' subsidiaries in India, that wanted to import drugs from their respective countries of origin. Post-independence, the first public sector drug company, Hindustan Antibiotics Limited (HAL), was established in 1954 with the help of the World Health Organization, and Indian Drugs and Pharmaceutical Limited (IDPL) was established in 1961 with the help of the then Soviet Union.

The 1970s saw several changes that would dramatically change the intellectual property regime and give rise to the emergence of local manufacturing companies. Two such key changes were the passage of the Patents Act 1970 (effective April 1972) and the Drug Price Control Order (DPCO). The Patents Act, in essence abolished the product patents for all pharmaceutical and agricultural products, and permitted process patents for five to seven years. The DPCO instituted price controls, by which a government body stipulated prices for all drugs. Subsequently, this list was revised in 1987 to 142 drugs (which accounted for 72 per cent of the turnover of the industry). Indian drug prices were estimated to be five per cent to 20 per cent of the U.S. prices and among the lowest in the world.[3] The DPCO also limited profits pharmaceutical companies could earn to approximately six per cent of sales turnover. Also, the post-manufacturing expenses were limited to 100 per cent of the production costs. At the World Health Assembly in 1982, Indira Gandhi, then Prime Minister of India, aptly captured the national sentiment on the issue in an often-quoted statement:

> The idea of a better-ordered world is one in which medical discoveries will be free of patents and there will be no profiteering from life and death.

With the institution of both the DPCO and the 1970 Patent Act, drugs became available more cheaply, and local firms were encouraged to make copies of drugs by developing their own processes, leading to bulk drug production. The profitability was sharply reduced for multinational companies, many of which began opting out of the Indian market due to the disadvantages they faced from the local competition. Market share of multinational companies dropped from 80 per cent in 1970 to 35 per cent in the mid-1990s as those companies exited the market due to the lack of patent protection in India.

In November 1984, there were changes in the government leadership following Gandhi's assassination. The dawn of the 1990s saw India initiating economic reform and embracing globalization. Under the leadership of Dr. Manmohan Singh, then finance minister, the government began the process of liberalization and moving the economy away from import substitution to an export-driven economy. Foreign direct investment was encouraged by increasing the maximum limit of foreign ownership to 51 per cent (from 40 per cent) in the drugs and pharmaceutical industry (see Exhibit 2). It was in this environment that Eli Lilly was considering getting involved.

Eli Lilly and Company

Colonel Eli Lilly founded Eli Lilly and Company in 1876. The company would become one of the largest pharmaceutical companies in the United States from the early 1940s until 1985, but it began with just $1,400 and four employees, including Lilly's 14-year-old son. This was accomplished with a company philosophy grounded in a commitment to scientific and managerial excellence. Over the years, Eli Lilly discovered, developed, manufactured and sold a broad line of human health and agricultural products. Research and development was crucial to Lilly's long-term success.

Before 1950, most OUS (a company term for "Outside the United States") activities were export focused. Beginning in the 1950s, Lilly undertook systematic expansion of its OUS activities, setting up several affiliates overseas. In the mid-1980s, under the leadership of then

---

[3] According to a study from Yale University, Ranitidine (300 tabs/10 pack) was priced at Rs18.53, whereas the U.S. price was 57 times more, and Ciprofloxacin (500 mg/4 pack) was at Rs28.40 in India, whereas the U.S. price was about 15 times more.

Exhibit 2
India's Economy at a Glance

	1992	1994	1996	1998	2000
Gross domestic product (GDP) at current market prices in US$	244	323	386	414	481
Consumer price index (June 1982=100) in local currency, period average	77.4	90.7	108.9	132.2	149.3
Recorded official unemployment as a percentage of total labor force	9.7	9.3	9.1	9.2	9.2
Stock of foreign reserves plus gold (national valuation), end-period	8,665	23,054	23,784	29,833	48,200
Foreign direct investment inflow (in US$ millions)[1]	252	974	2,525	2,633	2,319
Total exports	19,563	25,075	33,055	33,052	43,085
Total imports	23,580	26,846	37,376	42,318	49,907
Population (millions)	886	938	973	1,008	1,042

[1] United Nations Commission on Trade and Development.
Source: The Economist Intelligence Unit.

chairman Dick Wood, Lilly began a significant move toward global markets. A separate division within the company, Eli Lilly International Corporation, with responsibility for worldwide marketing of all its products, took an active role in expanding the OUS operations. By 1992, Lilly's products were manufactured and distributed through 25 countries and sold in more than 130 countries. The company had emerged as a world leader in oral and injectable antibiotics and in supplying insulin and related diabetic care products. In 1992, Lilly International was headed by Sidney Taurel, an MBA from Columbia University with work experience in South America and Europe, and Gerhard Mayr, an MBA from Stanford with extensive experience in Europe. Mayr wanted to expand Lilly's operations in Asia, where several countries, including India, were opening up their markets for foreign investment. Lilly also saw opportunities to use the world for clinical testing, which would enable it to move forward faster, as well as shape opinion with leaders in the medical field around the world; something that would help in Lilly's marketing stage.

Ranbaxy Laboratories

Ranbaxy began in the 1960s as a family business, but with a visionary management grew rapidly to emerge as the leading domestic pharmaceutical firm in India. Under the leadership of Dr. Parvinder Singh, who held a doctoral degree from the University of Michigan, the firm evolved into a serious research-oriented firm. Singh, who joined Ranbaxy to assist his father in 1967, rose to become the joint managing director in 1977, managing director in 1982, and vice-chairman and managing director in 1987. Singh's visionary management, along with the operational leadership provided by Brar, who joined the firm in 1977, was instrumental in turning the family business into a global corporation. In the early 1990s, when almost the entire domestic pharmaceutical industry was opposing a tough patent regime, Ranbaxy was accepting it as given. Singh's argument was unique within the industry in India:

The global marketplace calls for a single set of rules; you cannot have one for the Indian market and another for the export market.

Exhibit 3
Top 20 Pharmaceutical Companies in India by Sales (Rs billions)

Company	1996*	Company	2000
Glaxo-Wellcome	4.97	Ranbaxy	20.00
Cipla	2.98	Cipla	12.00
Ranbaxy	2.67	Dr. Reddy's Labs	11.30
Hoechts-Roussel	2.60	Glaxo (India)	7.90
Knoll Pharmaceutical	1.76	Lupin Labs	7.80
Pfizer	1.73	Aurobindo Pharma	7.60
Alembic	1.68	Novartis	7.20
Torrent Pharma	1.60	Wockhardt Ltd.	6.80
Lupin Labs	1.56	Sun Pharma	6.70
Zydus-Cadila	1.51	Cadilla Healthcare	5.80
Ambalal Sarabhai	1.38	Nicholas Piramal	5.70
Smithkline Beecham	1.20	Aventis Pharma	5.30
Aristo Pharma	1.17	Alembic Ltd.	4.80
Parke Davis	1.15	Morepen Labs	4.70
Cadila Pharma	1.12	Torrent Pharma	4.40
E. Merck	1.11	IPCA Labs	4.20
Wockhardt	1.08	Knoll Pharma	3.70
John Wyeth	1.04	Orchid Chemicals	3.60
Alkem Laboratories	1.04	E Merck	3.50
Hindustan Ciba Geigy	1.03	Pfizer	3.40

* 1996 figures from ORG, Bombay in Lanjouw, J.O., www.oiprc.ox.ac.uk/EJWP0799.html, NBER working paper No. 6366.
Source: "Report on Pharmaceutical Sector in India," *Scope Magazine*, September 2001, p.14.

Tomorrow's global battles will be won by product leaders, not operationally excellent companies. Tomorrow's leaders must be visionaries, whether they belong to the family or not. Our mission at Ranbaxy is to become a research-based international pharmaceutical company.[4]

By the early 1990s, Ranbaxy grew to become India's largest manufacturer of bulk drugs[5] and generic drugs, with a domestic market share of 15 per cent (see Exhibit 3).

One of Ranbaxy's core competencies was its chemical synthesis capability, but the company had begun to outsource some bulk drugs in limited quantities. The company produced pharmaceuticals in four locations in India. The company's capital costs were typically 50 per cent to 75 per cent lower than those of comparable U.S. plants and were meant to serve foreign markets in addition to the Indian market. Foreign markets, especially those in more developed countries, often had stricter quality control requirements, and such a difference meant that the manufacturing practices required to compete in those markets appeared to be costlier from the perspective of less developed markets. Higher prices in other countries provided the impetus for Ranbaxy to pursue international markets; the company had a presence in 47 markets outside India, mainly through exports handled through an international division. Ranbaxy's

---

[4] Quoted in *Times of India*, June 9, 1999.
[5] A bulk drug is an intermediate product that goes into manufacturing of pharmaceutical products.

R&D efforts began at the end of the 1970s; in 1979, the company still had only 12 scientists. As Ranbaxy entered the international market in the 1980s, R&D was responsible for registering its products in foreign markets, most of which was directed to process R&D; R&D expenditures ranged from two per cent to five per cent of the annual sales with future targets of seven per cent to eight per cent.

The Lilly Ranbaxy JV

Ranbaxy approached Lilly in 1992 to investigate the possibility of supplying certain active ingredients or sourcing of intermediate products to Lilly in order to provide low-cost sources of intermediate pharmaceutical ingredients. Lilly had had earlier relationships with manufacturers in India to produce human or animal insulin and then export the products to the Soviet Union using the Russia/India trade route, but those had never developed into on-the-ground relationships within the Indian market. Ranbaxy was the second largest exporter of all products in India and the second largest pharmaceutical company in India after Glaxo (a subsidiary of the U.K.-based firm).

Rajiv Gulati, at that time a general manager of business development and marketing controller at Ranbaxy, who was instrumental in developing the strategy for Ranbaxy, recalled:

> In the 1980s, many multinational pharmaceutical companies had a presence in India. Lilly did not. As a result of both the sourcing of intermediate products as well as the fact that Lilly was one of the only players not yet in India, we felt that we could use Ranbaxy's knowledge of the market to get our feet on the ground in India. Ranbaxy would supply certain products to the joint venture from its own portfolio that were currently being manufactured in India and then formulate and finish some of Lilly's products locally. The joint venture would buy the active ingredients and Lilly would have Ranbaxy finish the package and allow the joint venture to sell and distribute those products.

The first meeting was held at Lilly's corporate center in Indianapolis in late 1990. Present were Ranbaxy's senior executives, Dr. Singh, vice-chairman, and D.S. Brar, chief operating officer (COO), and Lilly's senior executives, including Gene Step and Richard Wood, the CEO of Lilly. Rickey Pate, a corporate attorney at Eli Lilly who was present at the meeting, recalled:

> It was a very smooth meeting. We had a lot in common. We both believed in high ethical standards, in technology and innovation, as well as in the future of patented products in India. Ranbaxy executives emphasized their desire to be a responsible corporate citizen and expressed their concerns for their employees. It was quite obvious Ranbaxy would be a compatible partner in India.

Lilly decided to form the joint venture in India to focus on the marketing of Lilly's drugs there, and a formal JV agreement was signed in November 1992. The newly created JV was to have an authorized capital of Rs200 million (equivalent of US$7.1 million), and an initial subscribed equity capital of Rs84 million (US$3 million), with equal contribution from Lilly and Ranbaxy, leading to an equity ownership of 50 per cent each. The board of directors for the JV would comprise six directors, three from each company. A management committee was also created comprising two directors, one from each company, and Lilly retained the right to appoint the CEO who would be responsible for the day-to-day operations. The agreement also provided for transfer of shares, in the event any one of the partners desired to dispose some or its entire share in the company.

In the mid-1990s, Lilly was investigating the possibility of extending its operations to include generics. Following the launch of the Indian JV, Lilly and Ranbaxy entered into two other agreements related to generics, one in India to focus on manufacturing generics, and the other in the United States to focus on the marketing of generics. However, within less than a year, Lilly made a strategic decision not to enter the generics market and the two parties agreed to terminate the JV agreements related to the generics. Mayr recalled:

> At that time we were looking at the Indian market although we did not have any particular time frame for entry. We particularly liked Ranbaxy, as we saw an alignment of the broad values. Dr. Singh had a clear vision of leading Ranbaxy to become an innovation driven company. And we liked what we saw in them. Of course, for a time we were looking at the generic business and wondering if this was something we should be engaged in. Other companies had separate divisions for generics and we were evaluating such an idea. However, we had a pilot program in Holland and that taught us what it took to be competitive in generics and decided that business wasn't for us, and so we decided to get out of generics.

The Start-up

By March 1993, Andrew Mascarenhas, an American citizen of Indian origin, who at the time was the general manager for Lilly's Caribbean basin, based in San Juan, Puerto Rico, was selected to become the managing director of the joint venture. Rajiv Gulati, who at the time spearheaded the business development and marketing efforts at Ranbaxy, was chosen as the director of marketing and sales at the JV. Mascarenhas recalled:

> Lilly saw the joint venture as an investment the company needed to make. At the time, India was a country of 800 million people: 200 million to 300 million of them were considered to be within the country's middle class that represented the future of India. The concept of globalization was just taking hold at Lilly. India, along with China and Russia, were seen as markets where Lilly needed to build a greater presence. Some resistance was met due to the recognition that a lot of Lilly's products were already being sold by Indian manufacturers due to the lack of patent protection and intellectual property rights, so the question was what products should we put in there that

could be competitive. The products that were already being manufactured had sufficient capacity; so it was an issue of trying to leverage the markets in which those products were sold into.

> Lilly was a name that most physicians in India did not recognize. Despite its leadership position in the United States, it did not have any recognition in India. Ranbaxy was the leader within India. When I was informed that the name of the joint venture was to be Lilly Ranbaxy, the first thing I did was to make sure that the name of the joint venture was Eli Lilly Ranbaxy and not just Lilly Ranbaxy. The reason for this was based on my earlier experience in India, where "good quality," rightly or wrongly, was associated with foreign imported goods. Eli Lilly Ranbaxy sounded foreign enough!

Early on, Mascarenhas and Gulati worked on getting the venture up and running with office space and an employee base. Mascarenhas recalled:

> I got a small space within Ranbaxy's set-up. We had two tables, one for Rajiv and the other for me. We had to start from that infrastructure and move towards building up the organization from scratch. Rajiv was great to work with and we both were able to see eye-to-eye on most issues. Dr. Singh was a strong supporter and the whole of Ranbaxy senior management tried to assist us whenever we asked for help.

The duo immediately hired a financial analyst, and the team grew from there. Early on, they hired a medical director, a sales manager and a human resources manager. The initial team was a good one, but there was enormous pressure and the group worked seven days a week. Ranbaxy's help was used for getting government approvals, licenses, distribution and supplies. Recalled Gulati:

> We used Ranbaxy's name for everything. We were new and it was very difficult for us. We used their distribution network as we did not have one and Lilly did not want to invest

heavily in setting up a distribution network. We paid Ranbaxy for the service. Ranbaxy was very helpful.

By the end of 1993, the venture moved to an independent place, began launching products and employed more than 200 people. Within another year, Mascarenhas had hired a significant sales force and had recruited medical doctors and financial people for the regulatory group with assistance from Lilly's Geneva office. Mascarenhas, recalled:

> Our recruiting theme was 'Opportunity of a Lifetime,' i.e., joining a new company, and to be part of its very foundation. Many who joined us, especially at senior level, were experienced executives. By entering this new and untested company, they were really taking a huge risk with their careers and the lives of their families.

However, the employee turnover in the Indian pharmaceutical industry was very high. Sandeep Gupta, director of marketing recalled:

> Our biggest problem was our high turnover rate. A sales job in the pharmaceutical industry was not the most sought-after position. Any university graduate could be employed. The pharmaceutical industry in India is very unionized. Ranbaxy's HR practices were designed to work with unionized employees. From the very beginning, we did not want our recruits to join unions. Instead, we chose to show recruits that they had a career in ELR. When they joined us as sales graduates, they did not just remain at that level. We took a conscious decision to promote from within the company. The venture began investing in training and used Lilly's training programs. The programs were customized for Indian conditions, but retained Lilly's values (see Exhibit 4).

Within a year, the venture team began gaining the trust and respect of doctors, due to the strong values adhered to by Lilly. Mascarenhas described how the venture fought the Indian stigma:

Lilly has a code of ethical conduct called the Red Book, and the company did not want to go down the path where it might be associated with unethical behavior. But Lilly felt Ranbaxy knew how to do things the right way and that they respected their employees, which was a very important attribute. So following Lilly's Red Book values, the group told doctors the truth; both the positive and negative aspects of their drugs. If a salesperson didn't know the answer to something, they didn't lie or make up something; they told the doctor they didn't know. No bribes were given or taken, and it was found that honesty and integrity could actually be a competitive advantage. Sales people were trained to offer product information to doctors. The group gradually became distinguished by this "strange" behavior.

Recalled Sudhanshu Kamat, controller of finance at ELR:

> Lilly, from the start, treated us as its employees, like all its other affiliates worldwide. We followed the same systems and processes that any Lilly affiliate would worldwide.

Much of the success of the joint venture is attributed to the strong and cohesive working relationship of Mascarenhas and Gulati. Mascarenhas recalled:

> We both wanted the venture to be successful. We both had our identities to the JV, and there was no Ranbaxy versus Lilly politics. From the very start when we had our office at Ranbaxy premises, I was invited to dine with their senior management. Even after moving to our own office, I continued the practice of having lunch at Ranbaxy HQ on a weekly basis. I think it helped a lot to be accessible at all times and to build on the personal relationship.

The two companies had very different business focuses. Ranbaxy was a company driven by the generics business. Lilly, on the other hand, was driven by innovation and discovery.

Exhibit 4
Values at Eli Lilly-Ranbaxy Limited

PEOPLE

"The people who make up this company are its most valuable assets"
- Respect for the individual
  - Courtesy and politeness at all times
  - Sensitivity to other people's views
  - Respect for ALL people regardless of caste, religion, sex or age
- Careers NOT jobs
  - Emphasis on individual's growth, personal and professional
  - Broaden experience via cross-functional moves

"The first responsibility of our supervisors is **to build men, then medicines**"

ATTITUDE

"There is very little difference between people. But that difference makes a BIG difference. The little difference is attitude. The BIG difference is... Whether it is POSITIVE or NEGATIVE"

"Are we part of the PROBLEM or part of the SOLUTION?"

TEAM

"None of us is as smart as all of us"

INTEGRITY

- Integrity outside the company
  a) "We should not do anything or be expected to take any action that we would be ashamed to explain to our family or close friends"
  b) "The red-faced test"
  c) "Integrity can be our biggest competitive advantage"
- Integrity inside the company
  - With one another: openness, honesty

EXCELLENCE

- Serving our customers
  "In whatever we do, we must ask ourselves: how does this serve my customer better?"
- Continuous improvement

"Nothing is being done today that cannot be done better tomorrow"
- Become the Industry Standard

"In whatever we do, we will do it so well that we become the Industry Standard"

Mascarenhas focused his effort on communicating Eli Lilly's values to the new joint venture:

I spent a lot of time communicating Lilly's values to newly hired employees. In the early days, I interviewed our senior applicants personally. I was present in the two-day training sessions that we offered for the new employees, where I shared the values of the company. That was a critical task for me to make sure that the right foundations were laid down for growth.

The first products that came out of the joint venture were human insulin from Lilly and several Ranbaxy products; but the team faced constant challenges in dealing with government regulations on the one hand and financing the affiliate on the other. There were also cash flow constraints.

The ministry of health provided limitations on Lilly's pricing, and even with the margin the Indian government allowed, most of it went to the wholesalers and the pharmacies, pursuant to formulas in the Indian ministry of health. Once those were factored out of the gross margin, achieving profitability was a real challenge, as some of the biggest obstacles faced were duties imposed by the Indian government on imports and other regulatory issues. Considering the weak intellectual property rights regime, Lilly did not want to launch some of its products, such as its top-seller, Prozac.[6] Gulati recalled:

> We focused only on those therapeutic areas where Lilly had a niche. We did not adopt a localization strategy, such as the ones adopted by Pfizer and Glaxo[7] that manufactured locally and sold at local prices. India is a high-volume, low price, low profit market, but it was a conscious decision by us to operate the way we did. We wanted to be in the global price band. So, we did not launch several patented products because generics were selling at 1/60th the price.

Product and marketing strategies had to be adopted to suit the market conditions. ELR's strategy evolved over the years to focus on two groups of products: one was off-patent drugs,

where Lilly could add substantial value (e.g. Ceclor), and two, patented drugs, where there existed a significant barrier to entry (e.g. Reopro and Gemzar). ELR marketed Ceclor, a Ranbaxy-manufactured product, but attempted to add significant value by providing medical information to the physicians and other unique marketing activities. By the end of 1996, the venture had reached the break-even and was becoming profitable.

The Mid-Term Organizational Changes

Mascarenhas was promoted in 1996 to managing director of Eli Lilly Italy, and Chris Shaw, a British national who was then managing the operations in Taiwan, was assigned to the JV as the new managing director. Also, Gulati, who was formally a Ranbaxy employee, decided to join Eli Lilly as its employee and was assigned to Lilly's corporate office in Indianapolis in the Business Development – Infectious Diseases therapeutic division. Chris Shaw recalled:

> When I went to India as a British national, I was not sure what sort of reception I would get, knowing its history. But my family and I were received very warmly. I found a dynamic team with a strong sense of values.

Shaw focused on building systems and processes to bring stability to the fast-growing organization; his own expertise in operations made a significant contribution during this phase. He hired a senior-level manager and created a team to develop standard operating procedures (SOPs) for ensuring smooth operations. The product line also expanded. The JV continued to maintain a 50–50 distribution of products from Lilly and Ranbaxy, although there was no stipulation to maintain such a ratio. The clinical organization in India received top-ratings in internal audits by Lilly, making it suitable for a wider range of clinical trials. Shaw also streamlined the sales and marketing activities around therapeutic areas to emphasize and enrich the knowledge capabilities of the company's sales force. Seeing the rapid change in the environment in India, ELR, with the support of Mayr, hired the management

---

[6] Used as an antidepressant medication.

[7] An industry study by McKinsey found that Glaxo sold 50 per cent of its volume, received three per cent of revenues and one per cent of profit in India.

Exhibit 5
Eli Lilly-Ranbaxy India Financials 1998 to 2001 (Rs'000s)

	1998–1999	1999–2000	2000–2001
Sales	559,766	632,188	876,266
Marketing Expenses	37,302	61,366	96,854
Other Expenses	157,907	180,364	254,822
Profit after Tax	5,898	12,301	11,999
Current Assets	272,635	353,077	466,738
Current Liabilities	239,664	297,140	471,635
Total Assets	303,254	386,832	516,241
No. of Employees	358	419	460
Exchange Rate (Rupees/US$)	42.6	43.5	46.8

Note: Financial year runs from April 1 to March 31.
Source: Company Reports.

consulting firm, McKinsey, to recommend growth options in India. ELR continued its steady performance with an annualized growth rate of about eight per cent during the late 1990s.

In 1999, Chris Shaw was assigned to Eli Lilly's Polish subsidiary, and Gulati returned to ELR as its managing director, following his three-year tenure at Lilly's U.S. operations. Recalled Gulati:

> When I joined as MD in 1999, we were growing at eight per cent and had not added any new employees. I hired 150 people over the next two years and went about putting systems and processes in place. When we started in 1993, and during Andrew's time, we were like a grocery shop. Now we needed to be a company. We had to be a large durable organization and prepare ourselves to go from sales of US$10 million to sales of US$100 million.

ELR created a medical and regulatory unit, which handled the product approval processes with government. Das, the chief financial officer (CFO), commented:

> We worked together with the government on the regulatory part. Actually, we did not take shelter under the Ranbaxy name but built a strong regulatory (medical and corporate affairs) foundation.

By early 2001, the venture was recording an excellent growth rate (see Exhibit 5), surpassing the average growth rate in the Indian pharmaceutical industry. ELR had already become the 46th largest pharmaceutical company in India out of 10,000 companies. Several of the multinational subsidiaries, which were started at the same time as ELR, had either closed down or were in serious trouble. Das summarized the achievements:

> The JV did add some prestige to Ranbaxy's efforts as a global player as the Lilly name had enormous credibility, while Lilly gained the toehold in India. In 10 years, we did not have any cannibalization of each other's employees, quite a rare event compared with the other JVs. This helped us build a unique culture in India.

The New World, 2001

The pharmaceutical industry continued to grow through the 1990s. In 2001, worldwide retail sales were expected to increase 10 per cent to about US$350 billion. The United States was expected to remain the largest and fastest growing country among the world's major drug markets over the next three years. There was a

Exhibit 6
Lilly Financials 1992 to 2000 (US$ millions)

	1992	1994	1996	1998	2000
Net sales	4,963	5,711	6,998	9,236	10,862
Foreign sales	2,207	2,710	3,587	3,401	3,858
Research and development expenses	731	839	1,190	1,739	2,019
Income from continuing operations before taxes and extraordinary items	1,194	1,699	2,131	2,665	3,859
Net income	709	1,286	1,524	2,097	3,058
Dividends per share*	1.128	1.260	0.694	0.830	1.060
Current assets	3,006	3,962	3,891	5,407	7,943
Current liabilities	2,399	5,670	4,222	4,607	4,961
Property and equipment	4,072	4,412	4,307	4,096	4,177
Total assets	8,673	14,507	14,307	12,596	14,691
Long-term debt	582	2,126	2,517	2,186	2,634
Shareholder equity	4,892	5,356	6,100	4,430	6,047
Number of employees*	24,500	24,900	27,400	29,800	35,700

* *Actual value*
Source: Company files.

consolidation trend in the industry with ongoing mergers and acquisitions reshaping the industry. In 1990, the world's top 10 players accounted for just 28 per cent of the market, while in 2000, the number had risen to 45 per cent and continued to grow. There was also a trend among leading global pharmaceutical companies to get back to basics and concentrate on core high-margined prescription preparations and divest non-core businesses. In addition, the partnerships between pharmaceutical and biotechnology companies were growing rapidly. There were a number of challenges, such as escalating R&D costs, lengthening development and approval times for new products, growing competition from generics and follow-on products, and rising cost-containment pressures, particularly with the growing clout of managed care organizations.

By 1995, Lilly had moved up to become the 12th leading pharmaceutical supplier in the world, sixth in the U.S. market, 17th in Europe and 77th in Japan. Much of Lilly's sales success through the mid-1990s came from its antidepressant drug, Prozac. But with the wonder drug due to go off patent in 2001, Lilly was aggressively working on a number of high-potential products. By the beginning of 2001, Lilly was doing business in 151 countries, with its international sales playing a significant role in the company's success (see Exhibits 6 and 7). Dr. Lorenzo Tallarigo recalled:

> When I started as the president of the intercontinental operations, I realized that the world was very different in the 2000s from the world of 1990s. Particularly, there were phenomenal changes in the markets in India and China. While I firmly believed that the partnership we had with Ranbaxy was really an excellent one, the fact that we were facing such a different market in the 21st century was reason enough to carefully evaluate our strategies in these markets.

Ranbaxy, too, had witnessed changes through the 1990s. Dr. Singh became the new CEO in 1993 and formulated a new mission for the company: to become a research-based international pharmaceutical company with $1 billion in sales by 2003. This vision saw Ranbaxy developing

Exhibit 7
Product Segment Information
Lilly and Ranbaxy 1996 and 2000

	Eli Lilly in 1996	Eli Lilly in 2000
Anti-infectives	35%	8%
Neurosciences	26%	48%
Diabetes care	13%	—
Animal health	9%	6%
Gastrointestinal (GI)	6%	3%
Other pharmaceutical	11%	1%
Endocrinology	—	24%
Cardiovascular	—	5%
Oncology	—	5%
	Ranbaxy in 1996	**Ranbaxy in 2000**
Anti-infectives	49%	56%
GI Tract	10%	9%
Nutritionals	8%	9%
NSAIDS	7%	—
Central Nervous System	3%	3%
Cardiovascular	1%	5%
Others	22%	5%
Orthopaedics/Pain management	—	9%
Dermatological	—	4%

new drugs through basic research, earmarking 20 per cent of the R&D budget for such work. In addition to its joint venture with Lilly, Ranbaxy made three other manufacturing/marketing investments in developed markets: a joint venture with Genpharm in Canada ($1.1 million), and the acquisitions of Ohm Labs in the United States ($13.5 million) and Rima Pharmaceuticals ($8 million) in Ireland. With these deals, Ranbaxy had manufacturing facilities around the globe. While China and Russia were expected to remain key foreign markets, Ranbaxy was looking at the United States and the United Kingdom as its core international markets for the future. In 1999, Dr. Singh handed over the reins of the company to Brar, and later the same year, Ranbaxy lost this visionary leader due to an untimely death. Brar continued Singh's vision to keep Ranbaxy in a leadership position. However, the vast network of international sales that Ranbaxy had developed created a large financial burden, depressing the

company's 2000 results, and was expected to significantly affect its cash flow in 2001 (see Exhibit 8). Vinay Kaul, vice-chairman of Ranbaxy in 2001 and chairman of the board of ELR since 2000, noted:

We have come a long way from where we started. Our role in the present JV is very limited. We had a smooth relationship and we have been of significant help to Lilly to establish a foothold in the market here in India. Also, we have opened up a number of opportunities for them to expand their network. However, we have also grown, and we are a global company with presence in a number of international markets, including the United States. We had to really think if this JV is central to our operations, given that we have closed down the other two JV agreements that we had with Lilly on the generics manufacturing. It is common knowledge that

Exhibit 8
Ranbaxy Financials 1992 to 2000 (Rs millions)

	1992–93	1994–95	1996–97	*1998	2000
Sales	4,607	7,122	11,482	10,641	17,459
Foreign sales	1,408	3,019	5,224	4,414	8,112
Profit before tax	358	1,304	1,869	1,240	1,945
Profit after tax	353	1,104	1,604	1,170	1,824
Equity dividend	66.50	199.80	379.10	560.10	869.20
Earnings per share (Rs)	16.21	25.59	32.47	13.46	15.74
Net current assets	1,737	5,790	9,335	8,321	8,258
Share capital	217.90	430.50	494.00	1,159.00	1,159.00
Reserves and surplus	1,028	6,000	11,056	12,849	16,448
Book value per share (Rs)	57.16	149.08	233.70	120.90	136.60
No. of employees	4,575	4,703	6,131	5,469	5,784
Exchange rate (US$1 = Rs)	29.00	31.40	35.90	42.60	46.80

The financial year for Ranbaxy changed from April 1 to March 31 to calendar year in 1998. Also, the company issued a 1:2 bonus issue (see the changes in share capital and book value per share). The 1998 figures are based on nine months April to December 1998.
Source: Company files.

whether we continue as a JV or not, we have created a substantial value for Lilly.

There were also significant changes in the Indian business environment. India signed the General Agreement on Tariffs and Trade (GATT) in April 1994 and became a World Trade Organization (WTO) member in 1995. As per the WTO, from the year 2005, India would grant product patent recognition to all new chemical entities (NCEs) (i.e., bulk drugs developed from then onward). Also, the Indian government had made the decision to allow 100 per cent foreign direct investment into the drugs and pharmaceutical industry in 2001.[8] The Indian pharmaceutical market had grown at an average of 15 per cent through the 1990s, but the trends indicated a slowdown in growth, partly due to intense price competition, a shift toward chronic therapies

and the entry of large players into the generic market. India was seeing its own internal consolidation of major companies that were trying to bring in synergies through economies of scale. The industry would see more mergers and alliances. And with India's entry into the WTO and its agreement to begin patent protection in 2004–2005, competition on existing and new products was expected to intensify. Government guidelines were expected to include rationalization of price controls and the encouragement of more research and development. Recalled Gulati:

The change of institutional environment brought a great promise for Lilly. India was emerging into a market that had patent protection and with tremendous potential for adding value in the clinical trials, an important component in the pharmaceutical industry. In Ranbaxy, we had a partner with whom we could work very well, and one which greatly respected Lilly. However, there were considerable signals from both sides that were forcing us to evaluate the strategy.

[8] In order to regulate the parallel activities of a foreign company, which had an ongoing joint venture in India, the regulations stipulated that the foreign partner must get a "No objection letter" from its Indian partner, before setting up a wholly owned subsidiary.

Dr. Vinod Mattoo, medical director of ELR, commented:

> We have been able to achieve penetration in key therapeutic areas of diabetes and oncology. We have created a high caliber, non-unionized sales force with world-class sales processes. We have medical infrastructure and expertise to run clinical trials to international standards. We have been able to provide clinical trial data to support global registrations, and an organization in place to maximize returns post-2005.

Evaluating Strategic Options

Considering these several developments, Tallarigo suggested a joint task force comprising senior executives from both companies:

> Soon after assuming this role, I visited India in early 2000, and had the pleasure of meeting Dr. Brar and the senior executives. It was clear to me that both Brar and I were in agreement that we needed to think carefully how we approached the future. It was there that I suggested that we create a joint task force to come up with some options that would help us make a final decision.

A task force was set up with two senior executives from Lilly's Asia-Pacific regional office (based in Singapore) and two senior executives from Ranbaxy. The task force did not include senior executives of the ELR so as to not distract the running of the day-to-day operations. Suman Das, the chief financial officer of ELR, was assigned to support the task force with the needed financial data. The task force developed several scenarios and presented different options for the board to consider.

There were rumors within the industry that Ranbaxy expected to divest the JV and invest the cash in its growing portfolio of generics manufacturing business in international markets. There were also several other Indian companies that offered to buy Ranbaxy's stake in the JV. With India recognizing patent protection in 2005, several Indian pharmaceutical companies were keen to align with multinationals to ensure a

pipeline of drugs. Although there were no formal offers from Ranbaxy, the company was expected to price its stakes as high as US$70 million. One of the industry observers in India commented:

> I think it is fair for Ranbaxy to expect a reasonable return for its investment in the JV, not only the initial capital, but also so much of its intangibles in the JV. Ranbaxy's stock has grown significantly. Given the critical losses that Ranbaxy has had in some of its investments abroad, the revenue from this sale may be a significant boost for Ranbaxy's cash flow this year.

Gerhard Mayr, who in 2001, was the executive vice-president and was responsible for Lilly's demand realization around the world, continued to emphasize the emerging markets in India, China and Eastern Europe. Mayr commented on Ranbaxy:

> India is an important market for us, and especially after patent protection in 2005. Ranbaxy was a wonderful partner and our relationship with them was outstanding. The other two joint ventures we initiated with them in the generics did not make sense to us once we decided to get out of the generics business. We see India as a good market for Lilly. If a partner is what it takes to succeed, we should go with a partner. If it does not, we should have the flexibility to reconsider.

Tallarigo hoped that Brar would be able to provide a clear direction as to the venture's future. As he prepared for the meeting, he knew the decision was not an easy one, although he felt confident that the JV was in good shape. While the new regulations allowed Lilly to operate as a wholly-owned subsidiary in India, the partnership has been a very positive element in its strategy. Ranbaxy provided manufacturing and logistics support to the JV, and breaking up the partnership would require a significant amount of renegotiations. Also, it was not clear what the financial implications of such a move would be. Although Ranbaxy seemed to favor a sell-out, Tallarigo thought the price expectations might be beyond what Lilly was ready to accept. This meeting with Brar should provide clarity on all these issues.

IVEY | Publishing

CASE 6.3 AMAZON AND FUTURE GROUP: RETHINKING THE ALLIANCE STRATEGY[1]

Meeta Dasgupta wrote this case solely to provide material for class discussion. The author does not intend to illustrate either effective or ineffective handling of a managerial situation. The author may have disguised certain names and other identifying information to protect confidentiality.

In 2014, Kishore Biyani, founder and chief executive officer (CEO) of Future Group, and Jeff Bezos, founder and CEO of Amazon, led their two companies in a business alliance: Amazon would sell Future Group's clothing brands and eventually retail other categories of goods for Future Group. The alliance started on an optimistic note, but by early 2016, the alliance partners were in conflict over discounts and who would bear the burden of those costs. Could the partners find a way to resolve the conflict or was it time for the companies to be independent again? Was the alliance continuing to deliver value for the companies?

The Global Retail Industry

The global retail industry had grown steadily from US$21.189 trillion in 2013 to $25.366 trillion in 2016, and was expected to reach $28.300

trillion in 2018.[2] Worldwide retail e-commerce sales had also grown. As a percentage of total retail sales, retail e-commerce sales grew from 5.1 per cent in 2013 ($1.077 trillion) to 5.9 per cent ($1.316 trillion) in 2014, 6.7 per cent ($1.592 trillion) in 2015 and 7.4 per cent in 2016 ($1.888 trillion). They were expected to reach 8.8 per cent ($2.489 trillion) in 2018. Interestingly, although a majority of American consumers were purchasing online, more than $10 out of every $11 were still spent in stores. In comparison, China and the United Kingdom, the other largest retail e-commerce markets, had much higher proportions of online to total retail sales (see Exhibit 1).

The Indian Retail Industry

By 2000, the retail sector had emerged in India as one of the largest sectors in the country's economy, registering a Compound Annual Growth Rate (CAGR) of 7.45 per cent. By 2014, the retail

---

[1] This case has been written on the basis of published sources. Consequently, the interpretation and perspectives presented in this case are not necessarily those of Future Group or Amazon or any of their employees.

[2] All currency amounts are in USD or INR unless otherwise specified; ₹ = INR = Indian rupee; US$1 = ₹66.235 on January 1, 2016.

Exhibit 1
E-Commerce Sales as a Percentage of Total Retail Sales

	2013	2014	2015	2016*	2017*	2018*
United Kingdom	11.6	13.0	14.4	15.6	16.9	18.0
China	8.3	10.1	12.0	13.8	15.5	16.6
United States	5.8	6.5	7.1	7.7	8.3	8.9
Brazil	3.4	3.8	4.1	4.4	4.6	4.8
Russia	2.0	2.2	2.4	2.6	2.8	3.0
Spain	3.6	4.1	4.8	5.4	6.0	6.5
India	0.6	0.7	0.9	1.1	1.3	1.4
Indonesia	0.5	0.6	0.8	1.0	1.2	1.4

Note: *The forecast is from September 2014.
Source: "Retail Sales Worldwide Will Top $22 Trillion This Year E-Commerce Eclipses $1.3 Trillion, Led by China and U.S.," eMarketer, December 23, 2014, accessed March 15, 2016, www.emarketer.com/Article/Retail-Sales-Worldwide-Will-Top-22-Trillion-This-Year/1011765.

sector had been showing a CAGR of about 15 per cent over the previous five years–a growth that exceeded the overall growth in India's gross domestic product during the same period.[3] As an industry, Indian retail grew from $204 billion in 2000 to $600 billion in 2015, and was expected to reach $1.3 trillion by 2020.[4] Retailing in India accounted for about 10 per cent of the country's gross domestic product and 8 per cent of employment.[5] Almost all of the retail business came from a fragmented, unorganized sector of individual and family-owned businesses.[6] The organized sector that accounted for 8 per cent of the market in 2015 was expected to account for 24 per cent of the overall retail market by 2020.

The Indian retail industry was attractive to investors, but Indian rules restricted foreign retailers' ability to sell directly to Indian consumers or invest on their own in a retail business.[7] Under its foreign direct investment policy, the government approved foreign direct investment of up to 51 per cent in multi-brand retail and up to 100 per cent in single-brand retail. However, both multi- and single-brand retailers had to source 30 per cent of their goods from Indian suppliers.[8]

Growth in organized retail was driven by, among other factors, a healthy growth in the Indian economy, changing demographic profiles, increased disposable incomes, and changes in the tastes and preferences of consumers.[9] The number of millennials were increasing, and it was expected that they would make up more than half of India's population by 2025. Shoppers increasingly depended on technology for consumption. In 2015, India had the third largest number of Internet users in the world (after China

[3] KPMG, Indian Retail: The Next Growth Story, 2014, 2, accessed March 15, 2016, www.kpmg.com/IN/en/IssuesAndInsights/ArticlesPublications/Documents/BBG-Retail.pdf.
[4] "Indian Retail Industry Analysis," India Brand Equity Foundation, January 2016, accessed March 15, 2016, www.ibef.org/industry/indian-retail-industry-analysis-presentation.
[5] "Retailing Sector Analysis Report," India Brand Equity Foundation, January 2016, accessed March 15, 2016, www.equitymaster.com/research-it/sector-info/retail/Retailing-Sector-Analysis-Report.asp.
[6] KPMG, op. cit.

[7] "Amazon India and Future Group Tie the Knot to Sell Fashion Online," Fashion United, October 13, 2014, accessed March 5, 2016, www.fashionunited.in/news/fashion/amazon-india-and-future-group-tie-the-know-to-sell-fashion-online-131020147656.
[8] "Indian Retail Industry Analysis," op. cit.   [9] Ibid.

and the United States), and was similarly ranked in penetration of smartphones.[10] Economic forecasters predicted that by 2020, India would be a $3 trillion economy with 5.8 per cent of global spending happening in the country–a significant increase from 2.6 per cent in 2015.[11] Anil Agarwal, then managing director of Amazon India, observed, "Everything is nascent in India–the seller ecosystem, the logistics, the payments.... We have to connect the dots on a massive scale that involves hundreds of cities, thousands of sellers, and millions of products."[12]

Even though the online retail industry in India occupied only about 2 per cent of the country's overall retail industry, online retailing was growing quickly, from less than $500 million in 2009 to about $5 billion in 2014.[13] According to a report by the consulting firm Technopak, the overall retail industry was expected to double by 2020. The online retailing market represented an increasing portion of that growth; the $2.3 billion online retail market in 2014 was expected to be $32 billion by 2020, an increase from 2 per cent to 3 per cent of the Indian retail sector.[14]

Growing Internet penetration, aggressive pricing strategies, and e-commerce companies with resources of investor cash spurred the growth. Young companies like Flipkart and Snapdeal dominated general e-commerce, and Myntra and Jabong dominated in apparels.[15] In FY2014/15, online retailers collectively captured $6 billion of the $40 billion organized retail market (excluding *kirana* or small neighbourhood stores). Regular retail stores were on the decline as evidenced by sales figures during the festival season in October to November 2014; visits at most of the bricks and mortar stores fell by 12 per cent.[16]

The growing energy around online retail was also reflected in the valuations of online retail companies (see Exhibit 2). At the end of 2014, India's biggest online retailer, Flipkart, was valued at $11 billion (₹700 billion) while Future Group's three listed companies were collectively valued at $1.2 billion (₹80 billion). The online retailer, Snapdeal, then just five years old, was already valued at $1.85 billion (about ₹117 billion), and after a round of fundraising in 2015, was valued at $4.9 billion (about ₹330 billion).[17]

Heavy discounting was leading to increased level of conflict between the online and offline retailers. Traditional retailers that were being hit by aggressive pricing or undercutting protested Flipkart's Big Billion Day Sale held on October 6, 2014. Flipkart promised to hold "the greatest sale ever in the history of our nation" on that day.[18] The government responded to retailers'

[10] "2BConsumers Worldwide to Get Smartphones by 2016," eMarketer, December 11, 2014, accessed March 23, 2016, www.emarketer.com/Article/2-Billion-Consumers-Worldwide-Smartphones-by-2016/1011694.

[11] Ajita Shashidhar and Nevin John, "The Rebirth of Kishore Biyani," *Business Today*, June 7, 2015, accessed March 22, 2016, www.businesstoday.in/magazine/cover-story/kishore-biyani-strategy-turnaround-future-group-bharti-retail/story/219409.html financials.

[12] Saritha Rai, "Amit Agarwal Leads Amazon India as Online Retail is Taking Off," *Forbes*, June 4, 2015, accessed June 13, 2016, www.forbes.com/sites/saritharai/2015/06/04/primed-for-battle/#35139af91c0e.

[13] "Why the Future Group–Amazon Tie-Up is a Win-Win for Both," Money Control, October 14, 2014, accessed March 5, 2016, www.moneycontrol.com/news/business/whyfuture-group-amazon-tie-up-iswin-win-for-both_1202970.html.

[14] Sagar Malviya, "Amazon and Future Group Ink Deal to Sell Goods Online; Starting With Apparel," *Economic Times*, October 13, 2014, accessed June 13, 2016, http://articles.economictimes.indiatimes.com/2014-10-13/

news/54970694_1_bangalore-based-flipkart-and-snapdeal-future-group-kishore-biyani.

[15] "Why the Future Group–Amazon Tie-Up is a Win-Win for Both," Money Control, October 14, 2014, accessed March 5, 2016, www.moneycontrol.com/news/business/whyfuture-group-amazon-tie-up-iswin-win-for-both_1202970.html.

[16] Shashidhar and John, op. cit.

[17] Shashidhar and John, op. cit.; T. E. Narasimhan, "Snapdeal, Flipkart Top Valuation Growth League Table in 2015," *Business Standard*, January 7, 2016, accessed June 13, 2016, www.business-standard.com/article/companies/snapdeal-flipkart-top-valuation-growth-league-table-in-2015-116010700020_1.html.

[18] Alok Soni, "How Big Was the Big Billion Day?," Your Story, October 6, 2014, accessed June 13, 2016, http://yourstory.com/2014/10/flipkart-big-billion-day.

Exhibit 2
Comparison of Large E-Commerce Retailers

Portal	Valuation	Gross Merchandise Value	Number of Items Stocked
Flipkart	$11 billion	$4 billion	20 million
Snapdeal	$1.85 billion	$3 billion	10 million
Amazon	$200 billion (market capitalization)	$1 billion	19 million

Source: Ajita Shashidhar and Nevin John, "The Rebirth of Kishore Biyani," *Business Today*, June 7, 2015, accessed March 22, 2016, www.businesstoday.in/magazine/cover-story/kishore-biyani-strategy-turnaround-future-group-bharti-retail/story/219409.html financials.

complaints by saying that the e-commerce policy would be reviewed.[19] Amazon, in response, offered Diwali sales but did not offer the kind of heavy discounts that Flipkart and Snapdeal offered.[20]

With the popularity of e-commerce, traditional, brick-and-mortar retailers had to change their approach to business by partnering with e-commerce entities in order to grow and survive. One of the major retailers, Cromā, owned by the Tata group, entered into an alliance with Snapdeal.[21] Just three companies in the offline retail market–Aditya Birla's Madura Fashion and Lifestyle, Arvind Lifestyle Brands, and Future Group–owned or sold more than two dozen brands each, thus qualifying to be a preferred partner for an online retailer (see Exhibit 3).[22]

Successful and faster delivery of products was the key to success for most of the e-commerce sector. Companies were trying to make their delivery networks increasingly efficient. Flipkart and Amazon had delivery networks: eKart Logistics and Amazon Transportation Solutions. Snapdeal acquired a stake in GoJavas; acquired an online order management start-up, Unicommerce; and made an investment of $3.7 million (₹250 million) in its own wholly-owned logistics unit, Vulcan Express.[23]

The battle in the Indian e-commerce industry was expected to intensify. Amazon's main rivals in India–Bangalore-based Flipkart and Delhi-based Snapdeal–sold goods worth more than $4 billion in 2014, with Flipkart alone estimated to have grossed $2 billion. Industry experts believed that the Indian e-commerce sector would undergo a spate of consolidation with smaller companies lacking the ability to sustain competition against a company like Amazon. Flipkart's acquisition of online fashion retailer Myntra in May 2014 set the trend.[24]

Amazon

Amazon.com, an e-commerce company, was incorporated in 1996. The company, operating

[19] Malviya, op. cit.
[20] Nivedita Bhattacharjee, "Biyani's Future Group Ties Up with Amazon India," ed. Stephen Coates, Reuters, October 13, 2014, accessed March 5, 2016, http://in.reuters.com/article/future-retail-amazon-idINKCN0I206E20141013.
[21] "Future Group, Amazon India Announce Strategic E-Commerce Alliance," *Business Standard*, October 14, 2014, accessed March 5, 2016, www.business-standard.com/article/reuters/future-retail-amazon-in-enter-into-strategic-partnership-114101300146_1.html.
[22] Malviya, op. cit.

[23] "Flipkart and Amazon Eyeing to Buy Stake in Biyani's Future Supply Chain Solutions," Inc42, April 9, 2015, accessed March 22, 2016, http://inc42.com/buzz/flipkart-amazon-eyeing-to-buy-stake-in-biyanis-future-supply-chain-solutions.
[24] "Amazon Future Group Deal Spurs E-tail Competition," CXO Today, October 13, 2014, accessed March 5, 2016, www.cxotoday.com/story/amazon-future-group-deal-spurs-e-commerce-competition.

Exhibit 3
Comparison of Large Offline Retailers

Name	Number of Stores	Size (million square feet)	Formats	FY2013/14 ($ millions)		FY2012/13 ($ millions)	
Reliance Retail	2,621	12.5	Value, hypermarket, digital, fashion, etc.	Revenue	190.41	Revenue	136.89
				PBDIT	9.78	PBDIT	2.18
				PAT	4.08	PAT	(2.03)
Aditya Birla Retail	2,371	7.1	Fashion, supermarket, hypermarket	Revenue	110.97	Revenue	73.86
				PBDIT	3.53	PBDIT	1.98
				PAT	NA	PAT	NA
Shoppers Stop	340	4.1	Fashion and lifestyle, hypermarket, furniture and home décor, consumer brands, books, airport duty-free, games	Revenue	43.10	Revenue	35.91
				PBDIT	2.79	PBDIT	2.4
				PAT	0.56	PAT	0.59

Note: "PBDIT" = profit before depreciation, interest, and taxes; "PAT" = profit after tax; US$1 = ₹66.235 on January 1, 2016; Ajita Shashidhar and Nevin John, "The Rebirth of Kishore Biyani," *Business Today*, June 7, 2015, accessed March 22, 2016, www.businesstoday.in/magazine/cover-story/kishore-biyani-strategy-turnaround-future-group-bharti-retail/story/219409.html financials.

in North America and internationally, offered a range of products and services through its websites.[25] Amazon's quarterly growth in international sales came down from 20 per cent in 2013 to 12 per cent in the second quarter of 2014 and then to 3 per cent in the second quarter of 2015.[26] In the United States over the past decade, Amazon entered into alliances with retailers such as Target Corporation (Target) and Toys R Us. After Target gained scale and attracted other large brands, the relationship with Amazon soured.[27] In November 2015, Amazon expanded beyond e-commerce to open its first physical bookstore in Seattle; it planned to open as many as 400 more.[28]

Amazon started its e-commerce operations in India in 2013 with its marketplace Amazon.in, selling in just two product categories: books and movies. It was quickly a major competitor for the top position in the country's growing e-commerce market.[29] In July 2014, within one year of its launch in India, Amazon announced that it would spend $2 billion on its Indian operations. The investment exceeded its gross merchandise sales in India of more than $1 billion.[30] In order to extend its reach and delivery speed,

[25] "Amazon.com Inc.," Reuters, http://in.reuters.com/finance/stocks/companyProfile?symbol=AMZN.O, accessed March 23, 2016.

[26] Jillian D'Onfro, "Amazon's Next Big Challenge: Winning India," *Business Insider*, July 24, 2015, accessed June 13, 2016, www.businessinsider.com/amazon-growth-in-india-2015-7.

[27] Malviya, op. cit.

[28] Greg Bensinger, "Amazon Plans Hundreds of Brick-and-Mortar Bookstores, Mall CEO Says," *Wall Street Journal*, February 2, 2016, accessed March 23, 2016, www.wsj.com/articles/amazon-plans-hundreds-of-brick-and-mortar-bookstores-mall-ceo-says-1454449475.

[29] "Future Group, Amazon India Announce Strategic E-Commerce Alliance," op. cit.

[30] Malviya, op. cit.

Amazon built two centres, one in Bangalore and the other in Bhiwadi on the outskirts of Mumbai.[31]

Sellers joined Amazon from all over India. In 2015, the number of sellers joining Amazon was two times more than those that joined in 2014. But the number of orders received by sellers in 2015 was three times the number of orders received in 2014, with sellers' total business increasing in the same period by $150,000 (₹10 million). The number of sellers using fulfillment centres–inventory storage space–increased by three times, with 86 per cent of those using the fulfillment centres increasing their sales volume. The storage space provided to sellers increased from 28,000 square metres in 2014 to 765,000 square metres in 2015.[32]

Amazon's logistics innovation for the Indian market, EasyShip, was paying off. Amazon picked up products from suppliers' outlets and distributed them to customers using its logistics services. The number of sellers using EasyShip increased three times, and the sellers using Amazon's Easy Ship increased their sales by 40 per cent. In response, Amazon increased the shipping service from covering 2,000 postal codes in 2014 to covering 20,000 postal codes in 2015 (see Exhibit 4).

Future Group

Future Group was controlled by Biyani, known in India as the man who introduced large scale retail to the country.[33] Central, Big Bazaar, Foodhall, Planet Sports, Brand Factory, Home Town, and eZone were some of India's most favourite retail chains operated by Future Group. The company had more than 75 of its own brands that earned the Group at least 15 per cent higher margins on average compared to other national brands.[34] The Group operated approximately 480,000 square metres (17 million square feet) of retail space in 98 urban, and 40 rural locations. Approximately 30,000 small, medium, and large enterprises were connected to its retail formats and about 300 million customers yearly visited them.[35] The company had 140,000 stock units across India.[36] See Exhibit 5 for Future enterprises financials.

The core value of the Group was "Indianness." Future Group believed in building a strong understanding of Indian consumers, and built its business based on Indian ideas. The Group's corporate principle was "Rewrite rules, retain values."[37] Future Group claimed to have a well-developed and well-equipped logistics system.[38] In addition to its own logistics chain, the Group also had a third-party logistics arrangement that it planned to leverage for its omni-channel strategy.[39]

In September 2014, Future Group entered into a collaboration with SAP Hybris, an e-commerce service, for an omni-channel retail strategy that would allow the Group to converge its digital and physical channels. According to Rakesh Biyani, the joint managing director at Future Retail, "The overall investment in this [business to consumer]

[31] Raghavendra Kamath, "Amazon Builds India Business Quietly," *Business Standard*, April 4, 2014, accessed March 23, 2016, www.business-standard.com/article/companies/amazon-builds-india-business-quietly-114040300984_1.html.

[32] Rasul Bailay and Chaitali Chakravartyl, "Amazon and Future Group Partnership on Rocks Over Funding of Discounts," *Times of India*, January 13, 2016, accessed March 5, 2016, http://timesofindia.indiatimes.com/tech/tech-news/Amazon-and-Future-Group-partnership-on-rocks-over-funding-of-discounts/articleshow/50557364.cms.

[33] Nivedita Bhattacharjee, op. cit.

[34] Malviya, op. cit.

[35] "Future Group, Amazon India Announce Strategic E-Commerce Alliance," op. cit.

[36] "Future Group Ties Up with Hybris for Online Synergy," *Business Standard*, September 3, 2014, accessed March 16, 2016, www.business-standard.com/article/companies/future-group-in-pact-with-sap-company-hybris-for-omni-channel-technology-114090301134_1.html.

[37] Bhattacharjee, op. cit.

[38] "Future Group Ties Up with Hybris for Online Synergy," op. cit.

[39] The omni-channel retail strategy allowed customers to view products online, check store inventory and location, order the product to be delivered, or reserve the product for pickup at the nearest store. The strategy required significant inter-departmental cooperation from supply chain management, suppliers, stores, merchandising, logistics, and technology.

Exhibit 4

Amazon.com Financials

Annual Income Statement (excerpts), in US$ thousands

Period Ending December 31	2012	2013	2014	2015
Total Revenue	61,093	74,452	88,988	107,006
Cost of Revenue	45,971	54,181	62,752	71,651
Gross Profit	15,122	20,271	26,236	35,355
Sales, General & Administrative Expenses	14,446	19,526	26,058	33,122
Operating Income	676	745	178	2,233
Earnings Before Interest & Tax	636	647	99	2,027
Net Income	(39)	274	(241)	596

Balance Sheet (excerpts), in US$ thousands

Period Ending December 31	2012	2013	2014	2015
Total Current Assets	21,296	24,625	31,327	36,474
Long Term Assets (including fixed assets and goodwill)	32,555	40,159	54,505	65,444
Total Current Liabilities	19,002	22,980	28,089	33,899
Total Liabilities	24,363	30,413	43,764	52,060
Total Equity	32,555	40,159	54,505	65,444

Source: "AMZN Company Financials," Nasdaq, accessed March 31, 2016, www.nasdaq.com/symbol/amzn/financials?query=income-statement.

enabler (typically an e-commerce platform) is about ₹1 billion and is spread over the next 18 months. . . . This kind of omni-channel retail will change the way we interact and serve the customer."

Future Group had earlier launched the Big Bazaar Direct portal that allowed online purchasing of products, but failed in that initiative. It was planned to make the initiative part of the omni-channel strategy.[40] As part of the omni-channel strategy, Ezone, Future Group's electronic format, was expected to be the first to be available online. It would be followed by Foodhall and Big Bazaar, the food and hypermarket retail chains, respectively.

The omni-channel strategy became apparent as a promising alternative for the corporate retail chains that had been losing sales to online retailers who had already captured around 15 per cent of the retail market world-wide.[41] Govind Shrikhande, managing director of Shoppers Stop–another big player in the retail industry–argued for the importance of offline retailers in an omni-channel shopping experience:

A pure online player can never be an omni-channel retailer as they don't have a physical presence. A customer can go into a physical store, shop the physical store merchandise, and they can also use a kiosk or an iPad within the store to order online in the store, get it delivered in the same store next day, or get it delivered to their home or any other place.[42]

[40] "Future Group Ties Up with Hybris for Online Synergy," op. cit.

[41] Shashidhar and John, op. cit.　　[42] Ibid.

Over the next 18 months, Future Group aimed to earn approximately 20 per cent of revenue from online sales and around 40 per cent by 2020."[43]

Biyani's negotiations with Flipkart to jointly sell goods stretched over 20 days, then collapsed in October 2014. According to media sources, Future Group wanted a fee of $10 million for giving sole, online retail rights–a price that Flipkart found excessive. Flipkart maintained that it did not pay for exclusive rights to retail products. Instead, Flipkart wanted Future Group to pay a commission on every sale on its platform. Future Group would have preferred a lower commission fee. A person involved in the talks said, "There was no warmth between the two parties." Another source said, "The Flipkart team felt the terms were onerous."[44]

Biyani was not in favour of marketplace models used by companies such as Amazon, Flip-Kart, and Snapdeal. He strongly believed their models were "front-end retailing with smart accounting to dodge Indian laws that bar overseas investment in these ventures."[45] Biyani accused online marketplaces of trying to destroy competition by selling products below manufacturing costs. He pointed out that online retailers were spending huge sums on advertising and customer acquisition. Biyani maintained, "Just because [online retailers] have foreign funding, they can't kill local trade like that."[46]

The Amazon–Future Group Deal

In October 2014, Biyani and Bezos met to finalize a deal to sell brands from Future Group's portfolio on Amazon's marketplace in India. Amazon would be the exclusive online platform for the brands.[47] Fulfillment of orders and customer service of the products on its portal would be handled by Amazon.[48]

To provide visibility of its brands on Amazon. in, Future Group entered into an exclusive marketing arrangement with Amazon. Cloudtail, a 49:51 joint venture between Amazon and the Indian investment firm Catamaran Ventures, would sell brands owned by or licensed to Future Group, including Lee Coopers, Converse, Indigo Nation, Scullers, Jealous 21, and 40 other private label brands owned by Future Group. The products would be offered to customers at a discount of 30 per cent to 40 per cent.[49] Following the deal, more than 40 brands owned by Future Group were to be removed from other online marketplaces where they were presently being sold.[50] While the deal involved fashion and food labels first, Amazon was expected to pick up other categories from Future Group's portfolio in the future.[51]

The deal was meant to be an arrangement built on customer service. Biyani's strategy for Future Group retail was to know and cater to Indian consumers, "The bottom line in each of our retail success stories is 'know your customer.' Insights into the soul of Indian consumers–how they operate, think, dream, and live–helps us innovate and create functionally differentiating products and experiences."[52]

Biyani saw Amazon as an opportunity to extend that strategy to customers in about 19,000 postal codes in India served by Amazon, "Partnership with Amazon, which obsesses to be Earth's most customer-centric company, will enable us to leverage their strengths,

[43] Malviya, op. cit.

[44] Radhika P. Nair, "How Flipkart's Cold Response Sealed Future Group and Amazon's Deal," ETRetail.com, October 14, 2014, accessed March 5, 2016, http://jetairways.globallinker.com/bizforum/news/how-flipkart-039-s-cold-response-sealed-future-group-and-amazon-039-s-deal/13440805?indid=0.

[45] Bailay and Chakravarty, op. cit.

[46] Vikas SN, "One Week After Dissing E-Tailers, Future Group Ties Up with Amazon," Medianama, October 13, 2014, accessed March 5, 2016, www.medianama.com/2014/10/223-future-group-amazon.

[47] Bailay and Chakravarty, op. cit.   [48] Malviya, op. cit.

[49] Bailay and Chakravarty, op. cit.; Bhattacharjee, op. cit.

[50] Malviya, op. cit.

[51] "Future Group, Amazon India Announce Strategic E-Commerce Alliance," op. cit.

[52] Amazon.in, "Amazon.in and Future Group Enter Into a Strategic Partnership," press release, October 13, 2014, accessed March 5, 2016, www.amazon.in/b?ie=UTF8&node=8520579031.

investments, and innovations in technology to reach out to a wider set of consumers across India."[53]

Biyani's goals for the deal were considerable: "We are targeting gross merchandise sales of ₹60 billion in the next three years through the alliance."[54]

For Amazon, the partnership was an important growth opportunity in the Indian retail industry. Future Group helped to provide Amazon with the Indian sources it needed under India's foreign direct-investment policy. The partnership was also expected to be a crucial step for Amazon's growth in the much sought after fashion category. Because of high margins and growing demand, fashion was the focus category for most of the e-commerce retailers. Flipkart and Snapdeal were leading in terms of product assortment and number of sellers and brands, and Flipkart, Myntra, and Jabong had their own private labels in India, which Amazon did not have.[55]

Amazon acknowledged the strategic partnership with Future Group. Amit Agrawal, vice-president and country manager for Amazon India reported:

> We are excited to collaborate, leverage each other's unique strengths, and serve customers across India. The product portfolio of Future Group, their innate understanding of the Indian consumer mindset, and our ability to serve and deliver a convenient, easy, trusted, and reliable delivery experience to a nationwide set of customers is a win-win for all.[56]

The Amazon–Future Group partnership was evidence of the importance of combining product with technology in omni-channel retailing. Amazon India noted that the partnership would benefit customers "in making a purchase decision through rich product content, secure payments, fast delivery, and easy returns on the www.amazon.in platform."[57]

The media reported:

> The partnership ... is not one between two retailers but of vendor and technology platforms offering technology and logistics services. This will help in the growth of new brands and private labels.... . It establishes that leading brick and mortar retailers cannot be dismissive about e-commerce players, which have become a brand in the online space."[58]

News of the partnership triggered an intra-day jump in the shares of two of Future Group's listed companies: Future Retail Ltd. and Future Lifestyle Fashion Ltd.[59] However, industry experts felt there were also possible pitfalls in the deal. Devangshu Dutta, chief executive officer at the retail consultancy firm Third Eyesight, said, "If the business is not aligned in terms of orientation and customer service, then it could create issues going forward, especially when one of the biggest barriers for online sale is inconsistency of products."[60]

Under the deal, Amazon and Future Group would work together to navigate the discounting conflict between online and offline retailers. The two businesses would jointly develop the pricing and discounting strategy. To avoid a conflict between the online and offline channels that could, in the end, undermine the business efforts of both, Amazon and Future Group agreed that the online price of products under Future Group's

53 Bailay and Chakravarty, op. cit.; Malavika Velayanikal, "Amazon Now Has a Powerful Brick-and-Mortar Ally in India. Flipkart and Snapdeal, Your Move," *Tech in Asia*, October 13, 2014, accessed June 14, 2016, www.techinasia.com/amazon-partners-future-retail-to-become-click-and-mortar-in-india.

54 Ibid.

55 "Future Group, Amazon India Announce Strategic E-Commerce Alliance," op. cit.

56 "Amazon.in and Future Group enter into a strategic partnership," op. cit.

57 Ibid.

58 Insight attributed to Arvind Singhal, Chairman, Technopak; "Future Group, Amazon India Announce Strategic E-Commerce Alliance," op. cit.

59 "Amazon India and Future Group Tie the Knot to Sell Fashion Online," op. cit.

60 Malviya, op. cit.

brands would not be very different from the prices at the stores.[61]

The partnership was also expected to extend to exploring synergies in distribution, customer acquisition, and cross-promotions.[62] Amazon announced that Amazon.in would also partner with Future Group brands in promoting existing and new brands in the market, exploring co-branding opportunities, and accelerating development of new products in categories that were not presently served by retailers.[63]

Food was expected to be the next category of products for the partnership. Amazon was already offering ready-to-eat foods and similar products online, and Future Group had plans to begin retailing food brands as well.[64] Biyani had a big vision for retailing fast-moving consumer goods: he wanted to move beyond the 25 per cent to 30 per cent margin of Future Group's immediate competitors and, instead, earn a margin of 40 per cent on premium products. This would have put Future Group in a category with Hindustan Unilever, Nestlé, and Britannia.[65] Biyani admitted that he lacked the product development experience of consumer goods companies, but he hoped to bridge the gap by entering into collaborations with experts in various fields.[66]

Interestingly, even after partnering with Amazon, Biyani continued his previously established criticism of foreign-funded e-commerce companies.[67] Biyani boldly declared in an interview with *Business Standard* that "the mindspace [e-commerce stakeholders] have occupied is far larger than their share of the market."[68] Biyani was particularly critical of deep-discounting schemes, criticizing Flipkart and other e-commerce retailers for the deep discounts they offered during a Diwali promotional sale event.

Biyani feared deep discounting would hurt the other retail channels.[69]

The Downturn

In January 2016, the media reported that differences had emerged between Future Group and Amazon over the funding structure for discounts Amazon offered on products sold from Future Group's fashion brands. Discounting was a common practice with online retailers in India, but it affected the profitability of most e-commerce companies. Amazon asked Future Group to bear a portion of offered discounts by taking a reduced margin on sales.

Given Biyani's public criticism of deep online discounting and his reluctance to share the cost of rebates, the media didn't expect Biyani to accept Amazon's proposal. If Future Group did agree to Amazon's request, the result would be different prices for the products sold in Future Group's physical stores and sold online. The rumour was that Amazon, in turn, told Future Group to end the exclusive deal with Amazon and instead, like any other vendor, list its private labels online and pay Amazon a commission on sales.[70]

Industry experts criticized the Amazon–Future Group deal, alleging that it was a media strategy for attention. According to Harminder Sahni, founder of retail consultancy firm Wazir Advisors, "Discounts should be the first thing to be discussed [in an e-commerce arrangement]. What priority pricing Future [Group] will give to Amazon, what price differentiation will work between offline and online, should be the first things to be discussed."[71]

The Way Forward

Biyani felt that there was a limit to the number of physical stores Future Group could have. He planned to increase the number of stores to 260 by 2018, but added, "Even if we add another

---

[61] Ibid.   [62] Bhattacharjee, op. cit.
[63] Amazon.in, op. cit.
[64] "Future Group, Amazon India Announce Strategic E-Commerce Alliance," op. cit.
[65] Shashidhar and John, op. cit.   [66] Ibid.
[67] Bailay and Chakravarty, op. cit.
[68] "Future Group, Amazon India Announce Strategic E-Commerce Alliance," op. cit.

[69] Bhattacharjee, op. cit.
[70] Bailay and Chakravarty, op. cit.   [71] Ibid.

Exhibit 5
Future Enterprises Financials

Profit and Loss (excerpts), in $ millions

	June 2010	June 2011	December 2012	March 2014	March 2015
	12 months	12 months	18 months	15 months	12 months
Operating Profit	90.07	62.85	116.45	164.06	167.41
PBDIT	101.13	65.30	159.09	164.72	186.49
PBT	32.35	17.29	43.25	1.91	9.20
Reported Net Profit	26.93	11.50	40.99	0.42	11.11

Balance Sheet (excerpts), in $ millions

	June 2010	June 2011	December 2012	March 2014	March 2015
Net Worth	413.44	431.72	498.38	487.75	779.69
Total Debt	207.93	289.65	480.84	825.57	630.14
Total Liabilities	621.37	721.37	979.22	1,313.32	1,409.83
Net Block	168.32	220.05	342.33	651.04	724.75
Total Current Assets, Loans and Advances	292.15	377.58	574.45	794.40	932.21
Total Current Liabilities and Provisions	148.49	228.86	311.21	389.12	482.65

Note: Exchange rates on January 1, 2016: ₹1=US$0.015; US$1 = ₹66.235; PBDIT = profit before depreciation, interest, and taxes; PBT = profit before taxes.
Source: "Future Enterprises," Money Control, accessed June 17, 2016, www.moneycontrol.com/financials/futureen terprises/profit-loss/PR03.

30 to 40 more physical stores, we can go to 300 and not beyond that … So the next option is to take the help of technology to penetrate deeper into the market."[72]

In March 2016, the Government of India changed its foreign investment policy to allow 100 per cent foreign direct investment in the business-to-consumer online marketplace. However, the government restricted e-commerce companies from directly or indirectly effecting the selling price of goods on online marketplaces. This came as a big relief to offline, brick-and-mortar retailers.[73] According to the directive, no

[72] "Future Group Ties-Up with Hybris for Online Synergy," *Business Standard*, September 3, 2014, accessed June 14, 2016, www.business-standard.com/ article/companies/future-group-in-pact-with-sap-company-hybris-for-omni-channel-technology-114090301134_1.html.

[73] John Sarkar, Digbijay Mishra, and Shilpa Phadnis, "100% FDI in E-Commerce Marketplaces: Days of Huge Online Discounts May End Soon," *Times of India*, March 30, 2016, accessed March 31, 2016, http:// timesofindia.indiatimes.com/tech/tech-news/100-FDI-in-e-commerce-marketplaces-Days-of-huge-online-discounts-may-soon-end/articleshow/51610085.cms.

single vendor or their group of companies could account for more than 25 per cent of the overall sales on a platform.[74]

The policy change was a major blow to Amazon, which had been lobbying for foreign direct investment on an inventory-based model[75] of e-commerce. In 2015, Amazon's Cloudtail posted a loss of $4.7 million (₹317 million) on revenues of $170 million (₹11.5 billion), but was expected to turn profitable in 2016.[76]

Amazon and Future Group needed to sort out their differences in the context of the changing market and evolving policy. Should the companies nurture the partnership on the existing terms and conditions, look for alternate options for growing together, and adjust the terms of the partnership, or exit from the partnership altogether?

---

[74] Ibid.

[75] In an inventory based model one is in control of the of the physical inventory of products thereby enabling a superior post-purchase customer experience. It enables one to deliver faster and with higher accuracy. In a market place model buyers and sellers transact on a technology-based platform, with no physical inventory in the possession of the seller.

[76] Shilpa Phadnis and John Sarkar, "Flipkart, Amazon Need to Downsize Sellers," *Times of India*, March 30, 2016, accessed March 31, 2016, http:// timesofindia.indiatimes.com/tech/tech-news/Flipkart-Amazon-need-to-downsize-sellers/articleshow/ 51609319.cms; *BS Reporter*, "Cloudtail Reports Rs. 32-cr Loss on Rs.1,145 Cr-Sales in FY15", December 31, 2015, accessed March 31, 2016.

Chapter 6 Recommended Practitioner Readings

- Paul W. Beamish, *A Note on the Design and Management of International Joint Ventures* (Ivey Publishing, 2017).

   "A Note on the Design and Management of International Joint Ventures" examines the alliance form that typically requires the greatest level of inter-action, cooperation, and investment: the equity joint venture. The reading focuses on two primary issues. The first of these considers the reasons why companies create international joint ventures. These include strengthening the existing business, taking existing products to foreign markets, bringing for-eign products to local markets, and diversifying into a new business. The second of these considers the requirements for international joint venture success. These include testing the strategic logic, partnership and fit, shape and design, doing the deal, and making the venture work.

- Ulrich Wassmer, Pierre Dussauge, and Marcel Planellas, "How to manage alli-ances better than one at a time," *MIT Sloan Management Review*, 51:3 (2010), 77–94.

   In "How to manage alliances better than one at a time," Wassmer, Dussauge, and Planellas focus on how companies can employ a more strategic approach to configuring effective alliance portfolios. The authors advocate a two-stage alliance assessment process (which includes both individual alliance analysis and alliance portfolio analysis) that can be used when considering any new alliance opportunity. They contend that when a company adds a new alliance to its portfolio, the firm tends to focus on how much value the alliance will create as a standalone transaction, while ignoring the fact that the composition of its entire alliance portfolio is an important determinant of the value that will emerge from the new alliance relationship.

- Ha Hoang and Frank T. Rothaermel, "How to manage alliances strategically," *MIT Sloan Management Review*, 58:1 (2016), 69–76.

  In "How to manage alliances strategically," decisions by Daimler, Toyota, and Panasonic to collaborate with Tesla highlight that individual companies may not need to own all of the resources, skills, and knowledge necessary to undertake key strategic growth initiatives. When conditions are uncertain and the stakes are high, partnerships can be an attractive alternative to going it alone or to mergers and acquisitions. Accordingly, many companies now maintain alliance portfolios. As a result, executives must manage multiple alliances with diverse partners across the globe simultaneously. However, the skills required to develop and manage alliances are still not well understood. The authors offer an integrative and holistic framework of alliance management along with practical guidance.

The recommended readings in this chapter all underscore the need for collaboration for international success.

Part III
The Managerial Implications

7 Building New Management Capabilities
Key to Effective Implementation

Just as new transnational strategic imperatives put demands on MNEs' existing organizational capabilities, so have evolving transnational organization models defined new managerial tasks for those operating within them. In this chapter, we examine the changing roles and responsibilities of three typical management groups that find themselves at the decision-making table in today's transnational organizations: the global business manager, the worldwide functional manager, and the national subsidiary manager. Although different organizations may define the key roles differently (bringing global account managers or regional executives to the table, for example), the main challenge facing all MNEs is to allocate their major strategic tasks and organizational roles among key management groups. Just as important is the subsequent need to give each of those groups the appropriate legitimacy and influence within the organization's ongoing decision-making process. The focus of this chapter is to provide an overview of the new roles and responsibilities of these key executives before concluding with a review of the role of top management in integrating their diverse interests and perspectives, and engaging them around a common direction.

As earlier chapters have made clear, the twenty-first century MNE is markedly different from its twentieth century predecessors. It has been transformed by an environment in which multiple, often conflicting forces accelerate simultaneously. The globalization of markets, the acceleration of product and technology life cycles, the assertion of national governments' demands, and, above all, the intensification of global competition have created an environment of complexity, diversity, and change for most of today's MNEs.

As we have seen, the ability of a company to compete based on a single dominant competitive advantage has morphed into a need to develop multiple strategic assets: global-scale efficiency and competitiveness, national responsiveness and flexibility, and worldwide innovation and learning capabilities. In turn, these new strategic demands have put pressure on existing organization structures and management processes. Traditional hierarchical structures, with their emphasis on either/or choices, have evolved toward organizational forms that we have described as transnationals. Such organizations are characterized by their abilities to manage integrated networks of assets and resources, multi-dimensional management perspectives and capabilities, and flexible coordinative processes.

The managerial implications of all these changes are enormous. To succeed in today's international operating environment, transnational managers must be able to sense and interpret complex and dynamic environmental changes; they must be able to develop and integrate multiple strategic capabilities; and they must be able to build and manage complicated yet controllable organizations capable of delivering coordinated action on a worldwide basis. Unless those in key management positions are highly skilled and knowledgeable, their companies simply cannot respond well to the major new challenges they face.

Yet surprisingly little attention has been devoted to the implications of these changes on the roles and responsibilities of those who manage today's MNEs. Academics, consultants, and even managers themselves focus an enormous amount of time and energy on analyzing the diverse international environmental forces, on refining the concepts of global strategy, and on understanding the characteristics of effective cross-border organizations. But without capable managers in place, sophisticated strategies and organizations will almost certainly fail. In simple terms, the great risk for most MNEs today is that they are often trying to implement third-generation strategies through second-generation organizations with first-generation managers.

In this chapter, we examine the management roles and responsibilities implied by the new challenges facing MNEs – those roles and responsibilities that take the manager beyond the first-generation assumptions. But because management tasks in transnational organizations differ widely by location, level, and assigned duties, it's impossible to generalize about appropriate duties. Instead, we focus on the distinctly different roles and responsibilities of three specific groups in the transnational company: the global business manager, the worldwide functional manager, and the country subsidiary manager. After reviewing the three core roles and responsibilities, we will close the chapter by examining the role of top management in integrating these often-competing perspectives and capabilities.

(Before proceeding further, it's helpful to recall that in Chapter 4, we suggested that transnational organizations come in many forms. It is hardly surprising therefore that similar variations also occur in the division of management roles. So, although we focus on the three typical roles described in the following paragraphs, other key executives – global account managers or regional managers, for example – may also have a seat at the table.)

Global Business Management

The challenge of developing global efficiency and competitiveness requires that management capture the various scale and scope economies available to the MNE as well as capitalize on the potential competitive advantages inherent in its worldwide market positioning. These requirements demand management with the acumen to see opportunities and risks across national boundaries and across functional specialties. Furthermore, management needs the skill to coordinate and integrate diverse activities across these barriers in order to minimize the risks and capture the potential benefits. This is the fundamental task of the global business manager.

In implementing this important responsibility, the global business manager will be involved in a variety of activities that vary significantly by the nature of the business and the company's administrative heritage. Nonetheless, there are three core roles and responsibilities that almost always fall to this key manager: he or she will be a global strategist, an architect of worldwide asset and resource configuration, and a coordinator and controller of cross-border transfers.

Global Business Strategist

Because competitive interaction increasingly takes place on a global chessboard, in any given business only a manager with a worldwide perspective and responsibility can assess the strategic position and the organizational capability to respond. To allow such assessment, companies must configure their information, planning, and control systems so that they can be consolidated into consistent, integrated reports available to the global business manager.

This does not imply that this individual is the only person with the perspective and capability to formulate strategic priorities, or that he or she should undertake that vital task unilaterally. Depending on the nature of the business, there will almost certainly be some need to incorporate the perspectives of geographic and functional managers who represent strategic interests that may run counter to the business manager's drive to maximize global efficiency. Equally important, the business strategy that is developed must fit within the broader corporate strategy, which should provide a clear vision of what the company wants to be, and explicit values pertaining to how it will accomplish its mission. In the final analysis, however, it is the global business manager who should have the responsibility to reconcile the different views and prepare an integrated strategy of how the company will compete in his or her particular business.

Because of this important responsibility, it is vital to assign a qualified person to the global business management role. Yet this position is sometimes created simply by elevating an otherwise unprepared domestic product division manager to a global responsibility. It is an appointment that can compromise the credibility of the position. Overseas subsidiary managers often feel that these managers are not only insensitive to non-domestic perspectives and interests but also biased toward the domestic organization in making key strategic decisions such as market positioning, product development, and capacity plans.

In many cases, these concerns are justified. For example, in 2001, when US-based building supplies chain Home Depot sold its operations in Chile and Argentina, industry experts suggested that the failure was largely due to an assumption by US management that it could transfer its successful domestic business model abroad. But its sophisticated logistical systems that allowed central warehouses to support low store inventories did not translate to smaller, less developed countries. Five years later, when it entered China, Home Depot thought it could overcome these logistical problems by purchasing an established Chinese chain. In 2012, however, as the company closed its doors taking a loss of $160 million, management acknowledged that the do-it-yourself homeowner on which their domestic model was built was flawed in countries where labor costs were low – leading consumers to hire outside services rather than buying the tools and equipment to do it themselves.

To minimize such strategy problems, the ideal career path for a global business manager may well involve some experience as a country manager. Such experience may help him or her develop a richer understanding of the ways in which national infrastructure, local consumer behavior, and national culture need to be considered in global strategy. Indeed, in the true transnational company, the global business manager may not even be located in the home country. Indeed, great benefits can accrue to relocating several such management groups abroad.

Even well-established MNEs with a tradition of close control of their worldwide business strategy have recognized this. The head of IBM's $6 billion telecommunications business moved her division headquarters to London. She explained that the rationale was not only to move the command center closer to the booming European market for computer networking but also "[to] give us a different perspective on all our markets." And when General Electric acquired Amersham, the British-based life sciences and diagnostics leader, it relocated its health care business headquarters to the UK to better leverage the technology, management talent, and entrepreneurial culture that came with this key acquisition.

Architect of Asset and Resource Configuration

Closely tied to the challenge of shaping an integrated business strategy is the global business manager's responsibility for overseeing the worldwide location of key assets and resources. Again, we do not mean to imply that he or she should make such decisions unilaterally. To ensure the input of interested geographic and functional managers is considered, several companies have used a global strategy committee while another large organization created an internal world business board with membership drawn from key geographic and functional management groups. However, on the issue of where to locate key plants or develop vital resources, it is the global business manager who is normally best placed to initiate and lead the debate and who also must make the final decision.

However, the business manager should never assume that such decisions can be made from a zero base on a blank canvas. He or she should recognize that all such decisions are rooted in the company's administrative heritage and must build on it rather than ignore it. In multinational companies such as Philips, Unilever, ICI, or Nestlé, this inevitably means recognizing that the assets and resources that permitted them to expand internationally are often deeply embedded in the national companies that are the foundation of their decentralized federation organization model. It would be unwise for any business manager trying to reposition the future configurations of such companies to ignore or destroy the valuable assets and resources on which they were built. That does not mean that the existing configuration should become a constraint, but any reconfiguration involving closures or layoffs must be handled with social sensitivity and political dexterity to avoid the loss of goodwill and to respond to inevitable resistance from longtime local stakeholders.

In this context, the challenge to the business manager is to shape the future configuration by leveraging existing resources and capabilities, and linking them in a configuration that resembles the integrated network form. When GE Medical Systems (GEMS) reconfigured its global structure, it did so by scaling up operations in its most efficient production centers around the world, making them global sources. This led to plants in Budapest, Shanghai, and Mexico City being designated "Centers of Excellence" supplying their specialized medical products to GE's operations worldwide. Meanwhile, operations in Paris, Tokyo, and Milwaukee were scaled back to become specialized assembly operations. The same process redefined the roles of its research and development centers, making GEMS a classic model of a distributed yet integrated transnational structure.

Cross-Border Coordinator

The third key role played by most global business managers is that of a cross-border coordinator. Although less overtly strategic than the other two responsibilities, it is nonetheless a vital operating function, because it involves deciding on sourcing patterns and managing cross-border transfer processes.

As companies build transnational structures and capabilities, the task of coordinating flows of materials, components, and finished products becomes extremely complex.[1] Rather than producing and shipping all products from a fully integrated central plant (the centralized hub model) or allowing local subsidiaries to develop self-sufficient capabilities (the decentralized federation model), as the GEMS example above illustrates, transnational companies specialize their worldwide operations, building on the most capable national activities and capitalizing on locations of strategic importance.

But the resulting integrated network of specialized operations is highly interdependent. For example, the structure that GEMS created linked its high labor content component plants in Eastern Europe and China with its highly skilled subassembly operations in Germany and Singapore. In turn, each of these operations supply specialized components and finished products to assembly plants in the United States, England, France, and Japan.

In GEMS as in many other transnational operations, the coordination task is further complicated by the fact that it involves both corporate-owned and out-sourced supply. Both sources require the resolution of issues ranging from

---

[1] K. Roth, "Managing international interdependence: CEO characteristics in a resource-based framework," *Academy of Management Journal*, **38**:1 (1995), 200–31.

    This study argued that the level of a firm's international interdependence influences the pattern of CEO characteristics ideal for enabling a CEO to contribute to firm performance. The influence of locus of control, information evaluation style, and international experience on firm performance varied with interdependence.

controlling the quality of the final product to carefully managing the transfer of proprietary design and production knowledge to subcontractors.

The simplest coordination mechanism available to the global business manager is the ability to exercise direct central control over quantities shipped and prices charged. This is the model most likely to be used for products of high strategic importance (e.g., Pfizer's central coordination of quantities and pricing of the active ingredients of Viagra®, or Coca-Cola's tight corporate control of the supply of Coke syrup worldwide).

As products become more commodity-like, however, global product managers recognize that internal transfers should reflect the competitive conditions set by the external environment. This recognition has led many to develop internal quasi-markets as the principal means of coordination. For example, in the consumer electronics giant Panasonic, the product development group at the parent company works with the relevant domestic marketing organization to develop prototypes of the following year's models of products from video cameras to TVs. But to ensure that the new models are adapted to Panasonic's many overseas markets, global product managers present them to internal buyers at the company's annual merchandise meetings. These are, in effect, huge internal trade fairs at which national sales and marketing directors from the company's sales companies around the world enter into direct discussions with the global product managers, negotiating modifications in product design, price, and delivery schedule to meet their local market needs.

Worldwide Functional Management

In most companies, there are two types of worldwide functional managers – those with specialist oversight responsibility for activities like R&D, manufacturing, and marketing, and those with responsibility for support activities, such as the chief financial officer and the chief information officer. Broadly speaking, the job of both these groups is to provide support to line managers, particularly by diffusing innovations and transferring knowledge on a worldwide basis. This vital task is built on their access to knowledge that is highly specialized by function – technological capability, marketing expertise, manufacturing know-how, and so on. To implement this role effectively requires that functional managers evolve from the secondary support roles they may have played in the past and take their place as active managers with a seat at the transnational decision-making table.

The role, responsibility, and relative importance of functional managers vary widely by business. For example, in a biotech company the nature and importance of technology transfer may be more critical than the transfer of marketing expertise, while the opposite would be true for a company in fast-moving consumer goods. Furthermore, companies in transnational industries such as telecommunications will require more functional linkages and transfers than those in multinational industries such as retailing. Nonetheless, we highlight three basic roles and responsibilities that most worldwide functional managers should play: worldwide scanner of specialized information and intelligence, cross-pollinator of "best practices," and champion of transnational innovation.

Worldwide Intelligence Scanner

Most innovations are triggered by a stimulus that drives the company to respond to a perceived opportunity or threat. It may be a revolutionary technological break-through, an emerging consumer trend, a new competitive challenge, or a pending government regulation. And the company may first encounter such new developments anywhere in the world.

A typical example occurred with the birth and rapid emergence of a viable commercial market for alternative energy, a trend that appeared in Europe in the early years of the new millennium. Strong public support backed by widespread government incentives and legislative requirements resulted in explosive growth in the demand for generators powered by wind, solar, and other non-carbon emitting sources. Particularly in Europe, the subsequent transformation was rapid. By 2015, renewable energy accounted for 16.4% of all power generation in the EU, well along the way to the EU's commitment of 20% by 2020. Even more impressive was that in 2016, 86% of new EU energy capacity was from wind, solar, hydro, and biomass.

Those power generation companies and equipment manufacturers that had good sensory mechanisms in Europe at the turn of the century soon recognized the significance of these developments and became first-mover competitors in several segments. Early awareness of the growing trend allowed them to make appropriate adjustments to their market positioning, technological capabilities, and product-line configuration.

For example, Siemens leveraged its recognition of the evolving energy revolution to develop the dominant European wind turbine business, quickly accumulating significant experience at meeting the fast-growing new demands. With that knowledge and expertise, in 2008, it opened a wind turbine research center in Colorado, partnering with the National Wind Technology Center (NWTC). This created a strong base from which to expand into the growing US demand for energy from renewable sources, and allowing the company to become the number two competitor in wind-powered generation by 2015.

In contrast, those companies that had not been monitoring the European development as an advance warning system found themselves at a disadvantage as those trends spread to developed and developing countries worldwide. They found themselves scrambling to respond to the growing political and consumer pressures while simultaneously having to defend against challengers from more responsive competitors that had several years' head start in developing alternative energy technologies, products, and strategies.

But global awareness alone is not sufficient. Historically, even when strategically important information was sensed in the foreign subsidiaries of classic multi-national or global companies, it was rarely transmitted to those who could act on it. Worse yet, when it did get through, it was often ignored. The communication problem was due primarily to the fact that the intelligence was usually of a specialist nature, not always well understood by the geographic- or business-focused generalists who controlled the line organization. To capture and transmit such information across national boundaries required the establishment of functional specialist information channels to link local technologists, marketers, and production experts with others who understood their needs and shared their specialized perspective.

In transnational companies, functional managers are often most effectively linked through informal networks that are nurtured and maintained through frequent meetings, visits, and transfers. Through such personal linkages, these managers develop the contacts and relationships that enable them to transmit information rapidly around the globe. In this way, the functional managers at the corporate level become the linchpins in a worldwide intelligence scanning effort. In addition, they also play a vital role as facilitators of communication and as the corporate repositories of specialist information.

Procter & Gamble provides a good example of such a process. By his leadership in supporting the implementation of the digital strategy, P&G's corporate CIO, Fillippo Passorini, built a close relationship with all the company's global business managers. Because the process aggregates consumer feedback collected from tweets, blogs, emails, and call center records worldwide, P&G's business managers found great value in the system's real-time digital dashboard that displayed current information on consumer perceptions. By analyzing a massive amount of data from around the world, the CIO and his staff were also able to provide global business executives and local subsidiary managers with a sales forecasting tool that has allowed the company to redeploy 5,000 staff who had been engaged in demand planning, replacing their spreadsheets with computer models that provide more accurate and timely aggregated demand forecasts.

Cross-Pollinator of "Best Practices"

Overseas subsidiaries can be more than sources of strategic intelligence, however. In a truly transnational company, they can also be the source of capabilities, expertise, and innovation that can be transferred to other parts of the organization. For instance, Caterpillar's leading-edge flexible manufacturing first emerged in its French and Belgian plants, and much of P&G's liquid detergent technology was developed in its European Technology Center. In both cases, this expertise was transferred to the company's operations in other countries with important strategic impact.

Such an ability to transfer new ideas and developments requires a considerable amount of management time and attention to break down the not-invented-here (NIH) syndrome that often thrives in international business. In breaking down the NIH barriers, those with worldwide functional responsibilities are ideally placed to play a cross-pollination role. Not only do they have the specialist knowledge required to identify and evaluate leading-edge practices, they also tend to have a well-developed informal communications network developed with others in their functional area.

Traditional ways of transferring leading-edge processes and practices from one part of the organization to another typically relied on formal structures and systems. For example, plant design blueprints and operating manuals from the company's best practice operating facility might be transferred to plants and other countries. But embedded NIH barriers frequently prevented the successful implementation of the expertise, regardless of how well documented it might have been.

In contrast, corporate functional managers who engage in frequent travel, conduct regular reviews, and develop networks of informal contacts are often the first to identify where best practices are being developed and implemented. Furthermore, they are also in a position to arrange cross-unit visits and transfers, host conferences, form task forces, or take other initiatives that will expose others to the best new ideas. And once personal contacts have been made, relationships developed, and trust built, the ability to move ideas and initiatives from one unit to another becomes much easier. In this way, the functional managers become the midwives of the practice transfer process.

For example, in preparation for GE's planned US launch of a highly successful 2.5 MW wind turbine it had developed in Europe, the company decided to move production to its plant in Florida. To ensure that the US operations captured all the vital technical expertise developed in its plants in Germany and Spain, the transfer task was assigned to a global manufacturing technology group in GE's power generation business. After the process was successfully completed, the team concluded that the complex transfer had only been possible due to the personal links they had carefully created between managers in the European operations and those in the new manufacturing site in Florida.

Champion of Transnational Innovation

The two previously identified roles ideally position the functional manager to play a key role in developing what we have called transnational innovations. As described in Chapter 5, these are different from the predominantly local activity that dominated the innovation process in multinational companies or the centrally driven innovation in international and global companies. But as we emphasized, the successful implementation of transnational innovations is built on a set of sophisticated organizational linkages.

Corporate functional managers have a key role to play in managing what we called locally leveraged innovations, the simplest form of transnational innovation. These managers are in an ideal position to scan their companies' worldwide operations and identify local innovations that have applications elsewhere. In Unilever, for example, product and marketing innovation for many of its global brands originated in national subsidiaries. Snuggle fabric softener was born in Unilever's German company, Timotei herbal shampoo originated in its Scandinavian operations, and Impulse body spray was first introduced by its South African unit. Recognizing the potential that these local innovations had for the wider company, the parent company's marketing and technical groups created the impetus to spread them to other subsidiaries.

The second type of transnational innovation is one that we called globally linked, a model that requires functional managers to play a more sophisticated role. This type of innovation fully exploits the company's access to worldwide information and expertise by linking and leveraging intelligence sources with internal centers of excellence, wherever they may be located. For example, the revolutionary design of GE's 2.5 MW wind turbine generator described above drew on jet engine turbine expertise from GE's transportation group in the United States, carbon composite materials technology that came out of its corporate R&D facility, blade design developed in its engineering center in Warsaw, Poland, and software written in its Indian R&D facility that could locate wind towers and feed power into the grid. The coordination required to identify these diverse capabilities and bring them together to create a sophisticated new generator could only be executed by functional technical experts with perspectives and responsibilities that reached across countries and across businesses.

Geographic Subsidiary Management

In many MNEs, a successful tour as a country subsidiary manager is often considered the acid test of general management potential. Indeed, in many companies, it can be a vital qualification on the résumé of any candidate for a top management position.[2] Not only does it provide frontline exposure to the realities of the current international business environment, but it also puts the individual in a position where he or she must deal with unending strategic complexity from an organizational position that is severely constrained. Indeed, as more MNEs move toward structures dominated by global business units and global customers, the role of "country manager" is, if anything, becoming more intricate and challenging. Despite having only limited formal authority over local assets and resources, the manager of the national operation is inevitably held fully accountable for results within his or her country.

We have described the strategic challenge facing the MNE as one that requires resolving the conflicting demands for global efficiency, multinational responsiveness, and worldwide learning. On the frontlines of the operation, it is typically the country manager who is located at the nexus of this strategic tension. He or she must simultaneously defend the company's market positions against global competitors, satisfy the demands of the host government, respond to the needs of local

---

[2] A. Yan, G. Zhu, and D. T. Hall, "International assignments for career building: a model of agency relationships and psychological contracts," *Academy of Management Review*, **27**:3 (2002), 373–91.

The authors present a theoretical model of international assignments, which examines the alignment or non-alignment of the organization's and the individual's expectations of an assignment and its effect on assignment success. Four basic configurations were considered: mutual loyalty, mutual transaction, agent opportunism, and principal opportunism. A matrix of organization–individual alignment was developed to help predict varying degrees of success in expatriate assignment and in repatriation.

customers, serve as the "face" of the organization at the national level, and leverage its local resources and capabilities to strengthen the company's competitive position worldwide.

There are many vital tasks the country manager must play. We identify three that capture the complexity of the task and highlight its important linkage role: acting as a bicultural interpreter, becoming the chief advocate and defender of national needs, and executing the vital frontline responsibility of implementing the company's strategy.

Bicultural Interpreter

All country managers realize they must become the local expert who understands the needs of the local market, the strategy of competitors, and the demands of the host government. But his or her responsibilities are also much broader. Because managers at corporate headquarters rarely understand all the complex subtleties of environmental and cultural differences across the MNE's diverse foreign markets, the country manager must be able to analyze the information gathered, interpret its implications, and even predict the range of feasible outcomes. This role suggests an ability not only to act as an efficient sensor of the national environment but also to become a cultural interpreter able to communicate the importance of that information to those whose perceptions may be obscured by ethnocentric biases.[3]

Fast-food company KFC learned an important lesson in 1980, one that it regarded as key to its subsequent successful international expansion. That was the year when Loy Weston, the general manager of KFC's Japanese subsidiary, suggested that the chain's classic "bucket of chicken" was too large for Japanese appetites; his request to introduce a new line of chicken pieces in a small serving size was rejected by corporate headquarters. It was a proposal that violated the corporate strategy of rolling out KFC's successful US menu as it expanded around the world. It was only after McDonald's introduced its wildly successful Chicken McNuggets that the company recognized that the failure to learn in Japan had left a gap for its giant competitor to move in on KFC's previously impregnable chicken franchise.

Being a bicultural interpreter implies another aspect to the country manager's role as an information broker. Not only must the individual have a sensitivity to and understanding of the *national* culture, he or she must also be comfortable in the

---

[3] A. Schotter and P. W. Beamish, "Performance effects of MNC headquarters–subsidiary conflict and the role of boundary spanners: the case of headquarter initiative rejection," *Journal of International Management*, **17**:3 (2011), 243–59.

Conflict is a normal consequence of organizing and managing across national borders. This study considered the case of headquarter initiative rejection by foreign subsidiaries. It focused on subsidiary conflict negotiation tactics, the effects of organizational and individual managerial power, and the characteristics and roles of MNC managers that act as boundary spanners during intra-organizational conflict processes. New theory was developed pertaining to the phenomenon. In the presence of boundary spanners, dysfunctional conflict was less common and better overall organizational performance was achieved for both the subsidiary and the MNC as a whole.

corporate culture at the MNE. Again, this second aspect of the bicultural role implies much more than being an information conduit to communicate the corporation's goals, strategies, and values to a group of employees located far away from the parent company. The country subsidiary manager must also interpret those broad goals and strategies so they become meaningful objectives and priorities at the local level of operation. Equally important, they must translate the core corporate values in a way that is sensitive to local cultural norms. And in the opposite direction, they must also be able to present to corporate headquarters the ideas and proposals generated in their local environment in a way that reflects an appreciation of the company's strategy and values.

So although the KFC corporate executives had to accept much of the blame for missing the chicken nugget opportunity, country manager Loy Weston also bore partial responsibility. In a location far removed from headquarters, Weston had established himself as a rebel willing to ignore the standard systems and challenge corporate directives. By distancing himself from corporate policies and procedures, and openly resisting headquarters attempts to control him, he effectively undermined his credibility as a bicultural interpreter.

National Defender and Advocate

As important as the communication role is, the effective country manager is obviously more than just an intelligent mailbox. Information and analysis conveyed to corporate headquarters must not only be well understood but also be acted upon. This is particularly true in MNEs where strong global business managers are arguing for a more integrated worldwide approach and corporate functional managers are focusing on cross-border linkages. The country manager's role is to counterbalance these centralizing tendencies and ensure that the needs and opportunities that exist in the local environment are understood and reflected in the decision-making process.

As the national organization evolves from its early independence to a more mature interdependent role as part of an integrated worldwide network, the country manager's drive for national self-sufficiency and personal autonomy (recall Loy Weston's motivation in KFC) must be replaced by a less parochial perspective and a more corporate-oriented identity. This shift does not imply, however, that he or she should stop presenting the local perspective to headquarters management or stop defending national interests. Indeed, the company's ability to become a true transnational depends on having strong country management advocates of the need to differentiate its operations locally and be responsive to national demands and pressures.

Two distinct but related tasks are implied by this important role. The first requires that the country manager ensure the overall corporate strategies, policies, and organization processes are appropriate from the national organization's perspective. If the interests of local constituencies are violated or the subsidiary's position risks being compromised by the global strategy, it is the country manager's responsibility to become the defender of national needs and perspectives.

For example, when Ericsson, the Swedish-based telecommunications company, was rolling out its new digital switching system worldwide, the general manager of the Australian subsidiary strongly advocated for a smaller, more flexible switching system adaptable to rural locations. Initially, management at the corporate center resisted this challenge to their global strategic plan, but eventually relented. The result was a rural switch that was not only a success in Australia, but also a new product that the company rolled out worldwide.

In addition to defending national differentiation and responsiveness, the country manager must become an advocate for his or her national organization's role in the corporation's worldwide integrated system of which it is a part. As MNEs develop a more transnational strategy, national organizations compete not only for corporate resources but also for roles in the global operations. To ensure that each unit's full potential is realized, country managers must be able to identify and represent their national organization's particular assets and capabilities, as well as the ways in which they can contribute to the MNE as a whole.

In the Ericsson example we just described, to help develop the rural switch the subsidiary manager linked up his Australian engineers to the corporate group. The working relationship exposed Ericsson's corporate engineers to the capability of this team on the other side of the world. As a result, the Australian R&D operation became part of the global design team and was assigned increasingly important roles in designing several key components in other corporate development projects.

This example also illustrates how the country manager's job is to mentor local employees and support them in their fight for corporate resources and recognition. In doing so, they build local capability that can be a major corporate asset. This responsibility was expressed passionately by the former head of the Scottish subsidiary of a major US computer company. He observed, "It is my absolute obligation to seek out new investment. No one else is going to stand up for these workers at head office. They are doing a great job, and I owe it to them to build up this operation. I get very angry with some of my counterparts in other parts of the company who just toe the party line. They have followed their orders to the letter, but when I visit their plants I see unfulfilled potential everywhere."

Frontline Implementer of Corporate Strategy

Although the implementation of corporate strategy may seem the most obvious of tasks for the manager of a frontline operating unit, it is far from the easiest. The first challenge stems from the multiplicity of constituents whose demands and pressures compete for the country manager's attention. In some countries, being a subsidiary company of some distant MNE seems to bestow a special status on national organizations and subject them to a different and a more intense type of pressure than that put on local companies. Governments may be suspicious of their motives, unions may distrust their national commitment, and customers may misunderstand their way of operating. The problem is compounded in many instances in which the corporate management fails to understand or appreciate the significance of these demands and pressures.

The country manager's implementation task is also complicated by the corporate expectation that he or she will be able to translate the broad corporate goals and strategies into specific actions that are responsive to the needs of the national environment. As we have seen, these global strategies are usually complex and finely balanced, typically reflecting multiple conflicting demands. Having been developed through subtle internal negotiation, they often leave the country manager with very little room to maneuver.

Pressured from without and constrained from within, the country manager needs a keen administrative sense to plot the negotiating range in which he or she can operate. The action decided on must be sensitive enough to respect the limits of the diverse local constituencies, pragmatic enough to achieve the expected corporate outcome, and creative enough to balance the diverse internal and external demands and constraints.

This delicate balancing act is made even more difficult by the fact that the country manager does not act solely as the implementer of predetermined corporate priorities. As we discussed previously, it is important that he or she also plays a key role in the shaping of those priorities. Thus the strategy the country manager is required to implement will often reflect some decisions against which he or she lobbied hard. Once the final decision is taken, however, the country manager must be able to convince his or her national organization to implement it with commitment and enthusiasm.

When Australian winemaker BRL Hardy wanted to introduce a new entry-level wine brand worldwide, the company's UK subsidiary general manager, Christopher Carson, developed a detailed marketing strategy for a proposed brand he called Kelly's Revenge, which he believed would fit well in a market niche for a fun product appealing to young people. When his proposal was rejected in favor of an Australian-originated idea for an environmentally conscious brand called Banrock Station, Carson was disappointed but recognized his responsibility to put his organization's full efforts behind the new global roll-out. With that commitment, Banrock Station eventually became the top-selling wine brand in the UK.

Top-Level Corporate Management

Nowhere are the challenges facing management more extreme than at the top of an organization that is evolving toward becoming a transnational. Not only must these senior executives integrate and provide direction for the diverse management groups we have described but, in order to succeed, they must do so while redefining many of the norms and traditions that had traditionally framed the top management role.

Historically, as increasingly complex hierarchical structures forced top management further and further from the frontlines of their businesses, in many companies its role became bureaucratized in a rising sea of systems, committees, and staff reports. As layers of management slowed decision making and the corporate headquarters role of coordination and support evolved to one of control and interference, top management's attention was often distracted from the external demands of customers and competitive pressures and began to focus internally on an increasingly bureaucratic process.

The transnational organization of today cannot afford to operate in this way. Like executives at all levels of the organization, top management must add value, which means liberating rather than constraining the organization below them. For those at the top, this means more than just creating management groups to represent business, functional, and geographic perspectives and assigning them specific roles and responsibilities. It also means maintaining the organizational legitimacy of each group, balancing and integrating their often divergent influences, and maintaining a unifying sense of purpose and direction in the face of often conflicting needs and priorities.[4]

This constant balancing and integrating role is perhaps the most vital aspect of a top-level executive's job. It is reflected in the tensions these managers continually feel – between ensuring long-term viability and achieving short-term results, or between providing a clear overall corporate direction and leaving sufficient room for experimentation.

The three core top management tasks we highlight here reflect these tensions. The first focuses on the key role of providing long-term direction and purpose. In some ways, this role is counterbalanced by the second, which highlights the need to achieve current results by leveraging performance. The third core top management task is subtler. It focuses on ensuring continual renewal by drawing the organization's attention again to long-term needs, but simultaneously challenging those directions and priorities. We explore each of these key top management tasks in the following paragraphs.

Providing Direction and Purpose

In a well-functioning transnational organization built around multidimensional strategic capabilities and competing management perspectives, the embedded diversity and internal tension creates a free market of competing ideas and generates a powerful source of individual and group motivation. But without strong top management leadership, these same strong centrifugal forces can pull the company apart. This makes the conception of a common vision of the future and a shared set of values a vital top management task. In doing so, it can, in effect, create a corporate lightning rod to capture otherwise disparate and diffused sources of energy and channel them toward powering a single company engine.

---

[4] B. B. Nielsen and S. Nielsen, "Top management team nationality diversity and firm performance: a multilevel study," *Strategic Management Journal*, **34**:3 (2013), 373–82.

This study combined upper echelons theory with institutional theory, to establish a new dimension of top management team diversity – nationality diversity – and develop an integrated multilevel framework explaining how its performance implications vary across contextual settings. Nationality diversity was positively related to performance; and this effect was stronger in (a) longer tenured teams, (b) highly internationalized firms, and (c) munificent environments.

There are a few key characteristics of a strategic vision that distinguish it from a catchy but ineffective public relations slogan. First, the vision must be clear – and here simplicity, relevance, and continuous reinforcement are the key. NEC's long-held strategy recognizing the importance of integrating computers and communications – its C&C philosophy – is a good example of how clarity can make a vision powerful and effective. For almost four decades, NEC's top management has applied the C&C concept so completely and effectively that it is understood not only to describe the company's enduring vision, but also to define its distinctive source of competitive advantage over more entrenched companies such as IBM and AT&T. Throughout the company, the many rich interpretations of C&C have been deeply embedded and are both understood and believed.

Second, continuity of a vision can provide direction and purpose. Despite shifts in leadership and continual adjustments in short-term business priorities, top management must remain committed to the company's core set of strategic objectives and organizational values. Without such continuity, the unifying vision takes on the transitory characteristics of the annual budget or quarterly targets – and engenders about as much organizational enthusiasm. Since first being articulated in 1977, NEC's concept of C&C has remained at the core of the company's strategy, and is now embodied into its well-articulated underlying corporate philosophy.

Third, in communicating the vision and strategic direction, it is critical that top management establish consistency across organizational units – in other words, to ensure that the vision is shared by all. The cost of inconsistency can be horrendous. At a minimum, it can result in confusion and inefficiency; at the extreme, it can lead individuals and organizational units to pursue agendas that are mutually debilitating.

Leveraging Corporate Performance

Although the persistent priorities of aligning the company's resources, capabilities, and commitments to achieve long-term objectives is vital, to remain viable among competitors and credible with stakeholders top management must also achieve results in the short term. Top management's key role in this task is to provide the controls, support, and coordination to leverage resources and capabilities to their highest level of performance.

In doing so, the leaders of transnational companies must abandon old notions of control that often saw their role reduced to routine tasks such as monitoring and responding to below-budget financial results. Today's most effective top managers rely much more on control mechanisms that are personal and proactive. In discussions with each management group, they ensure that its responsibilities are understood in relation to the overall goal, and that strategic and operational priorities are clearly identified and agreed upon. They set demanding standards and use frequent informal visits to discuss operations and quickly identify new problems or opportunities.

When such problems or opportunities are identified, the old model of top-down interference is replaced by one driven by corporate-level support. Having created an organization staffed by experts and specialists, the most successful transnational top managers resist the temptation to send in the "headquarters experts" to take charge at the first sign of difficulty. Far more effective is an approach of delegating clear responsibilities, backing those responsibilities with rewards that align them with the corporate goals, then supporting the relevant management group with the resources, specialized expertise, and other forms of support necessary to succeed.

As top management tries to leverage the overall performance of the corporation, perhaps the most challenging task it faces is to coordinate the activities of an organization deliberately designed around diverse perspectives and responsibilities. As we described in Chapter 4, there are three basic cross-organizational flows that must be carefully managed – the flows of goods, resources, and information – and each demands a different means of coordination. We described how goods flows can normally be routinized and managed through formal systems and procedures, a process we characterized as *formalization*. In contrast, decisions involving the allocation of scarce resources – capital allocation and key personnel assignments, for example – are usually ones in which top management wants to be involved directly and personally, a process we called *centralization*. And flows of information and knowledge are most effectively generated and diffused through the management of personal contacts in a process we described as *socialization*.

These three flows are the lifeblood of any company, and any organization's ability to make them more efficient and effective depends on top management's ability to develop a rich portfolio of coordinative processes we described in Chapter 4. By balancing the formalization, centralization, and socialization processes, they can fully exploit the company's assets and resources, and greatly leverage its performance.

Ensuring Continual Renewal

Despite the enormous value of both of these top management roles, if pursued to the extreme, either can result in a company's long-term demise. A fixation on an outmoded long-term mission can be just as dangerous as a preoccupation with short-term performance – since emphasis in either can focus management only on maintaining a company's ongoing current performance. The risk is that successful strategies can become elevated to the status of unquestioned wisdom and effective organizational processes become institutionalized as embedded routines. As strategies and processes ossify, management loses its flexibility. Eventually, the organization sees its role as protecting its past heritage.

It is top management's role to prevent this ossification from occurring, and there are several important ways it can ensure that the organization moves beyond just reinventing its past, and sees its challenge as continually renewing itself. First, top management must ensure the organization's external orientation by constantly reinforcing the need to focus on customers and to benchmark against the best competitors. For example, when Jin Zhiguo became the president of China's massive

Tsingtao Brewery Company Ltd, he felt the company had become too self-satisfied and inwardly focused. As his first priority, Jin immediately began implementing internal reforms to encourage management to challenge conventional wisdom and focus on the company's significant external competitive challenges. As he noted, "Tsingtao Brewery has been an arrogant company. We must have an open mind and learn from other companies. Only a strong learning ability will lead to powerful innovations."

An equally important top management role is to constantly question, challenge, and change things in a way that forces adaptation and learning. It is by creating a "dynamic imbalance" among those with different objectives that top management can prevent a myopic strategic posture from developing. It is a delicate process requiring a great deal of time to prevent it from degenerating into internal anarchy or corporate politics. But as Steve Jobs exhibited when he regained the leadership position of Apple in 1997, it's a skill that can turn around the company. Through his ability to question, to push, and, above all, to challenge, Jobs created the necessary internal dynamic imbalance that turned Apple from a loss-making company with a shrinking worldwide market share into a market-sensitive, technology-driven global dynamo.

Third, top management can ensure renewal by defining the corporate mission and values so that they provide some strategic stretch and maneuverability while simultaneously legitimizing innovative new initiatives. More than this, those at the top must monitor the process of dynamic imbalance they have created in order to identify and support the most promising entrepreneurial experimentation and challenges to the status quo that emerge from the deliberately created instability. The champion of such adaptation must be Nokia, a company that started its life in the nineteenth century as a forestry-based paper mill company. In the post-World War II era, it diversified into electric cable production, which in turn led it to become a television set manufacturer. Then, in the 1990s, it evolved into a global mobile phone company – an impressive final transformation that led to decades of success in markets around the world.

CONCLUDING COMMENTS

Having earlier focused on the changing nature of the business environment, the conflicting strategic imperatives facing the MNE, and the organizational model needed to implement them, in this chapter we shifted the level of analysis down to the level of the individual manager. We examined the new roles of three groups of managers – those responsible for a global business (e.g., a product SBU or division), a worldwide function (e.g., finance, marketing, or technology), and a geographic territory (e.g., a country or region). And to understand how these diverse roles and responsibilities were reconciled, we reviewed the role of top-level corporate management in integrating and providing direction for these three groups.

These new roles and responsibilities are challenging to implement, primarily because they require managers to rethink many of their traditional assumptions about the nature of their work. Indeed, this is ultimately the biggest challenge facing the transnational organization – to create a generation of managers that have the requisite skills and the sense of perspective needed to operate in a multibusiness, multifunctional, multinational system.

HARVARD | BUSINESS | SCHOOL   REV: FEBRUARY 26, 2013

BRIEF CASES

Christopher A. Bartlett and Arar Han

CASE 7.1 LEVENDARY CAFÉ: THE CHINA CHALLENGE

HBS Professor Christopher A. Bartlett and writer Arar Han prepared this case solely as a basis for class discussion and not as an endorsement, a source of primary data, or an illustration of effective or ineffective management. This case, though based on real events, is fictionalized, and any resemblance to actual persons or entities is coincidental. There are some references to actual companies in the narration.

Levendary Café was spun out from private equity ownership in January 2011, and the following month, Mia Foster was named as its new CEO. The departing CEO, Howard Leventhal, was the beloved founder of the popular chain of 3,500 cafés. He had grown a small Denver soup, salad, and sandwich restaurant into a $10 billion business, but after 32 years was moving on to new interests.

This was Foster's first job as CEO. Previously, the 47-year-old had been president of the U.S. business of a large American fast food company for seven years. She had started her career at a major global accounting firm, leaving to earn an MBA from Wharton. Upon graduation, she had become a consultant at McKinsey before taking a job in product management at P&G, where she worked her way up the ranks. Foster was known for her frank communication style and strong execution.

In spite of the promise held by the Levendary brand and Foster's strong track record, Wall Street was cautious about the stock. While the company's fundamentals were strong and its performance generally in line with management forecasts, its shares traded at a discount to comparable restaurant stocks. There were two reasons for this. First, analysts were concerned that Levendary's domestic business was nearly tapped out. Second, given Foster's lack of previous international management experience, they were skeptical of her ability to build a multi-national brand.

Foster felt challenged by Wall Street's skepticism and wanted to address it head-on. In particular, she knew that Levendary's recent entry into the fast-growing China market would be closely watched. So she was concerned by reports that recently opened China locations incorporated some dramatic departures from Levendary's

U.S. concept, particularly in store design and menu selection. She was also frustrated by the apparent unwillingness of Louis Chen, Leventhal's hand-picked president of Levendary China, to conform to the company's planning and reporting processes. To address these concerns, Foster decided she needed to visit the Chinese operations.

On May 25, 2011, Foster stepped out of the limo that Chen had arranged to pick her up at the Shanghai Pudong airport. Heading in to her first in-person meeting with Chen, she knew there were big decisions to be made. Indeed, they would determine the future of Levendary China.

The Multi-Unit Restaurant Business

In 2010, the U.S. restaurant and contract food-service industry was a $600 billion industry with 960,000 locations.[1] Multi-unit restaurant concepts represented approximately 30% of the industry by units, with independent operators as the balance. The restaurant and foodservice industry was highly fragmented, and even industry giant McDonald's generated just 2% of total revenues.

Multi-unit concepts were generally categorized into three industry segments:

- **Specialty Establishments** like Starbucks, Dunkin' Donuts, and Baskin-Robbins primarily served snacks and beverages under $5.
- **Quick Service Restaurants**, or so-called "fast food" concepts like McDonald's, Taco Bell, and Wendy's, provided counter or drive-through service with average tickets between $4 and $10.
- **Casual Dining** included brands like Olive Garden, Applebee's, and Outback, and offered table service for dinner entrees priced between $8 and $20. Within this group, fine dining concepts like Ruth's Chris and Capital Grille featured entrées into the $40 range.

While some concepts had bridged these categories for years (e.g., Friendly's offered casual dining coupled with a strong takeaway ice cream business), more recently several concepts had clustered around an emerging category often called "Quick Casual." For example, Panda Express was a quick service format of Chinese casual dining, while Chipotle offered a quick casual Mexican-American dining experience. Like other quick casual restaurants, Levendary promised more wholesome choices than its quick service cousins and a more informal self-serve dining experience than its casual dining relatives. Quick casual restaurants typically had average checks in the $8 to $12 range.

Restaurant Cost Structure

Restaurants had relatively simple cost structures which one industry expert defined as follows:[2]

- **Occupancy:** These costs included real estate rental, common area maintenance, and energy and waste disposal. In the United States, they hovered around 10% of revenues.
- **Labor:** Even at minimum wage, labor was typically the largest cost element. High turnover in the industry required restaurant companies to continually source and train new employees and to manage employee attrition. Labor typically represented 25% to 35% of total revenues.
- **Food:** Food costs accounted for 28% to 32%. This expense was influenced by not only the cost of the ingredients purchased, but also the amount of waste.
- **Supply:** About 1% to 4% of revenues typically went to paper products at quick service restaurants or to linen and uniform cleaning at higher-end casual dining restaurants.

In a best case scenario, a restaurant might make up to 35% gross margin, but 20% to 25% was more typical. Franchised restaurants also paid a royalty, adding a 3% to 6% cost line, and a marketing fee which added a further 2% to 10% in costs. Depending on the size of the franchise organization, overhead might account for another 5% to 15% of cost.

---

[1] "Freedonia Focus on Restaurants," *Freedonia Group.* February 2011.

[2] http://www.bakertilly.com/userfiles/BT_Retail_ RestaurantBenchmarks_web_small.pdf.

Exhibit 1 Levendary Organizational Chart

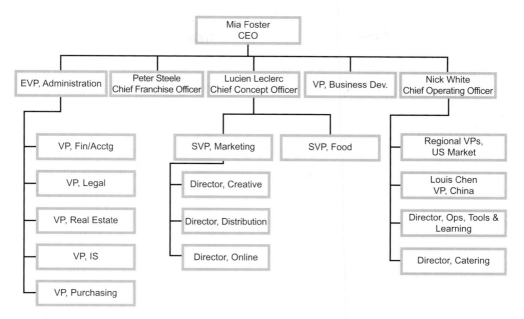

Restaurants typically operated on razor-thin margins, with profitability a direct function of their ability to generate high traffic, execute consistently, and control costs. Traffic, in turn, was a function of the brand's appeal, marketing effectiveness, real estate location, and store experience.

Levendary Café: The Foundations

In the quick casual restaurant segment, Levendary Café was distinguished by two elements: wholesome soups, salads, and sandwiches using high-quality ingredients, and a commitment to service in a comfortable, friendly environment. Its corporate chefs were highly trained artisans from the Culinary Institute of America and other top cooking schools who took pride in creating everyday versions of gourmet fare. Customers raved, "Eating at Levendary makes me feel rich."

Levendary was also distinguished by its willingness to take risks, especially those that helped evolve its concept over time. It was an entrepreneurial characteristic traced to founder Howard Leventhal. The most recent risky change occurred five years before Foster became CEO, when the company decided to use only organic grains in its breads and hormone-free naturally raised meats in its sandwiches. To management's delight, customers willingly paid the premium price, resulting in increased revenues and margins and a simultaneous boost in customer trust in the brand.

The Organizational Foundation: Blending Concepts and Operations

A complex organization supported Levendary's primarily U.S. business. The Denver headquarters housed the following activities (see **Exhibit 1** for a basic organizational chart):

- **Concept:** For 23 years, Howard Leventhal had relied on Chief Concept Officer (CCO) Lucian Leclerc to keep Levendary a top U.S. restaurant concept. Leclerc managed both the food development group and the marketing team that together determined what Levendary represented to the customer. With Leclerc's uncanny ability to sense nascent food trends and Leventhal's willingness to take calculated risks, the pair had kept the company at the forefront of changing tastes. Their shared commitment to healthful, wholesome eating was embedded in the company's culture and reflected in its well-known advertising slogan "Tasty Fresh Goodness" or TFG as insiders referred to it.

- **Marketing:** The Marketing group reported to the CCO. Its creative team worked with outside advertising agencies to convey the TFG concept through advertising copy and images. The logo, store decor, and media images used a palette of earth tones to communicate natural, wholesome goodness. The distribution team ensured that banners, table tents, window decals, and menu boards were properly placed in all 3,500 company and franchised stores, appropriately modified for differences in store size and layout. Preparing menus and menu boards was complicated by variations in menu items to respond to local market preferences and by pricing differences to meet local competition. But the comfortable, welcoming, and homey "look and feel" of stores always remained consistent.

- **Food:** A fully scaled test kitchen and food science laboratory also reported to the CCO, taking the items developed by the CCO's executive chefs and making the adaptations necessary to supply their components with quality and consistency to each of Levendary' 3,500 cafés. The food team was also responsible for conducting quality checks in the field.

- **Operations:** Led by Chief Operating Officer (COO) Nick White, who had 30 years of operating experience in U.S. franchised restaurant companies, this group managed the day-to-day restaurant business. Store managers at the 1,200 company-owned cafés reported to district managers, who in turn reported in to area directors, then market vice presidents. This structure allowed tight control of store level expenses and close monitoring of operations against the company's detailed and strict operating standards, policies, and practices. It also relayed any recommendations for modifications to the menu or variations in the store "look and feel" to the Concept group for consideration and approval.

Operations was also responsible for Operating Tools and Learning (OTL). As retail employees were often high school-aged or minimally educated, OTL set operating standards and provided materials to enhance employees' learning. Acting as a bridge between the Concept team and the stores, OTL also developed the training materials and processes to break down food preparation into steps that ensured quality local delivery of the chefs' gourmet creations. In general, OTL functioned as both an internal school and a standards enforcer.

- **Franchise:** About two-thirds of Levendary's 3,500 stores were franchised. Headed by Chief Franchise Officer Peter Steele, the franchise team recruited new franchisees, supported existing franchisees, and enforced brand and operating standards in franchised stores.

- **Business Development:** Staffed by former strategy consultants, this department sourced new revenue opportunities such as Levendary branded grocery items like coffee, cold cuts, and soups. This group also led research for the company's nascent international expansion and was responsible for an experimental licensing deal in Dubai. Launched in 2009, this opportunistic venture was run by a Saudi Arabian restaurant company owned by an old friend of Leventhal's. Aside from China, Dubai was Levendary's only international operation.

- **Administrative Staff Groups:** Real estate, finance and accounting, legal, purchasing, and information systems all reported to an Executive Vice President (EVP) of Administration.

Headquarters staff totaled approximately 300 in all. There was no separate international division.

The Strategic Base: Serving the U.S. Market

Levendary was built on a culture that emphasized "delighting the customer." As founder, Howard Leventhal was fond of telling store staff, "Forget

Exhibit 2
Levendary Income Statement 2010 (dollars in 000s)

	Year Ending December 31, 2010
Revenues	
Sales	9,248,134
Royalties	603,365
Ingredient & paper good sales to franchisees	945,924
Total	10,797,423
Costs and Expenses	
Food & Paper	2,623,712
Labor	2,933,980
Occupancy	706,790
Total	6,264,482
Food and paper good inventory	776,902
Depreciation and amortization	480,711
G&A	710,458
Marketing	1,239,413
Pre-opening expenses	29,974
Total costs and expenses	3,237,458
Operating profit	1,295,483
Interest expense	4,725
Other expense	29,624
Income before tax	1,261,134
Income tax	480,571
Net income	**780,563**

today's profit. Have a positive impact on customers' lives. Make them want to come back. That's how we'll win in the long run." Day-to-day, this philosophy translated into a personalized approach that would accommodate customer requests such as removing sprouts from a sandwich or serving a soup extra hot. Such service appealed to Levendary's customer base of white-collar professionals and upper-middle-class women. "Heavy user" customers in these groups visited Levendary five or six times a week.

But this approach taxed Levendary's store-level operations. The two key store operating metrics of speed of service and order accuracy were driven by standardization, and personalization threatened both. In response to store operators who questioned his relentless drive to provide personal service,

Leventhal would simply point to the company's impressive results. (See **Exhibit 2**.)

Leventhal's philosophy of delighting the customer also translated into local menu adaptions. With stores in urban, suburban, and rural environments across all 50 states, Levendary believed there was no such thing as "the American consumer." While McDonald's created one menu for its entire system, Levendary was more flexible. It offered fewer soup items and more drink options in the South, allowed one or two regional specialties to be added to its core menu, and listed its menu items in order of local popularity. While appreciated by customers, the menu variations represented a challenge for the Food, Operations, and Marketing teams.

To keep the brand fresh in the eyes of the customer, the company was also committed to evolving menu choices, typically by featuring in-trend healthy ingredients like pomegranates or quinoa. The Concept team rolled out a suite of new products five times a year, often with minor variants adapted to the South's appetite for fat-tier, sweeter formulations, or the Northeast's love of turkey and cheddar cheese. Each new release was accompanied by a marketing program and new menu boards.

In truth, the new items boosted the company's image more than its sales. Systemwide sales were driven by a small number of core items. For 80% of locations, those included such Levendary clas-sics as its turkey and avocado sandwich with cranberry dressing, its award-winning cheese soup, and its chicken Caesar salad. For the other 20% of outlets, the core sales drivers could be as diverse as espresso beverages, Howard's Famous Cookies, or a local seasonal special.

Expanding Abroad: China Dreams

In 2008, the company's domestic growth was slowing. Its geographic expansion strategy (jok-ingly referred to within the company as "follow the mommies," later adapted to "follow the yuppies") had plateaued. Recognizing that its concept did not translate well into small towns, particularly in the Midwest and South, the board of directors began discussions about overseas expansion. At the board's urging, management instructed its strategy team to research opportunities in China, a market that had attracted a great deal of atten-tion among U.S. restaurant companies.

Opportunities in China

With a population of 1.4 billion people and annual GDP growth of 14.5% over the past decade, China was ripe for investment. Two add-itional trends attracted U.S. restaurants: China's urban population rose from 36.2% of the total in 2000 to 46.6% in 2009, and a strong middle class emerged whose per capita income surged from RMB 6,282 to RMB 17,175. (In 2010, RMB 1 = USD 0.15.)

An affluent middle class, a large increase of women in the workforce, and a growing lifestyle

trend to eat out all supported growth in the Chi-nese food services industry, which increased from RMB 1.106 trillion in 2004 to RMB 1.996 trillion five years later. Independent full-service restaur-ants still dominated the industry (there were 2,723,000 nationally), but the highly competitive quick service sector was growing the fastest, from RMB 254 billion in 2004 to RMB 471 billion in 2009.

While foreign fast food companies attracted the most attention, restaurants serving Asian food, primarily Chinese, took the biggest share of the quick service segment. These mostly independent restaurants appealed to locals' preference for rice-based dishes and low prices. However, due to low margins, wide variation in regional food tastes, and most of all, the difficulty independents had experienced in standardizing operations, there were few successful local chains.

The most successful foreign fast food chain was KFC, which had more than 3,000 restaurants in 450 Chinese cities. In 2010 KFC opened on average one new store every day. Through its Chinese joint venture partners and local manage-ment, it had learned to adapt. It added a few items such as congee rice porridge and even altered the famous seasoning on its core fried chicken offering.

McDonald's entered China in 1992, five years after KFC, and by 2010 operated 1,100 restaur-ants in 110 cities. Its restaurants retained a con-sistent worldwide look and feel, and a menu featuring its Big Mac, McNuggets, and french fries. While its core menu was the same, localized specials such as the China Mac with black pepper sauce, pork burgers, and red bean ice cream had been added. Despite the fact that a plate of six pork buns cost 25 cents at a Chinese street stall, McDonald still charged $2.50 for its large fries, appealing to Chinese youth's willingness to indulge in foreign fare.

Pizza Hut's China strategy was notable for its departure from its U.S. original. Its 560 outlets were positioned as high-end casual dining res-taurants, and its menu extended well beyond pizza to include scallop croquettes and escargot. Wine was served, reservations were accepted, and a 45-minute wait for a table was not uncommon.

Young affluent Chinese went to Pizza Hut to impress their dates.

Despite these successes, many other American restaurants had struggled in China. When Applebee's replanted itself in Shanghai, the concept fizzled. So too did California Pizza Kitchen, forcing the founders to personally intervene to relaunch the effort. Many attributed Pretzel Time's failure in China to its white tile décor that reminded people of a bathroom.

More recently, Chinese chains had begun to learn from foreign competition and began to focus on standardization and tight control of raw materials, food preparation, and in-store service. After overtaking McDonald's as Hong Kong's leading chain, Dar Jia Le ("*Big Happy House*") took its tightly controlled operations to China. Other successful Asian chains in China included U.S.-listed Country Style Cooking (2009 Chinese sales of $495 million) serving Sichuan food, Hong Kong-based Little Sheep ($235 million) featuring Mongolian hot pot, and Japan's Ajisen ($256 million) ramen shops.

Leaping into China

After reviewing the research, Levendary's board and top management decided to enter China. The decision was hastened by the appearance of Louis Chen as a viable candidate to lead the effort. Chen heard about Levendary's interest in China through a Stanford MBA classmate who had become a partner at the private equity firm that had owned the company prior to its 2011 IPO. Chen gradually earned the confidence of CEO Leventhal and other key stakeholders. In time, Leventhal dropped his original idea of a joint venture with an established Chinese operator, and entrusted Levendary China to Chen, whose energy and entrepreneurial spirit reminded him of an earlier version of himself.

Chen's formal contract provided a two-year term starting in September 2009 with an option for annual renewal, but his relationship with the company was best described as a handshake agreement. While Chen formally reported to Leventhal, the CEO managed him with a very light touch. He asked Chen to establish a strong market position as a base for franchising outlets throughout China, but apart from a requirement to "do right by the concept," gave him broad latitude to execute.

To prepare for his assignment, Chen became a rotational intern in each of the major departments in Levendary's Denver headquarters as well as in a handful of stores. Over six weeks, his mandate was to pick up as much as he could and replicate it in China. The Denver team invited him to tap into their resources and expertise, interpreting and adapting them for use in the local Chinese stores. Before his departure for China, the board asked Chen about his plans. He was confident:

> It won't be easy but others have succeeded and we can too. I believe we have a good chance of building a credible foundation of stores and breaking even within a year. We just have to be flexible. For example, Chinese eat few dairy products, so we should downplay our cheese soup. But a new generation now gives milk to its children, so tastes are evolving. And most people aren't familiar with turkey, but they love chicken, so we'll adapt the menu, just as we do in the States. It may take time, but I believe Levendary will connect with Chinese youth, and that's the future.

In spite of the monumental work ahead, the board was convinced that Chen was the right choice. The 34-year-old was bilingual in English and Mandarin Chinese, and his decade-long experience as a retail property developer gave him intimate familiarity with neighborhoods in Shanghai and Beijing–a valuable asset given the powerful impact of store location on profitability. Chen also had a network of contacts to help speed up the process of permitting, incorporating, and staffing stores. Finally, he was passionate about good food, and had long wanted to work in the restaurant industry.

Chen opened his first location in the expatriate-heavy Pudong region of Shanghai in January 2010, just three months after returning to China in his new role. Occupying the corner ground floor location of a new high-rise office building, the first restaurant was both prominent and luxurious. It was an instant hit among white-collar employees of the global financial firms housed above it. Taking a page from Pizza Hut's China playbook, Chen positioned the new location as casual dining with table service and higher prices than local fast food concepts. But with the real estate markets in Beijing and Shanghai heating up, and KFC and McDonald's snapping up sites, Chen wanted to move fast. His local knowledge and connections helped him lock in prime locations at good prices, and within a year, his initial location had grown into a chain of 23 restaurants.

Expansion in China: Key Decisions

During her interview process, Foster heard much about the great hopes for Levendary China. However, she had not had the opportunity to meet Chen or to closely examine the China business. When she became CEO in February 2011, the new CEO was surprised to find that the Chinese subsidiary submitted all management and financial reports to Denver in its own format. The finance group then "massaged" them to apply U.S. Generally Accepted Accounting Principles (GAAP) and adapt them to Levendary's internal monthly reporting format. Foster felt strongly that this would not be a sustainable practice as the China operations grew into a larger portion of total revenue.

The First Meeting: Raising the Questions

In considering her options for bringing the China reporting in line with the U.S., Foster favored hiring an international financial analyst for the Denver finance team, and thought Levendary's auditor should also manage the China audit. Both steps were expensive but seemed necessary for a publicly traded company that intended to stake its future on growth in the China market. During a video conference that Foster set up to meet Chen in her first week at Levendary, she shared these thoughts with him. He bristled at her suggestions, claiming that both changes would not only incur unnecessary costs but would also greatly inconvenience his local operations.

Chen's resistance struck Foster as either naïve or antagonistic, and she responded firmly: "You're going to have to make a change, Louis. We have to protect the integrity of our reporting structure." "Fine," Chen shot back. "But to operate here, we have to be compliant with local tax laws or we'll get shut down. If you need those changes, you're going to have to spend the money to set it up right." Saying she would follow up, Foster left the virtual meeting with a nagging feeling that developing a productive relationship with Chen was not going to be easy.

The next day, Foster added the China operations as an agenda item in the weekly executive meeting she held with her direct reports in Denver. The EVP of Administration agreed that using non-GAAP numbers from China in the financial reports was a risk, and that formalizing the reporting process was a necessary change. As the discussion broadened, COO Nick White, the person to whom Chen had reported since Leventhal's departure, spoke up:

> I talk to Louis every week or two. I'm floored by how quickly he got a couple dozen stores up and running. It's an amazing achievement. But the reality is that no senior executive has visited China since Howard officiated at the opening ceremony for the Pudong store a year ago. I'm sure a lot has changed since then, but I haven't been able to get Louis to give me much. Howard gave Louis a lot of freedom to establish the Chinese operations, and frankly, it shows. Louis is a great asset but I confess managing him has been a frustrating exercise.

By the end of the meeting, the executive team had agreed it was time to obtain more information about the China operations. Chief Franchise Officer Peter Steele agreed to conduct a comprehensive review of the 23 Levendary Cafés in that market. White said he would advise Chen of Steele's plans, emphasizing that this was a routine process regularly undertaken in all franchised and licensed cafés in the U.S. market, and that Steele had recently completed such a review in Dubai.

Steele spent 10 days in China, and at a weekly executive meeting in late March, presented his findings. He provided detailed descriptions of the 23 China locations, all in or around Beijing and Shanghai. Chen had taken many liberties with the look and feel of the cafés. While the first location in Pudong largely conformed to Levendary's design standards and menu selection, other locations held surprising and sometimes alarming changes. For example, the second location, located in Shanghai's historic Yu Garden area, was a takeaway counter with no seating. The third location, on Beijing's embassy row, was similar to the first store in both design and offering, but the fourth, at the north entrance to Beijing's Forbidden City, not only had no salads on its menu, it replaced Levendary's classic wooden framed upholstered chairs with a plastic framed alternative from a local furniture supplier. By the opening of the 23rd location in a Korean expatriate-heavy suburb of Shanghai, all but one sandwich item had been removed from the menu, and replaced by a variety of local dumplings.

Immediately after the meeting, an irate Lucian Leclerc appeared in Foster's office. She was not surprised, given his visible agitation during Steele's presentation. "Plastic chairs and dumplings! This is a pure disaster," he exploded. "What's going on in China could destroy everything I've worked for over the past 23 years. Our customers travel a lot, and in one visit to just one of those places, our carefully nurtured concept and image will be ruined. Mia, you need to stop Louis now."

After letting him vent, Foster reassured Leclerc that she would give the issue her full attention. She turned to examine a chart comparing several Levendary locations in the United States and China (Exhibit 3). Inwardly, she knew that resolving this issue would be a big test for her.

Meeting Two: Confronting the Issues

In early April, Foster sent Chen a copy of Steele's findings in advance of a second video conference to which she also invited White. Foster opened the discussion by explaining that China was critical to Levendary's growth, so she wanted to be involved in discussions about its plans. She explained how concerned she and White had been about Steele's report. Chen's response sounded angry:

> I don't think you guys appreciate the difficulty of managing a business in this environment. We've worked like crazy this past year and half. And in a tough market with minimum support from Denver, we've built a business that works in China. But now that we've opened 23 locations in just over a year and are about to turn a profit, you want me to change everything? Why would you do that?
>
> Levendary as it exists in the U.S. simply will not work in China. Have you seen Denny's in Japan? It's wildly successful but it serves *ton-katsu* [a Japanese breaded and fried pork cutlet] and *ramen*. They understand that nobody wants pancakes and BLTs in Tokyo. People want the food they know but with cool American branding.
>
> The only places where we can do what Levendary does in the U.S. are Pudong and Beijing's embassy row. Those locations are up and running using the American model. Everywhere else, we have to adapt our store design and menu. Otherwise, we won't be profitable. I think our performance speaks for itself (Exhibit 4).

Having reviewed the research, Foster was keenly aware of the difficulties of localizing a chain restaurant concept in a foreign market and the major tradeoffs entailed. She was aware that the Japanese company operating Denny's Japan had great success by radically changing its entire menu while keeping the stores' look and feel. But she also knew that the McDonald's approach was much more standardized worldwide. A McDonald's in Shanghai varied from one in New York City only in local marketing practices and some limited menu deletions and insertions. Indeed, Foster had been amazed to learn that McDonald's had even imported bricks to new markets it entered in Eastern Europe so that its restaurants would be as consistent as possible to its U.S. standards.

These were two opposite approaches, and Foster was not sure either model was appropriate

Exhibit 3
Comparison of Two Levendary U.S. and Two Levendary China Locations

	Metro U.S./ NYC	Suburban U.S./ Denver Area	Metro China/ Beijing Embassy	Metro-suburb China/ Shanghai Koreatown
Annualized 2010 sales (USD)	$10,320,000	$2,126,000	$806,000	$288,000
Square footage	2,500	4,000	1,500	500
Seats	84	120	80	0 (counter only)
Staff (full-time equivalent)	24	26	20	13
Average traffic (guests per day)	3,210	560	260	430
Average check (USD)	$15	$12	$10	$2
Top 5 menu items	Turkey sand. Cheese soup Salmon salad Chicken sand. Caesar salad	Denver Melt sand. Cheese soup Turkey sand. Caesar salad Howard's cookie	Chicken soup Chicken sand. Roast beef sand. BBQ chicken sand. Thai veggie soup	Chicken dumpling Pork dumpling Chicken sand. BBQ chicken sand. Pu-erh tea
Outdoor seating?		Yes	Yes	
Personalized service?	Yes	Yes	(simplified table service)	
Free WiFi?	Yes	Yes	Yes	

for Levendary. She had yet to be convinced by Chen's assertion that growth in China required that the stores and menus be as different as they had become, and responded carefully:

Louis, I think Peter's report gives us a good starting point to think about that issue going forward. You've provided us a great platform for our future growth in China. Now it's time for us to think through how we want to do that. The home office will probably need to step up and do more to support you. We'll also have to ensure the Levendary brand is positioned for growth, and that will require some consistency across borders. Nick and I will both commit to working with you to support your efforts. But we first need to fully understand your strategic plan for growth in China.

A more conciliatory-sounding Chen responded:

Mia, you speak from a place of ideas, best practices, and compliance. But I'm here in the trenches running 23 restaurants that I've built one by one by reading market needs and sensing opportunities. I'm proud of Levendary's presence here. When you send in headquarters analysts and start telling me things need to change, I don't think you have a good sense of what it took to get us to where we are.

You asked me about my strategic plan. Well I don't have one. And frankly, if I'd had one, I don't think we would have grown so quickly because we wouldn't have been as nimble or responded as flexibly to market needs. I'm willing to work with you to make some changes. But understand that I was given free

Exhibit 4
Levendary China Income Statement (2010)

	Year Ending October 31, 2010
Sales (US$)	$ 3,261,598
Costs and Expenses	
Food & Paper	1,663,415
Labor	382,720
Occupancy	782,784
Total	2,828,919
Depreciation and amortization	6,523
G&A	163,080
Marketing	65,232
Pre-opening expenses	391,392
Total costs and expenses	3,455,145
Operating profit	-193,547
Interest expense	0
Other expense	5,925
Income before tax	-199,472
Income tax	-55,852
Net income	**-143,620**

rein for 18 months. If you start putting in new controls and tying local operations to the home office, I can't be held responsible if growth slows. If you make changes, we'll need to be very clear about what I'm responsible for, and what can I expect from Denver.

Foster found herself annoyed at what she sensed to be Chen's continued resistance and negative attitude. But there was no time for that now. Thoughts racing, she thanked Chen for his candor and expressed a desire to visit China to see in person what he had built, and also to finally meet him face-to-face. Chen welcomed her planned visit and offered his sympathy for the pressure she must be feeling from Wall Street. "Mia, I love what I'm doing, and I hope we can work things out. I really want to stay on when my contract expires in a few months," he said.

After ending the video conference, Foster reviewed the exchange with White. The conversation had raised some big issues that needed to

be resolved: What strategy should Levendary adopt to drive its expansion in China? Who should have responsibility to make and implement those decisions? And what changes, if any, should be made in the roles, responsibilities, and relationships that linked China's management team to the home office? Acknowledging the importance of these issues, White agreed it was vital for Foster to get closer to the China business. A visit was set for May.

Meeting Three: Deciding the Future

On May 25, as her plane landed at Shanghai's Pudong International Airport, Foster felt a mix of excitement and concern. She was thrilled to finally visit this market that held such great potential for the Levendary brand and for her new role as CEO. But she was also grappling with some nagging doubts about whether Chen was right person for the job.

An old mentor had once told Foster that there were three types of managers in a new business's evolution to greater scale: the go-getter, the local baron, and the professional manager. All three types could be entrepreneurial in spirit, but not all were equally well suited for the various stages of a business's growth. Chen was clearly a go-getter who had evolved to become a local baron. The question in Foster's mind was whether he could transition to become a professional manager.

Two hours later, Mia Foster got out of the limousine that Louis Chen had arranged to pick her up at the airport. As she strode toward the entrance of Levendary's Shanghai office, she felt confident and prepared. Foster was ready for this conversation.

H A R V A R D │ B U S I N E S S │ S C H O O L   REV: MARCH 8, 2017

Christopher A. Bartlett

CASE 7.2 UNILEVER'S LIFEBUOY IN INDIA: IMPLEMENTING THE SUSTAINABILITY PLAN

Emeritus Professor Christopher A. Bartlett prepared this case. It was reviewed and approved before publication by a company designate. Funding for the development of this case was provided by Harvard Business School and not by the company. Certain details have been disguised. HBS cases are developed solely as the basis for class discussion. Cases are not intended to serve as endorsements, sources of primary data, or illustrations of effective or ineffective management.

In early 2013, Samir Singh faced a challenge—in fact, a double challenge. When he was named Global Brand VP for Lifebuoy soap in early 2010, this iconic Unilever brand was suffering. Its global market share had fallen from 11.2% in 2005 to 9.7% in 2009. In India, its largest market, the situation was even worse: its 2009 share had dropped to 15.5% from 18.4% four years earlier. But just as Singh and his team managed to reverse the decline, his boss challenged them to double sales in five years.

As large as this task was, it was made even more demanding by another commitment Singh had made—to improve the health and hygiene of a billion people by 2015. This ambitious goal was part of the Unilever Sustainable Living Program (USLP), an initiative introduced by the company's newly appointed CEO, Paul Polman. Aiming to decouple Unilever's growth from its impact on earth, USLP challenged the company to halve the environmental footprint of its products, to source 100% of its agricultural raw materials sustainably, and to help improve the health and well-being of a billion people worldwide. Singh's challenge was to make Lifebuoy the standard-bearer of this last goal while simultaneously doubling sales and meeting ambitious profit objectives. It would be quite a test.

Unilever's History, Lifebuoy's Heritage

Despite an uneven performance in recent decades, by 2012 Unilever had reemerged as a very effective global competitor challenging

Exhibit 1
Unilever Financial Performance, 1990–2012 ($ millions)

	2012	2011	2010	2005	2000	1995	1990
Unilever							
Revenues	67,669.6	60,366.4	59,352.3	45,488.0	44,694.7	45,651.4	39,620.0
Europe	18,299.2	17,529.1	17,753.9	17,697.2	17,816.1		24,169.0
Americas	22,530.2	19,812.9	19,526.7	15,611.2	27,790.8		8,247.0
Developing Countries	26,840.3	23,024.4	22,071.7	12,179.6	16,640.6		7,204.0
Earnings from continuing operations	6,376.2	5,834.4	6,165.6	3,950.5	1,239.9	2,066.3	3,650.0
Loss from discontinued operations	-	-	-	(758.1)	-	(361.4)	-
Net earnings	5,759.1	5,352.4	5,690.9	4,461.0	1,037.9	2,325.4	2,081.0
Dividends declared	(3,558.6)	(3,228.3)	(3,115.0)	(2,136.9)	(1,320.7)	(970.7)	(3,172.0)
Earned on average shareholder's equity	5,758.7	5,519.7	5,693.5	3,884.3	996.2	2,277.7	2,138.4
Per share: (US$)							
Net earnings	$2.04	$1.9	$2.02	$1.53	$0.34	$0.77	
Net earnings-diluted	$1.98	$1.84	$1.96	$1.48	$0.33	$0.75	
Dividends declared	$1.25	$1.21	$1.11	$0.78	$0.43	$0.28	
Stock price range (US$)							
High	$39.45	$34.32	$32.29	$23.58	$19.02	$11.47	$7.43
Low	$30.87	$28.79	$25.75	$20.23	$11.86	$9.91	$5.55
Total assets of continuing operations (Current assets)	16,443.0	18,886.7	17,232.1	13,508.2	16,537.7	15,807.0	13,434.7
Long-term borrowings	9,727.7	9,990.3	9,479.0	7,648.7	12,273.2	3,406.4	3,394.9
Shares outstanding-average (in thousands)	2,997.8	2,966.1	2,879.4	2,791.7	2,820.4	2,831.8	
Employees at year-end: (in thousands)							
Europe	35	35	29	41	80	101	114
Americas	43	42	40	47	39	29	35
Developing Countries	94	92	96	118	176	178	155
Total employees	172	169	165	206	295	308	304

Source: Capital IQ, ThomsonOne (accessed 4/29/14) and company financial statements.
Researcher: E. McCaffrey, Baker Research Services

companies like Procter & Gamble and Nestlé for a share of the fast-moving consumer goods (FMCG) industry. (For financial results, see **Exhibit 1**.) But its business and management philosophies still had deep roots in the company's origins.

Lifebuoy's Origins: Born of a Company with a Conscience

Born in the north of England in 1851 at the height of the Industrial Revolution, William Hesketh Lever grew up in an era when Britain's squalid urban environments were a breeding ground for typhoid, cholera, and smallpox. In his early 20s, he left a thriving family grocery store to start his own business making soap, a product he felt could help ameliorate the wretched conditions.

In 1888, Lever built Port Sunlight as a model village for employees working at his nearby Sunlight soap factory. By today's values, Port Sunlight would be viewed as paternalistic, but at the time, it was celebrated as a benevolent offering of a generous employer. Lever expressed strong ideals for his fledgling Lever Brothers Ltd.: "I believe that nothing can be greater than a business, however small it may be, that is governed by conscience," he said. "And that nothing can be meaner or more petty than a business, however large, governed without honesty and without brotherhood."

The philosophy gave rise to Lever's conviction that business success went hand-in-hand with ethical practices and a sense of social responsibility. He believed that if he took care of his workers, they would be more productive, and if he sold innovative products that benefited the public, the business would prosper. It was a philosophy he described as "doing well by doing good."

These values were evident at the birth of the company's iconic Lifebuoy soap in 1894. Lever held that Joseph Lister's discovery of antiseptic properties in carbolic acid offered a solution to the disease rampant in Britain's grimy urban centers. At a time when soap was still regarded as a luxury, he introduced Lifebuoy at a price the working class could afford. Within a year, he was exporting his "soap that could save lives" to the United States and much of the British Empire.

Managing Global Expansion: New Strategic and Organizational Challenges

In 1930, seeking sourcing economies for their common raw material of palm oil, Lever Brothers and Dutch margarine producer Margarine Unie merged to create a new company called Unilever. As the company expanded abroad, it managed its offshore operations through a classic geographic organization in which strong, independent, national operating companies (referred to internally as Opcos) held prime responsibility. Opco country managers typically had the final decision on key issues, while business and product groups played support and advisory roles.

But as competitive forces demanded new technologies, distribution systems, and marketing skills, the need for more cross-market, product-based coordination became clear. Over the following four decades, Unilever struggled to retain the Opcos' historic local responsiveness while also capturing these regional- and global-scale efficiencies. In the process, it developed a complex multilayered organization structure that made flexible decision-making difficult. By the end of the 20th century, the company had come to be regarded as a formidable but slow-moving giant in the FMCG industry.

100-Year-Old Lifebuoy Enters 21st-Century India

In 1995, as Lifebuoy celebrated its 100th-year anniversary on the Indian market, the familiar red, carbolic soap brick was the country's leading health soap. But its age was beginning to show.

Marketplace Upheavals: Threat or Opportunity?

In 2000, after a decade of rapid growth, the Indian economy stalled and its FMCG market ground to a halt. In 2001, total demand in the personal soap market declined 9.3%.[1] Aggressive new local competitors began offering attractive beauty soaps, particularly in the lower-priced segment where Lifebuoy had long been dominant. The result was that Lifebuoy became seen as a cheap old-fashioned soap, and its market share fell from 15.4% in 1997 to 12.1% in 2001.[2]

---

[1] HUL, 2001 Annual Report, page XXI.
[2] "A Fresh Lease of Lifebuoy?," *Business Standard*, February 25, 2002.

Alarmingly, its sales value declined by more than 20% in a single year between 2000 and 2001.[3]

Since most of this decline occurred in rural areas–markets accounting for nearly 70% of Lifebuoy sales–executives at Hindustan Unilever (HUL) decided to focus rebuilding efforts on the more than 50% of India's population that lived in its 635,000 villages. It was a bold move since the residents of these rural communities, with an average population of 1,000, were largely illiterate. Furthermore, they had limited access to schools, telephones, electricity, or media.

Critics claimed it made little sense to try boosting share in locations where HUL soap brands (Lux, Dove, etc.) already had a market share of almost 60%. But the Lifebuoy team had data showing that soap was used on only 20% of rural bathing occasions.[4] Also, current distribution reached only 46% of rural residents.[5] Far from being saturated, they believed the growth potential was huge.

One innovative response was to recruit women as local distributors in these remote communities, appointing them as *Shakti Ammas* ("strength mothers"). The company offered them training, microcredit, and products in small pack sizes affordable to people on low incomes. These Shakti women entrepreneurs could earn Rs. 1,000 a month or more, often doubling their household income.

But better distribution could not solve Lifebuoy's core problem, and in 2001 management decided to relaunch the 107-year-old brand. In a break from tradition, they replaced the chunky carbolic brick soap with a shaped, milled toilet bar that promised a "contemporary health fragrance" and "better germ protection." (See **Exhibit 2**.) Supported by extensive advertising, Lifebuoy was repositioned from a male-oriented personal hygiene bar to a family health soap. Advertising and promotion were aimed at women, and the new package featured a family on the wrapper. But price remained largely unchanged at an economical nine Indian rupees (Rs. 9)–about $0.18–for a 125-gram bar.[6]

Rural Outreach through Swasthya Chetna

The company also launched a rural outreach program called *Swasthya Chetna* (SC) that translated as "Health Awakening." In addition to reaching new markets, SC aimed to reduce a major public health problem. According to the World Health Organization (WHO), diarrhea killed 2.2 million people every year. In India, it took the lives of 600,000 children under age five annually. Yet WHO claimed that by washing hands properly, half of the deaths could be avoided, making handwashing the single most cost-effective health intervention available to developing countries.

Launched in May 2002, SC's objective was to contact remote, media-inaccessible communities, and grow Lifebuoy's sales through education. With a primary target of schoolchildren, teams of trained "health development facilitators" each visited 72 villages quarterly, delivering their scripted health and hygiene messages through a variety of illustrated stories, visual aids, and quizzes with prizes.

Their most powerful tool was the "Glo-Germ" demonstration in which children rubbed white UV powder on their hands before being told to wash them clean with only water. When they then held their hands under an ultraviolet light, the powder glowed, showing how germs remained even when hands looked clean. A follow-up Glo-Germ inspection of hands washed with soap verified that all dirt and germs were removed, illustrating the central message that "visibly clean is not really clean."

[3] "HLL Uses Health Card to Push Lifebuoy Sales in Rural Areas," *Business Standard*, October 25, 2002.

[4] HUL, 2001 Annual Report, page XXI.

[5] HUL, "Repositioning Strengthens Lifebuoy's 107-Year Heritage," press release 312, 2002.

[6] "HLL Relaunches Lifebuoy, Eyes Healthy Sales Numbers," *Business Standard*, February 13, 2002.

Exhibit 2 Lifebuoy's Indian Relaunch, February 2002

LIFEBUOY'S 2002 TRANSFORMATION:
FROM A CARBOLIC SOAP TO A MILLED SOAP

Transition to Milled soap in 2002

Red, Chunky, & Powerful
Lifebuoy's Iconic Germicidal Carbolic Soap

Source: Unilever internal company document.

The Turnaround: Some Wins, Some Worries

The impact of these initiatives was mixed. On the sales front, Lifebuoy's revenues grew by 20% in 2003–2004, and the following year, by an additional 10%.[7] By 2005, the brand had an 18.4% share in the $880 million Indian personal soap market, and was again the brand leader. However, because no price increase accompanied its relaunch, profit margins continued to decline.

The social impact of the SC rural outreach program was also initially impressive. By mid-decade, it had reached more than 120 million people in 50,600 villages. Immediate post-visit awareness of germs grew by 30%, and short-term soap use increased among 79% of parents and 93% of children.[8] But no sustained change in handwashing habits was found, and while Lifebuoy's brand recognition increased, sales rose only modestly. As a result, the program's cost significantly exceeded its returns.

Late-Decade Reversals: New Market Challenges

Any glimmer of a turnaround was extinguished when a combination of strategic miscalculations and market forces resulted in Lifebuoy's renewed decline in the second half of the decade.

Serial Missteps: Repositioning and Relaunch Failures

Buoyed by the sales boost following the 2002 relaunch, management decided to reposition the

---

[7] "Lifebuoy Swasthya Chetna: Unilever's Social Marketing Campaign," ICFAI Case Study MKTG/147, 2006.

[8] "Lifebuoy – Swasthya Chetna," posted by bsaikrishna on October 3, 2010, Brandalyzer, http://brandalyzer.wordpress.com/2010/10/03/lifebuoy-swasthya-chetna/, accessed May 18, 2013.

brand again in 2005. A "Life without Fear" campaign was built around the theme that mothers need not worry about sending their children outside to get dirty. But while the TV ads were emotionally engaging, they failed to communicate product advantages or to motivate consumers to buy. From 2005 to 2007, Lifebuoy's germ-protection attribute scores dropped from 59.5 to 50.5, and market share declined from 18.4% to 17.6%.[9] Meanwhile, the category was assaulted by mounting competition and steep cost increases, particularly a 50% rise in vegetable oil prices.

The crisis led to yet another relaunch, this time based on data rather than emotions. In 2007, HUL sponsored a clinical trial that collected evidence of the effect of handwashing on disease. A scientific study involving 2,000 Mumbai families showed that children who practiced handwashing had 26% fewer days of school absence, due to 25% fewer diarrhea events, 15% fewer cases of respiratory infection, and 46% fewer eye infections.[10]

Excited by these findings, the HUL team used them to support a product relaunch. But it proved difficult to communicate research results connecting soap usage to school attendance. It was simply too big a conceptual leap for people who were unaware of the basic concept of germs, let alone the link between germs and disease. So Lifebuoy's market share kept falling–to 15.5% by 2009.

Rejuvenating Lifebuoy Liquid

At about this time, a worldwide swine flu pandemic broke out, ultimately resulting in the death of more than 18,000 people in South Asia and Africa. When public health officials began stressing the importance of handwashing, it triggered a widespread switch from beauty bars to health soaps. Moreover, the Lifebuoy team discovered that when consumers were assured of germ protection, they became price insensitive. It was an important insight that the team planned to exploit.

Serendipitously, at this time, the Indian-based R&D team responsible for Lifebuoy was working on a new liquid soap formulation. (In Unilever's network of R&D centers, the Bangalore center had global responsibilities for Lifebuoy.) As a late entrant to the fast-growing liquid handwash segment, Lifebuoy Liquid Handwash had met with only moderate success. Responding to research showing that the average time spent washing hands was far less than the recommended 20 to 30 seconds, the R&D team developed a new formulation able to get hands germ free in 10 seconds.

The innovation instantly caught the attention of Lifebuoy's marketing team, and in 2010, Lifebuoy Liquid Handwash was relaunched with a campaign highlighting its germ-killing capability. The product was an immediate success, not only for its formulation but also its futuristic package that became a symbol identifying homes in which it was displayed as "modern households." However, management knew that overtaking liquid handwash pioneer Dettol would be quite a challenge.

An Emerging Competitor: Dettol's Challenge

Launched in India in 1933 as an antiseptic liquid, Dettol had remained focused on its first-aid segment for half a century. But as growth stalled in the early 1980s, management extended the brand into soap, a market 50 times larger than its original mature segment. Exploiting Dettol's antiseptic heritage and an instantly identifiable smell associated with hospitals, the new soap was positioned as providing protection from germs. Its advertising slogan "Be 100% Sure" reinforced the message.

Rather than struggling to claim a share of the mass market that Lifebuoy had long dominated, this new soap brand was launched at almost

[9] Shailesh Oururani, "The Lifebuoy Story: Repositioning of a Brand," November 3, 2012, http://www.slideshare.net/shaileshgururani/lifebuoy-15005646.

[10] "Sustainable Living: Handwashing Behavior Change," http://www.unilever.com/sustainable-living/healthandhygiene/handwashing/handwashing behaviourchange/index.aspx, accessed July 13, 2013.

twice the price of its established competitor and soon grew to become Dettol's main product line. But by 2000, its market share was stagnating. To expand beyond its established use as "a soap for special bathing occasions," product variations were introduced–a white soap in 2004, and a menthol soap in 2006. However, in 2007, Life-buoy's new rival sent a strong signal when it vacated its traditional mid-price segment by offering a small 35-gram pack for Rs. 6 (about $0.12)–clearly positioned against Lifebuoy's 42-gram pack at Rs. 5.

It was an unusual move for Dettol, which had always nurtured its brand equity, rarely engaging in price or promotional competition. As a result, the brand had always been very profitable, and despite a 5.2% market share that was less than one-third of Lifebuoy's, it could match the leading brand's advertising spending. Also, unlike local competitors, Dettol was backed by Reckitt Benckiser, its German-based parent, whose brands such as Lysol, Calgon, Woolite, and Clearasil generated sales of $6 billion in 180 countries. Together, these elements suggested that the fast-growing liquid handwash segment would be the arena where the two brands would soon go head-to-head.

New CEO, New Directions

In January 2009, a new CEO took charge of Unilever. The strategic and organizational changes he introduced had an immediate impact companywide–including for Lifebuoy in India.

Shaking the Tree: Instilling Discipline, Infusing Energy

When Unilever's board appointed Paul Polman as the first outside CEO in the company's history, it signaled a major shakeup in its underperforming culture. The 52-year-old Dutchman was not just an outsider, he had spent 27 years at archrival Procter & Gamble, reaching that company's most senior executive levels before joining Nestlé as its CFO.

Assuming his new Unilever role during a global recession, Polman's actions confirmed his belief in the motto "never waste a crisis." In his first week, he announced that he would no longer provide earnings guidance or publish quarterly reports. When the share price fell almost 10%, he attributed the decline to the departure of hedge funds, a group that he felt "would sell their own grandmothers if they thought they could make a profit."[11] When analysts queried him about the stock price drop, he responded: "We need to know why we are here. The answer is, for consumers not sharehold-ers. If we are in sync with consumer needs and the environment in which we operate, and take responsibility for society as well as our employees, then the shareholder will also be rewarded."[12]

To shake up a culture that was "internally focused and self-serving after years of restructur-ing,"[13] Polman froze all salaries and cut overseas travel. Then, to implement his belief that "execu-tion is strategy in our business," he installed 30-day action plans to increase the company's speed to market and consumer-led innovation. And, to instill discipline, he insisted all managers be held accountable.

Polman claimed that he was not just driving for short-term effect, but was positioning Unilever for long-term growth: "It is easy for me to get tremendous results very short term, get that translated into compensation and be off sailing in the Bahamas. But the goal for this company . . . is to follow a four or five year pro-cess. We need to change the strategy and the structure as well as the culture."[14]

Redefining the Strategy: Committing to Sustainability

In keeping with these beliefs, the new CEO announced an ambitious goal of doubling

---

[11] "Sustainable Living: Handwashing Behavior Change."
[12] Andrew Saunders, "The MT Interview: Paul Polman of Unilever," *Management Today*, March 1, 2011.
[13] Andrew Saunders, "The MT Interview: Paul Polman of Unilever."
[14] Stefan Stern, "Outsider in a hurry to shake up Unilever," *Financial Times*, April 4, 2010.

Unilever's sales volume. But he also acknowledged that "growth at any cost is not viable," and committed to achieving this goal while decoupling growth from the company's environmental impact. To translate his bold vision into specific objectives, in October 2010 the company unveiled the Unilever Sustainable Living Plan (USLP).

USLP had three goals: to halve the environmental footprint of making and using its products, to source 100% of its agricultural raw materials sustainably, and to help a billion people improve their health and well-being. Polman emphasized that USLP was no mere corporate social responsibility program, but was totally aligned with its commercial interests. It was Unilever's core strategy built on its long-held mission to "do well by doing good."

As the broad goals were broken into 50 measurable objectives, management found that Unilever's own operations accounted for only 6%–7% of its environmental footprint. So the company committed to taking responsibility for its entire value chain, and over the full product life cycle. For example, it began working with tea and palm oil suppliers (responsible for a quarter of Unilever's footprint) to help them meet USLP's 100% sustainable sourcing commitment. Meanwhile, on the consumption end, product development and marketing programs began working to reduce the two-thirds of their footprint generated by consumers' use of Unilever products, and to increase their positive social impact. (See Exhibit 3.)

Reshaping the Organization: New Roles, New Players

In parallel, Polman continued to implement "One Unilever," an in-process program aimed at streamlining its complex, multilevel matrix by assigning responsibility to three regional heads and three global category presidents. This reorganization had already shifted the power balance from country-based Opco chairmen (who reported to the regional heads) to global brand leaders (who reported to the category presidents). Opcos were still accountable for the profitability of their local operations, but were now responsible for implementing strategies developed by global brand teams.

Building on "One Unilever," Polman made the regional head for Asia his Chief Operating Officer (COO), giving him responsibility for all regions. Simultaneously, the new CEO expanded the three category divisions to four–personal care, home care, food, and refreshment–and, in a signal that reinforced the earlier power shift, had all of them report directly to himself. (See Exhibit 4.)

With strategy in the hands of global brand leaders, Polman wanted to ensure that Unilever was still responsive to local consumer needs, particularly in emerging markets that now accounted for half the company's turnover. As a result, global brand management resources and responsibilities were now distributed worldwide, including in the developing world. For example, Lifebuoy's Global Brand Vice President was located in Singapore, and his global brand teams responsible for bar soaps, liquids, and social mission were based in Mumbai, Singapore, and Nairobi, respectively.

Through all this, Polman insisted that USLP targets be embedded in all key business decisions. "This is at the core of our business strategy," he said. "It's not a separate CSR agenda. We believe that responsible companies that make contributions to society a central part of their business model will be successful." So while most managers' incentive compensation was still tied primarily to financial objectives, USLP targets were monitored and independently audited by PricewaterhouseCoopers (PwC) and were reported in detail through the company's management reporting system.

Lifebuoy Rebooted: New Players, New Priorities

As part of the restructuring, Samir Singh was appointed as Lifebuoy's Global Brand VP with a mandate to revitalize this iconic brand that had now retreated to a few developing countries and

Exhibit 3
Unilever Sustainable Living Program (USLP): Original Targets 2010

Press Release:

Unilever announces plans to decouple future growth from environmental impact.

Global firm announces plans to:

- halve the environmental footprint of its products
- help 1 billion people improve their health and wellbeing
- source 100% of its agricultural raw materials sustainably

At the launch of Unilever's Sustainable Living Plan, announced simultaneously in London, Rotterdam, New Delhi and New York, CEO Paul Polman explained: "We have ambitious plans to grow the company. But growth at any price is not viable. We have to develop new ways of doing business which will ensure that our growth does not come at the expense of the world's diminishing natural resources."

He also announced plans to help over 1 billion people take action to improve their health and wellbeing, mostly in developing countries, over the next 10 years.

The Sustainable Living Plan sets out over 50 social, economic and environmental targets. It will see Unilever, whose global brands include Dove, Omo, Knorr and Lipton, halve the greenhouse gas emissions, water and waste used not just by the company in its direct operations, but also by its suppliers and consumers.

Over two-thirds of greenhouse gas emissions and half the water used in Unilever products' lifecycle come from consumer use, so this is a major commitment on an unprecedented scale. . .

Other key goals Unilever plans to achieve by or before 2020 include:

- sourcing 100% of its agricultural raw materials sustainably including, by 2015, 100% sustainable palm oil;
- changing the hygiene habits of 1 billion people in Asia, Africa and Latin America so that they wash their hands with Lifebuoy soap at key times during the day—helping to reduce diarrhoeal disease, the world's second biggest cause of infant mortality;
- making safe drinking water available to half a billion people by extending sales of low-cost in-home water purifier, Pureit, from India to other countries;
- improving livelihoods in developing countries by working with Oxfam, Rainforest Alliance and others to link over 500,000 smallholder farmers and small-scale distributors into its supply chain.

Commenting that Unilever wants to be sustainable 'in every sense of the word', Polman said: "There are billions of people who want the improvements to their health and wellbeing and who want to live sustainably. Our aim is to help people in developing countries improve their quality of life without a big increase in their environmental impacts, and to help those in developed markets maintain a good standard of living while reducing theirs."

Paul Polman sees no conflict between Unilever achieving its sustainability goals and growing its business. "We are already finding that tackling sustainability challenges provides new opportunities for sustainable growth: it creates preference for our brands, builds business with our retail customers, drives our innovation, grows our markets and, in many cases, generates cost savings."

Polman emphasised that Unilever did not have all the answers and that the company would need to work in partnership with customers, suppliers, governments and NGOs if it was to achieve its goals.

Source: Unilever press release, November 15, 2010.

Exhibit 4 Unilever Corporate Organization Structure

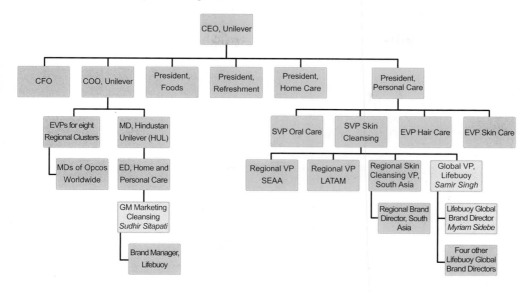

Source: Casewriter's construction from company documents.

was struggling in several of them, including India. Singh, a 12-year company veteran with extensive brand management experience, soon built a team and defined a strategy to drive Lifebuoy's renewal.

Defining a Global Strategy: Reclaiming the Heritage

The new global team's first priority was to complete what Singh called "an archaeological review" of Lifebuoy's past successes and problems. Concluding that the core of the problems lay in Lifebuoy's history of continual reinvention, repositioning, and relaunch, Singh decided to return the brand to its roots–offering protection from diseases spread by germs. The first element of the strategy was to educate consumers on the consequences of germs by assuring mothers that Lifebuoy provided their families superior protection from 10 infections from flu to diarrhea. (See Exhibit 5.)

Next, marketing efforts focused on "hot spots"–times of the year such as monsoon season, school re-entry, or crowded religious festivals when infection risk was high. Tailored messages reassured mothers that Lifebuoy could help protect their family at these times of high anxiety. The advertising and promotional activities were customized to each country's specific calendar of hot-spot events as well as its competitive situation and stage of hygiene development.

Finally, these activities were supported by a program of product development that resulted in innovations such as Clinicare 10, a premium product claiming germ protection 10 times better than any other soap, and Lifebuoy Color Changing Handwash aimed at encouraging children to wash their hands for a full 10 seconds, at which time the soap changed color.

The approach proved successful, and from 2009 to 2012, Lifebuoy's global sales increased by 17% per annum (p.a.), and gross profit by 22% p.a. Indeed, Singh's boss became so confident that his five-year plan forecast that Lifebuoy's global sales would surge from €408 million in 2010 to become a €1 billion brand by 2015. But Polman's rollout of USLP presented an even more difficult goal. With

Exhibit 5 Lifebuoy Core Claim: Protection against Germs

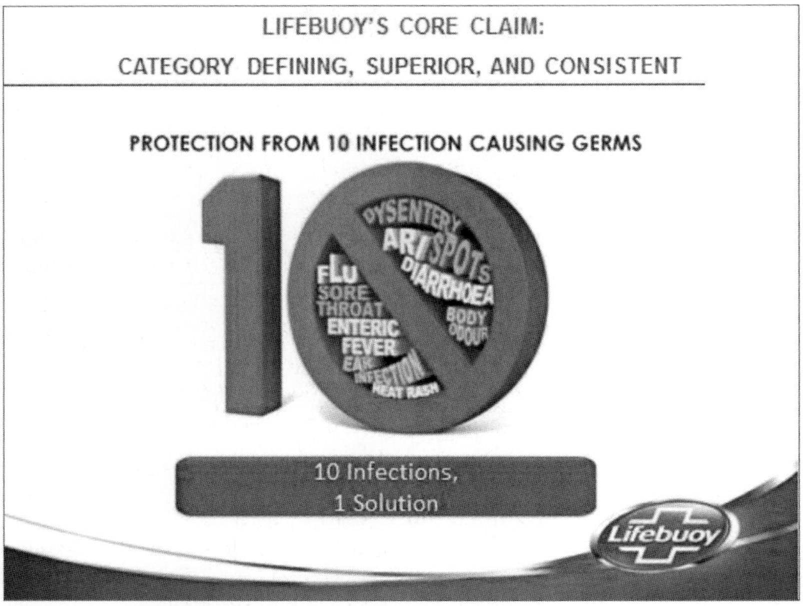

LIFEBUOY'S CORE CLAIM:
CATEGORY DEFINING, SUPERIOR, AND CONSISTENT

PROTECTION FROM 10 INFECTION CAUSING GERMS

10 Infections,
1 Solution

Lifebuoy

Source: Unilever internal company document.

all Unilever brands expected to contribute to the USLP objectives, Singh volunteered Lifebuoy to assume the main role in fulfilling the global health and hygiene target. And because India was Lifebuoy's largest market, the Indian team would need to make a significant contribution.

Integrating the Social Mission: Beyond Pilots to Performance

When Singh was appointed Lifebuoy's Global Brand VP, Dr. Myriam Sidibe joined his team as Global Brand Director, Social Mission. A world expert on the public health impact of handwashing, Sidibe had been recruited to the corporate office in 2006 as Lifebuoy's Global Partnership Manager. In that role, she had become the champion of handwash behavior-change programs, initiating numerous activities, including the Mumbai clinical trial that led to India's 2008 product relaunch.

In their discussions, Singh suggested that while Sidibe's campaigning had inspired many new initiatives, the high cost of her "pristine" forms of handwash programs had slowed implementation and limited transferability. Stressing his belief that Lifebuoy's social mission must be fully aligned with its commercial interests, he challenged her to take her behavior-change initiatives beyond clinical studies, conferences, and pilots and focus on leveraging her exciting research results into commercially viable programs that would open up new market segments for the brand.

On her part, Sidibe urged Singh to make the goal of reaching a billion people with handwashing programs a strategic priority. She explained that when she was in her corporate partnership role, she had publicly committed Lifebuoy to this target in support of the United Nations Millennium Development Goals, aligning her pledge with the UN goals' 2015 target date.

Others were concerned, however. They told Singh that the 1 billion USLP goal had been set for Unilever's entire product line, not just Lifebuoy. And they pointed out that USLP targets had a 2020 time horizon, not a 2015 target. But Singh decided to embrace Sidibe's commitment: "I'd rather set a goal of a billion for 2015 and 'fail' by only reaching 650 million than take on a safe 100 million target for 2020 and over-deliver with 200 million," he said. "Only bold stretching goals generate passion."

It was a brave decision. Singh knew that USLP targets were closely monitored by PwC, and that results were not only tracked by top management but were also highlighted in Unilever's annual report as well as in its widely circulated annual USLP report. Both documents provided information and presented data that was explicit and detailed–celebrating achievements, identifying shortfalls, and outlining proposed adjustments and corrective action.

Selling the Strategy: Engaging Operating Companies

In late 2010, Singh convened a workshop in Jakarta to which he invited brand directors from all Opcos with large Lifebuoy sales to identify the most effective ways to meet the brand's USLP target. In open sessions, they shared models, compared costs, quantified benefits, and identified what worked. In the end, two programs attracted the most interest: an Indonesian partnership program built on "training the trainer," and an Indian multibrand rural outreach initiative. With credibility that he had built through the sales and profit turnaround, Singh was now ready to ask the Opcos to invest in these projects.

In early 2011, with the endorsement of the Cleansing Category SVP (Singh's boss) and Unilever's Chief Operating Officer (the Opco chairmen's boss), Singh took his USLP business case to a meeting of Opco chairmen. Conceding that previous handwashing behavior-change programs had struggled, he assured them that these two models were worth investing in. Without disrupting existing programs, he suggested that

they take them on as pilots, funding them by reinvesting some of the enhanced profits generated by the brand's recent turnaround.

Because India accounted for almost half of Lifebuoy's global sales, Singh was gratified that HUL's chairman became a strong supporter of his proposal. Although subsequent discussions within the Indian Opco revealed pockets of skepticism and even some resistance, he was confident that the support of Unilever's top man in the country would allow his global brand team to implement their agenda. And HUL's local Lifebuoy team would need that help: they had been allocated 450 million of the 1 billion USLP behavior-change target.

Implementation in India: Reviewing the Options

When Singh offered to help the Indian team implement the two Jakarta models, Sudir Sitapati, HUL's Category Manager for Lifebuoy in India, told him he had a third model to consider.

The First Option: The KKD Rural Outreach Initiative

One of the models endorsed in Jakarta was based on a rural program first launched in India in 2010. It emerged as a replacement for the SC "Health Awakening" program that had petered out due to its unacceptable payback of almost 10 years compared to the Unilever norm of one to three years to recoup marketing expenses. The innovative *Khushiyon Ki Doli* (KKD)–or "Caravan of Happiness"–was a collaborative, multibrand, rural outreach effort in which brand managers for Surf detergent, Close Up toothpaste, Sunsilk shampoo, Vim dishwashing liquid, and Lifebuoy soap pooled resources to create a direct contact program to reach remote rural villages with all their products.

KKD involved teams visiting villages and hosting meetings at which all sponsoring products were presented. Lifebuoy's KKD component was a scaled-back version of its SC routine, retaining the "Glo-Germ" demonstration but focusing on housewives rather than children. Supported by videos, games, and prizes, the presentations were received enthusiastically by residents of these media-dark villages. Later, promoters went door-to-door with coupons and offers, while other team members ensured prominent product placement at village shops.

The Second Option: The MP Partnership Initiative

The second program endorsed in Jakarta was the Indonesian partnership program, a clinically proven 21-day intervention built on the Unilever Handwashing Program that Sidibe and her co-developers had published as "Five Levers for Change." (See **Exhibit 6**.) Lifebuoy Indonesia had integrated this scientifically based behavior model into a national schools program in partnership with the Indonesian government and some NGOs. The program trained teachers and provided them with tools to deliver the behavior change in their schools. It then leveraged that impact by requiring each teacher to cascade the program to three other schools.

With the endorsement of HUL's chairman, Singh had convinced Sitapati to sign an agreement with UNICEF to bring a similar handwashing program to Madhya Pradesh (MP), an extremely poor Indian state with a literacy rate of 80% for males and 60% for females.[15] Under the agreement, HUL would create the materials, deliver the training, provide the soap, and manage the evaluation process; the MP government would provide school access and support; and UNICEF would print activity kits and link the partners. As a condition of its support, however, the MP government insisted that the training and materials could not be branded with Lifebuoy's name.

This pilot program would adapt Indonesia's proven "School of Five" materials for the 900,000 children initially targeted in 5,700

government schools. Implementation would conform with the "five non-negotiables" of Sidibe's change program: the four key phases of behavior change–awareness, commitment, reinforcement, and reward–all applied over a 21-day program, the fifth key element.

The Third Option: The Urban Schools Liquids Initiative

While Sitapati was ready to consider expanding these two programs in 2013, he also wanted to offer a third option. He felt that Lifebuoy Liquid Handwash had the potential to change behavior while also boosting revenue and profits. Arguing that liquid soap had a higher usage rate, and potentially a much higher margin, in 2011 he had launched a new urban schools liquids initiative.

Like KKD, this program was designed primarily as a marketing initiative, but differed from KKD on several dimensions: it was focused solely on Lifebuoy, not on multiple products; it was aimed at urban markets rather than rural locations; it targeted children not housewives; and most critically, its objective was to increase the use of Lifebuoy Liquid Handwash rather than Lifebuoy soap bars.

To implement the program, Indonesia's "School of Five" educational program was adapted for urban schools by employing interactive games, songs, dances, and the classic Glo-Germ demon-stration. Because children found the use of a pump more fun, they washed their hands more frequently. And as School of Five research had shown, they took the lessons home and influenced the handwashing behavior of the whole household.

The Decision: Singh's Balancing Act

In early 2013, Singh was pleased that Lifebuoy's three-year 17% average annual growth rate not only made it Unilever's fastest-growing brand, but also outpaced Dettol's growth for the first time. But he worried that its handwash program had only reached 119 million people globally. If Lifebuoy was to achieve its 1 billion USLP

---

[15] United Nations Development Program, "Madhya Pradesh: Economic and Human Development Indicators," http://www.undp.org/content/dam/india/docs/madhyapradesh_factsheet.pdf.

Exhibit 6
Unilever Behavior-Change Model

FIVE LEVERS FOR CHANGE

Lifebuoy has used Unilever's Five Levers for Change methodology to develop a series of interventions to ensure that people understand why handwashing with soap is important. The model sets out five principles, which, if applied to behaviour change interventions, will have a positive and lasting impact.

LEVER 1: MAKE IT UNDERSTOOD

Visibly Clean Not Necessarily Clean: One key element of Lifebuoy's behaviour change approach is the 'glo-germ' demonstration. This counters the common misconception that 'visibly clean' is 'hygienically clean'. When held under ultra-violet light, 'glo-germ' powder illuminates the germs left behind on hands washed only with water. This makes it clearly understood that handwashing with soap provides greater protection against germs than washing with water alone.

LEVER 2: MAKE IT EASY

Mother and Child Interaction: As part of our programmes we encourage interaction between children and their mothers. This helps to ensure that new habits start and stick. For example with our school programmes, mothers play a role in tracking their child's handwashing compliance via a daily sticker chart. This is important in helping to reinforce the behaviour in the home environment as well as at school.

LEVER 3: MAKE IT DESIRABLE

Pledging: Studies show that people who commit to a future action in public are more likely to deliver on this commitment. Our school programme uses the Classroom Soap Pledge, where children pledge to wash their hands on the five occasions that matter, for the duration of the programme. This is done in class so that peer pressure and teacher approval makes the behaviour more likely. The use of aspirational comic book characters in our schools programmes and local celebrities in our campaigns is also key. When well-known celebrities emphasise the importance of handwashing with soap for a healthy nation, people are encouraged to practise the habit and emulate the behaviour of people they admire.

LEVER 4: MAKE IT REWARDING

Positive Reinforcement: Lifebuoy understands the power of the positive influences to motivate social change. Positive reinforcement runs throughout the school programme—a strong rewards system makes mothers and children feel good for taking positive steps in changing their habits.

LEVER 5: MAKE IT A HABIT

21 Days Practice: Habits build up over time through repetitive behaviour. This is why practising handwashing with soap for a minimum of 21 days is a critical element in our programmes. Our classroom materials—comic books, posters, quizzes and songs—all work over 21 days to remind students about the message of handwashing at key occasions. A 21-day compliance diary is also used to record handwashing behaviour over the course of the intervention.

Source: Company document, "Unilever's Five Levers for Change."

Exhibit 7
Lifebuoy India P&L: 2006 to 2012 (€ thousands)

	2006	2007	2008	2009	2010	2011	2012
Turnover	125,191	136,658	166,424	162,266	169,751	189,855	238,629
Growth %		*9.2%*	*21.8%*	*-2.5%*	*4.6%*	*11.8%*	*25.7%*
Supply Chain Costs	88,271	97,879	123,062	127,638	127,063	158,149	188,832
Gross Margin	36,920	38,779	43,363	34,628	42,688	31,705	49,798
Gross Margin %	*29.5%*	*28.4%*	*26.1%*	*21.3%*	*25.1%*	*16.7%*	*20.9%*
Advertising and Promotion	8,693	8,438	9,698	15,157	13,945	13,536	17,199
Profit Before Overheads	28,227	30,341	33,664	19,471	28,744	18,169	32,598
PBO %	*22.5%*	*22.2%*	*20.2%*	*12.0%*	*16.9%*	*9.6%*	*13.7%*

Source: Unilever internal company documents (all data disguised).

target, India would have to step up to the challenge.

Lifebuoy India's Achievements–and Shortfalls

Lifebuoy's excellent global performance had been greatly helped by strong growth in India, its largest market. (See Exhibit 7.) But despite strong recovery in sales and profitability, hand-washing behavior-change programs in India had reached just 17 million people in 2012, taking its total to 47 million since 2010. While impressive, the performance was well below the trajectory necessary to achieve the country's allocated behavior-change target of 450 million by 2015.

Singh knew that Sitapati also had to meet HUL financial objectives, and accepted that most of his advertising and promotion (A&P) budget would be allocated to media expenditure, typically with a payback of one to three years. Nonetheless, since 2010 Sitapati had boosted the share of A&P budget that he allotted to behavior-change programs from zero to 5%. Singh felt that such programs offered a great opportunity to reach the 40% of the population in media-dark locations unreachable by traditional broadcast or print media. For this reason, he hoped that Sitapati would at least double the behavior-change A&P percentage. But because the payback on these programs was three or four times that of traditional marketing outlays, it was a tough sell. (See Exhibit 8.)

Evaluating Progress, Focusing Investments:

As the team discussed the three behavior-change options, different perspectives emerged:

In its first two years, KKD had reached 25 million people in 70,000 villages, with research showing that soap consumption increased by 8% following a KKD visit. In rural Utter Pradesh, after two years of KKD visits, Lifebuoy's market share increased from 13.9% to 15.6%. While the cost per contact had fallen to Rs. 6 (about $0.10), Sitapati was concerned that as KKD moved to smaller, more remote villages, such visits were now becoming decreasingly cost effective.

Singh's global team was more concerned that brief KKD Lifebuoy demonstrations to housewives were not resulting in sustainable behavior change that would satisfy the PwC auditors. To ensure that KKD estimates counted towards India's 450 million target, Sidibe's team was helping add a school component to KKD visits and the "five non-negotiables" into its presentations. But as Sitapati noted, such efforts further slowed KKD's delivery and increased its cost.

In 2013, for Rs. 54.5 million (about $780,000), KKD could bring its handwashing message to 8.5 million people. But it would take Lifebuoy India 8.6 years to break even on the investment. Sitapati had marketing investments that would yield much higher returns much faster.

Exhibit 8
Lifebuoy Behavior-Change Program Options: 2013 Projected Costing (values in Rs.)

2013 Program Parameters	KKD Outreach	MP Partnership	Urban Liquids	Assumptions/Comments
	(All values in Indian Rupees)			
Estimated number of contacts in 2013	8,500,000	4,500,000	1,500,000	KKD and MP usage impact assume that they both influence family behavior, justifying an X5 multiplier.
Total Program Cost for Lifebuoy (in Rs.)	54,500,000	28,000,000	35,000,000	Lifebuoy's Share of costs (KKD: 20%; MP: 33%; Urban Liquid: 100%.)
Cost per Contact (in Rs.)	6.4	6.2	23.3	
Incremental Lifebuoy Revenue (in Rs.)	25,250,000	8,285,000	19,800,000	Post-program soap consumption assumptions: Lifebuoy obtains 30% of forecast post-KKD increase; 20% of post-MP's increase (due to unbranded soap); Urban Liquids program converts 12% of households to Lifebuoy Handwash averaging Rs. 110 use p.a.
Gross Margin (in Rs.)	6,312,500	2,071,250	9,900,000	25% for bar soap; 50% for liquid.
Investment Payback for Lifebuoy	8.6 years	13.5 years	3.5 years	
Investment Payback for Unilever	5.7 years	8.9 years	3.5 years	Post-KKD and MP programs, Unilever retains 45% rural market share for its soap brands.

Source: Internal documents (all data disguised).
Note: Exchange rate January 2013: 70 INR = €1.

Although Sitapati knew that the **MP Partnership** would be time consuming, with a long payback period, he was willing to consider it as a pilot. But he was troubled that it would reach only 900,000 children. He also worried about relying on external funding, and was unhappy about delivering it as an unbranded program. Finally, he felt that 13.5 years was just far too long a payback period.

The global brand team was more excited. Because studies proved that training made children effective change agents who could influence family behavior, they estimated that 900,000 kids could change the behavior of 4.5 million people. Moreover, the team believed that a successful pilot could lead to the program's adoption by all 47 MP districts, and eventually by other Indian states. The huge potential impact of rolling out this program across India had led Singh to initiate negotiations with a potential new funding partner that could significantly leverage this important initiative.

The **Urban Schools Liquids** program targeted 25 cities with a population of 1 million or more where liquid soap had achieved 7% to 10% penetration, and where Sitapati hoped to build brand preference for Lifebuoy. Although India's total liquid handwash market was only about $65 million–5% of the total personal soap market–it was growing at up to 40% annually.

While Singh accepted that education was also valuable to urban populations, he was concerned that liquids were too expensive for the poor rural mass market that was the target of behavior change, and worried that the initiative would distract the organization's attention. But knowing that the brand had to be profitable in order to support its ambitious handwash programs, he had agreed to support the urban schools initiative if implemented, and his team had offered to help integrate "the five non-negotiables" into the design.

Although the program was expected to reach only 1.5 million people, Sitapati believed the higher margins of liquid handwash would translate into a payback period of 3.5 years–not as good as alternative marketing investments, but the most attractive of the behavior-change options.

***

It was a complex decision with important implications both locally and globally. In India, Sitapati would have to decide which, if any, of these three behavior-change projects he should include in his Indian budget; in Singapore, Singh had to decide whether to intervene in the decision, and if so, how; and in London, Polman would be considering whether this tension reflected the shift in strategic process he had envisioned when he introduced his USLP goals.

HARVARD | BUSINESS | SCHOOL

REV: NOVEMBER 6, 2006

Perry L. Fagan, Michael Y. Yoshino, and Christopher A. Bartlett

CASE 7.3 SILVIO NAPOLI AT SCHINDLER INDIA (A)

Senior Research Associate Perry L. Fagan and Professor Michael Y. Yoshino prepared the original version of this case, "Silvio Napoli at Schindler India (A)," HBS No. 302-053 (Boston: Harvard Business School Publishing, 2002). This version was prepared by Professor Christopher A. Bartlett. HBS cases are developed solely as the basis for class discussion. Cases are not intended to serve as endorsements, sources of primary data, or illustrations of effective or ineffective management.

"Monsieur Napoli, si vous vous plantez ici vous êtes fini! Mais si vous réussissez, vous aurez une très bonne carrière." (Translation: "Mr. Napoli, if you fall on your face here you are finished! But if you succeed, you will have a very nice career.") The words echoed off the walls of Silvio Napoli's empty living room and disappeared down the darkened hallway like startled ghosts. The parquet was still wet from the five inches of water that had flooded the first floor of the Napoli home in suburban New Delhi several days before, during one of the sewer system's periodic backups. Standing in the empty room were Napoli and Luc Bonnard, vice chairman, board of directors of Schindler Holdings Ltd., the respected Swiss-based manufacturer of elevators and escalators. It was November 1998, and Bonnard was visiting New Delhi for the first time to review progress on the start-up of the company's Indian subsidiary, which Napoli had been dispatched to run eight months earlier. Things were not going according to plan.

Napoli, a 33-year-old Italian former semiprofessional rugby player, had arrived in March with his pregnant wife and two young children and had quickly set about creating an entirely new organization from scratch. Since March, he had established offices in New Delhi and Mumbai, hired five Indian top managers, and begun to implement the aggressive business plan he had written the previous year while head of corporate planning in Switzerland. The plan called for a $10 million investment and hinged on selling "core, standardized products," with no allowance for customization. To keep costs down and avoid India's high import tariffs, the plan also proposed that all manufacturing and logistics activities be outsourced to local suppliers.

Shortly before Bonnard's visit, however, Napoli was confronted with three challenges to his plan. First, he learned that for the second time in two months, his Indian managers had submitted an order for a nonstandard product–calling for a glass rear wall in one of the supposedly standard elevators. At the same time, his business plan had come under intense cost pressures, first from a large increase in customs duties on imported elevator components, then from an unanticipated rise in transfer prices for the "low-cost" components and materials imported from Schindler's European factories. Finally, as Napoli began accelerating his strategy of developing local sources for elevator components, he found that his requests for parts lists, design specifications, and engineering support were not forthcoming from Schindler's European plants.

As the implementation of his business plan stalled, Napoli wondered what he should do. Eight months in India and he still had not installed a single elevator, while his plan showed first-year sales of 50 units. And now Bonnard was visiting. Should he seek his help, propose a revised plan, or try to sort out the challenges himself? These were the thoughts running through Napoli's head as the vice chairman asked him, "So, how are things going so far, Mr. Napoli?"

Schindler's India Explorations

Schindler had a long and rather disjointed history with the Indian market. Although its first elevator in India was installed in 1925, the company did not have a local market presence until it appointed a local distributor in the late 1950s. Almost 40 years later, Schindler decided it was time to take an even bolder step and enter the market through its own wholly owned subsidiary.

The Growing Commitment

Established in 1874 in Switzerland by Robert Schindler, the company began manufacturing elevators in 1889. Almost a century later, the 37-year-old Alfred N. Schindler became the fourth generation of the family to lead the company, in 1987. Over the next decade, he sought to transform the company's culture from that of an engineering-based manufacturing company to one of a customer-oriented service company.

By 1998, Schindler had worldwide revenues of 6.6 billion Swiss francs (US$4 billion) and was widely perceived as a technology leader in elevators. It was also the number one producer of escalators in the world. The company employed over 38,000 people in 97 subsidiaries but did not yet have its own operations in India, a market Alfred Schindler felt had great potential.

Although the first Schindler elevator in India was installed in 1925, it was not until 1958 that the company entered into a long-term distribution agreement with ECE, an Indian company. In 1985, Schindler terminated that agreement and entered into a technical collaboration with Mumbai-based Bharat Bijlee Ltd. (BBL) to manufacture, market, and sell its elevators. After acquiring a 12% equity stake in BBL, Schindler supported the local company as it became the number two player in the Indian elevator market, with a 10%–15% share a decade later.

On assuming the role of chairman in 1995, Alfred Schindler decided to take a six-month "sabbatical" during which he wanted to step back and review the long-term strategy of Schindler. As part of that process, he undertook to travel through several markets–China, Japan, and several other Far Eastern markets–that he felt were important to the company's growth. He spent several weeks in India, traveling over 3,000 kilometers in a small Ford rental car. "After his trip Mr. Schindler saw India as a second China," said a manager in Switzerland. "He saw huge growth potential. And once he targets something, he's like a hawk."

With the objective of raising its involvement, Schindler proposed to BBL that a separate joint venture be created solely for the elevator business, with Schindler taking management control. But negotiations proved difficult and eventually collapsed. In late 1996, collaboration with BBL ended, and Schindler began considering options to establish its own operation in India.

Silvio Napoli's Role

Meanwhile, after graduating from the MBA program at Harvard Business School, Silvio Napoli had joined Schindler in September 1994. He accepted a position at the company's headquarters in Ebikon, Switzerland, reporting directly to the CEO as head of corporate planning.

With its 120 years of history, Schindler was a formal Swiss company where the hierarchy was clear, politeness important, and first names rarely used. Napoli's office was on the top floor of the seven-story headquarters building, a floor reserved for the three members of the company's executive committee and the legal counsel. (For profiles of top management, see Exhibit 1.) "As soon as I arrived, I was aware that people were very responsive to my requests," said Napoli. "Just by my physical location, I generated fearful respect, and I realized I would have to manage my situation very carefully." A 20-year Schindler veteran recalled his reaction to Napoli's arrival: "He was the assistant to Mr. Schindler, so I knew I'd better be nice to him."

As head of corporate planning, Napoli was responsible for coordinating the annual strategic review process and undertaking external benchmarking and competitor analysis. But his most visible role was as staff to the corporate executive committee, the Verwaltungsrat

Ausschuss (VRA)–which was composed of Alfred Schindler, Luc Bonnard, and Alfred Spöerri, the chief financial officer. As the only nonmember to attend VRA meetings, Napoli was responsible for taking meeting minutes and for following up on action items and special projects defined by the VRA.

The Swatch Project

In 1995, Napoli took on the Swatch Project, a major assignment that grew out of a concern by VRA members that margins on new product sales were eroding as each competitor strove to expand its installed base of elevators. Since such sales were a vital source of profitable long-term maintenance and service contracts, the project's goal was to develop a standardized elevator at a dramatically lower cost than the existing broad line of more customized products. It was an assignment that involved the young newcomer in sensitive discussions with Schindler's plants in Switzerland, France, and Spain to discuss design, determine costs, and explore sourcing alternatives. Napoli described the process and outcome of the Swatch Project:

> As you might imagine, I was viewed with some suspicion and concern. Here was this young MBA talking about getting costs down or outsourcing core tasks that the plants felt they owned. . . . In the end, we developed the S001, a standard elevator that would not be customized, incorporated processes never before seen in the group, and used many parts sourced from outside suppliers. All of this was unthinkable in the past. We redesigned the entire supply chain and in doing so, halved the industry's standard 20- to 30-week cycle time.

The Indian Entry Project

Meanwhile, as negotiations with BBL broke down in India, the VRA engaged Boston Consulting Group to identify and evaluate alternative local partners with whom Schindler might build its business in India. As the company's point man

Exhibit 1
Schindler Top Management Profiles

Name:	Alfred N. Schindler	Luc Bonnard	Alfred Spöerri
Position:	Chairman and Chief Executive Officer	Vice Chairman of the Board and Member of the Executive Committee	Member of the Board of Directors Member of the Executive Committee
Date of Birth:	March 21, 1949	October 8, 1946	August 22, 1938
Education:	*1976–1978:* MBA, Wharton, USA *1974–1976:* Certified Public Accountant School, Bern *1969–1974:* University of Basel–Law School (lic. jur.), Abschluss:lic.iur.	*1971:* Diploma in Electrical Engineering at ETH (Technical University), Zurich	
Experience:	*Since 1995:* Chairman of the Board and Chief Executive Officer *1985–1995:* Chairman of the Corporate Executive (CEO) *1984–1985:* Member of Corporate Management *1982–1984:* Head of Corporate Planning *1978–1979:* Deputy Head of Corporate Planning	*1996:* Vice Chairman *1991–1996:* Member of the Executive Committee *1986–1990:* COO Elevators and Escalators, Member Corporate Executive Committee *1985–1986:* Member, Executive Committee *1983–1985:* Group Management Member, North Europe *1973:* Management, Schindler, in France	*1991–1998:* Member, Executive Committee *1997–1998:* Chief Financial Officer *1979–1988:* Corporate Controller–Treasurer *1975–1979:* COO of Mexico *1971–1974:* Area Controller, Latin America *1968–1974:* Financial Officer of Mexico *1968:* Joined Schindler Group

Source: Schindler India.

on the project, Napoli worked with the consultants to narrow the list of 34 potential partners to eight candidates for review by the VRA. As the team pursued the final choices, however, it concluded that there was no ideal partner. But it learned that it was now legally feasible to start up a 100% wholly owned company in India. The VRA then asked Napoli and the head of Schindler's mergers and acquisitions department to explore that option.

Napoli contacted experts in India who helped him expand his understanding of the situation. Through discussions with market experts and studies by local consultants, Napoli spent nine months developing a detailed analysis of the market size, legal environment, and competitive situation in the Indian elevator market. He integrated this into a business plan for Schindler's market entry and submitted it to the VRA. The plan was approved in October. Soon after, Napoli was offered the job of creating the Indian subsidiary. Napoli recalled his reaction:

> I realized that the future manager of the new company would be key to the success of the business plan I had been working on. I was conscious that my early involvement in the project made me a candidate, so when the offer came, I was not surprised. Deep down, I knew I could do it. More surprising was the reaction of my headquarters' colleagues, who thought I was crazy to take such a high-risk career move that involved dragging my family to a developing country.

Bonnard explained the choice of Napoli:

> There are two possible profiles in a country like India. The first is a young guy who knows the company, people, and products; the second is someone who is 55 years old with grown kids looking for a new challenge. ... Mr. Napoli knew lots of people. He was open to go new ways. We needed someone who could handle different cultures, who was young and flexible. We needed to trust the person we sent, and we trusted him 100%. And we needed a generalist, not a pure specialist. We needed someone who had courage. Finally, I believe that the people who make the business plan should have to realize it. Of course, we also needed to have someone who was willing to go.

In November Napoli and his wife Fabienne, a French-German dual national, made their first trip to India. "We went on a 'look and see' visit, starting in Mumbai," Napoli recounted. "When we arrived in Delhi my wife looked around and said she would be more comfortable living here. After reaching an agreement on the relocation package back in Switzerland, I accepted the job."

Over the next several months, Napoli made three more trips to India to lay the groundwork for the move. In one key move, he engaged the executive search firm Egon Zehnder to identify candidates for his top management team. Although he had to await government approval to start the new company, when he moved to India, he wanted to have key managers in place.

Forming Schindler India

As vice president for South Asia, Napoli was responsible for India and a few nearby export markets in Schindler's elevators and escalators division (see Exhibit 2). In March, Napoli relocated to India and began the task of building the company that would implement his business plan.

New Culture, New Challenges

On his first day in the Delhi office, Napoli got stuck in one of BBL's elevators. As he recalled, it proved to be an omen of things to come:

> On our first morning in Delhi, six hours after the family had landed, my two-year-old daughter opened her forehead falling in the hotel room. The deep wound required hospitalization and stitching under total anesthesia. Two weeks later, my wife Fabienne got infectious food poisoning, which required

Exhibit 2 Schindler Organization Chart, Elevator and Escalator Division

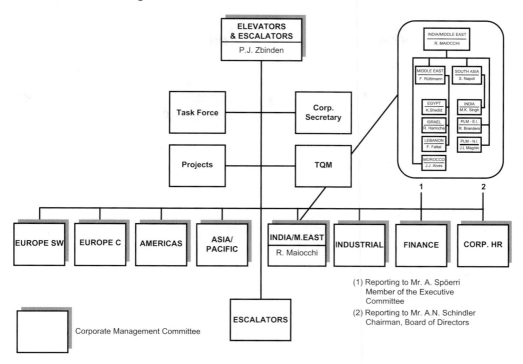

Source: Schindler Management Ltd.

one-week hospitalization, even threatening a miscarriage. The day she came back from hospital, my three-year-old son fell in the hotel bathroom and broke his front tooth. Rushing to an emergency dentist in a hotel car, I really wondered, for the only time in my life, whether I could stand this much longer.

Although Napoli and his family were in New Delhi, where he had opened a marketing and service office, he spent most of a typical week at the company's headquarters in Mumbai. "The first two months were really a hard-fought battle between family relocation and company start-up," he recalled. "Weeks were consumed shuttling between Delhi and Mumbai, hunting for office space, filing government registrations, and completing legal paperwork. On the family front, I had to get them started in a totally different system: housing, schools, doctors, grocery

shopping... all things which are totally different in India."

In the process, Napoli found he had to adapt his management approach. "For example," he recalled, "all types of characters started to approach me offering their services. They had heard that I was representing a Swiss firm about to invest in India. I soon learned to be careful in deciding who I could trust."

Recruiting the Team

Over the previous couple of months, Egon Zehnder had identified several promising candidates who became the pool from which Napoli recruited for his top positions in the new company. Mehar Karan ("M.K.") Singh, 42, was tapped for the role of managing director, a position that reported to Napoli but was viewed as a stepping stone to heading the subsidiary. (For profiles of key Indian managers, see Exhibit 3). "At some point in your career you will report to someone younger than yourself," said Singh. "I decided that Schindler was an exciting opportunity to test this scenario."

Napoli explained the choice of Singh: "Having led construction projects for some of India's largest hotels, M.K. had firsthand experience in building an organization from scratch. But most of all, he had been on our customers' side. He would know how to make a difference in service." In addition, being 10 years older and having grown up in India, Singh brought valuable experience and a different perspective. He was also more sensitive to organizational power and relationships, as Napoli soon recognized:

> The first question M.K. asked me after joining the company was, "Who are your friends inside the company? Who doesn't like you?" I never thought about it this way. And I said to him: "Listen, you will have to develop a sense of that yourself. As far as I know, probably people are a little bit cautious of me because they know I used to work for the big bosses at headquarters. But we will have to wait and see."

To head field operations (sales, installation, and maintenance) Napoli hired T.A.K. Matthews, 35, who had worked for nine years at Otis India. Matthews recalled: "I had been approached before by elevator people, but after hearing a bit about Schindler's plans, I realized that you don't have a chance to get involved with a start-up every day." For Napoli, Matthews brought the business expertise he needed: "With M.K. and I as generalists, I absolutely needed someone with in-depth elevator experience to complement our management team. T.A.K. came across as a dynamic and ambitious hands-on manager waiting for the chance to exploit his potential."

Next, Napoli hired Ronnie Dante, 39, as his general manager for engineering. Dante had 24 years of experience at Otis. "Even with T.A.K., we missed a real hard-core elevator engineer capable of standing his ground in front of his European counterparts," said Napoli. "Such people are the authentic depositories of an unpublished science, and they are really very hard to find. Honestly, nobody in the group expected us to find and recruit someone like Ronnie. He is truly one of the best."

Hired to head the company's human resources department, Pankaj Sinha, 32, recalled his interview: "Mr. Napoli and Mr. Singh interviewed me together. There was a clarity in terms of what they were thinking that was very impressive." Napoli offered his assessment of Sinha: "Mr. Schindler had convinced me that the company really needed a front-line HR manager who was capable of developing a first-class organization. But I certainly did not want a traditional Indian ivory tower personnel director. Pankaj convinced us to hire him through his sheer commitment to care about our employees."

Finally, he recruited Jujudhan Jena, 33, as his chief financial officer. (See Exhibit 4 for an organization chart.) Napoli explained his approach to hiring: "You try to see whether the character of the person is compatible with yours, whether you have a common set of values, which in our case range from high ethical standards, integrity, assiduousness to work, and drive. Mostly we were looking for people with the right attitude and energy, not just for elevator people."

Developing the Relationships

As soon as the senior managers were on board, Napoli began working to develop them into an effective team. He recalled the early meetings with his new hires:

> Because some of them were still finishing up their previous jobs, the first Schindler India staff meetings were held at night, in the Delhi Hotel lounge. I'll never forget working together on our first elevator project offer, late after holding a series of interviews for the first employees who would report to the top team. But most of those "undercover" sessions were dedicated to educating the new team about their new company and building consensus around our business plan. ... The team was really forged through days of late work, fueled by the common motivation to see our project succeed.

Exhibit 3
Schindler India: Key Managers' Profiles

Name:	Silvio Napoli	Mehar Karan (M.K.) Singh	T.A.K. Matthews	Ronnie Dante	Jujudhan Jena
Position:	Vice President, Schindler South Asia	Managing Director	Vice President–Field Operations	General Manager–Engineering	Chief Financial Officer
Date of Birth:	August 23, 1965	April 12, 1955	March 12, 1964	November 3, 1959	March 3, 1967
Education:	*1992–1994:* MBA, Harvard University Graduate School of Business Administration, Boston, Massachusetts *1984–1989:* Graduate degree in Materials Science Engineering, Swiss Federal Institute of Technology (EPFL), Lausanne, Switzerland; Lausanne University rugby captain (1987) *1983–1984:* Ranked among top 20% foreign students admitted to EPFL, one-year compulsory selection program, Swiss Federal Institute of Technology (EPFL), Cours de Mathematiques Special, Lausanne, Switzerland	*1977:* B.E.–Mechanical Engineering; ranked top of his class in Indian Institute of Technology, Delhi, India *1979:* MBA, Indian Institute of Management, Ahmedabad, India (Awarded President of India's Gold Medal)	*1986:* B.Sc.–Civil Engineering, University of Dar-E-Salaam, Tanzania *1989:* MBA, Birla Institute of Technology, Ranchi, India	*1977:* HSC, D.G. Ruparel College, Mumbai, India	*1990:* Chartered Accountant, Institute of Chartered Accountancy, India
Experience:	*Since 1998:* Vice President, South Asia, Schindler Management Ltd. *1994–1997:* Vice President, Head of Corporate Planning,	*Since 1998:* Managing Director, Schindler India Pvt. Ltd., Mumbai, India *1979–1998:* Head of Projects and Development Group, Taj Group	*Since 1998:* Vice President–Field Operations, Schindler India Pvt. Ltd., Mumbai	*Since 1998:* General Manager–Engineering, Schindler India Pvt. Ltd., Mumbai	*Since 1998:* Chief Financial Officer, Schindler India Pvt. Ltd., Mumbai

Exhibit 3 (*cont.*)

Name:	Silvio Napoli	Mehar Karan (M.K.) Singh	T.A.K. Matthews	Ronnie Dante	Jujudhan Jena
	Schindler, Switzerland *1991–1992:* Technical Market Development Specialist, Dow Europe, Rheinmuenster, Germany *1989–1991:* Technical Service & Development Engineer, Dow Deutscheland, Rheinmuenster, Germany *1989–1992:* French Semi-Pro Rugby League (Strasbourg)	of Hotels, India (setting up hotels in India and abroad; joint ventures with state governments, local authorities, and international investors, including the Singapore Airlines, Gulf Co-operation Council Institutional investors. Responsible for financial restructuring of the international operations after the Gulf War, culminating with the successful 1995 GDR offering).	*1998:* Modernization Manager, Otis Elevator Company, Mumbai *1989–1998:* Otis Elevator Company, New Delhi • Service & Service Sales Manager • Construction Manager • Assistant Construction Manager • Management Trainee *1986–1987:* Civil Engineer, Construction Companies, Tanzania	*1995–1998:* National Field Engineering Manager, Otis Elevator, Mumbai *1991–1995:* National Field Auditor, Otis Elevator, Mumbai *1989–1991:* Supervisor, Otis Elevator *1984–1989:* Commissioning of New Products, Otis Elevator, Singapore, Malaysia, and Mumbai *1982–1984:* Commissioning Engineer, Otis Elevator Company, Gujarat *1977–1982:* Apprentice, Otis Elevator Company, Maharashtra	*1997–1998:* Financial Controller, Kellogg India Ltd., Mumbai *1996–1997:* Group Manager, Procter & Gamble India Ltd., Mumbai *1995–1996:* Treasury Manager, Procter & Gamble India Ltd. *1990–1995:* Financial Analyst, Procter & Gamble India Ltd.

Source: Schindler India.

Exhibit 4 Schindler India Organization Chart

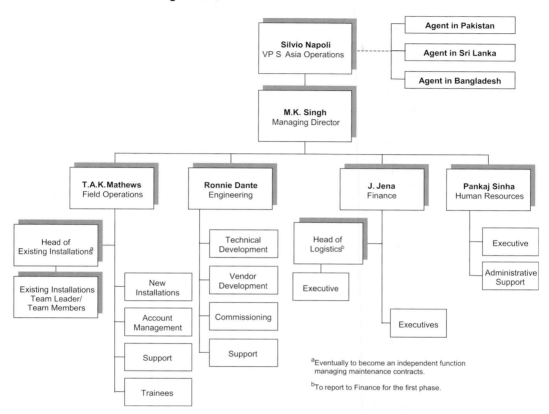

Source: Schindler India.

In the team-forming process, the different management styles and personal characteristics of Schindler India's new leaders became clear. Even before he was assigned to India, Napoli was recognized as a "strong-headed and single-minded manager," as one manager at Swiss headquarters described him. "There couldn't have been a better environment to send Silvio than India," said another Swiss colleague. "He wants everything done yesterday. And in India, things don't get done yesterday."

Napoli acknowledged the personal challenge. "To survive in India you have to be half monk and half warrior," he said. "I was certainly more inclined to the warrior side, and when I left Switzerland, Mr. Bonnard told me, 'You will have to work on your monk part.'"

Napoli's Indian staff and colleagues described him as "driving very hard," "impulsive," "impatient," and at times "over-communicative." "Mr. Napoli gets angry when deadlines are not met," added a member of his New Delhi staff. "He's a pretty hard taskmaster." The HR director, Sinha, was more circumspect: "Silvio has a lot of energy. When he focuses on an issue he manages to get everybody else's focus in that direction."

Descriptions of Napoli contrasted sharply with those of Singh, whom one manager saw as "friendly and easygoing." Another described him as "much more patient, but he can also be tough." Jena, the finance director, reflected on his first encounter with the two company leaders: "During the interview Silvio came across banging on the table, but I don't think that concerned me. Still,

Exhibit 5 Indian Elevator Market, Structure, and Product Segmentation

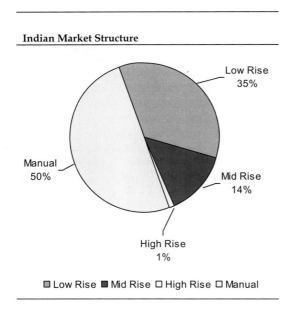

Indian Market Structure

Low Rise 35%
Mid Rise 14%
High Rise 1%
Manual 50%

☐ Low Rise ■ Mid Rise ☐ High Rise ☐ Manual

Segment	Stops	Speeds MPS	Schindler Products
Manual	2–8	0.5–0.7	NIL
Low rise	2–15	0.6–1.5	S001
Mid rise	16–25	1.5	S300P
High rise	>25	>1.5	S300P

Source: Schindler India.

I remember wondering during the interview how two guys as different as M.K. and Silvio would fit together in a start-up." Matthews, the field operations manager, added another perspective:

> It's true that if you look at Silvio, M.K., and me we are all very different. At first we had sessions where the discussion would get pulled in every direction, but I think in the end, it did bring about a balance... I would put it this way. Silvio came to India from Switzerland. But things here are very different: You can't set your watch by the Indian trains. M.K. came from the hotel industry where even if you say "no," it's always made to sound like "yes."

"Silvio was the driver and clearly was the boss," said another Indian executive. "M.K. was great in helping Silvio understand the Indian environment. Having worked in the hotel industry he had a very good network. He had been on the customer side. But he had to learn the elevator business."

Out of this interaction emerged a company culture that employees described as "informal,"

"open," "responsive," and "proactive." It was also a lean, efficient organization. For example, furniture and office space were rented, and there were only two secretaries in the company–one for the Delhi office and one for Mumbai. "People must do their own administrative work or they won't survive," said Singh.

The India Business Plan

As soon as his team was in place, Napoli worked to gain their commitment to his business plan. At its core were two basic elements: the need to sell a focused line of standard products, and the ability to outsource key manufacturing and logistics functions. This plan had been built on an analysis of the Indian market and competitive environment that Napoli also communicated to his team (see Exhibits 5 and 6 for data from the plan).

The Indian Elevator Market

Economic liberalization in India in the early 1990s had revived the construction industry,

Exhibit 6 Market Research on Indian Elevator Market, 1996

Unprompted Recall of Elevator Brands — Builders

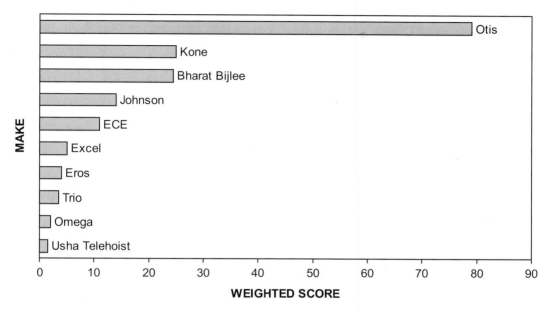

Factors Influencing Elevator Purchase — Unprompted Listing — Builders

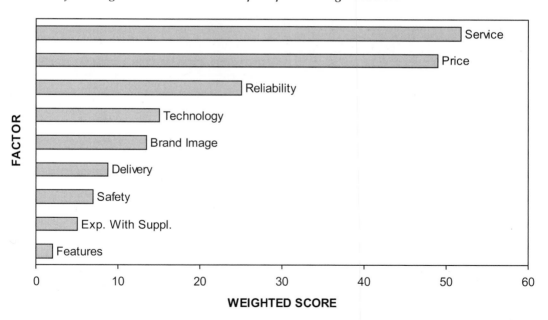

Exhibit 6 (*cont.*)

Comparative Rating of Elevator Makes — Builders

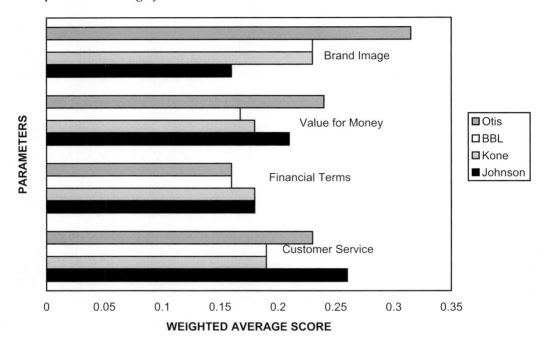

Preferred Communication Channels — Builders

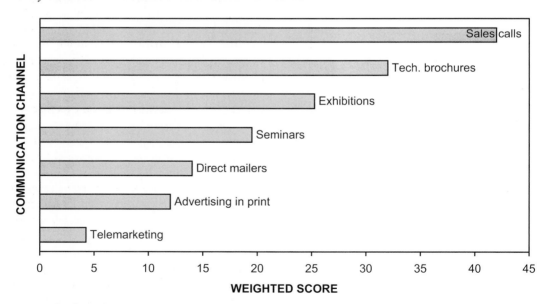

Source: Schindler India.

and along with it, the fortunes of the elevator industry. Roughly 50% of demand was for low-tech manual elevators, typically fitted with unsafe manual doors (see Exhibit 5). But a ban on collapsible gate elevators had been approved by the Indian Standards Institute, and, at the urging of the Indian government, individual states were making the ban legally enforceable. This low end of the market was characterized by intense competition among local companies, but was expected to make this market segment more interesting to major international players when the ban was fully implemented.

The middle segment of low- and mid-rise buildings was promising due to India's rapid urbanization which had led to a shortage of space in Mumbai and fast-growing cities such as Bangalore, Pune, and Madras. Concurrently, traditional builders were becoming more sophisticated and professionalized, leading to an emphasis on better services and facilities and on higher quality, safer, and more technologically advanced elevators.

At the top end of the market, there was small but growing demand for top-quality, high-rise office facilities, particularly from multinational companies. Tourism was also expanding, greatly aiding the domestic hotel industry, a major buyer of top-line elevators. The average value per top end elevator was five to six times that of low end installations.

At the end of 1997, the installed base of elevators in India was 40,000, with an estimated 5,600 units sold during the year. Although this installed base was small compared with those of China (140,000 units) and Japan (400,000 units), India's growth potential was significant. The rapidly expanding residential segment accounted for 70% of the Indian market, followed by the commercial segment (office buildings and shopping centers) with a 20% share. The balance was accounted for by hotels (4%) and others (6%). Total revenues for the industry were US$125 million, including service income. For the first half of the decade, the market grew at a compound annual rate of 17% in units and 27% by value, but due to a slump in the real estate market, the unit growth

forecast for 1998 was just 5%. It was expected to rise to 8%–12% in subsequent years. Together, Mumbai and New Delhi represented 60% of the total Indian elevator market.

In India, most sales were of single-speed elevators (65%), followed by two-speed (20%), variable frequency (13%), and hydraulic (2%). Sales of single-speed elevators dominated the residential market, while variable frequency was most commonly used in higher-end commercial applications. Although the Indian market was biased toward the simplest products, it was expected to shift gradually toward two-speed or higher technology in the future.

Competition

Napoli's business plan also documented that four major players accounted for more than three-quarters of the Indian market value: Otis (50%), BBL (8.6%), Finland's Kone (8.8%), and ECE (8.4%). Mitsubishi had recently begun importing premium elevators for hotels and commercial developments, and Hyundai Elevators had entered into a joint venture to manufacture high-end elevators in India. At this stage, however, they accounted for only 1% of sales. With the exception of Mitsubishi, all multinational players relied on local manufacturing for the majority of their components. The remaining 23% of the market—mostly the price-sensitive low end—was controlled by 25 regional players characterized by a lack of technical expertise and limited access to funds.

Otis India had an installed base of 26,000 elevators, 16,000 of which were under maintenance contracts. It manufactured its own components, spare parts, and fixtures at an aging plant in Mumbai and a new state-of-the art manufacturing plant near Bangalore. The company staffed 70 service centers, including a national service center in Mumbai, and held an estimated 85% of the high-end hotels and commercial segment. ("You couldn't name any building over 15 floors that did not have an Otis elevator," said ex-Otis employee Matthews. "Otis, Otis, Otis. Any special equipment, it goes Otis. Any fast elevator goes Otis.") Otis was reportedly one of the most profitable industrial companies in India, and its 3,500 employees had an average tenure of 20 years.

The Indian market was highly price sensitive, and most analysts agreed that elevators were becoming commodity products and that price pressures would increase. However, surveys indicated that service was also important in the buying decision, as were the financial terms (Exhibit 6).

The elevator life cycle had seven distinct phases: engineering, production, installation, service, repair, modernization, and replacement. Over the 30-year life cycle of an elevator, the first three stages accounted for about one-third of the labor content but only 20% of the profits. In contrast, the latter four accounted for two-thirds of labor content but 80% of profits. As a result, annual maintenance contracts covering routine maintenance and breakdown service were vital. (High-margin spare parts were billed separately.) Service response time varied across segments. Most five-star hotels with multiple installations had a technician on call or on-site; for important commercial buildings and hospitals, the response time was usually within two hours, but many residential and some commercial customers reported an average response time of between six and eight hours.

The Standard Product Strategy

Napoli felt that Schindler could not compete just by matching what others did. It had to find its own unique source of advantage. His analysis of the Indian environment coupled with his work on the Swatch Project led him to conclude that, although it was a radically different approach from that of his key competitors, the most effective way for Schindler to enter this market would be to focus on a narrow product line of simple, standardized elevators.

He proposed building the business around the Schindler 001 (S001)–the product developed in the Swatch Project–and the Schindler 300P (S300P), a more sophisticated model being manufactured in Southeast Asia. The plan was to use the S001 to win share in the low-rise segment as a primary target, then pick up sales opportunistically in the mid-rise segment with the S300P. Both products could be adapted to meet Indian requirements with only minor modifications (e.g., adding a ventilator, a fire rescue controller function, a stop button, and different guide rails). Equally important, as long as the company stuck to the principle of no customization, both products could be priced appropriately for the local market. The plan called for Schindler India to sell 50 units in the first year and to win a 20% share of the target segments in five years. It also projected Schindler India would break even after four years and eventually would generate double-digit margins.

After communicating this strategy to his Indian management team, Napoli was pleased when they came back with an innovative approach to selling the standard line. If the product was standardized, they argued, the sales and service should be differentiated. Singh's experience with hotel construction led him to conclude that projects were more effectively managed when one individual was responsible for designing, planning, contracting, and implementing. Yet, as Matthews knew, the traditional sales structure in the elevator industry had different specialists dedicated to sales, technical, and installation, each of whom handed the project off to the next person. Together, these managers proposed to Napoli that Schindler organize around an account-management concept designed to give the customer a single "hassle-free" point of contact.

The Outsourcing Strategy

India's high import duties had forced most foreign elevator companies to manufacture locally. But again, Napoli chose a different approach. To keep overheads low, his business plan proposed a radical sourcing concept for the S001 that was expected to account for 75% of sales: Schindler India would have no in-house manufacturing, no centralized assembly, and no logistics infrastructure. Instead, the production of most components for the dominant S001 model would be outsourced to approved local suppliers. (The S300P would be wholly imported from Southeast Asia.) Only safety-related components (the safety gear and speed governor, together representing 10% of the value), would be imported from Schindler plants in Europe. In addition, the entire logistics function would be handled by to an internationally reputed logistics service provider. And some basic installation work–part of the on-site assembly of the drive, controller, car, doors, rails, and counter-weight–would also be outsourced. However, maintenance contracts resulting from new sales would stay with Schindler.

Inspired by the local automotive industry–Mercedes outsourced most components of its Indian vehicles–Napoli believed he could set up a local manufacturing network that would pre-serve Schindler's quality reputation. To ensure this, localization of each component would follow the same "product-creation process" criteria used by Schindler worldwide. Furthermore, before the first pre-series batch could be released, it would face an additional hurdle of testing and approval by experts from Schindler's European factories and competence centers.

From Analysis to Action: Implementing the Plan

By June, Napoli's management team members had settled into their roles, and the newly hired sales force was in the field. Almost immediately, however, the young expatriate leader began to experience questions, challenges, and impediments to his carefully prepared business plan.

Business Challenges

From the outset, several of Napoli's new management team had questioned him on the feasibility of his plan. In particular, those from the elevator industry wondered how the company would survive selling only standard elevators. They also worried about the outsourcing strategy, since no other company in the industry worked this way. "Some of the doubts were expressed as questions," said Napoli. "Many more were unspoken. My guess is they thought, 'We'll soon convince this crazy guy from Europe that we have to do something a bit less unusual.'"

In August, Napoli traveled to Italy to be with his wife when she gave birth to their third child. On one of his daily telephone calls to key managers in India, he discovered that the company had accepted an order for an expensive custom glass pod elevator that was to be imported from Europe. "I was at first just surprised, and then pretty angry, since it clearly was a violation of the strategy we had all agreed on," said Napoli. "The project was committed, and it was too late to stop it. But I had a long talk with M.K. and followed it up with an e-mail reminding him and the others of our strategy."

After his return to India, Napoli was delighted when he heard that the company was ready to accept another order for four S001 elevators for a government building in Mumbai. But in later conversations with a field salesman he discovered that there was a good possibility that each of the elevators would be specified with a glass wall. Although the managers insisted that this was really a minor modification to the standard S001 product, Napoli believed that, especially for a new team, installing it would be much more difficult than they expected.

The next challenge to his plan came when price estimates for the proposal was received to Schindler's plants in Europe. (Sources had not yet been qualified for local production.) Napoli was shocked when he saw the transfer prices on the basic S001 elevators at 30% above the costs he had used to prepare his original plans. "When I called to complain, they told me that my calculations had been correct six months ago, but costs had increased, and a new transfer costing system had also been introduced," recalled Napoli.

The impact of the transfer price increase was made worse by the new budget the Indian government had passed during the summer. It included increased import duties on specific "noncore goods" including elevators, whose rates increased from 22% to 56%. Napoli recalled the impact:

This was devastating to our planned break-even objectives. The first thing I did was to accelerate our plans to outsource the S001 to local suppliers as soon as possible. We immediately started working with the European plants to get design details and production specifications. Unfortunately, the plants were not quick to respond, and we were becoming frustrated at our inability to get their assistance in setting up alternative local sources.

Reflections of a Middle Manager

As darkness enveloped the neighborhood surrounding his townhouse, Napoli sat in his living room reflecting on his job. Outside, the night was filled with the sounds of barking dogs and the piercing whistles of the estate's security patrol. "Each family here has its own security guard," he explained. "But because guards fall asleep at their posts, our neighborhood association hired a man who patrols the neighborhood blowing his whistle at each guard post and waiting for a whistle in response. But now the whistling has gotten so bad that some families have begun paying this man not to whistle in front of their houses. Incredible, isn't it?"

Thinking back on his eight months in his new job, Napoli described the multiple demands. On one hand, he had to resolve the challenges he faced in India. On the other, he had to maintain contact with the European organization to ensure he received the support he needed. And on top of both these demands was an additional expectation that the company's top management had of this venture. Napoli explained:

When we were discussing the business plan with Mr. Schindler, he said, "India will be our Formula One racing track." In the auto industry, 90% of all innovations are developed for and tested on Formula One cars and then reproduced on a much larger scale and adapted for the mass market. We are testing things in India–in isolation and on a fast track–that probably could not be done anywhere else in the company. The expectation is that what we prove can be adapted to the rest of the group.

While the viability of the Formula One concept was still unclear, Alfred Schindler commented on Napoli's experience:

This job requires high energy and courage. It's a battlefield experience. This is the old economy, where you have to get involved in the nitty-gritty. We don't pay the big salaries or give stock options. We offer the pain, surprises, and challenges of implementation. The emotions start when you have to build what you have written. Mr. Napoli is feeling what it means to be in a hostile environment where nothing works as it should.

Napoli reflected, "You know the expression, 'It's lonely at the top?' Well, I'm not at the top, but I feel lonely in the middle. ... Somehow I have to swim my way through this ocean. Meanwhile, we have yet to install a single elevator and have no maintenance portfolio." At this point, Napoli's reflections were interrupted by the question of visiting vice chairman Luc Bonnard, "So, how are things going so far, Mr. Napoli?"

⊗IVEY | Publishing

CASE 7.4 LARSON INC. IN NIGERIA

Professor Paul W. Beamish revised this case (originally prepared by Professor I.A. Litvak) solely to provide material for class discussion. The authors do not intend to illustrate either effective or ineffective handling of a managerial situation. The authors may have disguised certain names and other identifying information to protect confidentiality.

David Larson, vice-president of international operations for Larson Inc., was mulling over the decisions he was required to make regarding the company's Nigerian operation. He was disturbed by the negative tone of the report sent to him on January 04, 2015, by the chief executive officer (CEO) of the Nigerian affiliate, George Ridley (see Exhibit 1). Larson believed the future prospects for Nigeria were excellent and was concerned about what action he should take.

Company Background

Larson Inc. was a New York-based multinational corporation in the wire and cable business. Wholly-owned subsidiaries were located in Canada and the United Kingdom, while Mexico, Venezuela, Australia, and Nigeria were the sites of joint ventures. Other countries around the world were serviced through exports from the parent or one of its subsidiaries.

The parent company was established in 1925 by David Larson's grandfather. Ownership and management of the company remained in the hands of the Larson family and was highly centralized. The annual sales volume for the corporation worldwide approximated $936 million in 2014. Revenue was primarily generated from the sale of power, communication, construction and control cables.

Technical service was an important part of Larson Inc.'s product package; therefore, the company maintained a large force of engineers to consult with customers and occasionally supervise installation. As a consequence, licensing was really not a viable method of serving foreign markets.

Background on Nigeria

Nigeria is located in the west-central part of the African continent. With 178.5 million people in 2014, it was the most populous country in Africa and the seventh most populous nation in the world. Population growth was estimated at 2.8 per cent annually. About 44 per cent of the population was under 15 years of age. A majority of the labor force in Nigeria worked in agriculture but there was a trend of more people moving to urban centres.

The gross domestic product in 2014 was about $510 billion, making it the largest economy in Africa. While per capita GDP was about $3000, on a purchasing power parity basis it was substantially higher at $5676. GDP had grown from 2005 to 2014 at about six per cent annually. This increase was fueled in part by growth in services and the export sales of Nigeria's oil reserves.

During the 2005 to 2014 period, Nigeria's average annual inflation rate had been 10.3 per cent. This high level had contributed to the change in the value of the naira from about 132 to the U.S. dollar in 2005 to about 165 to the U.S. dollar in 2014.

The Nigerian Operation

Larson Inc. established a joint venture in Nigeria in 2005 with a local partner who held 25 per cent of the joint venture's equity. Sales revenue for the Nigerian firm totalled $45 million in 2014. Of this revenue, $39.4 million was realized in Nigeria, while $5.6 million was from exports. About 40 per cent of the firm's Nigerian sales ($16 million) were made to various enterprises and departments of the government of Nigeria. The company was making a reasonable profit of 10 per cent of revenue, but with a little bit of luck and increased efficiency, it was believed it could make a profit of 20 per cent.

The Nigerian operation had become less attractive for Larson Inc. in recent months. Although it was widely believed that Nigeria would continue to be one of the key economic

Exhibit 1
The Ridley Report

In response to the request from head office for a detailed overview of the Nigerian situation and its implications for Larson Inc., Ridley prepared the following report in December, 2014. It attempts to itemize the factors in the Nigerian environment that have contributed to the problems experienced by Larson's joint venture in Nigeria.

Repatriation of Capital

1. While the Nigerian Investment Promotions Commission (NIPC) has removed time constraints and ceilings on repatriation, the divesting firm still has to submit evidence of valuation. In most cases the valuation is unrealistically low. This has represented substantial real-capital asset losses to the overseas companies concerned.

Remittance

2. A problem regarding remittances has arisen as a result of the 2003 Nigerian Insurance Act, section 67, under which cargoes due for import to Nigeria have to be insured with a Nigerian-registered insurance company. For cargoes imported without confirmed letters of credit, claims related to cargo loss and damage are paid in Nigeria; however, foreign exchange for remittance to pay the overseas suppliers is not being granted on the grounds that the goods have not arrived.

Problems Affecting Liquidity and Cash Flow

3. A number of problems have arisen during the last two years that are having a serious effect upon liquidity and cash flow, with the result that the local expenses can be met only by increasing bank borrowing, which is not only an additional cost but also becoming more difficult to obtain.

   a) Serious delays exist in obtaining payment from federal and state government departments for supplies and services provided, even in instances where payment terms are clearly written into the contract concerned. This is particularly true for state governments where payment of many accounts is 12 months or more in arrears. Even after payment, further delays and exchange-rate losses are experienced in obtaining foreign currency for the part that is remittable abroad. This deterioration in cash flow from government clients had, in turn, permeated through to the private clients.
   b) There is a requirement that a 100 per cent deposit be made on application for foreign currency to cover letters of credit.
   c) In order to clear the cargo as soon as possible and to avoid possible loss at the wharf, importers normally pay their customs duty before a ship arrives.
   d) Most company profits are taxed at a flat rate of 30 per cent. Firms operating in Nigeria must contend with a number of arbitrary levies and taxes, imposed mainly by state governments eager to augment their extremely thin revenue bases. The federal government attempted to put a halt to such practices by specifying which taxes all three (federal, state and local) tiers of government can collect, but it has not been entirely successful in enforcing compliance. Tax authorities are constantly trying to "trip up" companies in the course of inspections or audits, through their "interpretation" of the tax legislation. Consequently, net earnings after tax are insufficient to cover increased working capital requirements.

Incomes and Prices Policy Guidelines

4. Many of the guidelines issued by the Productivity, Prices and Incomes Board are of direct discouragement, as they make operations in Nigeria increasingly less attractive in comparison with other areas in the world. Although these guidelines were removed, increases for wage, salary, fees for professional services and auditing are still subject to final government approval.

Offshore Technical and Management Services

5. Restrictions on the reimbursement of expenses to the parent company for offshore management and technical services are a cause of great concern, since such services are costly to provide.

Professional Fees

6. The whole position regarding fees for professional services provided from overseas is most unsatisfactory. Not only are the federal government scales substantially lower than those in most other countries, but also the basis of the project cost applied in Nigeria is out of keeping with normally accepted international practice. The arbitrary restriction on the percentage of fees that may be remitted is a further disincentive to attracting professional services. Moreover, payment of professional fees in themselves produces cash flow problems exacerbated by long delays in payments and remittance approvals.

Royalties and Trademarks

7. The National Office of Technology Acquisition and Promotion (NOTAP) restricts the payment of royalties for the use of trademarks for a period of 10 years, which is out of keeping with the generally accepted international practice. This can be extended only under special cases. Limits for licensing and technical service fees are between one per cent to five per cent of net sales. Management fees are chargeable at two per cent to five per cent of a company's profit before tax (or one per cent to two per cent of net sales when no profits are anticipated during the early years). The maximum foreign share of consulting fees is five per cent. Such applications, however, are only granted for advanced technology projects for which indigenous technology is not available. Further, service agreements for such projects have to include a schedule of training for Nigerian personnel for eventual takeover and Nigerian professionals are required to be involved in the project from inception.

Quotas, Work Permits, and Entry Visas

8. It must be recognized that expatriate expertise is a very important element for this business, but expatriate staff is very costly. Unfortunately, at the present time there are a number of difficulties and frustrations, such as the arbitrary cuts in expatriate quotas, the delays in approving quota renewal, and in some cases, the refusal of entry visas and work permits for individuals required for work in Nigeria. Expatriate quotas are usually granted for two to three years subject to renewal.

Expatriate Staff

9. In general, the conditions of employment and life in Nigeria are regarded as unattractive when compared with conditions in many other countries competing for the same expertise. These differences are due to: the general deterioration of law and order; the rising security threats from the Boko Haram insurgency; the restrictions on salary increase and home remittance; the difficulties in buying air tickets; the poor standard of health care; the unsatisfactory state of public utilities such as electricity and water; the harassment from the police, airport authorities and other government officials; the general frustrations related to visas and work permits mentioned above. The situation has now reached a stage where not only is recruitment of suitably qualified, skilled experts becoming increasingly difficult, but we are also faced with resignations and refusals to renew contracts even by individuals who have worked and lived here for some years. Furthermore, the uncertainty over the length of time for which employment in Nigeria will be available (due to doubts whether the necessary expatriate quotas will continue to be available to the employer) is most unsettling to existing staff. This and the restriction of contracts to as little as two years are

(continued)

Exhibit 1 (*cont.*)

important factors in deterring the more highly qualified applicants from considering posts in Nigeria. These factors are resulting in a decline in the quality of expatriate staff it is possible to recruit.

Local Staff

10. Nigeria has one of the strongest national unions in Africa – the Nigeria Labour Congress (NLC). It is almost impossible to discipline a worker without attracting confrontation with the union. On certain occasions, some union members can be very militant. The union is also continuously attacking the employment of expatriates and trying to replace them with Nigerian staff.
11. Inadequate local technical training leads to low quality workers who tend to be lazy and not quality conscious.
12. The desirability of maintaining a tribal balance in the work force limits the options in recruiting the best workers.
13. Nigerian companies suffer heavily from pilferage, which normally accounts for two per cent of sales.

Public Utilities

14. The constant interruption in public utility services not only affects the morale of all employees but also has a very serious impact upon the operation of the business itself. Unless reasonable and continuing supplies of electricity, water, and petroleum products can be assured, and the highway adequately maintained, the costs related to setting up and operating escalate.

Continuity of Operating Conditions

15. The general and growing feeling of uncertainty about the continuity of operating conditions is a matter of considerable concern. It would seem that this uncertainty is engendered by a whole range of matters related to: short notice changes (sometimes even retrospective) in legislation and regulations; imprecise definition of legislation and regulations, which leads to long periods of negotiation and uncertainty; delays between public announcement of measures and promulgation of how they are to be implemented; and sometimes inconsistent interpretation of legislation and regulations by Nigerian officials.

Government Officials

16. Foreign partners have to rely on their Nigerian counterpart to handle the government officials. But it is impossible to measure its performance nor to control its expense in these activities. In addition, carefully cultivated relationships with officials could disappear, as they are transferred frequently.

Bribery

17. Surrounding many of the problems previously listed is the pervasive practice of bribery, known locally as the *dash*. Without such a payment it is very difficult to complete business or government transactions with native Nigerians.

Terrorism

18. Since 2009, Boko Haram's activities have caused a significant threat to our operation and to the security of our employees, especially expatriates. The militancy and strength of the terrorist group have been on a steady rise and foreign companies and nationals have traditionally been its main targets.

players in Africa in the years to come and that the demand for Larson's products would remain very strong there, doing business in Nigeria was becoming more costly. Furthermore, Larson Inc. had become increasingly unhappy with its local partner in Nigeria, a lawyer who was solely concerned with quick "paybacks" at the expense of reinvestment and long-term growth prospects.

David Larson recognized that having the right partner in a joint venture was of paramount importance. The company expected the partner or partners to be actively engaged in the business, "not business people interested in investing money alone." The partner was also expected to hold a substantial equity in the venture. In the early years of the joint venture, additional funding was often required and it was necessary for the foreign partner to be in a strong financial position.

The disillusionment of George Ridley, the Nigerian firm's chief executive officer (CEO), had been increasing since his early days in that position. He was an expatriate from the United Kingdom who, due to his background as a military officer, placed a high value upon order and control. The chaotic situation in Nigeria proved very trying for him. His problems were further complicated by his inability to attract good, local employees in Nigeria, while his best expatriate staff requested transfers to New York or Larson Inc.'s other foreign operations soon after their arrival in Nigeria. On a number of occasions, Ridley was prompted to suggest to head office that it reconsider its Nigerian commitment.

The Decision

David Larson reflected on the situation. He remained convinced that Larson Inc. should maintain its operations in Nigeria. Larson also wondered what should be done about Ridley. On the one hand, Ridley had been with the company for many years and knew the business intimately; on the other hand, Larson felt that Ridley's attitude was contributing to the poor morale in the Nigerian firm and wondered if Ridley had lost his sense of adaptability. Larson knew Ridley had to be replaced, but he was unsure about the timing and the method to use, since Ridley was only two years away from retirement.

Larson had to come to some conclusions fairly quickly. He had been requested to prepare an action plan for the Nigerian operation for consideration by the board of directors of Larson Inc. in a month's time. He thought he should start by identifying the key questions, whom he should contact, and how he should handle Ridley in the meantime.

Chapter 7   Recommended Practitioner Readings

- Tsedal Neeley, "Global teams that work," *Harvard Business Review*, 93:10 (2015), 74–81.

  In "Global teams that work," Neeley discusses how geographically dispersed teams face a big challenge: physical separation and cultural differences can create social distance, or a lack of emotional connection, that leads to misunderstandings and mistrust. To help manage this effectively, Neeley provides a SPLIT framework for mitigating social distance. It has five components: (1) Structure. If a team is made up of groups with different views about their relative power, the leader should connect frequently with those who are farthest away and emphasize unity. (2) Process. Meeting processes should allow for informal interactions that build empathy. (3) Language. Everyone, regardless of language fluency, should be empowered to speak up. (4) Identity. Team members must be active cultural learners and teachers to understand one another's identity and avoid misinterpreting behaviors. (5) Technology. When choosing between videoconferencing, email, and other modes of communication, leaders should ask themselves if real-time conversation is desirable, if their message needs reinforcement, and if they are opting for the technology they want others to use.

- Julian Birkinshaw, Cyril Bouquet, and Tina C. Ambos, "Managing executive attention in the global company," *MIT Sloan Management Review*, **48**:4 (2007), 39–90.

  In "Managing executive attention in the global company," Birkinshaw, Bouquet, and Ambos describe how "executives can prioritize their time to ensure that they are focusing on the countries and subsidiaries that need the most attention." The authors describe two key strategies a subsidiary can use to attract parent company attention: by using its "weight" as a player in an important market, and by exerting its "voice" and working through company channels.

- Christopher A. Bartlett and Sumantra Ghoshal, "Tap your subsidiaries for global reach," *Harvard Business Review*, **64**:6 (1986), 87–94.

  In "Tap your subsidiaries for global reach," Bartlett and Ghoshal introduce a simple conceptualization of the important roles for national subsidiaries in overall MNE success. In balancing the strategic importance of the local environment with the competence of the local organization, the authors define four very different roles for managers of country subsidiaries: strategic leader, contributor, implementer, and black hole.

- Rick Lash, "The collaboration imperative," *Ivey Business Journal*, January/February (2012).

  In "The collaboration imperative," Lash emphasizes the need for leaders who are able to achieve results even where they do not have direct control or authority over resources. The article describes the competencies required by these collaborative managers, able to lead diverse groups across functional disciplines, regions, and cultures.

- Mansour Javidan, Mary B. Teagarden, and David Bowen, "Making it overseas," *Harvard Business Review*, **88**:4 (2010), 109–13.

  In "Making it overseas," Javidan, Teagarden, and Bowen present two scenarios in which executives are employed overseas and focus on the characteristics and skills needed to be an effective manager in a foreign country. The idea that successful leaders have a global mindset that is based on intellectual, psychological, and social capital is discussed. The article mentions how to take the Global Mindset Inventory and evaluate one's ability to be a business leader in a culturally different environment. A strategy is explained for creating a plan that will develop the three types of capital and nine attributes that define global leaders.

- Morten Hansen and Nitin Nohria, "How to build collaborative advantage," *MIT Sloan Management Review*, **46**:1 (2004), 22–30.

    In "How to build collaborative advantage," Hansen and Nohria note that for many years, MNCs could compete successfully by exploiting scale and scope economies or by taking advantage of imperfections in the world's goods, labor, and capital markets. But these ways of competing are no longer as profitable. The new economies of scope are based on the ability of business units, subsidiaries, and functional departments within the company to collaborate successfully by sharing knowledge and jointly developing new products and services. Collaboration can be an MNC's source of competitive advantage because it does not occur automatically – far from it. And in order to overcome those barriers, companies will have to develop distinct organizing capabilities that cannot be easily imitated. A framework is presented that links managerial action, barriers to interunit collaboration, and value creation in MNCs to help managers understand how collaborative advantage can work.

All of these readings emphasize the multidimensional capabilities that must be built for effective strategy implementation in the transnational organization.

8 Shaping the Transnational's Future
Defining an Evolving Global Role

As powerful forces of globalization continued driving the growth and expansion of multinational enterprises (MNEs), questions were increasingly raised about what responsibilities came with the power that these large companies had accumulated. Indeed, some of these questions and concerns have been behind a slowdown and even reversal of some of the earlier globalizing dynamics. In this final chapter, we address this issue by examining the evolving role of the MNE in the dynamic political economy of the twenty-first century.

The recent decades of growth in the global economy have also advanced the development of most large nation-states in which MNEs operated, as their economic and social infrastructure benefited from the value created through booming cross-border trade and investment. However, another group of countries has remained largely in the backwash of the potent developmental forces of globalization. While the richest nations argued that the rising tide of globalization would lift all boats, to those in the poorest countries, it appeared to be lifting mainly the luxury yachts. And despite half a century of effort, government-sponsored aid programs designed to narrow the growing gap between rich and poor nations have exhibited surprisingly little positive impact. With 71% of the world's population subsisting on less than $10 a day (and 11% on less than $1.90 a day), many have begun to feel that the MNEs that benefited so greatly from global economic expansion now have a responsibility to help deal with the unequal distribution of those benefits.

After discussing this evolving situation, this chapter will describe four different postures that MNEs have adopted in recent decades, ranging from the exploitative and the transactional to the responsive and the transformational. Although these are presented as descriptive generalizations rather than definitive normative categories, in today's global environment, there is a strong push to have companies move away from the exploitative end of the spectrum toward the responsive and even transformative end. These expectations are set out in documents ranging from the UN Global Compact to the voluntary industry norms and standards that have been established to provide guidance to the way the MNEs might think about their responsibilities abroad as they expand their operations into the twenty-first century.

For most transnational companies, the dawning of a new millennium offered exciting prospects of continued growth and prosperity. Yet, in the poorest nations on Earth, the reputation of large MNEs from the world's most developed countries was shaky at best in 2000, and in some quarters, in complete tatters. Indeed, a series of widely publicized events in the closing years of the twentieth century led many to ask what additional constraints and controls needed to be placed on their largely unregulated activities.

- In Indonesia, Nike employed children in unhealthy work environments, paying them $1.80 a day to make athletic shoes being sold for a $150 a pair to affluent Western buyers.
- In Europe, Coca-Cola refused to take responsibility when consumers of soft drinks produced at its Belgian plant reported getting sick, then finally acknowledging the problem only after 100 people had been hospitalized and five countries had banned the sale of its products.
- In India, a regional government was trying to cancel a contract with Enron for the construction of the Dabhol power station and the supply of power, citing the company's "fraud and misrepresentation" during the original negotiations.
- In South Africa, 39 Western pharmaceutical companies jointly sued the government and President Nelson Mandela to prevent the importation of cheap generic versions of patented AIDS drugs to treat the country's 4.5 million HIV-positive patients.

Each of these situations involved complex, multifaceted issues to which intelligent managers apparently believed that they were responding in a logical, justifiable manner – conforming to local labor laws and practices at Nike, conducting quality tests and communicating the data at Coco-Cola, enforcing legal contract provisions at Enron, and protecting intellectual property rights of the drug companies. Yet in the court of public opinion, their rational, abstract, and legalistic arguments were swamped by an overarching view of Western multinational companies operating out of greed, arrogance, and self-interest. They were seen as powerful hammers driving home a widening wedge between the "haves" and the "have nots."

The Growing Discontent

Partly because of this growing distrust of MNEs, a popular groundswell against globalization began to gather strength in the early years of the twenty-first century. Prior to this movement, globalization had been widely viewed as a powerful engine of economic development, spreading the benefits of free market capitalism around the world. Yet the increasingly apparent reality was that far fewer developing countries had seen the benefits of this much-discussed tidal wave of trade and investment. Indeed, to some living in these countries, the growing gap between the rich and the poor offered clear evidence that "globalization" was just the latest term for their continued exploitation by the developed world through the agency of MNEs.

This growing sense of dissatisfaction gained global attention in November 1999 when a huge crowd of protesters prevented delegates from entering a meeting of the World Trade Organization (WTO) in Seattle. In what became known as "The

Battle in Seattle," riot police fired tear gas and the non-violent protest turned violent. Predictably, the visible storefront presence of MNEs soon became a target, resulting in windows at Starbucks being smashed and a Niketown store being looted.

This widely reported event was followed the following year by a series of demonstrations around the world. First in Washington DC and then Prague in the Czech Republic, tens of thousands demonstrated against meetings of the World Bank and the International Monetary Fund (IMF), organizations that were also seen as agents of globalization. Then, in 2002, 300,000 demonstrators gathered at the Group of Eight (G8) Summit in Genoa, Italy, leading to a violent confrontation with police that resulted in the death of a young Genoese demonstrator. Again, MNEs became a focus of the demonstrations, with high-profile storefronts such as McDonald's and Starbucks becoming prime targets.

The arguments of the protesters were being buttressed by powerful allies, including the Nobel laureate Joseph Stiglitz, a former chairman of the Council of Economic Advisors and chief economist at the World Bank. In his book *Globalization and Its Discontents*, Stiglitz submitted that previous actions of the WTO, the IMF, and the World Bank had often damaged developing countries' economies more than they had helped them.[1] He pointed out that although the First World preached the benefits of free trade, it still protected and subsidized agricultural products, textiles, and apparel – precisely the goods exported by Third World countries. Rather than seeing MNEs as creating value in developing countries, Stiglitz suggested that their effect was often to crowd out local enterprise, and then use their monopoly power to raise prices.

While data compiled by the World Bank indicates that the percentage of the world's population living on less than $1.90 a day in constant 2011 purchasing price parity (the level defined as "extreme poverty") decreased from 41.9% in 1981 to 10.7% in 2013, there was still widespread concern that after three decades of globalization-driven growth, 767 million people were still barely surviving at this near-starvation income level. Indeed, many pointed to other data showing that during the same period, the gap between those living in rich and poor nations continued to widen. At the national level, the Maddison Project showed that in the 50 years since 1960, the absolute gap between the real income per capita of people in the richest and poorest countries has grown by 135%. But the number that attracted most attention was the Oxfam figures that showed that the world's richest 1% had more wealth than the rest of the world's population combined. It was all more fuel to stoke the continued uprising against the forces of globalization.

In the subsequent worldwide anti-establishment movement, there was an increasing recognition that globalization's shift required "adaptation and adjustment" that was largely being borne by low-skilled workers and those living in developing countries. And the villain in that transformation was the MNE.

---

[1] Joseph E. Stiglitz, *Globalization and Its Discontents* (New York: W.W. Norton & Company, 2002).

The Challenge Facing MNEs

Regarding the issue of global poverty, a view began to emerge that it was time to radically rethink an approach that relied so heavily on government-funded aid programs. William Easterly, a former research economist at the World Bank, pointed out that after developed countries had provided $2.3 trillion of aid to developing countries over the five decades immediately preceding the new millennium, it had become clear that the West's model of development had failed.[2] He argued that a large portion of foreign aid had taken a paternalistic view in defining both the problems and the solutions, and had provided for neither accountability nor feedback. A classic example was provided by the Ajaokuta Steel Complex in Nigeria, which despite receiving $4.5 billion of internationally funded aid since 1979, had never produced any steel. Finally, in 2016, the complex was handed over to private operators.[3]

In contrast to such underperformance and failure, the outstanding success stories in India and China have been achieved largely by unleashing the power of their market economies rather than through massive aid programs. In what the World Bank has called "the greatest poverty reduction program in human history," hundreds of millions of people in China have moved out of poverty since the late 1970s. In large part, this transformation has been due to the cumulative investment of $1,765 billion in 864,304 foreign investment projects approved in the 35 years following the announcement of China's open-door policy in 1979. Included in that total are 490 of the world's top 500 companies, who not only see China providing them access to low-cost labor and a huge fast-growing market, but also as a technology source in which they have established 1,300 R&D centers. Such a win–win consequence is due to one undeniable reality: the faster the poor gain wealth, the faster they become customers.

Considering this impressive record, the eyes of many in the international community began to turn toward the MNEs to provide at least a part of the solution to the intractable problems that numerous developing countries faced.[4] But this has required more than just a public relations exercise extolling the benefits of free trade and openness to foreign investment. It has meant understanding what role MNEs might play in dealing with some of the underlying causes of the widespread

---

[2] William Easterly, *White Man's Burden* (New York: Penguin Press, 2006).

[3] Antony Sguazzin, "Nigeria seeks to revive dormant $4.5 billion steel mill in 2016," *Bloomberg News*, February 9, 2016. Accessed April 25, 2017, www.bloomberg.com/news/articles/2016-02-09/nigeria-seeks-to-revive-dormant-4-5-billion-steel-mill-in-2016.

[4] For a discussion of such problems, see Joshua Margolis and James Walsh, "Misery loves companies: rethinking social initiatives by business," *Administrative Science Quarterly*, 48:2 (2003), 268–305. Companies are increasingly asked to provide innovative solutions to deep-seated problems of human misery, even as economic theory instructs managers to focus on maximizing their shareholders' wealth. This paper assesses how organization theory and empirical research have thus far responded to this tension over corporate involvement in wider social life.

discontent in the developing world. In financial power alone, the World Bank estimated that the net inflows of FDI into low and middle income countries in 2015 was about $1.4 trillion, nearly five times the amount of foreign aid and development funding flowing into that same group of countries.

For the MNEs, the immediate challenge has been to decide how to respond to widespread public questioning of the legitimacy of their rapid expansion and growing power over the previous half-century. Their longer term challenge is to determine whether they are willing to take a leadership role in dealing with the problems that are the underlying causes of the antiglobilization movement.

Responding to Developing World Needs: Four MNE Postures

To understand how MNEs have faced such issues in the past and how they might in the future, we will describe four somewhat archetypical responses along a spectrum of possible action, ranging from an approach we label "exploitative" to one we describe as "transformative." (The main characteristics of these four archetypes are summarized in Table 8.1.) Our observations suggest that the great majority – but clearly not all – MNEs have long since abandoned the former model; many believe that it is in their long-term interest to move rapidly toward embracing the latter.

The Exploitative MNE: Taking Advantage of Disadvantage

As we saw in Chapter 1, because a strong and enduring motivation for a company to internationalize is its desire to access low-cost factors of production, the ability to locate cheap labor has long encouraged MNEs to enter emerging markets. On entering these environments, it soon became clear that not only were the wages significantly below those in developed countries, but so were the health and safety standards, the working conditions, and even the human rights of the workers. The question facing MNE management was how to respond to that situation.

For a subset that we describe as "exploitative MNEs," the lower the labor rate, the longer the working week, the fewer the restrictions on working conditions, and the less regulation on workers' rights, the better. The companies that we categorize this way believe that cross-country differences in wages, working conditions, legal requirements, and living standards all represent unregulated opportunities for them to capture competitive advantage.

In the 1970s, such attitudes received strong support in the writings of University of Chicago economist Milton Friedman. Guided by the view that companies had a responsibility to maximize profits and that shareholders were their only legitimate stakeholder, he argued that "[those who believe that] business has a 'social conscience' and takes seriously its responsibilities for providing employment,

Table 8.1 MNE–stakeholder relationships in emerging markets: a typology

	Stakeholders					
	Economics			Societal	Political/regulatory	
MNE Responses and Attitudes	Shareholders	Customers	Employees/ suppliers	Local communities	Governmental and supranational agencies/ regulators (e.g., UN agencies)	NGOs
Exploitative *Views differences in wages, working conditions, and living standards as exploitable opportunities.*	Adopts classic Milton Friedman view: its only legitimate role is to maximize returns to shareholders.	Sells existing products and services, even if they have negative social or economic impact.	Exploits existing local wages, working conditions, and suppliers, driving them lower if possible.	Accepts no community responsibility for its social or environmental impact.	Seeks concessions and subsidies, using bargaining power to play national investment boards against each other. If bribery and corruption exist, engages in local practices to win benefits.	An adversary: NGOs actively work to force the MNE to change its behavior through protests, boycotts, political activism, etc.

Table 8.1 (*cont.*)

	Stakeholders				
	Economics		Societal	Political/regulatory	
	Shareholders	Customers	Employees/suppliers	Local communities	Governmental and supranational agencies/regulators (e.g., UN agencies)	NGOs
MNE Responses and Attitudes						
Transactional *Engages in law-abiding, non-exploitative, commercial interactions.*	Focus on shareholder returns, but believes a pure Friedman approach is inconsistent with the long-term interests of its shareholders.	Treats it as any other market. Makes product adaptations if they are economically viable and can increase market share.	Complies with local labor laws and workplace regulations. Uses cost-efficient local sources, pressuring them on price.	Adopts a Hippocratic oath approach toward communities: (i.e., "First, do no harm").	Obeys local laws and regulations, but uses country differences to gain competitive advantage.	A watchdog: NGO monitors the MNE's actions, urging or pushing it to do more.

Responsive *Acts in a way that is sensitive and responsive to the needs of all its immediate stakeholders.*	Feels a responsibility to be a "good corporate citizen" in the environments in which it operates.	Invests in potentially significant product or service developments and/or adaptations to meet local needs.	Committed to caring for its employees and developing their skills. Actively engages local sources, using its buyer power to improve working conditions for employees.	Aims to affect positively those whose lives it touches in communities in which it operates.	Sets its standard of behavior above minimum local legal requirements. Conforms to higher international standards (e.g., set by ILO or UNESCO).	An observer: NGO may be neutral or partially engaged with MNE. Limited mutual trust.
Transformative *Commits to leading initiatives to bring life-enhancing changes to the broader society.*	Persuades investors of the need for companies to be part of the solution by bringing their resources to bear on the root causes of problems.	Believes that by helping to move people out of poverty, it will create stability and goodwill and help grow the world's customer base. Develops products or services specifically to meet local needs.	Committed to upgrading the lives of its employees, inside and outside the workplace. Brings work-standard-compliant local suppliers into global supply chain networks.	Leads in developing the quality of life in the broad community (e.g., upgrading health education).	Actively raises local standards (e.g., transferring developed world workplace health and safety standards). Supports change agenda of international agencies (e.g., WHO, UNESCO).	A partner: NGO works with and supports the MNE working toward the same objectives.

eliminating discrimination, avoiding pollution... are preaching pure and unadulterated socialism."[5] Such absolutes from a Nobel laureate in economics provided the exploitative MNEs all the legitimacy they needed to embrace their oppressive stance, and during the 1960s and 1970s, many did. Surprisingly, a few still operate this way today.

One of the most commonly held negative images of MNEs relates to the use of "sweatshops" – workplaces characterized by some combination of hot, crowded, poorly ventilated, poorly lit, and unsafe environments – in which the labor force, sometimes including children, works long hours for less than a "living wage." Unfortunately, these are not extreme examples from an era long past. Following an in-depth investigation, *The New York Times* reported that workers from Bangladesh were paying between $1,000 and $3,000 to agents in return for the promise of work in Jordanian factories producing garments for Target and Wal-Mart. After they arrived at their new place of work, their passports were confiscated to ensure that they did not quit. Not only were they paid less than promised (far less than the country's minimum wage), they were forced to work 20-hour days and were hit by supervisors if they complained.[6]

Most MNEs have tried to avoid criticism around the sweatshop issue by outsourcing manufacturing. But as Nike, Wal-Mart, and many other high-profile companies found, such tactics are no longer effective in insulating the MNE from responsibility. Stories such as the one in *The New York Times* have resulted in widespread consumer outrage and public demands that MNEs take responsibility for the suppliers with whom they contract to make their products. In recent years, companies such as Apple, Nike, and Wal-Mart have yielded to the pressure of consumer boycotts and public criticism to step up their monitoring of suppliers.

Yet despite the pressure from consumers, governments, and non-governmental organizations (NGOs), there are still some MNEs that will simply shut down and move their factory to another city, state, or country. Understanding that many government agencies are desperately trying to attract investment to develop employment and increase their tax base, these exploitative MNEs will often play countries against one another. A classic example was provided by companies making soccer balls in Pakistan. When publicity about the widespread use of child labor forced them to change their practices, some decided to provide employees with materials that could be stitched by children in their homes. Others simply responded to government incentives to relocate to Bangladesh where their use of child labor continued.

In countries where corruption and bribery are common, pressure from local government officials and regulators to provide questionable subsidies and concessions has led some exploitative MNEs to engage in illegal activities. Justifying

---

[5] Milton Friedman, "The social responsibility of business is to increase its profits," *New York Times Magazine*, September 13, 1970.

[6] Steven Greenhouse and Michael Barbaro, "An ugly side of free trade: sweatshops in Jordan," *The New York Times*, May 3, 2006.

their actions with an attitude of "when in Rome. . ." some firms have been willing to engage in such practices in the name of maximizing profits. In one example, a report presented to a meeting of the G8 in 2013 documented how Glencore, a London Stock Exchange-listed company, had acquired mining assets valued at $1.63 billion that had been sold by officials of the Democratic Republic of the Congo (DRC) for $275 million. The deal, which had been conducted through intermediary offshore companies, also minimized DRC's tax income from the mines. The report concluded that the cost of the deal to the DRC was equivalent to the country's total annual health and education budgets for two years – a huge price to pay in a state with extremely high child mortality rates and 7 million children out of school.

Government regulations that have tried to eliminate such behavior have not been entirely successful. In 1977, in response to several high-profile examples of corrupt behavior by US-based MNEs, the US Congress passed the Foreign Corrupt Practices Act (FCPA). Yet such unethical payments have continued, as confirmed by the 2016 assessment of a $600 million penalty against Wal-Mart to resolve probes by the Justice Department and the Securities and Exchange Commission into allegations of bribes made by the company to government officials in Mexico, Brazil, India, and China. Because this penalty – one of the largest in FCPA history – is still under appeal, it is not included in the tally of $9.4 billion in FCPA fines collected by the US government in the decade up to 2016.

Beyond the relentless pursuit of low-cost labor and subsidized investment, unethical global practices have led some exploitative MNEs to seek market expansion regardless of whether it was likely to result in social, economic, or cultural damage. One definitive example unfolded in the mid-1970s, when Nestlé and other infant formula manufacturers became concerned that birth rates in most industrialized countries were flattening and declining. Shifting their attention to what they saw as huge opportunities in the emerging-country markets, they began a major marketing push in those countries. Marketing tactics included employing sales promoters dressed as nurses to hand out samples and providing hospitals with discharge kits of bottles and baby milk powder.

Subsequent reports of increases in infant mortality and malnourishment soon raised concerns that the practice was having negative health consequences. It was discovered that because mothers saw infant formula as "modern and Western," the practice of breastfeeding declined. But because many could not afford to use the formula at the recommended level, they diluted it. Not only was the baby not receiving necessary nutrients, the water being used to mix the formula often was unsanitary, leading to diarrhea, dehydration, and malnutrition. Furthermore, the immunities normally transferred from the mother via breastfeeding were lacking in formula, making the child less resistant to sickness.

The case proved important as one of the first examples in which public outrage was channeled into a worldwide boycott of Nestlé products. Even today, four decades later, that boycott continues, supported by major NGOs including Save the Children, CARE, and World Vision, protesting what they believe to be continued unethical practices promoting infant formula in Laos, Bangladesh, and other developing countries.

Beyond the direct way that it affects the lives of its employees and customers, the MNE can also have an impact – positive or negative – on the local communities in which it operates. In its single-minded focus on maximizing profit, the exploitative MNE is unlikely to accept responsibility for the social or environmental consequences of its actions. One of the most severe industrial tragedies in history involved a massive gas leak from a Union Carbide facility in Bhopal, India, an accident that resulted in 18,000 deaths and 50,000 permanent disabilities. The company was fined $470 million, and criminal proceedings were initiated against its key executives. In 2010, 26 years after the tragedy, the case was finally resolved in Indian courts, but it was immediately appealed by the government, which felt that a sentence of two years in prison for seven Indian company executives was too lenient.[7]

Subsequent decades have been punctuated by similar disasters for which MNEs have been held responsible. Some, such as BP's 2010 Deep Horizon oil rig explosion in the Gulf of Mexico, have been highly publicized. Others, such as the ongoing series of spills in the Niger Delta – at least 50 times the impact of the 1989 *Exxon Valdez* oil spill, according to the World Wildlife Fund (WWF) – go largely unreported. Shell and Exxon claim that most of the Nigerian spills have been the result of oil pipeline thieves and militant activists.

Because MNEs can operate outside the legal framework of any single government, some believe that they need to be better regulated and controlled. However, most supranational organizations and agencies (e.g., ILO, UNCTAD, and UNESCO) have been relatively ineffective in providing such oversight. As a result, many global NGOs have assumed the role of monitors and controllers of exploitative MNEs. As Nestlé, Nike, and Shell learned firsthand, these NGOs could exercise their power effectively through their ability to organize protests, boycotts, or political action, targeting the MNE's customers, stock owners, or regulators.

Not surprisingly, exploitative MNEs soon developed adversarial attitudes toward NGOs, and that relationship was reciprocated. Consider the example of the multinational tobacco companies that had been targeting developing-country markets for decades as regulatory pressure and consumer education shrank their markets in the West. During the early 1990s, when the former Soviet Union split into a dozen independent countries, the laws previously in place banning tobacco advertising, forbidding smoking in many public places, and requiring health warnings on cigarette packages were no longer binding in the newly created states. According to researchers, "post-transition, the tobacco companies exploited confusion over the legality of this Soviet legislation by advertising heavily to establish their brands."[8] Subsequent surveys indicated that in a part of the world where tobacco was already responsible for twice the number of deaths among men as in the West, there has been a significant increase in youth smoking.

---

[7] See www.bhopal.com and www.responsiblecare.org.

[8] A. B. Gilmore and M. McKee, "Tobacco and transition: an overview of industry investment, impact, and influence in the former Soviet Union," *Tobacco Control* 13 (2004), 136–42.

Similar tactics were being employed in many developing countries in Africa and Asia. To fight this growing trend, public health researchers and anti-smoking NGOs have mounted a sustained response. But while they lobby governments to establish anti-smoking controls and publicize the negative implications of MNE activities in the region, the tobacco companies counter this by emphasizing the job creation and increased taxes that their industry generates.

The adversarial relationship between the groups continues. In 2011, when British American Tobacco (BAT) threatened to sue the Namibian government over its plan to require warning statements and photos on cigarette packages, NGOs from 50 countries banded together to communicate their support of the government's actions and their willingness to help it defend against what they described as BAT's "bullying." Although Namibia eventually folded to the legal pressure of BAT, in 2016 Uruguay won a six-year battle against a $25 million suit brought by Philip Morris to prevent the government requiring graphic warnings on cigarette packages.

Overall, the picture of the exploitative MNE is a distressing one. It is an organization that is willing to collude with political elites, violate environmental norms, ignore the welfare of consumers and employees, and expose emerging market communities to potential harm. Fortunately, it seems to be a species in decline.

The Transactional MNE: Doing Deals, Respecting Laws

Although the examples cited in the previous section indicate that some companies still exhibit elements of the exploitative MNE, fortunately few companies today are still driven only by the objective of maximizing profit in the sole service of the shareholder. In the pure form articulated by economist Milton Friedman, this philosophy was opposed to corporations making charitable donations or acting in response to any social issue. Today, most publicly owned corporations demonstrate at least a little charitable generosity and show at least some sensitivity toward their communities. In part due to widespread public rejection of extreme profit maximization behavior, the minimum expectation of MNE behavior today tends to be based on what we describe as a "transactional attitude."

The difference between the transactional MNE and the exploitative one is that the former adopts an approach that is both legally compliant and socially aware in its emerging market dealings. Yet despite adopting a relationship with its environment that is almost exclusively commercial, the transactional MNE, unlike its exploitative counterpart, does not pursue the bottom line at all costs. Indeed, many companies that once were insensitive to the serious problems that their aggressive or indifferent attitudes created have evolved from their exploitative approach to adopt a more responsible transactional posture.

The transactional MNE's relationship with its emerging market customers avoids the egregious missteps highlighted in the Nestlé experience. This implies having the sensitivity to recognize that products originally developed for consumers with very different needs or markets with very different characteristics should not be promoted where they are socially, culturally, or economically inappropriate. Typically, these companies are willing to make minor product or service adaptations to meet local needs or preferences, but only if such a change is likely to expand market share, increase profits, or meet some other commercial need.

For example, global fast-food giants such as McDonald's and KFC are often willing to make minor changes to their product offering or service approach on a country-by-country basis as long as they don't stray too far from their standard menus. Yet while such fast-food companies may be regarded as law-abiding, taxpaying corporate citizens in the countries in which they operate, they have also been accused of cultural insensitivity or worse. Because of their ability to change eating habits of those in developing countries from the high-fiber, natural foods of their local diets to high-fat fast-food offerings, the impact of such companies has often been to increase the health risks of those they are influencing.

Regarding employee relations, because the transactional MNE respects local labor laws and International Labor Organization (ILO) guidelines, it usually relates to its employees in a much less oppressive way than the exploitative company. For example, the transactional MNE would not be willing to have its own employees, or those of its subcontractors, work in the sweatshop-like conditions that we described in the previous section. Yet, although they conform to labor laws and workplace regulations, these companies still would be likely to maintain pressure on employees and suppliers to maximize the value of the legally lower cost labor that attracted their original investment.

In one widely publicized recent example, in the face of growing reports of harsh working conditions in its suppliers' plants, Apple was forced to move some way along this learning curve from exploitative to transactional MNE. For many years, Apple had sidestepped pressure from NGOs about labor practices employed in the manufacture of its products, arguing that it was the subcontractors, not Apple, that employed the workers. Finally, in response to pressure, in 2007 it began publishing audits of factories where its products were sourced. But in May 2010, the press reported that a Foxconn factory producing Apple products in southern China had admitted that nine suicides had occurred at its facility so far that year. In response to the resulting public outrage, Foxconn's initial insensitive response was to erect safety nets to prevent further jumps from dormitories resulting in death. Yet despite commitments to improve factory conditions and raise wages, a year later a watchdog group reported that the Apple subcontractor was still forcing employees to work up to 100 hours a week without proper compensation.

In response, Apple committed to ensuring greater compliance and transparency. It became the first high-tech company to join the Fair Labor Association, inviting that non-profit group to conduct inspections of its suppliers' factories. In its 2012 annual report on conditions in its suppliers' factories, Apple released the names of its 156 suppliers and their compliance with its standards. Foxconn subsequently raised the wages of workers by 25% and promised its employees that they would no longer have to work beyond the 49-hour working week limit set by Chinese law. The monitoring process continued, and in 2016, the teams of Apple and third-party inspectors conducting 705 audits reported that all but 3.4% of its suppliers complied with the company's code of conduct, which it regarded as the highest in the industry.

Compared to the exploitative MNE, the transactional MNE's attitude toward local communities no longer exhibits the indifference and irresponsibility of its less developed forebear. One lesson that transactional-oriented MNEs appear to have learned from the experiences of Nestlé in Africa, Union Carbide in Bhopal, and tobacco companies in the former Soviet Union is that it usually makes economic sense to obey both the letter and the spirit of local and international laws and regulations.

Following the signing of the North American Free Trade Agreement (NAFTA) in 1993, many had predicted that Mexico would become a pollution haven for MNEs with dirty chemical, metals, or paper plants hoping to take advantage of that country's low environmental standards or lax enforcement. Yet more than two decades later, research concluded that "no discernible migration of dirty industry has occurred."[9] The absence of such large-scale migration of companies fleeing tightening US regulations suggests that most North American MNEs appeared to practice a law-abiding, non-exploitative attitude toward emerging markets.

At a minimum, the transactional-oriented MNE takes the equivalent of a Hippocratic oath to communities. (The ancient Greek physician Hippocrates is credited with the expression "First, do no harm," which forms part of the oath taken by physicians.) When adopted by MNEs, such an attitude may increase the likelihood that the worst potential corporate abuses will be avoided, but that does not mean that transactional MNEs will be fully trusted or that their actions will not be carefully monitored by regulators or NGOs. And in recent years, it has often been the global NGOs that have taken the more active role in pushing MNEs to take more responsibility for their social, economic, and environmental impact.

Take the case of Nike. Despite the major concessions that the company made to the NGOs' demands in the late 1990s – to increase its working minimum age for footwear manufacture from 14 to 16, and eventually to 18, for example – it was clear that NGOs would remain interested in the company's practices. This is largely because Nike is a highly visible, highly profitable industry leader, dealing with 700 factories that collectively employ over half a million people, mostly in emerging markets. But Nike's relationship with the many NGOs with which it sparred through the 1990s has slowly changed. Although a few remnants of the activist-driven boycotts and protests remain, the heat has gradually reduced as the company created transparent reports on the pay scales, working conditions, and compliance in its supplying factories. In the process, the NGOs' relationship with Nike evolved from active adversary to vigilant watchdog.

Although not always enthusiastically embracing each other, this relationship between NGOs and transactional companies is based less on confrontation and

---

[9] Gustavo Alanis-Ortega, "Is global environmental governance working?" *The Environmental Forum*, May/June (2006), 23.

accusation and more on monitoring and challenging. And while the NGOs might agree that "doing no harm" is certainly a positive characteristic, they also challenge companies to consider whether that is a sufficient role for the MNE of the twenty-first century.

The Responsive MNE: Making a Difference

In the past, a large number – perhaps a majority – of MNEs might have exhibited behavior that was significantly or even predominantly exploitative or transactional, as we have described those terms. In recent years, however, management's concept of a responsible strategy has migrated from a passing acknowledgment of the need to develop socially sensitive corporate policies to a recognition that companies must articulate a philosophy that reflects their long-term viability as both participants in and contributors to the broader social, economic, and environmental practices in every environment in which they operate. This perspective requires managers to take a broader view of their constituencies and their roles and responsibilities.

There are some indications that companies are moving in this direction. A 2016 PwC global survey of 1,379 CEOs found that 64% of them said that corporate social responsibility was "core to their business rather than being a stand-alone program."[10] The data support the findings of a similar McKinsey survey of 4,238 executives from 116 countries that reported that only 16% of respondents saw their responsibility as being to focus on the maximization of shareholder returns compared to 84% expressing the opinion that high returns to shareholders must be balanced with contributions to a broader good.[11]

The responsive MNE, as we have dubbed it, reflects this view and undertakes to be more than just a law-abiding entity: it makes a conscious commitment to be a contributing corporate citizen in all the environments in which it operates. In contrast to its exploitative and transactional counterparts, the responsive MNC is more sensitive to the different needs of the stakeholders in developing countries and manifests this behavior more proactively in the way in which it deals with its customers, employees, and the community at large.

In his influential book *The Fortune at the Bottom of the Pyramid*, C. K. Prahalad argued that MNEs have a responsibility to contribute to development in the poorest nations of the world. In his words, "Big corporations should solve big problems." But he also made the case that in doing so, they can avail themselves of a huge opportunity to access a largely untapped market of 4 billion people. By investing in developing markets, creating jobs, generating wealth, and catering to underserved consumers, Prahalad contends that MNEs have an opportunity to bring into

---

[10] "20 years inside the mind of the CEO... what's next?" PwC 20th CEO survey. Accessed September 1, 2017. www.pwc.com/gx/en/ceo-agenda/ceosurvey/2017/us.

[11] "McKinsey global survey of business executives: business and society," *McKinsey Quarterly*, January (2006).

the marketplace millions of consumers from the two-thirds of the global population that earns less than $2,000 per year.[12]

Some companies have understood this opportunity for decades, none more so than Hindustan Lever. As Unilever's operating company in India for more than a century, this company has long understood that the key to developing scale and driving growth in that densely populated country is to expand its target market well beyond the middle- and upper-class consumers that are the focus of most MNEs in India. For many decades, Hindustan Lever has aimed at expanding its operations to serve the rural poor by adapting the company's products and technologies to their very different needs and economic means. Decades ago, for example, it developed a way to incorporate Unilever's advanced detergent technology into simple laundry bars, thereby providing superior washing capabilities in the cold-water hand-washing methods that characterize India's widespread practice of doing laundry in the local stream or village washhouse. The company also adapted to local economic realities and social structures by selling through small rural shops and a network of 50,000 *shakti* women who make a living on sales commissions earned by selling products from their homes in remote villages.

Even in sophisticated product markets, such as medical diagnostic equipment, there is the opportunity for MNEs to adopt a more responsive approach that can bring advanced technology to developing countries. For example, GE Healthcare's Indian R&D center invested $60 million to develop a range of products adapted to the simpler needs and more cost-constrained budgets of developing country health care systems. The resulting stripped-down model of GE's computed tomography (CT) scanner sells for about one-tenth of the top end $2 million Revolution CT that the company supplies to customers in advanced markets like the United States. GE's Indian engineers subsequently adapted its latest positron emission tomography (PET) technology and, in 2015, introduced an advanced PET–CT scanner that offered improved diagnosis for cancer, heart disease, and brain disorders. The Discovery IQ scanner designed for emerging countries cost 40% less than the original models and its market potential was expected to be huge.

Beyond adapting its current product line to meet the needs of these large, previously under-served developing-country markets, GE has created a new business it calls its Gold Seal Program. Through this program, the company acquires used x-ray machines and CT scanners, refurbishes them to their original specifications, and then resells them to developing-country markets. While not the latest models with the most up-to-date technological features, these machines are in high demand, and GE's initiative has earned it a 30% share of a $1 billion global market for refurbished diagnostic equipment, a market growing at 15% per year.

---

[12] C. K. Prahalad, *The Fortune at the Bottom of the Pyramid* (Upper Saddle River, NJ: Wharton School Publishing/Pearson, 2005).

But the responsive MNE accepts a role beyond that of a commercial participant in developing countries' economies, no matter how flexible and responsive. These companies also feel the responsibility to be good corporate citizens that have a positive impact on those whose lives they touch. For example, Starbucks has accepted the responsibility to help its farmer suppliers obtain higher prices for their coffee while simultaneously enhancing local environmental and labor practices. In 2004, it collaborated with Conservation International to create its Coffee and Farmer Equity (CAFE) practices, an initiative that planned a new agreement between Starbucks and the farmers. In return for farmers' compliance with labor and environmental standards independently set and monitored by Conservation International, they would be offered "preferred supplier" status, including long-term contracts and a price premium. In 2015, the company announced that over 99% of its coffee was ethically sourced under the CAFE standards. In 2016, along with other industry leaders, the company engaged in a new initiative coordinated by Conservation International to make coffee the world's first sustainable agricultural product. An initial priority of the initiative was to replace aging trees and, in 2017, Starbucks committed to provide 100 million trees to farmers by 2025.[13]

Many of the actions of these and other responsive MNEs reflect the aspirational standards of behavior contained in the voluntary Global Compact introduced in 1999 by Kofi Annan, then Secretary General of the United Nations (UN). Since then, the contract has been signed by more than 9,000 companies from 160 countries.[14] (See Table 8.2 for a summary of the key principles of the Global Compact.) Although it is a voluntary, self-regulated set of aspirational norms rather than a legislated and enforceable code, the Global Compact offers a way forward by encouraging MNEs to embrace a more responsive and constructive role in the developing world.

The Transformative MNE: Leading Broad Change

In recent years, there has been a growing number of examples of private sector organizations not only being sensitive and responsive to the problems and needs of the developing world, but also taking the lead in broad-scale efforts to deal

---

[13] More examples of such strategies are available in Michael Porter and Mark Kramer, "Strategy and society: the link between competitive advantage and corporate social responsibility," *Harvard Business Review*, 84:12 (2006), 78–92. This article proposes a new way to look at the relationship between business and society that does not treat corporate growth and social welfare as a zero-sum game. They introduce a framework that individual companies can use to identify the social consequences of their actions; to discover opportunities to benefit society and themselves by strengthening the competitive context in which they operate; to determine which CSR initiatives they should address; and to find the most effective ways of doing so.

[14] More recently, the Global Compact has helped establish the Principles for Responsible Management Education (PRME). Its mission is to "inspire and champion responsible management education, research, and thought leadership globally."

Table 8.2 The Global Compact's ten principles

Human rights
1. Businesses should support and respect the protection of internationally proclaimed human rights; and
2. make sure that they are not complicit in human rights abuses.

Labor standards
3. Businesses should uphold the freedom of association and the effective recognition of the right to collective bargaining;
4. the elimination of all forms of forced and compulsory labor;
5. the effective abolition of child labor; and
6. the elimination of discrimination in respect of employment and occupation.

Environment
7. Businesses should support a precautionary approach to environmental challenges;
8. undertake initiatives to promote greater environmental responsibility; and
9. encourage the development and diffusion of environmentally friendly technologies.

Anti-corruption
10. Businesses should work against all forms of corruption, including extortion and bribery.

Source: www.unglobalcompact.org/AboutTheGC/TheTenPrinciples/index.html.

with their root causes. Because of the cost and commitment required to take such action, it is hardly surprising that the boldest and most visible of such initiatives have been those taken by private individuals or their foundations. Highly visible current era global philanthropists, such as Bill Gates and George Soros, have created foundations that have committed billions of dollars to attacking some of the biggest problems of health, education, and welfare among the world's neediest populations.

However, several large companies have also stepped up to the challenge. Despite the huge commitment required, these pioneering transformative MNEs are leading major initiatives to help deal with problems facing the developing world. Beyond being good corporate citizens, they have concluded that they can and should take a larger role in the less advantaged countries in which they operate by bringing their resources to bear on the massive problems that the populations and governments of these countries face.

Most transformative MNEs evolve to this high level of commitment from the more modest business-linked activities that characterized those companies we described as responsive MNEs. For example, Heineken responded to the AIDS epidemic in Africa in the 1990s by creating a prevention and education program for its 6,000 African employees. In 2001, the company expanded the program to offer free anti-retroviral drugs to all infected employees, later extending the benefit to cover all their family members. In subsequent years, however, Heineken expanded the program to 21 public treatment centers. Then, in 2007, it created the Heineken Africa Foundation, providing it with initial funding of €10 million to fund prevention, treatment, and research programs in eight sub-Saharan African countries. In 2016, the Foundation provided €1.1 million to support such programs.

Another company whose recent commitments have vaulted it into the transformational MNC category is Unilever. Its Sustainable Living Plan (USLP), described in more detail in a case accompanying this chapter, provides a commitment that by the year 2020, the company will improve the health and well-being of 1 billion people worldwide, will cut the environmental impact of its products by 50%, and will source 100% of its agricultural products from sustainable producers. The bold plan is broken down into more than 60 social, economic, and environmental targets, each of which is monitored and reported on annually. Early progress has been impressive. By 2015, the company's externally audited USLP performance report described how the program had reached 482 million people through its programs to improve health and hygiene, achieved sustainable sourcing on 60% of its raw materials, and engaged with 2.4 million smallholder farmers and small-scale retailers in the company's commitment to enhance their livelihoods. Paul Polman, Unilever's CEO, explained that he simply believed that this is the way responsible companies should act: "I'm not interested whether the plan brings competitive advantage... It's the only way to do business in the long term."

Because such transformational programs often deal with long-term problems or challenge deeply embedded practices, they can be difficult to implement, particularly when social and economic environments are governed by very different cultural norms and legal frameworks. As a result, it often requires a long process of learning, adaptation, and, above all, commitment to achieve results. One of the most sustained examples of transformational change has been the commitment by the pharmaceutical company Merck to eradicate river blindness, a disease that exists almost entirely in the developing world. When the pharmaceutical giant developed a drug to prevent river blindness in 1987, it recognized that few of the 18 million sufferers of this debilitating disease or the 100 million who were at risk could afford the treatment. So the company decided to make the drug freely available for as long as it was needed to anyone suffering from or at risk of becoming exposed. Over the past 30 years, in partnership with numerous UN and governmental agencies, NGOs, and local communities, the program has provided for patients in Africa and South America Mectizan® tablets for 2.5 billion treatments, all without charge. It currently reaches 250 million people annually and prevents an estimated 50,000 cases of blindness each year.

As the preceding examples have shown, in implementing these activities, MNEs often find themselves working in partnership with NGOs or supragovernment agencies that can provide expertise in social program delivery that the companies typically lack. In doing so, they develop very different relationships with these groups than the adversarial or defensive exchanges that characterize exploitative or transactional MNEs' experiences with such organizations. It is a partnership that leverages the resources and capabilities of both groups and may well prove to be the engine that can drive the changes that have been so elusive in attempts to accelerate economic and social development in the world's poorest nations. If so, it will create a future role for the MNE that will make it an even more important and respected player on the world stage.

CONCLUDING COMMENTS

Over time, there has been an evolution in the roles, responsibilities, and expectations of MNEs operating in host countries around the world. In his seminal books *Sovereignty at Bay* and *Storm Over the Multinationals,* both published in the 1970s, Harvard Professor Ray Vernon expressed concerns about the "economic hegemony and economic dependence" that often characterized the relationship between MNEs and host-country governments in the developing world in that era.[15] And various corrupt or exploitative acts by those companies during this time period created what Vernon described as a sense of "tension and anxiety on the part of many nation-states."

As the anecdotes that open this chapter illustrate, MNEs are still susceptible to charges of insensitivity and irresponsibility. But in the four decades since Vernon's research was published, while the concern that MNEs were holding "sovereignty at bay" has not entirely disappeared, it has significantly subsided. And although there has been little success in creating the effective supranational agencies that once were thought vital to reigning in the unfettered power of the MNE, the rise of numerous, highly effective global NGOs has filled the role of the active "watchdog." As the several examples cited in this chapter show, NGOs have become very effective at using their clout with consumers, shareholders, and other company stakeholders to bring about change.[16]

But the biggest change has occurred in the evolving attitudes of companies toward their sense of corporate social responsibility and their commitment to a strategy of sustainability. Although a few firms have remained stuck in an exploitative mode, most have adopted, at a minimum, a transactional approach. And with the growing influence of government and NGO pressure, consumer demands, and increasingly rising shareholder expectations, the trend is clearly moving toward responsive and even transformative models.

The social needs in emerging markets are great, and MNEs and their managers are feeling both pressure and encouragement to respond. In addition to transforming the lives of those at the "bottom of the pyramid," their commitment of resources to such activities may very well represent one of the most important investments that the MNE will ever make.

[15] Raymond Vernon, *Sovereignty at Bay* (New York: Basic Books, 1971); Raymond Vernon, *Storm Over the Multinationals: The Real Issues* (Cambridge, MA: Harvard University Press, 1977).

[16] For more discussion on the roles of NGOs, see Michael Yaziji, "Turning gadflies into allies," *Harvard Business Review*, 82:2 (2004), 110–15.

HARVARD | BUSINESS | SCHOOL   REV: NOVEMBER 14, 2006

Christopher A. Bartlett, Vincent Dessain, and Anders Sjöman

CASE 8.1 IKEA'S GLOBAL SOURCING CHALLENGE: INDIAN RUGS AND CHILD LABOR (A)

Professor Christopher A. Bartlett, Executive Director of the HBS Europe Research Center Vincent Dessain, and Research Associate Anders Sjöman prepared this case. HBS cases are developed solely as the basis for class discussion. Certain details have been disguised. Cases are not intended to serve as endorsements, sources of primary data, or illustrations of effective or ineffective management.

In May 1995, Marianne Barner faced a tough decision. After just two years with IKEA, the world's largest furniture retailer, and less than a year into her job as business area manager for carpets, she was faced with the decision of cutting off one of the company's major suppliers of Indian rugs. While such a move would disrupt supply and affect sales, she found the reasons to do so quite compelling. A German TV station had just broadcast an investigative report naming the supplier as one that used child labor in the production of rugs made for IKEA. What frustrated Barner was that, like all other IKEA suppliers, this large, well-regarded company had recently signed an addendum to its supply contract explicitly forbidding the use of child labor on pain of termination.

Even more difficult than this short-term decision was the long-term action Barner knew IKEA must take on this issue. On one hand, she was being urged to sign up to an industry-wide response to growing concerns about the use of child labor in the Indian carpet industry. A recently formed partnership of manufacturers, importers, retailers, and Indian nongovernmental organizations (NGOs) was proposing to issue and monitor the use of "Rugmark," a label to be put on carpets certifying that they were made without child labor. Simultaneously, Barner had been conversing with people at the Swedish Save the Children organization who were urging IKEA to ensure that its response to the situation was "in the best interest of the child"–whatever that might imply. Finally, there were some who wondered if IKEA should not just leave this hornet's nest. Indian rugs accounted for a tiny part of IKEA's turnover, and to these observers, the time, cost, and reputation risk posed by continuing this product line seemed not worth the profit potential.

The Birth and Maturing of a Global Company[1]

To understand IKEA's operations, one had to understand the philosophy and beliefs of its 70-year-old founder, Ingvar Kamprad. Despite stepping down as CEO in 1986, almost a decade

---

[1] This section draws on company histories detailed in Bertil Torekull, *Leading by Design–The IKEA Story* (New York: Harper Business, 1998), and on the IKEA website, available at http://www.ikea.com/ms/en_GB/about_ikea/splash.html, accessed October 5, 2005.

later, Kamprad retained the title of honorary chairman and was still very involved in the company's activities. Yet perhaps even more powerful than his ongoing presence were his strongly held values and beliefs, which long ago had been deeply embedded in IKEA's culture.

Kamprad was 17 years old when he started the mail-order company he called IKEA, a name that combined his initials with those of his family farm, Elmtaryd, and parish, Agunnaryd, located in the forests of southern Sweden. Working out of the family kitchen, he sold goods such as fountain pens, cigarette lighters, and binders he purchased from low-priced sources and then advertised in a newsletter to local shopkeepers. When Kamprad matched his competitors by adding furniture to his newsletter in 1948, the immediate success of the new line led him to give up the small items.

In 1951, to reduce product returns, he opened a display store in nearby Älmhult village to allow customers to inspect products before buying. It was an immediate success, with customers traveling seven hours from the capital Stockholm by train to visit. Based on the store's success, IKEA stopped accepting mail orders. Later Kamprad reflected, "The basis of the modern IKEA concept was created [at this time] and in principle it still applies. First and foremost, we use a catalog to tempt people to visit an exhibition, which today is our store. ... Then, catalog in hand, customers can see simple interiors for themselves, touch the furniture they want to buy and then write out an order."[2]

As Kamprad developed and refined his furniture retailing business model he became increasingly frustrated with the way a tightly knit cartel of furniture manufacturers controlled the Swedish industry to keep prices high. He began to view the situation not just as a business opportunity but also as an unacceptable social problem that he wanted to correct. Foreshadowing a vision for IKEA that would later be articulated as "creating a better life for the many people," he wrote: "A disproportionately large part of all resources is used to satisfy a small part of the population. ... IKEA's aim is to change this situation. We shall offer a wide range of home furnishing items of good design and function at prices so low that the majority of people can afford to buy them. ... We have great ambitions."[3]

The small newsletter soon expanded into a full catalog. The 1953 issue introduced what would become another key IKEA feature: self-assembled furniture. Instead of buying complete pieces of furniture, customers bought them in flat packages and put them together themselves at home. Soon, the "knockdown" concept was fully systemized, saving transport and storage costs. In typical fashion, Kamprad turned the savings into still lower prices for his customers, gaining an even larger following among young postwar householders looking for well-designed but inexpensive furniture. Between 1953 and 1955, the company's sales doubled from SEK 3 million to SEK 6 million.[4]

Managing Suppliers: Developing Sourcing Principles

As its sales took off in the late 1950s, IKEA's radically new concepts began to encounter stiff opposition from Sweden's large furniture retailers. So threatened were they that when IKEA began exhibiting at trade fairs, they colluded to stop the company from taking orders at the fairs and eventually even from showing its prices. The cartel also pressured manufacturers not to sell to IKEA, and the few that continued to do so often made their deliveries at night in unmarked vans.

Unable to meet demand with such constrained local supply, Kamprad was forced to look abroad for new sources. In 1961, he contracted with several furniture factories in Poland, a country still in the Communist eastern bloc. To assure quality output and reliable delivery, IKEA

[2] Ingvar Kamprad, as quoted in Torekull, *Leading by Design–The IKEA Story*, p. 25.

[3] Quoted in Christopher A. Bartlett and Ashish Nanda, "Ingvar Kamprad and IKEA," HBS No. 390–132 (Boston: Harvard Business School Publishing, 1990).

[4] Ibid.

brought its know-how, taught its processes, and even provided machinery to the new suppliers, revitalizing Poland's furniture industry as it did so. Poland soon became IKEA's largest source and, to Kamprad's delight, at much lower costs—once again allowing him to reduce his prices.

Following its success in Poland, IKEA adopted a general procurement principle that it should not own its means of production but should seek to develop close ties by supporting its suppliers in a long-term relationship.[5] Beyond supply contracts and technology transfer, the relationship led IKEA to make loans to its suppliers at reasonable rates, repayable through future shipments. "Our objective is to develop long-term business partners," explained a senior purchasing manager. "We commit to doing all we can to keep them competitive—as long as they remain equally committed to us. We are in this for the long run."

Although the relationship between IKEA and its suppliers was often described as one of mutual dependency, suppliers also knew that they had to remain competitive to keep their contract. From the outset they understood that if a more cost-effective alternative appeared, IKEA would try to help them respond, but if they could not do so, it would move production.

In its constant quest to lower prices, the company developed an unusual way of identifying new sources. As a veteran IKEA manager explained: "We do not buy products from our suppliers. We buy unused production capacity." It was a philosophy that often led its purchasing managers to seek out seasonal manufacturers with spare off-season capacity. There were many classic examples of how IKEA matched products to supplier capabilities: they had sail makers

make seat cushions, window factories produce table frames, and ski manufacturers build chairs in their off-season. The manager added, "We've always worried more about finding the right management at our suppliers than finding high-tech facilities. We will always help good management to develop their capacity."

Growing Retail: Expanding Abroad

Building on the success of his first store, Kamprad self-financed a store in Stockholm in 1965. Recognizing a growing use of automobiles in Sweden, he bucked the practice of having a downtown showroom and opted for a suburban location with ample parking space. When customers drove home with their furniture in flat packed boxes, they assumed two of the costliest parts of traditional furniture retailing—home delivery and assembly.

In 1963, even before the Stockholm store had opened, IKEA had expanded into Oslo, Norway. A decade later, Switzerland became its first non-Scandinavian market, and in 1974 IKEA entered Germany, which soon became its largest market. (See Exhibit 1 for IKEA's worldwide expansion.) At each new store the same simple Scandinavian-design products were backed up with a catalog and offbeat advertising, presenting the company as "those impossible Swedes with strange ideas." And reflecting the company's conservative values, each new entry was financed by previous successes.[6]

During this expansion, the IKEA concept evolved and became increasingly formalized. (Exhibit 2 summarizes important events in IKEA's corporate history.) It still built large, suburban stores with knockdown furniture in flat packages the customers brought home to assemble themselves. But as the concept was refined, the company required that each store follow a predetermined design, set up to maximize customers' exposure to the product range. The concept mandated, for instance, that the living room

---

[5] This policy was modified after a number of East European suppliers broke their contracts with IKEA after the fall of the Berlin Wall opened new markets for them. IKEA's subsequent supply chain problems and loss of substantial investments led management to develop an internal production company, Swedwood, to ensure delivery stability. However, it was decided that only a limited amount of IKEA's purchases (perhaps 10%) should be sourced from Swedwood.

[6] By 2005, company lore had it that IKEA had only taken one bank loan in its corporate history—which it had paid back as soon as the cash flow allowed.

Exhibit 1
IKEA Stores, Fiscal Year Ending August 1994

a. Historical Store Growth

	1954	1964	1974	1984	1994
Number of Stores	0	2	9	52	114

b. Country's First Store

Year	First Store (with city) Country	City
1958	Sweden	Älmhult
1963	Norway	Oslo
1969	Denmark	Copenhagen
1973	Switzerland	Zürich
1974	Germany	Munich
1975	Australia	Artamon
1976	Canada	Vancouver
1977	Austria	Vienna
1978	Netherlands	Rotterdam
1978	Singapore	Singapore
1980	Spain	Gran Canaria
1981	Iceland	Reykjavik
1981	France	Paris
1983	Saudi Arabia	Jeddah
1984	Belgium	Brussels
1984	Kuwait	Kuwait City
1985	United States	Philadelphia
1987	United Kingdom	Manchester
1988	Hong Kong	Hong Kong
1989	Italy	Milan
1990	Hungary	Budapest
1991	Poland	Platan
1991	Czech Republic	Prague
1991	United Arab Emirates	Dubai
1992	Slovakia	Bratislava
1994	Taiwan	Taipei

Source: IKEA website, http://franchisor.ikea.com/txtfacts.html, accessed October 15, 2004.

interiors should follow immediately after the entrance. IKEA also serviced customers with features such as a playroom for children, a low-priced restaurant, and a "Sweden Shop" for groceries that had made IKEA Sweden's leading food exporter. At the same time, the range gradually expanded beyond furniture to include a full line of home furnishing products such as textiles, kitchen utensils, flooring, rugs and carpets, lamps, and plants.

Exhibit 2
IKEA History: Selected Events

Year	Event
1943	IKEA is founded. Ingvar Kamprad constructs the company name from his initials (**I**ngvar **K**amprad), his home farm (**E**lmtaryd), and its parish (**A**gunnary**d**).
1945	The first IKEA ad appears in press, advertising mail-order products.
1948	Furniture is introduced into the IKEA product range. Products are still only advertised through ads.
1951	The first IKEA catalogue is distributed.
1955	IKEA starts to design its own furniture.
1956	Self-assembly furniture in flat packs is introduced.
1958	The first IKEA store opens in Älmhult, Sweden.
1961	Contract with Polish sources, IKEA's first non-Scandinavian suppliers. First delivery is 20,000 chairs.
1963	The first IKEA store outside Sweden opens in Norway.
1965	IKEA opens in Stockholm, introducing the self-serve concept to furniture retailing.
1965	IKEA stores add a section called "The Cook Shop," offering quality utensils at low prices.
1973	The first IKEA store outside Scandinavia opens in Spreitenbach, Switzerland.
1974	A plastic chair is developed at a supplier that usually makes buckets.
1978	The BILLY bookcase is introduced to the range, becoming an instant top seller.
1980	One of IKEA's best-sellers, the KLIPPAN sofa with removable, washable covers, is introduced.
1980	Introduction of LACK coffee table, made from a strong, light material by an interior door factory.
1985	The first IKEA Group store opens in the U.S.
1985	MOMENT sofa with frame built by a supermarket trolley factory is introduced. Wins a design prize.
1991	IKEA establishes its own industrial group, Swedwood.

Source: Adapted from IKEA Facts and Figures, 2003 and 2004 editions, and IKEA internal documents.

The Emerging Culture and Values[7]

As Kamprad's evolving business philosophy was formalized into the IKEA vision statement, "To create a better everyday life for the many people," it became the foundation of the company's strategy of selling affordable, good-quality furniture to mass-market consumers around the world. The cultural norms and values that developed to support the strategy's implementation were also, in many ways, an extension of Kamprad's personal beliefs and style. "The true IKEA spirit," he remarked, "is founded on our enthusiasm, our constant will to renew, on our cost-consciousness, on our willingness to assume responsibility and to help, on our humbleness before the task, and on the simplicity of our behavior." As well as a summary of his aspiration for the company's behavioral norms, it was also a good statement of Kamprad's own personal management style.

Over the years a very distinct organizational culture and management style emerged in IKEA reflecting these values. For example, the company operated very informally as evidenced by the open-plan office landscape, where even the CEO did not have a separate office, and the familiar and personal way all employees addressed one another. But that informality often

[7] Ibid.

masked an intensity that derived from the organization's high self-imposed standards. As one senior executive explained, "Because there is no security available behind status or closed doors, this environment actually puts pressure on people to perform."

The IKEA management process also stressed simplicity and attention to detail. "Complicated rules paralyze!" said Kamprad. The company organized "anti-bureaucrat week" every year, requiring all managers to spend time working in a store to reestablish contact with the front line and the consumer. The workpace was such that executives joked that IKEA believed in "management by running around."

Cost consciousness was another strong part of the management culture. "Waste of resources," said Kamprad, "is a mortal sin at IKEA. Expensive solutions are often signs of mediocrity, and an idea without a price tag is never acceptable." Although cost consciousness extended into all aspects of the operation, travel and entertainment expenses were particularly sensitive. "We do not set any price on time," remarked an executive, recalling that he had once phoned Kamprad to get approval to fly first class. He explained that economy class was full and that he had an urgent appointment to keep. "There is no first class in IKEA," Kamprad had replied. "Perhaps you should go by car." The executive completed the 350-mile trip by taxi.

The search for creative solutions was also highly prized with IKEA. Kamprad had written, "Only while sleeping one makes no mistakes. The fear of making mistakes is the root of bureaucracy and the enemy of all evolution." Though planning for the future was encouraged, overanalysis was not. "Exaggerated planning can be fatal," Kamprad advised his executives. "Let simplicity and common sense characterize your planning."

In 1976, Kamprad felt the need to commit to paper the values that had developed in IKEA during the previous decades. His thesis, *Testament of a Furniture Dealer*, became an important means for spreading the IKEA philosophy, particularly during its period of rapid international expansion. (Extracts of the *Testament* are given in Exhibit 3.) Specially trained "IKEA ambassadors" were assigned to key positions in all units to spread the company's philosophy and values by educating their subordinates and by acting as role models.

In 1986, when Kamprad stepped down, Anders Moberg, a company veteran who had once been Kamprad's personal assistant, took over as president and CEO. But Kamprad remained intimately involved as chairman, and his influence extended well beyond the ongoing daily operations: he was the self-appointed guardian of IKEA's deeply embedded culture and values.

Waking up to Environmental and Social Issues

By the mid-1990s, IKEA was the world's largest specialized furniture retailer. Sales for the IKEA Group for the financial year ending August 1994 totaled SEK 35 billion (about $4.5 billion). In the previous year, more than 116 million people had visited one of the 98 IKEA stores in 17 countries, most of them drawn there by the company's product catalog, which was printed yearly in 72 million copies in 34 languages. The privately held company did not report profit levels, but one estimate put its net margin at 8.4% in 1994, yielding a net profit of SEK 2.9 billion (about $375 million).[8]

After decades of seeking new sources, in the mid-1990s IKEA worked with almost 2,300 suppliers in 70 countries, sourcing a range of around 11,200 products. Its relationship with its suppliers was dominated by commercial issues, and its 24 trading service offices in 19 countries primarily monitored production, tested new product ideas, negotiated prices, and checked quality. (See Exhibit 4 for selected IKEA figures in 1994.) That relationship began to change during the 1980s, however, when environmental problems emerged with some of its products. And it was even more severely challenged in the mid-1990s when accusations of IKEA suppliers using child labor surfaced.

[8] Estimation in Bo Pettersson, "Han släpper aldrig taget," *Veckans Affärer*, March 1, 2004, pp. 30–48.

Exhibit 3
"A Furniture Dealer's Testament"–A Summarized Overview
In 1976, Ingvar Kamprad listed nine aspects of IKEA that he believed formed the basis of the IKEA culture together with the vision statement "To create a better everyday life for the many people." These aspects are given to all new employees through a pamphlet titled "A Furniture Dealer's Testament." The following table summarizes the major points:

Cornerstone	Summarize Description
1. The Product Range–Our Identity	IKEA sells well-designed, functional home furnishing products at prices so low that as many people as possible can afford them.
2. The IKEA Spirit–A Strong and Living Reality	IKEA is about enthusiasm, renewal, thrift, responsibility, humbleness toward the task and simplicity.
3. Profit Gives Us Resources	IKEA will achieve profit (which Kamprad describes as a "wonderful word") through the lowest prices, good quality, economical development of products, improved purchasing processes and cost savings.
4. Reaching Good Results with Small Means	"Waste is a deadly sin."
5. Simplicity is a Virtue	Complex regulations and exaggerated planning paralyze. IKEA people stay simple in style and habits as well as in their organizational approach.
6. Doing it a Different Way	IKEA is run from a small village in the woods. IKEA asks shirt factories to make seat cushions and window factories to make table frames. IKEA discounts its umbrellas when it rains. IKEA does things differently.
7. Concentration–Important to Our Success	"We can never do everything everywhere, all at the same time." At IKEA, you choose the most important thing to do and finish that before starting a new project.
8. Taking Responsibility–A Privilege	"The fear of making mistakes is the root of bureaucracy." Everyone has the right to make mistakes; in fact, everyone has an obligation to make mistakes.
9. Most Things Still Remain to be Done. A Glorious Future!	IKEA is only at the beginning of what it might become. 200 stores is nothing. "We are still a small company at heart."

Source: Adapted by casewriters from IKEA's "A Furniture Dealer's Testament"; Bertil Torekull, *Leading by Design: The IKEA Story* (New York: Harper Business, 1998, p. 112); and interviews.

The Environmental Wake-Up: Formaldehyde

In the early 1980s, Danish authorities passed regulations to define limits for formaldehyde emissions permissible in building products. The chemical compound was used as binding glue in materials such as plywood and particleboard and often seeped out as gas. At concentrations above 0.1 mg/kg in air, it could cause watery eyes, headaches, a burning sensation in the throat, and difficulty breathing. With IKEA's profile as a leading local furniture retailer using particleboard in many of its products, it became a prime target for regulators wanting to publicize the new standards. So when tests showed that some IKEA products emitted more formaldehyde than was allowed

Exhibit 4
IKEA in Figures, 1993–1994 (fiscal year ending August 31, 1994)
a. Sales

Country/region	SEK billion	Percentage
Germany	10.4	29.70%
Sweden	3.9	11.20%
Austria, France, Italy, Switzerland	7.7	21.90%
Belgium, Netherlands, United Kingdom, Norway	7.3	20.80%
North America (U.S. and Canada)	4.9	13.90%
Czech Republic, Hungary, Poland, Slovakia	0.5	1.50%
Australia	0.4	1.00%
	35.0	

b. Purchasing

Country/region	Percentage
Nordic Countries	33.4%
East and Central Europe	14.3%
Rest of Europe	29.6%
Rest of the World	22.7%

Source: IKEA Facts and Figures, 1994.

by legislation, the case was widely publicized and the company was fined. More significantly–and the real lesson for IKEA–was that due to the publicity, its sales dropped 20% in Denmark.

In response to this situation, the company quickly established stringent requirements regarding formaldehyde emissions but soon found that suppliers were failing to meet its standards. The problem was that most of its suppliers bought from subsuppliers, who in turn bought the binding materials from glue manufacturers. Eventually, IKEA decided it would have to work directly with the glue-producing chemical companies and, with the collaboration of companies such as ICI and BASF, soon found ways to reduce the formaldehyde off-gassing in its products.[9]

A decade later, however, the formaldehyde problem returned. In 1992, an investigative team from a large German newspaper and TV company found that IKEA's best-selling bookcase series, Billy, had emissions higher than German legislation allowed. This time, however, the source of the problem was not the glue but the lacquer on the bookshelves. In the wake of headlines describing "deadly poisoned bookshelves," IKEA immediately stopped both the production and sales of Billy bookcases worldwide and corrected the problem before resuming distribution. Not counting the cost of lost sales and production or the damage to goodwill, the Billy incident was estimated to have cost IKEA $6 million to $7 million.[10]

These events prompted IKEA to address broader environmental concerns more directly. Since wood was the principal material in about

[9] Based on case study by The Natural Step, "Organizational Case Summary: IKEA," available at http://www.naturalstep.org/learn/docs/cs/case_ikea.pdf, accessed October 5, 2005.

[10] Ibid.

half of all IKEA products, forestry became a natural starting point. Following discussions with both Greenpeace and World Wide Fund for Nature (WWF, formerly World Wildlife Fund) and using standards set by the Forest Stewardship Council, IKEA established a forestry policy stating that IKEA would not accept any timber, veneer, plywood, or layer-glued wood from intact natural forests or from forests with a high conservation value. This meant that IKEA had to be willing to take on the task of tracing all wood used in IKEA products back to its source.[11] To monitor compliance, the company appointed forest managers to carry out random checks of wood suppliers and run projects on responsible forestry around the world.

In addition to forestry, IKEA identified four other areas where environmental criteria were to be applied to its business operations: adapting the product range; working with suppliers; transport and distribution; and ensuring environmentally conscious stores. For instance, in 1992, the company began using chlorine-free recycled paper in its catalogs; it redesigned the best-selling OGLA chair–originally manufactured from beech–so it could be made using waste material from yogurt cup production; and it redefined its packaging principles to eliminate any use of PVC. The company also maintained its partnership with WWF, resulting in numerous projects on global conservation, and funded a global forest watch program to map intact natural forests worldwide. In addition, it engaged in an ongoing dialogue with Greenpeace on forestry.[12]

The Social Wake-Up: Child Labor

In 1994, as IKEA was still working to resolve the formaldehyde problems, a Swedish television documentary showed children in Pakistan working at weaving looms. Among the several Swedish companies mentioned in the film as importers of carpets from Pakistan, IKEA was the only high-profile name on the list. Just two months into her job as business area manager for carpets, Marianne Barner recalled the shockwaves that the TV program sent through the company:

> The use of child labor was not a high-profile public issue at the time. In fact, the U.N. Convention on the Rights of the Child had only been published in December 1989. So, media attention like this TV program had an important role to play in raising awareness on a topic not well known and understood–including at IKEA. ... We were caught completely unaware. It was not something we had been paying attention to. For example, I had spent a couple of months in India learning about trading but got no exposure to child labor. Our buyers met suppliers in their city offices and rarely got out to where production took place. ... Our immediate response to the program was to apologize for our ignorance and acknowledge that we were not in full control of this problem. But we also committed to do something about it.

As part of its response, IKEA sent a legal team to Geneva to seek input and advice from the International Labor Organization (ILO) on how to deal with the problem. They learned that Convention 138, adopted by the ILO in 1973 and ratified by 120 countries, committed ratifying countries to working for the abolition of labor by children under 15 or the age of compulsory schooling in that country. India, Pakistan, and Nepal were not signatories to the convention.[13] Following these discussions with the ILO, IKEA added a clause to all supply contracts–a "black-and-white" clause, as Barner put it–stating simply that if the supplier employed children under legal working age, the contract would be cancelled.

To take the load off field trading managers and to provide some independence to the monitoring process, the company appointed a third-party

[11] "IKEA–Social and Environmental Responsibility Report 2004," p. 33, available at http://www.ikea-group.ikea.com/corporate/PDF/IKEA_SaER.pdf, accessed October 5, 2005.

[12] Ibid., pp. 19–20.

[13] Ratification statistics available on ILO website, page titled "Convention No. C138 was ratified by 142 countries," available at http://www.ilo.org/ilolex/cgi-lex/ratifce.pl?C138, accessed December 4, 2005.

agent to monitor child labor practices at its suppliers in India and Pakistan. Because this type of external monitoring was very unusual, IKEA had some difficulty locating a reputable and competent company to perform the task. Finally, they appointed a well-known Scandinavian company with extensive experience in providing external monitoring of companies' quality assurance programs and gave them the mandate not only to investigate complaints but also to undertake random audits of child labor practices at suppliers' factories.

Early Lessons: A Deeply Embedded Problem

With India being the biggest purchasing source for carpets and rugs, Barner contacted Swedish Save the Children, UNICEF, and the ILO to expand her understanding and to get advice about the issue of child labor, especially in South Asia. She soon found that hard data was often elusive. While estimates of child labor in India varied from the government's 1991 census figure of 11.3 million children under 15 working[14] to Human Rights Watch's estimate of between 60 million and 115 million child laborers,[15] it was clear that a very large number of Indian children as young as five years old worked in agriculture, mining, quarrying, and manufacturing, as well as acting as household servants, street vendors, or beggars. Of this total, an estimated 200,000 were employed in the carpet industry, working on looms in large factories, for small subcontractors, and in homes where whole families worked on looms to earn extra income.[16]

Children could be bonded–essentially placed in servitude–in order to pay off debts incurred by their parents, typically in the range of 1,000 to 10,000 rupees ($30 to $300). But due to the astronomical interest rates and the very low wages offered to children, it could take years to pay off such loans. Indeed, some indentured child laborers eventually passed on the debt to their own children. The Indian government stated that it was committed to the abolition of bonded labor, which had been illegal since the Children (Pledging of Labour) Act passed under British rule in 1933. The practice continued to be widespread, however, and to reinforce the earlier law, the government passed the Bonded Labour System (Abolition) Act in 1976.[17]

But the government took a less absolute stand on unbonded child labor, which it characterized as "a socioeconomic phenomenon arising out of poverty and the lack of development." The Child Labour (Prohibition and Regulation) Act of 1986 prohibited the use of child labor (applying to those under 14) in certain defined "hazardous industries" and regulated children's hours and working conditions in others. But the government felt that the majority of child labor involved "children working alongside and under the supervision of their parents" in agriculture, cottage industries, and service roles. Indeed, the law specifically permitted children to work in craft industries "in order not to outlaw the passage of specialized handicraft skills from generation to generation."[18] Critics charged that even with these laws on the books, exploitive child labor–including bonded labor–was widespread because laws were poorly enforced and prosecution rarely severe.[19]

Action Required: New Issues, New Options

In the fall of 1994, after managing the initial response to the crisis, Barner and her direct

[14] Indian Government Policy Statements, "Child Labor and India," available at http://www.indianembassy.org/policy/Child_Labor/childlabor_2000.htm, accessed October 1, 2005.

[15] Human Rights Watch figures, available at http://www.hrw.org/reports/1996/India3.htm, accessed October 1, 2005.

[16] Country Reports in Human Rights, U.S. State Department, February 2000, available at http://www.state.gov/g/drl/rls/hrrpt/2000/, accessed October 1, 2005.

[17] Indian Government Policy Statements, "Child Labor and India," available at http://www.indianembassy.org/policy/Child_Labor/childlabor_2000.htm, accessed October 1, 2005.

[18] Ibid.

[19] Human Rights Watch data, available at http://www.hrw.org/reports/1996/India3.htm, accessed October 1, 2005.

Exhibit 5
The U.N. Convention on the Rights of the Child: Article 32

1. States Parties recognize the right of the child to be protected from economic exploitation and from performing any work that is likely to be hazardous or to interfere with the child's education, or to be harmful to the child's health or physical, mental, spiritual, moral, or social development.
2. States Parties shall take legislative, administrative, social, and educational measures to ensure the implementation of the present article. To this end, and having regard to the relevant provisions of other international instruments, States Parties shall in particular:

   (a) Provide for a minimum age for admission to employment
   (b) Provide for appropriate regulation of hours and conditions of employment
   (c) Provide for appropriate or other sanctions to ensure the effective enforcement of the present article.

Source: Excerpt from "Convention on the Rights of the Child," from the website of the Office of the United Nations High Commissioner for Human Rights, available at http://www.unhchr.ch/html/menu3/b/k2crc.htm, accessed October 2005.

manager traveled to India, Nepal, and Pakistan to learn more. Barner recalled the trip: "We felt the need to educate ourselves, so we met with our suppliers. But we also met with unions, politicians, activists, NGOs, U.N. organizations, and carpet export organizations. We even went out on unannounced carpet factory raids with local NGOs; we saw child labor, and we were thrown out of some places."

On the trip, Barner also learned of the formation of the Rugmark Foundation, a recently initiated industry response to the child labor problem in the Indian carpet industry. Triggered by a consumer awareness program started by human rights organizations, consumer activists, and trade unions in Germany in the early 1990s, the Indo-German Export Promotion Council had joined up with key Indian carpet manufacturers and exporters and some Indian NGOs to develop a label certifying that the hand-knotted carpets to which it was attached were made without the use of child labor. To implement this idea, the Rugmark Foundation was organized to supervise the use of the label. It expected to begin exporting rugs carrying a unique identifying number in early 1995. As a major purchaser of Indian rugs, IKEA was invited to sign up with Rugmark as a way of dealing with the ongoing potential for child labor problems on products sourced from India.

On her return to Sweden, Barner again met frequently with the Swedish Save the Children's expert on child labor. "The people there had a very forward-looking view on the issue and taught us a lot," said Barner. "Above all, they emphasized the need to ensure you always do what is in the best interests of the child." This was the principle set at the heart of the U.N. Convention on the Rights of the Child (1989), a document with which Barner was now quite familiar. (See **Exhibit 5** for Article 32 from the U.N. Convention on the Rights of the Child.)

The more Barner learned, the more complex the situation became. As a business area manager with full profit-and-loss responsibility for carpets, she knew she had to protect not only her business but also the IKEA brand and image. Yet she viewed her responsibility as broader than this: She felt the company should do something that would make a difference in the lives of the children she had seen. It was a view that was not universally held within IKEA, where many were concerned that a very proactive stand could put the business at a significant cost disadvantage to its competitors.

A New Crisis

Then, in the spring of 1995, a year after IKEA began to address this issue, a well-known

German documentary maker notified the company that a film he had made was about to be broadcast on German television showing children working at looms at Rangan Exports, one of IKEA's major suppliers. While refusing to let the company preview the video, the filmmaker produced still shots taken directly from the video. The producer then invited IKEA to send someone to take part in a live discussion during the airing of the program. Said Barner, "Compared to the Swedish program, which documented the use of child labor in Pakistan as a serious report about an important issue without targeting any single company, it was immediately clear that this German-produced program planned to take a confrontational and aggressive approach aimed directly at IKEA and one of its suppliers."

For Barner, the first question was whether to recommend that IKEA participate in the program or decline the invitation. Beyond the immediate public relations issue, she also had to decide how to deal with Rangan Exports' apparent violation of the contractual commitment it had made not to use child labor. And finally, this crisis raised the issue of whether the overall approach IKEA had been taking to the issue of child labor was appropriate. Should the company continue to try to deal with the issue through its own relationships with its suppliers? Should it step back and allow Rugmark to monitor the use of child labor on its behalf? Or should it recognize that the problem was too deeply embedded in the culture of these countries for it to have any real impact and simply withdraw?

⊗IVEY | Publishing

CASE 8.2 BARRICK GOLD CORPORATION – TANZANIA[1]

Professors Aloysius Newenham-Kahindi and Paul W. Beamish wrote this case solely to provide material for class discussion. The authors do not intend to illustrate either effective or ineffective handling of a managerial situation. The authors may have disguised certain names and other identifying information to protect confidentiality.

By March 2009, Canadian mining company Barrick Gold Corporation (Barrick) had only been operating in the Lake Victoria Zone in Tanzania for a decade. In the same year, Barrick had adopted a new name for its business in Tanzania,

African Barrick Gold plc (ABG), which was also listed on the London Stock Exchange. The company was widely considered to be one of the more "responsive" global corporations in the mining industry.[2] Its extensive mining activities in the region employed thousands of local people, and Barrick was engaged in social development

---

[1] This case has been written on the basis of published sources only. Consequently, the interpretation and perspectives presented in this case are not necessarily those of Barrick Gold Corporation or any of its employees.

[2] www.barrick.com/CorporateResponsibility/BeyondBorders/default.aspx, accessed March 24, 2009.

projects in various Tanzanian communities.[3] By October 2010, the company operated four main gold mining sites in the country.[4]

Despite Barrick's efforts to support social development initiatives in the Lake Victoria Zone over the past decade, discontent and resistance at one of its mining sites in North Mara still remained. This area posed challenges. A key question was why the tension and violence had not stopped in certain mining sites in the North Mara mining area, and whether there was much more Barrick could reasonably be expected to do to resolve the problem.

Background on Tanzania

Tanzania was a developing country located in East Africa, with a total land size of 945,087 square kilometres. It had one of the highest levels of unemployment and poverty in Sub-Saharan Africa. Its economy was heavily dependent on agriculture, which accounted for half of the gross domestic product (GDP), provided 85 per cent of the country's exports and employed 90 per cent of the work force. Topography and climatic conditions, however, limited cultivated crops to only four per cent of the land area. Industry was mainly limited to processing agricultural products and light consumer goods.

Like most developing nations, Tanzania had a very weak national institutional and legal system. It also had a very high rate of corruption.[5] The country needed support from foreign direct investment (FDI) and transnational corporations (TNCs) in order to promote businesses, employment, and other opportunities for its citizens. Tanzania wanted its institutions to be more transparent and accountable, and to regulate the activities of FDI and TNCs in addressing the country's social and ecological issues. Both local and international not-for-profit organizations

(NFOs), however, had continued to create a significant impact with respect to promoting responsive behaviour in corporate governance practices, positively influencing all involved stakeholders and other social actors to address social issues.

Following independence in 1961, Tanzania opted for a socialist command economic and institutional system, with socialist policies ("*Ujamaa*" in Swahili) being implemented in 1967. The emphasis of these policies was to promote co-operative institutions and collective villages with the aim of building an egalitarian society, eliminating ethnic and gender barriers, and creating a common language of Swahili for all. Within the practice of Ujamaa, the country had managed to unite its ethnic groups under a common language, with the result that the central government had created strong post-colonial nationalistic ideologies, unity, ethnic harmony and peace among its people. Compared to many post-colonial Sub-Saharan African countries that went through civil and ethnic strife and conflicts after independence in the 1960s and 1970s, Tanzania under Ujamaa appeared to be a successful model.

Towards the end of the 1980s, however, Tanzania began to experience significant economic stagnation and social problems. To combat these issues, in the early 1990s the government sought to privatize its economy and reform its institutions in order to attract foreign investment. The introduction of the famous post-Ujamaa Investment Act of 1997 was intended to encourage free market and trade liberalization in the country. Investment in various private sectors such as mining, tourism, fishing, banking and agriculture under foreign-owned TNCs served to bolster the country's reforms by creating employment opportunities for the local economy.

As the country continued to privatize and reform its national institutional and legal systems, many foreign companies sought to invest in its economy. The Tanzania Investment Centre (TIC) was created in the early 2000s as a tool for identifying possible investment opportunities and aiding potential investors in navigating any procedural barriers that might exist

---

[3] www.barrick.com/News/PressReleases/PressRelease Details/2010/Barrick-Named-to-Dow-Jones-Sustainability-World-Index-for-Third-Consecutive-Year/default.aspx, accessed September 27, 2010.

[4] www.tanzaniagold.com/barrick.html, accessed October 1, 2010.

[5] See data on Tanzania at www.transparency.org.

during the process of investment in the country.[6] The liberalization of the banking industry in 2002, for example, saw the former Ujamaa Cooperative and Rural Development Bank replaced by the Commercial Rural Development Bank (CRDB) and the National Microfinance Bank (NMB), which promoted community investments across the country. In February 2009, the Tanzania Private Sector Foundation (TPSF) was created with the aim of strengthening the entrepreneurial culture among its citizens by providing communities and individuals across the country with entrepreneurial business ideas and grants. In June 2009, the government started an ambitious national resolution under the so-called "Kilimo Kwanza" policies (meaning "Agriculture First" in Swahili) to boost the standard of living among the *eighty per cent* of citizens who relied on agriculture for their livelihood.[7] It was based on Green Revolution principles aimed at boosting Tanzania's agriculture into the modern and commercial sector, and mobilizing for-profit organizations (FPOs) such as local private businesses and foreign-owned TNCs in the country to increase their investment engagement with the agriculture sector, both at the macro and micro levels (i.e. along with local communities).

In order to ensure that there was sufficient security and peace for private and foreign-owned investors (i.e. TNCs), in 2005 the government introduced a new entity called "Tanzania Security Industry Association." The association was based on local, professional private security firms and groups whose main tasks were to safeguard business firms' activities rather than letting the firms rely on local police forces. The largest and best-known local security firm was "Moku Security Services Limited," based in Dar Es Salaam, which had over 13,000 employees across the country. Other security groups with over 400 employees were "Ultimate Security Company," "Dragon Security," "Tele-security Company Limited," and "Group Four Security Company."

Private security employees were mainly retired army and police officers; young people who had lost their previous jobs following the collapse of the Ujamaa policies that provided "jobs for everyone and for life"; and individuals who sought better remuneration in the security sector than in the government public sector. However, due to increased demand for better security across businesses, many foreign-owned TNCs sought the services of security firms from abroad, mainly from South Africa's professional security firms such as the South African Intruder Detection Service Association (SAIDS). Some security personnel had combat experience, which helped them handle sophisticated forms of crime and intrusion.

The Tanzanian economy continued to grow and create job opportunities, training and innovative development prospects for its people. Earlier, the country had introduced new mining legislation such as the Mining Act of 1998 and the Mining Regulation Act of 1999 in order to harmonize investment relations between FDI and local interests. However, in April 2010 the government passed another new mining Act, following consultations with civil society groups such as the Foundation for Civil Society Tanzania (FCST), companies and other stakeholders. The legislation of a new mining Act imposed a new form of royalties that required all TNCs and local companies to be listed in the country and gave the state a stake in future projects.[8]

The country possessed vast amounts of natural resources like gold, diamond, copper, platinum, natural gas, and zinc deposits that remained underdeveloped. It was one of the more peaceful countries in Sub-Saharan Africa. In order to attract and protect the interests of FDI and TNCs and, of course, its own people, Tanzania had attempted to harmonize its investment practices and labour legislation. In order to create responsible institutional policies, in February 2010 the National Assembly of Tanzania enlisted a group of local environmental and toxicity experts to investigate environmental and toxic

[6] www.tic.co.tz, accessed April 1, 2009.

[7] www.actanzania.org/index.php?option=com_content&task=view&id=121&Itemid=39, accessed February 12, 2010.

[8] www.mining-journal.com/finance/new-tanzanian-mining-act, accessed September 27, 2010.

effects on the people and livestock in the North Mara gold mine in Tarime District, Mara Region, by the Tigithe River.[9]

For a number of reasons, Tanzania was a willing host nation for FDI. The country needed the input of TNCs in order to create employment and prosperity. In return, Tanzania could provide TNCs with low-cost labour and a readily available labour force. Low labour costs were an opportunity to support a host nation's development policy in attracting FDI and ultimately in creating a knowledge-based society in the midst of the globalization challenges that were faced by so many developing countries. Furthermore, Tanzania continued to create a local business environment in conjunction with various TNCs' global business interests in order to generate sustainable development policies and practices. It also engaged in market development initiatives that represented innovative learning opportunities and entrepreneurship ventures for its citizens.

Lake Victoria Background

Tanzania's Lake Victoria was surrounded by the three East African countries of Kenya, Tanzania and Uganda. The lake itself was named after the former Queen of England, Queen Victoria, and stood as the world's largest tropical lake and the second-largest freshwater lake after Lake Superior in North America. Covering a total of 69,000 square kilometres, the lake was as large as the Republic of Ireland and lay in the Rift Valley of East Africa, a 3,500-mile system of deep cracks in the earth's crust, running from the Red Sea south to Mozambique. Lake Victoria was the source of the Nile River, which passed through the Sudan and Egypt and finally reached the Mediterranean Sea.

Lake Victoria Zone in Tanzania

The Lake Victoria Zone consisted of the three regions of Mwanza, Mara (formerly called Musoma) and Kagera (formerly called Bukoba), and was one of the most densely populated

regions in Africa. Population growth around Lake Victoria was significantly higher than in the rest of Sub-Saharan Africa. During the last five decades, population growth within a 100-kilometre buffer zone around the lake had outpaced the continental average, which had led to growing dependency and pressure on the lake's resources.

Prior to the mining extraction boom in the early 1990s and following the collapse of Ujamaa, most people living in this region were mainly engaged in rudimentary forms of fishing, agricultural farming and keeping cattle, as well as other forms of co-operative activities that had been engineered by the country's former Ujamaa policies. Irrigation was limited to a small scale and often used rudimentary technologies to support both individual and co-operative farming activities. Noted for its temperate climate, the area had a mean temperature of between 26 and 30 degrees Celsius in the hot season and 15 and 18 degrees Celsius in the cooler months. The area was rich with tropical vegetation and fruits such as bananas, mangoes, corn, pineapple and many others. The lake was essential to more than 15 million people, providing potable water, hydroelectric power, and inland water transport, as well as support for tourism and wildlife.

The area remained one of the most fertile for farming activities and continued to attract immigrants from other regions of the country, as well as from Tanzania's neighbors in the war-torn populations of Burundi, Rwanda and the Democratic Republic of Congo. The presence of hundreds of TNCs engaged in various activities in the area was the main "draw" for these immigrants, who came seeking employment and new sources of livelihood.

The resulting population increase in the Lake Victoria Zone created several problems with respect to the lake and the environment. According to a report by World Watch Institute in Washington, D.C., the once clear, life-abounding lake had become murky, smelly and choked with algae. It had been reported that:

> The ecological health of Lake Victoria has been affected profoundly as a result of a rapidly growing population, clearance of natural vegetation along the shores, a booming

---

[9] www.dailynews.co.tz, accessed February 10, 2010.

fish-export industry, the disappearance of several fish species native to the lake, prolific growth of algae, and dumping of untreated effluent by several industries. Much of the damage is vast and irreversible. Traditional lifestyles of lakeshore communities have been disrupted and are crumbling.[10]

As a result of the overuse of natural resources in the area, the traditional lifestyles of the lakeshore communities were significantly disrupted, a situation that prompted both social and ecological concerns for the area and its residents.

The fishing industry was badly affected in the region following the introduction of Nile perch (Lates Niloticus) and Nile tilapia (Oreochromis Niloticus) into the lake. For example, in the 1980s a survey of the lake revealed an abrupt and unexpected increase in numbers among the Nile perch, constituting 80 per cent of all fish in the lake. In spite of working harder, local fishermen caught fewer fish since the populations of smaller fish, which traditionally had been the fishermen's primary source of livelihood, became decimated. In addition, the big oily Nile perch, generally referred to as "Mbuta," swam too far out in the open waters for the little local fishing boats and was too big to be caught in the locals' unsophisticated nets.

In response to an increased international demand for the Nile perch, commercial fishing fleets owned by foreign firms displaced local fishermen and many women in lakeside communities who worked as fish processors. The processing of fish, traditionally performed by women, was gradually taken over by large filleting plants. The women resorted to processing fish waste, commonly referred to as *mgongo-wazi*, or "bare-back" in Swahili. The waste, comprised of fish heads, backbones and tails, was sun-dried and then deep-fried and sold to local people who were drawn to its low price and nutritional value. Many fishermen were forced to look for alternative sources of livelihood, mainly seeking employment in extractive mining

corporations and other industries as manual labourers.

The water hyacinth posed another threat to the health of Lake Victoria. With the deceptive appearance of a lush, green carpet, the hyacinth was in fact a merciless, free-floating weed, reproducing rapidly and covering any uncovered territory. First noticed in 1989, the weed spread rapidly and covered areas in all three surrounding countries. It formed a dense mat, blocking the sunlight from reaching the organisms below, depleting the already-low concentrations of oxygen and trapping fishing boats and nets of all sizes. The hyacinth was also an ideal habitat for poisonous snakes and disease-carrying snails that caused bilharzias. The government, in partnership with other international agencies, had tried desperately to control the weed. Its most promising approach involved harvesting the hyacinth and using it either for compost or for biogas production.

The health implications associated with the declining state of the lake were extensive. Dumping untreated sewage in the lake and nearby rivers exposed people to waterborne diseases, such as typhoid, cholera and diarrhea, and chronic forms of malaria. The Lake Victoria Zone was known to have the most dangerous types of malaria in the world. As fish prices soared, protein malnutrition became a significant threat for communities living in the zone. Lack of regular income also meant that many people in the area could not afford to be treated for waterborne typhoid, yellow fever, and various forms of tropical worms such as tapeworms and hookworms.

Mining in Tanzania

Gold mining activities around the Lake Victoria Zone in Tanzania started during the German colonial period in 1894, when Tanzania was called Tanganyika. The First and Second World Wars accelerated the demand for gold production in the region and, following the introduction of Ujamaa in 1967, mining became a state-directed activity. By nationalizing the industry, the government hoped to capture more benefits from mining through the creation of local employment, direct spending on social services for

---

[10] www.cichlid-forum.com/articles/lake_victoria_sick.php, accessed April 1, 2009.

mining communities, and higher budget revenues from having a direct stake in the business. However, despite these high hopes, the mining sector failed to stimulate the industrialization of the country's economy. During Ujamaa, the production of gold declined significantly due to limited government funding and limited technological know-how within the industry. Mining activities that were performed illegally by small-scale operators contributed to several environmental and social problems.[11]

The collapse of Ujamaa in the 1990s, however, resulted in new opportunities for the country to attract mining companies from Canada, the United Kingdom, Australia and South Africa, all of whom were interested in gold exploration and development activities. Following successful exploration mining activities that began in 1995, Barrick invested in Tanzania in 1999 at the Lake Victoria Zone. It acquired gold reserves in the Bulyanhulu mine, located in northwest Tanzania, East Africa, approximately 55 kilometres south of Lake Victoria and approximately 150 kilometres from the city of Mwanza; Buzwagi near Kahama District; Tulawaka in Biharamulo, Kagera Region; and later at the North Mara gold mine in the northwestern part of Tanzania in Tarime District of Mara Region, approximately 100 kilometres east of Lake Victoria and 20 kilometres south of the Kenyan border.

According to the Tanzanian Mineral Authority and Tanzania Chamber of Minerals and Energy (TCME), since 2000 production of gold had been growing, making the Lake Victoria Zone one of the most attractive areas for employment opportunities as well as for business opportunities in other industries. Tanzania was Africa's third-largest producer of gold, after Ghana and South Africa.[12] Tanzania was also richly endowed with other minerals, including cobalt, copper, nickel, platinum group metals, and silver, as well as diamonds and a variety of gemstones. The energy sector was dominated by natural gas. Commercial quantities of oil had yet to be discovered. In 2008, TCME reported that a total of US$2 billion in the past decade had been injected into the Tanzanian economy by mining TNCs, and in total mining TNCs had paid the government over US$255 million in taxes within the same period.[13]

In 2002, Tanzania joined the African Union's development blueprint, an endeavour that was governed by the New Economic Partnership for African Development (NEPAD), to oversee an African Mining Partnership (AMP) with global mining corporations. The goal of this partnership was to promote sustainable development and best-practice guidelines for African governments as a way to ensure that their mining laws protected ecological and community welfare while maximizing remittances from the mining TNCs to the government budgets in a transparent and accountable way.

The country did, however, develop competitive tax packages and incentives to attract TNCs to invest in high-risk and complex exploration areas such as the Lake Victoria Zone. The government did not devise a practical and engaging strategy to utilize mining resources and revenues paid by TNCs to support the local communities that were situated around mining sites and who had lost their livelihood, homes, health, natural resources and recreation with little or no compensation.[14] Also, the government did not come up with a concrete strategy to deal with the chronic sewage and environmental issues in the area.

Like any TNC engaged in extractive mining activities in a developing country such as Tanzania with so many social problems and legal and institutional weaknesses, Barrick had faced conflicting pressures with regard to the way it engaged in locally based community social partnership (see Exhibit 1). Such partnerships were meant to address the social problems of unemployment, poverty, diseases and environmental concerns in a sustainable way. Barrick

---

[11] www.douglaslakeminerals.com/mining.html, accessed February 26, 2009.

[12] www.mineweb.co.za/mineweb/view/mineweb/en/page67?oid=39782&sn=Detail, accessed May 1, 2009.

[13] Ibid.

[14] "The Challenge of Mineral Wealth in Tanzania: using resource endowments to foster sustainable development," International Council on Mining & Metals, 2006.

Exhibit 1
Three Types of Engagement Behaviors

Dimension	Transactional	Transitional	Transformational
Corporate Stance	"Giving Back" Community Investment	"Building Bridges" Community Involvement	"Changing Society" Community Integration
Communication	One-Way	Two-Way	Two-Way
# of Community Partners	Many	Many	Few
Nature of Trust	Limited	Evolutionary	Relational
Frequency of Interaction	Occasional	Repeated	Frequent
Learning	Transferred from Firm	Transferred to Firm	Jointly Generated
Control over Process	Firm	Firm	Shared
Benefit & Outcomes	Distinct	Distinct	Joint

Source: F. Bowen, A. Newenham-Kahindi and H. Irene, "Engaging the Community: A Synthesis of Academic and Practitioner Knowledge on Best Practices in Community Engagement," Canadian Research Network for Business Sustainability, Knowledge Project Series, Ivey School of Business, 1:1, 2008, pp. 1–34.

strictly followed Western legal and property approvals to legitimize its mining activities in the country. It also continued to face challenges with respect to its efforts to strike a balance between its global strategies and those of the local subsidiary operations in Tanzania. Mineral wealth continued to fuel and prolong violent behaviour by local communities mainly in North Mara, thus failing to diversify economic growth and contribute to the development of communities in the Lake Victoria Zone. Corruption and weak institutional capabilities to enact or enforce the democratic, transparent and agreed-upon rules and laws that governed the operation and taxation of mining activities were a source of ongoing problems.[15] Also, some local communities did not see the potential benefits of large corporations in their communities.

Barrick Gold Corp in Tanzania

As a gold producer on the world stage, Barrick used advanced exploration technological systems for its mining development projects.[16]

The company owned one of the world's largest gold mineral reserves and a large land position across its subsidiary mining extraction activities. These were located across the five continents of North America, South America, Africa, Australia and Asia. As one of the largest Canadian mining companies, Barrick shares were traded on the Toronto and New York stock exchanges and on other major global stock index centres in London, as well as on the Swiss Stock Exchanges and the Euronext-Paris. It was a shareholder-driven firm. Barrick invested in Tanzania in 1999, following the completion of exploration activities that had started in 1995. The company's initial mining activities were limited to Bulyanhulu in Kahama Dictrict until 2004, when it expanded to other areas surrounding the Lake Victoria Zone.

Socialization was part of the corporate culture used to manage human resources (HRM)[17] in Tanzania. Each mining site had a training department. Barrick recruited university graduates who worked on administrative activities in corporate offices, and assigned manual labourers to mining

[15] www.revenuewatch.org/our-work/countries/ tanzania.php, accessed May 1, 2009.

[16] www.tanzaniagold.com/barrick.html, accessed, May 1, 2009.

[17] www.barrick.com/CorporateResponsibility/Employees/ AttractingRetaining/default.aspx, accessed April 24, 2009.

sites to work along with expatriates and locals who had experience in mining activities. Also, the company was involved in developing the so-called Integrated Mining Technical Training (IMTT) program, a joint project with the Tanzania Chamber of Minerals and Energy and the Tanzanian government. The goal was to offer locals the skills they needed to participate in the country's burgeoning mining sector and to reduce the industry's reliance on foreign-trained expatriates.[18] Barrick used its Global Succession Planning Program (GSPP) that provided expatriates with a chance to increase their knowledge and expertise by transferring them into assignments at other Barrick sites in Tanzania, and sites in other countries where the company operated.[19] The major role of GSPP was to instill the corporate culture through the training of employees regarding various mining technology skills, and to run the company's daily practices in accordance with the corporate business interests of the company.

Mission, Vision and Values

Given the questionable reputation of some global mining corporations with respect to sustainable development projects in developing societies, Barrick's core vision and values were to continue finding, acquiring, developing and producing quality reserves in a safe, profitable and socially responsible manner. Barrick claimed to promote long-term benefits to the communities in which it operated and to foster a culture of excellence and collaboration with its employees, governments and local stakeholders.

The company followed global corporate social responsibility standards as part of its larger global business strategies, using the vocabularies of business ethics, human rights and development. Among these strategies, the company placed significant emphasis on its social relationships with local communities and the right to operate in their land.[20]

Building Social Development Initiatives

Barrick was committed to making a positive difference in the communities where it operated. The company focused on responsible behaviour as its duty, as well as creating opportunities to generate greater value for its shareholders, while at the same time fostering sustainable development in the communities and countries where it operated. As a global TNC, Barrick strove to earn the trust of its employees, of the communities where its subsidiary operations were based, of the host nations' governments, and of any other persons or parties with whom the company was engaged in the sustainable development of mineral resources.[21]

In 2008, the corporation established a locally based mining institution in Moshi, Kilimanjaro Region. The aim of the institute was to provide training skills and opportunities for Barrick's mining sites and other mining TNCs in the country.[22] Local individuals involved in the training program included fresh university graduates in engineering and geology, and dedicated individuals from local communities where Barrick operated. Such an initiative supported Barrick's sense of corporate responsibility towards these two groups of people by providing tangible benefits to their communities in the form of employment opportunities and co-operative relationships.

Yet among community leaders and NFOs, there was clear discontent regarding the various foreign companies:

"The government has not addressed the role of foreign companies in our communities. Some

[18] www.barrick.com/Theme/Barrick/files/docs_csr/ BeyondBorder2008July.pdf#page=4, accessed September 27, 2010.

[19] www.barrick.com/CorporateResponsibility/Employees/ AttractingRetaining/default.aspx, accessed September 27, 2010.

[20] www.barrick.com/CorporateResponsibility/ OurCommitment/default.aspx, accessed September 27, 2010.

[21] www.barrick.com/CorporateResponsibility/ default.aspx, accessed March 25, 2009.

[22] www.ippmedia.com/ipp/guardian/2008/04/11/ 112164.html, accessed February 13, 2009.

communities have been compensated by the government to clear land for the mining company, but some did not receive any money. Most communities would tell you what was given to them by the government, which is very little. They cannot build a house and send children to school and so on. They feel their livelihood is gone forever."

"The mining corporation does not compensate people nor does it explain why it is operating in our communities. Of course, these companies have official binding contracts and the right to operate in our communities from the government. Local communities are in despair . . . the government is nowhere to be seen! The people are angry with the government and the mining company."

"People are not happy with the government. They are aware of the extent of corruption among the government officials in the region and districts, but they cannot confront the government the way they are now confronting the mining company. They think that the company might be more sympathetic to them than the government would be with respect to offering them jobs and other opportunities."

"The company has initiated several development projects in our communities [North Mara] in education, health and infrastructure. But we do not have jobs to access these better equipped services (education and health) nor essential means to support us to build community enterprises where we could apply our local skills in many activities. Though the company is doing very good projects here, we are still unhappy with the company. Our problems are long-term; they need serious engagement with us."

"The company discharges water to the land, which is causing lots of environmental problems on our farms such as land erosion and polluting of the rivers. We have more mosquitoes, snakes and snails at the moment than any time in our lives because of stagnant water caused by the company's water discharge. The exploration and explosive activities conducted at night on mining sites have caused shockwaves, panic and sleepless nights among neighborhood villages, making big cracks on community farms and land."

Two community leaders (representing local stakeholders' interests) commented:

"The other night we were all suddenly shaken by the mining blast tremor. Initially, we thought it was the so-called earthquake ("Tetemeko la Ardhi" in Swahili). What is on all the people's minds here in Bulyanhulu is, 'When will all this end?'"

"We need a mutual partnership with foreign companies investing in our communities. There are so many potential benefits we can get from the company with respect to jobs and skill development; also, the company can learn a lot from us when it comes to negotiation strategies with our communities. If the company responds positively to our concerns, we will strive to protect its business interests here and it will operate in harmony in our communities. But the government needs to sit with local communities and tell them why the government has allowed the company to come to practice mining in their land and tell us what potential benefit it will bring in our communities. For the time being, the company is left to itself to address these issues with the local communities."

Amid this climate of discontent among the native Tanzanians, Barrick's mining operations were subject to some hostilities from local stakeholders. In response, the company put into place several CSR initiatives that were aimed at developing sustainable benefits within the communities and around its business operations in the core mining sites of Tulawaka, Bulyanhulu and Buzigwa. Two NFO officials in Mwanza cut to the nature of the problem:

"The company initially attempted to collaborate with local communities and the local government to address the social and ecological issues during its initial stage of entry into the country. But it was not easy to find serious stakeholders right away. Because of the nature of the local institutions, it was also not easy to have things done quickly due to the degree of bureaucracy and the culture of corruption."

"The recent protests in North Mara from local communities can be resolved only if the government, company and other social awareness groups sit together to address this situation. Shooting protestors, closing the mining site and sending employees home without pay won't solve the problem in the long run. And the company's legal insistence of its right to operate in the communities isn't enough to convince these angry communities."

"The company is not wrong at all … it has followed all legal procedures and has the right to be here [in the Lake Victoria Zone], but for local communities, legal papers are NOTHING. The company finds people very unpredictable. The answer is so simple: it is all about deep understanding, integration, and building a trusting relationship."

"Mining companies are granted too many tax contracts and subsidies in order to create jobs. During this process, it is very possible for companies to avoid paying taxes that would actually benefit poor countries. There are often 'secret contracts' with corrupt government officials. The lack of institutional capacity is also a major problem; the people have not been made to see how these companies can benefit our poor societies. That's why there is still so much poverty, and that's why communities around the mining sites are angry and desperate."

Several local communities felt they were isolated when it came to the social issues that concerned them, e.g., land issues, compensation, employment, and how the presence of the company in their communities would benefit them generally. According to community leaders, few projects were initiated by the company within the various neighbourhood communities, and the ones that were enacted showed a lack of any significant sense of local ownership and influence; they did not possess the diverse forms of institutional infrastructure that fostered accountability values in communities and in the management of the company itself. As a consequence, local communities lost interest in pursuing most of the developmental projects that Barrick had initiated.

Following community tensions with Barrick between 2007 and 2009, a different strategy was developed. Implementing a locally based interaction model that promoted mutual partnership with communities seemed like the best strategic legitimacy approach. In early 2009, Barrick encountered discontent from the local communities, as well as from the local media, activists groups and lobby groups, who felt that the company had not done enough to promote sustainable and inclusive development in the communities where it operated. Barrick's new mining site at North Mara was featured several times in the media.[23] Two local NFOs commented on the dispute:

> "The government needs to educate its people as to what benefits TNCs would bring to its citizens; the mining company is extracting our natural resources, causing environmental degradation and pollution, and displacing people, all with a lack of accountability, and is not doing enough for the host communities to create prosperity, jobs, local innovation and entrepreneurship initiatives."

> "The source of discontent is from local communities and small-scale miners who feel neglected by the government. We strongly feel that their livelihoods have been destroyed with little or no compensation. They also feel that the government and local authorities have been giving foreign investors much attention at the expense of local people. Corruption and lack of accountability on the government side is the source of all these problems. The company is caught in the middle!"

---

[23] Several protests by local communities against Barrick's mining activities in Tanzania had been reported. See www.protestbarrick.net/article.php?list=type&type=12, accessed February 17, 2009.

Exhibit 2 Barrick Spending on Corporate Social Responsibility in Tanzania

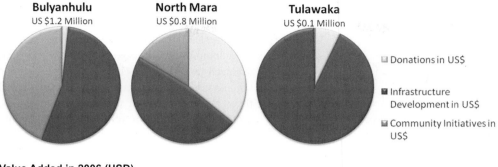

Bulyanhulu
US $1.2 Million

North Mara
US $0.8 Million

Tulawaka
US $0.1 Million

☐ Donations in US$

■ Infrastructure Development in US$

☐ Community Initiatives in US$

Value Added in 2006 (USD)

Donations	$321,000
Infrastructure Development	$1,110,000
Community Initiatives	$655,000
Local/Regional Procurement	$104,900,000

2006 Environmental, Health & Safety Performance

Note: Total amount of money in U.S. dollars spent on health & safety training and emergency response training in 2006.

Source: www.barrick.com/Theme/Barrick/files/docs_ehss/2007%20Africa%20Regional%20Rpt.pdf, accessed April 30, 2009.

Creating a Corporate Responsive Agenda

Barrick developed a responsive initiative to deal with the company's challenges in its international business activities abroad, including Tanzania. It established a community department in all four mining areas to oversee development initiatives. It also adopted standardized global CSR strategies as part of its larger international and localization business strategies, stating that "as a global corporation, we endorse the definition of Corporate Social Responsibility as proposed by the World Bank – Corporate Social Responsibility is the commitment of business to contribute to sustainable economic development – working with employees, their families, the local community and society at large to improve the quality of life, in ways that are both good for business and good for development."[24]

---

[24] www.barrick.com/CorporateResponsibility/Ethics/
PoliciesStandards/default.aspx, accessed February 17, 2009.

1. Education in partnership with local communities

Through its newly established community department, Barrick had made a concerted attempt to identify self-employment opportunities to the communities around the Bulyanhulu gold mine. In partnership with local governments, NFOs and communities, the company had used educated locals to promote a broad array of social entrepreneurship skills in a variety of areas such as finance, accounting and marketing (see Exhibit 2).

The communities surrounding the mine needed a great deal of support in terms of education in order to be able to exploit the area's potential. By 2008, Barrick had committed to working closely with eight villages before expanding to another eight villages along the Bulyanhulu-Kahama road in Bulyanhulu. Seven of the eight villages were in the Bugarama ward and one was in the Mwingilo ward, but all were located in the Bulyanhulu mining area.

2. Community-based entrepreneurship

In collaboration with local community authorities, Barrick went on to assist several community groups that already possessed local skills and entrepreneurship initiatives and which had local resources to generate business activities. Other community development projects had also been started and were engineered under the same procedure of governance.

3. Health

Barrick committed itself to upgrading the Sungusungu Health Centre into what became called the Nyamongo Hospital in the Bulyanhulu area under the so-called phase I. Organized by the Evangelical Lutheran Church in the area, several NFOs had entered into an agreement with the local District Office and the Village Councils to provide health care that was affordable to the many local residents to treat diseases such as malaria, waterborne diseases, typhoid, yellow fever and other epidemiology problems. The community trust committed $30,000 towards beds and fittings and for a general upgrade to the hospital. Barrick's overall objective was to make health services available to many disadvantaged communities, and to attempt to curb the number of deaths that occurred among pregnant women when they travelled from the poor communities to the district hospital.

4. Environment

The Lake Victoria Zone was one of the most densely populated areas in Sub-Saharan Africa, but it was also one of the most polluted and environmentally affected places in the world. Barrick, in cooperation with local government authorities, had been working to provide opportunities to the residents of the mining areas to orient themselves with mining operations. The company was creating environmental awareness in order to create local "ambassadors" who could then go out and speak positively about the mining sites to other communities. Adequately addressing the issues of water toxins on rivers

and the lake and land degradation had been the major challenge for Barrick.

Protests from so-called "secondary" stakeholders that included local communities, artisanal miners, peasant farmers and their families, and local not-for-profit organizations (NFOs) had occurred to address specific social, environmental, and land heritage and resettlement issues. All these stakeholders had widely varying claims, interests and rights. In addition, subgroups and individuals with multiple and changing roles and interests existed. They included manual mining workers who felt they had been unfairly dismissed from their jobs with little or no compensation, and felt unjustly treated by either Barrick or the Tanzanian labour court system. Local communities also had expressed anger at the level of noise caused by heavy machines during mining explorations at night and the extent of the company's impact on land in their neighborhoods. There were also individuals, mainly unemployed youths, who were engaged in intrusion, vandalism and theft at the mining sites.

Barrick had relied on the Tanzanian anti-riot police force, known as "Field Force Unit" (FFU), to quell large-scale mob criminal behaviour and demonstrations at the mining sites. Also, Barrick had relied on the Tanzanian legal system and government to protect its business activities in the region. However, the behaviour of the FFU, the weak government institutional system, and the loyalty of administrative workers to Barrick had increased anger, frustration, and resentment among communities, small-scale artisan miners and NFOs. The FFU had been regarded by local communities as brutal and uncompromising during confrontations. Responses by the FFU had even led to death,[25] long-term imprisonment of community campaigners' leaders, intimidation and harassment.[26] The government had been

[25] A recent incident at a Barrick mining site in the Mara region had led the Tanzanian FFU to kill an intruder (see www.protestbarrick.net/article.php?list=type&type=12, accessed April 17, 2009).

[26] For the behaviour of Tanzania's FFU in quelling demonstrations, see www.protestbarrick.net/article.php?id=369, accessed April 17, 2009.

Exhibit 3
Total Amount of Money Spent on Community Development Projects, 2006 (in US$)

COMMUNITY	2006	2005	2004	2003
Donations in US$				
Bulyanhulu	20,193	14,000	410,000	485,000
North Mara	294,220	50,000	0	0
Tulawaka	6,778	7,662	5,894	n/a
Infrastructure Development in US$				
Bulyanhulu	631,222	3,570,000	4,374,000	572,000
North Mara	389,384	360,000	350,000	100,000
Tulawaka	89,020	43,697	6,250	n/a
Community Initiatives in US$				
Bulyanhulu	519,793	609,000	0	0
North Mara	135,015	0	not measured	
Tulawaka	304	0	0	n/a
Regional Purchases of Goods & Services in US$				
Bulyanhulu	65,600,000		not measured	
North Mara	37,700,000		not measured	
Tulawaka	1,600,000		not measured	

Source: www.barrick.com/Theme/Barrick/files/docs_ehss/2007%20Africa%20Regional%20Rpt.pdf, accessed April 30, 2009.

viewed as lacking vision and leadership to reap the benefits of the mining activities in the region and had been criticized for failing to protect the interests of its citizens.

Conclusion

By 2010, a variety of corporate social responsibility (CSR) initiatives were established based on ABG's commitment to building a sustainable relationship with local communities. The overall aim was to ensure that the company would build mutual respect, active partnerships, and a long-term commitment with its secondary stakeholders who tended to have disparate goals, demands and opinions. Mutual respect, it was argued, was important if such relationships were to be lasting, beneficial and dynamic. In addition, the company had used its social development department in each of the mining sites to develop practical guidelines in order to facilitate the implementation of its organizational values and mission, including building long-term relationships of mutual benefit between the operations and their host communities, and to avoid costly disputes and hostilities with local stakeholders.[27] Although significant progress and successful collaborations had evolved across local communities at its mining sites, African Barrick Gold still faced serious, unique problems and increased pressure to manage conflicts and reconcile stakeholders' demands in places such as North Mara.

[27] Further CSR programs are available at www.barrick.com/CorporateResponsibility/default.aspx, accessed February 24, 2009.

HARVARD | BUSINESS | SCHOOL REV: AUGUST 24, 2016

Christopher A. Bartlett

CASE 8.3 UNILEVER'S NEW GLOBAL STRATEGY: COMPETING THROUGH SUSTAINABILITY

Emeritus Professor Christopher A. Bartlett prepared this case. It was reviewed and approved before publication by a company designate. Funding for the development of this case was provided by Harvard Business School and not by the company. HBS cases are developed solely as the basis for class discussion. Cases are not intended to serve as endorsements, sources of primary data, or illustrations of effective or ineffective management.

In January 2015, CEO Paul Polman announced Unilever's financial results for 2014. (See **Exhibit 1.**) It was hardly a celebration. Despite outperforming competitors, the company's 2.9% sales growth was its lowest in a decade, and had actually slowed to just 2.1% in the final quarter. The gloomy results were due to depressed growth in the developed world reinforced by shrinking demand in emerging markets, long the engine of Unilever's growth. But more disturbing than the 2014 results was the news that Polman was not predicting significant improvement in market conditions in 2015.

This already challenging situation was complicated by the fact that the company was in the midst of implementing a transformational strategy driven by the Unilever Sustainable Living Plan (USLP). Despite its impressive results to date, this bold initiative had not been fully embraced by some parts of the organization. One problem was that in order to achieve the expected long-term positive impact, USLP's shift to a sustainability-focused strategy typically required Unilever's businesses to make significant upfront investments that could be recouped only in the longer term. In an operating environment that Polman characterized as having "more head-winds than tailwinds," some wondered how far

he could push this transformational strategic agenda at such a difficult time.

Complicating the issue was the fact that despite making good progress, USLP was well off-target on two key metrics. While reporting a 40% reduction in its own internal greenhouse gases (GHG) emissions and a 31% drop in its water use, Unilever was far short of objectives that encompassed its whole value chain, from sourcing to consumer use and disposal. In fact, against its target to halve the entire environmental footprint of making and using Unilever products by 2020, GHG impact per consumer had actually increased 4% since 2010, and water use per consumer had fallen by only 2%. Even some USLP supporters wondered if it was time to reassess some of its goals and priorities.

It was a complex set of challenges that Polman and his top team faced. Until now, the company had been able to deliver on both its financial expectations and its environmental and social commitments. The question was, could it continue that delicate balancing act into the future.

Behind the Change: Unilever's Rich History

When he became Unilever's CEO, Polman realized that, as the first outsider ever brought in to lead

Exhibit 1
Unilever Financial Performance, 1995–2014 ($ millions)

	2014	2013	2012	2011	2010	2005	2000	1995	1990
Total Revenue	58,628.6	68,576.7	67,669.6	60,366.4	59,352.3	45,488.0	44,694.7	45,651.4	39,620.0
Europe	23,849.2	18,599.5	18,299.2	17,529.1	17,753.9	17,697.2	17,816.1		24,169.0
Americas	18,778.7	22,317.7	22,530.2	19,812.9	19,526.7	15,611.2	16,232.4		8,247.0
Developing Countries	16,000.7	27,659.6	26,840.3	23,024.4	22,071.7	12,179.6	10,646.3		7,204.0
Earnings from Cont. Ops.	6,675.5	7,247.8	6,376.2	5,834.4	6,165.6	3,950.5	1,239.9	2,066.3	3,650.0
Loss from Discontinued Ops.						(758.1)		(361.4)	
Net Income	6,259.2	6,668.0	5,759.1	5,352.4	5,690.9	4,461.0	1,037.9	2,325.4	2,081.0
Total Dividends Paid	(3860.1)	(4121.7)	(3558.6)	(3228.3)	(3115.0)	(2136.9)	(1320.7)	(970.7)	(3172.0)
NI to Common, Incl. Extra Items	6,259.2	6,668.0	5,759.1	5,352.4	5,690.9	4,461.0	996.6	2,316.0	1,124.5
Per Share: (US$)									
Basic EPS	$2.20	$2.35	$2.04	$1.90	$2.02	$1.53	$0.34	$0.77	
Diluted EPS	$2.17	$2.29	$1.98	$1.84	$1.96	$1.48	$0.33	$0.69	
Dividends per Share	$1.38	$1.49	$1.28	$1.17	$1.12	$0.78	$0.45	$0.36	
Stock Price Range (US$)									
High	$44.28	$42.94	$38.80	$35.20	$33.07	$24.20	$21.16	$13.52	$8.43
Low	$36.75	$37.19	$30.59	$29.24	$26.27	$20.92	$13.29	$10.76	$6.76
Total Current Assets	14,945.2	16,693.5	16,015.6	18,565.8	16,807.2	13,198.3	18,952.7		9,051.4
Long-Term Debt	8,473.0	10,054.4	9,727.7	9,990.3	9,479.0	7,648.7	12,273.2		2,463.3
Total Shares Outstanding ('000)	2,836.8	2,840.0	2,831.8	2,820.4	2,809.8	2,879.4	2,966.1	2,997.8	
Employees: Average per Year ('000)									
Europe	32	34	35	29	29	41	80	101	114
Americas	42	43	43	42	40	47	39	29	35
Developing Countries	99	97	94	98	96	118	176	178	155
Full-Time Employees	172	174	172	169	165	206	295	308	304

Source: Capital IQ, accessed August 21, 2015; and Unilever financial statements. (Researcher: E. McCaffrey, Baker Research Services.)

this venerable consumer goods giant, he needed to understand the company's rich cultural values as well as its long history of adaptive struggle. Both factors, he knew, would shape his options.

Birth and Evolution: From Global Growth to Static Stall

Unilever traced its origins to three family businesses of the late 19th century. In the Netherlands in the 1870s, two butter merchants, Jurgens and Van den Berg, both decided to expand into margarine, a new butter alternative. A decade later in the north of England, William Lever started making an inexpensive household soap that he hoped could reduce sickness and disease in the crowded cities of the Industrial Revolution. These young companies first encountered each other on global commodity markets as they sought out sources of their common ingredient, palm oil.

Their initially benign relationships deteriorated when the Dutch diversified into soap making and built factories in England. Lever countered by launching a brand of margarine. But after Jurgens and Van den Berg merged to create Margarine Unie, Lever initiated negotiations that eventually evolved into a merger agreement in 1927. On January 1, 1930, Unilever was established, pursuing William Lever's founding belief that a business would prosper only if it operated ethically and responsibly–a philosophy he described as "doing well by doing good."

After surviving the 1930s depression, Unilever saw its overseas operating companies (OpCos in company terminology) become increasingly independent during World War II. In the postwar consumer boom, OpCos used that independence to respond to fast-growing local markets, driving Unilever's growth through the 1950s and 1960s. But the company over-diversified, and declining profitability led to many restructurings, with much of that effort focused on offsetting the OpCos' power with business-oriented teams called Category Coordinations. In the 1990s, three decades after making these changes, management still struggled to balance the Categories' quest for global and regional efficiencies with the OpCos' responsiveness to national markets. The

resulting slow and adversarial decision-making process led to stagnant growth.

In 2004, as market share and financial performance continued to deteriorate, the company issued its first-ever profit warning. Four years later, ongoing profitability declines led a major trade magazine to report, "P&G has powered ahead of Unilever over the past five years."[1] Finally, for the first time in Unilever's history, the board decided to bring in an outsider to lead the company.

New CEO, New Directions

In January 2009, when Paul Polman became Unilever's new CEO, observers expected a major shakeup. More than just an outsider, the 52-year-old Dutchman had been a competitive adversary. In 27 years at Procter & Gamble, he had reached P&G's most senior levels before joining Nestlé in 2006 as CFO. While familiar with Unilever, he was not bound by its established practices or its embedded assumptions. Indeed, he took on his new role ready to challenge much of the conventional wisdom.

Shaking the Tree: Challenging the Culture, Changing the Team

Assuming leadership in the midst of a global financial crisis and with Unilever's stock price declining 35% in the previous year, Polman's actions confirmed his belief in the motto "never waste a crisis." In his first meeting with financial analysts, he told them he would no longer provide earnings guidance or publish full quarterly reports. ("I figured I couldn't be fired on my first day," he said.[2]) When the share price fell a further 8%, he attributed the decline to hedge funds that he claimed "would sell their own grandmothers if they thought they could make money."[3]

He reinforced his message to the investment community by noting his hierarchy of

---

[1] David Benady, "Will putting a P&G man in charge work for Unilever?," *Marketing Week*, September 10, 2008.
[2] Paul Polman and Adi Ignatius, "Captain Planet," *Harvard Business Review*, June 2012.
[3] Kamal Ahmed, "Davos 2011: Unilever's Paul Polman believes we need to think long term," *Telegraph*, January 15, 2011.

Exhibit 2 Unilever's Compass Vision and USLP Goals

OUR VISION **IS TO DOUBLE THE SIZE OF THE BUSINESS, WHILST REDUCING OUR ENVIRONMENTAL FOOTPRINT AND INCREASING OUR POSITIVE SOCIAL IMPACT**

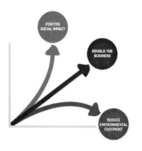

UNILEVER SUSTAINABLE LIVING PLAN

In an uncertain and volatile world, we cannot achieve our vision to double our size unless we find new ways to operate that do not just take from society and the environment.

Launched in 2010, the Unilever Sustainable Living Plan is our blueprint for sustainable growth.

The Plan is helping to drive profitable growth, reduce costs and fuel innovation.

Our Plan sets out three big goals. Underpinning these goals are nine commitments supported by targets spanning our social, environmental and economic performance.

IMPROVING HEALTH AND WELL-BEING FOR MORE THAN 1 BILLION

By 2020 we will help more than a billion people take action to improve their health and well-being.

REDUCING ENVIRONMENTAL IMPACT BY 1/2

By 2020 our goal is to halve the environmental footprint of the making and use of our products as we grow our business.

ENHANCING LIVELIHOODS FOR MILLIONS

By 2020 we will enhance the livelihoods of millions of people as we grow our business.

Our plan is distinctive in three ways.

It spans our entire portfolio of brands and all countries in which we sell our products.

Secondly, it has a social and economic dimension – our products make a difference to health and well-being and our business supports the livelihoods of many people.

Finally, when it comes to the environment, we work across the whole value chain – from the sourcing of raw materials to our factories and the way consumers use our products.

21%	2%	2%	4%	70%	1%
Raw Materials	Manufacture	Transport	Retail	Consumer	Disposal

Unilever's Greenhouse Gas Footprint

Source: USLP, Summary of Progress, 2014 ("Scaling for Impact"), p. 5.

stakeholders: "We need to know why we are here. The answer is, for consumers not shareholders. If we are in sync with consumer needs and the environment in which we operate, and take responsibility for society as well as our employees, then the shareholder will also be rewarded."[4]

To shake up a culture he saw as "internally focused and self-serving,"[5] Polman froze salaries and cut overseas travel. He then initiated a management shakeup, replacing the Chief Financial Officer, the Chief Marketing Officer, and the Global Head of Foods, Home, and Personal Care. Within a year, he had changed a third of the top 100 executives.

Redefining the Strategy: Committing to Sustainability

While he was tightening operations and making structural and personnel changes, Polman was also preparing a radically new corporate strategy. One of his first commitments was to double the size of Unilever's business. He felt that 80% of the growth needed to meet that target of €80 billion in revenues would come from developing countries–markets that already accounted for more than half of the company's sales, a larger share of those markets than any of its competitors.

But the big surprise was in how the new CEO planned to achieve that growth. "We think that businesses that are responsible and actually make contributing to society a part of their business model will be successful," he said.[6] So he announced a "Compass Vision" that aimed to double the size of Unilever's business while simultaneously reducing its environmental footprint and increasing its positive social impact. The boldness of the commitment took many by surprise.

In November 2010, the company unveiled the USLP–the key to achieving its new Compass Vision. (See **Exhibit 2**.) The plan had three goals

[4] Andrew Saunders, "The MT Interview: Assuming his new role in the midst of a global recession," *Management Today*, March 1, 2011.

[5] Saunders, "The MT Interview."

[6] Polman and Ignatius, "Captain Planet."

for 2020: to help a billion people improve their health and well-being, to halve the environmental footprint of making and using Unilever products, and to enhance the livelihoods of those in its value chain. Far from a PR-driven corporate social responsibility program, USLP was introduced as a core strategy that Polman believed would stimulate growth, cut costs, engage consumers, and motivate employees. He saw it as fully aligned with Unilever's commercial interests and its mission of "doing well by doing good."

What made USLP unusual was its breadth. The commitment not only applied to every Unilever business, function, and country under its direct control, but also extended across its value chain and over the product life cycle. This ambitious scope was revealed in an analysis at that time showing that Unilever's own manufacturing activities generated less than 5% of its products' total greenhouse gas (GHG) footprint. Its suppliers contributed 21%, and consumers of its products accounted for 70%. Accepting responsibility to halve that entire footprint represented a huge undertaking.

Communicating the Vision: Aligning Support, Allaying Skepticism

Because management had been developing USLP parameters for more than a year before the initiative was formally announced, its detail was well defined. The three core goals were expanded into seven commitments ("pillars" in Unilever terminology) and further broken into more than 50 specific, measurable targets (e.g., to source 100% of palm oil from certified sustainable sources, to reduce salt to a recommended 5 grams a day, etc.). The broad goals and specific targets not only gave credibility to Unilever's new corporate purpose "to make sustainable living commonplace," but were also translated into its operating business model that it depicted as "A Virtuous Circle of Growth" with sustainable living at its core. (See **Exhibit 3**.)

Polman knew that USLP required a radical new way of thinking not only from Unilever's 165,000 employees, but also by the 5 million people in its supply chain, and eventually by the 2 billion people worldwide who used one of its products on any given day. It was a huge task, and internally the new strategy was greeted with nervous anticipation. While the idea of doubling revenues seemed exciting, some found USLP's less familiar environmental and social goals harder to grasp. Having seen several previous corporate initiatives bloom and die, many adopted a "wait and see" attitude.

Externally, press reaction was a mixture of cautious admiration, lingering doubt, and outright skepticism. A column in *Marketing Week*, a generally sympathetic industry publication, reflected some of the questions and concerns expressed elsewhere: "So what makes the Unilever sustainability program so high risk? First, the sheer ambition of the targets compared with the relatively achievable goals of enhanced quarterly earnings or brand share.... The second caveat is that there are inherent contradictions between the conventional marketing objectives and the sustainability targets."[7]

A *Financial Times* columnist was more blunt and direct: "I listened for something I wasn't hearing. Where were the figures on cost savings? Where were the promises about results flowing to the bottom line?"[8] The journalist concluded, "Mr. Polman's appeal to shareholders to take the long view is admirable, but I felt nervous about his own long-term prospects. Even the most patient investor eventually needs a decent return."

Implementing USLP: From Aspiration to Action

Polman understood that it was one thing to create a bold vision, and quite another to implement it–particularly as an outsider upsetting the comfortable status quo. Indeed, when asked about his biggest risk, the new CEO replied, "The biggest challenge, to be honest, is surviving the transition."[9]

---

[7] Stuart Smith, "Is Unilever's sustainability drive a hostage to fortune?," *Marketing Week*, December 9, 2010.

[8] Michael Skapinker, "Corporate plans may be lost in translation," *Financial Times*, November 22, 2010.

[9] Polman and Ignatius, "Captain Planet."

Exhibit 3 Unilever's Virtuous Cycle Business Model

HOW WE CREATE SUSTAINABLE VALUE

OUR BUSINESS MODEL AND STRATEGY COME TOGETHER TO
DELIVER VALUE FOR SHAREHOLDERS. HERE WE EXPLAIN
THEIR ELEMENTS AND HOW THEY ARE COMBINED.

OUR BUSINESS MODEL

OUR CORE PURPOSE

MAKING SUSTAINABLE LIVING COMMONPLACE
Our business model starts with our core Purpose which is a clear
expression of what we believe to be the best long-term way for
Unilever to grow. It is a simple Purpose to help us meet changing
consumer preferences and the challenges of a volatile, uncertain,
complex and ambiguous world.

KEY INPUTS

BRANDS, OPERATIONS, PEOPLE
Our business model works by combining three key inputs and
filtering them through the lens of the Unilever Sustainable Living
Plan (USLP). Our brands have significant value and succeed
through products that meet the needs of consumers. Our people
identify social and consumer needs to grow our brands, market
them and manufacture and distribute them. Our operations are the
essential supply chain functions and assets of raw material supply,
factories, logistics, go-to-market expertise and marketing. We
invest financial capital to support all these assets and activities.

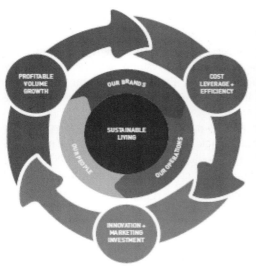

HOW WE DRIVE PROFIT

PROFITABLE VOLUME GROWTH, COST LEVERAGE +
EFFICIENCY, INNOVATION + MARKETING INVESTMENT
Unilever aims for a virtuous circle of growth. Profitable volume
growth is driven by investment in innovation and brands to deliver
products which 2 billion consumers use every day. We can leverage
this scale to spread fixed costs and improve profitability while
further investing in the business. This investment funds R&D
and innovation to create new and improved products backed by
marketing to create even stronger brands. This drives profitable
volume growth and the virtuous circle continues.

Source: Unilever, 2014 Annual Report, p. 14.

Leveraging History, Building Momentum

Unilever's "doing well by doing good" philosophy meant that the seeds of USLP were planted in fertile soil. In 2006, its Corporate Social Responsibility (CSR) group had initiated "brand imprint" workshops to help all brand leaders examine the environmental, social, and economic impact of their brands. After reviewing working conditions and environmental practices on its tea plantations, for example, Lipton invited the Rainforest Alliance to certify its tea as sustainably grown and responsibly sourced. And Lifebuoy soap responded to the UN's Millennium Development Goals by committing to positively affect the health and hygiene of a billion people through handwashing education.

Realizing that not all brand managers had responded to the "brand imprint" initiative, Unilever's category heads commissioned a team to measure the environmental footprint of the company's entire product portfolio. Karen Hamilton, the leader of the team, recalled the outcome: "By 2009 we had identified the major sources of our greenhouse gases, water and waste. This was soon after Paul became CEO and just before the UN's 2009 Copenhagen Climate Change Conference, so the data became vital input for the change that followed." But while the study's recommendations provided a strong basic platform, Polman knew he would need a lot more support to implement USLP.

Consolidating Power, Focusing Responsibility

Rather than giving USLP oversight responsibility to Unilever's CSR office, in 2010 Polman named Keith Weed to a new role he created on the Unilever Leadership Executive (ULE), combining the role of Chief Marketing Officer (CMO) with responsibility for the leadership of both Communications and Sustainability. In addition to heading the marketing function, the CMO would also coordinate the development and implementation of the new USLP sustainability strategy. (See **Exhibit 4**.) Weed described how he saw the role: "In many companies, the head of sustainability is a guy with a beard and sandals urging people to save the planet. We wanted to signal that sustainability was not about 'corporate social responsibility' as an isolated activity. It was everyone's responsibility. So we abolished the CSR office to underline our belief that marketing and sustainability were two sides of the same coin. It was a belief [that] became reflected in our strategy."

Weed's elevation to the ULE gave him a seat at the table where strategy was discussed, and where the company's heads of categories, countries, and functions became aligned around future priorities. "Beyond that level, gaining acceptance was tough," Weed acknowledged. "We realized that it was going to take a long time to embed something on this scale deeper in the organization."

The new CMO's implementation task was greatly facilitated by his inheritance of an established 12-person corporate sustainability group, most with deep operating and marketing backgrounds. Hamilton, VP of Sustainable Business since 2008, recalled the change: "We had been working on measuring our environmental footprint for a couple of years. But after Paul joined, we started getting a lot more attention from the ULE leadership team. They asked us about environmental targets and metrics, but they were particularly interested in what USLP would mean for the business."

Simultaneously, an intensive communication campaign began. Internally, the new CEO and his management team held meetings, hosted forums, and visited operations to outline the vision, answer questions, and celebrate early achievements. Externally, Polman gave interviews to the media, met with analysts, and spoke at meetings from UN conferences to the World Economic Forum at Davos. Within a year, few in the business world were unaware of Unilever's USLP strategy.

Delivering Results, Confronting Shortfalls

By late 2013, Polman was generally satisfied with USLP's progress in its first three years. He was particularly pleased with the imagination and passion shown by the supply chain function, whose early embrace of the new strategic challenges had resulted in positive change on many

Exhibit 4 Unilever Corporate Organization Chart

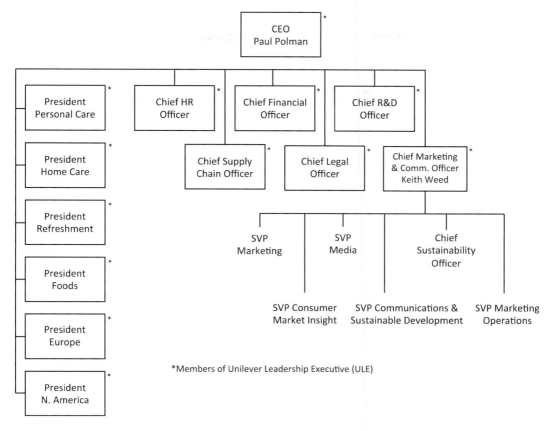

Source: Casewriter's representation.

fronts ranging from implementing sustainable sourcing policies to championing smallholder farmers. In addition to dramatically reducing Unilever's environmental footprint, such actions also played a lead role in creating a platform on which brand management could build consumer-facing claims. These achievements were highlighted in Unilever's annual report and also celebrated in a separate USLP report that was published annually beginning in 2011.

Three years into USLP's rollout, Unilever sustainably sourced 48% of its agricultural products, up from 14% in 2010. The company was also on track to meet the goal of doubling the proportion of its food products meeting the highest globally recognized nutritional standards, with 31% of the portfolio by volume already meeting that standard. And its efforts to improve the health of a billion

people had reached 303 million with handwashing, oral health, and safe drinking water programs.

Indeed, of USLP's more than 50 specific defined targets, at the end of 2013 only five were regarded as being "off-target." But of those, two were of particular concern: GHG emissions and water usage. Rather than shrinking, over the previous two years, Unilever's GHG footprint per consumer use had actually increased by 5%, while its water impact had grown by 15%. Given the size and environmental sensitivity of these shortfalls, they clearly represented major stumbling blocks to the achievement of the USLP goal of halving Unilever's environmental impact.

Having accepted responsibility for the whole value chain of its products, USLP's early analysis had calculated that consumer use accounted for 68% of Unilever's GHG impact and 85% of its water footprint. Unsurprisingly, the majority of both off-target metrics was due to consumers' use of hot water for bathing, hair washing, and laundry. The discouraging increase in these two key metrics was due to two main factors–the impact of acquiring Alberto Culver's shower and hair products in 2011 and Unilever's lack of progress in reducing the impact of consumer use.

Redoubling its efforts, management underlined the need for impactful innovations. The company introduced laundry detergents that required shorter wash cycles, minimum rinse fabric conditioners, and dry shampoos. The latter, for example, were sold in 10 countries under brands including Dove, Suave, TRESemmé, and VO5. But despite data indicating that dry shampoo users replaced wet shampoos 60% of the time, management recognized that it could only achieve its ambitious GHG and water usage objectives by changing other energy-efficiency variables, particularly those affecting domestic hot water use. And so they tried. For example, in one multi-country experiment, Unilever offered low-flow showerheads and aerators as an incentive with the purchase of its shampoos.

But the impact of such innovations was limited, and management understood that much bigger initiatives were needed to meet its GHG and water use targets. So management committed to using Unilever's influence to reduce carbon intensity in the energy supply infrastructure. Company representatives became active in a variety of industry and government organizations to influence public policy, measure environmental footprints, and develop uniform reporting standards.

As anti-smoking and seatbelt education programs had shown, however, changing ingrained habits took decades. As this reality became clearer, some began questioning whether some of USLP's bold 2020 objectives were simply unrealistic. Polman disagreed.

Reinforcing the Mission: New Leaders, New Initiatives

Although USLP's early successes were impressive, the top ULE team felt that many had been achieved by picking "low hanging fruit." Despite strong results in manufacturing efficiencies,

sustainable sourcing, and some brands with existing USLP-linked programs, they were concerned about a lack of initiative, innovation, and even engagement in other parts of the organization. They felt a need to reinforce the resources and capabilities dedicated to supporting USLP.

New CSO: Refreshing USLP's Mandate

In 2012, when Gail Klintworth was appointed Chief Sustainability Officer, she identified several impediments to implementation: some people were unclear about their roles, others viewed USLP as a separate initiative that was unconnected to their strategy, and a good number were concerned about the cost of shifting to a sustainability-based strategy.

Everyone was very familiar with success stories such as Lifebuoy, the venerable soap brand that had built a successful business on the promise of improving family health. But they also knew that by shifting promotional expenditures from TV advertising to handwashing education programs in schools, Lifebuoy had to be willing to extend the payback on its marketing investments by several years.[10] Many marketing managers felt they could not do so and still meet their budget targets.

Convinced that her small corporate team had to become catalysts to help businesses recognize the feasibility and potential of change, Klintworth launched an initiative she called "USLP Refresh." Assigning leaders for each of USLP's seven pillars, she charged them with working with category and brand teams to evaluate their business models, connect them with resources, and help build the capability to take action. They reviewed three levels of sustainability-linked opportunities: "must do" initiatives critical to the business (e.g., reducing fat, sugar, and salt content); growth or cost-cutting opportunities (e.g., new products to respond to water scarcity in developing countries); and opportunities where Unilever could take leadership on important environmental or

---

[10] For a detailed description, see Christopher A. Bartlett, "Unilever's Lifebuoy in India: Implementing the Sustainability Plan," HBS No. 914–417 (Boston: Harvard Business School Publishing, 2016).

social issues (e.g., managing its supply chain to help close human rights gaps).

In a typical example, the designated leader for sustainable sourcing met with the Knorr soups and sauces team to review how USLP-linked opportunities could support their business objectives. The team agreed to explore new opportunities for sustainable sourcing that could also cut costs, drive growth, or reduce risk. After setting a baseline of current performance versus target metrics, the team developed a program for tomatoes, Knorr's largest vegetable purchase. Implementing the program, they found that drip irrigation could halve water consumption, improve yields, and lower fertilizer and pesticide use. To spread such practices, Knorr established a €1 million annual Sustainability Partnership Fund to support best practices on "landmark farms" from which other growers could learn. By 2013, the program boosted Knorr's purchase of tomatoes from sustainable sources to 84%.

New Marketing SVP: Linking Brands to Purpose

While Klintworth's team was implementing USLP Refresh, Marc Mathieu, the newly recruited Senior Vice President of Marketing, initiated a program he called "Crafting Brands for Life" (or CB4L for short). With an objective of closely linking brand strategy to USLP principles, CB4L had three principles: "We put people first, recognizing them as individuals, not just consumers," said Mathieu. "Then we aim to build 'brand love' so people identify with our brands, not just purchase our products. And finally, we want to unlock the magic–not just the logic–in our execution."

To implement CB4L, he rolled out a series of 1½-day workshops designed to engage Unilever's 6,000 marketers on how their brands were linked to USLP. Using prepared frameworks, they debated how to develop not just a brand position, but also a brand purpose that could be embedded into their strategy. The "Brand Key" that had long defined each brand's competitive positioning was adapted to become a "Brand Love Key" that embodied what the brand stood for.

The CB4L workshops were followed by "Brand Deep Dives" to engage marketers with end-users in their homes. Unlike typical focus groups, these were a series of two-hour conversations to explore the human themes that connected the individual to the brand, and how it fit into their lives. "People today expect transparency and real-time engagement with their brands," said Mathieu. "To develop a personal relationship with end users, the role of marketing has to change from creating a myth and telling it to finding a truth and sharing it."

Through this process, many more brands linked their strategies to USLP priorities. For example, the laundry brand Persil (sold in other countries as Omo, Skip, Surf, and Rinso) was no longer built on the platform that "Persil Washes Whiter" but instead had developed a Brand Love Key linked to a mother's strong interest in her child's development. Building on research showing that hands-on play and trial-and-error discovery were vital to a child's development, the brand built its strategy around a "Dirt Is Good" campaign. This reversed the traditional fear-based laundry detergent advertising message that dirt was bad. Instead, it projected a positive life-celebrating message inspiring mothers to encourage their children to play outside, explore, and get dirty, knowing that it was good for their development, and that Persil/Omo would remove the stains. (See **Exhibit 5**.)

But Mathieu acknowledged that some brands were "more challenging" than others. For example, Axe, the very successful men's deodorant had been built on macho themes of helping men attract women. To reposition Axe as a product with a positive societal impact was proving difficult. "The question we eventually will have to ask is whether we ask each category to identify a few flagship brands and allow other brands not to participate," said Mathieu. "Or might you risk becoming only as strong as your weakest link? Some have even proposed divesting such non-conforming brands. It's an open debate."

New VP of Social Impact: Broadening USLP's Ambition

Meanwhile, UN Secretary General Ban Ki-moon had invited Polman to join the board of the UN Global Compact, an initiative designed to commit global businesses to the environment, human rights, and anti-corruption actions.

Exhibit 5 Persil/ Omo "Dirt Is Good" Campaign

Source: Company documents.

He also appointed the Unilever CEO to an elite group of 27 global leaders–the only corporate representative invited–to advise on a Post-2015 Development Agenda, a vital initiative to follow the UN's Millennium Development Goals that would expire in 2015.

In part influenced by discussions in these forums, Polman began to feel that Unilever was focused on environmental goals more than on a social agenda, and urged his team to consider expanding USLP's commitments. To lead this new emphasis, the company brought in Marcella Manubens as its first VP of Social Impact and charged her with implementing the UN Guiding Principles on Business and Human Rights by expanding on USLP's existing "Enhancing Livelihoods" pillar.

In 2013, her focus led to three new USLP commitments: to drive fairness in the workplace (e.g., 100% of procurement from suppliers committed to promoting fundamental human rights by 2020), to advance opportunities for women (e.g., empower 5 million women both inside and outside Unilever by 2020), and to develop inclusive business (e.g., positively affect 5.5 million people by improving the livelihoods of smallholder farmers, small-scale retailers, and young entrepreneurs by 2020). To some, USLP's expansion from seven to nine pillar commitments seemed a stretch. Just as they were grappling with the first round of objectives, a new set of challenges had been added to the agenda.

Adapting and Adjusting: Transformational Partnerships

Beyond these structural changes, USLP's implementation also benefited from an ongoing process of learning and adaptation. For example, the company's continuing struggle to meet GHG and water usage targets reinforced the belief of the ULE leadership team that many USLP objectives could not be achieved without changes in the wider system. The expanding commitments that followed led to a significant evolution in Unilever's sustainability agenda.

New Partnerships: Collaborating for Change

Since the outset, Unilever had understood that it could not achieve its bold objectives by itself. Indeed, in the very first USLP Progress Report, Polman had emphasized, "Delivering these commitments won't be easy. . . . We will have to work in partnership with governments, NGOs, suppliers and others to address the big challenges that confront us all. Ultimately, we will only succeed if we inspire billions of people around

the world to take the small, everyday actions that add up to a big difference–actions that will enable us all to live more sustainably."[11]

Over time, partnerships became embedded in USLP's implementation. For example, Unilever's "Partner to Win" program resulted in hundreds of agreements being signed with scores of suppliers, many linked to sustainable sourcing. Unilever also brought sustainability programs to consumers by partnering with retail chains like Tesco and Walmart. And it created entirely new initiatives such as "innovation eco-systems" based on open innovation teams with academics and small and medium-sized enterprises.

Beyond such partnerships in its own value chain, the company also took leadership roles in industry organizations such as the Consumer Goods Forum, the Tropical Rainforest Alliance, and the World Business Council for Sustainable Development. It also partnered with scores of NGOs including Oxfam, Unicef, Save the Children, WWF, and Rainforest Alliance. And it had dozens of collaborative programs with governments at national and local levels worldwide.

Rather than being peripheral, many of these partnerships played key roles in developing USLP strategies. For example, in early 2013, when Oxfam advised the new VP of Social Impact of its plans to investigate labor practices in Vietnam, the company welcomed its involvement and opened the organization to a full review. Despite Unilever paying above Vietnam's legal minimum wage, the study found that its factory wages were below the international poverty level. Rather than challenging or ignoring the report, the company engaged the findings and used the criticisms to review working conditions in its factories worldwide. The Oxfam spokesman described Unilever's response as "the most transparent and forward thinking example I've seen."[12]

[11] Paul Polman, Introduction, "Unilever Sustainable Living Plan: Small Actions, Big Difference," Unilever 2011 document, p. 3.

[12] Tim Smedley, "Unilever's labour practices in Vietnam found wanting by Oxfam report," http://www.the guardian.com/sustainable-business/blog/unilever-labour-practices-vietnam-oxfam-report, accessed April 2, 2015.

Strategy Adjustments: Leading Systemwide Transformational Change

Although partnerships proved effective, it became clear that the company would need even more support to meet its goals. It was time for a new emphasis that management first outlined in the 2013 USLP Progress Report: "We have been asking ourselves how we can make a bigger difference to those big issues that matter most to our business.... We are only one company among many and the change needed to tackle the world's major social environmental and economic issues is big and urgent.... What's really needed are changes to the broader systems of which we are a part."[13]

Behind this announcement was a commitment for Unilever to take a leadership role to make a "transformational impact" in key areas relevant to its businesses. While not giving up on its USLP agenda, management decided that in order to achieve its goals, it had to leverage its scale, its influence, and its resources to bring about a market transformation and engage other companies to take broader responsibility.

This expansion of the sustainability agenda put new demands on the Chief Sustainability Officer (CSO) role, and the decision was taken to divide it in two. While most of the corporate sustainability group remained focused on the internal agenda under Sue Garrard as Senior Vice President for Sustainable Business Development, Jeff Seabright was recruited as the company's new CSO. As Garrard's staff worked on accelerating the integration of sustainability into all aspects of Unilever's business, especially its brand portfolio, Seabright and his small team focused on three objectives at the core of Unilever's new externally oriented, transformational change agenda. (See Exhibit 6.)

The first target for transformational change was deforestation, chosen because Unilever was a major buyer of palm oil, a key driver of the problem. Beyond its own commitment to source 100% of its palm oil from certified and traceable sources by 2020, management committed to lead worldwide efforts to eliminate deforestation by working with governments, NGOs, and others in the industry. In September 2014, it led members of the Consumer Goods Forum at the UN Climate Summit in New York in obtaining the commitment of 170 governments, companies, and NGOs to cut forest loss by half by 2020, and eliminate it completely by 2030.

Unilever's second transformational agenda priority was to champion sustainable agriculture and the development of smallholder farmers. Again, the company wanted others to join it in making sustainable agriculture mainstream while enhancing the livelihoods of smallholder farmers. In one initiative, it partnered with Solidaridad to improve the lives of a million smallholders in developing countries by offering them training and funds to grow sustainable tea, cocoa, sugar, and other crops.

The third area in which Unilever believed it could lead changes in the broader system was in improving health and hygiene, particularly for the 2.5 billion people without access to adequate sanitation or safe drinking water. Taking its expertise in consumer behavior change, the company partnered with governments, NGOs, and other companies to leverage its initiatives in handwashing, sanitation, and safe drinking water, tied to brands such as Lifebuoy, Domestos, and Pureit. In one initiative, Unilever partnered with NGOs, social entrepreneurs, academics, and other businesses to create the Toilet Board Coalition, whose mission was to develop commercial, scalable toilet facilities for the world's 2.5 billion people without adequate sanitation. And it trained entrepreneurs to supply, install, and maintain 50,000 toilets in India and Vietnam by 2015.

Looking Back to Look Ahead: Next Steps

In early 2015, four years into USLP's implementation, Polman and his ULE leadership team were pleased with progress and with the process that had helped the company's sustainability strategy to adapt and improve. But they wanted to evaluate whether further adjustments were needed, particularly in light of current operating conditions.

---

[13] USLP, 2013 Report, p. 14.

Exhibit 6 Unilever's Transformational Change Priorities

WE HAVE SET OUT TO **MAKE A DIFFERENCE**
TO THOSE BIG ISSUES THAT MATTER MOST

Scaling for impact is ever more critical in 2015 as the United Nations prepares to adopt a set of Sustainable Development Goals and broker a climate deal to reduce emissions. Success for both will require input and active leadership by business.

By combining our own actions with external advocacy on public policy and joint working with partners, we are seeking to create what we call 'transformational change' – that is fundamental change to whole systems, not simply incremental improvements.

We are focusing on three areas where we have the scale, influence and resources to make this big difference:

 ELIMINATING DEFORESTATION

Eliminating deforestation from commodity supply chains by 2020, to help combat the threat from climate change

 SUSTAINABLE AGRICULTURE & SMALLHOLDER FARMERS

Making sustainable agriculture the mainstream, and so increase food yields and enhance the livelihoods of smallholder farmers

 **WATER, SANITATION & HYGIENE**

Working towards universal access to safe drinking water, sanitation and hygiene

In all three areas, the role of women is crucial, both as partners in change and as beneficiaries. Empowering women is critical to eradicating poverty and accelerating global development.

To achieve change at scale, we need to go beyond what we can achieve in our own operations and with our suppliers. We are stepping up our engagement with governments, NGOs and others in our industry and forming partnerships to demonstrate the change we want to see. Often our partners become the best advocates of system-wide change.

By focusing on these three areas, we believe we can help address the twin goals of combating climate change and promoting human development.

Source: USLP, Summary of Progress, 2014 ("Scaling for Impact"), p. 11.

Sustainability as Strategy: Measuring the Impact

From the outset, Polman had visualized USLP at the core of Unilever's strategy–driving growth, cutting costs, reducing risks, stimulating innovation, inspiring employees, and engaging consumers. But these were assertions rather than proven outcomes, and some still viewed USLP mainly in corporate social responsibility terms, and remained skeptical that its benefits exceeded its costs.

To respond, the SVP of Sustainable Development, the CSO, and the Group Financial Controller all committed to developing tools that could measure the business impact of the USLP strategy. Beginning in 2014, they subjected all Unilever products to an analysis not only to determine their growth rate and profitability, but also to show if they had contributed measurably to USLP objectives. It required a huge effort, but was felt to be worthwhile if it could remove skepticism and help expand the integration of the sustainability agenda into more business strategies.

One outcome of the analysis was the identification of what the group called "sustainable living brands"–those whose product not only contributed to one or more USLP goal (e.g., sustainably sourced, reduces environmental impact, makes a health contribution, etc.), but also whose brand built on a sustainable living purpose (e.g., positioned to engage consumers to take sustainable behavior). Of Unilever's top 30 brands, 11 were classified as "sustainable living brands."

In April 2015, the analysis was complete, and the company announced that it now had evidence that integrating sustainability into its business strategy was driving growth, reducing costs, and increasing business resilience. Indeed, it found that its "sustainable living brands" accounted for half the company's growth and had grown at twice the rate of the rest of the business.[14]

[14] "New Unilever report points to success in all target areas," *Guardian* online, May 13, 2015, http://www.theguardian.com/sustainable-business/unilever-partner-zone/2015/may/13/new-unilever-report-points-to-success-in-all-target-areas.

Performance to Date: Achievements and Challenges

However, as all ULE members knew, the future of USLP depended on how the total business was performing. In reporting on Unilever's 2014 results, Polman proudly highlighted that the company had continued to grow ahead of its slowing markets worldwide, that it had recorded its fifth consecutive year of top- and bottom-line growth, and that cost savings programs had lifted core operating margins from 14.1% to 14.5%, continuing the upward trend from 13.6% in 2009.[15]

When asked what pleased him most about those results, the CEO identified the ability to deliver them while balancing the needs of multiple stakeholders. Not only had investors been rewarded with an 18% rise in total shareholder return, but employee engagement scores tracking job satisfaction, pride, loyalty, and so on were also very strong at 75%, well ahead of the 63% level of 2009. (The high scores were validated by Unilever's third-place position on LinkedIn's list of "The World's Most In-Demand Employers in 2014," just behind Google and Apple, and ahead of Microsoft, Facebook, and Amazon.[16]) Furthermore, Unilever's sustainability record was recognized by its continued inclusion in the Dow Jones Sustainability Index, as well as by its position as number one on the 2014 list of "Sustainability Leaders" in GlobeScan's annual survey of worldwide sustainability experts.[17]

However, Polman also expressed concern about the business environment, characterizing it as "volatile and complex ... with more headwinds than tailwinds."[18] Developed markets had stalled and emerging market growth slowed. So, despite gaining share by growing faster than its markets, Unilever's underlying sales growth rate declined from 6.9% in 2012 to 4.3% in 2013 and just 2.9% in 2014. And due to foreign exchange impact, its 2014 revenues were actually down 2.7% from 2013. Indeed, after years of seeing its shares outperform its key competitor P&G, by 2014 Unilever's stock price growth seem to have stalled. (See **Exhibit 7**.)

In the company's 2014 USLP Progress Report, Polman again reported strong results before recognizing some concerns. The company reported "on-track" performance on seven of its nine USLP pillars, with detailed results showing that 12 of 67 specific metrics had already been achieved, 48 were tracking to plan, and only 7 were off plan. (See **Exhibit 8**.)

Yet, once again, the CEO was transparent about the shortfalls. He acknowledged that because both of the "off-track" USLP pillars were linked to consumers' use of its products, they would be hard to fix. In contrast to a goal of halving its environmental footprint, in part due to its merger and acquisition activity, Unilever's GHG impact per consumer use had actually increased by 4% since 2010, and consumer water use impact had been reduced by only 2%.

Decision Time: Possibilities and Priorities

Looking back over the previous four years, Polman's top ULE team realized how far Unilever's sustainability strategy had come. Yet, while the company's overall vision remained clear, and its commitment stayed constant, USLP's implementation had been characterized by continuous adaptation, adjustment, and learning. So, once again, they had an opportunity to assess where their future priorities should lie, and whether further adjustments might be necessary.

There certainly was no shortage of views within the company–from those who were deeply committed to others more generally skeptical. To the former, this was the time to double down and make an even stronger effort to achieve USLP's objectives by 2020. Now that evidence existed supporting the business value of the sustainability agenda, they felt that management should push lagging parts of the business to increase the number of "sustainable living brands" in the portfolio.

[15] Unilever, 2014 Annual Report, p. 7.

[16] "The World's 100 Most InDemand Employers: 2014," LinkedIn, https://www.linkedin.com/indemand/global/2014, accessed January 15, 2015.

[17] "The 2014 Sustainability Leaders: A GlobeScan Survey," GlobeScan, http://www.globescan.com/component/edocman/?view=document&id=103&Itemid=591, accessed May 20, 2015.

[18] Unilever, 2014 Annual Report, p. 4.

Exhibit 7 Unilever's Stock Price vs. DJIA and P&G, 2009–2014

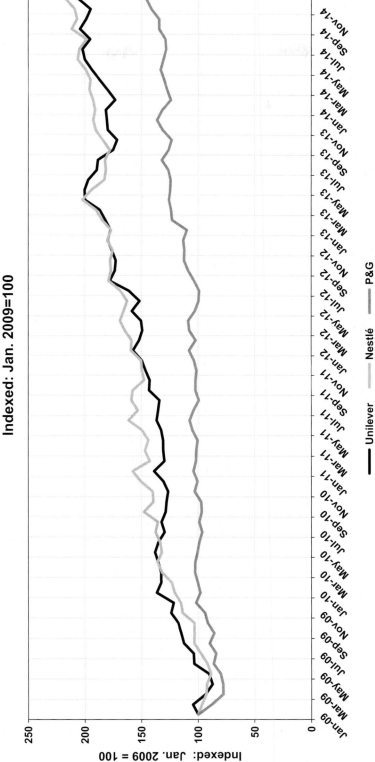

Unilever, Nestle & P&G Stock Prices 2009–2014
Indexed: Jan. 2009=100

— Unilever   — Nestlé   — P&G

Source: Capital IQ, accessed August 21, 2015. (Researcher: E. McCaffrey, Baker Research Services.)

Exhibit 8 Unilever's USLP Achievements, 2014

The Unilever Sustainable Living Plan sets out to decouple growth from our environmental impact, while increasing our positive social impact.

Our Plan has three big goals to achieve by 2020, underpinned by nine commitments and targets spanning our social, environmental and economic performance across the value chain.

We will continue to work with others to focus on those areas where we can drive the greatest change.

More detail on our progress can be found in the Sustainable Living section of www.unilever.com.

IMPROVING HEALTH AND WELL-BEING

FOR MORE THAN 1 BILLION

By 2020 we will help more than a billion people take action to improve their health and well-being.

We have helped 397 million people take action to improve their health and well-being.

HEALTH AND HYGIENE

By 2020 we will help more than a billion people to improve their health and hygiene. This will help reduce the incidence of life-threatening diseases like diarrhoea.

397M people reached by end 2014

- Reduce diarrhoeal and respiratory disease through handwashing †
- Provide safe drinking water †
- Improve access to sanitation
- Improve oral health
- Improve self-esteem

NUTRITION

We will continually work to improve the taste and nutritional quality of all our products. The majority of our products meet, or are better than, benchmarks based on national nutritional recommendations. Our commitment goes further: by 2020, we will double the proportion of our portfolio that meets the highest nutritional standards, based on globally recognised dietary guidelines. This will help hundreds of millions of people to achieve a healthier diet.

33% † of our portfolio by volume met highest nutritional standards in 2014

- Reduce salt levels

Saturated fat:
- ⊘ Reduce saturated fat
- ⊘ Increase essential fatty acids
- Reduce saturated fat in more products
- ◯ Improve heart health
- Remove trans fat
- Reduce sugar

Reduce calories:
- ⊘ In children's ice cream
- In more ice cream products
- Provide healthy eating information

REDUCING ENVIRONMENTAL IMPACT

BY 1/2

By 2020 our goal is to halve the environmental footprint of the making and use of our products as we grow our business.*

GREENHOUSE GASES

Our products' lifecycle:
Halve the greenhouse gas (GHG) impact of our products across the lifecycle by 2020.

4% † our greenhouse gas impact per consumer use has increased by around 4% since 2010*

Our manufacturing:
By 2020 CO₂ emissions from energy from our factories will be at or below 2008 levels despite significantly higher volumes.

37% † reduction of CO₂ from energy per tonne of production since 2008

Reduce GHG from manufacturing:
- Renewable energy
- New factories
- Reduce GHG from skin cleansing and hair washing

Reduce GHG from washing clothes:
- ⊘ Concentration
- ⊘ Reformulation
- Consumer behaviour
- Reduce GHG from transport
- Reduce GHG from refrigeration
- Reduce energy consumption in our offices
- ⊘ Reduce employee travel

WATER

Our products in use:
Halve the water associated with the consumer use of our products by 2020.*

2% † our water impact per consumer use has reduced by around 2% since 2010*

Our manufacturing:
By 2020 water abstraction by our global factory network will be at or below 2008 levels despite higher volumes.

32% † reduction in water abstraction per tonne of production since 2008

Reduce water use in manufacturing process:
- New factories

Reduce water use in the laundry process:
- Easy rinse products
- Products that use less water
- Reduce water use in skin cleansing and hair washing
- Reduce water use in agriculture

UNILEVER SUSTAINABLE LIVING PLAN 2014 PROGRESS

Source: USLP, Summary of Progress, 2014 ("Scaling for Impact"), p. 20.

Exhibit 8 (*cont.*)

ENHANCING LIVELIHOODS

FOR MILLIONS

By 2020 we will enhance the livelihoods of millions of people as we grow our business.

85% of our strategic suppliers met our Responsible Sourcing Policy's mandatory criteria. We helped 800,000 smallholder farmers and 238,000 women gain access to training, support and skills.

WASTE

Our products:
Our greenhouse gas impact has increased and our water and waste impact per consumer use has reduced since 2010.

Halve the waste associated with the disposal of our products by 2020.

12%
our waste impact per consumer use has reduced by around 12% since 2010*

Our manufacturing:
By 2020 total waste sent for disposal will be at or below 2008 levels despite significantly higher volumes.

85%† reduction
in total waste per tonne of production since 2008

Reduce waste from manufacturing:
- ✓ Zero non-hazardous waste to landfill
- New factories
- Reduce packaging

Recycle packaging:
- Increase recycling and recovery rates
- Increase recycled content
- Reuse packaging
- Tackle sachet waste
- ⊛ Eliminate PVC

Reduce office waste:
- Recycle, reuse, recover
- Reduce paper consumption
- Eliminate paper in processes

SUSTAINABLE SOURCING

By 2020 we will source 100% of our agricultural raw materials sustainably.

55%
of agricultural raw materials sustainably sourced by end 2014

Palm oil:
- ● Sustainable
- ● Traceable
- ● Paper and board
- ● Soy beans and soy oil
- ● Tea
- ● Fruit
- ● Vegetables
- ● Cocoa
- ● Sugar
- ● Sunflower oil
- ● Rapeseed oil
- ● Dairy
- ⊘ Fairtrade Ben & Jerry's
- ● Cage-free eggs
- ● Increase sustainable sourcing of office materials

FAIRNESS IN THE WORKPLACE

By 2020 we will advance human rights across our operations and extended supply chain.

85%
of our strategic suppliers met our Responsible Sourcing Policy's mandatory criteria by March 2015

- Implement UN Guiding Principles on Business and Human Rights
- Source 100% of procurement spend in line with our Responsible Sourcing Policy
- Create framework for fair compensation
- Improve employee health, nutrition and well-being
- ✓ Reduce workplace injuries and accidents †

OPPORTUNITIES FOR WOMEN

By 2020 we will empower 5 million women.

238,000
women provided with access to training and skills, including 70,000 Shakti micro-entrepreneurs trained in India

- Build a gender-balanced organisation with a focus on management
- Promote safety for women in communities where we operate
- Enhance access to training and skills
- Expand opportunities in our value chain

INCLUSIVE BUSINESS

By 2020 we will have a positive impact on the lives of 5.5 million people.

800,000
smallholder farmers gained access to training and support via partnerships with our agricultural suppliers and other partners

- Improve livelihoods of smallholder farmers
- Improve incomes of small-scale retailers
- Increase participation of young entrepreneurs in our value chain

† PricewaterhouseCoopers (PwC) assured. For details and the basis of preparation, see www.unilever.com

* Our environmental targets are expressed on a per consumer use basis. This means a single use, portion or serving of a product.

* In seven water-scarce countries representing around half the world's population.

KEY
- ✓ Achieved by target date
- ● On-plan for target date
- ● Off-plan for target date
- ⊛ % achieved by target date
- ○ Target discontinued

Source: USLP, Summary of Progress, 2014 ("Scaling for Impact"), p. 21.

To achieve that objective, they felt the new metrics offered an opportunity to evaluate and reward managers on their effectiveness in meeting USLP goals. Because this had previously been difficult to do, current evaluations and rewards were biased toward financial performance. But recently, parts of the organization had experimented with holding managers as accountable for their sustainability objectives as for their financial targets. Some felt it was time to expand that practice companywide.

However, others worried that because "strong headwinds" were slowing growth, shrinking margins, and depressing the stock price, the company should hunker down and show financial restraint. Their concern was that creating "sustainable living brands" typically involved significant upfront investment to shift the brand positioning and implement the product or process changes needed to deliver on environmental and social goals. They felt that the current environment did not support making such large investments that promised mostly long-term pay-offs. In their view, this might be the time to scale back and acknowledge that despite the company's best efforts, some objectives like reductions in GHG and water usage were beyond its reach.

Still others believed that Unilever should pivot toward its transformation agenda and focus on building external partnerships to support and amplify the company's good work over the past four years. In this view, management should acknowledge that while Unilever would not meet its GHG and water usage objectives through internal efforts, its leadership in forging partnerships to reduce global deforestation could well achieve those goals through different means.

These were large and complex questions facing Polman and his ULE team. At a minimum, they had to decide what, if any, fine-tuning adjustments needed to be made in its USLP strategy. But they also recognized that Unilever could well be at a major inflection point in the program. The question was, where to next?

Chapter 8 Recommended Practitioner Readings

- Lynn S. Paine, Rohit Deshpandé, and Joshua D. Margolis, "A global leader's guide to managing business conduct," *Harvard Business Review*, September (2011).

  In "A global leader's guide to managing business conduct," Paine, Deshpandé, and Margolis use the results of a large-scale survey to challenge multinational corporations to reconsider their current internal standards of business behavior. Their findings suggest that there is surprising agreement on what those standards should be, as well as a consensus that companies are falling short of their basic responsibilities in the international environment. They provide guidance on the development and monitoring of an appropriate set of standards.

- C. K. Prahalad and Allen Hammond, "Serving the world's poor, profitably," *Harvard Business Review*, 80:9 (2002), 48–57.

  In "Serving the world's poor, profitably," Prahalad and Hammond detail how multinationals can build businesses aimed at the bottom of the economic pyramid in order to build competitive advantage. They argue that such investments in the world's poorest markets can result in both tangible business benefits and major contributions to poverty reduction. The roles and responsibilities of the MNE continue to evolve, as these readings suggest. MNEs have much to contribute.

- Joseph L. Bower, Herman B. Leonard, and Lynn S. Paine, "Global capitalism at risk: what are you doing about it?" *Harvard Business Review*, 89:9 (2011), 104–12.

  In "Global capitalism at risk," Bower, Leonard, and Paine argue that market capitalism, a remarkable engine of wealth creation, is poised for a breakdown. Increasing income inequality, migration, weaknesses in the global financial system, environmental degradation, and inadequate government and international institutions are just a few of the forces that threaten to disrupt global market capitalism in the decades ahead. The authors call for business to be both innovator and activist in protecting and strengthening market capitalism. Instead of seeing themselves as narrowly self-interested players in a system that is overseen by others, business leaders must spearhead entrepreneurial activity on a massive scale – devising strategies that provide employment for the billions now outside the system, inventing business models that make better use of scarce resources, and creating institutional arrangements for coordinating and governing neglected and dysfunctional aspects of market capitalism.

- Bill Drayton and Valeria Budinich, "A new alliance for global change," *Harvard Business Review*, 88:9 (2010), 56–64.

  In "A new alliance for global change," Drayton and Budinich note that the citizen sector, composed of millions of groups worldwide that are attempting to address critical social needs, has long been regarded as understaffed and inefficient. But it has grown and matured over the past three decades. Citizen sector organizations (CSOs) are attracting talented and creative leaders, and their work is changing the game in critical industries such as energy and health care. For-profit companies now have an opportunity to collaborate with CSOs to create new markets for reaching the 4 billion people who are not yet part of the world's formal economy. The power of such collaborations lies in the complementary strengths of the partners. Business offers scale, expertise in manufacturing and operations, and financing; social entrepreneurs offer lower costs, strong social networks, and deep insights into potential customers and communities. The authors call this framework the hybrid value chain.

- Ben W. Heineman, Jr., "Avoiding integrity land mines," *Harvard Business Review*, 85:4 (2007), 100–8.

  In "Avoiding integrity land mines," Heineman explains how a large multinational keeps thousands of employees, operating in hundreds of countries, honest in a high-pressure business environment. The chief legal officer at GE for nearly 20 years describes a set of systems that combine the communication of clear expectations with oversight, deterrence, and incentives. Nowhere are the expectations higher – and the sanctions more powerful – than for top executives. General Electric has systematically sought to set uniform standards that stay well ahead of current legal developments and stakeholders' changing attitudes about corporate accountability. Responsibility for implementing those standards, which are embedded in GE's operating practices, rests with the business leaders in the field. Oversight is both methodical and multifaceted. A host of auditing and assessment systems enables GE to compare the performance of its various business units against one another and against industry benchmarks. The company's ombudsman system doesn't just allow but requires employees to lodge concerns. Failures to report into the system or up the line, or retaliation in any form, are firing offenses.

The recommended readings discuss how the roles and responsibilities of the MNE continue to evolve.

TRANSNATIONAL MANAGEMENT INDEX (CODED)